Lecture Notes of the Institute
for Computer Sciences, Social Informatics
and Telecommunications Engineering 227

Xuemai Gu · Gongliang Liu
Bo Li (Eds.)

Machine Learning and Intelligent Communications

Second International Conference, MLICOM 2017
Weihai, China, August 5–6, 2017
Proceedings, Part II

 Springer

Editors
Xuemai Gu
Harbin Institute of Technology
Harbin, Heilongjiang
China

Bo Li
Shandong University
Weihai, Heilongjiang
China

Gongliang Liu
Harbin Institute of Technology
Weihai, Heilongjiang
China

ISSN 1867-8211   ISSN 1867-822X (electronic)
Lecture Notes of the Institute for Computer Sciences, Social Informatics
and Telecommunications Engineering
ISBN 978-3-319-73446-0   ISBN 978-3-319-73447-7 (eBook)
https://doi.org/10.1007/978-3-319-73447-7

Library of Congress Control Number: 2017963764

Printed on acid-free paper

This Springer imprint is published by Springer Nature
The registered company is Springer International Publishing AG
The registered company address is: Gewerbestrasse 11, 6330 Cham, Switzerland

Preface

We are delighted to introduce the proceedings of the second edition of the 2017 European Alliance for Innovation (EAI) International Conference on Machine Learning and Intelligent Communications (MLICOM). This conference brought together researchers, developers, and practitioners from around the world who are leveraging and developing machine learning and intelligent communications.

The technical program of MLICOM 2017 consisted of 141 full papers in oral presentation sessions at the main conference tracks. The conference tracks were: Main Track, Machine Learning; Track 1, Intelligent Positioning and Navigation; Track 2, Intelligent Multimedia Processing and Security; Track 3, Intelligent Wireless Mobile Network and Security; Track 4, Cognitive Radio and Intelligent Networking; Track 5, Intelligent Internet of Things; Track 6, Intelligent Satellite Communications and Networking; Track 7, Intelligent Remote Sensing, Visual Computing and Three-Dimensional Modeling; Track 8, Green Communication and Intelligent Networking; Track 9, Intelligent Ad-Hoc and Sensor Networks; Track 10, Intelligent Resource Allocation in Wireless and Cloud Networks; Track 11, Intelligent Signal Processing in Wireless and Optical Communications; Track 12, Intelligent Radar Signal Processing; Track 13, Intelligent Cooperative Communications and Networking. Aside from the high-quality technical paper presentations, the technical program also featured three keynote speeches. The three keynote speeches were by Prof. Haijun Zhang from the University of Science and Technology Beijing, China, Prof. Yong Wang from Harbin Institute of Technology, China, and Mr. Lifan Liu from National Instruments China.

Coordination with the steering chairs, Imrich Chlamtac, Xuemai Gu, and Gongliang Liu, was essential for the success of the conference. We sincerely appreciate their constant support and guidance. It was also a great pleasure to work with such an excellent Organizing Committee who worked hard to organize and support the conference, and in particular, the Technical Program Committee, led by our TPC co-chairs, Prof. Xin Liu and Prof. Mingjian Sun, who completed the peer-review process of technical papers and created a high-quality technical program. We are also grateful to the conference manager, Katarina Antalova, for her support and to all the authors who submitted their papers to MLICOM 2017.

We strongly believe that the MLICOM conference provides a good forum for researchers, developers, and practitioners to discuss all the science and technology aspects that are relevant to machine learning and intelligent communications. We also hope that future MLICOM conferences will be as successful and stimulating, as indicated by the contributions presented in this volume.

December 2017

Xuemai Gu
Gongliang Liu
Bo Li

Organization

Steering Committee

Steering Committee Chair

Imrich Chlamtac   University of Trento, Create-Net, Italy

Steering Committee

Xin-Lin Huang   Tongji University, China

Organizing Committee

General Chairs

Xuemai Gu   Harbin Institute of Technology, China
Z. Jane Wang   The University of British Columbia, Canada
Gongliang Liu   Harbin Institute of Technology (Weihai), China

General Co-chairs

Jianjiang Zhou   Nanjing University of Aeronautics and Astronautics, China

Xin Liu   Dalian University of Technology, China

Web Chairs

Xuesong Ding   Harbin Institute of Technology (Weihai), China
Zhiyong Liu   Harbin Institute of Technology (Weihai), China
Xiaozhen Yan   Harbin Institute of Technology (Weihai), China

Publicity and Social Media Chair

Aijun Liu   Harbin Institute of Technology (Weihai), China

Sponsorship and Exhibits Chair

Chenxu Wang   Harbin Institute of Technology (Weihai), China

Publications Chairs

Xin Liu   Dalian University of Technology, China
Bo Li   Harbin Institute of Technology (Weihai), China

Posters and PhD Track Chair

Xiuhong Wang   Harbin Institute of Technology (Weihai), China

Local Chair

Bo Li   Harbin Institute of Technology (Weihai), China

Conference Manager

Katarina Antalova   EAI - European Alliance for Innovation

Technical Program Committee

Technical Program Committee Chairs

Z. Jane Wang   University of British Columbia, Canada
Xin Liu   Dalian University of Technology, China
Mingjian Sun   Harbin Institute of Technology (Weihai), China

TPC Track Chairs

Machine Learning
Xinlin Huang   Tongji University, China
Rui Wang   Tongji University, China

Intelligent Positioning and Navigation
Mu Zhou   Chongqing University of Posts
                                     and Telecommunications, China
Zhian Deng   Dalian Maritime University, China
Min Jia   Harbin Institute of Technology, China

Intelligent Multimedia Processing and Security
Bo Wang   Dalian University of Technology, China
Fangjun Huang   Sun Yat-Sen University, China

Wireless Mobile Network and Security
Shijun Lin   Xiamen University, China
Yong Li   Tsinghua University, China

Cognitive Radio and Intelligent Networking
Yulong Gao   Harbin Institute of Technology, China
Weidang Lu   Zhejiang University of Technology, China
Huiming Wang   Xi'an Jiaotong University, China

Intelligent Internet of Things
Xiangping Zhai   Nanjing University of Aeronautics and Astronautics,
                                     China
Chunsheng Zhu   The University of British Columbia, Canada
Yongliang Sun   Nanjing Tech University, China

Intelligent Satellite Communications and Networking
Kanglian Zhao   Nanjing University, China
Zhiqiang Li   PLA University of Science and Technology, China

Intelligent Remote Sensing, Visual Computing, and Three-Dimensional Modeling
Jiancheng Luo   Institute of Remote Sensing and Digital Earth,
                         Chinese Academy of Sciences, China
Bo Wang   Nanjing University of Aeronautics and Astronautics,
                         China

Green Communication and Intelligent Networking
Jingjing Wang   Qingdao University of Science and Technology, China
Nan Zhao   Dalian University of Technology, China

Intelligent Ad-Hoc and Sensor Networks
Bao Peng   Shenzhen Institute of Information Technology, China
Danyang Qin   Heilongjiang University, China
Zhenyu Na   Dalian Maritime University, China

Intelligent Resource Allocation in Wireless and Cloud Networks
Feng Li   Zhejiang University of Technology, China
Jiamei Chen   Shenyang Aerospace University, China
Peng Li   Dalian Polytechnic University, China

Intelligent Signal Processing in Wireless and Optical Communications
Wei Xu   Southeast University, China
Enxiao Liu   Institute of Oceanographic Instrumentation,
                         Shandong Academy of Sciences, China
Guanghua Zhang   Northeast Petroleum University, China
Jun Yao   Broadcom Ltd., USA

Intelligent Radar Signal Processing
Weijie Xia   Nanjing University of Aeronautics and Astronautics,
                         China
Xiaolong Chen   Naval Aeronautical and Astronautical University,
                         China

Intelligent Cooperative Communications and Networking
Deli Qiao   East China Normal University, China
Jiancun Fan   Xi'an Jiaotong University, China
Lei Zhang   University of Surrey, UK

Contents – Part II

Intelligent Radar Signal Processing

Intelligent Cooperative Communications and Networking

The Second Round

Contents – Part I

Intelligent Multimedia Processing and Security

Wireless Mobile Network and Security

Cognitive Radio and Intelligent Networking

Intelligent Internet of Things

Intelligent Satellite Communications and Networking

Intelligent Remote Sensing, Visual Computing and Three-Dimensional Modeling

Green Communication and Intelligent Networking

Intelligent Ad-Hoc and Sensor Networks

Intelligent Resource Allocation in Wireless and Cloud Networks

The Application of Equivalent Mean Square Error Method in Scalable Video Perceptual Quality

Daxing Qian[✉], Ximing Pei, and Xiangkun Li

Dalian Neusoft University of Information,
Software Park Road 8, Dalian 116023, Liaoning, China
{qiandaxing, peiximing, lixiangkun}@neusoft.edu.cn

Abstract. Scalable video is a stream video over heterogeneous networks to different clients. To provide the better quality of service (QoS) or quality of experience (QoE) to customer, we propose an Equivalent Mean Square Error (Eq-MSE) method which is developed based on spatial and temporal frequency analysis of input video content. Eq-MSE is used to calculate minimal frame rate (MinFR) for different videos to guarantee motion without jitter. The proposed scheme in this paper can provide better perceptual video quality than without considering the video content impact.

Keywords: SVC · Eq-MSE · MinFR · Perceptual quality

1 Introduction

With the advances of semi-conductor and access network technologies, real-time video streaming becomes more and more popular in our daily life. We can enjoy the videos service at famous website through different networks using heterogeneous devices. How to provide the high quality of service (QoS) or quality of experience (QoE) to different users over heterogeneous networks is a crucial problem for the success of video streaming application. Scalable video coding (SVC) [1, 2] is a full resolution scalable video stream which can be truncated to adapt different requirements imposed by the subscribed users and underlying access networks.

SVC includes temporal, spatial, SNR and combined scalabilities. Temporal scalability is realized by the hierarchical-B prediction [3]. Spatial scalability is achieved by encoding each supported spatial resolution into one layer. SNR scalability includes coarse grain scalability (CGS) and medium grain scalability (MGS) [4]. To achieve the SNR refinement, we usually use different quantization steps at different SNR layers. In this paper, we study the temporal and SNR joint scalability, and the spatial scalability is not mentioned.

Video content have a significant impact on the perceptual quality. For example, a motion intensive video need a larger frame rate to maintain the continuity of the object movement and avoid jitter and guarantee the motion smoothness, while for stationary video, a relatively lower frame rate is enough to provide the decent video quality. For motion-intensive content, bit stream extracted at higher frame rate is favored. On the

© ICST Institute for Computer Sciences, Social Informatics and Telecommunications Engineering 2018
X. Gu et al. (Eds.): MLICOM 2017, Part II, LNICST 227, pp. 3–7, 2018.
https://doi.org/10.1007/978-3-319-73447-7_1

other hand, if there are larger high-frequency components (i.e., rich texture) in a single frame of the video, a finer quantization to reach better spatial quality is typically preferred. To solve the problem, we study the spatial and temporal frequency of the input video content, and propose an Equivalent Mean Square Error (Eq-MSE) scheme to derive the minimal frame rate (MinFR) for different video sources to guarantee the motion smoothness and excellent QoE of the decoded video.

This paper is organized as follows. Section 2 introduces the temporal frequency in a video sequence (i.e., motion). In Sect. 3 we introduce the Eq-MSE method to derive the minimal frame rate without jitter for different input video sources. Subjective test evaluation and experimental results are shown in Sect. 4. Section 5 concludes the paper and discusses the future directions.

2   Temporal Frequency

The concept of spatial frequency is introduced in [5].

We can use the function [6, 7]:

$$
\begin{aligned}
\Psi\left(f_x, f_y, f_t\right) \\
&= \iiint \psi(x, y, t) \exp\left(-j2\pi\left(f_x x + f_y y + f_t t\right)\right) dx\,dy\,dt \\
&= \iint \psi_0\left(x - v_x t, y - v_y t\right) \cdot \exp\left(-j2\pi\left(f_x(x - v_x t) + f_y(y - v_y t)\right)\right) dx\,dy \\
&\quad \cdot \int \exp\left(-j2\pi\left(f_t + f_x v_x + f_y v_y\right)t\right) dt \\
&= \Psi_0\left(f_x, f_y\right) \int \exp\left(-j2\pi\left(f_t + f_x v_x + f_y v_y\right)t\right) dt \\
&= \Psi_0\left(f_x, f_y\right)\delta\left(f_t + f_x v_x + f_y v_y\right)
\end{aligned}
\tag{1}
$$

where $\Psi_0\left(f_x, f_y\right)$ indicates the 2D CSFT of $\psi_0(x, y)$. This function means that a spatial pattern characterized by $\left(f_x, f_y\right)$ in the object will lead to a temporal frequency, i.e.,

$$
f_t = -f_x v_x - f_y v_y
\tag{2}
$$

For a video signal, the temporal frequency is 2D position dependent. For a fixed 2D position (x, y), its temporal frequency is defined as the number of cycles per second usually denoted by Hertz (Hz).

From (2) we can draw a conclusion that the temporal frequency depends on not only the motion, but also the spatial frequency [6] of the object.

3   Equivalent Mean Square Error (Eq-MSE)

We propose an Eq-MSE method to calculate the SF of general objects in a picture and find the appropriate frame rate [6, 7].

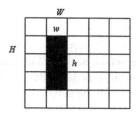

Fig. 1. Illustrative figure for object in general picture.

Figure 1 illustrates that the size of black column is $w \times h$ and picture size is $W \times H$. We use f_{tB} to represent the induced frame rate by the object, which is defined as:

$$f_{tB} = -\frac{MSEf\left(\frac{h}{H},0\right)}{MSEf(1,0)} \cdot v_x - \frac{MSEf\left(0,\frac{w}{W}\right)}{MSEf(0,1)} \cdot v_y \tag{3}$$

where $MSEf(f_x,0)$ is $MSE(x,y)$ when the picture SF is $(f_x,0)$, and $MSEf(0,f_y)$ is $MSE(x,y)$ when the picture SF is $(0,f_y)$. v_x and v_y are velocities in horizontal and vertical directions.

We regard the SF of a general picture is:

$$(f_x,f_y) = \left(\frac{MSEf\left(\frac{h}{H},0\right)}{MSEf(1,0)}, \frac{MSEf\left(0,\frac{w}{W}\right)}{MSEf(0,1)}\right) = \left(\frac{h}{H},\frac{w}{W}\right) \tag{4}$$

The objects in a picture that induce the frame rate from moving from arbitrary directions are:

$$f_t = \sum f_{tB} = \sum\left(-\frac{MSEf\left(\frac{h}{H},0\right)}{MSEf(1,0)}v_x - \frac{MSEf\left(0,\frac{w}{W}\right)}{MSEf(0,1)}v_y\right) = \sum\left(-\frac{h}{H}v_x - \frac{w}{W}v_y\right) \tag{5}$$

where $\sum$ is all the MBs in the picture. v_x and v_y are velocities in horizontal and vertical directions of corresponding MB. We get the mode and number of MB in a picture, and then choose the other picture within the same GOP to get MVs according to every MB. The ratio between MVs number in MB and the time interval between two frames are v_x and v_y. For example, the $\sum\frac{h}{H}v_x$ and $\sum\frac{w}{W}v_y$ of sequence Mobile are 12.2, 9.4, respectively. Its MinFR is $12.2 + 9.4 = 21.6$. Note that with a real signal, the CSFT is symmetric, so that for every frequency component at (f_x,f_y), there is also a component at $(-f_x,-f_y)$ with the same magnitude. The corresponding temporal frequency caused by this other component is $f_x v_x + f_y v_y$ [5].

Equation (5) is the function of minimal frame rate (MinFR) that makes the video motion smoothness without jitter.

4 Experimental Results

We invite 15 experimenters to give the decoded video subjective ratings for evaluate the subjective quality. Sub0 is the default scalable video adaptation without considering the video content impact, while sub1 is scalable adaptation with dependent video content. We use 11 ranks (i.e., 0–10) for the subjective tests ranging. The worst is 0 and the best is 10. The subjective assessment follows [8]. The results show in Table 1.

Table 1. Sequences subjective test comparative results

Sequences	Sub0	Sub1
Akiyo	6.6	6.8
City	4.9	7.7
Mobile	5.7	7.1
Football	6.1	7.9

Table 1 depicts the subjective test results of four sequences. It is obviously that "City", "Mobile" and "Football" have better perceptual rating for sub1 session, while "Akiyo" is quite similar between sub1 and sub0. We can draw a conclusion that the Eq-MSE method is providing better-decoded video quality at a given bit rate.

5 Conclusions

In this paper, we propose the Eq-MSE scheme, which is developed based on the spatial and temporal frequency analysis of the video content. This scheme is used to derive the MinFR for different videos and in consequence, so as to guarantee the motion smoothness for decent decoded video quality. Compared with the default scalable video adaptation without considering the video content impact, our proposed scheme can provide better perceptual video quality at the same bit rate according to the subjective quality assessments.

References

1. Text of ISO/IEC 14496-10:2005/FDAM 3 Scalable Video Coding, Joint Video Team (JVT) of ISO-IEC MPEG and ITU-T VCEG, Lausanne, N9197 (2007)
2. ISO/IEC ITU-T Rec. H264: Advanced Video Coding for Generic Audiovisual Services, Joint Video Team (JVT) of ISO-IEC MPEG and ITU-T VCEG, International Standard (2003)
3. Schwarz, H., Marpe, D., Wiegand, T.: Hierarchical B pictures. In: Joint Video Team, Doc. JVT-P014 (2005)
4. Schwarz, H., Marpe, D., Wiegand, T.: Overview of the scalable video coding extension of the H.264/AVC standard. IEEE Trans. Circ. Syst. Video Technol. **17**(9), 1103–1120 (2007)
5. Wang, Y., Ostermann, J., Zhang, Y.-Q.: Video Processing and Communications (2001)

6. Qian, D., Wang, H., Niu, F.: Scalable video coding bit stream extraction based on equivalent MSE method. In: Advanced Materials Research, vol. 204–210, pp. 1728–1732 (2011)
7. Qian, D., Wang, H., Sun, W., Zhu, K.: Bit stream extraction based on video content method in the scalable extension of H.264/AVC. J. Softw. **6**, 2090–2096 (2011)
8. ITU-R Rec. BT.500-11: Methodology for the subjective assessment of the quality of television pictures (2002)

Spectrum Allocation in Cognitive Radio Networks by Hybrid Analytic Hierarchy Process and Graph Coloring Theory

Jianfei Shi[1], Feng Li[1(✉)], Xin Liu[2], Mu Zhou[3],
Jiangxin Zhang[1], and Lele Cheng[1]

[1] Zhejiang University of Technology, Hangzhou 310023, Zhejiang, China
{sjf,fenglzj,zjx}@zjut.edu.cn, 478708892@qq.com
[2] Dalian University of Technology, Dalian 116024, Liaoning, China
liuxinstar1984@dlut.edu.cn
[3] Chongqing University of Posts and Telecommunications, Chongqing 400065, China
zhoumu@cqupt.edu.cn

Abstract. In this paper, a graph coloring-based spectrum allocation algorithm in cognitive radio networks combined with analytic hierarchy process is proposed. By analyzing several key factors that affect the quality of the leased spectrum, the algorithm combines the graph algorithm and analytic hierarchy process to assign the optimal spectrum to cognitive users orderly. Simulation results show that the proposed algorithm can effectively improve the network efficiency compared with original algorithms and arose inconspicuous loss to the whole network's fairness. The proposal not only improves the efficiency of spectrum allocation, but also balances the requirements of the overall fairness of cognitive radio networks.

Keywords: Cognitive radio · Graph coloring · Spectrum allocation
Analytic hierarchy process

1 Introduction

Spectrum sharing is the key technology in cognitive radio which attracts the increasing interest [1–3]. Graph theory, as a classical optimization theory, has been introduced to solve the difficulty of spectrum allocation in cognitive radio. [4] proposed a list-coloring algorithm based on the graph coloring theory, which includes distributed greedy algorithm and distributed fairness algorithm. In [5], as the list coloring algorithm can allocate only one spectrum once, the authors proposed a spectrum allocation algorithm to assign channels to multiple users at the same time without incurring interference. Based on [5], authors in [6] proposed an improved graph coloring algorithm for spectrum allocation with regards to the maximum weighted independent set to improve the spectrum utilization by combining the power control technology.

© ICST Institute for Computer Sciences, Social Informatics and Telecommunications Engineering 2018
X. Gu et al. (Eds.): MLICOM 2017, Part II, LNICST 227, pp. 8–14, 2018.
https://doi.org/10.1007/978-3-319-73447-7_2

In this paper, we apply analytic hierarchy process (AHP), one of the multi-objective decision method to proceed spectrum decision and provide a reasonable spectrum access strategy according to the heterogeneous idle spectrum. The improved proposal takes into account diverse spectral characteristics to meet the actual needs of the spectrum allocation in cognitive radio networks. In addition, by combining the advantages of the methods of AHP and coloring theory, the proposal not only improves the efficiency of spectrum allocation, but also satisfies the requirements of the overall benefits of cognitive radio networks.

2   Spectrum Allocation

2.1   Spectrum Selection Based on AHP

In spectrum selection, secondary users always want to switch to the spectrum with high bandwidth, low delay, low jitter and packet loss rate, etc. Therefore, this paper selects four indexes of bandwidth, delay, jitter and packet loss rate as the judgment criterion of spectrum selection. During the course, secondary users should also take their own preferences into account. When the number of considering factors become increasing, secondary users will struggle to make a rational choice by qualitative analysis. We thus introduce the method of AHP to analyze this problem. The selection problem can decomposed into three levels as shown in Fig. 1. In more complex environment, more evaluation criteria can be introduced to make it closer to realize.

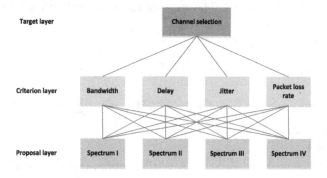

Fig. 1. Hierarchical graph of optimal spectrum decision based on AHP algorithm

To compare the impacts of factors $C_1, C_2, \cdots, C_n$ of one layer on a factor S_i of another layer, such as the importance of different choice criterions on final channel selection, it is essential to make a comparison between only two factors rather than multiple factors at the same time. Selecting two factors C_i and C_j each time, we use a_{ij} to denote the impact ratio of C_i and C_j on S_i, all the comparison results can be expressed in matrix as following

$$A = (a_{ij})_{n \times n}, \quad a_{ij} > 0, \quad a_{ij} = \frac{1}{a_{ji}}. \tag{1}$$

We can rewrite (1) as

$$A = \begin{pmatrix} \omega_1/\omega_1 & \omega_1/\omega_2 & \cdots & \omega_1/\omega_n \\ \omega_2/\omega_1 & \omega_2/\omega_2 & \cdots & \omega_2/\omega_n \\ \vdots & \vdots & \ddots & \vdots \\ \omega_n/\omega_1 & \omega_n/\omega_2 & \cdots & \omega_n/\omega_n \end{pmatrix}, \tag{2}$$

where $\omega = (\omega_1, \omega_2, \cdots)^T$ is the weighted coefficient vector satisfying $\sum_{i=1}^{n} \omega_i = 1$. Thus, as mentioned above, proper selection of the weighted coefficients in the secondary user's utility function is significant. In subsequent simulation tests, we will provide numerical results to testify the effects of different parameter selection in spectrum trading.

2.2   Single Hierarchical Arrangement and Consistency Check

Single hierarchical arrangement refers to the same level of the corresponding factors for the relative importance of the upper level of a factor ranking weight, it can be obtained by normalizing the eigenvector (weighted vector) W of the largest eigenvalue λ_{max} of judgment matrix A. So the essence is to calculate the weight vector. The calculation of the weight vector has the characteristic root method, the sum method, the root method, the power method and so on. In this paper, we use the sum method. The steps of the sun method are as follows:

1. Normalize each column vector of A : $\tilde{W}_{ij} = a_{ij}/\sum_{i=1}^{n} a_{ij}$.

2. Make summation for each row of A : $\tilde{W}_{ij} = a_i/\sum_{j=1}^{n} \tilde{W}_{i,j}$.

3. Normalize above matrix vector $W = \tilde{W}_i/\tilde{W}_{ij} = a_i/\sum_{i=1}^{n} \tilde{W}_i$, then obtain $W = (W_1, W_2, \cdots, W_n)^T$ as weight vector.

4. Calculate AW.

5. Calculate $\lambda_{max} = \frac{1}{n} \sum_{i=1}^{n} \frac{(AW)_i}{W_i}$, this is the approximate value of the largest eigenvalue.

The procedure for the consistency check is as follows:
Step 1: Calculate the consistency index (CI).

$$CI = \frac{\lambda_{max} - n}{n - 1}. \tag{3}$$

Step 2: Seek table to determine the corresponding random index (RI). According to the different order of the judgment matrix, we get the average random index RI.

Table 1. Random index RI

Matrix order	1	2	3	4	5	6	7	8	9	10
RI	0	0	0.58	0.9	1.12	1.24	1.32	1.41	1.45	1.40

Step 3: Calculate the consistency ratio (CR) and make judgments.

$$CR = \frac{CI}{RI}. \tag{4}$$

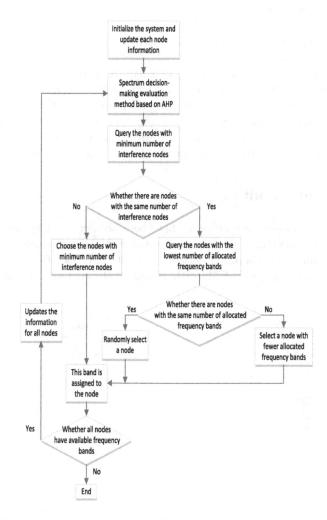

Fig. 2. Diagram of greedy spectrum allocation algorithm combined with AHP

When $CR < 0.1$, the consistency of the judgment matrix is acceptable, when $CR > 0.1$, it is considered that the judgment matrix does not meet the consistency requirement, the judgment matrix should be revised again. To test the consistency. We take matrix A as an example. First, we use (3) to calculate the consistency index $CI = 0.0083$, and then obtain $RI = 0.9$ via Table 1. Finally, due to the fact that $CR = 0.0092 < 0.1$, we can conclude that A is verified to pass consistency check.

2.3 Improved Spectrum Allocation Algorithm Model

According to the analysis above-mentioned, by selecting the optimal spectrum and then using the graph algorithm to allocate idle spectrum, we can make full use of spectrum resources, enhance the spectrum utilization and improve the overall efficiency.

Combining the distributed greedy algorithm and the method of AHP, the spectrum decision diagram is shown in Fig. 2.

The improved spectrum allocation algorithm can be described as follows: After initializing the system and updating the node information, according to the measured values of bandwidth, delay, jitter and packet loss rate of each spectrum, the hierarchical structure is established by using AHP; Set up the corresponding comparison matrix, and obtain the spectrum efficiency; Finally, the selected optimal spectrum is allocated using the coloring algorithm.

3 Numerical Results

In the simulation process, we suppose that there are six primary users in given region of $1000\,\text{m} \times 1000\,\text{m}$, and the initial number of idle channels is 10. In this simulation environment, the total network benefits and user fairness of the two algorithms and their improved algorithms are analyzed and compared. Using

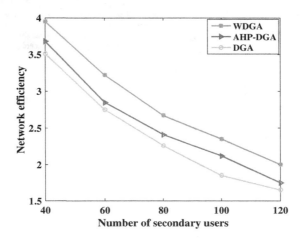

Fig. 3. Network utility curves of the three algorithms in greed mode

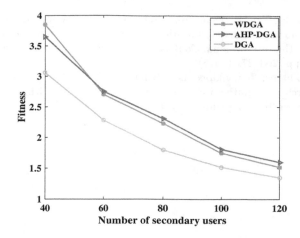

Fig. 4. Changing curves of the three algorithms in greedy mode

$U(R)$ to measure the network efficiency, with the variance to measure the fairness between users. In the simulation, randomly generate the network topology diagram. Furthermore, we randomly set the values in available spectrum matrix L, interference matrix C and utility matrix B within $[0, 1]$.

The parameters including bandwidth, delay, jitter and packet loss rate meet the data transmission standard of wireless networks proposed by ITU-T [7]. From Figs. 3 and 4, our proposed method using AHP and distributed greed algorithm (AHP-DGA) is compared with the results obtained by original distributed greedy algorithm (DGA) and weighted distributed greedy algorithm (WDGA). It can be concluded that AHP-DGA can receive high network efficiency and decent network fairness.

References

1. Fadeel, K.Q.A., Elsayed, D., Khattab, A., Digham, F.: Dynamic spectrum access for primary operators exploiting LTE-A carrier aggregation. In: IEEE ICNC, pp. 143–147 (2015)
2. Li, F., Tan, X., Wang, L.: A new game algorithm for power control in cognitive radio networks. IEEE Trans. Veh. Technol. **60**(9), 4384–4392 (2011)
3. Liu, X., Jia, M., Tan, X.: Threshold optimization of cooperative spectrum sensing in cognitive radio network. Radio Sci. **48**(1), 23–32 (2013)
4. Wang, W., Liu, X.: List-coloring based channel allocation for open-spectrum wireless networks. In: IEEE VTC-Fall, pp. 690–694 (2005)
5. Liu, Y., Jiang, M., Tan, X., et al.: Maximal independent set based channel allocation algorithm in cognitive radios. In: IEEE Youth Conference on Information, Computing and Telecommunication, pp. 78–81 (2009)

6. Bao, Y., Wang, S., Yan, B., et al.: Research on maximal weighted independent set-based graph coloring spectrum allocation algorithm in cognitive radio networks. In: Proceedings of the International Conference on Communications, Signal Processing and Systems, pp. 263–271 (2016)
7. ITU-T (2016). https://en.wikipedia.org/wiki/ITU-T
8. Li, M.: Research of cognitive radio spectrum allocation algorithm based on graph theory. Southwest Jiaotong University, pp. 45–47 (2012)

Spectrum Pricing in Condition of Normally Distributed User Preference

Li Wang[1], Lele Cheng[1], Feng Li[1(✉)], Xin Liu[2], and Di Shen[1]

[1] Zhejiang University of Technology, Hangzhou 310023, Zhejiang, China
{liwang2002,fenglzj}@zjut.edu.cn, 478708892@qq.com, 814120631@qq.com
[2] Dalian University of Technology, Dalian 116024, Liaoning, China
liuxinstar1984@dlut.edu.cn

Abstract. During secondary user's dynamic access to authorized spectrum, a key issue is how to ascertain an appropriate spectrum price so as to maximize primary system's benefit and satisfy secondary user's diverse spectrum demands. In this paper, a scheme of pricing-based dynamic spectrum access is proposed. According to the diverse qualities of idle spectrum, the proposal applies Hotelling game model to describe the spectrum pricing problem. Firstly, establish a model of spectrum leasing, among which the idle spectrum with different qualities forms a spectrum pool. Then, divide the idle spectrum into equivalent width of leased channels, which will be uniformly sold in order. Secondary users can choose proper channels to purchase in the spectrum pool according to their spectrum usage preferences which are subject to normal distribution and affected by the spectrum quality and market estimation. This paper analyzes the effect of spectrum pricing according to the primary system's different tendencies to spectrum usage and economic income.

Keywords: Spectrum pricing · Cognitive radio · User preference
Spectrum quality

1 Introduction

With the rapid development of wireless communication technology and the establishment of next-generation 5g communication standard, high-quality idle spectrum is more scarce which has become one of the bottlenecks restricting the development of wireless communication technology [1]. Cognitive radio which is based on dynamic spectrum access has attracted more and more attention of academe and engineering recent years [2]. Various kinds of emerging network technology have begun to adopt dynamic spectrum detection and dynamic spectrum access to improve the efficiency of spectrum utilization. In the process of dynamic spectrum access, primary users owning licensed spectrum can lease the idle channels to secondary user to gain incomes. For primary users, how to identify an optimal channel pricing to maximize its own profit has become a significant issue. In this paper, we directly price the idle spectrum of authorized users according to the secondary user's diverse preferences. The spectrum

© ICST Institute for Computer Sciences, Social Informatics and Telecommunications Engineering 2018
X. Gu et al. (Eds.): MLICOM 2017, Part II, LNICST 227, pp. 15–22, 2018.
https://doi.org/10.1007/978-3-319-73447-7_3

pricing scheme has a prior estimate to the spectrum market. Compared with the spectrum auction, it doesn't need many overheads and improves the convenience of the spectrum access.

Spectrum trading provides an efficient way for secondary users to dynamically access licensed bands while the financial gains can encourage primary users to lease unused spectrum temporarily. Generally, the participants can perform the deal by auction-based method or pricing-based method. The spectrum auction mechanism can be divided into many kinds according to different application circumstances, such as trust-based auction which relaxes the credit limit appropriately in return for a higher economic efficiency to balance the honesty and the efficiency [3,4]. On the other hand, to lower the overhead and time cost for spectrum pricing, pricing-based spectrum trading has also been widespread concerned either [5,6].

In this paper, we investigate how to price the spectrum when heterogeneous spectrum and stochastic secondary user's preference are under consideration. A concept of spectrum pool is introduced to facilitate the following spectrum deal. A secondary spectrum customer will pick a high-quality channel for usage when its capital is ample or wide band is required to support essential service. We adopt Hotelling model which is proper to describe the product pricing issue in heterogeneous market. By analyzing the secondary user's preference parameter, an iterative algorithm for spectrum pricing is obtained by fixing the Nash equilibrium. Numerical results are further provided to evaluate how the pricing parameters affect the primary system's profits.

2 System Model

Suppose the idle spectrum leased by the primary system consists a spectrum sharing pool, where the spectrum can be divided into many uniform channels for selling. Besides, the qualities of these channels are not homogeneous. For high-quality channels, the secondary users suffers lower channel fading or adjacent channel interference. Thus, secondary users choose these channels according to their diverse preferences. The preference parameter is determined by the channel quality and channel price.

2.1 Utility Functions

In this paper, we consider the spectrum trading is performed without auction activities. During the course, primary systems have no prior knowledge of the secondary customer's spectrum preference. In spectrum trading, the utility function of a secondary user can be expressed as

$$U = \theta s - p, \tag{1}$$

where θ denotes the secondary user's preference, s denotes the channel quality and p denotes the channel price. In the spectrum sharing pool, it is assumed that two kinds of channels with diverse qualities can be chosen by secondary users as shown in Fig. 1. We use s_1 to denote the channel quality of high-quality channel and s_2 the low-quality channel. Then, we have $s_1 > s_2 > 0$. Here, different channel qualities means various transmission capacities. Furthermore, we suppose the secondary user's preference parameter θ is subject to normal distribution expressed as $g(\theta)$. θ locates in the region of $[\theta_L, \theta_H]$, and ρ is the corresponding probability distribution function denoted as $\rho = G(\theta)$. We adopt θ_0 to express the non-preference parameter of a cognitive user which means no demand difference existing between the high-quality channel and low-quality channel. Then, it can be calculated as $\theta_0 = \frac{p_1 - p_2}{s_1 - s_2}$, where p_1 and p_2 represent the two kinds of channels' prices. When a secondary user's spectrum preference θ_i is higher than θ_0, the user prefers to choose the high-quality channel. Otherwise, it would rather to choose the low-quality channel to lease.

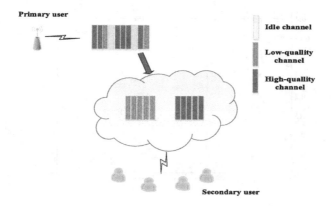

Fig. 1. Spectrum pool

2.2   Spectrum Pricing

Secondary user's preference parameter is considered to be non-uniform and obey normal distribution in practical application. Figure 2 shows the density curve of the standard normal distribution. The probability density can be given as

$$\varphi(x) = \frac{1}{\sqrt{2\pi}e^{-\frac{x^2}{2}}} \tag{2}$$

Then, the distribution function is

$$f(x) = \int \varphi(x) = \frac{1}{2\pi} \int_{-a}^{a} e^{-\frac{t^2}{2}}. \tag{3}$$

According to [7], $f(a)$ can be simplified as

$$f(a) = \sqrt{1 - e^{\frac{-a^2}{1.6058}}}. \tag{4}$$

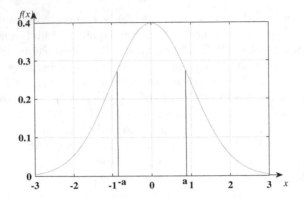

Fig. 2. Standard normal distribution

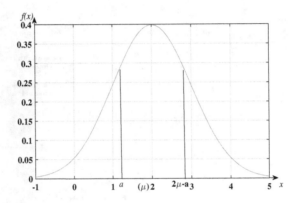

Fig. 3. General normal distribution

Thus, the probability can be approximately calculated in given region $[-a, a]$.

The conclusion can also be applied to the case of general normal distribution as shown in Fig. 3. When the distribution mean is μ, the probability calculated approximately in $[a, 2\mu - a]$ is obtained as

$$f(a) = \sqrt{1 - e^{-\frac{(u-a)^2}{1.6058}}}. \tag{5}$$

Furthermore, as shown in Fig. 4, the secondary customer whose preference parameters θ locates in $[\theta_L, \theta_0]$, will purchase low-quality channels. The user with preference parameters $\theta \in [\theta_0, \theta_H]$ chooses a high-quality channel.

Then, in order to obtain the specific solution, divide the red shadow part in Fig. 4 into two parts, where we have $\theta_0' = \theta_0 + \mu$ and $\theta_H - \theta_H' = \mu$.

According to the various regions of high-quality and low-quality channels in Fig. 4, we achieve the following equations

$$p_H = \frac{1}{2} \times (\sqrt{1 - e^{-\frac{(\mu-\theta_0)^2}{1.6058}}} + \sqrt{1 - e^{-\frac{(\theta_H-\mu)^2}{1.6058}}}), \tag{6}$$

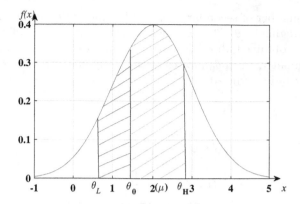

Fig. 4. Divide the channels into two kinds of qualities

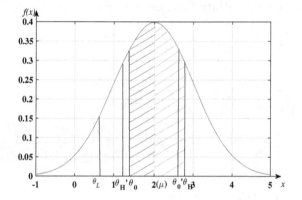

Fig. 5. Divide the high-quality channels into two parts

$$p_H = \frac{1}{2} \times (\sqrt{1 - e^{-\frac{(\mu - \theta_L)^2}{1.6058}}} + \sqrt{1 - e^{-\frac{(\mu - \theta_0)^2}{1.6058}}}). \tag{7}$$

Assume the marginal cost of the primary user is related to the quality of the channel which can be expressed as $c_i = \alpha s_i (i = 1, 2)$, where α is the marginal cost factor. Formulating the problem by Berland game model, the profit functions of system H and L can be given as

$$\pi_H(p_1, p_2) = N(p_1 - \alpha s_1) \times \frac{1}{2} \times$$
$$= (\sqrt{1 - e^{-\frac{(\mu - \theta_0)^2}{1.6058}}} + \sqrt{1 - e^{-\frac{(\theta_H - \mu)^2}{1.6058}}}), \tag{8}$$

$$\pi_L(p_1, p_2) = N(p_2 - \alpha s_2) \times \frac{1}{2} \times$$
$$= (\sqrt{1 - e^{-\frac{(\mu - \theta_L)^2}{1.6058}}} + \sqrt{1 - e^{-\frac{(\mu - \theta_0)^2}{1.6058}}}), \tag{9}$$

where N is the number of secondary users. The non-preference parameter θ_0 is not fixed and changing in $[\theta_L, \theta_H]$. Besides, whether $\theta_0 > \mu$ will affect the deductions. The profits obtained above is under the situation when θ_0 locates at the left side of μ. Similarly, when θ_0 locates at the right side of μ, the corresponding profit functions can be deduced as

$$
\pi_H(p_1, p_2) = N(p_1 - \alpha s_1) \times \frac{1}{2} \times
$$
$$
= (\sqrt{1 - e^{-\frac{(\theta_H - \mu)^2}{1.6058}}} + \sqrt{1 - e^{-\frac{(\theta_0 - \mu)^2}{1.6058}}}),
$$
$$(10)$$

$$
\pi_L(p_1, p_2) = N(p_2 - \alpha s_2) \times \frac{1}{2} \times
$$
$$
= (\sqrt{1 - e^{-\frac{(\mu - \theta_L)^2}{1.6058}}} + \sqrt{1 - e^{-\frac{(\theta_0 - \mu)^2}{1.6058}}}).
$$
$$(11)$$

Based on the marginal utility function, we can achieve the optimal channel pricing as

$$
p_1^{(t+1)} = p_1 + \beta \times N \times \frac{1}{2} \times
$$
$$
= (\sqrt{1 - e^{-\frac{(\mu - \theta_0)^2}{1.6058}}} + \sqrt{1 - e^{-\frac{(\theta_H - \mu)^2}{1.6058}}}) +
$$
$$
\beta \times N \times e^{-\frac{(\mu - \theta_0)^2}{1.6058}} \times (2\alpha - p_1^{(t)}) \times \frac{2\mu - 2p_1^{(t)} - 2p_2^{(t)}}{6.4232\sqrt{1 - e^{-\frac{(\mu - \theta_0)^2}{1.6058}}}},
$$
$$(12)$$

$$
p_2^{(t+1)} = p_2 + \beta \times N \times \frac{1}{2} \times
$$
$$
= (\sqrt{1 - e^{-\frac{(\mu - \theta_L)^2}{1.6058}}} + \sqrt{1 - e^{-\frac{(\mu - \theta_0)^2}{1.6058}}}) +
$$
$$
\beta \times N \times e^{-\frac{(\mu - \theta_0)^2}{1.6058}} \times \frac{1}{6.4232} \times (2p_2^{(t)} - 2p_1^{(t)} + 2\mu)
$$
$$(13)$$

Similarly, we can obtain the optimal channel pricing when $\theta_0 > \mu$.

3   Numerical Results

In this section, numerical results are provided to testify the effects of the proposed pricing method. In the dynamic access networks, we suppose the idle spectrum is controlled by the licensed users and we ignore the internet interference caused by adjacent cells. The secondary users who are eager to access the spectrum must participant in the spectrum trading and pay for the cost to the primary systems. As the proposed pricing solution is an iterative algorithm, we thus give the initial spectrum pricing for two kinds qualities of channels to be $s_1 = 2$, $s_2 = 1$, $N = 100$, $\alpha = 1$, $\mu = 2.2$, $\beta \in (0, 0.028)$. The cognitive user's preference locates at $[1, 3]$ which means $\theta_L = 1$, $\theta_H = 3$. Furthermore, since the

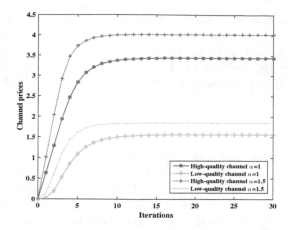

Fig. 6. Channel prices with different marginal factors

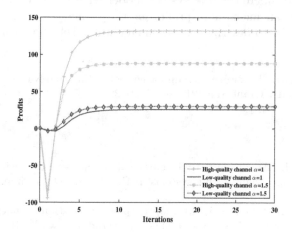

Fig. 7. System profits with different marginal factors

proposed pricing method is an iterative algorithm, we set the initial spectrum pricing for two kinds qualities of channels as $p_i^{(0)} = 0.01$. Then, we give the performances of the channel prices and system profits of the proposed method in the following tests.

In Fig. 6, we present the performances of the channel prices obtained in this paper with different marginal factors α. We can achieve from the figure that the optimal price of high-quality channel is much higher than that of low-quality channel. Furthermore, the channel pricing rises with increasing marginal factor α since higher marginal cost needs to be compensated for the primary system. We also can get the iterative algorithm converges very fast which will attain a stable value within 15 iterations. In the counterpart, Fig. 7 gives the performances of the system profits in optimal pricing with different marginal factors. We can obtain from Fig. 7 that the system profits decrease with increasing marginal factor α which means the close relationship between spectrum cost and system profit. Besides, it is obvious that the profit received on the high-quality channel overcomes that on the low-quality channel. It can be understandable that the primary system expects to reap more profits by its more excellent products.

4   Conclusion

In this paper, we investigate how to price the differential spectrum in respond to secondary users' stochastic selection preferences. The main contribution of this paper lies in that we introduce the Hotelling game model to formulate and address the differential spectrum pricing. In the paper, we assume the idle spectrum is collected and leased to potential secondary users centrally, then a centralized spectrum pricing by the primary system can be proceeded. Two kinds of spectrum is considered in the system model where it is foreseen the high-quality channels can incur more profits for the primary system. A preference factor is introduced to describe the secondary user's selection tendency on the spectrum leased.

Acknowledgement. This work was supported by the National Natural Science Foundation of China under Grant 51404211 and 61601221.

References

1. Yang, C., Li, J., Anpalagan, A.: Hierarchical decision-making with information asymmetry for spectrum sharing systems. IEEE Trans. Veh. Technol. **64**(9), 4359–4364 (2015)
2. Zhao, N., Yu, F.R., Sun, H., Li, M.: Adaptive power allocation schemes for spectrum sharing in interference-alignment-based cognitive radio networks. IEEE Trans. Veh. Technol. **65**(5), 3700–3714 (2016)
3. Gao, L., Huang, J., Chen, Y., Shou, B.: An integrated contract and auction design for secondary spectrum trading. IEEE J. Sel. Areas Commun. **31**(3), 581–582 (2013)
4. Zhu, K., Dusit, N., Wang, P., Han, Z.: Dynamic spectrum leasing and service selection in spectrum secondary market of cognitive radio networks. IEEE Trans. Wirel. Commun. **11**(03), 1136–1145 (2012)
5. Dixit, S., Periyalwar, S., Yanikomeroglu, H.: Secondary user access in LTE architectrur based on a base-station-centric framework with dynamic pricing. IEEE Trans. Veh. Technol. **62**(01), 284–285 (2013)
6. Zhong, W., Wang, J.: Energy efficient spectrum sharing strategy selection for cognitive MIMO interference channels. IEEE Trans. Sig. Process. **61**(14), 3705–3706 (2013)
7. Liang, C., Shi, X., Li, L.: Approximate calculation of standard normal distribution. In: National Conference on Microwave and Millimeter Wave, pp. 1–4 (2001)

Allocation Optimization Based on Multi-population Genetic Algorithm for D2D Communications in Multi-services Scenario

Xujie Li[1,2($\boxtimes$)], Xing Chen[1], Ying Sun[1], Ziya Wang[1], Chenming Li[1], and Siyang Hua[3]

[1] College of Computer and Information Engineering, Hohai University, Nanjing 210098, China
lixujie@hhu.edu.cn
[2] Hubei Key Laboratory of Intelligent Wireless Communications, South-Central University for Nationalities, Wuhan 430074, China
[3] Talent Science and Technology Co., Ltd., Nanjing 211800, China

Abstract. For D2D Communications in Multi-services scenario, fast resource allocation optimization is a crucial issue. In this paper, a resource allocation optimization method based on the multi-population genetic algorithm for D2D communications in Multi-services scenario is proposed. Due to the interference between the cellular user equipment (CUE) and D2D user equipment (DUE) which share the same frequency, the complexity of resource allocation increases. Firstly, the interference model of D2D communications is analyzed. Then the resource allocation problem is formulated and discussed. Next, a resource allocation scheme based on Multi-population genetic algorithm is presented. Finally, the analysis and simulation results show the Multi-population genetic algorithm can converge faster compared with standard genetic algorithm. Therefore, the Multi-population genetic algorithm is more suitable to the Multi-services scenario where the data rate demand varies quickly and frequently.

Keywords: D2D communications · Cellular network
Multi-population genetic algorithm · Resource allocation

1 Introduction

With the rapid development of modern communication technology, the demand for wireless data is increasing rapidly. The wireless spectrum becomes a scarce resource [1]. Device to Device (D2D) communications can effectively improve spectrum efficiency by licensed frequency sharing between the cellular user equipments (CUEs) and D2D user equipments (DUEs) [2]. D2D communication using the licensed band can guarantee the quality of communication [3]. The establishment of D2D communication link is divided into two modes: One is centralized mode, with the intervention of base station (BS). The BS can control the interference between the links by power control, resource allocation and other ways to achieve reasonable optimization. The other one is

© ICST Institute for Computer Sciences, Social Informatics and Telecommunications Engineering 2018
X. Gu et al. (Eds.): MLICOM 2017, Part II, LNICST 227, pp. 23–32, 2018.
https://doi.org/10.1007/978-3-319-73447-7_4

distributed mode. DUE pairs may bypass the BS and establish the link directly, but this approach requires more complex D2D devices to achieve the discovery and connection between the D2D pairs.

Recently, most researches mainly focus on resource allocation [4], interference coordination [8], power control [11] and so on. In paper [4], the authors propose a new resource allocation scheme to obtain higher throughput and save significant amount of energy. In order to maximize the sum rate of the cellular system while meeting the rate requirements of all users, an alternating optimization method is proposed in paper [5]. In paper [6, 7], the authors make full use of the spectrum resources through optimal power allocation to improve the system performance. Considering the capacity and power saving, the authors propose an incentive mechanism encouraging terminals to organize themselves into an optimal number of clusters and achieve a significant gain in terms of costs while increasing the capacity of the whole cell in [6]. The authors propose an algorithm which converges quickly, have low overhead, and maximizes network throughput, while maintaining the quality of CUEs in [7]. In order to improve the spectrum efficiency and the energy efficiency of the D2D-aided networks, a proper interference coordination scheme is proposed in [8]. In paper [9], the authors introduce the non-negligible distance of the interference between D2D pairs and the non-reusable distance of CUE, and propose a method which allocated the resource based on graph theory, and improve the total system capacity. In paper [10], the authors optimize the resource allocation of DUE and CUE one-to-one by genetic algorithm, and increase the total system throughput. The authors also use the genetic algorithm to reduce the transmission power and the energy consumption in [11]. Based on the genetic algorithm, the wireless frequency hopping technology with a reasonable resource allocation of DUE is adopted to reduce the interference between the same sub-channel in paper [12]. In paper [13], the authors define the interference limited region and control the D2D transmission power so as to improve the channel capacity. The authors formulate the joint power control and mode selection problem for D2D communications in LTE-A network to minimize the aggregate transmit power of users subject to a minimum target throughput for each cellular and D2D user in paper [14]. In paper [15], a two-stages relay selection and resource allocation joint method for relay-assisted D2D communication is proposed to maximize the total throughput of cellular uplink (UL) and D2D link. It can guarantee the quality of service (QoS) of the two links simultaneously [16–20].

However, few papers and works had been contributed to resource allocation optimization based on intelligent algorithm for D2D communications in multi-services scenario. To guarantee the QoS of all UEs, we need to allocate the applicable channel resources for UEs. In multi-services scenario, the service type of the UEs maybe transit from low data rate service to high data rate service. Then the resource allocation scheme needs to be adjusted frequently and rapidly. Therefore, a quick convergence algorithm needs to be presented. Based on above, a resource optimization scheme based on multi-population genetic algorithm for D2D communication in multi-services scenario is proposed. The proposed algorithm can rapidly allocate the channel resources for multi-services. And the performance of the algorithm is evaluated.

The structure of this paper is as follows. In Sect. 2, the system model is presented. Based on the system model, a resource optimization scheme based on multi-population genetic algorithm for D2D communication in multi-services scenario is proposed in Sect. 3. The simulation results are analyzed in Sect. 4. Finally, we summarize this work in Sect. 5.

2 System Model

In cellular networks, there are two types of mobile terminals: conventional cellular network mobile terminal CUEs and D2D mobile terminal DUEs. DUEs are in pairs, and a pair of DUEs includes a D2D transmitting mobile terminal DTUE and a D2D receiving mobile terminal DRUE. In a FDD network, each CUE is assigned a separate and mutually orthogonal sub-channel, and multiple DUE pairs can simultaneously share a sub-channel resource. This paper assumes that N CUEs and M DUEs share all channel resources. Figure 1 shows the application scenario that a D2D communication system in which N CUEs and M DTUEs are randomly distributed in a cell with the radius of R. DRUE uniformly locates in the circle with center at the DTUE and radius equal to L (the allowed maximum communication distance for D2D communications). The same colors in the figure represent that the users' spectral resources are the same.

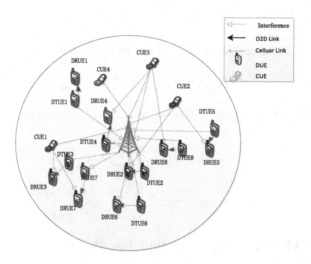

Fig. 1. D2D communications system model in multi-services scenario

Due to the complexity that power control scheme is applied to the D2D communications, we only consider that the power control scheme is applied to CUEs and the fixed transmission power is applied to DUEs. In other words, the transmitting powers for all DTUEs are the same and denoted as P_T. Next, we assume that the UE links follow a median path loss model with the form of $P_r/P_t = 1/r^\alpha$. Here P_r is the received power at the UE or BS. The transmitting power of UE denoted as P_t. r is the distance between the transmitter and receiver. α is path loss exponent.

In D2D communications, the SINR of CUE i can be written as

$$SINR_{c_i} = \frac{P_i/r_i^\alpha}{\sum\limits_{k\in\Re_i} P_T/d_{k,i}^\alpha + N_0} \qquad (1)$$

Here, P_i is the transmission power of CUE i, r_i is the distance between CUE i and the BS, $d_{k,i}$ is the distance between DTUE k and the BS, $\Re_i$ is ith package which includes the DTUEs using the same frequency with CUE i.

Similarly, the SINR of DRUE j can be written as

$$SINR_{d_j} = \frac{P_T/l_j^\alpha}{P_m/d_{m,j}^\alpha + \sum\limits_{k\in\Re_m} P_T/d_{k,j}^\alpha + N_0} \qquad (2)$$

Here, l_j is the distance between the DTUE j and DRUE j, P_m is the transmission power of CUE m, $d_{m,j}$ is the distance between CUE m and DRUE j, $d_{k,j}$ is the distance between DTUE k and DRUE j.

Next, we can get capacity of CUE i

$$R_{c_i} = \log_2(1 + SINR_{c_i}) \qquad (3)$$

In the same way, the capacity of DUE j can be calculated

$$R_{d_j} = \log_2(1 + SINR_{d_j}) \qquad (4)$$

Therefore, the fitness function is denoted as

$$C(U_x) = \sum_{i=1}^{N} R_{c_i} + \sum_{j=1}^{M} R_{d_j} \qquad (5)$$

Here, U_x represents some chromosome.

3   Resource Allocation Optimization Based on Multi-population Genetic Algorithm

In Multi-services Scenario, to satisfy the demand for varying transmission rate of UEs, we need to adjust the resource allocation schemes rapidly. As shown in Fig. 1, when the CUE4 requires a higher date rate, the DUE pair 7 which reuses the spectrum resources of CUE4 may be kicked out. DTUE7 sends a request to BS, and BS reallocates the other sub-channel resources to DTUE7. So we need a quick and effective resource optimization algorithm to reallocate channel resources. Then a resource optimization scheme based on multi-population genetic algorithm for D2D communication in multi-services scenario is proposed. The proposed algorithm can rapidly allocate the channel resources for multi-services.

Because a sub-channel can only be assigned to one CUE, and multiple DUEs can share a sub-channel, N CUEs and M DUEs need at least N sub-channels. We denote the set of sub-channels as $\Re_i(i = 1, 2\ldots N)$. For CUEs, CUE i is allocated to ith sub-channel (package i). For DUE pair j, the gene-bit is the sequence number of the assigned package for DUE pair j. Then every chromosome is coded as a M dimensional row vector like $G = (g_1, \cdots, g_j, \cdots, g_M)\, g_j \in (1, 2, \cdots, N)$. For example $N = 4$ and $M = 8$, chromosome (1,2,1,3,2,3,4,3) means that DUE pairs 1 and 3 share sub-channel 1 with CUE1, DUE pairs 2 and 5 share sub-channel 2 with CUE2, DUE pairs 4, 6 and 8 share sub-channel 3 with CUE3, DUE pair 7 share sub-channel 4 with CUE 4, as illustrated in Fig. 2.

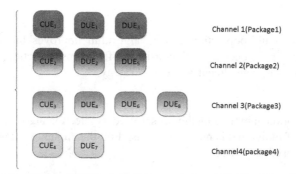

Fig. 2. Original channel resource allocation scheme

In multi-services scenario, the service type of the UEs is likely to change from low data rate service to high data rate service. Then we need to frequently and rapidly adjust resource allocation scheme. For example, DUE 2 needs higher data rate, and it maybe forces DUE 5 to change sub-channel from 2 to 4, as shown in Fig. 3.

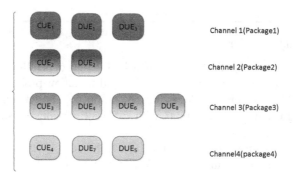

Fig. 3. Channel re-allocation scheme

The resource optimization scheme based on multi-population genetic algorithm can be divided into five main steps:

1. Parameter Initialization

We initialize system parameters including the radius of the cell, the threshold of SINR, the maximum power of CUE and DUEs, the number of UEs, and the positions of UEs.

2. Population Initialization

We initiate the number of populations as 10. Every population includes 30 chromosomes. For every chromosome, the element is a discrete random variable which takes value between 1 and N based on the equal probability.

3. Breeding Process

The population of multi-population genetic algorithm improves the system performance by the breeding process, which consists of five steps: selection, crossover and mutation, immigration, amendment and elite strategy.

(1) Selection

Generally, the rotation gambling method is selected as selection algorithm [10]. But the competitiveness of individual is not strong. Based on this, a new sorting and selection algorithm is proposed as follows:

Algorithm 1 Selection algorithm

Begin

    {Sorting the chromosomes in the population according to their fitness function value from largest to smallest, denoting the values as set A(i) ($i = 1...30$)}

    $i = 1; j = 1$;

    While $j <= 30$ do

    {B(j) = B(j+1)=A(i); $j = j + 2; i = i + 1$}

    Based on classical roulette wheel selection scheme, selecting the chromosome.

End

---

(2) Crossover and Mutation

We set the crossover probability as P_c, which is different depending on the different populations. The value of crossover probability and mutation probability determines the ability of global search and local search. Multi-population genetic algorithm co-evolves through multiple populations with different parameters, so it can get the optimal value faster.

    We denote the probability of mutation as P_m. If the gene bit is x, then the mutated value is randomly selected from the set $\bar{x}$ (The universal set is $S = 1 \cdots N$).

(3) Immigration

Immigration operator is adopted in the multi-population genetic algorithm. It introduces the optimal individual of each population in the evolution process into other populations periodically to realize the information exchange among the populations.

The multi-population genetic algorithm can achieve fast convergence by the introduction of immigration operator.

(4) Amendment

If we can't guarantee the QoS of UEs whose SINR must be greater than SINR threshold, we should repeat the process as mentioned above.

(5) Elite Strategy

The elite strategy is introduced into Multi-population genetic algorithm. In each generation of evolution, the best individuals of every population are selected and stored in the elite set. The individuals in elite set don't participate in crossover and mutation to ensure that the optimal individuals will not be affected by the following changes such as damage or loss.

4. Iteration Termination Condition

We set a minimum generation value Γ for optimal individual. The iterative process is terminated if optimal individual doesn't change in Γ iterations. Compared with standard genetic algorithm in which a fixed maximum generation value is set, Multi-population genetic algorithm has faster convergence ability.

4 Simulation and Discussion

In our simulations, we assume that there are four CUEs and thirty DUEs which follow a uniform distribution in the cell with the radius of R and DTUEs uniformly located in the circle with center at the corresponding DRUE and radius equal to L. Simulation parameters are as shown in Table 1.

Table 1. Simulation parameters

Parameter	Value
Cell radius (R)	600 m
The number of CUEs	4
Path loss factor (α)	4
SINR threshold (β)	6 dB
N_0	−105 dBm
L	20 m
The number of D2D pairs	30
The maximum transmission power of CUE	0.02 W
The transmission power of DTUE	0.001 W

Figure 4 shows the convergent speed comparison between standard genetic algorithm and Multi-population genetic algorithm. The Multi-population genetic algorithm can converge faster compared with standard genetic algorithm. This is because that migration and elite strategy are introduced into the Multi-population genetic algorithm.

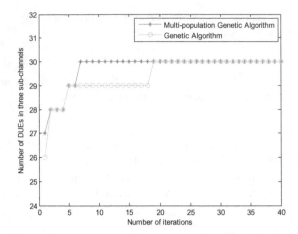

Fig. 4. Convergent speed comparison (standard genetic algorithm vs Multi-population genetic algorithm)

Migration ameliorates the diversity of populations, and elite strategy maintains the optimality of populations. Therefore, the Multi-population genetic algorithm is more suitable to the Multi-services scenario where the data rata demand varies quickly and frequently.

At the same time, Fig. 5 shows the capacity based on the two algorithms. We can get a slightly better capacity based on Multi-population genetic algorithm compared with that based on standard genetic algorithm. This is because that the introduction of elite strategy can maintain the better individual in population. Meanwhile, Multi-population genetic algorithm also has faster convergence ability.

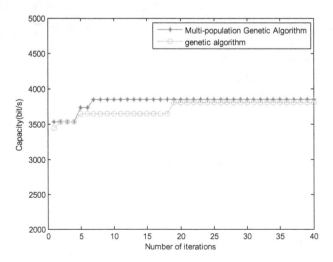

Fig. 5. The capacity of D2D communications

5   Conclusion

In this paper, the resource allocation problem for D2D Communications in Multi-services scenario is described and analyzed. Based on the analysis of interference model of D2D communications, the resource allocation problem in Multi-services scenario is formulated and analyzed. Then a resource allocation scheme based on Multi-population genetic algorithm is proposed. Finally, the analysis and simulation results show the Multi-population genetic algorithm has faster convergence ability compared with standard genetic algorithm. So, it is more suitable to the Multi-services scenario where the data rate demand varies quickly and frequently. This result can be applied for design and optimization of D2D communications in Multi-services scenario.

Acknowledgements. This work was supported in part by "Key technology integration and demonstration of optimum dispatching of pumping stations of east route of South-to-North Water Diversion Project" of the National Key Technology R&D Program in the 12th Five-year Plan of China (2015BAB07B01), "the Fundamental Research Funds for the Central Universities (No. 2017B14214)", the Project of National Natural Science Foundation of China (61301110), the Project funded by the Priority Academic Program Development of Jiangsu Higher Education Institutions.

References

1. Li, X., Shen, L.: Interference analysis of 3G/ad hoc integrated network. IET Commun. **6**(12), 1795–1803 (2012)
2. Li, X., Zhang, W., Zhang, H., Li, W.: A combining call admission control and power control scheme for D2D communications underlaying cellular networks. China Commun. **13**(10), 137–145 (2016)
3. Li, X., Wang, Z., Sun, Y., Gu, Y., Hu, J.: Mathematical characteristics of uplink and downlink interference regions in D2D communications underlaying cellular networks. Wirel. Pers. Commun. **93**(4), 917–932 (2017)
4. Mumtaz, S., Huq, K.M.S., Radwan, A.: Energy efficient interference-aware resource allocation in LTE D2D communication. In: IEEE International Conference on Communications, Sydney, NSW, pp. 282–287 (2014)
5. Zhao, W., Wang, S.: Resource allocation for device-to-device communication underlaying cellular networks: an alternating optimization method. IEEE Commun. Lett. **19**(8), 1398–1401 (2015)
6. Castagno, P., Gaeta, R., Grangetto, M., Sereno, M.: Device-to-device content distribution in cellular networks: a user-centric collaborative strategy. In: IEEE Global Communications Conference (GLOBECOM), San Diego, CA, pp. 1–6 (2015)
7. Ye, Q., Al-Shalash, M., Caramanis, C., Andrews, J.G.: Distributed resource allocation in device-to-device enhanced cellular networks. IEEE Trans. Commun. **63**(2), 441–454 (2015)
8. Cao, Y., Jiang, T., Wang, C.: Cooperative device-to-device communications in cellular networks. IEEE Wirel. Commun. **22**(3), 124–129 (2015)
9. Cai, X., Zheng, J., Zhang, Y.: A graph-coloring based resource allocation algorithm for D2D communication in cellular networks. In: IEEE International Conference on Communications (ICC), London, pp. 5429–5434 (2015)

10. Yang, C., Xu, X., Han, J., Tao, X.: GA based user matching with optimal power allocation in D2D underlaying network. In: IEEE 79th Vehicular Technology Conference (VTC Spring), Seoul, pp. 1–5 (2014)
11. Yang, C., Xu, X., Han, J., Tao, X.: Energy efficiency-based device-to-device uplink resource allocation with multiple resource reusing. Electron. Lett. **51**(3), 293–294 (2015)
12. Lee, Y.H., Tseng, H.W., Lo, C.Y., Jan, Y.G.: Using genetic algorithm with frequency hopping in device to device communication (D2DC) interference mitigation. In: International Symposium on Intelligent Signal Processing and Communications Systems, Taipei, pp. 201–206 (2012)
13. Sun, J., Zhang, T., Liang, X., Zhang, Z., Chen, Y.: Uplink resource allocation in interference limited area for D2D-based underlaying cellular networks. In: IEEE Vehicular Technology Conference, Nanjing, pp. 1–6 (2016)
14. Naghipour, E., Rasti, M.: A distributed joint power control and mode selection scheme for D2D communication underlaying LTE-A networks. In: IEEE Wireless Communications and Networking Conference, Doha, pp. 1–6 (2016)
15. Zhao, M., Gu, X., Wu, D., Ren, L.: A two-stages relay selection and resource allocation joint method for d2d communication system. In: IEEE Wireless Communications and Networking Conference, Doha, pp. 1–6 (2016)
16. Zhang, H., Dong, Y., Cheng, J., Hossain, M.J., Leung, V.C.: Fronthauling for 5G LTE-U ultra dense cloud small cell networks. IEEE Wirel. Commun. **23**, 48–53 (2016)
17. Zhang, H., Liu, N., Chu, X., Long, K., Aghvami, A., Leung, V.: Network slicing based 5G and future mobile networks: mobility, resource management, and challenges. IEEE Commun. Mag. **62**(7), 2366–2377 (2017)
18. Zhang, H., Jiang, C., Beaulieu, N.C., Chu, X., Wen, X., Tao, M.: Resource allocation in spectrum-sharing OFDMA femtocells with heterogeneous services. IEEE Trans. Commun. **62**, 2366–2377 (2014)
19. Zhang, H., Jiang, C., Beaulieu, N.C., Chu, X., Wang, X., Quek, T.Q.: Resource allocation for cognitive small cell networks: a cooperative bargaining game theoretic approach. IEEE Trans. Wirel. Commun. **14**, 3481–3493 (2015)
20. Zhang, H., Jiang, C., Mao, X., Chen, H.-H.: Interference-limited resource optimization in cognitive femtocells with fairness and imperfect spectrum sensing. IEEE Trans. Veh. Technol. **65**, 1761–1771 (2016)

Agricultural IoT System Based on Image Processing and Cloud Platform Technology

Yaxin Zheng[(⊠)] and Chungang Liu

Communication Research Center,
Harbin Institute of Technology, Harbin 150001, China
Asin_zheng@163.com, cgliu@hit.edu.cn

Abstract. Detection of crop disease and growth state have always been the key to ensure the yield and quality of agricultural products. The algorithms, which are in the field of pattern recognition or image recognition, have been using to crop-disease detection and growth-state detection, these algorithms undoubtedly have great significance, and with the development of IoT technology in recent years, the Internet of things technology combining with the existing technology will be the future direction of intelligent agriculture. This paper proposed an agricultural system, which based on the image processing technology and cloud platform of the Internet of things technology. The system can complete image recognition process real-time detection and recording of crop growth status and alarm crop disease in time based on the mutual connection with the cloud platform, and truly realize the unmanned detection in the field of intelligent agricultural system.

Keywords: IoT technology · Cloud platform · Pattern recognition

1 Introduction

China is one of the biggest country of agricultural production, the quality of these production is always people's focus. How to have an effectively detect about the disease and status of crops is the key to producing high quality crops. The disease status of crops can lead to visible changes in the leaves of the crop, and the identification of the crops' surface features can play a role in the detection and prevention of the disease.

The automatic detection of crop growth and disease status can be achieved through a long time real time image recognition process. Therefore, this paper proposes a system based on the cloud platform of the IoT technology and image recognition technology. The system can upload the crop state for a long time and display the crops' status after the process of image recognition to the cloud platform. In this way, we can detect the status of crops remotely through the telephone and websites. In addition, if the system detect the disease about the crops, the cloud platform can send an alarm about it to you immediately. Meanwhile, the system allows you to reverse control some equipments (such as lights, water sprayer, fertilizer application) to improve the environment of the crops in the field (Fig. 1).

© ICST Institute for Computer Sciences, Social Informatics and Telecommunications Engineering 2018
X. Gu et al. (Eds.): MLICOM 2017, Part II, LNICST 227, pp. 33–42, 2018.
https://doi.org/10.1007/978-3-319-73447-7_5

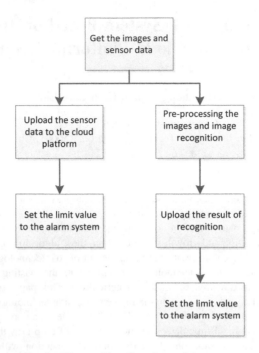

Fig. 1. The working flowchart of the system

2   Basic Process of the System

The system collect the data through the temperature and humidity sensor and the camera that are connected to the self-designed microchip circuit board. About the collected images, we need to use the image processing and get the result of the disease recognition. After that, we transfer the data about the sensors and the recognition results to the cloud platform through the MCU serial. Connect the output of the MCU and the input of the module of WIFI to transfer the data from the MCU to the WIFI module, and then send the data to the cloud platform through RF antenna, along with the connection about the antenna and the wireless router. After the operations about combine the cloud ID with the WeChat or Twitter, we can check the data remotely through the telephone. Moreover, the cloud can periodic send email, text-message and twitter message to the users. During the process of the data transfer, by changing the code about the MCU, we can realize send the sensor-data to the WIFI module successfully and periodic send data to the cloud platform to make sure the users can figure out the real-time situation about the crops and the field.

Then, switch the TCP short connection that we used during send data to the cloud to TCP long connection. In the way of holding the connection about the cloud platform and the MCU and refuse to disconnect it, we can make the cloud to give the orders to communicate with the MCU. So that, we can make the real-time reversal control to come true, to control the equipment in the field as we need.

2.1   The Acquisition of Images and Sensors

The collection of images based on the high-definition cameras, and then transfer the RGB images to HIS images. This color model, which is more close to the color-pattern in human eyes, can make the images more sensitive about the differences between colors and make the recognition more precisely.

About the sensor data, we get it through the temperature and humidity sensors among the field (also we can add any kinds of sensors as we need), this system use the DHT11 sensor to get two different variables, temperature and humidity. The sensor can change the variables to the data that can be upload to the cloud platform; you can just power it to make it work, and no need for other connections to make it more portable.

2.2   Upload Data of Sensors to the Cloud Platform

The design choose STM8 MCU and ESP8266 WIFI module to realize the data transformation. After the register about the cloud platform, we need to set the WIFI module to make sure the module and the cloud are connected. Then, by changing the code of the MCU to initialize the MCU modules and make it to get the sensor data periodically. Every 40 s to make the code into the interrupt routine and send the sensor to the cloud platform.

We have to consider the problems of timer, system clock, and baud rate; so need to set the timer of the MCU to make the system clock into 16 MHz and 128-frequency divider, the baud rate into 115200, enable the timer to make sure it can update the interrupt routine every 40 s.

The DTH11 temperature and humidity sensor used to get the environment data; we should initialize the IO port. To send the sensor data, have to receive the sensor data periodic and put it into the send-buffer. Lastly, recode the interrupt routine to make the MCU send the sensor to the cloud in the format, which the platform needed every 40 s.

2.3   Image Processing, Upload, Reverse Control

2.3.1   Image Processing

The accuracy of image recognition most depends on the pre-operation of the images and the feature extraction. To get a high precision, we used the mixed feature extraction, using color information, texture information, and morphological information to get a mixed feature information. Afterwards, using the SVM to recognize the images, in this way, we can detect the disease crop image.

Because most of the leaves of diseased plants' color will change, so color information is an essential part of the process of crop disease recognition, we can use color information as a part of the feature information. This design uses the color information features as the HSI color mode, that is, we need to converse the images the camera captured. Many cloud platforms have the corresponding image sensors, if the users need; they can save them to the platform. For a given RGB format image, each pixel corresponds to the H (hue) component can be obtained by the following equation, but the component is also needed to be divided by 360° normalized into [0,1] interval.

$$H = \begin{cases} \theta & (B<G) \\ 360 - \theta & (B \geq G) \end{cases} \tag{1}$$

$$\theta = \arccos\left\{ \frac{1/2[(R-G)+(R-B)]}{(R-G)^2 + (R-G)(G-B)^{1/2}} \right. \tag{2}$$

S (saturation) and I (intensity) components are expressed as follows, these two components have already been in the [0,1] interval between, so do not need normalization:

$$S = 1 - \frac{3}{(R+G+B)}[MIN(R,G,B)] \tag{3}$$

$$I = \frac{1}{3}(R+G+B) \tag{4}$$

Crop image via HSI conversion results as shown in Fig. 2; we can see that in the case of yellow diseased leaves area after transformation will appear darker effect, thus the conversion mode for effective detection.

Fig. 2. Images before and after the HIS transformation

If we only do the image recognition with color feature information, the recognize result will cause remarkable error. We figure that the crop disease occurs mostly the short plant and the spots on the leaves, so the texture information and morphological characteristics will also be the significant feature information. To mix these three kinds of information can get a higher accuracy.

All the feature information are getting from the gray level images, and need to process these images to make the information more efficient. In this paper, we use the Laplacian algorithm to sharpen the image, and then, using the Gauss filter to reduce the noise. Lastly, the histogram equalization make the needed information more significant.

The Laplacian operator is used to sharpen the image detail information of the crops, and the detail information of the disease is strengthened, after that, the effectiveness of the identification be improved. In the process of image acquisition and conversion, noise is inevitable. Because the main information of image recognition exists in the low frequency part, we can use the Gaussian filter to reduce the noise, which is almost in the high frequency part, and protect the low frequency part. This method will reduce the effect for the recognize process from the noise. Finally, the image texture features are well distributed by histogram equalization, and the texture image is clearer. The processed gray images were as shown in Fig. 3, and the images show that the processed imaged are obvious more effective than the untreated images in details, effectiveness, and display of gray images.

Fig. 3. The images after Laplacian algorithm sharpen the image process, the Gaussian filter process, and the histogram equalization process

Image texture feature obtained by gray level co-occurrence matrix, and save the texture feature vector as the corresponding matrix variables. The acquisition of simple morphological feature vectors are got by simple region descriptors. After obtaining the texture features of the image, the local binary pattern (LBP) is used to reduce the dimension of the texture feature firstly, which can produce the non-one order statistical features of the image structure information. The LBP algorithm is chosen for its superior texture ability, high classification ability and computational efficiency. The results show that the dimension reduction effect is obvious and the overall trend has not changed greatly, so the algorithm can play an important role in improving the utilization rate of resources, as shown in Fig. 4.

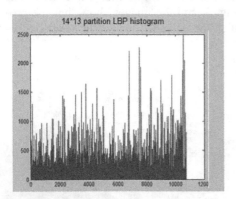 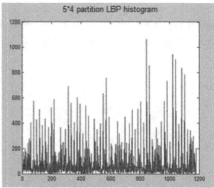

Fig. 4. The results of the dimensionality reduction, the left image shows that the result of 14*13 partition LBP histogram, and the right image shows that the result of 5*4 partition LBP histogram. The left one has more details and the right one has more efficiency.

The three feature vectors are combined to make the recognition process more than just one element, the combination prevent the error caused by the color, shape and other individual phenomena. In the second step of dimensionality reduction, the color feature information, the refined texture information and the morphological feature information will combine with each other and reproduce the new feature information matrix. Because of the high dimensionality of the feature vector and the relative invalid feature, the computing resources are wasted. In this process, we use the PCA algorithm to reduce the dimension of the combined matrix. This is the way to make the result more precisely and the computation more efficient.

After the refined step, which is the reducing dimension part, we use the SVM to train and test the images. The SVM technology based on the principle of structural risk minimization, give consideration to the training error and test error. This algorithm achieve the best classification results by selecting different kernel functions, and using parameter search tools to get the best parameters that we need to used. Also, it is also possible to avoid the over-training phenomenon that the artificial neural network technology has been happened, the SVM makes the classifier after full training has a higher classification effect. Through the acquisition of the image recognition, detection of the current gives the type of disease within the scope, to grasp the disease status of field crops.

2.3.2 Upload the Result of Recognition and Reverse Control

The identified category information is converted to ASCII code and send to the WIFI module through the serial port, WIFI module connected to the cloud platform can send data to it. Because image processing takes a relatively long time, to avoid the connection between the cloud and the WIFI module to released, the MCU can send some initialize value to fill the time. When identifying the disease category, send the designed number to present the disease, in the paper the designed number is 99. When the received number is bigger than the limit value we set on the cloud, the cloud will send the users an alarm to make the users to solve the disease problems.

The reverse control function also need to be realized by the TCP link. Make a connection about the cloud platform and the WIFI module to succeed the send/receive message with the STM8 MCU chip, and get the data at the specific location of a fixed format to control the pin into a low or high level to switch the status about the equipment in the field. In this method, the users can realize change the switch status to control the medicine, fertilize, water. In addition, the cloud not only turn the switch from on to off, but also can control the number controller from 0 to 255.

First, we need to send messages to the cloud platform through MCU chips, so the TCP connection about the cloud and the MCU will be created. After the connection has been created successfully, the MCU will send the register message to the cloud platform, the specific data can change along with the data the users used during the register ID process. Afterwards, the MCU can be coded to waiting the messages, which the cloud send back to the MCU chip. In this way, we can link the cloud ID to the MCU chip, and then, we have to send initialize information to the controller in the cloud when the MCU received the feedback message. In this paper, we decided to set the switch controller to on and the number controller to the number 1. After the operations above, we can set the initial state of the controllers, and then, when we click the controllers in the cloud through websites, the MCU will get different values with the fixed format. If we let the MCU to get data at the specific location, we can get the situation the equipment in the field need to be.

Take the switch controller as an example, if the switch controller were set the controller status to be off, the MCU will get the data 0 from the cloud, we should get the data 0 at the fixed location of the feedback message, and turn the pin PD4 (which we used to control the power of the equipment) to a low-level output to let the power of the equipment in the field to be off. When the data interaction between the cloud and the MCU be stopped for 40 s, the TCP link will released, if need to reverse control after that, should to reconnect it again.

3 Debugging the System

To test if the designed IoT system can truly realize the real-time collection about the crops' situations and complete the reversal control, we need to debug the system. During this experiment, we choose the DHT11 sensor to feel the difference about temperature and humidity. Then, we create the temperature/humidity sensor in the cloud platform; the platform will give your sensor an ID number when you finish the created. The ID number about our DHT11 sensor is 38416, and the data that we upload to the cloud platform are as follows:

```
POST /v1.0/device/21775/sensor/38416/datapoints
HTTP/1.1
Accept: */*
Host: api.yeelink.net
U-ApiKey:6ac5806f65203ce63a7bf39d604ae206
Content-Length: 14
Content-Type: application/json;cahrset=utf-8

{"value":59}
```

The platform can detect the data of the specified location to find out the temperature or humidity; this is because the format of the sending message is stationary.

When the sensor of cloud platform receive a number which is bigger than the designed limit value, the cloud can send an alarm to the user to make the situation of the crops can be improved. The sensors are not only about the temperature but also can use to send alarms when the crops were detected to be illness. When we need to upload the status of the crops, the created sensors in the cloud platform need to be generic sensors, which we can design the key word to display the status and the value. We designed the code of crops' disease to be 99, and then when the cloud platform received the value of 99, the users will get an alarm about the disease. In this way, the users can be more clearly to figure out the situation about the crops and the field. The data that the generic sensor will upload are as follows:

```
POST /v1.0/device/1/sensor/5/datapoints HTTP/1.1
Accept: */*
Host: api.yeelink.net
U-ApiKey:78195d42-df52-45ca-af5f-70a4c6777ef9
Content-Length: 97
Content-Type: application/json;cahrset=utf-8

{"key":"shibeiqingkuang","value":{99}}
```

When we need to control the equipment, which is in the field through the cloud platform, we will receive the data the platform send to are as follows:

```
GET /v1.0/device/1/sensor/3/datapoints HTTP/1.1
Host: api.yeelink.net
U-ApiKey:78195d42-df52-45ca-af5f-70a4c6777ef9
Content-Length: 0
Connection: close
```

The realization about the system as show in the figures, you can complete the data upload, check the real-time situation through the App in your phone, periodic send the sensor-data to the platform and use the platform to reverse control. Figure 5 is representing check the uploaded data through website, the WeChat and the website of telephones; and Fig. 6 shows that the website when you want to reverse control the power of the equipments in the field (the red means the switch is off, and when you click it you can change the switch to on).

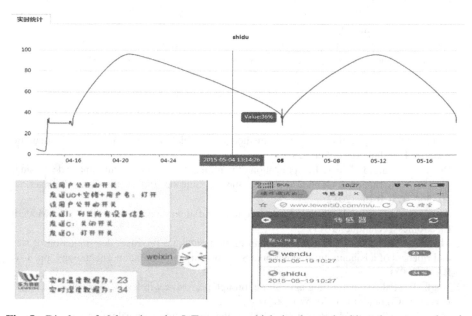

Fig. 5. Display of debugging the IoT system, which is about checking the sensor data in real-time.

Fig. 6. Display of debugging the IoT system, which is about reversing control the equipment in the field

Through the operations of the designed system, we can see that the system can realize the real-time monitor, the reverse control; the data uploaded and display the curve of the changing sensor-data.

4   Conclusion

To satisfy the needs about producing high-quality crops, we need to find out what status the crops are and how to fix the problematic situation in time. The system which the paper purposed realize the real-time control of crop growth environment, real time recognize disease image for the collected crop images and send an alarm about it. Make people can remotely through the mobile client, WeChat, micro-blog to get a full range of real-time understanding check on the growth state and disease situation of the crops. Moreover, can real-time reverse control based on different conditions of the environment that the crops are, so that crops grow more intelligent and flexible.

References

1. Liang, Y.Q.: Application of a new method of wavelet image denoising in agriculture picking. J. Anhui Agric. Sci. (2010)
2. Bu, Y.Q., Zhang, J., Xie, C.J.: Application of nonlinear filter in agriculture image de-noising. In: IEEE International Conference on Computer Science and Automation Engineering, pp. 368–371. IEEE (2012)
3. Song, H.Y.: Image de-noising based on total variation and median filter. In: Modern Electronics Technique (2011)
4. Mustafa, N.B.A., et al.: Image processing of an agriculture produce: determination of size and ripeness of a banana. In: International Symposium on Information Technology, pp. 1–7. IEEE (2008)
5. Wark, T., et al.: Transforming agriculture through pervasive wireless sensor networks. IEEE Pervasive Comput. **6**(2), 50–57 (2007)
6. Min, W.Z., Chao, Q.M.: Research of IOT in the application of wisdom agricultural. Appl. Mech. Mater. **511–512**, 714–718 (2014)
7. Liu, Z.Y., Chen, B.J., Men, W.J.: Application and research of Internet of Things technology in modern agricultural production. Heilongjiang Agricultural Sciences (2016)
8. Li, J., Long, Z.: Study on agriculture image processing based on discrete wavelet transform. In: Second Iita International Conference on Geoscience and Remote Sensing, pp. 384–387 (2010)
9. Fu, S., Ruan, Q., Wang, W.: Remote sensing image data enhancement based on robust inverse diffusion equation for agriculture applications. In: International Conference on Signal Processing, pp. 1231–1234. IEEE Xplore (2008)
10. Khirade, S.D., Patil, A.B.: Plant disease detection using image processing. In: International Conference on Computing Communication Control and Automation, pp. 768–771. IEEE (2015)
11. Sammouda, R., et al.: Adapting artificial hopfield neural network for agriculture satellite image segmentation. In: International Conference on Computer Applications Technology, pp. 1–7. IEEE (2013)
12. Guo, W., et al.: Image-based field plant phenotyping approaches for modern agriculture. In: Conference of the Society of Instrument and Control Engineers of Japan, pp. 1212–1215 (2015)

Extension of 2FSK Signal Detection Utilizing Duffing Oscillator

Dawei Chen[✉], Enwei Xu, Shuo Shi, and Xuemai Gu

School of Electronics and Information Engineering,
Harbin Institute of Technology, Harbin 150080, China
chen415963066@sina.com, xewmickey@gmail.com,
{crcss,guxuemai}@hit.edu.cn

Abstract. Based on the sensitivity of the chaotic system to the initial value and the characteristics of the noise immunity, this paper presents a method to detect the FSK signal of closed carrier frequency under the low signal-to-noise ratio based on the Duffing oscillator, and then give the principle of FSK signal and its modulation. Furthermore, a method to solve the problem that frequency overlapping occurred between two closed frequencies FSK signal is proposed. Based on the theoretical analysis, the simulation model is established by using MATLAB and Simulink. The simulation results show that the model can solve the frequency overlapping of the FSK signal effectively; meanwhile, it has good detection precision and anti-noise performance.

Keywords: Duffing oscillator · Chaos system · Frequency overlapping
Weak signal detection · FSK

1 Introduction

Signal detection plays an important role in the communication system, in which the identification and extraction of signal characteristics is particularly important. When the transmission signal is weak, the effect of the traditional signal detection method is not ideal. Chaotic systems are widely used to detect the weak signal of the noise background. The effect of the noise in the detection is often ignored because of the characteristics of sensitive to certain signals and inert to noise. The sensitivity of the chaos theory to the initial value and the immunity to the noise are gradually applied to the weak signal detection and the result is much better [1].

In the conventional detection method, the linear detection method [2] mainly including three aspects, such as the detection in time domain, the detection in frequency domain and the detection in time-frequency domain. These methods mainly including correlation method, sampling integral and time domain averaging method, which are widely used in the detection of periodic signals, however, they have shortage apparently, for example, the lower detection efficiency and higher detection threshold [3]. As the rapidly development of nonlinear theory in recent years, in which the duffing oscillator in chaos theory transforms the presence or absence of weak signal into obvious state change of the system, that is to say, the chaotic state changes to large-scale periodic state, in that way can detect weak signal accurately [4].

© ICST Institute for Computer Sciences, Social Informatics and Telecommunications Engineering 2018
X. Gu et al. (Eds.): MLICOM 2017, Part II, LNICST 227, pp. 43–52, 2018.
https://doi.org/10.1007/978-3-319-73447-7_6

The traditional detection method of FSK signal is to improve the signal to noise ratio of the input signal by filtering, then detect FSK signal by conventional method. Indeed, that way can reduce the noise in the weak FSK signal. Meanwhile, the useful signal in noise can also be affect in the process by filtering the noise, thereby the detection accuracy is affected [5]. On the contrary, chaos system detects the weak signal directly by utilizing the sensitivity of weak signal of the system without filter out the noise, in this way, it can be used in a lower signal to noise ratio [6, 7] situation. In the practical application, due to the characteristics of the communication channel, it will cause a higher bit error rate phenomenon at the receiving terminal as result of the delay of transmission signal.

In this paper, we present a new system aim at solve the phenomenon of frequency overlapping, in which is general in FSK signal detection. The proposed approach can identify the frequency overlapping phenomenon of FSK signal, then has good performance in distinguish the code overlapping, thereby reducing the bit error rate in the communication system, which is successfully shown in this paper through Simulink simulation.

2 Duffing Oscillator System Model

As the most classic oscillator in all kinds of chaotic systems, Duffing oscillator is often used by researchers to detect weak signal.

Now, the mature Duffing-Holmes equation as follow:

$$\ddot{x}(t) + k\dot{x}(t) - x(t) + x^3(t) = F\cos(\omega t) \tag{1}$$

Where $-x(t) + x^3(t)$ is non-linear restoring force; k is damp ratio; $F\cos(\omega t)$ is main sinusoidal driving force; F is amplitude of driving force.

When k is fixed, the system state enters the monoclinic orbit state, the periodic bifurcation state, the chaotic state and the large state periodic with the increase of F.

Let $t = \omega\tau$, then $x(t) = x(\omega\tau)$,

$$\dot{x}(t) = \frac{dx(t)}{dt} = \frac{dx(\omega\tau)}{d(\omega\tau)} = \frac{dx(\omega\tau)}{d(\tau)} \cdot \frac{d\tau}{d(\omega\tau)} = \frac{1}{\omega}\frac{dx(\omega\tau)}{d\tau} \tag{2}$$

$$\ddot{x}(t) = \frac{d\dot{x}(t)}{dt} = \frac{d\dot{x}(\omega\tau)}{d(\omega\tau)} = \frac{1}{\omega} \cdot \frac{dx(\omega\tau)}{d\tau} \cdot \frac{d\tau}{d(\omega\tau)} = \frac{1}{\omega^2}\frac{dx(\omega\tau)}{d\tau} \tag{3}$$

We can get:

$$\frac{1}{\omega^2}\ddot{x}(\omega\tau) + \frac{k}{\omega}\dot{x}(\omega\tau) - x(\omega\tau) + x^3(\omega\tau) = F\cos(\omega\tau) \tag{4}$$

Let $\dot{x}_\tau = \omega y$, then the equation became as follow:

$$\frac{1}{\omega}\ddot{y} + ky - x + x^3 = F \cos(\omega\tau) \tag{5}$$

The Duffing equations is:

$$\begin{cases} \dot{x}_\tau = \omega y \\ \dot{y}_\tau = \omega(-ky + x - x^3 + F \cos(\omega\tau)) \end{cases} \tag{6}$$

Now, we make a research on the chaotic characteristics of Duffing system by building the Duffing system model through the Matlab/Simulink tool. The fourth-order Runge-Kutta method is used to simulate the Duffing oscillator, as shown in Fig. 1.

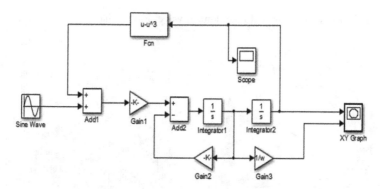

Fig. 1. Duffing oscillator Simulink model in Matlab

Where *Sine Wave* is the sinusoidal driving force, *Fcn* is the nonlinear restoring force, the integrator model *integrator* 1 and *integrator* 2 are used for closed-loop calculation of the first and second order, the multiplier *Gain* 1 adjust the coefficients of the integrator output in the Duffing oscillator, *Gain* 2 also represents the damp ratio, the multiplier *Gain* 3 adjusts the integrator coefficient when drawing the phase diagram. After the simulation runs, the oscilloscope *Scope* displays the time-domain waveform of the oscillator. The *XY Graph* shows the phase diagram of the oscillator, which is used to analyze and compare the properties of the vibrator in different environments and different parameters.

The value of the k is set to 0.5, and the amplitude F of the Duffing system cycle is gradually increased from a certain value. When running the Simulink module, we can find that the Duffing system will go through three system states, namely chaotic state, critical state (chaotic state transition to large-scale periodic state) and large-scale periodic state. After simulation experiments, the output state of the system can be seen equivalently from the x output waveform of the system. The specific system output state phase diagram and the time domain waveform of x are shown in Figs. 2, 3 and 4.

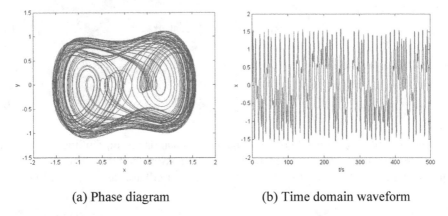

(a) Phase diagram   (b) Time domain waveform

Fig. 2. Phase diagram and time domain waveform in chaos state $(F = 0.7)$

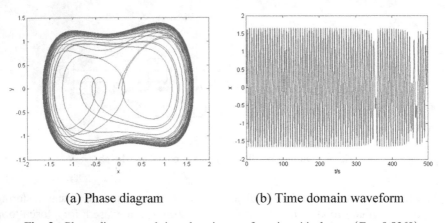

(a) Phase diagram   (b) Time domain waveform

Fig. 3. Phase diagram and time domain waveform in critical state $(F = 0.8260)$

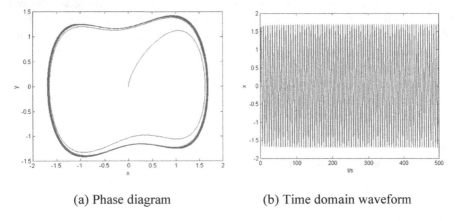

(a) Phase diagram   (b) Time domain waveform

Fig. 4. Phase diagram and time domain waveform in large scale period state $(F = 0.83)$

In summary, the signal detection method utilizing Duffing oscillator is make the system stay at the critical state, when the weak signal input to the right side of the Duffing equation, the amplitude of driving force will increases to higher than the critical value, the oscillator will enter the large-scale periodic state; If there is no signal input, the amplitude of the driving force is still at the critical value, the oscillator state remains as it is, so that it can distinguish whether there is a weak signal whose frequency similar to the oscillator frequency or not, then detect the weak signal.

3 Spectrum Overlapping Signal Detection Through System

Frequency shift keying (FSK) is use the variation of carrier frequency to transfer digital information, the carrier frequency changed between the binary baseband signal frequency points, the expression of 2FSK signal is as follow:

$$e_{2FSK}(t) = \left[\sum_n a_n g(t - nT_s)\right] \cos \omega_1 t + \left[\sum_n \bar{a}_n g(t - nT_s)\right] \cos \omega_2 t \tag{7}$$

Where, $\omega_1 = 2\pi f_1$, $\omega_2 = 2\pi f_2$, $\bar{a}_n$ is the reverse code of a_n, $g(t)$ is single rectangular pulse. The detection of the 2FSK signal utilizing Duffing oscillator is based on the sensitivity of the chaotic system to the specific frequency weak signal. The phase change of the system output can be used as a standard for the existence of the special signal that to be detected, then output the code. But in the actual transmission process, it can't be avoided to exist the error code under the influence of communication channel. In the communication system, there are two main factors of error code, one is the channel additive noise, the other one is inter-symbol interference. Using the chaotic system as the signal detection tool, the additive noise of the channel does not affect the system discrimination, it is only changed the trajectory of the chaotic state, the oscillator is still in the chaotic state; however, the inter-symbol interference became the core reason that affects whether the receiver can get the correct information directly.

The 2FSK signal with inter-symbol interference is detected by using an array of two Duffing oscillators. When the carrier frequency is the same as the frequency of the system, the corresponding Duffing oscillator will be changed from the initial chaotic state to the large-scale periodic state, and the Duffing oscillator with different frequencies will still be in the chaotic state. Thus, it is judged whether or not the received symbol signal is "1" or "0" based on the state of the system in each symbol period. Due to the other factors such as communication channel, the number n code transmits delay, when the number $n + 1$ symbol arrives at the receiver, it contains information of the both frequency f_1 and f_2, so at this moment, the oscillator 1 and oscillator 2 will both be changed the chaotic state to large-scale periodic state. Further, the number n code can be obtained according to the time at which the oscillator state changes, thereby solving the problem of inter-symbol interference. The flow chart of the principle as shown in Fig. 5.

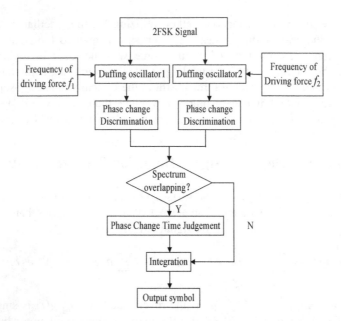

Fig. 5. The flow chart of the principle of 2FSK detection utilizing Duffing oscillator array

4 Simulation

According to the flow chart of the previous section, we can know that the step of detecting the spectrum overlapping 2FSK signal based on Duffing oscillator is:

Step 1: Set the 2FSK signal as shown in Fig. 6.

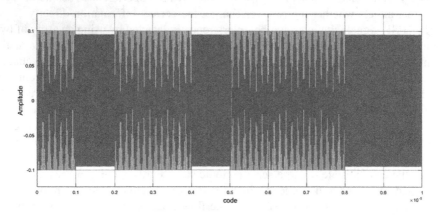

Fig. 6. The waveform of 2FSK signal

The binary symbol of 2FSK signal to be transmitted is [1,0,1,1,0,1,1,1,0,0], where $\omega_1 = 2\pi f_1$, $\omega_2 = 2\pi f_2$, $f_2 = 10 f_1$, f_1 represents signal "1" and f_2 represents "0".

Step 2: Set the frequency of driving force in oscillator 1 and the oscillator 2 is f_1 and f_2, meanwhile, set its amplitude is the amplitude of critical state. Then input 2FSK signal to the duffing oscillator system. When the 2FSK signal input to the oscillator 1 and oscillator 2, the corresponding signal waveform and time domain waveform of output are shown in Figs. 7 and 8.

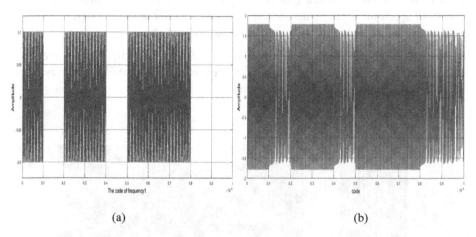

(a)   (b)

Fig. 7. (a) The waveform of transmission code of f_1 and (b) the time domain waveform of duffing oscillator1

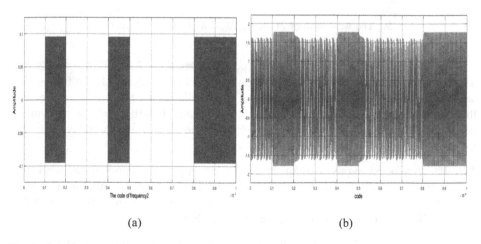

(a)   (b)

Fig. 8. (a) The waveform of transmission code of f_2 and (b) the time domain waveform of duffing oscillator2

When the frequency of 2FSK signal is the same as the frequency of the oscillator, in this symbol period, the amplitude of the oscillator becomes larger than the critical state, the oscillator enters the large-scale periodic state, however, the oscillator whose frequency is different form the oscillator frequency is still in chaotic state.

Step 3: Due to the delay caused by the communication channel, the two adjacent signals in the transmission process are overlapped. There are two cases in the spectrum overlapping in 2FSK signal transmission. One is that the adjacent symbols of spectrum overlapping code are same, at this point the integration signal is not continuous, moreover the state of oscillator changed only one. The other one is that the adjacent symbols of spectrum overlapping code are not same, at this time, although the receive signal not continuous, but the two oscillators both changed.

[1]. For example, the 2FSK binary symbol is [1,0,1,1,0,1,1,1,0,0], when the third symbol "1" and the fourth symbol "1" generate inter-symbol interference, the received signal is discontinuous. As shown in Fig. 9.

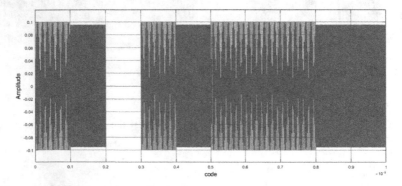

Fig. 9. The waveform of 2FSK signal with inter-symbol interference

The oscillator state of the third symbol period of oscillator 1 is still in chaotic state. The received signal and its time-domain waveforms of f_1 and f_2 are shown in Figs. 10 and 11. It can be seen that the system state of two oscillators are not changed during the third symbol period, while only one oscillator changed during the fourth symbol period. It can be concluded that the third symbol is the same as the fourth symbol, and the two symbols of spectrum overlapping occurs.

[2]. If the adjacent symbols of spectrum overlapping code are not same, when the second symbol "0" and the third symbol "1" generate inter-symbol interference, the received signal is not continuous. The output time domain waveforms of the oscillator 1 and the oscillator 2 are shown in Fig. 12.

It can be seen that the two oscillators are not changed during the second symbol period and both are changed during the third symbol period. It can be concluded that the second symbol is not the same as the third symbol, and the two symbols of spectrum overlapping occurs.

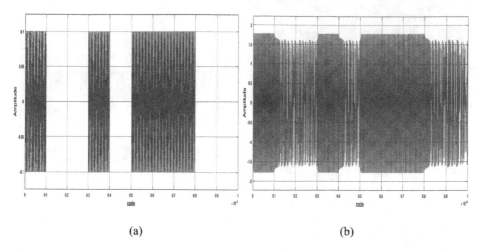

(a)   (b)

Fig. 10. (a) The waveform of received signal code of f_1 and (b) the time domain waveform of duffing oscillator1

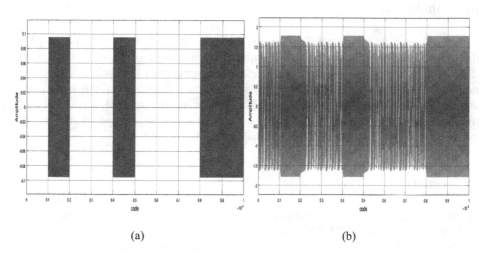

(a)   (b)

Fig. 11. (a) The waveform of received signal code of f_2 and (b) the time domain waveform of duffing oscillator2

Step 4: According to the time point at which the oscillator changed, the exact value of the two symbols can be discriminated, and the signal detection is completed.

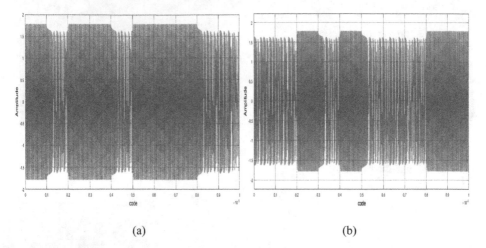

(a)   (b)

Fig. 12. The time domain waveform of duffing oscillator1 (a) and oscillator2 (b)

5 Conclusions

Compared with the traditional 2FSK signal detection method, the method proposed in this paper can solve the spectrum overlapping phenomenon of adjacent symbols in 2FSK caused by delay effectively. Through the research and simulation of this phenomenon, we improve the duffing oscillator accurate detection of the modulation signal. At the same time, it is proposed to determine the symbol when spectrum overlapping occurs according to the time point of the state change of the chaotic system, so as to determine the 2FSK signal further accurately.

References

1. Zhang, S., Rui, G.-S.: Chaotic detector for BPSK signals in very low SNR conditions. Int. J. Bifurc. Chaos **22**(6), 223–225 (2012)
2. Poor, H.V.: An Introduction to Signal Detection and Estimation. Springer Science & Business Media, Heidelberg (2013)
3. Huang, C., Zhou, Y.: Cyclic correlation detection method applied to weak LFM signals in multiplicative noise. In: 2004 7th International Conference on Signal Processing: Proceedings ICSP 2004, vol. 1, pp. 5–8 (2004)
4. Nan, L.I., Fu, L.I.U.: Three nonlinear methods of weak signal detection. Electr. Power Autom. Equip. **4**, 021 (2008)
5. Lai, Z., Leng, Y., Sun, J.: Weak characteristic signal detection based on scale transformation of duffing oscillator. Acta Phys. Sin. **61**(5), 050503-1–050503-9 (2012)
6. Wang, G., He, S.: A quantitative study on detection and estimation of weak signal using chaotic duffing oscillators. IEEE Trans. Circuits Syst. **50**(7), 945–953 (2003)
7. Qin, H.L., Sun, X.L., Jin, T.: Weak GPS signal detect algorithm based on duffing chaos system. In: IEEE 10th International Conference on Signal Processing, Beijing, p. 2501 (2010)

An Efficient DOA Estimation and Network Sorting Algorithm for Multi-FH Signals

Xin-yong Yu[1(✉)], Ying Guo[1,2], Kun-feng Zhang[1], Lei Li[1],
Hong-guang Li[1], and Ping Sui[1]

[1] Information and Navigation College, Air Force Engineering University,
Xi'an 710077, China
yuxinyong99@163.com
[2] Science and Technology on Information Transmission and Dissemination
in Communication Networks Laboratory, Shijiazhuang 050081, China

Abstract. In order to use the spatial characteristic parameter of frequency hopping (FH) signal to realize FH sorting, an efficient FH signal DOA estimation algorithm is proposed in this paper. Firstly, the effective hop of signal is extracted from time and frequency domain and the spatial-time-frequency distribution matrix of this hop is established; then the SCMUSIC spatial spectrum is constructed using descending dimension method of noise sub-space based on MUSIC algorithm; finally we realize fast DOA estimation through half-spectrum searching so that FH sorting can be achieved using DOA information. Theoretical analysis and simulation results show that this algorithm has good effectiveness and estimation performance.

Keywords: Frequency-hopping (FH) · SCMUSIC spatial spectrum
Direction of arrival (DOA) · Morphological filtering · Network sorting

1 Introduction

Frequency-hopping signals have been widely used in military communication because of their characteristics of good security, strong anti-interference ability, low probability of interception and strong networking capability [1]. How to realize the correct network sorting for multiple frequency hopping signals with different frequency hopping parameters without prior knowledge is the essential issue of frequency hopping signal reconnaissance and countermeasure.

Signal direction of arrival (DOA) plays an important role in the separation of frequency hopping signals. In [2, 3], a novel space-time approach is developed for estimating the DOA of FH signals. However, it is only applicable to over-determined conditions; Electromagnetic vector antenna is used to estimate the DOA of frequency hopping signal in [4], but this approach can only deal with a limited number of frequency hopping signals; The concept of spatial-time-frequency was first proposed

This work was supported by the National Natural Science Foundation of China under Grant 64601500.

by Belouchrani in [5, 6], and then it was used in linear frequency modulation signal estimation and blind source signal separation; Chen [7] introduces the space-time-frequency analytical method into the FH signals by constructing the spatial-time-frequency distribution matrix of each hop and using the MUSIC algorithm, however this approach is very complicated; In [8, 9], root-music approach is proposed in order to replace the MUSIC algorithm, which reduced the complexity of the MUSIC algorithm, but the algorithm has high demand for the array and is not suitable for engineering applications; A spatial-polarimetric-time-frequency distributions and ESPRIT algorithm was proposed in [10, 11], to estimate DOA and polarization of FH signals, however the ESPRIT algorithm needs parameter matching, which increases the complexity of the algorithm.

Based on the above issues, the STFD&SCMUSIC algorithm is proposed in this paper to estimate DOA of multiple FH signals. Firstly, the effective hop of signal from time and frequency domain is extracted and the spatial-time-frequency distribution matrix of this hop is established; Then we introduce a conjugate noise subspace to construct the spatial spectral function of SCMUSIC algorithm based on the idea of noise subspace reduction, and realize the estimation of multi-frequency hopping signal; Finally, achieve FH signal network sorting according to the estimated DOA information using clustering algorithm; At the same time, the time-frequency map is amended via morphological filtering method in order to enhance performance of low SNR algorithm. The proposed method can not only adapt to different network information, but also can greatly reduce the complexity of the original algorithm.

2   Snapshots Model of FH Signal

Suppose that the hopping period of FH signal $s_n(t)$ is T_n, there are K hops within time of Δt in total. ω_{nk} and φ_{nk} represent the carrier frequency and initial phase of K-th hop respectively and the time of initial hop is Δt_{0n}. Then the $s_n(t)$ can be defined as:

$$s_n(t) = v_n(t) \sum_{k=0}^{K-1} \exp[j(\omega_{nk}t' + \varphi_{nk})] rect\left(\frac{t'}{T_n}\right) \tag{1}$$

Where $t' = t - (k-1)T_n - \Delta t_{0n}$, v_n stands for the complex envelope of base band of signal $s_n(t)$, $rect$ is the unit rectangle pulse.

Assume that N FH signals impinge instantaneously onto an M-element array, the FH signal is not correlated with the noise between the array, the bandwidth of the receiver $B = f_{max} - f_{min}$, and the elements spacing $d < c/2f_{max}$ (c denotes the speed of light), f_{max} and f_{min} denote the upper and lower limits of the receiver bandwidth respectively. Let the azimuth angle of the FH incident wave is θ and the wavelength is λ, then the steering vector of the array can be expressed as:

$$a(\theta) = [1, e^{-j2\pi d \sin\theta/\lambda}, \cdots, e^{-j2\pi(M-1)d \sin\theta/\lambda}]^T \tag{2}$$

The array flow pattern matrix can be formulated as:

$$A = [a_1, a_2, \cdots, a_N] \tag{3}$$

Assume the data vector is $X(t) = [x_1(t), x_2(t), \cdots, x_M(t)]^T$, noise vector is $N(t) = [n_1(t), n_2(t), \cdots n_M(t)]^T$, and FH source data vector is $S(t) = [s_1(t), s_2(t), \cdots s_N(t)]^T$, so snapshot vector model for array can be defined as:

$$X(t) = Y(t) + N(t) = AS(t) + N(t) \tag{4}$$

3   Construction of Space-Time-Frequency Matrix of FH Signal

The FH signal is a wide-band signal, and the carrier frequency of each hop jumps randomly, so the steering vector and manifold matrix of array jump with the carrier frequency, but it can be simplified as a narrow-band signal when studying one hop. So we establish the spatial-time-frequency distribution matrix of one effective hop of signal.

Cohen discrete time frequency distribution of signal $x_i(t)$ is expressed as:

$$D_{x_i x_i}(t,f) = \sum_{\tau=-\infty}^{\infty} \sum_{l=-\infty}^{\infty} \varphi(l,\tau) x_i(t+l+\tau) x_i^*(t+l-\tau) e^{-j4\pi f\tau} \tag{5}$$

Where $\varphi(l,\tau)$ denotes kernel function. So the discrete cross-time-frequency distribution of signal $x_i(t)$ and $x_j(t)$ can be defined as:

$$D_{x_i x_j}(t,f) = \sum_{\tau=-\infty}^{\infty} \sum_{l=-\infty}^{\infty} \varphi(l,\tau) x_i(t+l+\tau) x_j^*(t+l-\tau) e^{-j4\pi f\tau} \tag{6}$$

So the spatial-time-frequency distribution of signal $x(t)$ can be defined as:

$$D_{XX}(t,f) = \sum_{\tau=-\infty}^{\infty} \sum_{l=-\infty}^{\infty} \varphi(l,\tau) X(t+l+\tau) X^H(t+l-\tau) e^{-j4\pi f\tau} \tag{7}$$

Where $[D_{XX}(t,f)]_{ij} = D_{x_i x_j}(t,f)$ $(i,j = 1,2,\cdots,M)$ denotes the time frequency distribution between the output signals of each array. According to (4) and (7), the covariance matrix of time frequency domain can be written as:

$$E[D_{XX}(t,f)] = AD_{SS}(t,f)A^H + E[D_{NN}(t,f)] \tag{8}$$

4 DOA Estimation and Network Sorting

4.1 Construction of SCMUSIC Spatial Spectrum

Suppose that the number of sources for each hop is L. According to eigenvalue decomposition of array covariance matrix, we can obtain the signal subspace U_S whose dimensional is L, and noise subspace U_N whose dimensional is $M - L$. The spatial spectral function $P_{MUSIC}(\theta)$ of MUSIC algorithm can be expressed as:

$$P_{MUSIC}(\theta) = \frac{1}{a^H(\theta)U_N U_N^H a(\theta)} \tag{9}$$

According to $P_{MUSIC}(\theta)$, seek the spectrum peak in θ domain, and the extreme value θ of $P_{MUSIC}(\theta)$ is the desired DOA, however, the MUSIC algorithm needs to seek the spectrum peak in the whole field, which makes the algorithm too complex to be realized. We can get (10) from the orthogonal subspace principle, i.e.

$$a^H(\theta)U_N = O \tag{10}$$

According to the conjugate principle, (2) can be rewritten as:

$$a^*(\theta) = [1, e^{j2\pi d \sin\theta/\lambda}, \cdots, e^{j2\pi(M-1)d \sin\theta/\lambda}]^T = a(-\theta) \tag{11}$$

According to the relationship in formula (11), (13) can be rewritten as:

$$[a^H(\theta)U_N]^* = a^T(\theta)U_N^* = a^H(-\theta)U_N^* = O \tag{12}$$

Where U_N^* denotes the conjugate of noise subspace U_N. Suppose that the DOA of the signal source S is θ_s, from (12) we can see that there is a mirror source S' in the time-frequency domain whose DOA is $-\theta_s$, its steering vector is conjugated to steering vector of source S and orthogonal to U_N^*. Therefore, U_N^* is introduced into the spatial spectrum of MUSIC algorithm, and the spatial spectrum function $P_{SCMUSIC}(\theta)$ of SCMUSIC can be defined as:

$$P_{SCMUSIC}(\theta) = \frac{1}{a^H(\theta)U_N U_N^H U_N^* U_N^T a(\theta)} \tag{13}$$

From (13), $P_{SCMUSIC}(-\theta)$ can be defined as:

$$P_{SCMUSIC}(-\theta) = \frac{1}{a^H(-\theta)U_N U_N^H U_N^* U_N^T a(-\theta)} = P_{SCMUSIC}(\theta) \tag{14}$$

We can see from (14) that $P_{SCMUSIC}(\theta)$ is an even function. If the noise subspace is $U_N = [U_{N_1}, U_{N_2}, \cdots, U_{N_{M-L}}]$, we can obtain

$$U_N^H U_N^* = \begin{bmatrix} U_{N_1}^* \\ U_{N_2}^* \\ \vdots \\ U_{N_{M-L}}^* \end{bmatrix} [U_{N_1}^*, U_{N_2}^*, \cdots, U_{N_{M-L}}^*]$$

$$= \begin{bmatrix} U_{N_1}^* U_{N_1}^* & U_{N_1}^* U_{N_2}^* & \cdots & U_{N_1}^* U_{N_{M-L}}^* \\ U_{N_2}^* U_{N_1}^* & U_{N_2}^* U_{N_2}^* & \cdots & U_{N_2}^* U_{N_{M-L}}^* \\ \vdots & \vdots & \ddots & \vdots \\ U_{N_{M-L}}^* U_{N_1}^* & U_{N_{M-L}}^* U_{N_2}^* & \cdots & U_{N_{M-L}}^* U_{N_{M-L}}^* \end{bmatrix} \tag{15}$$

Substitute (15) into (13), we have:

$$P_{SCMUSIC}^{-1}(\theta) = [a^H(\theta)U_N](U_N^H U_N^*)[U_N^T a(\theta)]$$

$$= [a^H(\theta)U_{N_1} \quad a^H(\theta)U_{N_2} \quad \cdots \quad a^H(\theta)U_{N_{M-L}}] \begin{bmatrix} U_{N_1}^H U_{N_1}^* & U_{N_1}^H U_{N_2}^* & \cdots & U_{N_1}^H U_{N_{M-L}}^* \\ U_{N_2}^H U_{N_1}^* & U_{N_2}^H U_{N_2}^* & \cdots & U_{N_2}^H U_{N_{M-L}}^* \\ \vdots & \vdots & \ddots & \vdots \\ U_{N_{M-L}}^H U_{N_1}^* & U_{N_{M-L}}^H U_{N_2}^* & \cdots & U_{N_{M-L}}^H U_{N_{M-L}}^* \end{bmatrix} \tag{16}$$

$$\begin{bmatrix} U_{N_1}^T a(\theta) \\ U_{N_2}^T a(\theta) \\ \vdots \\ U_{N_{M-L}}^T a(\theta) \end{bmatrix} = \sum_{i=1}^{M-L}\sum_{j=1}^{M-L} [a^H(\theta)U_{N_i}](U_{N_i}^H U_{N_j}^*)[U_{N_j}^T a(\theta)]$$

From (10), (11) and (12), we can obtain:

$$\begin{cases} a^H(\theta_s)U_{N_i} = O \\ U_{N_j}^T a^H(-\theta_s) = [a^H(\theta_s)U_{N_i}]^T = O \end{cases} \tag{17}$$

Substitute (16) into (17), we have:

$$P_{SCMUSIC}^{-1}(\pm\theta_s) = 0 \quad (s = 1, 2, \cdots L) \tag{18}$$

Therefore, the spatial spectrum function $P_{SCMUSIC}(\theta)$ of the SCMUSIC algorithm takes the extremum at $\pm\theta_s$, so $P_{SCMUSIC}(\theta)$ is the symmetric spatial spectrum.

4.2 DOA Estimation and Network Sorting Based on SCMUSIC

When constructing the spatial spectral function $P_{SCMUSIC}(\theta)$, the noise subspace decreases with the L dimension, and the signal subspace increases with L dimension. Suppose that the new noise subspace is U_N', and new signal subspace is U_S'. So U_N' is the intersection of the noise subspace U_N with its conjugate U_N^*, and U_S' is the union of the signal subspace U_S with its conjugate U_S^*.

Let $R = I - U_N U_N^H U_N^* U_N^T$, the zero space of R is R°, (i.e. $R^\circ = \{x|Rx = O, x \in C^M\}$), the new noise subspace U_N' is the same as the zero space R° [12], i.e. $U_N' = R^\circ$.

We can obtain the Singular value decomposition for R:

$$R = UAV^H \tag{19}$$

Where $A = diag(\sigma_1, \sigma_2, \cdots, \sigma_M)$ is a diagonal matrix, and $V = [V_{2L} \ \tilde{V}_{M-2L}]$, V_{2L} is composed of $2L$ nonzero singular value of V, $\tilde{V}_{M-2L}$ is composed of $M - 2L$ zero singular value of V. We can see that $\tilde{V}_{M-2L}$ is the standard orthogonal basis of R°, the spatial spectrum function $P_{SCMUSIC}(\theta)$ can be rewritten as:

$$P_{SCMUSIC}(\theta) = \frac{1}{a^H(\theta)U_N U_N^H U_N^* U_N^T a(\theta)} = \frac{1}{a^H(\theta)\tilde{V}_{M-2L}\tilde{V}_{M-2L}^H a(\theta)} \tag{20}$$

According to (20), the half-spectral peak search is carried out in the θ domain to obtain the $\pm\theta_s$, which makes the extremum of $P_{SCMUSIC}(\theta)$. If $\|a^H(\theta_s)U_N\| \approx 0$, then θ_s is the required DOA, otherwise $-\theta_s$ is the required DOA. Therefore, the complexity of the full spectrum peak search in the MUSIC algorithm is reduced to half of that, which greatly reduces the complexity of the algorithm. Through the clustering analysis of the obtained DOA, the network sorting of multi-FH signal can be achieved.

5 Simulation and Analysis

There are three frequency hopping signal FH1, FH2, FH3 in the space, the incident angle is $\theta_1 = 20°$, $\theta_2 = 40°$, $\theta_3 = 60°$ respectively, the hopping period is 10 µs, the carrier frequency jumps between 0–0.5, the sampling rate is 100 MHz, the number of receiving array is 4 and the number of snapshots is 3000.

100 Monte Carlo experiments were performed, the root mean square error of DOA, and estimated success rate were used as the performance criterion. The root mean square error (RMSE) of DOA is defined as:

$$RMSE = \sqrt{\frac{1}{L}\sum_{i=1}^{L}(\tilde{\theta}_i - \theta)^2} \tag{21}$$

Where L denotes the source number, $\tilde{\theta}$ and θ denote the estimated and true values of the DOA respectively. The estimated success rate η is defined as:

$$\eta = N_1/N \tag{22}$$

Where N_1 denotes the number of successful experiments with DOA estimated deviations less than $2°$, and N denotes the total number of experiments.

5.1   Experiment 1

Figure 1 shows the performance comparison of DOA estimation in proposed algorithm and MUSIC algorithm when SNR increase from −10 dB to 30 dB.

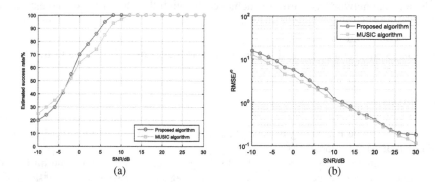

(a)   (b)

Fig. 1. Performance comparison of DOA estimation. (a) The success rate of experiment 1, (b) the RMSE of experiment 1

It can be seen from Fig. 1(a) that with the increase of SNR, the η of the proposed algorithm and the MUSIC algorithm are gradually increased; the RMSE are both gradually decreased; when SNR is greater than −2 dB, the η of the proposed algorithm is larger than the MUSIC algorithm, and when the SNR reaches 8 dB, the η of the proposed algorithm is close to 100% while the MUSIC algorithm needs to reach about 12 dB.

It can be seen from Fig. 1(b) that with the increase of SNR, the RMSE of the proposed algorithm and the MUSIC algorithm are gradually decreased; the RMSE of the proposed algorithm is slightly larger than MUSIC algorithm in general; When the SNR is greater than 15 dB, the RMSE of the proposed algorithm is close to the MUSIC algorithm.

5.2   Experiment 2

The time required for the DOA estimation of the two algorithms SNR increase from −8 dB to 20 dB is shown in Table 1.

Table 1. Comparison of two algorithms for DOA estimation time required (s)

Algorithm type	−8 dB	−4 dB	0 dB	4 dB	8 dB	12 dB	16 dB	20 dB
Proposed algorithm	6.413	6.214	6.804	6.384	6.501	6.320	6.449	6.423
MUSIC algorithm	12.908	12.840	12.857	12.807	12.856	12.874	12.783	13.196

It can be seen from Table 1 that the time required for the DOA estimation of the proposed algorithm is about 6.43 s, while the MUSIC needs 12.85 s. Therefore, the complexity of the MUSIC algorithm can be reduced to half of that.

6 Conclusion

The DOA information of the frequency hopping signals can be effectively used to complete multi-FH signal network sorting. The STFD&SCMUSIC algorithm is deduced and explained in this paper to estimate the DOA information of multiple FH signals, and the networking sorting is achieved through the clustering of the estimated DOA. Theoretical analysis and simulation results show that the proposed algorithm can reduce the computational complexity of the traditional MUSIC algorithm by 50% while the RMSE is equivalent to it and the estimated success rate is higher than it.

References

1. Sha, Z.C.: Online hop timing detection and frequency estimation of multiple FH signals. ETRI J. **35**(5), 748–756 (2013)
2. Liu, X., Sidiropoulos, N.D., Swami, A.: Blind high-resolution localization and tracking of multiple frequency hopped signals. J. IEEE Trans. Signal Process. **50**(4), 889–901 (2002)
3. Liu, X., Li, J., Ma, X.: An EM algorithm for blind hop timing estimation of multiple FH signals using an array system with bandwidth mismatch. J. IEEE Trans. Veh. Technol. **56**(5), 2545–2554 (2007)
4. Wong, K.T.: Blind beamforming/geolocation for wide band-FFHs with unknown hop-sequences. J IEEE Trans. Aerosp. Electr. Syst. **37**(1), 65–76 (2001)
5. Belouchrani, A., Amin, M.G.: Time-frequency MUSIC. J. IEEE Signal Process. Lett. **6**(5), 109–110 (1999)
6. Belouchrani, A., Amin, M.G.: Blind source separation based on time-frequency signal representations. J. IEEE Trans. Signal Process. **46**(11), 2888–2897 (1998)
7. Chen, L.H., Wang, Y.M., Zhang, E.Y.: Directions of arrival estimation for multicomponent frequency-hopping/direction sequence spread spectrum signals based on spatial time-frequency analysis. J. Signal Process. **25**(8), 1309–1313 (2009)
8. Chen, L.H.: Directions of arrival estimation for multicomponent frequency-hopping signals based on spatial time-frequency analysis. J. Syst. Eng. Electr. **33**(12), 2587–2592 (2011)
9. Zhang, D.W., Guo, Y., Qi, Z.S., et al.: Joint estimation algorithm of direction of arrival and polarization for multiple frequency-hopping signals. J. Electr. Inf. Technol. **37**(7), 1695–1701 (2015). (in Chinese)
10. Zhang, D., Guo, Y., Qi, Z., et al.: A joint estimation algorithm of multiple parameters for frequency hopping signals using spatial polarimetric time frequency distributions. J. Xi'an Jiaotong Univ. **49**(8), 17–23 (2015). (in Chinese)
11. Zhang, D., Guo, Y., Qi, Z., et al.: A joint estimation of 2D-DOA and polarization estimation for multiple frequency hopping signals. J. Xi'an Jiaotong Univ. **49**(8), 17–23 (2015)
12. Yan, F.G., Liu, S., Jin, M., et al.: Fast DOA estimation based on MUSIC symmetrical compressed spectrum. J. Syst. Eng. Electr. **34**(11), 2198–2202 (2012)

Study on Correlation Properties of Complementary Codes and the Design Constraints of Complementary Coded CDMA Systems

Siyue Sun[1(✉)], Guang Liang[1], and Kun Wang[2]

[1] Shanghai Engineering Center for Micro-satellites, Shanghai, China
sunsiyue@hit.edu.cn
[2] Huawei Technologies Co., Ltd., Shanghai, China

Abstract. Complementary codes (CCs) are a kind of two-dimensional spreading codes with ideal correlation properties to resolve the interference-limited problem of traditional CDMA systems. This paper proves the ideal correlation properties of CCs with non-integral chip delay under the definition of aperiodic correlation functions. The comparisons of CCs with traditional spreading codes on auto- and cross-correlation properties under different definitions of correlation functions will also present to verify the correctness of the proof work and to show that a CC-CDMA system is able to achieve MPI- and MAI-free communication owning to the proved ideal aperiodic correlation properties.

Keywords: Complementary codes · CDMA · Correlation properties Multiple access interference · Multi-path interference

1 Introduction

Owning to better anti-interference ability, higher frequency efficiency, higher security and lower radiation, Code Division Multiple Access (CDMA) with spread spectrum technique has been widely applied in wireless communication systems in the last 50 years, since its origins in the military field and navigation systems. Till now, CDMA is still the preferred multiple access technique in satellite communications, although it has lost competitiveness compared with Frequency Division Multiple Access (FDMA) in cellular systems [1,2].

Now, we are interested in exploring reasons for the decline and walk-off of CDMA from a technical perspective. It is well known that all existing CDMA-based 2-3G standards are interference-limited, particularly in the presence of multiple access interference (MAI) and multi-path interference (MPI). It has to be admitted that the immediate cause is the unsatisfactory properties of

This work was partly supported by National Nature Science Foundation Program of China (No. 61601295) and Shanghai Sailing Program (16YF1411000).

© ICST Institute for Computer Sciences, Social Informatics and Telecommunications Engineering 2018
X. Gu et al. (Eds.): MLICOM 2017, Part II, LNICST 227, pp. 61–70, 2018.
https://doi.org/10.1007/978-3-319-73447-7_8

the spreading sequences, while the primary cause is the uncoupled design of spreading codes with the systems and environment of communication.

The study on spreading codes for CDMA applications is a traditional research topic and many candidate codes have been found in the literature, however, they were generated and applied to the systems only based on the knowledge of seemly acceptable properties in their periodic auto- and cross-correlation functions. Due to the poor properties of spreading codes, a great deal of auxiliary sub-systems or techniques should be added to CDMA systems, such as the power control and multiuser detection, to mitigate the problems associated with the spreading codes, such as near-far effect, MAI and MPI, etc.

In order to bring CDMA back on track and to speed up the evolution of CDMA technologies, a possible solution has been proposed with the help of a new spreading technique based on complementary codes (CCs)[3]. Different from all traditional spreading sequences, the orthogonality of CCs is established based on a "flock" of element sequences jointly. As a result, ideal auto- and cross-correlation properties are realizable at the same time, while it never happens for any traditional spread sequences as proved by the Welch bound [4] and Sarwate bound [5].

In the work [6], we have present a survey on the history of CCs. However, a deeply studies on the correlation properties of CCs, especially with realistic communication environment has not been presented. Taking complete CCs [3] as a classic example, this paper proves the ideal correlation properties of CCs with non-integral chip delay under the definition of aperiodic correlation functions. Comparisons of CCs and traditional spreading codes on auto- and cross correlation properties are also presented in this paper to verify correctness of the proof work. Finally, an analysis on the detecting process of a complementary coded CDMA (CC-CDMA) system is presented with the design constraints of CC-CDMA systems concluded at the end of this paper.

2   Definitions and Code Construction

2.1   Definitions of CCs

Different from all traditional spreading sequences, the orthogonality of CCs is established based on a "flock" of element sequences jointly. A family of CCs, denoting as $\mathcal{C}(K, M, N)$, contents K CCs each with M element sequences. Due to its two-dimensional feature, let $\mathbf{C}^{(k)} = \{\mathbf{c}_m^{(k)}\}_{m=1}^M$ be a CC with M element sequences $\mathbf{c}_m^{(k)} = [c_{m,1}^{(k)}, c_{m,2}^{(k)}, \cdots, c_{m,N}^{(k)}]$. M is called flock size (which determines the number of element sequences used by the same user), and N is the code length. In this way, MN is the "congregated length" of a CC, and it determines the processing gain of the corresponding CC-CDMA system. For the CDMA application, K CCs are needed as signature codes for K users.

2.2   Construction of Complete Complementary Codes

Complete Complementary Codes (CCCs) [3] is one of the most popular CCs and this section gives the construction method of CCCs to facilitate the following proof and simulation work.

Let $\mathbf{A} = [a_{i,j}]$, $\mathbf{B} = [b_{i,j}]$, $\mathbf{D} = [d_{i,j}]$ be three $N \times N$ orthogonal matrices with $|a_{i,j}| = |b_{i,j}| = |d_{i,j}| = 1$, where $i, j \in \{1, 2, \cdots, N\}$. $\mathbf{a}_i = [a_{i,1}, a_{i,2}, \cdots, a_{i,N}]$ denotes i-th row of $\mathbf{A}$.

Step 1. Construct N sequences with length N^2, as

$$\mathbf{E}^{(k)} = [b_{k,1}\mathbf{a}_1, b_{k,2}\mathbf{a}_2, \cdots, b_{k,N}\mathbf{a}_N,] = [e_1^{(k)}, e_2^{(k)}, \cdots, e_{N^2}^{(k)}], \quad k = 1, 2, \cdots, N \tag{1}$$

Step 2. Construct m-th element sequence of k-th CCs in a family of CCCs using the above N sequences with matrix $\mathbf{D}$, as

$$\begin{aligned}
\mathbf{c}_m^{(k)} &= \big[d_{m,1}e_1^{(k)}, d_{m,2}e_2^{(k)}, \cdots, d_{m,N}e_N^{(k)}, d_{m,1}e_{N+1}^{(k)}, d_{m,2}e_{N+2}^{(k)}, \cdots, d_{m,N}e_{2N}^{(k)}, \\
&\qquad \cdots \quad d_{m,1}e_{N^2-N+1}^{(k)}, d_{m,2}e_{N^2-N+2}^{(k)}, \cdots, d_{m,N}e_{N^2}^{(k)}\big] \\
&= [c_{m,1}^{(k)}, c_{m,2}^{(k)}, \cdots, c_{m,N^2}^{(k)}], \qquad k, m = 1, 2, \cdots, N
\end{aligned} \tag{2}$$

The above construction method of a family CCCs $\mathcal{C}(N, N, N^2)$ can be visually described in Fig. 1.

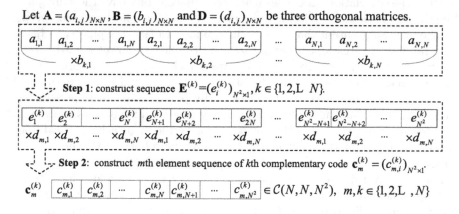

Fig. 1. The construction method of complete complementary codes.

3   Proof of Ideal Correlation Properties

3.1   Definitions of Complementary Correlation

Correlation properties of spreading codes are the key feature to effect the system performance of CDMA systems. Correlation function is usually used to describe

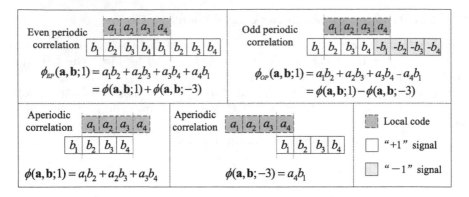

Fig. 2. Even periodic, odd periodic and aperiodic correlation functions and their relationships.

the correlation properties and three familiar definitions of correlation functions, even periodic, odd periodic and aperiodic correlation functions and their relationships, are visually described in Fig. 2.

When a and b is the same sequence, it is called auto-correlation function which is desired to be a delta function for a CDMA system to eliminate MPI, otherwise, it is called cross-correlation function which is desired to be a zero function for a CDMA system to eliminate MAI.

As can be seen from Fig. 2, the even periodic correlation function only describes the correlation properties when the adjacent bits have the same phase, while the odd periodic correlation function only describes the correlation properties when the adjacent bits have the positive phase. In fact, the phase of adjacent bits is random. Therefore, neither of them two is able to guarantee a MPI-free or MAI-free CDMA system, even though auto-correlation is a delta function and cross-correlation function is a zero function under the definitions of even or odd correlation functions. However, it can be easily proved that ideal aperiodic correlation properties are sufficient and necessary condition for both ideal even and odd correlation properties. Although it is more difficult to achieve ideal aperiodic correlation properties, but it is able to guarantee both MAI- and MPI-free in a CDMA system with any combination of adjacent bits.

Therefore, in this paper, the correlation properties of CCs are characterized by the complementary aperiodic correlation function which is calculated as the sum of the aperiodic correlation functions of all element sequences with the same delay δ, or

$$\rho(\mathbf{C}^{(k_1)}, \mathbf{C}^{(k_2)}; \delta) = \sum_{m=1}^{M} \phi(\mathbf{c}_m^{(k_1)}, \mathbf{c}_m^{(k_2)}; \delta) = \begin{cases} MN, & \delta = 0, k_1 = k_2 \\ 0, & \text{elsewhere} \end{cases} \quad (3)$$

where $\mathbf{C}^{(k_1)}, \mathbf{C}^{(k_2)} \in \mathcal{C}(K, M, N)$, $k_1, k_2 \in \{1, 2, \cdots, K\}$, and $\phi(\mathbf{c}_m^{(k_1)}, \mathbf{c}_m^{(k_2)}; \delta)$ is the aperiodic correlation function of $\mathbf{c}_m^{(k_1)}$ and $\mathbf{c}_m^{(k_2)}$. The ideal aperiodic correlation properties are described behind the second equal sign in (3).

3.2   Ideal Aperiodic Correlation Properties

The ideal aperiodic correlation properties of CCCs, as defined and constructed in the above sections, will be proved as followed.

As the construction method of CCCs, n-th chip of m-th element sequence of k-th CC can be expressed as

$$c_{m,n}^{(k)} = a_{x,y} b_{k,x} d_{m,y}, \quad k, m \in \{1, 2, \cdots, N\}, n \in \{1, 2, \cdots, N^2\} \tag{4}$$

where, $x = \lceil \frac{n}{N} \rceil, y = < n >_N + N\delta(< n >_N)$. The operator $< \cdot >_x$ means to calculate x-mod, $\lceil x \rceil$ denotes the ceil of x and $\delta(t)$ denotes a delta function.

According to (3), when $\delta \geq 0$, the complementary aperiodic correlation function of any two CCs in a family CCCs can be expressed as:

$$\rho(\mathbf{C}^{(k)}, \mathbf{C}^{(g)}; \delta) = \sum_{m=1}^{M} \sum_{n=1}^{N^2-\delta} c_{m,n}^{(k)} c_{m,n+\delta}^{(g)} = \sum_{m=1}^{M} \sum_{n=1}^{N^2-\delta} a_{x,y} b_{k,x} d_{m,y} a_{x',y'} b_{k,x'} d_{m,y'} \tag{5}$$

where $k, g \in \{1, 2, \cdots, N\}$, $x' = \lceil \frac{n+\delta}{N} \rceil$, $y' = < n+\delta >_N + N\delta(< n+\delta >_N)$.

It is easy to prove that when $i \neq i'$, $\sum_{j=1}^{N} a_{i,j} a_{i',j} = \sum_{j=1}^{N} b_{i,j} b_{i',j} = \sum_{j=1}^{N} d_{i,j} d_{i',j} = 0$.

Now we prove the ideal aperiodic correlation properties of CCCs in three cases:

(1) when $\delta \neq qN$ and $\delta \neq 0$, $q \in Z^+$, $y \neq y'$, we get

$$\rho(\mathbf{C}^{(k)}, \mathbf{C}^{(g)}; \delta) = \sum_{n=1}^{N^2-\delta} a_{x,y} a_{x',y'} b_{k,x} b_{g,x'} \sum_{m=1}^{M} d_{m,y} d_{m,y'} = 0 \tag{6}$$

(2) when $\delta = qN$, $y = y'$ and $x' = x + q$, we get

$$\begin{aligned}
\rho(\mathbf{C}^{(k)}, \mathbf{C}^{(g)}; \delta) &= \sum_{n=1}^{N^2-\delta} a_{x,y} a_{x',y} b_{k,x} b_{g,x'} \sum_{m=1}^{M} d_{m,y} d_{m,y} \\
&= N \sum_{x=1}^{N-q} \sum_{y=1}^{N} a_{x,y} a_{x+q,y} b_{k,x} b_{g,x'} \\
&= N \sum_{x=1}^{N-q} b_{k,x} b_{g,x+q} \sum_{y=1}^{N} a_{x,y} a_{x+q,y} \\
&= 0
\end{aligned} \tag{7}$$

(3) when $\delta = 0$, $y = y'$ and $x' = x$, we get

$$\begin{aligned}
\rho(\mathbf{C}^{(k)}, \mathbf{C}^{(g)}; \delta) &= \sum_{n=1}^{N^2} a_{x,y} a_{x,y} b_{k,x} b_{g,x} \sum_{m=1}^{M} d_{m,y} d_{m,y} \\
&= N \sum_{x=1}^{N} b_{k,x} b_{g,x} \sum_{y=1}^{N} a_{x,y} a_{x,y}
\end{aligned}$$

$$= N^2 \sum_{x=1}^{N} b_{k,x} b_{g,x}$$

$$= \begin{cases} N^3 & k = g \\ 0 & k \neq g \end{cases} \tag{8}$$

When $\delta < 0$, it is easy to prove that above conclusion is tenable. In conclusion, the CCCs constructed in Sect. 2.2 satisfies the ideal aperiodic correlation properties, as

$$\rho(\mathbf{C}^{(k)}, \mathbf{C}^{(g)}; \delta) = \begin{cases} N^3 & k = g, \delta = 0 \\ 0 & \text{elsewhere} \end{cases} \tag{9}$$

3.3   Ideal Correlation Properties with Non-integral Chip Delay

In practical CDMA systems, there exists non-integral chip delay between signals from multiple users or multiple paths. In this section, we will prove that the ideal aperiodic correlation properties of CCs still guarantee the interference-free communication even with non-integer chip-shift, taking the situation in Fig. 3 as an example.

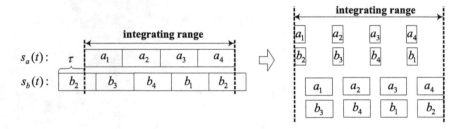

Fig. 3. The process of correlation with non-integral chip delay.

As shown in Fig. 3 the signal $s_a(t)$ and $s_b(t)$ are spread by the sequences $\mathbf{a} = [a_1, a_2, a_3, a_4]$ and $\mathbf{b} = [b_1, b_2, b_3, b_4]$ respectively. There exists chip delay τ between $s_a(t)$ and $s_b(t)$ due to multiple path transmission or asynchronous multi-user communication. When $\tau \neq q T_c$, $q \in Z^+$, T_c is the chip interval, we get

$$\int_0^{4T_c} s_a(t) s_b(t) dt = (T_c - \tau)(a_1 b_2 + a_2 b_3 + a_3 b_4 + a_4 b_1)$$

$$+ \tau(a_1 b_3 + a_2 b_4 + a_3 b_1 + a_4 b_2)$$

$$= (T_c - \tau)\phi_{EP}(\mathbf{a}, \mathbf{b}; 1) + \tau\phi_{EP}(\mathbf{a}, \mathbf{b}; 2)$$

$$= (T_c - \tau)[\phi(\mathbf{a}, \mathbf{b}; 1) + \phi(\mathbf{b}, \mathbf{a}; 3)] + \tau[\phi(\mathbf{a}, \mathbf{b}; 2) + \phi(\mathbf{b}, \mathbf{a}; 2)] \tag{10}$$

As shown in Fig. 3 and (10), correlation function with any non-integral chip delay equals to two correlation functions with integral chip delay. Therefore, the correlation properties of CCs with non-integral chip delay is still ideal owning to its ideal correlation properties with any integral chip delay.

4   Comparison on Correlation Properties with of Traditional Spreading Codes

In this section, taking a family of CCCs $\mathcal{C}(4,4,16)$ as an example, the simulated correlation properties of CCs are shown to verify correctness of the proof work. The congregated length of $\mathcal{C}(4,4,16)$ is 64, therefore, the correlation properties of Gold sequences with length 63 and Walsh codes with length 64 are also simulated.

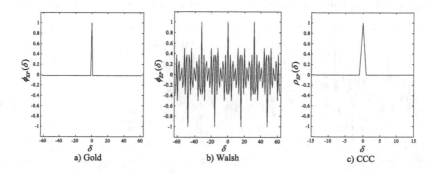

Fig. 4. Even periodic auto-correlation properties of different spreading codes.

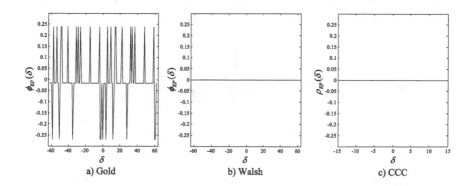

Fig. 5. Even periodic cross-correlation properties of different spreading codes.

The auto- and cross-correlation properties of the three spread codes under different definition of correlation functions: even periodic, odd periodic and aperiodic correlation functions are shown in Figs. 4, 5, 6, 7, 8 and 9 respectively. As can be seen from the simulated results, CCs are able to achieve ideal correlation properties (the auto-correlation is a delta function and the cross-correlation is a zero function) under all the three definitions. Gold code just achieves approximate

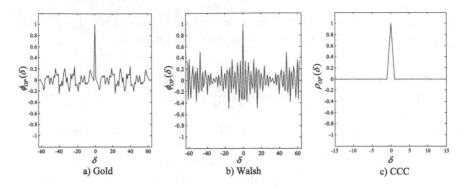

Fig. 6. Odd periodic auto-correlation properties of different spreading codes.

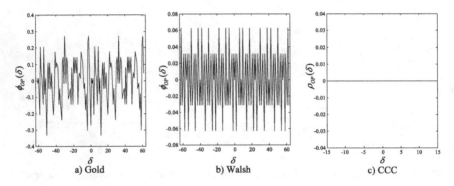

Fig. 7. Odd periodic cross-correlation properties of different spreading codes.

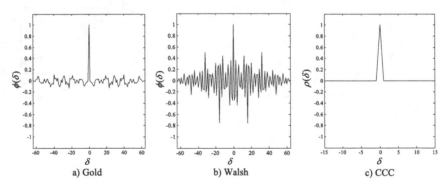

Fig. 8. Aperiodic auto-correlation properties of different spreading codes.

ideal auto-correlation property with even periodic correlation definition and Walsh code just achieves approximate ideal cross-correlation property with even periodic correlation definition. Therefore, a CDMA system with Gold code as its spreading sequence performs better under MPI, while it with Walsh code performs better under MPI. However, opposite phase between adjacent bits is

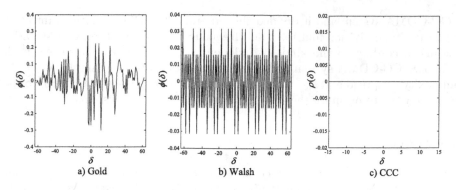

Fig. 9. Aperiodic cross-correlation properties of different spreading codes.

usual. In this situation, the non-zero sidelobe in odd periodic auto-correlation property of Gold, as shown in Fig. 6(a), will result in MPI, while the non-zero sidelobe in odd periodic cross-correlation property of Gold, as shown in Fig. 7(b), will result in MAI.

5   Conclusions and Discussions

This paper proves the ideal correlation properties of CCs with non-integral chip delay under the definition of aperiodic correlation functions. The above comparisons of CCs with traditional spreading codes on auto- and cross-correlation properties under different definitions of correlation functions verify the correctness of the proof work and show that a CC-CDMA system is able to achieve MPI- and MAI-free communication owning to the proved ideal aperiodic correlation properties.

However, due to the two-dimensional nature of CCs, the implementation of CC-CDMA system is a challenging work. In a direct sequence (DS) CC-CDMA system, each user will be allocated a particular CC from a code set as its signature code, and a user should spread its data with M element sequences of CC, respectively. In order to realize the spreading and de-spreading processes as definition of aperiodic correlation function, a CC-CDMA system must satisfies the following four conditions:

(1) M streams of spread signals of one user are required to be transmitted in M independent subchannels and separated at a receiver;

(2) each stream of spread signal should be de-spread using the right element sequence of the CC allocated to the user at a receiver;

(3) each stream of spread signal should be synchronized and therefore they have the same chip-delay;

(4) the de-spread signals with M element sequences should combined with equal gains.

Therefore, it's challenging to design and implement a CC-CDMA system. The work [7] has present a comprehensive survey of existing literature in the area of CC-CDMA system and it divided the existing CC-CDMA solutions into two categories: time division multiplex and frequency division multiplex CC-CDMA systems, according to the kinds of independent sub-channels. However, both of the two CC-CDMA system architecture have its problem on implementation complexity or spread and spectrum efficiency. Therefore, as for the future works, we will pursue to optimize the system deign of CC-CDMA systems.

References

1. Zhou, Y., Jiang, T., Huang, C., et al.: Peak-to-average power ratio reduction for OFDM/OQAM signals via alternative-signal method. IEEE Trans. Veh. Technol. **63**(1), 494–499 (2014)
2. Nguyen, H.C., de Carvalho, E., Prasad, R.: Multi-user interference cancellation schemes for carrier frequency offset compensation in uplink OFDMA. IEEE Trans. Wirel. Commun. **13**(3), 1164–1171 (2014)
3. Suehiro, N., Hatori, M.: N-shift cross-orthogonal sequences. IEEE Trans. Inf. Theory **34**(1), 143–146 (1988)
4. Welch, L.: Lower bounds on the maximum cross correlation of signals (corresp.). IEEE Trans. Inf. Theory **20**(3), 397–399 (1974)
5. Sarwate, D.V., Pursley, M.B.: Crosscorrelation properties of pseudorandom and related sequences. Proc. IEEE **68**(5), 593–619 (1980)
6. Sun, S.-Y., Chen, H.-H., Meng, W.: A survey of complementary coded wireless communications. IEEE Commun. Surv. Tutor. **17**(1), 52–69 (2015)
7. Sun, S., Han, S., Yu, Q., Meng, W., Li, C.: A survey of two kinds of complementary coded CDMA wireless communications. In: 2014 IEEE Global Communications Conference, pp. 468–472 (2014)

A Novel Structure Digital Receiver

Zijian Zhang[✉], Dongxuan He, and Yulei Nie

School of Information and Electronics,
Beijing Institute of Technology, Beijing, China
{2120150844, 2120130765, nieyulei}@bit.edu.cn

Abstract. This paper studies a novel structure digital receiver to demodulate signal with large frequency offset. When the carrier frequency offset is large, the matched filter will filter out part of the in-band signal, resulting in decrease of SNR and deterioration of BER. Different from traditional receiver structure, the novel receiver put a coarse frequency correction module before the matched filter, which will reduce the negative influence of matched filter under large frequency offset. Simulation results show that the new structure displays similar performance to the traditional structure under small frequency offset and great performance improvement when the frequency offset is large.

Keywords: Frequency offset · Matched filter

1 Introduction

The commonly used digital receiver structure is shown in Fig. 1. The baseband signal obtained after the digital down conversion and sampling rate conversion will pass through the matched filter, the timing module, the frequency synchronization module, phase synchronization module and the decoding module. After decoding we can get the bit stream [1]. Sometimes the received signal comes from different transmitters, so the feedback structure in reference [1, 2] can't be used. The structure shown in Fig. 1 has broader applicability.

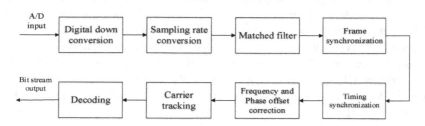

Fig. 1. The commonly used digital receiver structure

Matched filtering operation has two roles, the first is to ensure that the timing data has no inter symbol interference (ISI). The second is to make the SNR at the timing point has the largest value.

© ICST Institute for Computer Sciences, Social Informatics and Telecommunications Engineering 2018
X. Gu et al. (Eds.): MLICOM 2017, Part II, LNICST 227, pp. 71–78, 2018.
https://doi.org/10.1007/978-3-319-73447-7_9

The signal transmitter and receiver's crystal instability and other factors will cause the existence of the carrier frequency offset and phase offset. The purpose of the frequency offset correction module and the phase correction module is to estimate the frequency offset and phase offset on the signal and then compensate it respectively. Based on whether the pilot sequence is used, frequency offset estimation algorithm can be divided into DA (data aided) and NDA (non-data aided) estimation algorithm, which is the same in phase offset estimation.

For DA algorithm, The KAY algorithm [3], LR algorithm [4], Fitz algorithm [5] are commonly used. The KAY algorithm has larger frequency offset estimation range but lower accuracy compared to the LR algorithm. Therefore, in practical applications, we could first use the KAY algorithm to do a coarse frequency offset correction, and then use the LR algorithm to do a fine frequency offset correction. The signal after these two frequency corrections will only have a small residual frequency offset [6].

ML algorithm is commonly used in phase correction, after the phase compensation, there will be a small residual phase offset on the signal.

Usually a carrier tracking is performed to further reduce the residual frequency offset and residual phase offset, and tracking the carrier frequency and phase's changes, the PLL (phase-locked loop) is commonly used for tracking, the output of the PLL is the data symbols.

After decoding, the data symbols are transformed to bit stream.

With the increase of the carrier frequency offset, the receiver's performance will drop. To solve this problem, they use a feedback structure for more accurate digital down conversion in DVB-S2 [1], but if the received signal comes from different transmitters, this method can't be used. In this paper, a novel structure is proposed to solve the problem.

2 Performance Degradation Due to Frequency Offset

In this part, we discuss why the receiver's bit error rate increase significantly due to the large frequency offset.

Through the investigation of the receiver modules, it's found that when the carrier frequency offset is large, the matched filter will cause a great deterioration of the SNR.

This phenomenon can be visually observed in the frequency domain, as shown in Fig. 2, when the signal has no carrier frequency offset, all the signals filtered out by matched filter are out band noise, but when carrier frequency offset exists, part of the signal spectrum will appear outside the band of the matched filter, the filtering operation will filter out this part of signal spectrum, which will cause a significant deterioration of the SNR.

The Fig. 3 further demonstrates the phenomenon.

The E_S/N_0 value is fixed to 18 dB before match filtering. The SNR of the matched filter's output decreases gradually as the increase of normalized frequency offset, which will cause the rising of the system's BER.

We can also explain the problem through another perspective, for the sake of simplicity, we choose ideal low pass filter to be pulse-shaping filter and matched filter

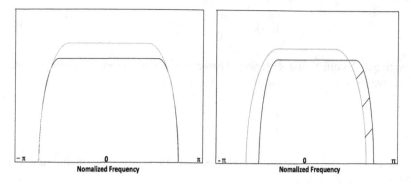

Fig. 2. Frequency domain of signal and matched filter. The red part represents the matched filter, the black part represents the signal. (Color figure online)

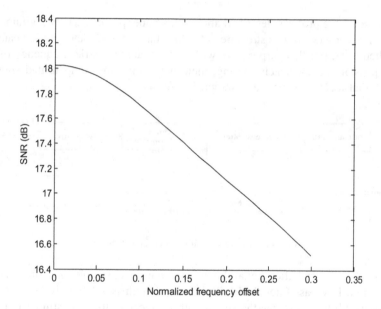

Fig. 3. The SNR of the match filter's output

(In practical applications we use root-raised cosine filter). If the total transfer function of baseband system satisfies the Nyquist first criterion:

$$\sum_i H(\frac{w + 2\pi}{T_s}) = T_s \quad |w| \leq \frac{\pi}{T_S},$$ (1)

the optimum sampling points have no ISI (inter symbol interfere). When there is no frequency offset, the transfer function is:

$$H(w) = \begin{cases} T_S & |w| \le \frac{\pi}{T_s} \\ 0 & \text{otherwise} \end{cases}, \tag{2}$$

which satisfies Nyquist first criterion. However, when carrier frequency exists, the transfer function is:

$$H(w) = \begin{cases} T_S & -\frac{\pi}{T_p} < w < \frac{\pi}{T_s} \quad T_p > T_s \\ 0 & \text{otherwise} \end{cases}, \tag{3}$$

Nyquist first criterion can't be satisfied anymore, thus producing the ISI and degrading the performance.

3   New Digital Receiver Structure

In order to solve the problem described above, this paper presents a new digital receiver structure. The core idea of this structure is to eliminate the SNR deterioration caused by the matched filter. For this purpose, we will compensate the carrier frequency offset as much as possible before match filtering, then match filter the compensated signal.

The digital receiver structure is shown in Fig. 4:

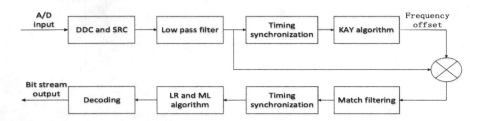

Fig. 4. The new digital receiver structure

The baseband signal after digital down conversion and sample rate conversion will pass through a low pass filter (LPF), whose bandwidth is sufficiently larger than the signal bandwidth to ensure that the signal with frequency offset can still lie in the pass band of the low pass filter, which ensures that the spectrum of the signal will not be filtered by the low-pass filter and out-of-band noise is filtered as much as possible. Commonly, the passband bandwidth can be set as the sum of the signal bandwidth and the maximal frequency offset.

The KAY algorithm is used to calculate the carrier frequency offset first due to its large estimates range. Before the frequency offset estimation, we use the OM timing algorithm to get the optimum sample point which is needed by the KAY algorithm. Since we use a LPF instead of matched filter, the best sample point is less accurate and has more noise, but it is enough for coarse frequency offset estimation.

We use the frequency offset calculated by the KAY algorithm to compensate the output signal of the low-pass filter. This operation aims to move the spectral center of the signal to zero frequency as much as possible. And then we use the compensated signal to do the match filtering, which will not filter out the spectrum of the signal anymore, thus further enhancing the SNR.

After match filtering, we do timing operation and carrier recovery with higher precision to get the data symbols. We use the OM timing algorithm to do the timing operation, the LR algorithm to do the frequency offset compensation with higher accuracy and ML algorithm to compensate the phase offset. Finally we get the bit stream.

The Fig. 5 shows the SNR curve of the match filter's output.

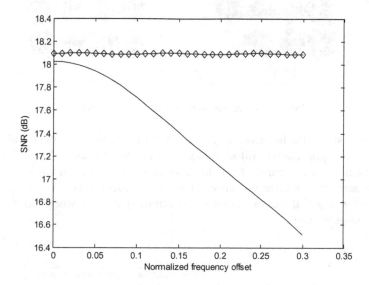

Fig. 5. The SNR of the match filter's output

The E_S/N_0 value of the system's input is fixed to 18 dB and the normalized carrier frequency offset changes. In this figure the ordinary line represents the SNR in the old structure receiver and the line with diamond marks represents the SNR in the new structure receiver. Compared with the old structure, we can see the SNR in the new structure has been greatly improved, and the receiver with new structure can work under a larger carrier frequency offset. Thus the performance of the new structure digital receiver can be significantly improved.

4   Simulation Results

The simulation results compare the performance of the two different structures of digital receiver. Test signal is 16QAM. Each frame contains the unique word portion and the data portion. The channel is an additive white Gaussian noise channel.

When the normalized frequency offset between the transceivers is fixed to 0.07 [7], E_S/N_0 is set to 18 dB, the output constellation of the two kinds of digital receivers is

shown in Fig. 6. It can be seen in the case of relatively small frequency offset, constellation quality improves slightly.

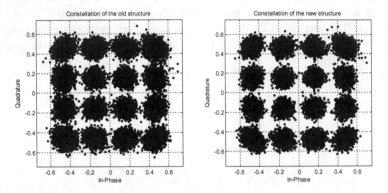

Fig. 6. The constellation of the two receivers.

The Fig. 7 shows the bit error rate curve of the two receivers. For convenience, we
use the hard decision method [8] to demodulate the constellation. The ordinary line
indicates the bit error rate curve of the old structure receiver, and the line with diamond
marks represents the bit error rate curve of the new structure receiver. It can be seen
that the performance of the two receivers is almost the same when the normalized
frequency offset is small.

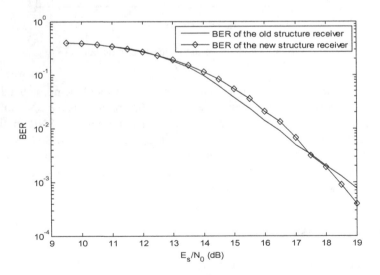

Fig. 7. The BER of the two receivers.

When the normalized frequency offset between the transceivers is increased to 0.15
while E_S/N_0 is still 18 dB, the constellation of the two receivers is shown in Fig. 8. It

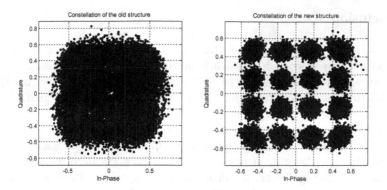

Fig. 8. The constellation of the two receivers.

can be seen that in the case of large frequency offset, the traditional structure receiver can't work normally, but the new structure receiver still shows perfect performance.

The Fig. 9 shows the bit error rate curves of these two different receivers. The ordinary line represents the bit error rate curve of the old structure receiver, and the line with diamond marks represents the bit error rate curve of the new structure receiver. We can see that when the frequency offset is relatively large, the new structure receiver's bit error rate has been significantly improved.

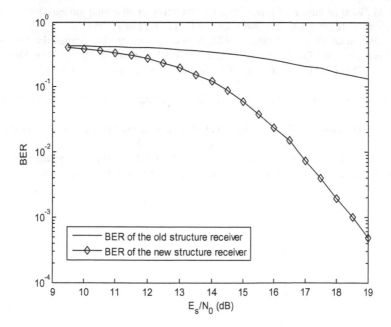

Fig. 9. The BER of the two receivers.

5 Conclusion

The new structure receiver shows similar performance to the old one when the frequency offset is small enough. But when the frequency offset increases, the match filtering operation will cause the damage to the signal spectrum and reduce the SNR, so that the bit error rate will increase. In this paper, a new structure of digital receiver is proposed. The front end uses a low-pass filter and a frequency compensation module to reduce the frequency offset, and then uses match filtering to improve the SNR, followed by carrier synchronization with higher accuracy. This new structure digital receiver can work normally under large frequency offset. When the normalized frequency offset is larger than 0.07, the performance will be better compared to the traditional digital receiver, while the cost is very little. The new structure receiver has a high value of engineering use.

References

1. Casini, E., Gaudenzi, R.D., Ginesi, A.: DVB-S2 modem algorithms design and performance over typical satellite channels. Int. J. Satell. Commun. Netw. **22**(3), 281–318 (2004)
2. Cioni, S., Corazza, G.E., Vanelli-Coralli, A.: Antenna diversity for DVB-S2 mobile services in railway environments. Int. J. Satell. Commun. Netw. **25**(5), 443–458 (2010)
3. Kay, S.: A fast and accurate single frequency estimator. IEEE Trans. Acoust. Speech Signal Process. **37**(12), 1987–1990 (1989)
4. Luise, M., Reggiannini, R.: Carrier frequency recovery in all-digital modems for burst-mode transmissions. IEEE Trans. Commun. **43**(2/3/4), 1169–1178 (1995)
5. Fitz, M.P.: Planar filtered techniques for burst mode carrier synchronization. In: 1991 Global Telecommunications Conference, GLOBECOM 1991. Countdown to the New Millennium. Featuring a Mini-Theme on: Personal Communications Services, vol. 1, pp. 365–369. IEEE (1992)
6. Mengali, U., D'Andrea, A.N.: Synchronization Techniques for Digital Receivers. Plenum Press, New York (1997)
7. Albertazzi, G., Cioni, S., Corazza, G.E., et al.: On the adaptive DVB-S2 physical layer: design and performance. IEEE Wirel. Commun. **12**(6), 62–68 (2005)
8. Baldi, M.: Low-density parity-check codes. QC-LDPC Code-Based Cryptography. SECE, pp. 5–21. Springer, Cham (2014). https://doi.org/10.1007/978-3-319-02556-8_2

Analysis of Passive Intermodulation Effect on OFDM Frame Synchronization

Yi Wang, Xiangyuan Bu[✉], Xiaozheng Gao, and Lu Tian

School of Information Science and Electronics, Beijing Institute of Technology,
No. 5 of South Zhong-guan-cun Avenue, Beijing 100081, China
wangyi9301@gmail.com, bxy@bit.edu.cn,
gxz6789@163.com, tianlu218@gmail.com

Abstract. Passive intermodulation can lead to a decrease in the performance of frame synchronization for the orthogonal-frequency-division multiplexing (OFDM) systems. In this paper, the Schmidl&Cox algorithm of frame synchronization is simplified by difference calculation to avoid overly complicated analysis. The statistical properties of time metric function in the presence of passive intermodulation interference are obtained by Gaussian distribution fitting. The closed form of false and missing detection probabilities are derived to evaluate the frame synchronization performance. Finally, simulations are conducted to demonstrate the validity of the analysis results.

Keywords: Passive intermodulation · Frame synchronization
Orthogonal-frequency-division multiplexing (OFDM) · Statistical properties

1 Introduction

As the demand of propagation rate rises, multicarrier modulation has been used in wireless communication systems. The orthogonal-frequency-division multiplexing (OFDM) system is one of the most successful implementations of multicarrier modulation. But when the system transmits the multiple carriers, the carriers which pass through the passive device can generate the combination products of the multi-frequencies due to nonlinearity [1]. Thus the passive intermodulation (PIM) products are formed. PIM has become a threat for these multicarrier systems, especially for the OFDM system with high transmitting power [2, 3].

PIM can lead to a degradation of the sensitive receivers when falling into the receiving band. The degradation in the performance of the communication systems can be quantified by bit error rate (BER) and synchronization probabilities. The PIM effects on the BER of M-PSK modulations were investigated in [4]. However, there is no complete model to characterize the PIM effect on synchronization. The OFDM frame synchronization is to find the start position of every frame in OFDM systems. The classical Schmidl&Cox synchronization algorithm was proposed for OFDM system by Schmidl and Cox in 1997 [5]. Based on the Schmidl&Cox algorithm, the influence of narrowband interference on timing synchronization was investigated by Marey and Steendam [6]. However, the broadband characteristic of PIM interference brings difficulty to the analysis on frame synchronization [7, 8].

© ICST Institute for Computer Sciences, Social Informatics and Telecommunications Engineering 2018
X. Gu et al. (Eds.): MLICOM 2017, Part II, LNICST 227, pp. 79–86, 2018.
https://doi.org/10.1007/978-3-319-73447-7_10

Motivated by the above observations, the frame synchronization performance in the presence of PIM using the simplified Schmidl&Cox method was investigated in this paper. To avoid complicated calculation of analysis, the Schmidl&Cox algorithm is simplified by the difference calculation at first. Among various models of PIM, the non-analytic behavioral model proposed by Jacques Sombrin is used for its simple and effective property [9]. The statistical properties of the time metric function falling into or outside the cyclic prefix (CP) are analyzed in presence of PIM. According to the predefined decision threshold, the false and missing detection probabilities analysis of OFDM systems interfered by PIM are obtained. Simulation results demonstrate the validity of the approximations with the analysis.

This paper is organized as follows. In Sect. 2, we describe the simplified Schmidl&Cox algorithm. In Sect. 3, the statistical properties of the time metric function are analyzed under the influence of PIM. We discuss the false and missing detection probabilities of OFDM systems in presence of PIM in Sect. 4. Finally conclusions are given in Sect. 5.

2   Frame Synchronization Algorithm of OFDM Systems

Here we adopt the typical frame structure of the OFDM system from the Schmidl&Cox algorithm, which uses two training sequences as the frame header [5]. It is shown in Fig. 1. Due to the fact that the first training symbol is used for frame synchronization at the receiver [5], we only focus on the first training symbol in this paper.

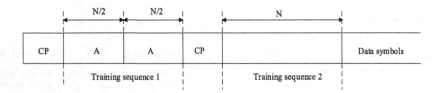

Fig. 1. The typical frame structure of OFDM in Schmidl&Cox algorithm

The first training symbol can transmit sequence PN_1 on the even frequency, and transmit "0" on the odd frequency. Through IFFT, we can obtain the training symbols with two same parts in the time domain.

Since the characteristics of the training symbol in time domain basically remain unchanged at the receiver, we adopt difference method to find the start position of the frame based on the accordance of the two parts of the training symbol.

Define the time metric function as

$$M(d) = \frac{1}{N} \sum_{m=0}^{N/2-1} [r(d+m) - r(d+m+N/2)]^2 \tag{1}$$

where $r(d)$ is the demodulated signal sample, N is the length of training symbol, d is the time indication of the first sample in the N-sample window. The window slides in the time domain to search for the first training symbol.

The iteration of the time metric function is

$$M(d+1) = M(d) + \frac{1}{N}[r(d+N/2) - r(d+N)]^2 - \frac{1}{N}[r(d) - r(d+N/2)]^2 \quad (2)$$

When $M(d)$ is minimum, the start position d is correctly acquired. Therefore, the start position of the signal is estimated as

$$\hat{d} = \arg\min M(d). \quad (3)$$

3 Statistical Properties of Time Metric in the Presence of Passive Intermodulation

The statistical properties of the time metric function in presence of PIM are the basis for analyzing the false or missing probability of the OFDM system. If the locating start position of the signal is behind the actual start position, it will inevitably introduce intersymbol interference (ISI). On the contrary, if the locating position falls into CP, the data can also be correctly received after amendment [10]. Therefore, it is generally considered that the frame can be correctly grabbed when falling into CP. Motivated by the above observations, we will elaborate the statistical properties of time metric function in two cases, i.e., falling into and not falling into CP.

If s_m is the sampled useful signal with the variance σ_s^2, and z_m is the PIM interference with the variance σ_z^2, the signal at the receiver can be expressed as $r_m = s_m + z_m$. The signal-to-interference power ratio SIR at the receiver is σ_s^2/σ_z^2.

For convenience, we define $(r_{d+m} - r_{d+m+N/2})^2$ as P_m.

3.1 Statistical Analysis of Time Metric Function Falling into Cyclic Prefix

When falling into the CP, P_m is denoted as P_{m_in}, and it only contains PIM interference z_m, then the time metric function $M(d_{in})$ can be expressed as

$$M(d_{in}) = \frac{1}{N} \sum_{m=0}^{N/2-1} P_{m\_in} = \frac{1}{N} \sum_{m=0}^{N/2-1} [z_{d+m} - z_{d+m+N/2}]^2 \quad (4)$$

According to the CLT, when N is larger, the time metric function $M(d_{in})$ follows the Gaussian distribution. Assuming that each sampling point is independent of each other and the mean value is 0, the mean of P_{m_in} is $2\sigma_z^2$ and the variance is

$$\text{var}(P_{m\_in}) = E[P^2_{m\_in}] - E^2[P_{m\_in}] = E[(z_{din+m} - z_{din+m+N/2})^4] - 4\sigma^4_z$$
$$= 2E[z^4_m] + 6E^2[z^2_m] - 2\sigma^2_z = 2E[z^4_m] + 2\sigma^4_z \qquad (5)$$

We consider the PIM interference model by non-analytic model as $z_m = \alpha x_m |x_m|^{0.6}$ [9], where x_m is the input signal of passive device. In OFDM system, x_m can be verified by simulation to approximately follow the Laplace distribution. Considering $E[z^2_m] = \sigma^2_z$, we have $E[z^4_m] = E[\alpha^4 x^4_m |x_m|^{2.4}] \approx 20\sigma^4_z$ through high order moment of Laplace distribution. Then the variance of P_{m_in} is about 42 σ^4_z. By the CLT, $M(d_{in})$ follows the Gaussian distribution with the mean σ^2_z and the variance $21\sigma^4_z/N$.

Therefore, the probability density function (PDF) of $M(d_{in})$ can be given by

$$f_{Md\_in}(x) = \frac{1}{\sqrt{42\pi\sigma^2_z/N}} \exp\left(-\frac{N(x - \sigma^2_z)}{42\sigma^4_z}\right) \qquad (6)$$

When $N = 1024$ and $\sigma^2_z = 1$, the theoretical and simulated PDFs are shown in Fig. 2.

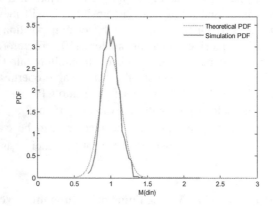

Fig. 2. Simulation and theoretical PDFs of $M(d)$ falling into the cyclic prefix

Figure 2 reflects that the PDF of $M(d_{in})$ is approximately consistent with the Gaussian distribution when falling into the CP. In general, the simulation and theoretical curves are both Gaussian distributions with mean value σ^2_z, but the variances exist little difference, which is caused by the approximation when solving $M(d_{in})$.

3.2   Statistical Analysis of Time Metric Functions Outside Cyclic Prefix

When the time metric function is outside the CP, P_m does not only contain the PIM interference z_m, but also includes the useful signal s_m. Replace P_m with P_{mout}, the time metric function $M(d_{out})$ can be written as

$$M(d_{out}) = \frac{1}{N} \sum_{m=0}^{N/2-1} P_{out} = \frac{1}{N} \sum_{m=0}^{N/2-1} \left((s_{d+m} + z_{d+m}) - (s_{d+m+N/2} + z_{d+m+N/2}) \right)^2 \quad (7)$$

Similar to Sect. 3.1, the time metric function $M(d_{out})$ follows Gaussian distribution when N is larger by CLT. Here we assume that each sampling point is independent of each other, the useful signal and PIM interference are independent of each other, and both the mean values of z_m and s_m are 0. Then the mean of P_{mout} is $2\sigma_s^2 + 2\sigma_z^2$.

Based on the fact that $E[s_m^2] = \sigma_s^2$, and s_m approximately follows Gaussian distribution, which has been verified by the simulation, the variance of P_{mout} can be given by

$$\begin{aligned} \text{var}(P_{mout}) &= E[P_{mout}^2] - E^2[P_{mout}] = 2E[r_m^4] + 6(\sigma_s^2 + \sigma_z^2)^2 - (2\sigma_s^2 + 2\sigma_z^2) \\ &\approx 8\sigma_s^4 + 16\sigma_s^2\sigma_z^2 + 42\sigma_z^4 \end{aligned} \quad (8)$$

$M(d_{out})$ follows the Gaussian distribution by CLT, and its mean is $\sigma_s^2 + \sigma_z^2$ and variance is $(4\sigma_s^4 + 8\sigma_s^2\sigma_z^2 + 21\sigma_z^4)/N$. Then the PDF of $M(d_{out})$ is

$$f_{Mdout}(x) = \frac{1}{\sqrt{2\pi/N \cdot (4\sigma_s^4 + 8\sigma_s^2\sigma_z^2 + 21\sigma_z^4)}} \exp\left(-\frac{N[x - (\sigma_s^2 + \sigma_z^2)]^2}{8\sigma_s^4 + 16\sigma_s^2\sigma_z^2 + 42\sigma_z^4} \right) \quad (9)$$

When $N = 1024$, $\sigma_s^2 = 1$, and $\sigma_z^2 = 1$ (that is, the SIR is 0 dB), the theoretical and simulated PDF are shown in Fig. 3.

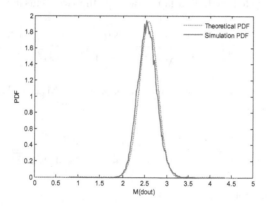

Fig. 3. Simulated and theoretical PDFs of $M(d)$ outside cyclic prefix

From Fig. 3, when $M(d)$ is outside the CP, the PDF is consistent with Gaussian distribution with the mean value $\sigma_s + \sigma_z$, the variance is also approximately equal. Therefore, we can conclude that the statistical property model for $M(d)$ is reasonable.

4 Probability of Missing/False Detection in Presence of Passive Intermodulation

During the process of frame capture, we predefined a threshold λ. When the time metric function $M(d)$ is larger than λ, we judge that the correct start position is not reached and the capture is not completed. Otherwise, we conclude that the correct start position has been found and the process of capture is completed.

From Eqs. (6) (9), the time metric functions $M\,(d_{in})$ and $M\,(d_{out})$ both follow the Gaussian distribution. When $M\,(d)$ is no more than the predefined threshold λ, but $M\,(d)$ does not fall into the CP, it causes a false detection [10]. The false probability can be expressed as

$$P_{false} = \int_{-\infty}^{\lambda} f_{Mout}(m)dm = \int_{-\infty}^{\lambda} \frac{1}{\sqrt{2\pi}\sigma_{out}} \exp\left[-\frac{(m-u_{out})^2}{2\sigma_{out}^2}\right]dm = \frac{1}{2} + \frac{1}{2}erf\left(\frac{\lambda-u_{out}}{\sqrt{2}\sigma_{out}}\right) \tag{10}$$

When $M\,(d)$ falls into the CP, but $M\,(d)$ is greater than the predefined threshold λ, a missing detection occurs [10]. The missing probability can be expressed as

$$P_{miss} = \int_{\lambda}^{\infty} f_{M\_in}(m)dm = \int_{\lambda}^{\infty} \frac{1}{\sqrt{2\pi}\sigma_{in}} \exp\left[-\frac{(m-u_{in})^2}{2\sigma_{in}^2}\right]dm = erfc\left(\frac{\lambda-u_{in}}{\sqrt{2}\sigma_{in}}\right) \tag{11}$$

Since $M\,(d_{in})$ and $M\,(d_{out})$ both follow the Gaussian distribution, the decision threshold λ is constructed by the variance ratio of the two Gaussian distributions.

$$\lambda = \sigma_z^2 \left[1 + \frac{SIR}{1 + \sqrt{(8SIR^2 + 16SIR + 42)/42}}\right] \tag{12}$$

For the sake of brevity, we normalize the power of PIM as 1. Therefore, the false detection probability is

$$P_{false} = \frac{1}{2} + \frac{1}{2}erf\left(\frac{\lambda - 1 - SIR}{\sqrt{(8SIR^2 + 16SIR + 42)/1024}}\right) \tag{13}$$

The missing detection probability is

$$P_{miss} = \frac{1}{2}erfc\left(\frac{\lambda - 1}{\sqrt{42/1024}}\right) \tag{14}$$

In the case of the influence of PIM, based on the synchronization method in Sect. 2 and the threshold λ predefined above, the false and missing detection probabilities are respectively shown in Figs. 4 and 5.

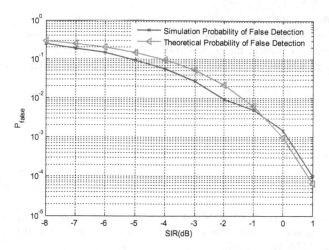

Fig. 4. The theoretical and simulated curves of false detection probability

In Figs. 4 and 5, the theoretical analysis is consistent with the simulation. And for the same false or missing detection probability, there is a less than 2 dB SIR gap between the theoretical and the simulation curves, which illustrates the rationality of the analysis model.

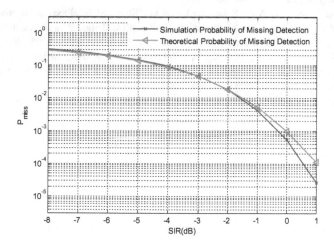

Fig. 5. The theoretical and simulated curves of missing detection probability

5   Conclusion

In this paper, we have analyzed the effects of PIM on the performance of OFDM frame synchronization. Based on the Schmidl&Cox algorithm, difference calculation method has been used to simplify analysis computation. The probabilities of both missing and false detections of a training sequence are derived by the statistical properties of time metric function. As the results shown, the theoretical analysis model of frame synchronization performance in the presence of PIM approximates the simulation result within 2 dB bias, which can provide useful guidance for the design of OFDM systems.

References

1. Lui, P.L.: Passive intermodulation interference in communication systems. Electron. Commun. Eng. J. **2**, 109–118 (1990)
2. Hoeber, F.C., Pollard, L.D., Nicholas, R.R.: Passive intermodulation product generation in high power communications satellites. In: The 11th Communication Satellite Systems Conference, pp. 361–374 (1986)
3. Liu, Y., Yu, R.M., Yong, J.X., Zhen, H.T.: Evaluation of passive intermodulation using full-wave frequency-domain method with nonlinear circuit model. IEEE Trans. Veh. Technol. **65**, 5754–5757 (2016)
4. Mudhafar, A., Hartnagel, H.: Bit error probability in the presence of passive intermodulation. J. IEEE Commun. Lett. **16**, 1145–1148 (2012)
5. Schmidl, T.M., Cox, D.C.: Robust frequency and timing synchronization for OFDM. J. IEEE Trans. Commun. **45**, 1613–1621 (1998)
6. Marey, M., Steendam, H.: Analysis of the narrowband interference effect on OFDM timing synchronization. J. IEEE Trans. Sig. Process. **55**, 4558–4566 (2007)
7. Zhao, P., Yang, D., Zhang, X.: Analysis of passive intermodulation generated by broadband signals. Electron. Lett. **52**, 564–566 (2015)
8. Kozlov, D.S., Shitvov, A.P., Schuchinsky, A.G., Steer, M.B.: Passive intermodulation of analog and digital signals on transmission lines with distributed nonlinearities: modelling and characterization. IEEE Trans. Microw. Theory Tech. **64**, 1383–1395 (2016)
9. Jacques, S., Geoffroy, S.P., Isabelle, A.: Relaxation of the multicarrier passive intermodulation specifications of antennas. In: 8th European Conference on Antennas and Propagation, pp. 1647–1650, The Hague (2014)
10. Goldsmith, A.: Wireless Communications. Cambridge University Press, Cambridge (2005)

Variable Tap-Length Multiuser Detector for Underwater Acoustic Communication

Zhiyong Liu[1,2(✉)], Yinghua Wang[1], and Yinyin Wang[1]

[1] School of Information and Electrical Engineering,
Harbin Institute of Technology, Weihai 264209, People's Republic of China
lzyhit@aliyun.com, xwc952684330@163.com,
WCUTEYY@163.com
[2] Key Laboratory of Science and Technology on Information Transmission
and Dissemination in Communication, Shijiazhuang 050081,
People's Republic of China

Abstract. In this paper, we propose a variable tap-length multiuser detector (VT-MUD) for multiuser underwater acoustic communications. The proposed scheme adopts interleave-division multiple access (IDMA) and dynamically adjusts tap-length based on the accumulated squared error (ASE) to achieve a good balance between performance and complexity. Simulation results demonstrate that the proposed scheme can converge to the optimum tap-length and achieve better bit error rate (BER) performance than traditional fixed tap-length multiuser detector (FT-MUD).

Keywords: Underwater acoustic communications
Interleave-division multiple access · Multiuser detector · Variable tap-length

1 Introduction

Underwater acoustic communication has become an important research hotspot for commercial and military applications. However, with the characteristics of limited bandwidth, enormous propagation delays and serious multipath effect, the underwater acoustic channel (UAC) brings great difficulties and challenges to reliable communications [1–3]. Furthermore, multiple-access interference (MAI) will exist in real underwater acoustic communication network because multiple users are present simultaneously in both time and frequency. To mitigate these effects, effective multiuser detection (MUD) scheme must be employed.

Interleave-division multiple access (IDMA) is considered as a special case of code-division multiple access (CDMA), which inherits many advantages from CDMA

The work was supported by Shandong Provincial Natural Science Foundation of China (ZR2 016FM02), National Natural Science Foundation of China (61201145), the Graduate Education and Teaching Reform Research Project in Harbin Institute of Technology (JGYJ-201625) and the Foundation of Key Laboratory of Communication Network Information Transmission and Dissemination.

and further improves performance and spectral efficiency with low computational complexity [4–6]. With the above characteristics, MUD schemes based on IDMA for underwater acoustic networks become the focus of studies in recent years. Two types' iterative receivers, employing adaptive decision feedback equalization (DFE) and conventional soft Rake for downlink multi-user underwater communications have been studied in [7]. It proved that the MUD strategy using DFE has performance improvements compared with Rake IDMA receiver. In order to remove MAI and ISI, two chip-level DFE-IDMA and DFE-CDMA receivers that utilize chip-level adaptive DFE are proposed in [8]. In [9], adaptive, chip-level, centralized decision feedback equalizer has been used to remove MAI and inter-symbol interference (ISI) for uplink IDMA shallow-water acoustic channels. The studies in [7–9] all employ fixed tap-length multiuser detection (FT-MUD). Unfortunately, the performance and computational complexity of the system are highly influenced by the tap-length of the filter. With too few taps, the system may not achieve well performance; in contrast, using too many taps, besides wasting computations, may increase the steady-state MSE [10]. There are no rules which can predict the optimal tap-length to obtain optimal performance of system for a specific UAC. Furthermore, for UAC, the optimum tap-length is likely to change with time. Hence, the existing FT-MUD strategies cannot accommodate to complicated UAC.

According to the above observations, a variable tap-length multiuser detector (VT-MUD) for underwater acoustic communication is presented based on IDMA in this paper. The proposed detector employs tap-length update algorithm that adaptively adjusts the number of taps for both complexity reduction and performance improvement.

2 System Model

Consider a typical multiuser underwater acoustic communication system with K simultaneous users, as shown in Fig. 1. Assume that IDMA is adopted. Spreader (repetition encoder) is same for all users and user-specific interleavers are used to distinguish users. The information bits $\mathbf{b}_k = [b_k(1), b_k(2), \cdots, b_k(N_b)]^T$ of the kth user are generated randomly, where N_b is the information bits frame length. The user's bits are spread by a simple repetitive scrambling sequence generating $\mathbf{c}_k = [c_k(1), c_k(2), \cdots, c_k(N)]^T$, where $N = N_b L_s$ is total number of chips, L_s represents the length

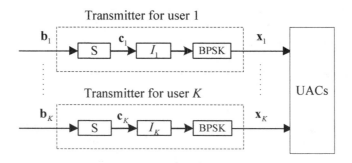

Fig. 1. Transmission system

of spreading sequence. Then the output of spreader is permuted by user-specific interleaver $I_k[\cdot]$. Finally, the output of $I_k[\cdot]$ is mapped to binary phase shift keying (BPSK) symbol

$$\mathbf{x}_k = [x_k(1), x_k(2), \cdots, x_k(N)]^T \qquad (1)$$

The received signal after transmission on the underwater acoustic channels (UACs), can be written as

$$r(n) = \sum_{k=1}^{K} \sqrt{P_k} h_k(n) * x_k(n) + v(n) \qquad (2)$$

where P_k is transmitted signal power of the kth user, $h_k(n)$ is underwater acoustic channel impulse response from the kth user to destination, which can be obtained by BELLHOP model [11]. $v(n)$ represents sample of the additive white Gaussian noise with zero mean and variance σ^2.

3   Variable Tap-Length Multiuser Detector

The proposed VT-MUD receiver after the acquisition stage is depicted in Fig. 2. MAI and ISI have been mitigated by jointly employing variable tap-length adaptive equalization and multiuser detection.

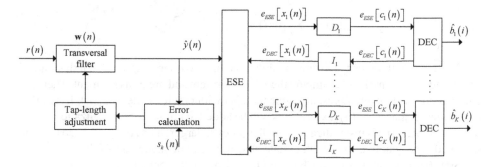

Fig. 2. The structure of VT-MUD

The VT-MUD scheme estimates the optimal tap-length by tap-length update algorithm and generates the estimation $\hat{y}(n)$ of the received signal. The key thought of tap-length adjustment is employing segmented equalization. Assuming that a M taps FIR filter is divided into L concatenated subfilters of P taps each ($M = LP$). Each part of the segmented equalization generates an estimate $\hat{y}_m(n)(1 \leq m \leq L)$ of the received data as

$$\hat{y}_m(n) = \mathbf{w}_m(n)\mathbf{u}(n) \qquad (3)$$

where $\mathbf{w}_m(n)$ is the tap-weight vectors of the filter, which is determined iteratively employing normalized least mean square (NLMS) algorithm [12] as

$$\mathbf{w}_m(n+1) = \mathbf{w}_m(n) + \frac{\mu}{\delta + \mathbf{u}^T(n)\mathbf{u}(n)} e_m(n)\mathbf{u}(n) \tag{4}$$

where μ $(0 < \mu < 2)$ is the step size factor, δ is a small correcting value to avoid numerical instabilities. $\mathbf{u}(n)$ is the observation vector

$$\mathbf{u}(n) = [r(n), r(n-1), \cdots r(n-l+1)] \tag{5}$$

where l is the tap-length of current moment. The corresponding error signal $e_m(n)$ for each segment is

$$e_m(n) = |s_k(n) - \hat{y}_m(n)| \tag{6}$$

where $s_k(n)$ is known training sequence. $e_m(n)$ can be used to compute mean square error (MSE) as

$$MSE_m(n) = E\left[|s_k(n) - \hat{y}_m(n)|^2\right] = \frac{\sum_{i=1}^{n} e_m(i)^2}{n} \tag{7}$$

In order to simplify the calculation, the accumulated squared error (ASE) is used to evaluate the performance of different segments. The ASE can be computed as

$$A_m(n) = \sum_{i=1}^{n} |s_k(i) - \hat{y}_m(i)|^2 = \sum_{i=1}^{n} e_m^2(i) \tag{8}$$

The tap-length update algorithm mainly contains two steps. Assume that there are F active segments. Firstly, we compute the ASE of present and previous segment. Then, we compare the ASE level of present segment $A_F(n)$ with previous one $A_{F-1}(n)$. If $A_F(n)$ is much smaller than $A_{F-1}(n)$, extra P taps will be added to improve the equalization effect. In contrast, if $A_F(n)$ is insignificantly smaller (or even larger) than $A_{F-1}(n)$, P taps will be removed. The adaptive tap-length update algorithm can be modeled as follows

Step (i): Estimation of ASE for present and previous segment

$$A_F(n) = \sum_{i=1}^{n} \gamma^{n-i} |s_k(i) - \hat{y}_F(i)|^2 \tag{9}$$

$$A_{F-1}(n) = \sum_{i=1}^{n} \gamma^{n-i} |s_k(i) - \hat{y}_{F-1}(i)|^2 \tag{10}$$

Step (ii): Adjustment of tap-length

$$\text{if } A_F(n) \leq \alpha_{up} A_{F-1}(n), \text{ add } P \text{ taps} \tag{11}$$

$$\text{if } A_F(n) \geq \alpha_{down} A_{F-1}(n), \text{ remove } P \text{ taps} \tag{12}$$

where γ is a forgetting factor ($\gamma \leq 1$), α_{up} and α_{down} need to satisfy $0 < \alpha_{up}, \alpha_{down} \leq 1$, $\alpha_{up} \leq \alpha_{down}$. The length of equalizer will change frequently if α_{up} is close to α_{down}.

The received signals $r(n)$ go through the variable tap-length adaptive equalizer, hence, achieving estimated signal $\hat{y}(n)$, we can express the equalized output signal as

$$\hat{y}(n) = x_k(n) + \eta_k(n) \tag{13}$$

where $\eta_k(n)$ is residual distortion, consists of residual MAI and the noise signal $v_r(n)$. The equalized signal is further processed by using Elementary Signal Estimation (ESE) and *a posteriori* probability (APP) decoders (DECs) to recover user's data bits.

The ESE generates logarithmic likelihood ratio (LLR) which can be expressed as in [8] as

$$e_{ESE}[x_k(n)] = \frac{2\{\hat{y}(n) - E[\hat{y}(n)] + E[x_k(n)]\}}{Var[\hat{y}(n)] - Var[x_k(n)]} \quad \forall k, n \tag{14}$$

where $E[\cdot]$ and $Var[\cdot]$ are the mean and variance functions, respectively. The mean and the variance of $\hat{y}(n)$ and $x_k(n)$ in (14) can be computed as

$$E[\hat{y}(n)] = \sum_{k=1}^{K} E[x_k(n)], \forall n \tag{15}$$

$$Var[\hat{y}(n)] = \sum_{k=1}^{K} Var[x_k(n)] + \sigma_v^2, \forall n \tag{16}$$

$$E[x_k(n)] = \tanh\{e_{DEC}[x_k(n)]/2\}, \forall k, n \tag{17}$$

$$Var[x_k(n)] = 1 - \{E[x_k(n)]\}^2, \forall k, n \tag{18}$$

where $e_{DEC}[x_k(n)]$ which is generated by DEC is extrinsic LLR of $x_k(n)$. Because the noise $v_r(n)$ is not available, σ_v^2 can be estimated as

$$\hat{\sigma}_v^2 = \sigma_e^2 = E\left[|s_k(n) - \hat{y}(n)|^2\right] \tag{19}$$

The output of ESE $e_{ESE}[x_k(n)]$ is then de-interleaving to achieve the *a priori* information of the DEC, which can be given as

$$e_{\text{ESE}}[c_k(n)] = D_k[e_{ESE}[x_k(n)]] \tag{20}$$

where $D_k[\cdot]$ represents de-interleaving function. Using the $e_{\text{ESE}}[c_k(n)]$ as input, the DEC adopts standard *a posteriori* probability (APP) decoding [13] to generate the *a posteriori* LLRs *LLR_d_APP*. After that the DEC generates the extrinsic LLR as

$$
\begin{aligned}
e_{\text{DEC}}[x_k(n)] &= I_k[e_{\text{DEC}}[c_k(n)]] \\
&= I_k[s(n) \cdot LLR\_d_{APP} - e_{\text{ESE}}[c_k(n)]]
\end{aligned}
\tag{21}
$$

where $s(n)$ is spreading sequence. $e_{\text{DEC}}[x_k(n)]$ is used as *a priori* information in ESE for the next iteration. After several iterations, the output of DEC is hard decision to construct the user's data bits $\hat{b}_k(i)$.

4 Simulation Results

In this section, the feasibility of proposed VT-MUD scheme is confirmed and analyzed by simulation results, meanwhile, the performance in terms of BER and MSE is evaluated. The Bellhop model is utilized to simulate UAC. Signal carrier frequency is 12 kHz. Two active users have been considered. The distances between transmitter and receiver are 500 m and 700 m, respectively. And they are placed in the position of water depth 10 m. The wave height is set to 0.5 m. The information bits frame length is set to 1024. Each frame contains 768 bits as the training sequence. Random interleavers [4] are adopted to separate users. The same spreading sequence $\{+1, -1, +1, -1, +1, -1, +1, -1\}$ is adopted as repetition code for all users as in [8]. The iteration times of MUD is set as 10. The initial length of variable tap-length method is 15. The tap-length increment P is 15.

Firstly, we verify the effect of tap-length on system performance and obtain the optimal tap-length for a specific channel profile through simulation. In Figs. 3 and 4, 200 data packets are transmitted. Figure 3 shows the effects of tap-length on signal-to-interference-and-noise ratio (SINR) where signal-to-noise ratio (SNR) is fixed at

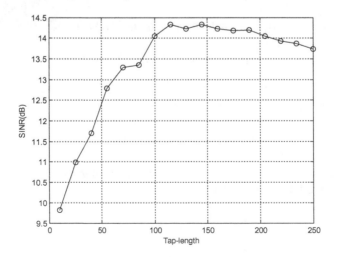

Fig. 3. The effects of tap-length on SINR at SNR = 15 dB

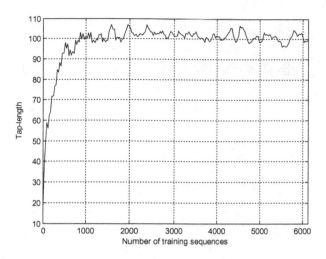

Fig. 4. Tap-length evolution for VT-MUD at SNR = 15 dB

15 dB. The output SINR is calculated according to [8]. As seen from the figure, the system cannot realize its full potential with few tap-length. In contrast, with too much tap-length, the SINR begins to deteriorate. It can be determined that the tap-length has significantly influence on the performance of the system. In this paper, considering the complexity, the optimal tap-length is defined as the minimum tap-length, which can let the system approximate the optimal SINR performance. It can be seen that the SINR is close to maximum when tap-length is set between 100 and 205. According to the definition of the optimum tap-length, we can identify the optimal tap-length in Fig. 3 is 100.

Then, we verify the feasibility of tap-length adjustment of the proposed detector. Figure 4 shows the automatic adjustment curve of tap-length in training mode. In (4), μ is set to 0.5, δ is set to 0.6. In (9) and (10), γ is set to 0.999. In (11) and (12), α_{up} is set to 0.998, α_{down} is set to 0.999. The channel in Fig. 4 is same as in Fig. 3. It is clear that the tap-length can eventually converge to the optimum value as in Fig. 3 as we expect.

Finally, we compare the BER performance and convergence performance of different schemes. A Monte-Carlo simulation is set up and 400 data packets are transmitted. Figure 5 shows the BER performance comparison between the proposed VT-MUD and existing FT-MUD scheme. As seen from the figure, VT-MUD can achieve better BER performance than existing FT-MUD scheme. At about BER = 10^{-3}, the proposed detector can achieve about 5 dB better than the FT-MUD. This is because there are no rules for FT-MUD to predict the optimal tap-length, while VT-MUD can converge to optimum tap-length. Convergence curves of two schemes has presented in Fig. 6. It is clear that the convergence rate of VT-MUD is close to FT-MUD, but VT-MUD can obtain lower MSE than FT-MUD. This is because tap-length is an important parameter on MSE performance, the tap-length can be adaptively adjusted by the VT-MUD.

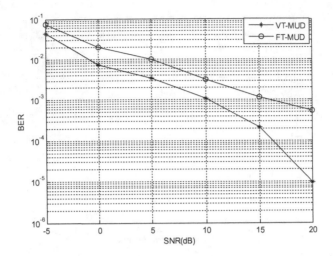

Fig. 5. BER performance comparison of proposed scheme and existing FT-MUD scheme

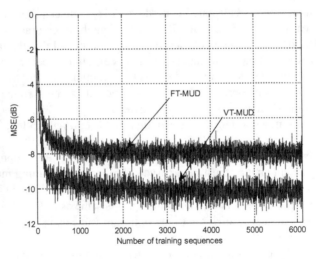

Fig. 6. MSE versus iteration number at SNR = 10 dB

5 Conclusion

In this paper, considering multiuser communication in UACs, we proposed a VT-MUD scheme. The proposed scheme utilizes adaptive tap-length update algorithm to converge to optimum tap-length with low computational complexity. The feasibility of proposed scheme has been confirmed and analyzed; meanwhile, the performances of the proposed VT-MUD and existing FT-MUD schemes have been compared. The results suggest remarkable performance improvements on VT-MUD as compared to FT-MUD.

References

1. Kilfoyle, D.B., Baggeroer, A.B.: The state of the art in underwater acoustic telemetry. IEEE J. Ocean. Eng. **25**(1), 4–27 (2000)
2. Jia, F., Cheng, E., Yuan, F.: Study on time-variant characteristics of under water acoustic channels. In: 2012 International Conference on Systems and Informatics (ICSAI 2012), Yantai, China, pp. 1650–1654. IEEE(2012)
3. Van Walree, P.A.: Propagation and scattering effects in underwater acoustic communication channels. IEEE J. Ocean. Eng. **38**(4), 614–631 (2013)
4. Kusume, K., Bauch, G., Utschick, W.: IDMA vs. CDMA: analysis and comparison of two multiple access schemes. IEEE Trans. Wirel. Commun. **11**(1), 78–87 (2012)
5. Ping, L., Wu, K.Y., Liu, L.H., Leung, W.K.: A simple, unified approach to nearly optimal multiuser detection and space-time coding. In: Proceedings of the IEEE Information Theory Workshop, Lausanne, Switzerland, pp. 53–56. IEEE (2012)
6. Ping, L., Liu, L., Wu, K., Leung, W.K.: Interleave-division multiple-access. IEEE Trans. Wirel. Commun. **5**(4), 938–947 (2006)
7. Aliesawi, S., Tsimenidis, C.C., Sharif, B.S., Johnston, M.: Soft rake and DFE based IDMA systems for underwater acoustic channels. In: Sensor Signal Processing for Defence (SSPD 2010), London, United Kingdom, pp. 1–5. IET (2010)
8. Aliesawi, S.A., Tsimenidis, C.C., Sharif, B.S., Johnston, M.: Iterative multiuser detection for underwater acoustic channels. IEEE J. Ocean. Eng. **36**(4), 728–744 (2011)
9. Qader, S.N., Tsimenidis, C.C., Sharif, B.S., Johnston, M.: Adaptive detection for asynchronous uplink IDMA shallow-water acoustic channels. In: Sensor Signal Processing for Defence (SSPD 2012), London, United Kingdom, pp. 1–5. IET (2012)
10. Riera-Palou, F., Noras, J.M., Cruickshank, D.G.M.: Linear equalizers with dynamic and automatic length selection. Electron. Lett. **37**(25), 1553–1554 (2001)
11. Ocean Acoustics Library. http://oalib.hlsresearch.com/Rays/index.html
12. Hsia, T.: Convergence analysis of LMS and NLMS adaptive algorithms. In: IEEE International Conference on ICASSP 1983, Boston, Massachusetts, USA, pp. 667–670. IEEE (1983)
13. Berrou, C., Glavieux, A.: Near optimum error correcting coding and decoding: turbo-codes. IEEE Trans. Commun. **44**(10), 1261–1271 (1996)

Two-Phase Prototype Filter Design for FBMC Systems

Jiangang Wen[1], Jingyu Hua[1(✉)], Zhijiang Xu[1], Weidang Lu[1],
and Jiamin Li[2]

[1] College of Information Engineering, Zhejiang University of Technology,
Hangzhou 310023, China
eehjy@163.com
[2] National Mobile Communications Research Laboratory, Southeast University,
Nanjing 210096, China

Abstract. FBMC has been taken as a candidate waveform for the next enhanced 5th generation (5G). To further improve its advantages over OFDM as well as to promote its application in burst transmission, a two-phase method is applied to design its prototype filter, i.e. a square-root Nyquist filter. In this method, the autocorrelation-based technique and a spectral factorization aimed at minimum stopband energy are successively exploited to acquire the final prototype filter. Through the relaxation of Nyquist condition and benefited from the nonlinear-phase, the frequency selectivity of our designed filters can be greatly improved. Furthermore, the performances of the proposed prototype filter brings a better BER in simulations, which demonstrates the effectiveness of our square-root Nyquist filter design for FBMC systems.

Keywords: FBMC · Prototype filter · Square-root Nyquist
Spectral factorization

1 Introduction

The evolution toward 5G includes an enhancement of the current cellular network, because the celebrated OFDM suffers from inefficiency for its tight synchronization and the use of cyclic prefix (CP) [1]. Besides, its large out-of-band (OOB) radiation makes it unattractive for flexible access to fragmented spectrum, which is crucial for efficient opportunistic communications in Internet of Things (IoT) [2].

To tackle above issues, a filter bank based multicarrier (FBMC) modulation is proposed as a promising candidate. Although FBMC was first investigated in the 1960s [3], it is experiencing renewed interest and has gained high attention in the recent years. In contrast to OFDM, this non-orthogonal waveform employs high quality filters on every subcarrier to produce better time-frequency localization and very low OOB radiation, and the offset quadrature amplitude modulation (OQAM) is usually employed to further reduce the inter-carrier interference [4]. Moreover, in the application of cognitive radios (CR), FBMC can simultaneously be used for data transmission as well as spectrum sensing [5]. However, the subcarrier-based shaping results in a prototype filter with long impulse response [6].

© ICST Institute for Computer Sciences, Social Informatics and Telecommunications Engineering 2018
X. Gu et al. (Eds.): MLICOM 2017, Part II, LNICST 227, pp. 96–105, 2018.
https://doi.org/10.1007/978-3-319-73447-7_12

The prototype filter for subcarrier shaping definitely determined the characteristics of the FBMC, and the nearly perfect reconstruction (NPR) is preferred in the design of prototype filter in discrete-time, such as the square-root raised-cosine (SRRC) filters [7]. There had been two typical design methods in [8, 9]. The frequency sampling technique was applied in the first method, and the obtained prototype filters had exact stopband zeros at the frequencies that were integer multiples of the sub-channel spacing. Nevertheless, the poor tradeoff between Nyquist condition and stopband performance made it inflexible. By contrast, in the second method, the filter could be designed through the minimization of a cost function that suitably struck a balance between stopband attenuation and residual inter-symbol interference (ISI).

Similar to above second method, we will design the square-root (SR) Nyquist filter as prototype filters in FBMC systems, where we straightly do tradeoff between stopband attenuation and residual ISI by constraining both the Nyquist condition and the stopband energy. Moreover, to address the nonconvex problem due to the convolution in transceivers, the autocorrelation-based technique [10] is employed in the construction of linear programming model, leading to linear inequations for ISI control. Besides, the original object and constraints in the stopband must be transformed to the ones about autocorrelation coefficients, i.e., the impulse coefficients of a Nyquist filter. Subsequently, to retrieve the SR Nyquist filter, from the optimized autocorrelation coefficients, a spectral factorization should be applied. Different from conventional minimum phase factorization [11] or the best stopband attenuation factorization [12], the minimum stopband energy is proposed here as the criteria. Such factorization would almost maintain the performances acquired in previous linear programming, and the obtained SR Nyquist filter is a nonlinear-phase one. Compared with the widely-used PHYDYAS filter [4], this resulted nonlinear-phase feature can benefit both the stopband attenuation and group-delay, or reduce the filter length. Thereby, the problems in realization complexity as well as low latency transmission might be alleviated. In our computer simulations, both the filter performances and the BER tests demonstrate a superiority of our designed prototype filters over the PHYDYAS filter.

2 Preliminaries

In the OQAM-FBMC system, the length of a prototype filter satisfies $N_p = KM + 1$, where M and K denote the subcarrier number and the overlapping factor. Thus, a FIR prototype filter can be presented by the real-valued impulse response coefficients $h(n)$, $0 \le n \le N_p - 1$, or its frequency response

$$H(\omega, \mathbf{h}) = \sum_{n=0}^{N_p-1} h(n)e^{-j\omega n} \qquad (1)$$

where $\mathbf{h} = [h(0), h(1), \cdots, h(N_p - 1)]$. The frequency response (1) is a general expression for either linear-phase or nonlinear-phase filter.

To design a NPR filter for the FBMC system, both the frequency selectivity and Nyquist condition should be taken into account. For the first purpose, the basic optimization model could be established as

$$
\min_{\mathbf{h}} f(\mathbf{h})
$$
$$
s.t. \begin{cases} |H(\omega, \mathbf{h})| \le 1 + \delta_p^m, & \omega \in [0, \omega_p] \\ -|H(\omega, \mathbf{h})| \le -1 + \delta_p^m, & \omega \in [0, \omega_p] \\ |H(\omega, \mathbf{h})| \le \delta_s^m, & \omega \in [\omega_s, \pi] \end{cases} \tag{2}
$$

where the amplitude ripples in both passband and stopband are constrained, and the choice of object function $f(\mathbf{h})$ could be the minimax cost or the least-square cost. In previous design [12], the minimax cost, i.e., the stopband attenuation is chosen, while our study chooses the least-square cost (the stopband energy) as the cost for improved OOB radiation reduction. To solve such an optimization problem (2), a number of algorithms [10, 11] could be exploited.

In practice, the interferences caused by relaxed Nyquist condition are small enough compared to the residual interferences due to transmission channel [13]. Therefore, a constraint for the control of Nyquist condition should be added into the basic model (2), but difficulty appears because of the convolution relation between the Nyquist filter $g(n)$ and its square-root Nyquist filter $h(n)$, i.e. $h(n) \otimes h(-n)$. This convolution makes the time-domain Nyquist constraints are nonconvex about $h(n)$

$$
\sum_{kM \ne (N-1)/2} |g(kM)|^2 \le \phi_t \tag{3}
$$

where ϕ_t represents the pre-specified threshold for relaxed Nyquist condition and $N = 2N_p - 1$ denotes the filter length of $g(n)$. In above constraints, M is an integer usually called the over-sampling factor, and it is exactly equal to the number of sub-carrier number.

In order to solve the above nonconvex issue of $h(n)$, we will design $g(n)$ first and then factorize it into $h(n)$'s, which is analogous to previous study [12]. However, our study employs the least-squares stopband ripples instead of the minimax in [12]. Moreover, the Nyquist condition in our study is established in frequency-domain based on the power-complementary property.

3 The Prototype Filter Design

The proposed method for prototype filter (SR Nyquist filter) design includes two steps. Firstly, the mathematical model is established and the optimization can be conducted with different constraint thresholds. In this step, the controllable inequation for Nyquist condition in the frequency-domain is expressed as a linear one, meanwhile the requirement for frequency selectivity is transformed to constrain the autocorrelation coefficient $g(n)$. In the second step, a spectral factorization is applied to the NYQ filter obtained in the previous step, resulting in the square-root Nyquist filter or the prototype filter ($h(n)$) equivalently. Note that the factorization also aims at the minimum stopband energy as we have done in the optimization step.

3.1 The NYQ Filter Design and Factorization

For Nyquist condition, we have the property of power complementary in the frequency-domain [9].

$$\sum_{k=0}^{M-1} \left| G(e^{j(\omega + \frac{2\pi}{M}k)}) \right| = 1, \ 0 \leq \omega \leq \pi/M \tag{4}$$

where $G(e^{j\omega})$ is the frequency response of the Nyquist filter $g(n)$. Due to its linear phase, $G(e^{j\omega})$ can be simplified to its zero-phase response $A(\omega, \mathbf{g})$ by abandoning the linear-phase term $e^{-j\omega(N-1)/2}$, which can be represented by using $\mathbf{g} = [g(0), g(1), \cdots, g((N-1)/2)]^T$, i.e.,

$$A(\omega, \mathbf{g}) = \mathbf{c}^T(\omega)\mathbf{g} \tag{5}$$

with $\mathbf{c}(\omega) = \left[2\cos(\omega \frac{N-1}{2}), 2\cos(\omega \frac{N-3}{2}), \cdots, 2\cos(\omega), 1 \right]^T$

According to the Nyquist condition in time-domain, a measurement to evaluate fitler's robustness against ISI was established in [12]. The better the Nyquist condition is satisfied, the smaller will this measurement be. Analogously, based on above power complementary, the measurement in frequency-domain is defined as the formula about $A(\omega, \mathbf{g})$, i.e.,

$$ISI_p = \int_0^{\frac{\pi}{M}} \left| \sum_{k=0}^{M-1} A(\omega + \frac{2\pi}{M}k, \mathbf{g}) - 1 \right|^p, p \geq 1 \tag{6}$$

For convenience, let

$$A_S(\omega, \mathbf{g}) = \sum_{k=0}^{M-1} A(\omega + \frac{2\pi}{M}k, \mathbf{g}) \tag{7}$$

And in our design, let $p \to \infty$, thus the formula (6) turns to

$$ISI = |A_S(\omega, \mathbf{g}) - 1|_{\max}, 0 \leq \omega \leq \pi/M \tag{8}$$

Then, it allows us to establish the frequency domain constraint by the simple forms

$$\begin{cases} A_S(\omega, \mathbf{g}) - 1 \leq \phi_f, & 0 \leq \omega \leq \pi/M \\ -A_S(\omega, \mathbf{g}) + 1 \leq \phi_f, & 0 \leq \omega \leq \pi/M \end{cases} \tag{9}$$

where ϕ_f is the pre-specified threshold for Nyquist control. As it is relaxed, better frequency selectivity would be traded for even the reduced filter length.

To keep consistency in the variable to be optimized, former model (2) must be transformed. First, the choice of object function should be done by representing it as

$$f(\mathbf{h}) = \int_{\omega_s}^{\pi} |H(\omega, \mathbf{h})|^2 d\omega \tag{10}$$

It means that the energy in stopband will be minimized in the design for prototype filter. The reason for this choice is that it has a similar effect as the minimization of OOB radiation, and the stopband attenuation is gradually promoted as the frequency far from the transition band. Besides, in following spectral factorization, this cost choice could produce a particularity that can reduce the complexity of finding the best SR Nyquist filter. Thanks to the relation between $A(\omega, \mathbf{g})$ and $H(\omega, \mathbf{h})$, i.e., $A(\omega, \mathbf{g}) = |H(\omega, \mathbf{h})|^2$, the object function can be readily transformed to the one aiming at $g(n)$

$$f(\mathbf{g}) = \int_{\omega_s}^{\pi} A(\omega, \mathbf{g}) d\omega = \mathbf{s}^T(\omega)\mathbf{g} \tag{11}$$

with the definition

$$\mathbf{s}(\omega) = \left[-4\frac{\sin(\omega_s \cdot \frac{N-1}{2})}{N-1}, -4\frac{\sin(\omega_s \cdot \frac{N-3}{2})}{N-3}, \cdots, -4\frac{\sin(\omega_s)}{2}, \pi - \omega_s \right]$$

Correspondingly, the constraint inequations for amplitude ripples are also modified, but just like many cases, in our final optimization model, only the stopband part is considered in constraints, and the ripples in passband is inherently shaped. Thus, the inequation for passband ripples is avoided, and the design problem could be expressed as to

$$\min_{\mathbf{g}} f(\mathbf{g}) = \mathbf{s}^T(\omega)\mathbf{g}$$

$$s.t. \begin{cases} A_S(\omega, \mathbf{g}) - 1 \le \phi_f, & \omega \in \left[0, \frac{\pi}{M}\right] \\ -A_S(\omega, \mathbf{g}) + 1 \le \phi_f, & \omega \in \left[0, \frac{\pi}{M}\right] \\ \mathbf{c}^T(\omega)\mathbf{g} \le \left(\delta_s^m\right)^2, & \omega \in [\omega_s, \pi] \\ \mathbf{c}^T(\omega)\mathbf{g} \ge 0, & \omega \in [0, \pi) \end{cases} \tag{12}$$

Among these constraint inequations, the third is the constraint for stopband attenuation, and the last one represents the condition for $g(n)$ to be the corresponding autocorrelation of $h(n)$. Consequently, this optimization problem can be easily solved by linear programming. Note that, though the design problem is with respect to $g(n)$, it is definitely optimized for the prototype filter as long as it could be retrieved by spectral factorization.

After getting the autocorrelation coefficients $g(n)$, the spectral factorization for minimum stopband energy is carried out to retrieve the prototype filter $h(n)$. which is analogous to those in [12]. An example with $M = 8$ and several different values of ϕ_f can be found in Fig. 1. In these figures, the nearly superposed zero pairs on the unit circle are partitioned into two different zero groups, which determine the frequency response of stopband. Meanwhile, the other reciprocal pairs are uniformly separated, which would limit the passband ripples. The final zero groups 'O' and '*' explicitly make up the obtained subfilter subfilters '**h1**' and '**h2**'.

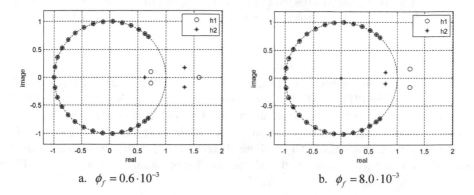

a. $\phi_f = 0.6 \cdot 10^{-3}$ b. $\phi_f = 8.0 \cdot 10^{-3}$

Fig. 1. The spectral factorization results for $M = 8$ and different ϕ_f's.

3.2   Filter Design Examples

First, we define the typical performance indicators include the passband ripples (R_p), the stopband attenuation (A_s), the stopband energy (E_s), the deviation of Nyquist in time-domain (ISI_t) [9] and in frequency-domain (ISI_f), viz.,

$$
\begin{cases}
R_p = -20\lg(1 - \delta_p) \,, \delta_p = \max_{\omega \in [0, \omega_p]} \left| |F(\omega)| - 1 \right| & (13) \\[2mm]
A_s = -20\lg(\delta_s) \,\,, \delta_s = \max_{\omega \in [\omega_s, \pi]} |F(\omega)| \\[2mm]
E_s = \mathbf{s}^T(\omega)\mathbf{g} \ or \ E_s = \int_{\omega_s}^{\pi} |H(\omega, \mathbf{h})|^2 d\omega \\[2mm]
ISI_t = \sum_{d=1}^{K} \frac{\left| \mathbf{g}\left(\frac{N-1}{2} + dM\right) \right| + \left| \mathbf{g}\left(\frac{N-1}{2} - dM\right) \right|}{\left| \mathbf{g}\left(\frac{N-1}{2}\right) \right|} , ISI_f = \max_{\omega \in [0, \frac{\pi}{M}]} \left| \sum_{k=0}^{M-1} A(\omega + \frac{2\pi}{M}k, \mathbf{g}) - 1 \right|
\end{cases}
$$

Referring to the FBMC setting in [13], we set $M = 8$ and $K = 4$, which leads to $N_p = 33$ for the prototype filter and $N = 65$ for the Nyquist filter. Due to the OQAM modulation, the roll-off factor is typically chosen as $\alpha = 1.0$, i.e., the same choice of PHYDYAS filter [13], which results in $\{\omega_c = \pi/M, \omega_s = 2\pi/M\}$. Meanwhile, the pre-specified threshold ϕ_f for Nyquist condition are relaxed to some different extent $\{0.6, 1, 4 : 4 : 12\} \cdot 10^{-3}$ for better frequency selectivity. The numerical results are listed in Table 1. Note that $F(\omega)$ in above formula should be chosen as $A(\omega, \mathbf{g})$ or $H(\omega, \mathbf{h})$ for $g(n)$ or $h(n)$.

From Table 1, we can clearly see the effectiveness of the Nyquist constraint in frequency-domain, where the resulted ISI_t and ISI_f are nearly the same. Moreover, a larger ϕ_f brings improvements both on A_s and E_s, which is beneficial for FBMC

Table 1. The performances of the Nyquist filter by optimization model (12) ($M = 8$).

ϕ_f	$R_p(dB)$	$A_s(dB)$	E_s	ISI_t	ISI_f
$0.6 \cdot 10^{-3}$	6.0258	105.1592	$1.6808 \cdot 10^{-7}$	$6.10 \cdot 10^{-4}$	$6.00 \cdot 10^{-4}$
$1.0 \cdot 10^{-3}$	6.0293	105.3603	$1.6283 \cdot 10^{-7}$	$1.00 \cdot 10^{-3}$	$1.00 \cdot 10^{-3}$
$4.0 \cdot 10^{-3}$	6.0554	106.9512	$1.2334 \cdot 10^{-7}$	$4.00 \cdot 10^{-3}$	$4.00 \cdot 10^{-3}$
$8.0 \cdot 10^{-3}$	6.0904	109.6685	$7.0680 \cdot 10^{-8}$	$8.00 \cdot 10^{-3}$	$8.00 \cdot 10^{-3}$
$1.20 \cdot 10^{-2}$	6.1255	116.8648	$3.3380 \cdot 10^{-8}$	$1.20 \cdot 10^{-2}$	$1.20 \cdot 10^{-2}$

prototype filter requiring better stopband suppression in FBMC. Such kind of tradeoff is exactly what the PHYDYAS does not achieve. Besides, we also show the spectral factorization results in Table 2, where the obtained A_s and R_p is nearly half of those in Table 1. Additionally, the resulted ISI_t and ISI_f in Table 2 are nearly the same as those before spectral factorization. All of those demonstrate that the two-phase method including constrained optimization and spectral factorization is effective for NPR prototype filter design.

Table 2. The performances of the subfilters after proposed spectral factorization ($M = 8$).

ϕ_f		$0.6 \cdot 10^{-3}$	$1.0 \cdot 10^{-3}$	$4.0 \cdot 10^{-3}$	$8.0 \cdot 10^{-3}$
$R_p(dB)$	h1	3.0009	3.0071	3.0313	3.0595
	h2	3.0301	3.0308	3.0588	3.1000
$A_s(dB)$	h1	52.2281	52.3485	53.1431	54.4826
	h2	52.9361	53.0204	53.8427	55.2551
E_s	h1	$1.6957 \cdot 10^{-7}$	$1.6394 \cdot 10^{-7}$	$1.2434 \cdot 10^{-7}$	$7.2396 \cdot 10^{-8}$
	h2	$1.6717 \cdot 10^{-7}$	$1.6206 \cdot 10^{-7}$	$1.2193 \cdot 10^{-7}$	$6.8386 \cdot 10^{-8}$
ISI_t		$6.10 \cdot 10^{-4}$	$1.00 \cdot 10^{-3}$	$4.00 \cdot 10^{-3}$	$8.00 \cdot 10^{-3}$
ISI_f		$5.94 \cdot 10^{-4}$	$0.99 \cdot 10^{-3}$	$4.00 \cdot 10^{-3}$	$7.90 \cdot 10^{-3}$

4   Simulation and Analysis

In this section, the prototype filter designed by the proposed two-phase method is compared with the PHYDYAS filter promoted by 5GNOW in terms of both the filter performance and the bit-error-ratio (BER).

4.1   The Comparison with the PHYDYAS Filter

In the first comparison of performances, only the retrieved subfilters 'h1' are adopted with the constraint thresholds $\phi_f = \{0.6, 4, 12\} \cdot 10^{-3}$, since subfilters 'h2' produces the same performances. The comparison results are presented in Table 3, and for convenience the PHYDYAS is abbreviated to PHY.

Explicitly, the proposed prototype filters outperform the PHYDYAS filter for the same K. Meanwhile, the E_s gaps of two kinds of filters could be up to two orders of

Table 3. The comparison between the prototype filters in our design and the PHY filters.

$M = 8$	N_p	$R_p(dB)$	$A_s(dB)$	E_s	ISI_t	ISI_f
PHY_A, $K = 4$	33	3.0103	39.8582	$1.0759 \cdot 10^{-5}$	$0.82 \cdot 10^{-3}$	$0.63 \cdot 10^{-3}$
PHY_B, $K = 3$	25	2.9946	32.5643	$8.0357 \cdot 10^{-5}$	$4.10 \cdot 10^{-3}$	$3.80 \cdot 10^{-3}$
$h1_A$, $K = 4$, $\phi_f = 0.6 \cdot 10^{-3}$	33	3.0009	52.2281	$1.6957 \cdot 10^{-7}$	$0.61 \cdot 10^{-3}$	$0.59 \cdot 10^{-3}$
$h1_B$, $K = 4$, $\phi_f = 4.0 \cdot 10^{-3}$	33	3.0313	53.1431	$1.2434 \cdot 10^{-7}$	$4.00 \cdot 10^{-3}$	$4.00 \cdot 10^{-3}$
$h1_C$, $K = 4$, $\phi_f = 1.2 \cdot 10^{-2}$	33	3.0947	58.1638	$3.3758 \cdot 10^{-8}$	$1.20 \cdot 10^{-2}$	$1.19 \cdot 10^{-2}$
$h1_D$, $K = 3$, $\phi_f = 0.6 \cdot 10^{-3}$	25	2.9870	38.8187	$4.6365 \cdot 10^{-6}$	$0.77 \cdot 10^{-3}$	$0.72 \cdot 10^{-3}$
$h1_E$, $K = 3$, $\phi_f = 4.0 \cdot 10^{-3}$	25	2.9871	38.9423	$4.4688 \cdot 10^{-6}$	$4.20 \cdot 10^{-3}$	$4.10 \cdot 10^{-3}$
$h1_F$, $K = 3$, $\phi_f = 1.2 \cdot 10^{-2}$	25	2.9874	39.2507	$4.0704 \cdot 10^{-6}$	$1.21 \cdot 10^{-2}$	$1.23 \cdot 10^{-2}$

magnitudes. Due to the nearly equivalent relation between E_s and OOB radiation, the improved E_s must be beneficial in many applications such as CR network. On the other hand, thanks to the flexible tradeoff in our method, it might be possible to reduce the filter length by replacing smaller value of K. In Table 3, it can be seen that the filter performances are sacrificed in our filter of $K = 3$, but it still produces comparable or even better performance than the PHYDYAS filter of $K = 4$.

4.2 The BER Test

The simulation parameters are set according to Table 4.1.6 of [14]. In simulations, two interference factors are taken into account.

(1) The carrier frequency offset (CFO) being set to 0.2 or a random number uniformly distributed in −0.2–0.2.
(2) In simulated CR-like scenarios, two users occupy half of the subchannels and posses power ratio 1:1 or 1:5. In the later case, the BER of the user with small power will be calculated.

Figures 2 and 3 show the BER simulations under different CFO effects and user power setup. In the case of power ratio 1:5, either 'CFO = 0.2' or random CFO will

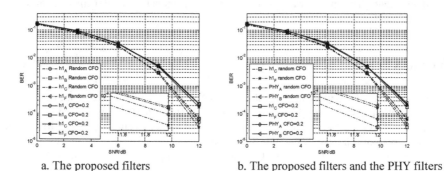

a. The proposed filters   b. The proposed filters and the PHY filters

Fig. 2. The BER comparison for the filters in Tab.III: the case for power ratio 1:1.

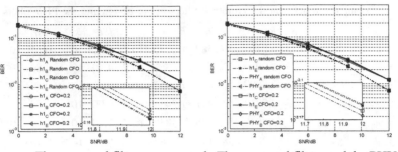

a. The proposed filters   b. The proposed filters and the PHY filters

Fig. 3. The BER comparison for the filters in Tab.III: the case for power ratio 1:5.

cause severe interference and degrade the BER performance, yet the proposed filters show some superiority to the PHYDYAS filters. While in the case of power ratio 1:1, it is clear to see the BER difference between our prototype filter and the PHYDYAS filter. Moreover, we can find that the frequency selectivity is more important than the Nyquist condition, since the interferences caused by relaxed Nyquist condition are smaller than the residual interferences by CFO. As a conclusion, the $\mathbf{h}1_C$ is the best one and the $\mathbf{h}1_F$ provides a suitable tradeoff with reduced filter length.

5 Conclusions

Combining the NYQ filter optimization and the spectral factorization aimed at minimum stopband energy, this paper provides a flexible design for prototype filter in FBMC systems. From the examples and BER simulations, it is evident that the resulted nonlinear-phase SR Nyquist filter with relaxed Nyquist condition are superior to the widely-employed PHYDYAS filters. These filters have a flexible tradeoff for better frequency selectivity, a strengthened robustness against ICI, and the ability to reduce the filter length, which may benefit FBMC practical application in such as CR networks and burst transmission.

Acknowledgement. This paper was sponsored by the National NSF of China under grant No. 61471322.

References

1. Chávez-Santiago, R., Szydełko, M., Kliks, A., Foukalas, F.: 5G: the convergence of wireless communications. Wirel. Pers. Commun. **83**(3), 1617–1642 (2015)
2. Bellanger, M.: Physical layer for future broadband radio systems. In: 2010 IEEE Radio and Wireless Symposium (RWS), pp. 436–439 (2010)
3. Doré, J.B., Cassiau, N., Kténas, D.: Low complexity frequency domain carrier frequency offset compensation for multiuser FBMC receiver. In: 2014 European Conference on Networks and Communications (EuCNC), pp. 1–5 (2014)

4. Bellanger, M., Le Ruyet, D., Roviras, D., Terré, M., et al.: FBMC physical layer: a primer. PHYDYAS report. http://www.ict-phydyas.org/teamspace/internal-folder/special-session-at-crowncom-2010

5. Premnath, S.N., Wasden, D., Kasera, S.K., Patwari, N., et al.: Beyond OFDM: best-effort dynamic spectrum access using filterbank multicarrier. IEEE/ACM Trans. Netw. **21**(3), 869–882 (2013)

6. Schaich, F., Wild, T.: Waveform contenders for 5G - OFDM vs. FBMC vs. UFMC. In: 6th IEEE International Symposium on Communications, Control and Signal Processing (ISCCSP), pp. 457–460 (2014)

7. Sahin, A., Guvenc, I., Arslan, H.: A survey on multicarrier communications: prototype filters lattice structures implementation aspects. IEEE Commun. Surv. Tutor. **16**(3), 1312–1338 (2014)

8. Mirabbasi, S., Martin, K.: Overlapped complex-modulated transmultiplexer filters with simplified design and superior stopbands. IEEE Trans. Circuits Syst. II: Analog Digit. Signal Process. **50**(8), 456–469 (2003)

9. Farhang-Boroujeny, B.: A square-root Nyquist (M) filter design for digital communication systems. IEEE Trans. Signal Process. **56**(5), 2127–2132 (2008)

10. Davidson, T.: Enriching the art of FIR filter design via convex optimization. IEEE Signal Process. Mag. **27**(3), 89–101 (2010)

11. Lai, X., Lin, Z.: Optimal design of constrained FIR filters without phase response specifications. IEEE Trans. Signal Process. **62**(17), 4532–4546 (2014)

12. Hua, J., Wen, J., Lu, W., Li, F., et al.: Design and application of nearly Nyquist and SR-Nyquist FIR filter based on linear programming and spectrum factorization. In: 9th IEEE Conference on Industrial Electronics and Applications (ICIEA), pp. 64–67 (2014)

13. Viholainen, A., Ihalainen, T., Stitz, T.H., Renfors, M., Bellanger, M.: Prototype filter design for filter bank based multicarrier transmission. In: 17th European Signal Processing Conference, pp. 1359–1363 (2009)

14. Germany F.E.H., France A.C.: Final 5GNOW transceiver and frame structure concept D3.3. 5GNOW report. https://www.is-wireless.com/fp7-5gnow/

A Fine Carrier Phase Recovery Method for 32APSK

Yulei Nie[(⊠)], Zijian Zhang, and Peipei Liu

School of Information and Electronics,
Beijing Institute of Technology, Beijing, China
{nieyulei,2120150844}@bit.edu.cn, 546641721@qq.com

Abstract. When 32-ary amplitude phase shift keying (32APSK) modulation is used in the communication system, carrier recovery is one of the most important technology. The decision-directed (DD) phase locked loop (PLL) is widely used for carrier recovery. Based on the decision-directed (DD) phase locked loop (PLL) algorithm, the paper proposes a new fine carrier phase recovery method, which is based on the constellation classification and different nonlinear operation. Simulation results show that the performance of the proposed method is much better than the traditional one.

Keywords: Carrier recovery · 32APSK · Constellation classification
PLL

1 Introduction

With the vigorous development of aerospace industry, broadband satellite communications have found wide applications. To settle the scarce problems of available spectrum resources, multi-level modulated signals are utilized to transmit over satellite channels for the improved spectral efficiency. The satellite channel is typically a nonlinear channel, mainly caused by amplifier imperfections. Since the envelopes of the traditional quadrature amplitude modulation (QAM) are not constant, they are very sensitive to channel nonlinearity due to amplitude levels. In contrast to quadrature amplitude modulation (QAM), the amplitude phase shift keying (APSK) is less vulnerable to nonlinear distortions, which is chosen for satellite communications. For example, in the new digital video broadcasting (DVB) standard for satellite communications [3], frequently denoted by DVB-S2, 32-ary amplitude-phase shift keying (32APSK) is recommended as a modulation scheme. However, 32APSK [2] signal is greatly influenced by the frequency offset, which makes the carrier recovery algorithm more complicated.

In digital communication [1], the frequency offset and phase offset are common problems. So the frequency offset and phase offset become key problems in carrier recovery. The frequency offset and phase offset often lead to degradation of communication system performance especially when higher order 32APSK modulation is applied. In order to compensate these two offsets, we have to use the carrier recovery technique. Two methods are often used for carrier recovery. The first method is to directly estimate the carrier information from the received signal. The second method

© ICST Institute for Computer Sciences, Social Informatics and Telecommunications Engineering 2018
X. Gu et al. (Eds.): MLICOM 2017, Part II, LNICST 227, pp. 106–114, 2018.
https://doi.org/10.1007/978-3-319-73447-7_13

needs to insert a pilot into the symbol. The carrier information is estimated by the pilot, which is more accurate. The method needs to use frequency estimation algorithm and phase estimation algorithm to eliminate most of the frequency offset and phase offset. In [6–8], the frequency estimation algorithm is introduced in detail. In [9], the phase estimation algorithm is introduced in detail. After the frequency estimation and phase estimation, the PLL is used for carrier recovery. In [3], a hybrid NDA/DD solution has been proposed. This solution performs same nonlinear operation for all the constellation symbols, then seeks the phase error estimation value, which is not accurate. In [4], all the constellation symbols are used. It performs different nonlinear operations on different rings to seek phase error estimation value. Therefore, the phase error estimation value is more accurate. Due to the characteristic of multiple amplitude, the phase error estimation value is affected by the amplitude of symbol, which will cause performance degradation.

To overcome these shortcomings, for the 32APSK fine carrier phase synchronization, we propose a new method. The new method will execute the constellation partitioning for 32APSK constellation firstly, then execute different nonlinear operation for different rings. After these operations, we will use the decision-directed (DD) algorithm to obtain the phase error estimation value which is not affected by the magnitude of the constellation points. For the 32APSK, if the points locate in the innermost ring, they have the smaller radii, and thus their signal-to-additive-plus-adaptation-noise ratio is smaller than the other points [10]. The phase error estimation value will be set to zero.

2 Signal Model and System Structure

Decision-directed PLL (DD-PLL) is a technique used for fine carrier phase synchronization widely. The Fig. 1 shows its structure. It is composed of phase detector, loop filter and NCO (Numerically Controlled Oscillator).

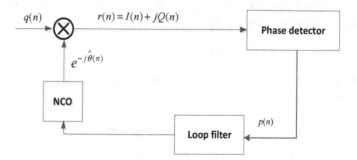

Fig. 1. Structure of carrier recovery loop

As shown in Fig. 1, it is assumed that the channel is an additive white Gaussian noise (AWGN) channel and the input signal $q(n)$ has been subjected to automatic gain control, timing synchronization [5], coarse frequency phase synchronization [6, 7]. The signal $r(n)$ is generated by using the signal $q(n)$ to multiply the NCO output. Assuming the signal $r(n)$ is written as

$$r(n) = I(n) + jQ(n) \tag{1}$$

The received signal $q(n)$ can be expressed as

$$q(n) = A(n)e^{-j\theta(n)} + v(n) \tag{2}$$

where $A(n)$ is the n-th transmitted complex data symbol, $v(n)$ is white Gaussian noise, $\theta(n)$ is the carrier phase, and it can be written as

$$\theta(n) = \Delta\theta + 2\pi\Delta f n T \tag{3}$$

where $\theta(n)$ is the carrier phase offset, Δf is the carrier frequency offset, and T is the symbol period. The received signal $q(n)$ is multiplied by the output of NCO to produce the phase compensated signal $r(n)$, so the signal $r(n)$ can be written as

$$r(n) = A(n)e^{-j(\theta(n)-\hat{\theta}(n))} + v(n)e^{-j\hat{\theta}(n)} \tag{4}$$

where $\hat{\theta}(n)$ is the estimated carrier phase caused. The phase error is $\theta(n) - \hat{\theta}(n)$, which is obtained by phase detector. The performance of the DD PLL can be improved by solving the output of the phase detector. In general DD PLL algorithm, the phase detector is designed as

$$p(n) = \text{Im}[\frac{r(n)}{\hat{r}(n)}] = \text{Im}[\frac{I(n)+jQ(n)}{\hat{I}(n)+j\hat{Q}(n)}] \tag{5}$$

where $\hat{r}(n)$ is the decision symbol of $r(n)$, $I(n)$ is the real part of the $r(n)$, $Q(n)$ is the imaginary part of the $r(n)$, $\hat{I}(n)$ is the real part of the $\hat{r}(n)$, $\hat{Q}(n)$ is the imaginary part of the $\hat{r}(n)$. But the phase error estimate $p(n)$ is affected by energy of signal. To solve this problem, the phase error estimate $p(n)$ can be written as

$$p(n) = angle(r(n)) - angle(\hat{r}(n)) \tag{6}$$

where $angle(x)$ represents the angle of the complex vector x.

For the QPSK signal, the $\hat{r}(n)$ can be written as

$$\hat{r}(n) = \hat{I}(n) + j\hat{Q}(n) = sgn(I(n)) + jsgn(Q(n)) \tag{7}$$

where $sgn(x) = -1$ when $x < 0$ and $sgn(x) = 1$ when $x \geq 0$.

And the phase error estimate $p(n)$ is computed as

$$p(n) = \tan^{-1}(\frac{I(n) * sign(Q(n)) - Q(n) * sign(I(n))}{I(n) * sign(I(n)) + Q(n) * sign(Q(n))}) \tag{8}$$

3 Carrier Recovery Algorithm

The algorithm proposed in this paper is described below. Figure 2 illustrates the normal constellation of 32APSK modulation. According to the figure, we can find that 32APSK constellation has three rings. We assume that r_1 represents the distance between the constellations of the innermost ring to the origin, r_2 represents the distance between the constellations of the middle ring to the origin, r_3 represents the distance between the constellations of the outermost ring to the origin.

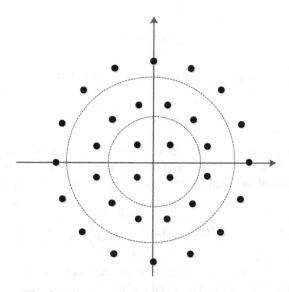

Fig. 2. The constellation of 32APSK modulation

The coordinates for the point of innermost ring can be expressed as

$$r_1 * \exp(j\frac{\pi}{2}k + \frac{\pi}{4})(k = 0, 1, 2, 3) \tag{9}$$

The coordinates for the point of middle ring can be expressed as

$$r_2 * \exp(j\frac{\pi}{6}k + \frac{\pi}{12})(k = 0, 1, 2, 3, 4, 5, 6, 7, 8, 9, 10, 11) \tag{10}$$

The coordinates for the point of outermost ring can be expressed as

$$r_3 * \exp(j\frac{\pi}{8}k)(k = 0, 1, 2, 3, 4, 5, 6, 7, 8, 9, 10, 11, 12, 13, 14, 15) \tag{11}$$

As shown in Fig. 3, assuming the signal $r(n)$ is written as

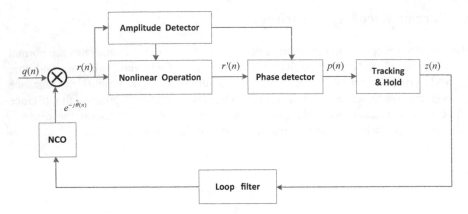

Fig. 3. Carrier recovery loop for 32APSK

$$r(n) = I(n) + jQ(n) \tag{12}$$

When the signal enters the phase-locked loop, firstly it is necessary to decide the position of signal. If the signal is located in the outermost ring, we first use four order operation for the signal and then rotate it with an angle of $\frac{\pi}{4}$, so the transformed signal can be written as

$$r'(n) = (r(n))^4 * \exp(j\frac{\pi}{4}) \tag{13}$$

After the transformation, the constellation on the outermost ring is similar to the QPSK constellation. If the signal is located in the middle ring, we will use three order operation for the signal, so the transformed signal can be written as

$$r'(n) = (r(n))^3 \tag{14}$$

After the transformation, the constellation on the middle ring is similar to the QPSK constellation. If the signal is located in the innermost ring, we will not process the signal. So that the 32APSK constellation is approximately converted into QPSK constellation whose amplitudes are different. Based on the above results, we can reference the QPSK signal to obtain the phase error estimation value.

In the following, we will reference Fig. 3 to introduce the process of obtaining the phase error estimate $p(n)$. After the nonlinear operation for 32APSK constellation. All the rings have become similar to the QPSK constellation. Because the 32APSK modulation is a high order modulation, using the point on the innermost ring to calculate phase error estimate $p(n)$ will increase the phase-locked loop jitter. That will influence the performance of the PLL. So if the point locates in the innermost ring, the phase error estimate $p(n)$ will be set to zero.

3.1   The Amplitude Detector and the Nonlinear Operation

The amplitude detector is used to calculate the amplitude of signal $r(n)$. The amplitude of signal $r(n)$ can be written as $|r(n)|$. Then the signal amplitude $|r(n)|$ is compared to two threshold values τ_1 and τ_2. According to the size of the $|r(n)|$, we will perform different nonlinear operation for signal $r(n)$. The $r'(n)$ can be calculated as

$$r'(n) = \begin{cases} (r(n))^4 * \exp(j\frac{\pi}{4}) & if\ |r(n)| > \tau_1 \\ (r(n))^3 & if\ \tau_1 > |r(n)| > \tau_2 \\ r(n) & if\ |r(n)| < \tau_2 \end{cases} \tag{15}$$

3.2   Phase Detector and Tracking and Hold

After the nonlinear operation, the signal will be processed by the phase detector (PD). Assuming the signal $r'(n)$ can be written as

$$r'(n) = I'(n) + jQ'(n) \tag{16}$$

The signal $p(n)$ can be written as

$$p(n) = \begin{cases} \tan^{-1}(\frac{I'(n)*sign(Q'(n)) - Q'(n)*sign(I'(n))}{I'(n)*sign(I'(n)) + Q'(n)*sign(Q'(n))})/4 & if\ |r(n)| > \tau_1 \\ \tan^{-1}(\frac{I'(n)*sign(Q'(n)) - Q'(n)*sign(I'(n))}{I'(n)*sign(I'(n)) + Q'(n)*sign(Q'(n))})/3 & if\ \tau_1 > |r(n)| > \tau_2 \\ 0 & if\ |r(n)| < \tau_2 \end{cases} \tag{17}$$

The Tracking & Hold output $z(n)$ is defined as

$$z(n) = \begin{cases} p(n) & if\ |p(n)| < \alpha \\ 0 & otherwise \end{cases} \tag{18}$$

4   Performance Analysis

The performance of the algorithm is verified by simulations. In the simulations, we use 32APSK signal, the symbol rate is 1 Mbps. Because the proposed algorithm is used for fine carrier phase synchronization, a frequency estimation algorithm and phase estimation algorithm are adopted to eliminate most of the frequency offset and part of the phase offset. The normalized residue frequency offset is 0.0004. Figure 4 shows the signal constellation diagram before the phase-locked loop. It can be observed signal constellation points are evenly distributed over three rings. However, Fig. 5 displays the signal constellation diagram after the phase-locked loop, discrete signal constellation points can be seen clearly. The bit error rate performance is illustrated in Fig. 6 for comparing with the other two methods. It can be seen that the proposed method has a lower bit error rate in the low SNR region.

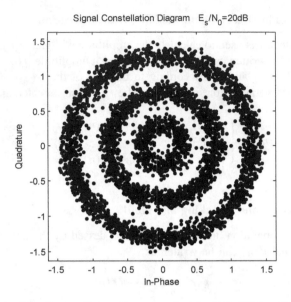

Fig. 4. Signal constellation diagram before the PLL (SNR = 20 dB)

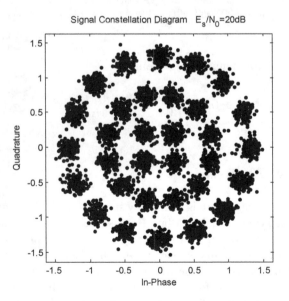

Fig. 5. Signal constellation diagram after the PLL (SNR = 20 dB)

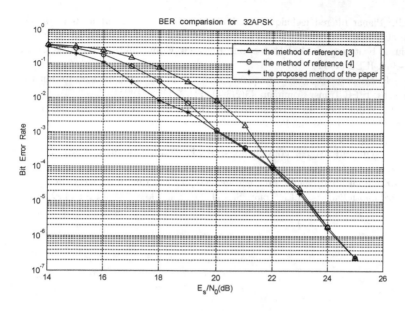

Fig. 6. BER comparison for different algorithms

5 Conclusion

In this paper, an improved decision-directed (DD) algorithm based on the phase-locked loop is proposed, which has a better performance in terms of bit error rate. This performance is especially good in the low SNR region. Compared to the traditional methods for 32APSK signal, the proposed method has better performance. The proposed method can be easily implemented and has a good practical significance.

References

1. Mengali, U., D'Andrea, A.N.: Synchronization Techniques for Digital Receivers. Applications of Communications Theory. Springer, New York (1997). https://doi.org/10.1007/978-1-4899-1807-9
2. DeGaudenzi, R., I Fàbregas, A.G., Martinez, A.: Performance analysis of turbo-coded APSK modulations over nonlinear satellite channels. IEEE Trans. Wirel. Commun. **5**(9), 2396–2407 (2006)
3. Casini, E., De Gaudenzi, R., Ginesi, A.: DVB-S2 modem algorithms design and performance over typical satellite channels. Int. J. Satell. Commun. Network. **22**(3), 281–318 (2004)
4. Xu, F., Qiu, L., Wang, Y.: Fine carrier phase recovery method for APSK signals. J. Chongqing Univ. Posts Telecommun. **25**, 281–284 (2013)
5. Oerder, M., Meyr, H.: Digital filter and square timing recovery. IEEE Trans. Commun. **COM-36**(5), 605–612 (1988)

6. Fitz, M.P.: Planar filtered techniques for burst mode carrier synchronization. In: Global Telecommunications Conference 1991, GLOBECOM 1991. Countdown to the New Millennium. Featuring a Mini-Theme on: Personal Communications Services, vol. 1, pp. 365–369. IEEE (1991)

7. Luise, M., Reggiannini, R.: Carrier frequency recovery in all-digital modems for burst-mode transmissions. IEEE Trans. Commun. **43**(2/3/4), 1169–1178 (1995)

8. Lovell, B.C., Williamson, R.C.: The statistical performance of some instantaneous frequency estimators. IEEE Trans. Signal Process. **40**(7), 1708–1723 (1992)

9. Moeneclaey, M., De Jonghe, G.: ML-oriented NDA carrier synchronization for general rotationally symmetric signal constellations. IEEE Trans. Commun. **42**(8), 2531–2533 (1994)

10. Jablon, N.K.: Joint blind equalization, carrier recovery and timing recovery for high-order QAM signal constellations. IEEE Trans. Signal Process. **40**(6), 1383–1398 (1992)

Intelligent Radar Signal Processing

Interferometric-Processing Based Small Space Debris Imaging

Yuxue Sun[1]([⊠]), Ying Luo[1,2], and Song Zhang[3]

[1] Institute of Information and Navigation, Air Force Engineering University,
Xi'an 710077, China
sunyuxuejiayou@163.com, luoying2002521@163.com
[2] Natural Laboratory of Radar Signal Processing, Xidian University,
Xi'an 710077, China
[3] Unit 95980 of the People's Liberation Army, Xiangyang 441000, China
zhangsong1949@163.com

Abstract. The detection and recognition of small space debris is an important task for space security. This paper proposed an interferometric-processing based imaging method for small space debris. First, based on L-shaped three antennas system, the signal model for interferometric imaging is established. Then aiming at the fact that the size of some space debris is smaller than range resolution, time-frequency analysis is adopted to separate echoes of different scatterers. The mechanism of time-frequency analysis for echo from three antennas is deduced in detail. It is proved that the phase for interferometric processing is reserved in the process of time-frequency analysis. Finally through interferometric processing, the positions and image of scatterers can be reconstructed. Simulations verify the validity of the proposed method.

Keywords: Radar imaging · Interferometric processing · Space debris
Time-frequency analysis · Sinusoidal frequency modulation

1 Introduction

The space debris is a big menace of space craft, satellite, and space stations with more and more explorations in aerospace [1]. If a collision between them, the surface properties of spacecraft may be changed and great damages will be brought about. Thus it is an important task to implement space surveillance for the safety of spacecraft. For space debris smaller than 1 cm, it is possible to protect spacecraft through an appropriately designed protector. For debris whose sizes are larger than 10 cm, the U.S. Space Command has employed the space surveillance networks which are situated all over the world to monitor them [2]. Thus an important target of space surveillance is space debris whose size is 1–10 cm.

High-resolution imaging needs wide bandwidth. In order to overcome the restriction of bandwidth, Ref. [3] firstly proposes a single-range Doppler interferometry (SRDI) imaging method for spinning space debris. The improved single-range matching filtering (SRMF) method is put up based on Ref. [3] to improve the range resolution and computation complexity [4]. Reference [5] proposed a single-range

© ICST Institute for Computer Sciences, Social Informatics and Telecommunications Engineering 2018
X. Gu et al. (Eds.): MLICOM 2017, Part II, LNICST 227, pp. 117–123, 2018.
https://doi.org/10.1007/978-3-319-73447-7_14

imaging (SRTI) method, which takes advantage of the phase trace to realize imaging of space debris. However, these methods can reconstruct the shape of target instead of the real position and size, since the angle between target spinning axis and radar LOS is hard to obtain.

This paper proposes an interferometric-processing based imaging method for space debris. Through time-frequency analysis, the echo of different scatterers can be separated which are inseparable in range profile for resolution restriction. Then based on three-antenna imaging system, echo of each scatter from three antennas is conducted interferometric processing on time-frequency plane. The phase information is then transformed into target position. Thus the real position and size of the target are obtained. The simulation results verify the validity of the proposed method.

2 Signal Model

L-shaped interferometric imaging system and 3-D spinning targets is given in Fig. 1. Antenna A transmits signal and antenna A, B and C receive signal. They are located in the radar coordinate system XYZ at $(0, 0, 0)$, $(L, 0, 0)$ and $(0, 0, L)$, respectively. Establish the target coordinate system xyz which is originated at point O whose position is (X_c, Y_c, Z_c) in the radar coordinate system. Space debris usually rotates around its axis. A scatterer P of the target, located at (x_p, y_p, z_p), rotates with angular rotation velocity $(\omega_x, \omega_y, \omega_z)$ when undergoing a translation. Radar transmits linear modulation frequency (LFM) pulse, which is represented as

$$s(\hat{t}, t_m) = \text{rect}\left(\frac{\hat{t}}{T_p}\right) \cdot \exp\left(j2\pi\left(f_c t + \frac{1}{2}\mu\hat{t}^2\right)\right). \tag{1}$$

where $\text{rect}\left(\frac{\hat{t}}{T_p}\right) = \begin{cases} 1, & -T_p/2 \leq \hat{t} \leq T_p/2 \\ 0, & \text{else} \end{cases}$, f_c is carrying frequency, T_p is pulse duration, μ is modulation rate, $\hat{t} = t - t_m$ denotes fast time and $t_m = mT$, $m = 0, 1, 2, \ldots M - 1$ denotes slow time, in which T is pulse repetition period and M is pulse

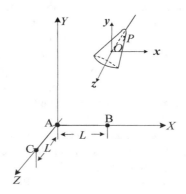

Fig. 1. Diagram of three-antenna interferometric imaging system and 3-D spinning targets.

number. After dechirp with reference range R_{AO} and Fourier transformation, the range profile of point P from antenna can be obtained as

$$
\begin{aligned}
S_A(f, t_m) &= \sigma_P T_p \mathrm{sinc}\left(T_p\left(f + \frac{2\mu}{c} R_{\Delta AP}(t_m)\right)\right) \cdot \\
&\quad \exp\left(-j\frac{4\pi}{c} f_c R_{\Delta AP}(t_m)\right).
\end{aligned}
\tag{2}
$$

where σ_P represents scattering coefficient and $R_{\Delta AP}(t_m)$ represents the range from P to antenna A. Suppose that the translation motion has been compensated. Since the size of target is small, the echo of target should be concentrated in one range cell, that is

$$
\begin{aligned}
S_A(t_m) &= \sigma_P T_p \exp\left(-j\frac{4\pi}{c} f_c R_{\Delta AP}(t_m)\right) \\
&= \sigma_A \exp(-j\Phi_A(t_m)).
\end{aligned}
\tag{3}
$$

where σ_A is a constant. Similarly, the echoes of antenna B and antenna C are

$$
\begin{aligned}
S_B(t_m) &= \sigma_P T_p \exp\left(-j\frac{2\pi}{c} f_c (R_{\Delta AP}(t_m) + R_{\Delta BP}(t_m))\right) \\
&= \sigma_B \exp(-j\Phi_B(t_m)).
\end{aligned}
\tag{4}
$$

$$
\begin{aligned}
S_C(t_m) &= \sigma_P T_p \exp\left(-j\frac{2\pi}{c} f_c (R_{\Delta AP}(t_m) + R_{\Delta CP}(t_m))\right) \\
&= \sigma_C \exp(\Phi_C(t_m)).
\end{aligned}
\tag{5}
$$

where σ_B and σ_C are constants. Through interferometric processing, the phase difference of the range profiles between echoes from three antennas can be abstracted.

$$
\begin{aligned}
\mathrm{angle}(s_A(t_m)^* s_B(t_m)) &= \Phi_B(t_m) - \Phi_A(t_m) \\
&= \Delta\Phi_{AB}(t_m) \\
&= \frac{2\pi}{\lambda}(R_{\Delta AP}(t_m) - R_{\Delta BP}(t_m)).
\end{aligned}
\tag{6}
$$

$$
\begin{aligned}
\mathrm{angle}(s_A(t_m)^* s_C(t_m)) &= \Phi_C(t_m) - \Phi_A(t_m) \\
&= \Delta\Phi_{AC}(t_m) \\
&= \frac{2\pi}{\lambda}(R_{\Delta AP}(t_m) - R_{\Delta CP}(t_m)).
\end{aligned}
\tag{7}
$$

where "angle" is abstracting-phase operation and λ is wave length.

Moreover, combined with the geometrical relationship in Fig. 1, the x-axis positions and z-axis positions are obtained as

$$x(t_m) = \frac{\Delta\Phi_{AB}(t_m)\lambda \cdot R_{AO}}{2\pi L} + \frac{L}{2} - X_c. \tag{8}$$

$$z(t_m) = \frac{\Delta\Phi_{AC}(t_m)\lambda \cdot R_{AO}}{2\pi L} + \frac{L}{2} - Z_c. \tag{9}$$

3   Interferometric Processing on the Time-Frequency Plane

When there is one more scatterer in the target, all of the range profiles are stacked together in one range cell due to low range resolution. The echo of all these scatterers cannot be separated. Thus the phases of them overlay each other, in which case, interferometric processing cannot be conducted since phase term is the key for interferometric imaging. Here time-frequency analysis is adopted to separate the echoes of different scatterers, meanwhile the phase term must be reserved. Short time Fourier transform (STFT) is chosen to conduct time-frequency analysis. The definition of STFT is

$$STFT(t,f) = \int_{-\infty}^{+\infty} s(\tau)g^*(\tau - t)e^{-j2\pi f\tau}d\tau. \tag{10}$$

where $g(t)$ is window function. Since the target undergoes spinning motion, $R_{AAP}(t_m)$ should be a sinusoidal modulation, that is, echo of space debris as (3)–(5) is in the form of sinusoidal frequency modulation (SFM). A SFM signal can be written as

$$x(t) = \sum_{m=-\infty}^{\infty} \{J_m(m_f)A \exp[j2\pi(f_c + mf_m)t]\}, f_m \neq 0 \quad . \tag{11}$$

where m is an integer and $J_m(\bullet)$ is the first-order Bessel function. In STFT, when a window with a relative short time width is added to SFM signal, the captured signal can be approximated as a form of LFM. For (3), the phase is

$$\Phi_A(\tau) = 2\pi f_c \frac{2R_{AAP}(\tau)}{c} = 2\pi\left(f_A(t_m)\tau + \frac{1}{2}\mu_A(t_m)\tau^2\right), \ \tau \in [t_m, t_m + T_W]. \tag{12}$$

where $f_A(t_m)$ represents the initial frequency, $\mu_A(t_m)$ represents the modulation rate and T_W is time width of the window. The STFT result of (3) is

$$\begin{aligned}
S_{Astft}(t_m,f) &= \int_{-\infty}^{+\infty} \sigma_A \exp(j\Phi_A(\tau))g^*(\tau - t_m)e^{-j2\pi f\tau}d\tau \\
&= \int_{-\infty}^{+\infty} \sigma_A \exp\left(j2\pi\left(f_A(t_m)\tau + \frac{1}{2}\mu_A(t_m)\tau^2\right)\right)g^*(\tau - t_m)e^{-j2\pi f\tau}d\tau.
\end{aligned} \tag{13}$$

where σ_A is a constant. According to principle of stationary phase, the approximate result of (13) is

$$S_{Astft}(t_m, f) = \sigma_A g^* \left(\frac{f - f_A(t_m)}{\mu_A(t_m)} - t_m \right) \exp\left(-j \frac{\pi (f - f_A(t_m))^2}{\mu_A(t_m)} \right). \tag{14}$$

Similarly, the STFT result of echo from antenna B denoted as $S_{Bstft}(t_m, f)$ and from antenna C denoted as $S_{Cstft}(t_m, f)$ can be obtained. It can be seen from (12) that the frequency of echo from antenna A is $f_A = f_A(t_m) + \mu_A(t_m) \cdot t_m$. Similarly the frequency of echo from antenna B is $f_B = f_B(t_m) + \mu_B(t_m) \cdot t_m$. Thus it yields

$$\left\{ \text{angle}\left(S_{Astft}(t_m, f_A)^* S_{Bstft}(t_m, f_B) \right) \right\}^* = \pi(\mu_B(t_m) - \mu_A(t_m)) t_m^2$$
$$= (\Phi_B(t_m) - \Phi_A(t_m)) - 2\pi(f_B(t_m) - f_A(t_m)) t_m. \tag{15}$$

The length of baseline is rather small compared with the range from target to radar, thus the time-frequency analysis result of echo from antenna A and that from antenna B are almost unanimous. Accordingly, for the same window section $[t_m, t_m + T_W]$, it yields $f_A(t_m) \approx f_B(t_m)$. In this case, (15) can be rewritten as

$$\left\{ \text{angle}\left(S_{Astft}(t_m, f_A)^* S_{Bstft}(t_m, f_B) \right) \right\}^* \approx \Phi_B(t_m) - \Phi_A(t_m). \tag{16}$$

Similarly, for antenna A and antenna C, it yields

$$\left\{ \text{angle}\left(S_{Astft}(t_m, f_A)^* S_{Cstft}(t_m, f_C) \right) \right\}^* \approx \Phi_C(t_m) - \Phi_A(t_m). \tag{17}$$

It can be seen from (16) and (17) that the interferometric phase term is still reserved after STFT analysis. And it can be abstracted directly from time-frequency plane.

4 Simulations and Analysis

Suppose that the length of baseline is $L = 100$ m. The carrier frequency is $f_c = 1$ GHz. Bandwidth is $B = 300$M and range resolution is 0.5 m. The imaging time is 1 s and pulse repetition frequency (PRF) is 800 Hz. The center of target is at $(0, 500, 0)$ km. There are two scatterers rotate with angular rotation velocity of $\omega = (\pi, 2\pi, \pi)^T \text{rad/s}$. The spinning period is $T = 2\pi/\|\omega\| = 0.2041$ s. The range profile of the target scatterers is shown in Fig. 2(a). It can be seen that range profiles of the two scatterers are concentrated in the same range cell. The STFT result is shown in Fig. 2(b).

Abstracting the phase information in STFT plane to conduct interferometric processing, the x-positions and z-positions can be reconstructed as shown in Fig. 3. It is shown in Fig. 3 that the reconstructed positions are not continuous and contain many break points. It is because that the frequency of scatterers overlaps at some seconds as shown in Fig. 2(b). At these seconds, the phase terms of different scatterers cannot be separated thus resulting failure in interferometric processing. The false reconstructed positions at these seconds are deleted. The theoretical positions are shown in Fig. 4. Compared reconstructed positions with theoretical ones, it shows that the reconstructed

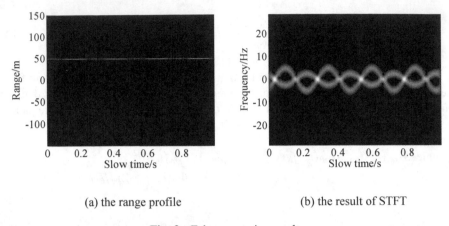

(a) the range profile　　　　　　　　(b) the result of STFT

Fig. 2. Echo processing results

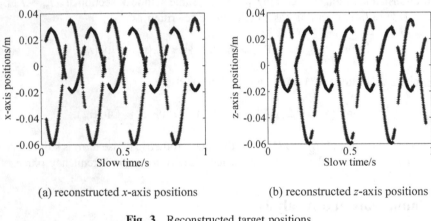

(a) reconstructed *x*-axis positions　　　　(b) reconstructed *z*-axis positions

Fig. 3. Reconstructed target positions

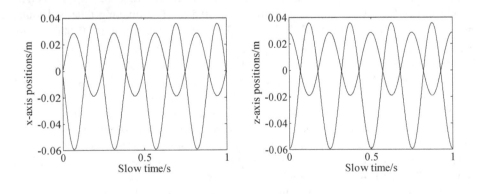

(a) theoretical *x*-axis positions　　　　　(b) theoretical *z*-axis positions

Fig. 4. Theoretical target positions

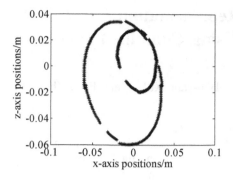

Fig. 5. Reconstructed motion trajectory

result is with good accuracy. Figure 5 is the two-dimensional motion trajectory of the target scatter. Through the motion trajectory, size and shape of the target can be scaled.

5   Conclusions

An interferometric-processing based imaging method for small space debris is offered in this paper. Through time-frequency analysis, echoes trajectories of all scatterers are segregated, which overcomes the difficulty of target size smaller than range resolution. What's more, time-frequency analysis does not destroy phase information for interferometric. Thus interferometric processing is successfully conducted to obtain the target position. The simulations verify the validity of the proposed imaging method. By comparison with existing ones, the proposed method shows the advantage that can get the real position and size of target. However, the phase information of echo is easily affected by noise. Although the space environment is in a low noise level, it is still an important task to abstract phase information in noise, which is also our next research direction.

Acknowledgments. This work was supported by the National Natural Science Foundation of China under Grant 61571457 and the Science Foundation for Post Doctorate of China under Grant 2015M570815.

References

1. Jiang, Z., Shengqi, Z., Guisheng, L.: High-resolution radar imaging of space debris base on sparse representation. J. IEEE Geosci. Remote Sens. Lett. **12**(10), 2090–2094 (2015)
2. Hongxian, W., Yinghui, Q., Mengdao, X.: Single-range image fusion for spinning space debris radar imaging. J. IEEE Geosci. Remote Sens. Lett. **7**(4), 626–630 (2010)
3. Sato, T.: Shape estimation of space debris using single-range Doppler interferometry. J. IEEE Trans. Geosci. Remote Sens. **37**(2), 1000–1005 (1999)
4. Qi, W., Mengdao, X., Guangyue, L.: Single range matching filtering for space debris radar imaging. J. IEEE Geosci. Remote Sens. Lett. **4**(4), 576–580 (2007)
5. Tao, S., Xiuming, S., Jing, C.: Three-dimensional imaging of spinning space debris based on the narrow-band radar. J. IEEE Geosci. Remote Sens. Lett. **11**(6), 1041–1045 (2014)

Sparse Representation Based SAR Imaging Using Combined Dictionary

Han-yang Xu[1(✉)] and Feng Zhou[1,2]

[1] School of Electronic Engineering, Xidian University, Xi'an 710071, China
xhy_xidian@163.com, fzhou@mail.xidian.edu.cn
[2] National Lab of Radar Signal Processing, Xidian University,
Xi'an 710071, China

Abstract. Sparse representation (SR)-based SAR imaging has shown its superior capability in high-resolution image formation. For SR-based SAR imaging task, a key challenge is how to choose a proper dictionary that can effectively represent the magnitude of the complex-valued scattering field. In this paper, we present a combined dictionary that simultaneously enhances multiple types of scattering mechanism. Trained by different kinds of SAR image patches with either strong point scatterers or smooth regions, the dictionary can represent both point-scattering and spatially distributed scenes sparsely. Finally, the SAR image is obtained by solving a joint optimization problem over the combined representation of the magnitude and phase of the observed scene.

Keywords: SAR imaging · Sparse representation · Dictionary learning
Combined dictionary

1 Introduction

Due to its day/night, all weather capabilities, synthetic aperture radar (SAR) has become one of the most promising remote sensing tools in military and civilian fields. Recently, compressive sensing (CS)-based SAR imaging has shown its superior capability in reducing sampling rate and improving image resolution compared to traditional Matched filtering (MF)-based imaging method. Baraniuk and Steeghs first demonstrated the CS theory in radar imaging in [1]. Later, Patel et al. introduced compressed SAR in [2]. Since then, CS-based SAR imaging has become a hot spot in SAR imaging community.

According to the CS theory, if the observed scene is sparse or can be sparsely represented in some space, then one can use limited radar measurements to reconstruct a high-resolution SAR image [3]. To sparsely represent the complex scene, the theory

This work was supported in part by the National Natural Science Foundation of China under Grant No. 61471284, 61522114, 61631019 and by the NSAF under Grant U1430123; it was also supported by the Young Scientist Award of Shaanxi Province under Grants 2015KJXX-19 and 2016KJXX-82.

of sparse signal reconstruction was introduced to CS-based SAR imaging. For instance, Samadi and Cetin proposed sparse representation (SR)-based SAR imaging method in [4], where the complex-valued signals were separated into real and imaginary parts to apply real-valued sparse representation methods directly to SAR imaging tasks.

In SR based SAR imaging, a key challenge is proper dictionary selection. In [4], the SR framework only focused on one type of scattering mechanism, and used common dictionaries such as discrete cosine transform (DCT) and wavelet transform coefficients. However, these dictionaries lack adaptivity in characterizing various scattering mechanisms for complex scenes.

Motivated by [5], we propose an SR-based SAR imaging method using a combined dictionary, which considers two types of most common scattering features in SAR images, i.e. strong point scatterers of man-made targets, and smooth regions of terrain or distributed natural regions. Firstly, two sub-dictionaries are trained using two types of SAR images separately. Then, we generate the third sub-dictionary by low-pass filtering for the enhancement of smooth regions. Finally, the combined-dictionary is obtained by concatenating the three sub-dictionaries, and therefore the new dictionary can represent all types of SAR scattering sparsely.

The reminder of this paper is organized as follows. Section 2 presents the framework of the proposed SAR imaging method. Section 3 shows the simulation results to verify the effectiveness of the proposed method. Section 4 provides the conclusion.

2 Framework of the Proposed SAR Imaging Method

This section describes the mathematical formulation of SR-based SAR imaging using the combined dictionary. We first introduce the observation model of SAR system and give a brief review of SR-based SAR imaging method. Then we propose our combined dictionary learning strategy. Finally, a joint iterative optimization method is presented.

2.1 SAR Observation Model

The observation geometry for spotlight SAR is shown in Fig. 1. The radar move along the straight path at constant speed v, and steers the antenna beam to the observation scene of interest. During imaging, the SAR system transmits pulses from a set of directions denoted by $\theta_k(k = 1, 2, \ldots, K$, and K is the total number of aspect angles in the azimuth dimension). The spotlight SAR transmits linear-frequency-modulated (LFM) signals $s(t) = \exp(j\omega_0 t + j\mu t^2)$ for $|t| \leq T_p/2$, where T_p is the pulse repetition interval, ω_0 is the carrier frequency and 2μ is the chirp rate. Assuming that the distance from radar to the scene center is much greater than the radius of ground patch, then the SAR echo $s_k(t)$ at θ_k can be described as:

$$s_k(t) = \iint\limits_{(x,y)\in D} f(x,y) \cdot \exp[-j\Omega(t)(x\cos\theta_k + y\sin\theta_k)]dxdy \tag{1}$$

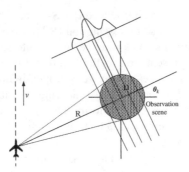

Fig. 1. SAR imaging geometry.

where D is the ground patch, (x, y) is the coordinates of scatterers in D, $f(x, y)$ is the complex-valued back-scattering coefficient at (x, y), $\Omega(t) = 2/c(\omega_0 + 2\mu(t - (2R_k/c)))$ is the radial spatial frequency, and c is the speed of light.

The imaging process can be described in a matrix form [13, 14], and the discrete observation model (1) is expressed as

$$s = \mathbf{H}f + n_0 \tag{2}$$

where s is the sampled echoes, f is the vectorized observation scene, n_0 is noise, and $\mathbf{H}$ is the SAR projection matrix containing the phase histories. For SAR imaging, the purpose is to reconstruct the unknown reflectivity f from s.

2.2   SR Based SAR Imaging

The recently emerged SR theory provides a feasible way for high-resolution SAR imaging. In an SR-based SAR imaging approach, an under-sampling strategy is carried on to the range and azimuth dimensions, and then the echo s is compressed by a sampling matrix $\mathbf{\Theta}$, so (2) can be written as:

$$y = \mathbf{\Theta}(\mathbf{H}f + n_0) = \mathbf{\Theta}\mathbf{H}f + n' \tag{3}$$

where y is the under-sampled measurements, and $n' = \mathbf{\Theta}n_0$ is the additive measurement noise. Our goal is to obtain the unknown observation scene f from the under-sampled measurements y. This ill-posed problem can be solved by a sparse signal reconstruction method. It is noticed that although f is complex-valued, we only care about its magnitude [6], thus the proposed SR-based imaging method only represents the magnitude of the complex-valued scene sparsely. In this case, we consider that:

$$
\begin{aligned}
y &= \mathbf{\Theta}\mathbf{H}f + n' = \mathbf{\Theta}\mathbf{H}\mathbf{P}|f| + n' \\
S.t \quad |f| &= \mathbf{\Phi}\alpha
\end{aligned}
\tag{4}
$$

where the complex-valued scene is separated into the magnitude $|f|$ and phase matrix $\mathbf{P} = diag(\exp(j\phi_i))$. $\mathbf{\Phi}$ is a dictionary that sparsely represents the magnitude $|f|$. Given

P, the scene f can be exactly recovered if we find a sparse coefficient α by solving the L1-norm regularization problem, i.e.

$$\hat{\alpha} = \arg\min_{\alpha}\left\{ \|y - \mathbf{H}\mathbf{P}\boldsymbol{\Phi}\alpha\|_p + \lambda\|\alpha\|_1 \right\} \tag{5}$$

where $\|\cdot\|_p$ is the Lp norm, and λ is the regularization parameter. In this way, the SR-based SAR imaging problem is converted to a joint optimization problem, which solves both the coefficient α and the phase matrix **P**. The joint optimization approach is as follows:

(1) Using conventional MF-based SAR imaging approach to get an initial estimate of f.
(2) Given f, obtain an initial estimate of **P** using the method in [4].
(3) Solve the optimization problem in (5) and get the estimate of $|f|$ though $|f| = \boldsymbol{\Phi}\alpha$.
(4) Update **P** using the new estimate of $|f|$.

Since $|f|$ is real-valued, we can use the state-of-art sparse representation methods for α estimation.

This made the selection of dictionary $\boldsymbol{\Phi}$ a key step of SR-based SAR imaging method. The dictionary should depend on the application and the type of objects or features of interest in our observation scene.

2.3 Combined Dictionary Learning

The selection of a proper dictionary $\boldsymbol{\Phi}$ is a key challenge in SR-based SAR imaging. There are many useful dictionaries that can sparsely represent $|f|$. Common dictionaries generated by scaling and translation of various basis, such as Gabor and wavelet, are appropriate for wide applications. Specialized dictionaries, intended to be used with a particular class of signals, can be learned from a large dataset. For SAR imaging task, the best way to get the sparsest result is to construct an overcomplete dictionary that includes all possible scattering features. However, such dictionary may lead to severe computation problems for large area imaging. To get sufficient sparse result with limited dictionary size, we present a combined dictionary learning method using 2D wavelet image decomposing and online dictionary learning strategy.

Instead of using a general dictionary constructed by a set of basis vectors (Fourier, curvelets, etc.) or an overcomplete dictionary generated by simple shapes (points, lines and squares, etc.) [6], we consider two types of scattering features in this paper: strong point scatterers of man-made targets; and smooth regions of terrain or distributed natural regions. Such features are most common in SAR images and of particular interest in SAR imaging task. In dictionary designing, we wish to combine these two features together so that the new dictionary can represent both strong scattering points and nature smooth scenes. Since the scene to be observed is unknown, we can select a set of SAR images having the similar scattering property as a training set based on prior knowledge, and such strategy has already been proved through transfer learning [7, 8]. Then, the dictionary $\boldsymbol{\Phi}$ can be constructed by two sub-dictionaries. The first sub-dictionary $\boldsymbol{\Phi}_p$ is trained by image patches with point-scattering features, such as tanks, vehicles and ships, etc., and the other sub-dictionary Φ_r is trained by image patches with smooth region features, such as cropland, mountain ridge and sea surface, etc.

To reduce the dictionary size, we use 2D discrete wavelet transform (DWT) to decompose the training SAR images into multi-resolutions. Figure 2 shows the results of DWT multi-resolution decomposition of two SAR images. Figure 2(b) shows the decomposition results after 2-level DWT using Haar wavelet, and Fig. 2(c) shows the zoomed out result of subband LL3 (the small image in the top left corner of Fig. 2(b)). It can be seen that almost all the magnitude information remains in subband LL3 while other subbands contain noise and a few ignorable high-frequency components. Meanwhile, the size of subband LL3 is only a quarter of the original SAR image. Therefore, we use subband LL3 as a training sample. By this means, we reduce the dictionary size while keep the effectiveness of the dictionary. To make the dictionary more overcomplete, we also select a small part of the high-frequency components as atoms of the sub-dictionary.

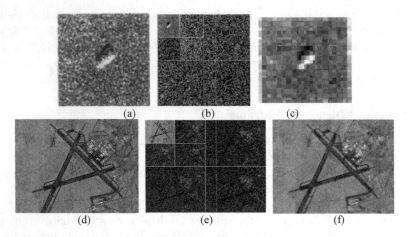

Fig. 2. 2D separable wavelet transform for SAR images. (a) original SAR images, (b) subbands after 2 level of Haar wavelet decomposition, (c) the zoom out image of subband LL3 (the small image in the top left corner of (b)), (d)–(f) results of another SAR image.

In dictionary learning, we apply the well-known recursive least squares dictionary learning algorithm (RLS-DLA). The training dataset is used iteratively to gradually improve the dictionary. Detailed information of RLS-DLA can be found in [9]. After the generation of Φ_p and Φ_r, we add another sub-dictionary Φ_f, which contains several local spatial smooth filters. Particularly, each column of Φ_f have the same number of elements as Φ_p and Φ_r, with all elements set to zeroes except for a local, vectorized region around a specific pixel. Φ_f can enhance the smooth regions because each atom in Φ_f takes the shape of the impulse response of a low pass filter. In the proposed method, we use a set of low-pass Gaussian filters as spatial smoothing filters.

In summary, the entire dictionary is given by:

$$\mathbf{\Phi} = \left[\mathbf{\Phi}_p, \mathbf{\Phi}_r, \mathbf{\Phi}_f\right] \tag{6}$$

3 Experiments

In this section, we demonstrate the validity of the proposed method. We first test the effectiveness of the proposed combined dictionary. Figure 3 visualizes the three sub-dictionaries. It can be seen that $\mathbf{\Phi}_r$ extracts shape features such as edges and corners, and $\mathbf{\Phi}_p$ extracts point features.

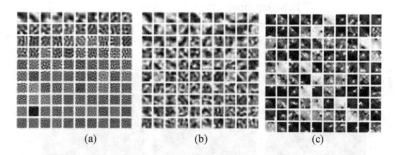

(a)   (b)   (c)

Fig. 3. Dictionary visualization. (a) Dictionary generated from randomly sampling raw training images, (b) learned sub-dictionary $\mathbf{\Phi}_r$, (c) learned sub-dictionary $\mathbf{\Phi}_p$.

Figure 4 shows the reconstruction error using different dictionaries. It can be seen that the proposed combined dictionary has achieved the lowest reconstruction error among other dictionaries. This is because the proposed combined dictionary can well represent all kinds of SAR images with different scattering mechanisms while other dictionaries lack completeness.

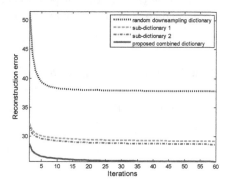

Fig. 4. Reconstruction error of different dictionaries.

Next, we test the validity of the proposed method using synthetic SAR scenes containing different kinds of scattering features. The radar parameters are shown in Table 1. We use a DCT dictionary for comparison. Figure 5 shows the final reconstructed results

Table 1. Parameters of simulated SAR system.

Carrier frequency	10 GHz
Slant range of radar center	14.14 km
Carrier frequency	10 GHz
Bandwidth	150 MHz
Pulse repetition frequency	500 Hz
Pulse repetition interval	10 us
Platform velocity	100 m/s

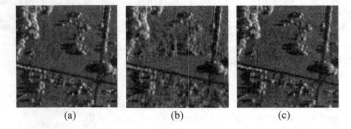

(a)   (b)   (c)

Fig. 5. Reconstruction of a SAR scene. (a) Observed scene, (b) reconstructed results using DCT dictionary, (c) reconstructed results using proposed combined dictionary.

Compared with the general dictionary like DCT, we see that using the proposed combined dictionary, the SR-based imaging method can suppress clutter more effectively and obtain better reconstruction result. We also use signal-to-noise ratio (SNR) and entropy of the full image (ENT) [10] for performance comparison. As is evident from Table 2, the proposed combined dictionary surpasses DCT in both SNR and ENT.

Table 2. SNR and ENT of the scene reconstructed by DCT dictionary and the proposed combined dictionary.

	DCT dictionary	Proposed combined dictionary
PSNR (dB)	28.44	31.53
ENT (dB)	0.733	0.405

4 Conclusion

In this paper, we have proposed a new approach for sparse representation based SAR imaging. Instead of using general dictionaries or single feature-based overcomplete dictionaries, we trained a combined dictionary that can enhance both strong point scattering and smooth region features. Compare to conventional dictionaries, the proposed combined dictionary can better represent the magnitude of the complex-valued scattering field. Finally, experimental results have demonstrated the validity of the proposed approach.

In the future, we intend to perform more detailed performance evaluation of our dictionary using simulated and experimental datasets.

References

1. Baraniuk, R., Steeghs, P.: Compressive radar imaging. In: Proceedings of IEEE Radar Conference, 17–20 April, Boston, MA, pp. 128–133 (2007)
2. Patel, V.M., Easley, G.R., Healy, D.M., Chellappa, R.: Compressed synthetic aperture radar. IEEE J. Sel. Topics Signal Process. 4(2), 244–254 (2010)
3. Donoho, D.L.: Compressed sensing. IEEE Trans. Inf. Theory 30(4), 1289–1306 (2006)
4. Samadi, S., Çetin, M., Masnadi-Shirazi, M.A.: Sparse representation based SAR imaging. IET Radar Sonar Navig. 5(2), 182–193 (2011)
5. Samadi, S., Cetin, M., Masnadi-Shirazi, M.: Multiple feature enhanced SAR imaging using sparsity in combined dictionaries. IEEE Geosci. Remote Sens. Lett. 10(4), 821–825 (2013)
6. Yang, J., Wright, J., Huang, T., Ma, Y.: Image super-resolution as sparse representation of raw image patches. In: Proceedings of IEEE Computer Society Conference on Computer Vision and Pattern Recognition (CVPR), 23–28 June, Anchorage, Alaska, USA, pp. 1–8 (2008)
7. Ben-David, S., Blitzer, J., Crammer, K., Pereira, F.: Analysis of representations for domain adaptation. In: Proceedings of Advances in Neural Information Processing Systems 19. MIT Press, Cambridge, pp. 137–144 (2007)
8. Luo, P., Zhuang, F.Z., Xiong, H., et al.: Transfer learning from multiple source domains via consensus regularization. In: Proceedings of the 17th ACM Conference on Information and Knowledge Management, 26–30 October, Napa Valley, California, USA, pp. 103–112 (2008)
9. Skretting, K.: Recursive least squares dictionary learning algorithm. IEEE Trans. Signal Process. 58(4), 2121–2130 (2010)
10. Wang, J., Liu, X.: SAR minimum-entropy autofocus using an adaptive order polynomial model. IEEE Geosci. Remote Sens. Lett. 3(4), 512–516 (2006)

Parametric Sparse Recovery and SFMFT Based M-D Parameter Estimation with the Translational Component

Qi-fang He[1(✉)], Han-yang Xu[2], Qun Zhang[1], and Yi-jun Chen[1]

[1] Information and Navigation College, Air Force Engineering University,
Xi'an 710077, China
qifanghe@163.com
[2] School of Electronic Engineering, Xidian University, Xi'an 710071, China

Abstract. The micro-Doppler effect (m-D effect) provides unique signatures for target discrimination and recognition. In this paper, we consider a solution to the m-D parameter estimation. This method mainly consists of two procedures, with the first being the radar returns decomposition to extract the m-D components in Bessel domain. Then the parameter estimation issue is transformed as a parametric sparse recovery solution. A parametric sparse dictionary, which depends on m-D frequencies, is constructed according to the inherent property of the m-D returns. Considering that the m-D frequency is unknown, the discretizing m-D frequency range for the parametric dictionary matrix is calculated by the sinusoidal frequency modulated Fourier transform (SFMFT). In this manner, the finer m-D frequency, initial phases, maximum Doppler amplitudes and scattering coefficients are obtained by solving the sparse solution of the m-D returns. The simulation results verify the effectiveness.

Keywords: Compressive Sensing (CS) · micro-Doppler effect (m-D effect)
Parametric sparse representation
Sinusoidal Frequency Modulated Fourier Transform (SFMFT)
K-resolution Fourier-Bessel (k-FB) series · Parameter estimation

1 Introduction

Micro-Doppler effects (m-D effects) depict targets' refined movement features, and provide the important information for target recognition and discrimination [1]. The rotation, vibration of a target induces the time-varying Doppler modulation on the received signals, which are most sinusoidal frequency-modulated (SFM) signals [2]. Hence, the parameters of the returned signals, including the scattering coefficients, modulation amplitudes, modulation frequencies and initial phases, suggest significant targets' m-D features.

This work was supported by the National Natural Science Foundation of China under Grant 61631019 and 61471386.

Time-frequency analysis (TF analysis) provides locations of such non-stationary signals in the TF plane, which has been widely utilized in m-D parameter estimation. However, most classic TF analyses either suffer from cross-term interferences, or are hardly to obtain the high resolution of time and frequency simultaneously [3]. Recently, some parametric methods which decompose signals into some different domain, such as the Bessel domain, are proposed and verified effective for the signal estimation and separation [4, 5]. Moreover, the sinusoidal frequency modulated Fourier transform (SFMFT) decomposes the phase term of a signal in the sinusoidal domain, so that the modulation frequency can be estimated by its projections on different sinusoids [6].

However, based on the Shannon-Nyquist theory, the received signals suffer from aliasing when the sampling frequency is less than twice of the maximum Doppler frequency shift, which makes it fail to estimate the motion features. In recent years, the compressive sensing (CS) technique is introduced to characterize the TF domain for m-D signatures extraction, and it is proved to be a promising tool with high-resolution [7–10]. CS theory supposes the sparsity of a signal in some transform domain, and the signal will be recovered from the limited samples. As the received signals induced by m-D are a sum of frequency modulated signals, they are sparse in TF domain [11]. As the approach proposed in [12], m-D signals can be first demodulated into some sinusoids, and then be reconstructed by exploiting their sparse solution in the Fourier domain. In [13], to extract accurate parameters, the demodulation procedure is conducted on the basis of a CS reconstruction process, but the initial phase cannot be obtained. In [14], the problem of m-D parameter estimation is transformed as a parametric sparse solution. It takes different m-D frequencies as the variables of the parametric dictionary matrix, and the sparse signal is solved by the pruned orthogonal matching pursuit (POMP) algorithm. Similarly, m-D signatures are extracted by parametric sparse recovery and OMP algorithm in passive radar systems [15]. In these methods, the m-D frequency is first being discretized as a frequency series. However, the estimation results are very sensitive to the m-D frequency, and meanwhile, the prior knowledge of the m-D frequency is unknown. In this case, the inaccurate division of m-D frequency series will lead to wrong estimation results. On the other hand, the wrong entries of the m-D frequency series are meaningless for estimation, which will lead to large computation amount. Additionally, some translational components induced by the bulk of non-rigid target or the scatters on the rotation axis, will make the traditional sparse recovery-based methods invalid for m-D parameter estimation.

To solve these problems, an approach based on the SFMFT in conjunction with the parametric sparse recovery and the k-resolution Fourier-Bessel (k-FB) series expansion is proposed. The received signal is first decomposed into different orders of k-FB series to extract the m-D signals of interest, and meanwhile, the phase shift ambiguity of the extracted m-D signals is revised. Considering the m-D frequency is unknown, it is first estimated coarsely by the SFMFT to provide a probable discretized frequency range for the parametric matrix. In this manner, the m-D frequency, as well as the initial phases and the modulation amplitudes are all discretized into series. The sparse representation model is solved by the OMP algorithm, and the finer modulation frequency, initial phases, modulation amplitudes and the scattering coefficients are obtained.

The following parts of the paper are organized as follows. In Sect. 2, the background of m-D signals and some basic theory is introduced. In Sect. 3 the proposed approach is described in details, while in Sect. 4 the simulation experimental results are analyzed. Section 5 draws the conclusion.

2   Background

In this section, some background including the m-D signal model and the basic theory of CS are briefly reviewed.

2.1   M-D Signal Model

The m-D effect is known as the time-varying Doppler modulations induced by the micro-motion of a target or its parts. The basic mathematical description of the m-D effect induced by rotation is discussed in this subsection.

The radar return of a target can be modeled as the signal reflected by a set of point scatters on the target. In this case, we suppose that there exist K point scatters on the target. Suppose that the target rotates with the angular frequency ω. The modulations induced by a rotation target consist of two parts: the m-D modulation induced by scatters rotating around the rotation axis; and the Doppler modulation induced by scatters on the rotation axis or the bulk of a non-rigid target. The received signal induced by rotation after the translation compensation is presented as

$$s(t) = \sum_{i=1}^{K} a_i \exp\left\{ j\frac{4\pi}{\lambda}[f_D t + d_i \sin(\omega t + \theta_i)] \right\}, t = t_1, \cdots, t_M \qquad (1)$$

where M denotes the signal sequence length, λ is the radar wavelength and f_D is the Doppler modulation frequency. d_i is the distance between the rotation axis and the scatter i in the LOS direction. φ_i and a_i are the initial phase and the scattering coefficient of scatter i, respectively. The Doppler frequency of scatter i can be given according to the derivative of the phase term in [1] as:

$$f_i(t) = \frac{2}{\lambda}[f_D + d_i\omega \sin(\omega t + \theta_i)] \qquad (2)$$

Note the fact that the rotation frequencies of all the scatters on one target are the same, with the rotation radius, initial phases and scattering coefficients are different. From (2) we can see that the translational component is different from that of the m-D component. The Doppler frequency of the translational component is constant, while the frequency of the m-D component is sinusoidal.

2.2   The CS Theory

The CS theory utilizes a signal's sparsity, so that the discrete sampling can be obtained under the sampling rate much less than the Nyquist sampling condition. In accordance with the CS theory, a signal can be recovered from the limited samples if it is sparse in some domain. The classic CS theory is described as

$$s = \boldsymbol{\Psi} g \tag{3}$$

where s is an $M \times 1$ observation vector, $\boldsymbol{\Psi}$ is an $M \times N$ matrix, and g is an $N \times 1$ sparse solution to be solved. The observation model in (3) can be solved under the constraint conditions, and thus, the sparse signal can be recovered from the observation vector by the following solution

$$\hat{g} = \arg\min_{g} \|g\|_0 \text{ s.t.} \|s - \boldsymbol{\Psi} g\|_2^2 < \varepsilon \tag{4}$$

where $\|\cdot\|_0$ and $\|\cdot\|_2$ denote the L_0. norm and the L_2 norm, respectively, and ε is the permitted error.

3   Parameter Estimation Method

As the modulation form of the translational component is different from that of the m-D component, the translational component will destroy the inherent property of the m-D signals, so that makes the sparse recovery based methods invalid. Hence, it requires an approach for the extraction of the m-D components from the received signals. Then the SFMFT and the parametric sparse recovery solution are adopted. The proposed parameter estimation method is introduced in the following subsections in detail.

3.1   Extraction of M-D Components

The discrete form $s(n)$ of the received signal in (1) with N samples is presented as

$$s(n) = \sum_{i=1}^{K} a_i \exp[j \, pha(n)], \, n = 1, \cdots, N \tag{5}$$

where $pha(n) = \frac{4\pi}{\lambda}[f_D n + d_i \cos(\omega n + \theta_i)]$ denotes the phase term.

As the discrete signals are mainly subjected to the problem of the phase shift ambiguity [16], the phase shift ambiguity should be revised for the received signal. Since the phase measurements are only possible in $(-\pi, \pi)$, the phase shift ambiguity occurs when the total phase shift is more than 2π when sampling, which can be revised by comparison of adjacent samples.

$$phar(n) = \begin{cases} pha(n) - 2\pi, & pha(n) - pha(n-1) > \pi \\ pha(n) + 2\pi, & phar(n-1) - phar(n) > \pi \\ pha(n), & |phar(n) - phar(n-1)| < \pi \end{cases} \tag{6}$$

where $i > 1$ and $phar(n)$ denotes the difference of the real phase shift and the phase shift measurement.

After the phase shift ambiguity is revised, the m-D returns are extracted on the basis of the Fourier-Bessel transform (FBT) and its related theories. A signal can be decomposed into a weighted sum of Bessel functions by FBT [4]. Similar to the Fourier transform and the Fourier series, FBT presents as the FB series within a finite interval. For a better resolution, a resolution metric k is introduced into the traditional FB series recently, which is called the k-FB series [5]. As the k-FB series has a one-to-one relationship between the order of the series and the frequency of a signal, it is effective for different signals separation overlapped in the TF domain.

Since the received signal $s(n)$ is in the neighborhood of zero-frequency after the translation compensation, the first several orders of the series correspond to the translational component. Expanded the signal by k-FB series and eliminate the first several orders of the series, the m-D signals $s_{m-D}(n)$ extracted from the radar returns can be reconstructed as follows

$$s_{m-D}(n) = \sum_{m=m_0}^{M} \sum_{n=1}^{N} C_m J_0 \left(\frac{\lambda_m}{kN} n \right) \tag{7}$$

where $J_0(\cdot)$ is the Bessel function of the zero order, λ_m is the m th positive root of the function $J_0(t) = 0$, m_0 is the maximum order of k-FB series corresponding to the translational component, and M is the order corresponding to the pulse repetition frequency (PRF). The series of order m in (7) can be calculated as

$$C_m = \frac{2PRF^2}{[NJ_1(\lambda_m)]^2} \sum_{n=1}^{N} ns(n) J_0 \left(\frac{\lambda_m}{kN} n \right) \tag{8}$$

3.2   Parameter Estimation

Considering that the parameters of the extracted m-D signals are $\{\omega, a, d, \theta\}$, discretize the candidates $\{d, \theta\}$ in a certain range as $d \in \{d_1, d_2, \cdots, d_P\}$ and $\theta \in \{\theta_1, \theta_2, \cdots, \theta_Q\}$, respectively. Then the received m-D signal can be presented as

$$s = \Psi(\omega) g(\omega) \tag{9}$$

where $s = [s(1), s(2), \cdots, s(N)]^T$, $g(\hat{\omega}) = [g(1), g(2), \cdots, g(PQ)]^T$ and $\Psi(\omega)$ is a $M \times PQ$ dictionary matrix. Then the sparse solution $g(\omega)$ can be obtained by

$$g(\omega) = \underset{g(\hat{\omega})}{\arg\min} \|g(\omega)\|_0 \text{ s.t.} \|s - \Psi(\omega)g(\omega)\|_2^2 \leq \varepsilon \tag{10}$$

$\Psi(\omega)$ is constructed by the m-D signal's intrinsic property

$$\Psi(\omega) = [\varphi(1, \omega), \cdots, \varphi(n, \omega), \cdots, \varphi(N, \omega)]^T \tag{11}$$

where

$$\varphi(n, \omega) = [\varphi_0(n, \omega, d_1, \theta_1), \cdots, \varphi_0(n, \omega, d_1, \theta_P), \varphi_0(n, \omega, d_2, \theta_1), \cdots, \varphi_0(n, \omega, d_Q, \theta_P)] \tag{12}$$

and

$$\varphi_0\left(n, \omega, d_p, \theta_q\right) = \exp\left[j\frac{4\pi}{\lambda} d_p \cos\left(\omega n + \theta_q\right)\right] \tag{13}$$

As the error of the sparse recovery solution is more sensitive to ω than $\{d, \theta\}$ in (9), serious recovery errors will be resulted in inaccurate or wrong ω [14]. However, without the prior knowledge of ω, the discrete values of ω will not be fine enough, so that inaccurate even wrong estimation results will be obtained. Meanwhile, to avoid the unnecessary computation amount of wrong ω in the sparse recovery process, the SFMFT is first utilized to obtain a coarse estimation of ω, which provides the candidate ω for a correct division range. In this manner, more accurate results of $\{\omega, a, d, \theta\}$ by the sparse recovery technique will be obtained.

SFMFT decomposes the modulation frequency ω on different sinusoidal basis, and the spectrum is obtained by the projections, referred to as the coefficient e_i on the different sinusoidal basis. The discrete SFMFT [6] of the signal $s_{m-D}(n)$ is presented as

$$s_{m-D}(n) = \left\langle \sum_{i=0}^{N-1} e_i\langle\times\rangle \exp[j \exp(j\omega_0 ni)] \right\rangle \tag{14}$$

where the coefficient e_i indicates the modulation spectrum of the signal, and $\omega_0 = 2\pi/N$ is the modulation frequency unit. Coefficient e_i can be calculated as

$$e_i = \langle\langle s_{m-D}(n), \exp[j \exp(j\omega_0 ni)]\rangle\rangle = \frac{1}{N}\sum_{n=0}^{N-1} \ln\{x(n)\} \cdot [-j\exp(-j\omega_0 ni)] \tag{15}$$

The frequency estimation of ω is obtained by e_i of the maximum value. Suppose that the maximum coefficient e_i locates at $i = i_0$. Then the estimation of the rotation angular frequency is $i_0\omega_0$, and the discrete range of the candidate ω is set as $[(i_0 - 1)\omega_0, (i_0 + 1)\omega_0]$.

One of the solutions of (10) is the OMP algorithm [17]. It makes the dictionary matrix orthogonal by the Schmidt orthogonalization method. And then the process of the signal decomposition is iterated on the over-complete orthogonal basis. In each round of iteration, the most matched atom is found as the sparse approximation of the signal. The OMP algorithm is widely used in sparse signal processing because of its advances in the decomposition efficiency. The OMP algorithm is selected to solve (10). For clarity, the m-D parameter estimation algorithm is stated as follows.

The M-D Parameter Estimation Algorithm

Input: The received signal $s(n)$ and the candidate set $\{d,\theta\}$.

Procedure:

1) Calculate the k-FB series of the received signal $s(n)$ and extract the m-D component $s_{\text{m-D}}(n)$ by (7).

2) Conduct the SFMFT of the signal $s_{\text{m-D}}(n)$, obtain the maximum coefficient $e_i = e_{i_0}$, and discretize the candidate ω as a $1 \times L$ vector $\omega_l \in \{\omega_1, \cdots, \omega_L\}$, where $\omega_1 = (i_0 - 1)\omega_0$ and $\omega_L = (i_0 + 1)\omega_0$.

3) For every ω_l, go through from 3-1) to 3-4).

   3-1) Initialization: residual vector $r_0 = s$, atom index set $\Lambda_0 = \phi$ and number of the iteration $t = 1$.

   3-2) Find $\lambda_t = \arg\max\limits_{j=1,\cdots,PQ} |r_{t-1}, \Psi_j|$, where Ψ_j denotes the column j of the matrix $\Psi(\omega_l)$, and update $\Lambda_t = \Lambda_{t-1} \cup \{\lambda_t\}$

   3-3) Update the sparse solution $\hat{g}(\omega_l)$, with nonzero elements being

$$\hat{g}_t(\omega_l) = \left(\Psi_t^H(\omega_l)\Psi_t(\omega_l)\right)^{-1}\Psi_t^H(\omega_l)s \text{ and the residual } r_t = s - \Psi_t(\omega_l)\hat{g}_t(\omega_l),$$

where $\Psi_t(\omega)$ is consisted by the different columns in $\Psi(\omega_l)$, and the column indices of $\Psi(\omega_l)$ belong to Λ_t.

   3-4) If $\|r\|_2^2 \leq \varepsilon$, stop the iteration and note the parameter ω_l. If not, set $t = t + 1$ and turn to 3-2).

4) Calculate the entropy $H(\hat{\omega}_l) = \sum\limits_n \hat{g}(\omega_l) \cdot \log_2\left[1/\hat{g}(\omega_l)\right]$ for every ω_l, and find the estimated m-D frequency $\hat{\omega} = \arg\min\limits_{\omega_l} H(\omega_l)$.

Output: The estimated m-D frequency $\hat{\omega}$ and the sparse solution $g(\hat{\omega})$.

---

4   Simulation Experiments

Suppose that the PRF of the radar is 1024 Hz, and with 1024 samples being collected. Considering that a target rotates with the angular velocity $\omega = 38.96$ rad/s with three scatters on it. One scatter locates at the rotation axis and thus induces a translational component. The rotation radiuses of other two scatters are 4 mm and 44 mm, the initial phases are 2.09 rad and 4.18 rad, and the scattering coefficients are 0.7 and 1, respectively. The received signal of the target under SNR = 12 dB is presented in Fig. 1(a).

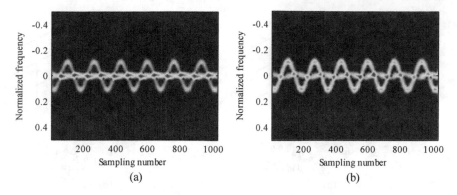

Fig. 1. TF analysis of the received signals. (a) The original received signal, (b) The extracted m-D signal.

From Fig. 1(a) we can see that the scatter with small rotation radius is almost contaminated by the translational component. The TF analysis of extracted the m-D signal is shown in Fig. 1(b), where the two m-D components can be both recognized. The m-D signals are extracted when the order is selected as $m_0 = 10$ and $k = 2$ in (7). After the m-D component extraction, the spectrum of the m-D frequency calculated by SFMFT is shown in Fig. 2.

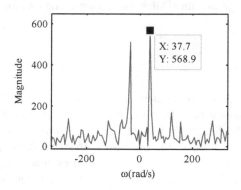

Fig. 2. The SFMFT spectrum of the m-D frequency.

It is shown in Fig. 2 that the extracted m-D components only contain a single modulation frequency at around $37.7\,\text{rad/s}$. The candidate ω is divided into the series of 40 entries between $[31.42, 43.98]$, and the candidates $\{d, \theta\}$ of the dictionary matrix are divided into 25×30. After the iteration, the estimation results of $\{d, \theta\}$ and a are shown in Fig. 3.

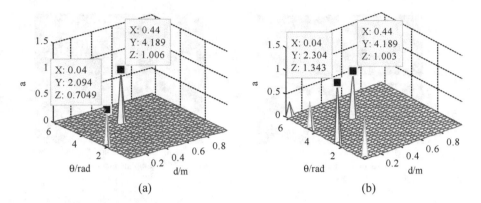

Fig. 3. The estimation result of $\{d, \theta\}$ and a. (a) The extracted m-D signal, (b) The original received signal.

As denoted in Fig. 3(a), the results of the two groups of the estimated parameters are $\{d_1, \theta_1\} = \{4 \text{ mm}, 2.094 \text{ rad}\}$ and $\{d_2, \theta_2\} = \{44 \text{ mm}, 4.189 \text{ rad}\}$. The estimated scattering coefficients are $\{a_1, a_2\} = \{0.7049, 1.006\}$, which reflect on the magnitude of the pinnacles. The estimated m-D angular frequency is 38.96 rad/s. The estimation results all agree well with the true values. On contrast, in Fig. 3(b), there are some interference pinnacles in the estimation results of the original received signal. The interference pinnacles are most in the location where the modulation amplitude approaches to zero. It agrees with (1) that the scatter on the rotation axis whose rotation radius is $d = 0$.

5 Conclusion

A novel approach of the m-D parameter estimation is proposed. We consider the m-D received signals containing both the m-D components and the translational components, which are invalid for the traditional sparse recovery based methods. The m-D components are first extracted in the procedure of signal decomposition and reconstruction by the k-FB series expansion. Then for finer estimation results, the SFMFT is adopted to provide the discretized modulation frequency range for parametric sparse recovery. By these means, interference pinnacles exist in traditional sparse recovery based methods are eliminated, and the accurate estimation results are obtained simultaneously.

References

1. Wang, D.C.: An overview of micro-doppler radar. J. CAEIT **7**(6), 575–580 (2012). (in Chinese)
2. Ruegg, M., Meier, E., Nuesch, D.: Vibration and rotation in millimeter-wave SAR. IEEE Trans. Geosci. Remote Sens. **45**(2), 293–304 (2007)

3. Liu, Z., Wei, X.Z., Li, X.: Aliasing-free micro-doppler analysis based on short-time compressed sensing. IET Sig. Process. **8**(2), 176–187 (2014)
4. Suresh, P., Thayaparan, T., Obulesu, T., Venkataramaniah, K.: Extracting micro-doppler radar signatures from rotating targets using fourier-bessel transform and time-frequency analysis. IEEE Trans. Geosci. Remote Sens. **52**(6), 3204–3210 (2014)
5. He, Q.F., Wang, J.D., Wang, K., Wu, Y.G., Zhang, Q.: Multi-component LFM signals detection and separation using fourier-bessel series expansion. In: RADAR 2016 Conference, Guangzhou, pp. 1749–1753. IEEE Press (2016)
6. Peng, B., Wei, X.Z., Deng, B., Chen, H.W., Liu, Z., Li, X.: A sinusoidal frequency modulation fourier transform for radar-based vehicle vibration estimation. IEEE Trans. Instrument. Measure. **63**(9), 2188–2199 (2014)
7. Luo, Y., Zhang, Q., Wang, G.Z., Guan, H., Bai, Y.Q.: Micro-motion signature extraction method for wideband radar based on complex image OMP decomposition. J. Radars. **1**(4), 361–369 (2012). (in Chinese)
8. Orovic, I., Stankovic, S., Thayaparan, T.: Time-frequency-based instantaneous frequency estimation of sparse signals from incomplete set of samples. IET Sig. Process. **8**(3), 239–245 (2014)
9. Stankovic, L., Orovic, I., Stankovic, S., Amin, M.: Compressive sensing based separation of nonstationary and stationary signals overlapping in time-frequency. IEEE Trans. Sig. Process. **61**(18), 4562–4572 (2013)
10. Flandrin, P., Borgnat, P.: Time-frequency energy distributions meet compressed sensing. IEEE Trans. Sig. Process. **58**(6), 2974–2982 (2010)
11. Chen, X.L., Dong, Y.L., Huang, Y., Guan J.: Detection of marine target with quadratic modulated frequency micromotion signature via morphological component analysis. In: 3rd International Workshop on Compressed Sensing Theory and its Applications to Radar, Sonar and Remote Sensing, Pisa, Italy, pp. 220–224 (2015)
12. Stankovic, S., Orovic, I., Pejakovic, T., Orovic, M.: Compressive sensing reconstruction of signals with sinusoidal phase modulation: application to radar micro-doppler. In: 22nd Telecommunications forum TELFOR, Belgrade, pp. 565–568 (2014)
13. Orovic, I., Stankovic, S., Amin, M.: Compressive sensing for sparse time-frequency representation of nonstationary signals in the presence of impulsive noise. In: Proceedings of SPIE, vol. 8717, United States (2013)
14. Li, G., Varshney, P.K.: Micro-doppler parameter estimation via parametric sparse representation and pruned orthogonal matching pursuit. IEEE J. Sel. Topic. Appl. Earth Obs. Remote Sens. **7**(12), 4937–4948 (2014)
15. Xia, P., Wan, X.R., Yi, J.X.: Micromotion parameters estimation for rotating structures on target in passive radar. Chin. J Radio Sci. **31**(4), 676–682 (2016)
16. Hasar, U.C., Barroso, J.J., Sabah, C., Kaya, Y.: Resolving phase ambiguity in the inverse problem of reflection-only measurement methods. Progr. Electromagn. Res. **129**, 405–420 (2012)
17. Tropp, J.A., Gilbert, A.C.: Signal recovery from random measurements via orthogonal matching pursuit. IEEE Trans. Inf. Theory **53**(12), 4655–4666 (2007)

A New Radar Detection Effectiveness
Estimation Method Based on Deep Learning

Feng Zhu[1,2(✉)], Xiaofeng Hu[1], Xiaoyuan He[1], Kaiming Li[3],
and Lu Yang[4,5]

[1] The Department of Information Operation and Command Training,
National Defense University, Beijing 100091, China
zhufeng_83@126.com
[2] No. 93682 Unit of PLA, Beijing 101300, China
[3] Information and Navigation Institute, AFEU, Xi'an 710077, Shaanxi, China
[4] Air and Missile Defense College, AFEU, Xi'an 710051, Shaanxi, China
[5] No. 91053 Unit of PLA, Beijing 100070, China

Abstract. Some of traditional analytical processes with non-linear characteristics are difficult to manage. For example, many issues of radar detection
effectiveness estimation relying on human experience are hardly to suggest by
using the traditional analytical methods. Therefore, some explored researches
aimed at this problem are carried out. The main purpose of the paper is some
reasonable ways are tried to designed to replace the analytical process, so as to
complete the radar detection effectiveness evaluation. As well known, Deep
Learning which is the typical models of deep neural network has a very good
capability for expressing non-linear contents. Hence, it could be brought into
studying the issue of the radar detection effectiveness evaluation, and this new
idea and relative new method are proposed in the paper. Furthermore, the CNN
as one of the typical network models or algorithms of the Deep Learning would
be employed to execute relative researches. In the proposed method, the input
sample data set which CNN needs can be constructed through designing the
spatial distribution images composed of the radar radiation domain and the
target location. And the labels for present or absent missing alarm can be
obtained according to some rules. Then, the CNN model with five hidden layers
is established to complete the non-linear mapping from input sample set to
output labels, in order to achieve the estimated results. Simulation results prove
the validity of the proposed method.

Keywords: Radar detection effectiveness estimation · Deep Learning
Convolution Neural Network · Missing alarm · Non-linear

1 Introduction

Radar as a tool to detect, identifying and tracking the targets, has played an increasingly important role in military and other fields. Radar detection effectiveness is a
comprehensive evaluation of discovery probability, target recognition rate, information
refresh rate of radar and so on. Through the valid evaluation of radar detection
effectiveness, the shortcoming of the using of radar can be detected in time, adjustment

© ICST Institute for Computer Sciences, Social Informatics and Telecommunications Engineering 2018
X. Gu et al. (Eds.): MLICOM 2017, Part II, LNICST 227, pp. 142–149, 2018.
https://doi.org/10.1007/978-3-319-73447-7_17

and deployment being carried out timely. It can be seen that radar detection effectiveness evaluation is an important prerequisite for commander's command decision, which is essential for guiding victory of battle [1].

For the evaluation of radar detection effectiveness, the non-linear analysis via the reasonable expression or calculation is usually used [2–4]. some analytical process is relatively simple, but with the continuous development of information technology, radar work mode more and more complex, The effectiveness of the play also becomes more difficult to grasp, which makes some difficult to analyze the expression, and even use the current analytical methods cannot be completed, such as many rely on human experience and intuitive assessment. In fact, the researches on the issues of radar detection effectiveness evaluation must be considered as the typical and explored studies for complex system. Therefore, the explored breakthroughs with new assessment methods which are from another new angle around the analytical process are necessary, in order to complete the assessment, especially some estimations are hardly to carried out by using the traditional analysis processes.

Deep Learning is a new field in artificial intelligence technology research in 2006 [5, 6], which originated in a typical technique of machine learning within artificial neural network, which is a process of simulating the study of human brain analysis, and has the deep network model. Based on this network model, the Deep Learning can complete the comprehensive study of a large number of samples by synthetically using multiple combinations, underlying information learning, finding correlation, layering, and so on, so as to discover the essential features of data, which is conducive to the extraction and classification of the deep features of things. At present, Deep Learning has been known as the closest to the human brain intelligent learning methods. It has a wide range of applications in many areas (including: classification, identification, assessment, etc.) [7, 8].

Some explored introduction of Deep Learning into the radar detection effectiveness evaluation study is given in the paper. Compared with the traditional effectiveness evaluation technology, the new ideas and ways are brought into executing relative researches. In the proposed method, the rich internal information within the complex system can be better described, mainly due to the good non-linear expression of Deep Learning. Therefore, the new ideas and ways can be provided from another new angle for assessing radar detection effectiveness which is difficult to express by the traditional nonlinear analytical process.

Convolution Neural Network (CNN) is an important and typical model in Deep Learning [9]. It has the advantages of powerful image processing and image information extraction. Therefore, CNN is used to construct the evaluation model of examining radar detection effectiveness. The new approach and the new idea of radar detection effectiveness evaluation based on Deep Learning are explored and studied in the paper. Finally, the validity of the proposed method can be verified by the simulation results.

2   Design of Radar Detection Effectiveness Evaluation Sample Set for CNN

2.1   Design of Radar Detection Effectiveness Data Set for CNN

Considering that the main advantages of CNN are to extract the image feature information, we intend to construct a matrix that characterizes the image as the input data set. And the image contains a lot of pixels, and these pixels can constitute the whole image matrix. According to the spatial distribution of the radar and its detection ability, the radar detection model is equivalent to the image matrix $S_{A \times B}$. The matrix shows the geographical distribution of the radar detection effectiveness in the north-south L_M km-wide and east-west L_N km wide range on a high-altitude plane. $S_{A \times B}$ has $A \times B$ elements total. Each element is the image of the pixels, the value of the integer value within $[0, 255]$, A is the number of pixels in the direction of the latitude, B is the number of pixels in the longitude direction, we can see

$$L_A = A \cdot D_A \tag{1}$$

$$L_B = B \cdot D_B \tag{2}$$

where D_A km, D_B km are the latitude and longitude resolutions, respectively.

Thus, we assume that there are N radars in the figure, the coordinates of each radar latitude and longitude is (Lat_n, Lon_n), the actual radiation radius of R_n km, $n = 1, 2, \cdots, N$. Assuming that there are I targets in the figure, each target latitude and longitude coordinates is (Lat_i, Lon_i), $i = 1, 2, \cdots, I$, respectively. The radar position and the radiation radius are all fixed, and the target position is randomly generated. The area where the actual radiation of the radar can be covered is filled with a pixel value P_1, each target is marked with another pixel value P_2, and the other pixel values are all P_3. Thus the sample set is assigned to generate.

2.2   Preprocessing the Input Dataset

We need to normalize the sample dataset in order to fit the unit dimension of the Deep Learning network training. The concrete details as follows.

For all elements of image matrix $S_{A \times B}$, i.e., x_i, $i = 1, 2, \cdots, A \times B$, the normalized processing can be expressed as follows.

$$\tilde{x}_i = \frac{x_i - x_{min}}{x_{max} - x_{min}} \tag{3}$$

where

$$x_{min} = \min\{x_1, x_2, \cdots x_{A \times B}\} \tag{4}$$

$$x_{max} = \max\{x_1, x_2, \cdots x_{A \times B}\} \tag{5}$$

$\tilde{x}_i$ is the result of normalized processing for x_i. From these results, we can see that the normalized method can be used to map different data into $[0, 1]$ space to unify the unit dimensions of different data, so as to construct the input sample set suitable for the Deep Learning network.

2.3   Design of Radar Detection Effectiveness Evaluation Label (i.e., Evaluation Criterion) for CNN

Taking into account the assessment of radar detection effectiveness is an important factor is the missing alarm situation, we have built the whether there is the missing alarm as an evaluation criterion of the radar detection effectiveness [10], assuming that the radar should be able to detect for reaching everywhere in the image $S_{A \times B}$, whether there is the missing alarm can be described as follows.

$$C = \begin{cases} 1, & \forall \text{ target is out of real detection domain of radar} \\ 0, & \text{all targets are in real detection domain of radar} \end{cases} \tag{6}$$

where the situation that the target is beyond the actual detection domain is occurred, i.e., $\exists i, n, i = 1, 2, \cdots, I, n = 1, 2, \cdots, N$, s.t.,

$$R_{in} \leq R_n \tag{7}$$

where

$$R_{in} = \sqrt{(Lat_n - Lat_i)^2 + (Lon_n - Lon_i)^2} \tag{8}$$

the situation that all targets are within the actual detection domain is shown, i.e., $\forall i, n, i = 1, 2, \cdots, I, n = 1, 2, \cdots, N$, s.t.,

$$R_{in} > R_n \tag{9}$$

According to these principles, the label of each image, i.e., the input sample set for CNN, can be achieved.

3   CNN Model

CNN is a multi-layer neural network. In CNN, each layer consists of multiple two-dimensional planes, and each plane consists of multiple independent neurons. Usually, the net structure of CNN contains the feature extraction layer, the down sampling layer and the full connection layer and so on. The feature extraction layer and the down sampling layer emerge alternately in the net structure, and the full connection layer is constructed in the end of the CNN to obtain the output results. The neurons of the feature extraction layer can extract the key features by the convolution operation aimed at the previous layer. And the adjacent pixels of the feature results obtained by the upper layer are averaged in the down sampling layer to obtain the new feature map. Furthermore, the above steps are repeated a number of times and then the resulted pixel values are rasterized and connected to become an input vector which can be brought into the conventional neural network to run and obtain the output results.

Based on this principle, we construct the radar detection effectiveness evaluation CNN model, as shown in Fig. 1.

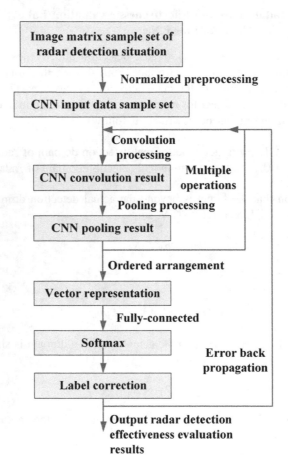

Fig. 1. Evaluation model of radar detection effectiveness based on CNN

4   Simulation Results

For the sake of validating the availability of the method proposed in the paper, the following simulation experiments are executed. Assuming that the rated detection radius of the X-band radar is 98 km, the actual detection radius is 65 km, and the resolution of the image matrix $S_{A \times B}$ is 5 km. Assuming that the 5 radars networking work to detect 10 targets, $P_1 = 200$, $P_2 = 100$, $P_3 = 0$, thus the sample images can be generated, as shown in Fig. 2. Figure 2(a) and (b) represent the radar detection situation and the input sample image, respectively, when there is the missing alarm, i.e., when some target is not detected, and the corresponding label is 1. Figure 2(b) and (c) represent the radar detection situation and the input sample image, where there is no missing alarm, that is, all targets are detected, and the corresponding label is 0.

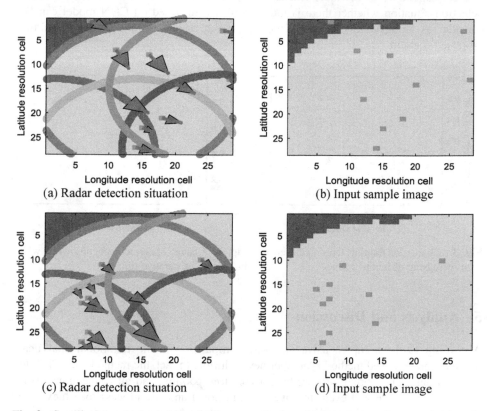

(a) Radar detection situation

(b) Input sample image

(c) Radar detection situation

(d) Input sample image

Fig. 2. Sample image, where (a) and (b) represent there is the missing alarm, and (c) and (d) represent there is no missing alarm

Thus, we constructed 70000 input sample data for CNN, as shown in Table 1.

Table 1. Input sample set for radar detection effectiveness evaluation with CNN

	Number of train sample	Number of test sample	Total
Label is 1	32998	5431	38429
Label is 0	27002	4569	31571
Total	60000	10000	70000

And next, the 5 layers of CNN, including two convolutions, two pooled layers and one full connected sensing layer is constructed. The sample number in each training group is 50, and the whole number for training is 1 to 5. The training termination error changing curve and the correct recognition rate corresponding to the label changing curve are shown in Figs. 3 and 4, respectively. From Figs. 3 and 4, we can see that on condition of the change of iteration number from little to large, the training termination error is gradually reduced and the correct recognition rate corresponding to the label is gradually increased. When the number of iterations reaches 5, the correct recognition rate corresponding to the label reaches 78%. At this time, the assessment for radar detection situation whether there is the missing alarm based on CNN model can be consider as being valid. Therefore, the simulation results show the validity of the proposed method.

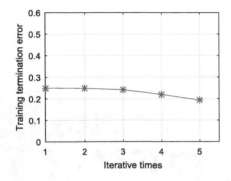 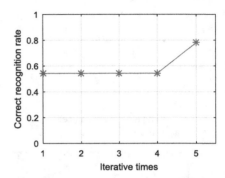

Fig. 3. Change of training termination error with increasing of iterative times

Fig. 4. Change of correct recognition rate with increasing of iterative times

5 Analysis and Discussion

According to the comprehensive analysis, compared with the traditional analytical method, the proposed method is another new solution. In fact, the method uses CNN to form a nonlinear mapping process by convolution, pooling, and all connections. This process can replace and even improve the traditional analytic process to achieve the more effective results beyond the traditional analytic process. This principle can be described and suggested in Fig. 5.

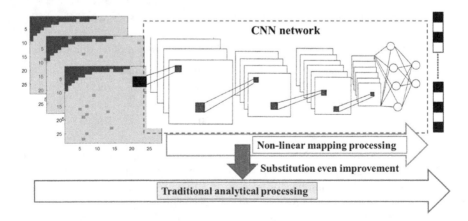

Fig. 5. Describing chart of principle within proposed method

6 Conclusions

This paper focuses on the current actual military needs, and puts forward a new method and new idea of radar detection effectiveness estimation which are engaged with Deep Learning. In the proposed method, the processes of convolution, pooling and full connection within CNN are used to complete the analysis process within the traditional evaluation, so as to realize the radar detection effectiveness evaluation. And even the proposed method has some important potential for improving and enriching the traditional assessment methods based on analytical processes. The simulation results show that the proposed method can achieve the correct recognition rate more than 78% at least aimed at the missing alarm labels. It also proves that the proposed method is valid to complete radar detection effectiveness estimations in certain extent. The research work of this paper can provide the new ideas and methods for the research on the relative issues of radar detection effectiveness evaluation, and it is also useful for studying and solving other evaluation problems. At the same time, it opens up some new spaces for the applications of Deep Learning.

Acknowledgement. This work is supported by the National Natural Science Foundation of China (No. 61374179, 61631019 and U1435218) and the China Postdoctoral Science Foundation (No. 2016M602996).

References

1. Wang, Z.-h., Li, X., Zhou, Q.-m., Zhou, J.-w.: Method to optimize cooperation deployment of GSR and AEW system. Mod. Radar **30**(4), 10–13 (2008)
2. Tong, L., Li, H.: Evaluation of combat capability for ground early warning detection system. Ship Electron. Eng. **35**(3), 24–27 (2015)
3. Feng, S., Yin, K., Yang, Z.: Research on modeling of early warning system based on complex system theory. J. Air Force Early Warn. Acad. **30**(12), 431–434 (2016)
4. Cai, W.-y., Li, X., Wan, F.-b., Wan, S.-h: Research on modeling and simulation for radar early warning detection system. J. Syst. Simul. **21**(3), 862–867 (2009)
5. Hinton, G.E., Deng, L., Dong, Yu., et al.: Deep neural networks for acoustic modeling in speech recognition. IEEE Sig. Process. Mag. **29**(6), 82–97 (2012)
6. Silver, D., Huang, A., Maddison, C.J., Guez, A., Sifre, L., van den Driessche, G., et al.: Mastering the game of go with deep neural networks and tree search. Nature **529**, 484–489 (2016)
7. Wei, O., Liu, S., Guo, S., He, X.: Study on the battlefield situation assessment model of simulation entity based on stacked auto-encoder network. In: 2016 International Simulation Multi-conference (Part II), 8–11 October 2016, Beijing, China, pp. 532–543 (2016)
8. Hui, G.: Auto target recognition technology based on deep learning. In: 4th Command and Control Conference, Beijing, 4 July 2016, pp. 319–324 (2016)
9. Huilin, G.: Military image classification based on convolutional neural network. Comput. Appl. Res. **34**(11), 3518–3520 (2017)
10. Si, G., Gao, X., Liu, Y., Wu, L.: Method for building effectiveness evaluation index system based on big simulation data. Big Data **42**(1), 57–68 (2016)

A Novel Parameter Determination Method for Lq Regularization Based Sparse SAR Imaging

Jia-cheng Ni[1(✉)], Qun Zhang[1,2], Li Sun[1], and Xian-jiao Liang[3]

[1] Information and Navigation College, Air Force Engineering University,
Xi'an 710077, China
littlenjc@sina.com
[2] Collaborative Innovation Center of Information Sensing and Understanding,
Xi'an 710077, China
[3] Unit 95100 of PLA, Guangzhou 510405, China

Abstract. Sparse SAR imaging based on $Lq(0 < q < 1)$ regularization has become a hot issue in SAR imaging. However, it can be difficult to determine a suitable value of the regularization parameter. In this paper, we developed a novel adaptive regularization parameter determination method for Lq regularization based SAR imaging. On the basis that the noise type in SAR system is mostly additive Gaussian white noise, we present a method for determining the regularization parameter through evaluating the statistics of noise. The parameter is updated through validating the statistical properties of the reconstruction error residuals in a suitable Noise Confidence Region (NCR). The experiment results illustrate the validity of the proposed method.

Keywords: SAR imaging · $Lq(0 < q < 1)$ regularization
Regularization parameter determination

1 Introduction

SAR imaging can be seen as an ill-posed inverse scattering problem whereby a spatial map of reflectivity is reconstructed from measurements of scattered fields [1]. In conventional SAR imaging, the data must be acquired at the Nyquist rate. The recently emerging of compressed sensing (CS) suggests that it is possible to recover a sparse signal from only a small number of random measurements, which permits signals to be sampled at the sub-Nyquist rate. More recently, another type of reconstruction algorithms called Lq norm regularization, have been utilized for radar imaging. Specially, when $q \leq 1$, many advantages over conventional radar imaging were demonstrated including enhanced features, increased resolution and reduced sidelobes. The L1 regularization is used in radar imaging in [2] as an alternative method for L0 regularization

The authors would like to express thanks for the support of the Aeronautical Science Foundation (Grant No. 20151996016) and Coordinate Innovative Engineering Project of Shaanxi Province (Grant No. 2015KTTSGY0406).

in CS [3, 4]. Since L1 regularization is a convex problem, it can be very efficiently solved. In [5], Lq $(0 < q < 1)$ regularization was introduced as a further improvement upon L1 regularization, it proves that Lq $(0 < q < 1)$ regularization can assuredly generate much sparser solutions than L1 regularization. Because of this, the Lq $(0 < q < 1)$ regularization has been accepted as a useful tool for solving the sparse SAR imaging problems.

In Lq regularization based SAR imaging approaches, the regularization parameter λ has a substantial impact on the imaging result. Inappropriate choice of these parameters can either trap the algorithm in local minima and/or lead to a lower convergence rate. Specifically, in SAR imaging task, if λ is too small, sidelobes are only partially reduced and there will still exist some noise. If λ is too large, the reconstruction image will be over-smoothed [6]. Usually, λ is set to be a fixed constant (greater than 0). However, the original setting of λ doesn't always apply to all imaging situations. There are also some methods been proposed to iteratively update the regularization parameters, such as use of the discrepancy principle [7] that seeks for the noise-only residual, and L-curve, which is based on the plot of the norm of the regularized solution versus the norm of the corresponding residual [8]. However, this type of methods suffers a time-consuming iterative process and may decreases the convergence of Lq reconstruction algorithms, which seriously limits the wide use of these methods.

In this paper, we present a regularization parameter determination method based on the properties of the additive noise. By assuming that the radar system noise and other additive noise follow the white Gaussian distribution, we define a probabilistic region of confidence for the noise coefficients. We update λ at the end of each iteration so that the statistical properties of the error residuals can fall into the noise confidence region. The updating algorithm stops when the residual has a Gaussian like structure. This method can avoid the over-smoothing without lowering the convergence speed.

The reminder of this paper is organized as follows. Section 2 presents the Sparse SAR imaging approach based on Lq regularization framework. Section 3 presents the regularization parameter determination method. Section 4 shows some simulation results to verify the effectiveness of the proposed approach. Section 5 provides the conclusion.

2 Sparse SAR Imaging Based on Lq Regularization

2.1 SAR Observation Model

The geometry of the SAR imaging system and the observation scene is shown in Fig. 1. Supposing the velocity of the platform is v. The transmitted signal of SAR imaging system is the linear-frequency-modulated (LFM) signals, which can be modeled by

$$s(\hat{t}, t_m) = \text{rect}\left(\frac{\hat{t}}{T_p}\right) \cdot \exp\left[j2\pi f_0 t + j\pi\gamma\hat{t}^2\right] \tag{1}$$

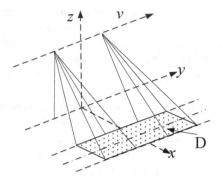

Fig. 1. SAR imaging geometry.

where $\hat{t}$ is the fast time, $t = \hat{t} + t_m$ is the full time, t_m is the slow time; $rect(\hat{t}/T_p)$ is the rectangular window with a width of T_p, T_p is the pulse repetition interval; f_0 is the carrier frequency and γ is the chirp rate. The received two dimensional SAR data can be written as:

$$s(\hat{t}, t_m) = \iint_D \sigma(x,y) \cdot rect\left(\frac{\hat{t} - \tau(x,y)}{T_p}\right) \cdot \exp\left[j\pi\gamma(\hat{t} - \tau(x,y))^2 - j2\pi f_0 \tau(x,y)\right] dxdy$$

$$(2)$$

where D is the imaging area, (x,y) is the coordinates of scatteres in D and $\sigma(x,y)$ denotes the scattering reflectivity coefficient at (x,y). $\tau(x,y) = 2\sqrt{y^2 + (x - u_m)^2}/c$ is the delay of the echo signal, $u_m = v \cdot t_m$ is the platform position and c is the speed of light. Now assume that the imaging scene is discrete into a point-scattering model, which includes $M \times N$ scatterers with the scattering coefficients $\sigma(x,y)$, $x = 1, 2, \ldots, M$ and $y = 1, 2, \ldots, N$. Therefore, (2) can be expressed as:

$$s(\hat{t}, t_m) = \sum_{x=1}^{M} \sum_{y=1}^{N} \sigma(x,y) \cdot rect\left(\frac{\hat{t} - \tau(x,y)}{T_p}\right) \cdot \exp\left[j\pi\gamma(\hat{t} - \tau(x,y))^2 - j2\pi f_0 \tau(x,y)\right]$$

$$(3)$$

Due to the sampling process, the radar fast and slow times are also discrete, so (3) can change into expression as:

$$s(\hat{t}_p, t_{m,q}) = \sum_{x=1}^{M} \sum_{y=1}^{N} \sigma(x,y) \cdot rect\left(\frac{\hat{t}_p - \tau(x,y)_q}{T_p}\right) \cdot \exp\left[j\pi\gamma\left(\hat{t}_p - \tau(x,y)_q\right)^2 - j2\pi f_0 \tau(x,y)_q\right]$$

$$p = 1, 2, \ldots, P; \qquad q = 1, 2, \ldots, Q;$$

$$(4)$$

where P is the samples of fast time and Q is the samples of slow time. $\tau(x,y)_q$ is the echo delay of scatterer (x,y) at slow time $t_{m,q}$.

2.2 Lq Regularization Based SAR Imaging

After the data discretization in (4), we put all the scattering coefficients $\sigma(x,y)$ into a column vector and change (4) into a more general matrix form as:

$$s = \mathbf{H}g + n_0 \tag{5}$$

where $s \in \mathbb{C}^{PQ \times 1}$ is the column vector of radar echo, $\mathbf{H} \in \mathbb{C}^{PQ \times MN}$ is the observation matrix, $g \in \mathbb{C}^{MN \times 1}$ is the column vector of scattering coefficients and $n_0 \in \mathbb{C}^{PQ \times 1}$ is the system noise. In (5) we have:

$$s = \left[s(\hat{t}_1, t_{m,1}), \ldots, s(\hat{t}_1, t_{m,Q}), s(\hat{t}_2, t_{m,1}) \ldots, s(\hat{t}_2, t_{m,Q}), \ldots, s(\hat{t}_P, t_{m,1}), \ldots, s(\hat{t}_P, t_{m,Q}) \right]^{\mathrm{T}}$$
$$g = \left[\sigma(1,1), \ldots, \sigma(M,1), \ldots, \sigma(1,N), \ldots \sigma(M,N) \right]^{\mathrm{T}}$$
$$\tag{6}$$

The observation matrix $\mathbf{H}$ can be expressed as:

$$\mathbf{H} = \left[h(\hat{t}_1, t_{m,1}), \ldots, h(\hat{t}_1, t_{m,Q}), h(\hat{t}_2, t_{m,1}) \ldots, h(\hat{t}_2, t_{m,Q}), \ldots, h(\hat{t}_P, t_{m,1}), \ldots, h(\hat{t}_P, t_{m,Q}) \right]^{\mathrm{T}} \tag{7}$$

where $h(\hat{t}_p, t_{m,q})$ contains the radar phase terms and rectangular window terms in (4), which can be written as:

$$h(\hat{t}_p, t_{m,q}) = \left[h(\hat{t}_p, t_{m,q}, 1), h(\hat{t}_p, t_{m,q}, 2), \ldots, h(\hat{t}_p, t_{m,q}, MN) \right]^{\mathrm{T}}$$
$$h(\hat{t}_p, t_{m,q}, i) = \mathrm{rect}\left(\frac{\hat{t}_p - \tau(x,y,i)_q}{T_p} \right) \cdot \exp\left[j\pi\gamma \left(\hat{t}_p - \tau(x,y,i)_q \right)^2 - j2\pi f_0 \tau(x,y,i)_q \right]$$
$$i = 1, 2, \ldots, MN$$
$$\tag{8}$$

From (8) we get the projection relationship between imaging scene g and radar echo s. In CS-based SAR imaging, s is compressed with a sampling matrix $\Theta \in C^{r \times PQ}$, $r \ll MN$, so (5) can be change into:

$$s_s = \Theta \mathbf{H}g + n_s \tag{9}$$

When g is a sparse scene, say, most of the scatters in g are zeros, the theory of CS tells when and how it can be recovered from the above ill-posed linear system. If the sensing matrix $\mathbf{A} = \Theta \mathbf{H}$ satisfies conditions like RIP [3], g can be exactly recovered using the Lq (quasi-norm) $(0 \le q \le 1)$ regularization optimization:

$$\hat{g} = \underset{g}{\text{argmin}}\left\{\|s_s - Ag\|_2^2 + \lambda\|g\|_q^q\right\} \tag{10}$$

where $\lambda > 0$ is the regularization parameter.

The first term in objective function (10) is called a data fitting term, which corresponds to model (9), and represents the observation geometry. The second term is called the regularization term regarding the behavior of the scene g. Regularization parameter λ controls the trade-off between data-fidelity and reconstruction sparsity, which plays a crucial role in the regularization optimization.

3   Regularization Parameter Determination Method

In this section we present a regularization parameter determination method using the statistics of noise. We first introduce the concept of Noise Confidence Region (NCR) and derive the upper boundary and lower boundary of NCR. We then present our regularization parameter updating method by control the reconstruction error residuals to obey a certain Gaussian distribution.

3.1   Noise Confidence Region Estimation

Note that the L2-norm term in (10) is under the assumption that the additive noise n_s is zero mean white Gaussian [9]. If $\hat{g}_i$ denotes the reconstruction result at ith iteration, then the reconstruction error residual $\Delta r = s_s - A\hat{g}$ at the end of ith iteration, ideally, should obey a white Gaussian distribution. Assume we choose an inappropriate λ that make the reconstruction result remove not only the noise but also parts of noiseless radar signal, then Δr will contain information that make its samples lager than white Gaussian noise. Based on this idea, we use a quantitative measure that verifies the similarity between the distribution of Δr and that of the noise.

Consider an additive noise random variable n with zero mean and finite variance σ. For any scalar value z, define a signature function $g(z, n)$:

$$g(z, n) = \frac{1}{m}\sum_{j=1}^{m} g(z, n_j), \quad g(z, n_j) = \begin{cases} 1 & |n_j| \leq z \\ 0 & |n_j| > z \end{cases} \tag{11}$$

where m is the length of noise n. $g(z, n)$ is equivalent to sorting the absolute value of the noise elements n_j. In this case, the mean and variance of $g(z, n)$ can be expressed as:

$$\begin{aligned} E\big(g(z, n_j)\big) &= F(z) \\ Var\big(g(z, n_j)\big) &= \frac{1}{m}F(z)(1 - F(z)) \end{aligned} \tag{12}$$

where $F(z) = 2\phi(z/\sigma) - 1$ is the cumulative distribution function (CDF) of absolute value of n, $\phi(.)$ represents the CDF of Gaussian distribution. The NCR is a proper confidence region around the noise signature. Due to the noise signature structure, the region is smaller than the corresponding confidence regions of the distribution of the additive noise itself. Since the additive noise n_s in radar system is zero mean white Gaussian noise, for each z and a high confidence probability p, the upper boundary $H(z)$ and lower boundary $L(z)$ of NCR can be derived using the Central Limit Theorem [10]:

$$H(z) = F(z) + \delta\sqrt{\frac{1}{m}F(z)(1 - F(z))}$$

$$L(z) = F(z) - \delta\sqrt{\frac{1}{m}F(z)(1 - F(z))} \tag{13}$$

where δ is a positive number that makes the probability p close to 1. In this case, if $g(z, n_j)$ is between the upper and lower boundary, it means that n_j has a Gaussian like structure.

3.2   Regularization Parameter Updating

Figure 2 shows the NCR of residual Δr, under confidence probability $p = 0.999$ and noise variance $\sigma = 0.9409$ (we add white Gaussian noise so that the SNR of radar system is 0 dB). It can be seen that the upper boundary and lower boundary have divided the $(z, g(z, n))$ space into three regions where the NCR in the middle. At the end of each iteration, we calculated $g(z, \Delta r_j)$ and see whether $g(z, \Delta r_j)$ falls into NCR. If $g(z, \Delta r_j)$ falls into the region below NCR, it means that λ is too big that the regularization term in (10) has removed not only the noise but also parts of noiseless

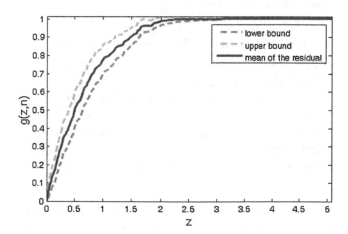

Fig. 2. NSR of the residual Δr, the upper bound and the lower bound are under confidence probability $p = 0.999$ with noise variance $\sigma = 0.9409$.

radar signal. If $g(z, \Delta r_j)$ falls into the region upon NCR, it means that λ is too small that only a part of noises are removed.

Here we proposed a simple regularization parameter updating method that force λ to moves toward NCR. We set a positive number $\alpha > 1$ and define λ_{j+1} as the regularization parameter in the next iteration:

$$
\lambda_{j+1} = \begin{cases} \alpha \cdot \lambda_j & g(z, \Delta r_j) \in \text{region upon NCR} \\ \lambda_j / \alpha & g(z, \Delta r_j) \in \text{region below NCR} \end{cases} \tag{14}
$$

If $g(z, \Delta r_j)$ falls into NCR, it means that the residual has a Gaussian like structure and the updating algorithm stops.

4 Experiments

In this section, we demonstrate the validity of the proposed method. We first conduct a simulation using single point scatterer to compare the reconstruction result. Table 1 lists the primary SAR parameters. Figure 3 shows the reconstruction results using Lq (q = 1/2) regularization optimization under different regularization parameters. These parameters are automatically chosen by our proposed method, start with $\lambda = 0.001$ and end with $\lambda = 0.1438$. We calculate the peak-to-sidelobe ratio (PSR) of different reconstruction results. It can be seen that the PSR increases monotonically with the update of λ, and the update stops when PSR is inf. The reconstruction result using the updated λ shows the absence of sidelobes as well as higher resolution than the result using initial λ. Figure 4 shows the reconstruction results using Lq (q = 2/3) regularization optimization, which get the same results.

Table 1. Parameters of SAR system and geometry.

Parameter	Simulation	RADARSAT-1
Slant range of radar center	50 km	1016.7 km
Radar center frequency	5000 MHz	5300 MHz
Platform velocity	110 m/s	7062 m/s
Pulse repetition frequency	175 Hz	1256.98 Hz
Pulse duration	2 µs	41.75 µs
Sampling rate	100 MHz	32.317 MHz

Next we test the validity of the proposed method on real SAR data from RADARSAT-1 in the fine mode-2 about Vancouver region. We applied our method to reconstruct the region of English Bay, where 6 vessels are sparsely distributed. The main radar parameters are shown in Table 1. Figure 5 shows the reconstruction results,

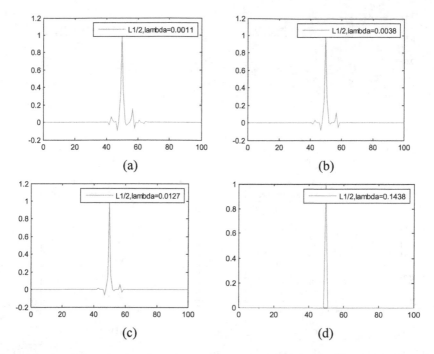

Fig. 3. Reconstruction results of a single point scatterer using Lq (q = 1/2) regularization optimization with different regularization parameters. (a) Imaging result with $\lambda = 0.0011$, PSR = 10.65 dB; (b) imaging result with $\lambda = 0.0038$, PSR = 11.55 dB; (c) imaging result with $\lambda = 0.0127$, PSR = 14.55 dB; (d) imaging result with $\lambda = 0.1438$, PSR = inf dB;

where the traditional SAR imaging result via Range Doppler Algorithm (RDA) under full sampling rate is shown in Fig. 5(a). Figure 5(b) shows the reconstructed result using L(1/2) regularization under $\lambda = 0.0038$ with 12.5% sampling rate than the Nyquist rate. Figure 5(c) shows the reconstructed result using L(1/2) regularization under the updated $\lambda = 0.01438$ with 12.5% sampling rate using the proposed method. Figure 6 shows the zoom in results of two vessels (in red boxes) in Fig. 5. It can be seen from Figs. 5 and 6 that the proposed method reconstructs higher quality images with reduced sidelobes at much lower sampling rate than traditional SAR imaging method and Lq regularization optimization method with fixed parameter.

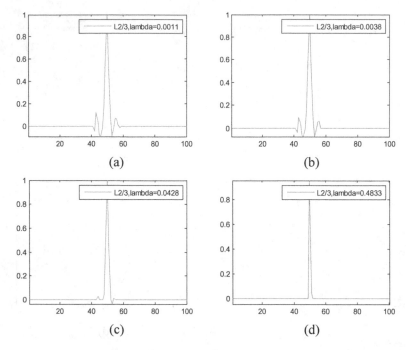

Fig. 4. Reconstruction results of a single point scatterer using Lq (q = 2/3) regularization optimization with different regularization parameters. (a) Imaging result with $\lambda = 0.0011$, PSR = 9.74 dB; (b) imaging result with $\lambda = 0.0011$, PSR = 10.32 dB; (c) imaging result with $\lambda = 0.0428$, PSR = 15.52 dB; (d) imaging result with $\lambda = 0.4833$, PSR = inf dB;

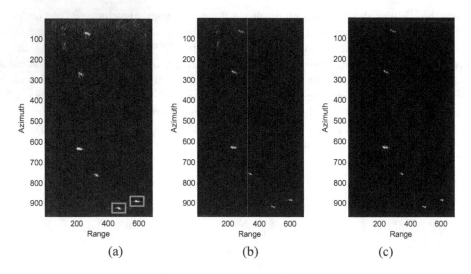

Fig. 5. Reconstructed results of RADARSAT-1 data. (a) The traditional radar image under the full sampling data, (b) reconstructed result using L(1/2) regularization under $\lambda = 0.0038$, (c) reconstructed result using L(1/2) regularization under $\lambda = 0.1438$. (Color figure online)

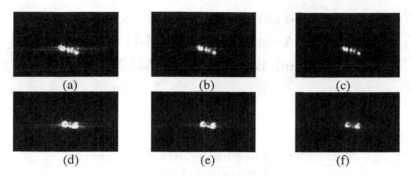

Fig. 6. Zoom in results of two vessels (in red boxes) in Fig. 5. (a) The traditional radar image under the full sampling data, (b) reconstructed result using L(1/2) regularization under $\lambda = 0.0038$, (c) reconstructed result using L(1/2) regularization under $\lambda = 0.1438$. (d)–(f) imaging results of another vessel.

5 Conclusion

In this paper, we present a regularization parameter determination method based on the properties of the additive noise. The proposed method is denoted by the noise confidence region (NCR), and validates the statistical properties of the error residuals. At the end of each iteration, the method categorizes the reconstruction result as well denoised, partially denoised, and over-smoothed. The method then updates the parameters so that the result falls into the well denoised region. The experiment results verify the validity of the new method.

References

1. Zeng, J., Fang, J., Xu, Z.: Sparse SAR imaging based on L1/2 regularization. Sci. China Inf. Sci. **55**, 1755–1775 (2012)
2. Logan, C.L.: An estimation-theoretic technique for motion-compensated synthetic-aperture array imaging. Ph.D. dissertation, Massachusetts Institute of Technology, Cambridge (2000)
3. Donoho, D.L.: Compressed sensing. IEEE Trans. Inf. Theory **30**(4), 1289–1306 (2006)
4. Candes, E., Romberg, J., Tao, T.: Robust uncertainty principles: exact signal reconstruction from highly incomplete frequency information. IEEE Trans. Inf. Theory **52**, 489–509 (2006)
5. Xu, Z.B., Zhang, H., Wang, Y., et al.: L1/2 regularizer. Sci. China Inf. Sci. **53**, 1159–1169 (2010)
6. Hashemi, S., Beheshti, S., Cobbold, S.C., et al.: Adaptive updating of regularization parameters. Sig. Process **113**, 228–233 (2015)
7. Vainikko, G.M.: The discrepancy principle for a class of regularization methods. USSR Comput. Math. Math. Phys. **22**(3), 1–19 (1982)
8. Hansen, P.: Analysis of discrete ill-posed problems by means of the L-curve. SIAM Rev. **34**(4), 561–580 (1992)
9. Samadi, S., Çetin, M., Masnadi-Shirazi, M.A.: Sparse representation based SAR imaging. IET Radar Sonar Navig. **5**(2), 182–193 (2011)
10. Beheshti, S., Hashemi, M., Zhang, X., Nikvand, N.: Noise invalidation denoising. IEEE Trans. Sig. Process. **58**(12), 6007–6016 (2010)

Downward-Looking Sparse Linear Array Synthetic Aperture Radar 3-D Imaging Method Based on CS-MUSIC

Fu-fei Gu[1], Le Kang[2,3(✉)], Jiang Zhao[1], Yin Zhang[1], and Qun Zhang[2,3]

[1] China Satellite Maritime Tracking and Control Department,
Jiangyin 214430, China
[2] Information and Navigation College, Air Force Engineering University,
Xi'an 710077, China
18810495946@163.com
[3] Collaborative Innovation Center of Information Sensing and Understanding,
Xi'an 710077, China

Abstract. In this paper, a three-dimensional imaging method for sparse multiple input multiple output (MIMO) synthetic aperture radar (SAR) is proposed. Due to the limitation of the antenna array length in DLSLA 3-D SAR, the cross-track resolution is poor than the resolution in high and along-track direction. To obtain high resolution in cross-track domain, the multiple signal classification (MUSIC) algorithm is introduced into the imaging problem. However, the MUSIC invalid under the condition of less snapshot numbers and presence of coherent sources, which may be caused by data missing or sparse sampling in practice. To overcome these limitations, after the preprocessing such as the range and along-track imaging with ordinary Nyquist based methods, the motion compensation and the quadratic phase compensation, this paper transform the process of cross-track direction into a multiple measurement vectors (MMV) model and applies compressive multiple signal classification (CS-MUSIC) algorithm rather than the conventional method or MUSIC algorithm. Based on CS-MUSIC algorithm, imaging result of high resolution with less snapshot numbers. Compared with the CS-based method, the proposed approach can obtain a better performance of anti-noise. The simulated results confirm the effect of the method and show that it can improve the imaging quality.

Keywords: Three-dimensional synthetic aperture radar · Sparse linear array
Compressive sensing · Multiple-signal-classification
Multiple Measurement Vectors

The authors would like to express thanks for the support of the National Natural Science Foundation of China (Grant No. 61501498, 61471386).

© ICST Institute for Computer Sciences, Social Informatics and Telecommunications Engineering 2018
X. Gu et al. (Eds.): MLICOM 2017, Part II, LNICST 227, pp. 160–168, 2018.
https://doi.org/10.1007/978-3-319-73447-7_19

1   Introduction

Downward-looking sparse linear array three-dimensional synthetic aperture radar (DLSLA 3-D SAR) obtains range resolution by pulse compression, azimuth resolution by virtual aperture synthesis with platform movement, and cross-track resolution by a linear array antenna [1]. Given the 3-D imaging capacity and downward-looking geometry, the problems in the conventional two-dimensional SAR can be solved by DLSLA 3-D SAR [2] ,which has attracted an increasing interest in recent years. Since ONERA [3] and ARTINO [4], as the real systems of MIMO-SAR, had been developed, a number of traditional 2D SAR imaging algorithms were extended into this 3D imaging mode such as chirp scaling algorithm [5], range migration algorithm [6] and polar format algorithm [7], which are based on matched filter (MF).

Due to the limitation of the space and capacity, the main problem of DLSLA 3-D SAR is that the resolution of cross-track direction is lower than the along-track and range direction. In addition, limited by the length of data, the resolution obtained by traditional MF method will be restricted because of Rayleigh limit To solve this problem, there are mainly two types super-resolution imaging methods, the methods respectively based on compressive sensing (CS) [8–10] and spatial spectrum estimation [11, 12], have been proposed for DLSLA 3-D imaging. However, the CS-based methods requires the sparsity of the target in observation scene and the resolution performance is noise sensitive, which limit the applications of DLSLA SAR. Besides, MUSIC invalids because of the coherence of scatterers in a realistic SAR imaging case, which can be solved by the spatial smoothing method with the reduction of real aperture and the dramatically decreased resolution [11, 12]. In addition, the data missing or sparse sampling resulted in the problem of less snapshot numbers and above-mentioned MUSIC-based method invalids in this case. To obtain the advantages of CS and MUSIC, CS-MUSIC [13] method have been proposed. The method has estimation accuracy under the condition of different snapshots and is robust to noise.

To solve these aforementioned problems of CS and MUSIC in DLSLA SAR, a novel imaging algorithm based on CS-MUSIC is proposed in this paper. The cross-track process is transformed into a Multiple Measurement Vectors (MMV) model, which will enhance the computational efficiency and elevate the performance of anti-noise compared with Single Measurement Vectors (SMV) model [14]. The cross-track location of the target is obtained by CS-MUSIC with constructing a new orthogonal space and searching peaks. The scattering intensity is recovered by the fast Fourier transform (FFT), which can also reduce the range of searching peaks. The super-resolution imaging result under the noise scenarios can be reconstructed by sparse sampling. Finally, we validate our theory by extensive numerical experiments.

2   Geometry and Signal Model

The geometry of DLSLA 3D SAR is shown in Fig. 1. The radar platform flies along the X-axis, at height H with velocity v. The array along the cross-track direction (Y-axis) is composed of N antenna elements with the equal distance d. At slow time t_m, the

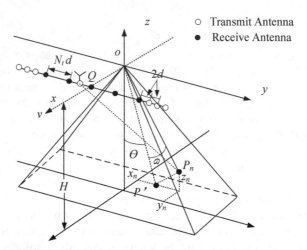

Fig. 1. DLSLA 3-D SAR imaging geometry model.

nth antenna element is located at $P_{mn} = (x_m, y_n, H)$, where $x_m = vt_m, y_n = -L_y d/2 + (n-1)d$. The linear array length is $L_y = (N-1)d$. The point scatterer $P_k(x_k, y_k, z_k)$, the instantaneous distance R between P_k and the nth transmitting antenna can be expressed as

$$R(t_m, y_n) = \sqrt{(vt_m - x_k)^2 + (y_n - y_k)^2 + (H - z_k)^2} \approx R_0 + \frac{x_m^2 - 2vt_m x_k}{2R_0} + \frac{y_n^2 - 2y_n y_k}{2R_0} \tag{1}$$

where R_0 is the projection of the range on the zero-Doppler plane.

The antenna element transmits a linear frequency modulation signal and the echo data can be expressed as

$$S(t, t_m, y_n) = \sum_K \sigma_k \exp\left(j2\pi K_r \left(t - \frac{R(t_m, y_n; K)}{c}\right)^2 - j4\pi \frac{R(t_m, y_n; K)}{\lambda}\right) \tag{2}$$

where σ_k is the backscattering coefficient, c is the light speed and, K_r is the chirp rate and λ is the wave length.

After the received signal are focused into two-dimensional points in the range and along-track domain, the rest phase obtain the cross-track information and two quadratic phase terms, which is about the flight distance and at slowtime t_m and the location of the nth antenna element. Therefore, echo signal can be rewritten as

$$S_n = \sum_K \gamma_k \exp\left(-j\frac{4\pi y_n y_k}{\lambda R_0}\right) + \omega \tag{3}$$

where γ_k is the coefficient of the kth point after two-dimensional focused, ω is the noise with zero mean and variance σ^2.

3 Proposed Imaging Algorithm

In this paper, in order to improve the resolution and enhance the computational efficiency for DLSLA 3-D SAR, a imaging method is proposed, in which the cross-track process is regard as a MMV model and solved by CS-MUSIC.

3.1 MMV Model for Cross-Track Reconstruction

As we can see, the grid points on the cross-track direction in DLSLA 3-D SAR can be discretized as $y_q = q\Delta y$, where $q = 1, 2, \ldots, Q$, Δy is the sampling intervals in the cross-track domain. Assuming $s_n = [s_n(t_1); \cdots; s_n(t_{M_1})] \in \mathbb{C}^{M_1 \times 1}$ is the measurement signal of nth antenna with M_1 sample number in cross-track direction. $\gamma_n = [\gamma_{n1}; \gamma_{n2}; \cdots; \gamma_{nQ}] \in \mathbb{C}^{Q \times 1}$ is the corresponding focused vector of the backscattering coefficient after cross-track focussing. Then, the signal shown in (3) is a linear measurement model, which can be written as

$$s_n = \boldsymbol{\Psi}_c \cdot \boldsymbol{\gamma}_n + \boldsymbol{\omega} \tag{4}$$

where

$$\boldsymbol{\Psi}_c = \left[\boldsymbol{\varphi}_1, \boldsymbol{\varphi}_2, \cdots, \boldsymbol{\varphi}_q \cdots, \boldsymbol{\varphi}_Q\right] \tag{5}$$

where

$$\boldsymbol{\varphi}_q = \left[\exp\left(-j2\pi\left(2y_q/\lambda R_0\right)y_1\right), \cdots, \exp\left(-j2\pi\left(2y_q/\lambda R_0\right)y_N\right)\right] \tag{6}$$

The structure of Eq. (4) is coincidence with the SMV mdoel. So, we can recover the azimuth signal γ from measurement vector s_n with CS theory. $\boldsymbol{\Psi}_c$ is the sparse dictionary. Next, we can get the low-dimensional measurement vector through down sampling. We choose the random partial unit matrix as sensing matrix $\boldsymbol{\Phi}_n \in \mathbb{R}^{M \times M_1}$. So the down sampling signal can be expressed as

$$s_n' = \boldsymbol{\Phi}_n s_n = \boldsymbol{\Phi}_n \boldsymbol{\Psi}_c \cdot \boldsymbol{\gamma}_n, \quad n = 1, \cdots, N \tag{7}$$

where s_n' is the down sampling signal.

Thus, for cross-track measurement vector, the sparse represent γ of signal s_n can be recovered by the following problem

$$\hat{\boldsymbol{\gamma}}_n = \min_{\boldsymbol{\gamma}_n} \|\boldsymbol{\gamma}_n\|_1, \quad \text{s.t.} \quad \left\|s_n' - \boldsymbol{\Phi}_n \boldsymbol{\Psi}_c \boldsymbol{\gamma}_n\right\|_2 < \varepsilon \tag{8}$$

In the reconstruction of cross-track signal, the cross-track direction is vertical with azimuth direction. Meanwhile, at the far field condition, with the length restriction of array antenna, there is no range migration to the same target for all antenna elements. It is implies that the sparse structure of each measurement is the same. Thus, the cross-track direction recovery can be implemented by MMV model. Additional, a same sensing matrix $\mathbf{\Phi}_c \in \mathbb{R}^{M \times M_1}$ should be adopted for the multiple measurement vectors. That is, we can take the $\mathbf{\Phi}_n$ as $\mathbf{\Phi}_c$ for any $n = 1, \cdots, N$.

Thus, the multiple measurement vectors can be denoted as $\mathbf{S} = [s_1, \cdots, s_N]$. M_1 can be regard as the snapshots number. The down sampling signal can be denoted as $\mathbf{\Xi} = \mathbf{\Phi}_a \mathbf{S}$. And the recovery signal can be denoted as $\gamma = [\gamma_1, \cdots, \gamma_N]$. Thus, the problem with MMV model can be reformulated as follows

$$\hat{\gamma} = \min_{\gamma} \|\gamma\|_{2,1} \quad \text{s.t.} \quad \|\mathbf{\Xi} - \mathbf{A}\gamma\|_2 < \varepsilon, \ \mathbf{A} = \mathbf{\Phi}_a \mathbf{\Psi}_c \tag{9}$$

where $\varepsilon \in \mathbb{C}^{M \times N}$. $\|\cdot\|_{2,1}$ is the (2, 1) norm which is defined by $\|\gamma\|_{2,1} = \sum_{i=1}^{N} \|\gamma^i\|_2$ and γ^i is the ith row of γ.

3.2   CS-MUSIC Algorithm

The signal subspace is $R(\mathbf{S})$ and the noise subspace is $R(\omega)$, where $R(\cdot)$ denotes the linear space. However, matrix $\mathbf{A}$, the measurement matrix after sparse sampling may not satisfy the above-mentioned property.

The support set of can be denoted by $\text{supp}(\gamma) = \{1 \leq q \leq Q : \gamma_q \neq 0\}$, where γ_q is the qth raw of γ. $\mathbf{A}_{I_{K-M_1}} \in \mathbb{C}^{M \times (K-M_1)}$ is composed of the columns of $\mathbf{A}$, and the indexes of the columns are belong to I_{K-M_1}, which is a subset of $\text{supp}(\gamma)$ and $|I_{K-M_1}| = K - M_1$. When $K > M_1$, the array manifold space $R(\mathbf{A}_{I_{K-M_1}})$ and noise subspace $R(\omega)$ are not orthogonal. $P_{R(\omega)}$ denotes the correlation matrix of noise subspace can be written as $\omega\omega^H$. Thus, the projection space is $R(\omega\omega^H \mathbf{A}_{I_{K-M_1}})$.

According to the above analysis, there are three steps in CS-MUSIC algorithm. Firstly, the indexes set I_{K-M_1} is reconstructed by SOMP or other CS methods. Secondly, the projection space $R(\omega\omega^H \mathbf{A}_{I_{K-M_1}})$ can be obtained by I_{K-M_1} and $\mathbf{A}$. Then the new noise subspace in is $R(P_{R(\omega)} - P_{R(\omega\omega^H \mathbf{A}_{I_{K-M_1}})})$. Then the spatial CS-MUSIC spectrum can be expressed as

$$P_{\text{CS-MUSIC}}(y_q) = \frac{1}{\mathbf{A}(y_q)^H \left(P_{R(\omega)} - P_{R\left(\omega\omega^H \mathbf{A}_{I_{K-M_1}}\right)} \right) \mathbf{A}(y_q)} \tag{10}$$

3.3   FFT in Cross-track Processing

Due to the SMV model, the spatial smoothing method and searching the peak of the spatial spectral in cross-track domain, the cost of computation in the traditional MUSIC algorithm is unacceptable. MMV model and the CS method have the less burden on peak searching rather than SMV model and spatial smoothing method, respectively. Thus, the FFT can decrease the spectral range of peak searching, which should be adopted.

And the coefficients can be obtained by the fast Fourier transform and be expressed as

$$g(\omega) = \sum_{n=1}^{N} S(y_n) \exp\left(-j2\pi \frac{\omega n}{N}\right), \quad \omega = 1, 2, \ldots N \tag{11}$$

The reduction of the computation can be expressed as

$$\mu = \frac{\cup_{i=1}^{P} \Delta f_i}{f_{all}} \tag{12}$$

where P is the major lobe numbers, Δf_i is the width of the peak lobe, $\cup_{i=1}^{P} \Delta f_i$ denotes the union of the 3 dB of each major lobe and f_{all} is the spatial spectral range in cross-track domain.

4   Simulations

To do further analysis, the simulations are provided. The parameters of platform and antenna, which are referenced the ARTINO system [4], are shown in Table 1.

Table 1. Parameters of platform and antenna.

Parameters	Value	Parameters	Value
Carrier frequency f_c (GHz)	37.5	Space distance of adjacent EPC d (m)	0.004
Bandwidth B_r (MHz)	300	Number of transmitting antenna N_t	10
Height of platform H (m)	500	Number of receiving antenna N_r	11
Velocity of platform v (m/s)	15	Cross-track resolution (m)	4.5
Pulse duration Tr (us)	0.1	Azimuth resolution (m)	0.5
Pulse repeat frequency PRF (Hz)	1000		

The algorithm is designed for 3D distributed scene in real use. So, 3D distributed imaging scene simulation must be added to make the imaging scene less sparse and check the performance. Figure 2 shows the imaging results of the L_1-CS method, MUSIC method and CS-MUSIC method. As we can see, the imaging result in Fig. 2(b) is complete and clear, the Fig. 2(c) misses some scattering points. That is caused by the scene is not sparse enough, which means the application of CS-based method is limited. The cross-track resolution in Fig. 2(d) is lower than the resolution in Fig. 2(b) and (c) because of the reduction of aperture in smoothing algorithm. The validity of the proposed method has been verified.

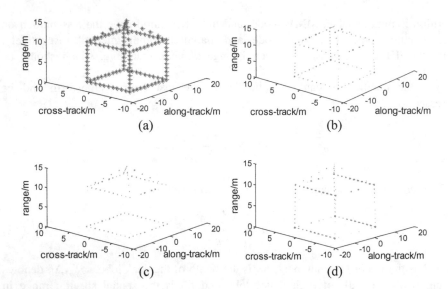

Fig. 2. Three dimensional imagery with SNR = 10 dB. (a) The distribution of the 3D imaging scene, (b) reconstructed by CS-MUSIC algorithm, (c) reconstructed by L_1-CS algorithm, (d) reconstructed by MUSIC algorithm.

To verify the anti-noise performance, the effects of signal-to-noise ratio (SNR), the point interval, and the probability of resolution are provided. In Fig. 3, it can be seen that the probability of resolution are improved with the point interval raised.

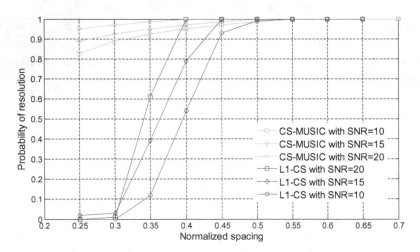

Fig. 3. Probability of separation versus different point interval. Two points are provided at $(0, 0, 0)$ and $(0, 0, 0.25\rho_y{-}1.2\rho_y)$ with interval $0.05\rho_y$. The times of Monte Carlo simulation is 500.

The spatial spectrum of proposed CS-MUISC-based method, the ordinary spatial smoothing and nearby spatial smoothing method are given. Figure 4 shows five points located at −7, −4, 0, 5, and 9 m in cross-track domain. The spatial spectrum of proposed CS-MUISC-based method has five peaks, however, the spatial spectrum of nearby spatial smoothing method has only four peaks, and the spatial spectrum of the ordinary spatial smoothing method has only three peaks.

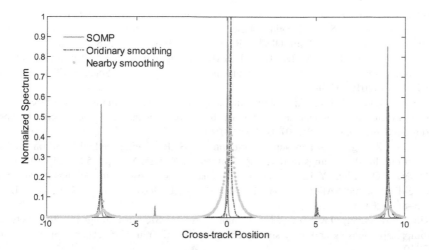

Fig. 4. Spatial spectrum in cross-track direction.

5 Conclusion

In this paper, we exploit the CS-MUSIC method for DLSLA 3-D SAR imaging at cross-track direction. The cross-track resolution can be improved compared with the conventional MUSIC-based imaging method, and the proposed method can obtain a better performance of anti-noise compared with the CS-based method. Finally, we validate our theory by extensive numerical experiments.

References

1. Giret, R., Jeuland, H., Enert, P.: A study of A 3D-SAR concept for a millimeter-wave imaging radar onboard an UAV. In: Proceedings of EURAD, Amsterdam, The Netherlands, pp. 201–204 (2004)
2. Klare, J., Cerutti-Maori, D., Brenner, A.: Image quality analysis of the vibrating sparse MIMO antenna array of the airborne 3D imaging radar ARTINO. In: Proceedings of IEEE IGARSS, Barcelona, Spain, pp. 5310–5314 (2007)
3. Nouvel, J., Jeuland, H., Bonin, G.: A Ka band imaging radar: DRIVE on board ONERA motorglider. In: Proceedings of IEEE IGARSS, Denver, CO, pp. 134–136 (2006)
4. Weib, M., Ender, J.H.G.: A 3D imaging radar for small unmanned airplanes-ARTINO. In: Proceedings of EURAD. Paris, France, pp. 209–212 (2005)

5. Zhang, D., Zhang, X.: Downward-looking 3-D linear array SAR imaging based on chirp scaling algorithm. In: Proceedings of APSAR, Xian, China, pp. 1007–1010 (2009)
6. Du, L., Wang, Y., Hong, W.: A three-dimensional range migration algorithm for downward-looking 3-D SAR with single-transmitting and multiple-receiving linear array antennas. EURASIP J. Adv. Sig. Process. **2010**, 1–15 (2010)
7. Peng, X., Hong, W., Wang, Y.: Polar format imaging algorithm with wave-front curvature phase error compensation for airborne DLSLA three-dimensional SAR. IEEE Geosci. Remote Sens. Lett. **11**(6), 1036–1040 (2014)
8. Zhang, S., Dong, G., Kuang, G.: Superresolution downward-looking linear array three-dimensional SAR imaging based on two-dimensional compressive sensing. IEEE J. Sel. Top. Appl. Earth Observ. Remote Sens. **9**(6), 2184–2186 (2016)
9. Bao, Q., Han, K., Peng, X.: DLSLA 3-D SAR imaging algorithm for off-grid targets based on pseudo-polar formatting and atomic norm minimization. Science **59**, 062310:1–062310:15 (2016). China
10. Bao, Q., Han, K., Lin, Y.: Imaging method for downward-looking sparse linear array three-dimensional synthetic aperture radar based on reweighted atomic norm. J. Appl. Remote Sens. **10**, 015008-1–015008-13 (2016)
11. Chen, C., Zhang, X.: A new super-resolution 3-D SAR imaging method based on MUSIC algorithm. In: Proceedings of RADAR Conference. Kansas, MO, pp. 525–529 (2011)
12. Zhang, S.Q., Zhu, Y.T., Kuang, G.Y.: Imaging of downward-looking linear array three-dimensional SAR based on FFT-MUSIC. IEEE Geosci. Remote Sens. Lett. **12**(4), 885–889 (2015)
13. Kim, J.M., Lee, O.K., Ye, J.C.: Compressive MUSIC: revisiting the link between compressive sensing and array signal processing. IEEE Trans. Inf. Theory **58**(1), 278–301 (2010)
14. Chen, J., Hu, X.: Theoretical results on sparse representations of multiple-measurement vectors. IEEE Trans. Sig. Process. **54**(12), 4634–4643 (2006)

Adaptive Scheduling Algorithm for ISAR Imaging Radar Based on Pulse Interleaving

Di Meng[1(✉)], Han-yang Xu[2], Qun Zhang[1], and Yi-jun Chen[1]

[1] Information and Navigation College, Air Force Engineering University,
Xi'an 710077, China
Mengdil105@163.com
[2] School of Electronic Engineering, Xidian University, Xi'an 710071, China

Abstract. Aiming at imaging task scheduling of multifunction phased array radar, this paper puts forward an adaptive scheduling algorithm for ISAR imaging radar based on pulse interleaving. Firstly, required resources for sparse aperture ISAR imaging were calculated according to initial cognition of target feature, based on that, a rational and optimized scheduling model of interleaving pulse dwelling is established, then radar resources can be allocated reasonably under the dual restraints of time and energy. At last, different targets were imaged respectively using compressed sensing-based sparse aperture ISAR imaging method and required imaging resolution is achieved while resource utilization rate is enhanced apparently. The simulation testified the feasibility of this algorithm.

Keywords: Phased array radar · Resource scheduling · Pulse interleaving
Sparse aperture imaging

1 Introduction

Recently, phased array radar (PAR) has been widely used. Compared with the conventional mechanical scanning radar, PAR has microsecond beam agile ability and controllable spatial resource allocation capability [1]. Reasonable, flexible and efficient scheduling strategy is the key to its advantage [2].

Scheduling method of phased array radar can be divided into two categories: template-based scheduling and adaptive scheduling. The adaptive scheduling method according to the environment and tasks adjust the resource scheduling strategy flexibly, which is the most effective, but also the most complex scheduling method [3]. In [4–7], a variety of adaptive scheduling algorithms are proposed for different radar tasks, such as target search and tracking. However, the resources of the system are not fully exploited. Pulse interleaving technology can improve the resource utilization of the radar system; its core idea is to schedule the transmitting or receiving pulse of other tasks in a single task pulse interval. Aiming at the time allocation of the PAR and

D. Meng—This work was supported by the National Natural Science Foundation of China under Grant 61631019.

© ICST Institute for Computer Sciences, Social Informatics and Telecommunications Engineering 2018
X. Gu et al. (Eds.): MLICOM 2017, Part II, LNICST 227, pp. 169–178, 2018.
https://doi.org/10.1007/978-3-319-73447-7_20

MIMO radar, some scheduling algorithm are proposed, which improves the time efficiency and energy utilization efficiency. A scheduling algorithm for digital array radar is proposed to solve the problem of dwell scheduling in [10]. The resource utilization of the traditional radar resource scheduling algorithm is optimized by using the pulse interleaving technique in [11–13]. However, most of the proposed algorithms only deal with the task of search and tracking, but don't take the imaging task into account. In fact, target imaging can provide important support information for target classification and recognition, and it is one of the important functions of PAR. Due to the imaging function need continuous time resources, so the resource utilization is low.

Under the framework of CS theory, continuous observation of the target image can be transformed into random sparse imaging, and in the sparse aperture condition, high-quality target ISAR image can be obtained [14]. This provides an effective technical support for incorporating imaging task requirements into the phased array radar resource scheduling model. Aiming at the imaging tasks, a resource scheduling algorithm is proposed in [15], but the algorithm only schedules from the beam, and does not utilize the time resource of the dwell waiting period.

Based on the above issues, a scheduling algorithm for ISAR imaging radar based on pulse interleaving is proposed in this paper, which can further improve the utilization ratio of radar resources.

2 Background

In this section, some background including the cognitive feature of target and the sparse aperture ISAR imaging are briefly reviewed.

2.1 The Cognitive Feature of Target

It is necessary to calculate the radar resources need for ISAR imaging tasks based on the results of target features to establish a reasonable pulse interleaved resource scheduling model. Sparse aperture ISAR imaging based on CS theory has made great achievements in recent years. In order to improve the adaptive ability of the radar imaging, the method in [15] can be used to recognize the characteristics of the target after entering the stable tracking phase. With the cognitive results of target features, the demand of radar resources for target imaging can be calculated. Using conventional tracking algorithms, the distance $\hat{R}$, speed $\hat{V}$, heading of the target $\hat{\theta}$ can be obtained; the target size $\hat{S}$ can be estimated; the azimuth sparsity $\hat{K}$ is defined as the number of distance units of azimuth direction is larger than the set threshold for each direction of the target rough resolution ISAR image; the observation time $\hat{T}_c$ is calculated from the reference azimuth resolution required for the reference target imaging; the relative priority P is calculated according to the distance, velocity and heading of the target.

2.2 Sparse Aperture ISAR Imaging

In the ISAR imaging process, the main position and amplitude information in the echo are mostly provided by strong scattering points while the weak scattering points contribute little to the echo. Therefore, using the recognition of target features, we can realize the sparse aperture cognitive ISAR imaging. Assume the accumulation time of the i-th target imaging is $\hat{T}_c$ after the feature recognition, $N = PRF \cdot \hat{T}_c$ pulses are transmitted, and the discretization of the full aperture is represented as $s_r(t, m)$, $m = 1, 2, \ldots, N$. There are $M(M < N)$ sub-pulses transmitted to the target, and the signal with sparse aperture is $s_r(t, m')$, $m' = 1, 2, \cdots, M$. For the i-th target, if the sparsity is $\hat{K}_i$, then the dimension M_i of azimuth observation after dimension reduction is expressed as:

$$M_i \geq c\hat{K}_i \ln(N_i) \qquad (1)$$

Where c is a constant associated with the recovery accuracy. The Fourier transform matrix is selected as the sparse transformation matrix $\boldsymbol{\Psi}$ of signal x. According to the sparse aperture distribution, the observation matrix $\boldsymbol{\Phi}$ can be designed as

$$\phi(m', m) = \left\{ \begin{array}{cc} 1, & \{(m', m) \mid m' = m\} \\ 0, & else \end{array} \right. \qquad (2)$$

It has been proved in [16] that the observation matrix is not related to the sparse transform matrix. Reconstructing azimuth information by solving the optimization problem:

$$\boldsymbol{\Theta} = \min \left\| \boldsymbol{\Psi}\boldsymbol{\Phi}^H S_r(f, \tau_m) \right\|_1, \quad s.t. S_r(f, \tau_m) = \boldsymbol{\Psi}\boldsymbol{\Phi}^H \boldsymbol{\Theta} \qquad (3)$$

The azimuth imaging of each distance unit is carried out according to the above method, and the matrix form is the ISAR image of the target.

3   Resources Scheduling of Radar Imaging Task

According to the sparse aperture cognitive ISAR imaging method, this paper proposes an adaptive scheduling strategy based on pulse interleaving. The proposed algorithm can significantly improve the resource utilization rate as well as obtain satisfying target imaging resolution.

3.1   Pulse Interleaving

The pulse dwell of the radar task is usually composed of the transmitting period, the waiting period and the receiving period. The radar can't be preempted in the process of transmitting and receiving pulses, but in the waiting period, the antenna is idle. Therefore, it is possible to take full advantage of the time resources of the waiting period for transmitting or receiving other tasks. This is the essence of pulse interleaving technique. By optimizing the beam level to the pulse level, the advantages of phased array radar beam agility can be further improved, as well as the utilization rate.

Pulse interleaving can be divided into the cross interleaving and the internal interleaving, which is shown in Fig. 1.

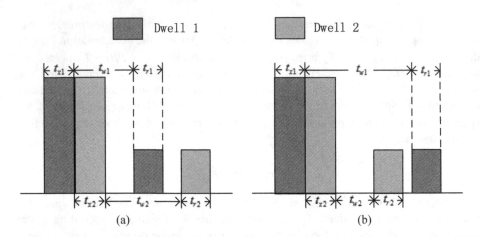

Fig. 1. Two forms of pulse interleaving. (a) The cross pulse interleaving, (b) the internal pulse interleaving.

Where t_{xj}, t_{wj}, t_{rj} denote the transmitting period, waiting period and receiving period of dwell $j(j = 1, 2)$ respectively. The time constraints of the two interleaving modes can be expressed as:

$$t_{w1} \geq t_{x2}, \ t_{w2} \geq t_{r1}, \ t_{x2} + t_{w2} \geq t_{x1} + t_{r1} \qquad (4)$$

$$t_{w1} \geq t_{x2} + t_{w2} + t_{r2} \qquad (5)$$

In the actual scheduling process, the number of the pulse interleaving is restricted by the energy constraint condition, so as to avoid the long working time of the transmitter. The energy constraint of radar system is divided into steady state energy constraint and transient energy constraint. Since the total energy consumption threshold of the steady-state energy constraint is constrained by the performance of the device, only transient energy constraint is usually considered. The transient energy at t moment can be defined as:

$$E(t) = \int_0^t P(x)e^{(x-t)/\tau}dx \qquad (6)$$

Where, $P(x)$ denotes the power parameter and τ denotes the back-off parameter which is related to the heat dissipation of the system.

In the process of pulse interleaving, the energy constraint can be defined as $E(t)$, which cannot exceed the maximum threshold E_{max} of instantaneous energy at any time, i.e.

$$E(t) \leq E_{max} \qquad (7)$$

In simulation, the energy consumption of radar beam and the variation of energy state in time Δt can be prior estimated by the parameters of antenna gain, transmission power, and pulse width and pulse number, so as to reduce the complexity of algorithm.

3.2   Resource Scheduling Algorithm for Radar Imaging Tasks

This paper presents an adaptive scheduling algorithm for radar imaging resources based on pulse interleaving. Firstly, the method in [10] is used to recognize the characteristics of the target, and then calculate the observation time $\hat{T}_{ci}$, azimuth observation dimension $\hat{M}_i$ and relative priority P_{ki} of each target imaging. On this basis, the pulse interleaving technology is used to allocate the radar resources from the high to the low. The waiting period t_{wi} of the mission dwell can be calculated from the distance between the radar and the targets which is obtained from the cognitive. The schematic of ISAR task scheduling based on pulse interleaving is shown in Fig. 2.

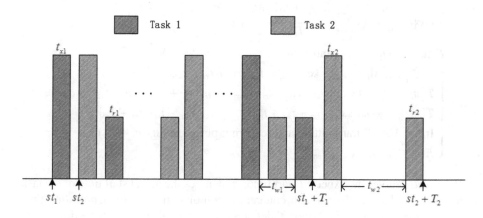

Fig. 2. The schematic of ISAR task scheduling based on pulse interleaving.

The scheduling success ratio (SSR), the hit value ratio (HVR), the time utilization ratio (TUR) and the energy utilization rate (EUR) are taken as the criterion.

(1) The scheduling success ratio (SSR): The number of imaging tasks performed to the actual number of imaging task. It can be expressed as:

$$SSR = \frac{N'}{N} \tag{8}$$

(2) The time utilization ratio (TUR): The ratio of the total dwell time to the total scheduling time. It can be expressed as:

$$TUR = \frac{\sum\limits_{i=1}^{N'} (t_{xi} + t_{ri}) \cdot M_i}{T_{\text{total}}} \tag{9}$$

(3) The energy utilization rate (EUR): The ratio of the energy consumed by all the transmit pulses to the total energy supplied by the system. It can be expressed as:

$$\text{EUR} = \frac{P_t \cdot \sum\limits_{i=1}^{N'} (t_{xi} \cdot M_i)}{P_{av} \cdot T_{\text{total}}} \tag{10}$$

Where N denotes the total number of tasks for request scheduling, N' denotes the successfully scheduled numbers, t_{xi} and t_{ri} denote the transmission time and the reception time of the pulse in the i-th task respectively; M_i is the dimension of azimuth observation; T_{total} is total simulation time, P_t is the peak power of each transmitted pulse and P_{av} is the average power delivered by the radar. So the radar imaging task model can be established as:

$$\max\{q_1 \frac{N'}{N} + q_2 \sum_{i=1}^{N'} \frac{\sum\limits_{i=1}^{N'} (t_{xi} + t_{ri}) \cdot M_i}{T_{\text{total}}} + q_3 \frac{P_t \cdot \sum\limits_{i=1}^{N'} (t_{xi} \cdot M_i)}{P_{av} \cdot T_{\text{total}}}\}$$

$$s.t. \begin{cases} \max(t_0, et_i) \leq st_i \leq \min(et_i + \omega_i, t_{end}), i = 1, 2, \cdots N' \\ \cap_{i=1}^{N'} [st_i, \ st_i + t_{wi}] \cup [st_i + t_{xi} + t_{wi}, \ st_i + t_{xi} + t_{wi} + t_{ri}] = \emptyset \\ T[st_i : st_i + t_{xi}] = T[st_i + T_{ci} - t_{ri} - t_{wi} - t_{xi} : st_i + T_{ci} - t_{ri} - t_{wi}] = a_i \\ T[st_i + t_{xi} + t_{wi} : st_i + t_{xi} + t_{wi} + t_{ri}] = T[st_i + T_{ci} - t_{ri} : st_i + T_{ci}] = -a_i \\ \text{Insert } M_i - 2 \text{ transmitting and receiving pulses in } (st_i, st_i + T_{ci}) \\ E(t) \leq E_{\max}, \ t \in [t_0, t_{end}] \end{cases} \tag{11}$$

Where et_i denotes the expected start time; st_i denotes the actual start time of the task scheduling; T_{ci} denotes the azimuth coherent accumulation time; ω_i denotes the time window of the i-th task; The vector T denotes the dispatching state of the discretized time interval; a_i is the task number of the i-th task; q_1, q_2, q_3 is the adjustment coefficient. The first and second constraints represent the time constraints that the task scheduling needs to satisfy; the third to fifth constraints represent the sparse aperture conditions and the observation time range that the imaging task needs to satisfy; the sixth constraint represent the energy constraints that the task scheduling needs to satisfy.

Discretize the system time, and the length of each time slot is Δt. Assuming that the target is to be imaged in the scheduling interval $[t_0, t_{end}]$, and the resource scheduling algorithm for ISAR imaging radar is described as follows:

Step 1: Sending a bit of pulse to recognize target features, and calculate the azimuth coherent accumulation time and the observation dimension according to the echo feedback information.

Step 2: Add the task of the latest scheduled start time less than t_0 and the task that the sum of the earliest scheduling start time and the azimuthal coherent accumulation time is greater than t_{end} to the delete list, According to the priority, join the remaining $N - K$ tasks to the application list (tasks with the same priority are arranged according to the expected execution time), and let $i = 1$.

Step 3: Let that t_{p_first} points to the first transmit pulse of the i-th imaging task, i.e. the expected start time of the task scheduling and t_{p_end} points to the last transmit pulse, so $t_{p\_end} = t_{p\_first} + T_{ci} - t_{w_i}$.

Step 4: If t_{p_first} and t_{p_end} determine the end of the transmission pulse to the interval, and $M_i - 2$ pulse pair is succeed inserted under the constraint of time and energy, then dispatch the imaging task in this manner and update the energy state of each time slot, $i = i + 1$, turn to step 5. Otherwise let $t_{p\_first} = t_{p\_first} + \Delta t_p$ and $t_{p\_end} = t_{p\_end} + \Delta t_p$ (Δt_p denotes the minimum step size). If $t_p < st_i + \omega_i$, return to step 4, otherwise the task cannot be scheduled and added to the delete list, let $i = i + 1$, and return to step 3.

Step 5: If $i \leq N - K$, return to step 3, otherwise, if $i > N - K$, return to step 6.

Step 6: Using the sparse aperture imaging method, the ISAR image can be obtained. Then end the schedule.

The flame of ISAR task resource scheduling is shown in Fig. 3.

Fig. 3. The flame of ISAR task resource scheduling.

4 Simulation Experiments

In the simulation, suppose the radar transmits LFM signals, in order to get more accurate simulation results, set both the transmit pulse width and the minimum pointer sliding step to 10 μs, the time window is 1 ms, the simulation time is 1 s, the pulse power is 4 kW, and the average power is 500 W. The distance between the target and the radar is 0 to 30 km.

It should be noted that the arrival time of radar echo is affected by the dimension of the target in rang direction. In order to ensure the imaging quality, the received pulse should be broadened properly. Suppose that the distance from the radar to the i-th target is R_i and the dimension of the target in rang direction is $\hat{S}_{y_i}$, the width of the actual received pulse of the i-th imaging task can be expressed as:

$$t'_{wi} = \frac{2(R_i + \hat{S}_{y_i})}{c} \tag{12}$$

Compare the traditional radar imaging task scheduling algorithm (traditional algorithm) in [15] and the radar imaging task scheduling algorithm proposed in this paper (proposed algorithm). In order to effectively receive echoes of all imaging targets, the dwell waiting period in the conventional algorithm is set as the round trip time between the radar and the farthest target. The results of the comparison are shown in Fig. 4.

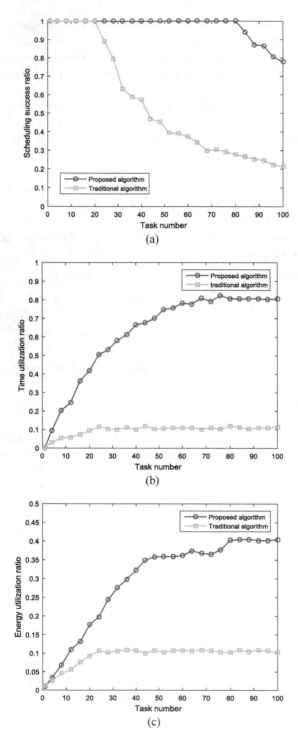

Fig. 4. The comparison of two scheduling algorithms. (a) The scheduling success ratio, (b) the time utilization ratio, (c) The energy utilization ratio.

From Fig. 4(a) we can see that when the number of tasks is small, both algorithms can successfully schedule all the imaging tasks, and the scheduling success rate is 100%. When the number of tasks is more than six, the scheduling success rate of the traditional algorithm begins to decline significantly, but the proposed algorithm can still successfully schedule all tasks until the task number reaches to 80. This is because the proposed algorithm takes full advantage of the idle time of the task pulse to schedule other tasks, which can take full advantage of the system time resources.

From Fig. 4(b) and (c), we can see that the proposed algorithm takes full advantage of the time resources of the pulse waiting period, and the number of tasks successfully scheduled in the same scheduling time is large, which makes the time utilization ratio and energy utilization ratio can reaches to 80% and 40%, and after the number of imaging tasks is more than 6, both the time utilization ratio and energy utilization ratio are far higher than the traditional algorithm.

5 Conclusion

In this paper, a scheduling algorithm for ISAR imaging radar based on pulse interleaving is proposed. The resource scheduling model for pulse interleaving is established and the realization method of online pulse interleaving under the constraint of time and energy resources is designed. Theoretical analysis and simulation results show that: the proposed algorithm can greatly improve the success rate and resource utilization of the system by reasonably utilizing the resource of the pulse waiting period.

References

1. Zeng, G., Lu, J.B., Hu, W.: Research on adaptive scheduling algorithm for multifunction phased array radar. J. Mod. Radar 26(6), 14–18 (2004). (in Chinese)
2. Zhang, J., Xia, Z.T.: An adaptive resource scheduling searching method based on information entropy. J. Mod. Radar 37(8), 33–36 (2015). (in Chinese)
3. Jang, D.S., Choi, H.L., Rohm, J.E.: A Time-window-based task scheduling approach for multi-function phased array radars. In: 2011 11th International Conference on Control, Automation and Systems, Deleon, pp. 1250–1255 (2011)
4. Lee, C.G., Kang, P.S., Shih, C.S.: Radar dwell scheduling considering physical characteristics of phased array antenna. In: Proceedings of 24th IEEE International Real-Time Systems Symposium (RTSS 2003), Columbus, pp. 14–24 (2003)
5. Lu, J.B., Hu, W.D., Yu, W.X.: Adaptive scheduling algorithm for real-time dwells in multifunction phased array radar. J. Syst. Eng. Electron. 27(12), 1981–1987 (2005). (in Chinese)
6. Ji, M.G., Zhang, Y.Y.: Research on adaptive integrated scheduling algorithm for multifunction phased array radar. In: Proceeding of 2006 Annual Conference of Electronic Technology Committee, pp. 309–317 (2006)
7. Zhao, Y., Li, J.X., Cao, L.Y.: Adaptive scheduling algorithm based on quadratic programming for multifunction phased array radars. J. Syst. Eng. Electron. 34(4), 698–703 (2012). (in Chinese)

8. Xie, X.X., Zhang, W., Chen, J.: A time pointer-based on-line pulse interleaving algorithm for phased array radar. J. Radar Sci. Technol. **4**(2), 185–191 (2013). (in Chinese)
9. Cheng, T., Liao, W.W., He, Z.S.: MIMO radar dwell scheduling based on novel pulse interleaving technique. J. Syst. Eng. Electron. **24**(2), 234–241 (2013)
10. Zhao, H.T., Cheng, T., He, Z.S.: Dwell scheduling algorithm based on analyzing scheduling interval for digital array radar. J. Inf. Electron. Eng. **9**(1), 17–21 (2011). (in Chinese)
11. Elshafei, M., Sherali, H.D., Smith, J.C.: Radar pulse interleaving for multi-target tracking. Naval Res. Logist. **51**, 72–94 (2004)
12. Cheng, T., He, Z.S., Li, H.H.: An adaptive dwell scheduling algorithm for digital array radar. J. Acta Electronica Sin. **37**(9), 2025–2029 (2009)
13. Tang, T., He, Z.S., Cheng, T.: A template-based adaptive radar dwell scheduling algorithm. J. Sig. Process. **26**(7), 998–1002 (2010). (in Chinese)
14. Li, W.J., Chen, H.W.: A kind of ISAR imaging algorithm based on compressed sensing. J. Comput. Simul. **32**(08), 10–13 (2015). (in Chinese)
15. Chen, Y.J., Zhang, Q., Luo, Y.: Adaptive scheduling algorithm for radar based on sparse aperture ISAR imaging. J. Project. Rockets Missiles Guid. **33**(4), 171–176 (2013). (in Chinese)
16. Li, J., Xing, M.D., Zhan, L.: High resolution imaging method for the sparse aperture of ISAR. J. Xi Dian Univ. **37**(3), 441–447 (2010). (in Chinese)

Direction of Arrive Estimation in Spherical Harmonic Domain Using Super Resolution Approach

Jie Pan$^{(\boxtimes)}$, Yalin Zhu, and Changling Zhou

College of Information Engineering, Yangzhou University,
Yangzhou 221000, China
panjie1982@nuaa.edu.cn

Abstract. Spherical array plays important role in 3D targets localization. In this paper, we develop a novel DOA estimation method for the spherical array with super resolution approach. The proposed method operates in spherical harmonic domain. Based on the atomic norm minimization, we develop a gridless L1-SVD algorithm in spherical harmonic domain and then we adopt the spherical ESPRIT method to two-dimensional DOA estimation. Compared to the previous work, the proposed method acquires better estimation performance. Numerical simulation results verify the performance of the proposed method.

Keywords: DOA estimation · Spherical harmonics · Atomic norm

1 Introduction

Direction-of-arrive (DOA) estimation is an attractive topic in array signal processing and finds a variety of application in acoustics and radio science [1]. In recent years, spherical array has received much attention because of the 3D array geometry configuration to estimation the azimuth and elevation of sources. The spherical array samples the wave-field by sensors distributed on a sphere. The manifold of the array can be transformed into Spherical Harmonic (SH) domain and analyze the wave-field with almost equal resolution in all directions [2, 3].

Several DOA estimation algorithms have been proposed in SH domain. In [4], conventional MUSIC method is implemented in terms of SH and ESPRIT method is extended for spherical array, called EB-ESPRIT, in [5]. In [6], the unitary transformations are proposed in real SH domain to reduce the computational complexity. Most of these methods rely on the spatial covariance matrix which decomposes the spatial covariance matrix into signal and noise subspace. However, in limited number of snapshots and coherent sources cases, the spatial covariance matrix will be distorted.

In [7], a discrete sparse recovery approach called variational sparse Bayesian learning (VSBL) is applied to SH domain. However, this approach needs discretizing the parameter space of interest with a grid and in practice the targets may locate off-grid. To alleviate this drawback, the off-grid sparse Bayesian inference (OGSBI) is extended to SH domain in [8], but this method is computationally prohibitive because of joint parameters optimization.

© ICST Institute for Computer Sciences, Social Informatics and Telecommunications Engineering 2018
X. Gu et al. (Eds.): MLICOM 2017, Part II, LNICST 227, pp. 179–187, 2018.
https://doi.org/10.1007/978-3-319-73447-7_21

Recently, several works on sparse recovery have been proposed to estimate parameters with continuous value. In [9], Candès develops a mathematical theory of continuous sparse recovery for 1-D frequency extrapolation which called Super Resolution approach. In [10] Candès' method is utilized to DOA estimation for spatial coprime arrays. In [11], an alternative discretization-free sparse DOA estimation method for linear array is proposed. In [12, 13], covariance domain DOA estimation methods with continuous sparsity approach are developed. In [14, 15] the continuous sparse recovery approach for 1-D parameters is extended to 2-D frequency models.

These methods mentioned above utilize the Vandermonde structure of the sampled data so as to be limited in case of linear or rectangular arrays. Mahata extend the super resolution approach to arbitrary linear array and planar array for 1-D parameter estimation in [16, 17] respectively. However, to the best of author's knowledge, super resolution approach in SH domain is not available in literature.

In this paper, we propose a novel 2-D DOA estimation method in SH domain with super resolution approach. We reformulate the array manifold in SH domain as a weighted Vandermonde structure matrix. By utilizing this model, we modify the atomic norm minimization algorithm to adapt the processing in SH domain and estimate azimuth and elevation of targets by spherical ESPRIT. The proposed method do not need predefined dense grid and joint parameters optimization. Simulation results show the improved performance of the proposed method.

Notations: $(\bullet)^{\mathrm{T}}$ denote the transpose, $(\bullet)^{\dagger}$ denote pseudo inverse of a matrix and $(\bullet)^{\mathrm{H}}$ denote conjugate transpose of a matrix or vector. $vec(\bullet)$ denotes the vectorization operator and $diag(x)$ denotes a diagonal matrix. $\|\bullet\|_2$ denotes the Euclidean l_2 norm of a vector. $\otimes$ denotes the Kronecker product.

2   Signal Model

There is a spherical array with I omnidirectional elements distributed on a sphere whose radius is R. The ith sensor is located at $r_i = (R, \Phi_i)$, where $\Phi_i = (\theta_i, \varphi_i)$. There are L narrowband far-field sources with wavenumber $k = \lambda/2\pi$ are imping the spherical array, where λ is the wavelength of the sources. The lth source location is defined as $\Psi_l = (\theta_l, \varphi_l)$, where θ is defined as elevation angle and φ is defined as azimuth respectively. The received signals of sensors can be described as:

$$X(t) = A(\Psi)s(t) + N(t). \tag{1}$$

where $X(t) = [x_1(t), \cdots, x_I(t)]^{\mathrm{T}}$ is the received data of sensors, $s(t) = [s_1(t), \cdots, s_L(t)]^{\mathrm{T}}$ is the emitting signal by sources, and $n(t)$ is additive Gaussian white noise and $E\{n(t)n^{\mathrm{H}}(t)\} = \sigma^2 I$.

$A(\Psi) = [a(\Psi_1), \cdots, a(\Psi_L)] \in \mathbb{C}^{I \times L}$ is the element-space manifold of the spherical array, where $a(\Psi_l) = [a_1(\Psi_l), \cdots, a_I(\Psi_l)]^{\mathrm{T}} \in \mathbb{C}^{I \times 1}$. The ith element of the steering vector $a_i(\Psi_l)$ can be represented in SH series as:

$$a_i(\mathbf{\Psi}_l) = \sum_{n=0}^{N} \sum_{m=-n}^{n} b_n(kR)[Y_n^m(\mathbf{\Psi}_l)]^H Y_n^m(\mathbf{\Phi}_i). \tag{2}$$

The far-field phase mode strength is given by:

$$b_n(kR) = \begin{cases} 4\pi i^n j_n(kR) & \text{open sphere} \\ 4\pi i^n(j_n(kR) - \frac{j_n'(kR)}{h_n'(kR)} h_n(kR)) & \text{rigid sphere} \end{cases}. \tag{3}$$

In (3), h_n is spherical Hankel function of second kind and j_n is spherical Bessel function of first kind. j_n' and h_n' are derivatives of j_n and h_n. $Y_n^m(\theta, \varphi)$ is the nth order and mth degree spherical harmonic function:

$$Y_n^m(\theta, \varphi) = \sqrt{\frac{(2n+1)(n-m)!}{4\pi(n+m)!}} P_n^m(\cos\theta)e^{jm\varphi} \quad \forall 0 \leq n \leq N,\ 0 \leq m \leq n. \tag{4}$$

where $P_n^m(\cos\theta)$ is the associated Legendre polynomial.

It is shown in [5] that for order $n > kR$, the phase mode coefficient $b_n(kR)$ decrease super-exponentially. Hence, for the high order n the phase mode $b_n(kR)$ will become small enough that we can truncate the steering vector in (2) to a limited order N with tolerable error.

Consider maximum order N, substituting (2) into (1), the array manifold of the spherical array can be written as:

$$A(\mathbf{\Psi}) = Y(\mathbf{\Phi})B(kR)Y^H(\mathbf{\Psi}) \tag{5}$$

where $Y(\mathbf{\Phi}) \in \mathbb{C}^{I \times (N+1)^2}$ is a spherical harmonic matrix. Its ith row vector can be given as:

$$y(\mathbf{\Phi}_i) = [Y_0^0(\mathbf{\Phi}_i), Y_1^{-1}(\mathbf{\Phi}_i), Y_1^0(\mathbf{\Phi}_i), Y_1^1(\mathbf{\Phi}_i), \cdots, Y_N^N(\mathbf{\Phi}_i)]. \tag{6}$$

$Y(\mathbf{\Psi})$ has the similar structure with (6). $B(kR) \in \mathbb{C}^{(N+1)^2 \times (N+1)^2}$ is the mode strength matrix defined as:

$$B(kR) = diag(b_0(kR), b_1(kR), b_1(kR), b_1(kR), \cdots, b_N(kR)) \tag{7}$$

Considering that the spherical harmonics are the orthonormal basis on unit 2-sphere, the spherical harmonics decomposition of the received data $X(t)$ can be written as:

$$P_{nm}(t) = Y^H(\mathbf{\Phi})\Gamma X(t) \tag{8}$$

where $P_{nm} = [P_{00}\ P_{1(-1)}\ P_{10}\ P_{11} \cdots P_{NN}]^T$ and $\Gamma = diag(\alpha_1, \alpha_2, \cdots, \alpha_I)$ is the weight matrix. For some special configurations of the spherical array and corresponding weight Γ introduced in [19], the spherical harmonic functions satisfy the orthogonality property:

$$Y^{\mathrm{H}}(\boldsymbol{\Phi})\boldsymbol{\Gamma}Y(\boldsymbol{\Phi}) = \boldsymbol{I} \tag{9}$$

Substituting (1) and (5) into (8), utilizing (9), the SH domain signal model can be written as:

$$\boldsymbol{P}_{nm}(t) = \boldsymbol{B}(kR)Y^{\mathrm{H}}(\boldsymbol{\Psi})\boldsymbol{s}(t) + \boldsymbol{V}_{nm}(t) \tag{10}$$

where $\boldsymbol{V}_{mn}(t) = Y^{\mathrm{H}}(\boldsymbol{\Phi})\boldsymbol{\Gamma}\boldsymbol{N}(t)$.

It is worth to note that the data model in SH domain can be described in weighted trigonometric polynomial form. This property will be useful for employing the super resolution approach in SH domain.

Considering the definition of the spherical harmonic function in (4), $P_n^m(\cos\theta)$ takes form of:

$$P_n^m(\cos\theta) = (\sin\theta)^{|m|}L_n^{(m)}(\cos\theta) \tag{11}$$

where $L_n^{(m)}$ is the kth derivative of the Legendre polynomial of degree n. Since $\cos\theta = (e^{j\theta} + e^{-j\theta})/2$ and $\sin\theta = (e^{j\theta} - e^{-j\theta})/2$, $P_n^m(\cos\theta)$ is a trigonometric polynomial of degree n which is given by $P_n^m(\cos\theta) = \sum\limits_{l=-n}^{n} \beta_{n,m,l}e^{jl\theta}$ with unique coefficients $\{\beta_{n,k,l}\}$. Then, we can write (4) as:

$$Y_n^m(\theta,\varphi) = \sum_{l=-n}^{n} A_{n.m}\beta_{n,m,l}e^{jl\theta}e^{jm\varphi} \tag{12}$$

where $A_{n.m} = \sqrt{\frac{(2n+1)(n-m)!}{4\pi(n+m)!}}$. Substituting (12) in (10), the SH domain data model can be given by:

$$\boldsymbol{P}_{nm} = \boldsymbol{B}(kR)\boldsymbol{G}\boldsymbol{D}(\boldsymbol{\Psi})\boldsymbol{s}(t) + \boldsymbol{V}_{nm}(t) \tag{13}$$

where $\boldsymbol{G} = [\boldsymbol{G}_{00}, \boldsymbol{G}_{1(-1)}, \boldsymbol{G}_{10}, \boldsymbol{G}_{11}\cdots\boldsymbol{G}_{NN}]^{\mathrm{T}}, \boldsymbol{G}_{mn} = [A_{n.m}\beta_{n,m,-n}, A_{n.m}\beta_{n,m,-(n-1)}, \cdots, A_{n.m}\beta_{n,m,n}], \boldsymbol{D}(\boldsymbol{\Psi}) = [\boldsymbol{d}(\boldsymbol{\Psi}_1), \cdots, \boldsymbol{d}(\boldsymbol{\Psi}_L)], \boldsymbol{d}(\boldsymbol{\Psi}_l)$ is written as:

$$\begin{aligned} \boldsymbol{d}(\boldsymbol{\Psi}_l) &= \boldsymbol{d}_\theta(\theta_l) \otimes \boldsymbol{d}_\varphi(\varphi_l) \\ \boldsymbol{d}_\theta(\theta_l) &= \left[e^{-jN\theta_l}, \cdots, 1, \cdots, e^{jN\theta_l}\right]^{\mathrm{T}} \\ \boldsymbol{d}_\varphi(\varphi_l) &= \left[e^{-jN\varphi_l}, \cdots, 1, \cdots, e^{jN\varphi_l}\right]^{\mathrm{T}} \end{aligned} \tag{14}$$

Considering the model described in (13) with K snapshots, we stack them in a matrix as:

$$\boldsymbol{P} = \boldsymbol{B}(kR)\boldsymbol{G}\boldsymbol{D}(\boldsymbol{\Psi})\boldsymbol{S} + \boldsymbol{V} \tag{15}$$

where $\boldsymbol{P} = [\boldsymbol{P}_{nm}(t_1), \boldsymbol{P}_{nm}(t_2), \cdots, \boldsymbol{P}_{nm}(t_K)], \boldsymbol{S} = [\boldsymbol{s}_1, \boldsymbol{s}_2, \cdots, \boldsymbol{s}_L]^{\mathrm{T}}$. The data model in (15) is utilized for the proposed SH domain DOA estimation method.

3   Super Resolution Approach in SH Domain

It is suggested in [12] that the noisy signal can be recovered by atomic norm minimization:

$$
\begin{aligned}
\min \quad & \|Z\|_A \\
s.t. \quad & \|Z - P\| \leq \varepsilon
\end{aligned}
\tag{16}
$$

where $A := \{B(kR)Gd(\Psi)s \mid \Psi = (\theta, \varphi), \theta \in [0, \pi], \varphi \in [-\pi, \pi), \|s\|_2 = 1\}$ denotes the atomic set. Due to L0-norm is not convex, we consider the convex relaxation and the atomic norm of Z which can be defined as:

$$
\begin{aligned}
\|Z\|_A &= \inf\{t > 0 : Z \in t \quad conv(A)\} \\
&= \inf\left\{\sum_l c_l \,\Big|\, Z = \sum_l c_l B(kR)Gd(\Psi_l)s_l, c_l \geq 0\right\}
\end{aligned}
\tag{17}
$$

The conventional atomic norm minimization methods are relying on the Vandermonde decomposition of Toeplitz matrices, hence they are limited to Vandermonde structure model. Here, we utilize the relationship between the data model in SH domain and a Vandermonde matrix shown in (15) to develop an atomic norm minimization method in SH domain with semidefinite programing (SDP):

$$
\begin{aligned}
\min_{T,W,Z} \quad & \frac{1}{2}\operatorname{tr}(S(T)) + \frac{1}{2}\operatorname{tr}(W) \\
s.t. \quad & \begin{bmatrix} S(T) & Z \\ Z^H & W \end{bmatrix} \geq 0 \\
& \|B(kR)GZ - P\|_2 \leq \varepsilon
\end{aligned}
\tag{18}
$$

where $T \in \mathbb{C}^{(4N+1)\times(4N+1)}$, $S(T)$ is a two-fold block Toeplitz defined from T as:

$$
S(T) = \begin{bmatrix}
T_0 & T_{-1} & \cdots & T_{-2N} \\
T_1 & T_0 & \cdots & T_{-2N+1} \\
\vdots & \vdots & \ddots & \vdots \\
T_{2N} & T_{2N-1} & \cdots & T_0
\end{bmatrix}
\tag{19}
$$

where each block $T_l, -2N < l < 2N$ is an $(2N+1) \times (2N+1)$ Toeplitz matrix constructed from the lth row of T:

$$
T_l = \begin{bmatrix}
x_{l,0} & x_{l,-1} & \cdots & x_{-2N} \\
x_{l,1} & x_{l,0} & \cdots & x_{l,-(2N-1)} \\
\vdots & \vdots & \ddots & \vdots \\
x_{2N} & x_{l,2N-1} & \cdots & x_{l,0}
\end{bmatrix}
\tag{20}
$$

For the large number of snapshots K, we can factorize the matrix P in terms of singular value decomposition $P = U\Sigma V$, we can construct $P' = U_L\Sigma_L$, where Σ_L is the diagram matrix consist of largest L singular value and U_L is the corresponding singular value vectors. It is shown in [17] that the SDP problem in (18) can be written as:

$$\min_{T,W,Z''} \quad \tfrac{1}{2}\mathrm{tr}(S(T)) + \tfrac{1}{2}\mathrm{tr}(W)$$

$$s.t. \quad \begin{bmatrix} S(T) & Z'' \\ Z''^{\mathrm{H}} & W \end{bmatrix} \geq 0 \qquad (21)$$

$$\|B(kR)GZ'' - P'\|_2 \leq \varepsilon$$

We argue that the choice of the parameter ε can done as $\sqrt{LK\sigma^2}$. The proposed method in (21) can be regarded as the atomic norm minimization based L1-SVD algorithm in spherical harmonic domain.

Then, we can apply spherical ESPRIT [5] to the recovered covariance matrix $R = B(kR)GS(\hat{T})G^{\mathrm{H}}B^{\mathrm{H}}(kR)$ to estimate DOAs of the targets, where $S(\hat{T})$ is the solution of (21). By expressing R in terms of eigenvalue decomposition, we can get:

$$R = U_s\Sigma_s U_s^{\mathrm{H}} + \sigma^2 U_N U_N^{\mathrm{H}} \qquad (22)$$

According to the property of the associated Legendre polynomials, the it can be given by:

$$D_1 U_s^0 = E\begin{bmatrix} \Delta^T \\ \Delta^H \end{bmatrix} \qquad (23)$$

where D_1, D_2, D_3 are auxiliary matrices with analytical expressions defined in [5], and E is given by:

$$E = \begin{bmatrix} D_2 U_s^{(-1)} & D_3 U_s^{(1)} \end{bmatrix} \qquad (24)$$

$U_s^{(-1)}, U_s^0, U_s^{(1)}$ is the first, middle and last sub-matrix from U_s as shown in [5]. Then Δ can be solved as:

$$\Delta = (E^H E)^{-1} E^H D_1 U_s^0 \qquad (25)$$

Compute the eigenvalues $u_l, l = 1, 2, \cdots, L$ of Δ. The estimation of the elevation and azimuth of the lth target are $\theta_l = \tan^{-1}|u_l|$ and $\varphi_l = \arg(u_l)$ respectively.

4 Simulation Results

In this section, simulations are presented to study the DOA estimation performance of proposed method compared with the spherical ESPRIT in [5]. The radius R of the spherical array used in the simulations is 0.042 m. There are 32 sensors mounted on the open sphere in a uniform way. The maximum order of the spherical harmonic is $N = 4$.

Firstly, we assume that there are two independent sources at $(\theta_1, \varphi_1) = (40°, 70°)$ and $(\theta_2, \varphi_2) = (50°, 120°)$ impinging the spherical array, where θ, φ are the elevation and azimuth respectively. 100 snapshots is collected. The RMSE of parameter estimation is defined as:

$$\text{RMSE} = \sqrt{\frac{1}{J}\sum_{j=1}^{J}(\hat{\theta}_{ij} - \theta_i)} \tag{26}$$

J the number of Monte Carlo trials is 200. The Fig. 1 shows that the proposed method achieve improved performance compared with the other methods especially in low SNR.

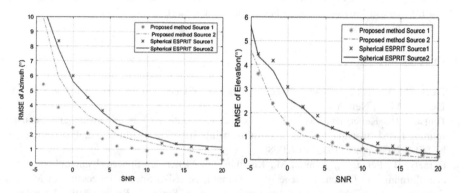

Fig. 1. RMSE of Azimuth and elevation versus SNR for uncorrelated sources

In the second example, we investigate the accuracy of our method in multipath environment. Considering two coherent sources at $(\theta_1, \varphi_1) = (40°, 70°)$ and $(\theta_2, \varphi_2) = (50°, 120°)$, SNR is 10 dB, the number of snapshot is 200. The number of Monte Carlo trials is 200. The simulation results of the proposed method and spherical ESPRIT are shown in Fig. 2.

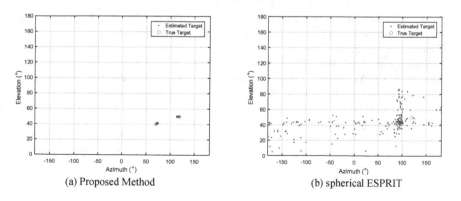

(a) Proposed Method   (b) spherical ESPRIT

Fig. 2. Spectrum using different methods for coherent sources

It is shown that the proposed method works well with coherent sources, while the spherical ESPRIT method can't work in multipath environment.

5 Conclusions

In this paper, we proposed a novel DOA estimation method for spherical array with super resolution approach. The proposed method does not need the grid discretization and multiple parameters optimization. This method works well in low SNR and multipath environment. Simulations show our method the superior performance compared with conventional techniques.

Acknowledgments. This work was supported by National Natural Science Foundation of China (61601402), Jiangsu Province Science Foundation of China (BK20160477).

References

1. Trees, H.L.V.: Optimum Array Processing: Part IV of Detection, Estimation and Modulation Theory. Wiley, New York (2002)
2. Teutsch, H., Kellermann, W.: Detection and localization of multiplewideband acoustic sources based on wavefield decomposition using spherical apertures. In: Proceedings of ICASSP 2008, pp. 5276–5279 (2008)
3. Rafaely, B., Peled, Y., Agmon, M., Khaykin, D., Fisher, E.: Spherical microphone array beamforming. In: Cohen, I., Benesty, J., Gannot, S. (eds.) Speech Processing in Modern Communication: Challenges and Perspectives, vol. 3. Springer, Berlin (2010). https://doi.org/10.1007/978-3-642-11130-3_11
4. Li, X., Yan, S., et al.: Spherical harmonics MUSIC versus conventional MUSIC. Appl. Acoust. **72**(9), 646–652 (2011)
5. Goossens, R., Rogier, R.: 2-D angle estimation with spherical arrays for scalar fields. IET Sig. Process. **3**(3), 221–231 (2009)
6. Huang, Q., Zhang, G., et al.: Unitary transformations for spherical harmonics MUSIC. Sig. Process. **131**, 441–446 (2016)
7. Huang, Q., Zhang, G., et al.: Real-valued DOA estimation for spherical arrays using sparse Bayesian learning. Sig. Process. **125**, 79–86 (2016)
8. Huang, Q., Xiang, L., et al.: Off-grid DOA estimation in real spherical harmonics domain using sparse Bayesian inference. Sig. Process. **137**, 124–134 (2017)
9. Candès, E.J., Fernandez-Granda, C.: Towards a mathematical theory of super-resolution. Commun. Pure Appl. Math. **67**(6), 906–956 (2014)
10. Tan, Z., Eldar, Y., et al.: Direction of arrival estimation using co-prime arrays: a super resolution viewpoint. IEEE Trans. Sig. Process. **62**(21), 5565–5576 (2014)
11. Yang, Z., Xie, L., et al.: A discretization-free sparse and parametric approach for linear array signal processing. IEEE Trans. Sig. Process. **62**(19), 4959–4973 (2014)
12. Hung, C.Y., Kaveh, M.: Super-resolution DOA estimation via continuous group sparsity in the covariance domain. In: IEEE International Conference on Acoustics, Speech and Signal Processing (2016)

13. Wu, X., Zhu, W.P., et al.: Direction-of-arrival estimation based on Toeplitz covariance matrix reconstruction. In: IEEE International Conference on Acoustics, Speech and Signal Processing (2016)
14. Tang, G., Bhaskar, B., Shah, P., Recht, B.: Compressed sensing off the grid. IEEE Trans. Inf. Theory 59(11), 7465–7490 (2013)
15. Chi, Y., Chen, Y.: Compressive two-dimensional harmonic retrieval via atomic norm minimization. IEEE Trans. Sig. Process. 63(4), 1030–1042 (2015)
16. Mahata, K., Hyder, M.M.: Frequency estimation from arbitrary time samples. IEEE Trans. Signal Process. 64(21), 5634–5643 (2016)
17. Mahata, K., Hyder, M.M.: Grid-less TV minimization for DOA estimation. Sig. Process. 132, 146–155 (2017)

Adaptive Mainlobe Interference Suppression in Sparse Distributed Array Radar Based on Synthetic Wideband Signal

Jian Luo, Honggang Zhang, and Yuanyuan Song[✉]

Beijing Key Laboratory of Embedded Real-Time Information Processing
Technology, Radar Research Laboratory, School of Information and Electronics,
Beijing Institute of Technology, Beijing 100081, China
beral@bit.edu.cn

Abstract. This paper proposes a mainlobe interference suppression method in distributed array radar (DAR) based on stepped frequency synthetic wideband signal. Due to the equivalent large aperture of DAR, it is possible to cancel the mainlobe interference without target signal suppression. The applying of stepped frequency synthetic wideband signal can avoid the different time delays arriving at each array compared with the traditional instantaneous wideband Chirp (linear frequency modulation) signal. Moreover, it can reduce the computational complexity. This method employs the narrowband adaptive processing to each sub-pulse of the stepped frequency signal, and then synthesizes the high resolution range profile (HRRP). As a result, mainlobe interference suppression under wideband signal is accomplished. Mainlobe interference suppression experiment is carried out by using an S-band experimental radar system, an S-band noise jammer and a target simulator. The measured data is processed employing the proposed method, and the result verifies the effectiveness of this algorithm.

Keywords: Distributed array radar
Stepped frequency synthetic wideband signal
Wideband adaptive beamforming · Mainlobe interference suppression

1 Introduction

In modern battlefield, due to the wide application of electronic interference equipment, the electromagnetic signals in the battlefield space are extremely dense, forming a very complex electromagnetic environment. Radar will be faced with serious problems such as power, accuracy decline and even can not work properly. As a result, radar interference suppression has gradually become a hot issue. The effective approach of radar sidelobe suppression is introduced [1]. With the adaptive beamforming method, the radar system can suppress sidelobe interference effectively [1]. But for the mainlobe interference, the traditional adaptive beamforming will produce a nulling in the mainlobe, which leads to the distortion of the antenna pattern and reduces the radar detection capability greatly.

© ICST Institute for Computer Sciences, Social Informatics and Telecommunications Engineering 2018
X. Gu et al. (Eds.): MLICOM 2017, Part II, LNICST 227, pp. 188–197, 2018.
https://doi.org/10.1007/978-3-319-73447-7_22

In recent years, scholars are beginning to recognize the importance of mainlobe interference suppression and begin to study it. A mainlobe interference suppression method based on eigen-projection algorithm (EMP) is proposed [2]. Elimination of mainlobe interference based on the sum and difference channel is introduced [3]. For a large aperture distributed array, Mainlobe interference suppression algorithm based on auxiliary array is introduced [4]. Fresnel based frequency domain adaptive beam-forming for large aperture distributed array radar is presented [5]. However, these methods only study the mainlobe interference suppression under narrowband signal, not including those under wideband signal.

For radar wideband signal, the conventional wideband adaptive beamforming algorithm includes incoherent subspace processing method (ISM) [6] and coherent subspace processing method (CSM) [7], which have a large amount of calculation.

Combining the above methods with my ideas, this paper presents a mainlobe inter-ference suppression method in sparse DAR based on stepped frequency synthetic wideband signal. The equivalent large aperture of sparse DAR can eliminate the mainlobe interference with little loss of target signal energy. The stepped frequency synthetic wideband signal is an instantaneous narrowband and synthetic wideband signal, so it can effectively eliminate the time delay problem. In addition, it can reduce the computational complexity compared with the traditional wideband adaptive beamforming method. This paper is divided into the following sections. Section 1 describes the problems faced by radar in today's electromagnetic interference environment. Section 2 introduces the signal model of the radar based on the stepped frequency synthetic wideband signal in case of the mainlobe interference. Section 3 put forwards the signal processing method. This method utilizes the narrowband adaptive processing to each sub-pulse of the stepped frequency signal, and synthesizes the high resolution range profile by an inverse Fourier transform (IFFT). Section 4 designs the mainlobe anti-jamming experimental system, collects the echo data and then confirms the validity of this algorithm by processing the collected data. Section 5 concludes the full paper at last.

2 Signal Model

This paper uses the stepped frequency synthetic wideband signal. The stepped synthetic wideband frequency signal can reduce the system's instantaneous bandwidth in the premise of synthesizing a large bandwidth. It transmits the total signal bandwidth of $N\Delta f$ in N pulses as a frequency interval of Δf. Finally, synthetic wideband results are obtained by matching processing.

The i th pulse in time domain of the stepped synthetic wideband frequency signal is expressed as:

$$s_i(t) = \text{rect}\left(\frac{t - iT_r}{\tau}\right)e^{j2\pi(f_0 + i\Delta f)t}. \tag{1}$$

Where, $i = 0, 1, 2, \ldots, N - 1$, T_r is the pulse repetition period, f_0 is the start frequency of the carrier frequency, Δf is the stepped frequency. N is the pulse number in a frame signal, M is the signal frame number, $\text{rect}(t)$ is the rectangular function. Figure 1 shows the time-frequency feature of stepped frequency synthetic wideband signal.

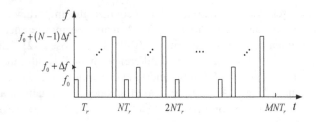

Fig. 1. Time-frequency feature of stepped frequency synthetic wideband signal

Supposing that DAR system has one transmitting antenna and m receiving antennas. The receiving antennas are on the same horizontal line, and their positions are respectively $\mathbf{d} = [d_1, d_2, \cdots, d_m]$, and $d_1 = 0$. The distance between the target and the transmitting antenna is R_0, and the distance between the target and m th receiving antenna are $R_1, R_2, \cdots, R_m$ respectively. For the i th pulse, the radar echo received by the 1st receiving antenna is:

$$s_{i1}(t) = s_i\left(t - \tau_1^s\right) = \text{rect}\left(\frac{t - iT_r - (R_0 + R_1)/c}{\tau}\right)e^{j2\pi(f_0 + i\Delta f)\left(t - \frac{R_0 + R_1}{c}\right)}. \qquad (2)$$

Assuming that the interference is R_{c0} away from the transmitting antenna, and the distance between the interference and m th receiving antenna are $R_{c1}, R_{c2}, \cdots R_{cm}$ respectively, so the actual signal received by the m th antenna is:

$$x_{im}(t) = s_i\left(t - \tau_m^s\right) + c\left(t - \tau_m^c\right) + w_m(t). \qquad (3)$$

Where, t is time, $s_i\left(t - \tau_m^s\right)$ is the echo of target, the interference is $c(t)$, the time delays of the target echo signal and the interference signal in the m th antenna are $\tau_m^s = (R_0 + R_1)/c + d_m \sin\theta_0/c$ and $\tau_m^c = (R_{c0} + R_{c1})/c + d_m \sin\theta_1/c$, the direction of target signal and interference signal are θ_0 and θ_1. c is the speed of light. $w_m(t)$ is the noise.

Considering that each sub-pulse of the stepped synthetic wideband frequency signal is narrowband signal, the time delay difference between target and each antenna can be ignored [5]. Accordingly, the array received data becomes:

$$x_i(t) = \mathbf{a}(\theta_0)s_{i1}(t) + X_{i+n}(t) = \mathbf{a}(\theta_0)s_{i1}(t) + \mathbf{a}(\theta_1)c_1(t) + w(t). \qquad (4)$$

Where, $x_i(t) = [x_{i1}(t), x_{i2}(t), \cdots, x_{im}(t)]^T$ is the vector of the echo signal, T expresses transpose. $\mathbf{a}(\theta_0) = \left[1, e^{-j2\pi d_2 \sin\theta_0/\lambda}, \cdots, e^{-j2\pi d_m \sin\theta_0/\lambda}\right]^T$ is the target steering vector, λ is the radar transmitting signal wavelength. $s_{i1}(t) = s_i\left(t - \tau_1^s\right)$ is the complex envelope representation of the target signal. $X_{i+n}(t)$ is the signal vector synthesized by interference and noise. $\mathbf{a}(\theta_1) = \left[1, e^{-j2\pi d_2 \sin\theta_1/\lambda}, \cdots, e^{-j2\pi d_m \sin\theta_1/\lambda}\right]^T$ is the interference steering vector. The interference vector is $c_1(t)$. The noise vector is $w(t) = [w_1(t), w_2(t) \cdots w_m(t)]^T$.

3 Signal Processing

3.1 Narrowband Adaptive Processing

The narrowband adaptive processing method is employed to the i th sub-pulse of the stepped frequency synthetic wideband signal. For the echo signal data model, the signal covariance matrix R_S and R_{i+n} can be computed as:

$$R_S = E\left[s_{i1}(t)\mathbf{a}(\theta_0)\mathbf{a}(\theta_0)^H s_{i1}^*(t)\right] = \sigma_s^2 \mathbf{a}(\theta_0)\mathbf{a}(\theta_0)^H. \tag{5}$$

$$R_{i+n} = E\left[X_{i+n}(t)X_{i+n}^H(t)\right] = \sigma_1^2 \mathbf{a}(\theta_1)\mathbf{a}^H(\theta_1) + \sigma_n^2 I. \tag{6}$$

Where, $\sigma_s^2 = E\left[|s_{i1}(t)|^2\right]$ is the signal power, $\sigma_1^2 = E\left[|c_1(t)|^2\right]$ is the interference signal power, σ_n^2 is the power of the noise. The optimal weight vector is obtained in accordance with the principle of the best output SINR.

$$W_{opt} = \alpha R_{i+n}^{-1} \mathbf{a}(\theta_0). \tag{7}$$

Where

$$\alpha = \sigma_s^2 \mathbf{a}^H(\theta_0)W_{opt}/\lambda. \tag{8}$$

However, in the realizable case, the covariance matrix of the optimal weight vector is hard to get. As a result, according to the temporal stability of the signal, the maximum likelihood estimation can be obtained from the snapshot data:

$$\hat{R}_{i+n} = \frac{1}{K}\sum_{k=1}^{K} X_{i+n}(nK+k)X_{i+n}^H(nK+k) = \frac{1}{K}XX^H. \tag{9}$$

$X = [X_{i+n}(nK+1), X_{i+n}(nK+2), \cdots, X_{i+n}(nK+k)]$, is n th snapshot data block, each block contains K snapshots. Replace R_{i+n} with $\hat{R}_{i+n}$, then we can obtain the adaptive weight vector of the SMI algorithm:

$$W_{smi} = \frac{\hat{R}_{i+n}\mathbf{a}(\theta_0)}{\mathbf{a}^H(\theta_0)\hat{R}_{i+n}^{-1}\mathbf{a}(\theta_0)}. \tag{10}$$

So the output signal is:

$$y_i(t) = W_{smi}^H x_i(t). \tag{11}$$

3.2   Synthesize HRRP

After the above process, we finish the interference suppression in each sub-pulse, then we synthesize the high resolution range profile (HRRP) with sub-pulses by an inverse Fourier transform (IFFT). For N pulses, the radar echo after the frequency mixing and the narrowband adaptive processing can be expressed as:

$$x'(t) = \sum_{i=0}^{N-1} \text{rect}\left[\frac{t - iT_r - (R_0 + R_1)/c}{\tau}\right] e^{-j2\pi i\Delta f(R_0 + R_1)/c} e^{-j2\pi f_0(R_0 + R_1)/c}. \tag{12}$$

For the echo of N PRT, the sampling points of the same distance are processed by an inverse Fourier transform (IFFT), then we derive:

$$
\begin{aligned}
y_{hrrp1}(l) &= \frac{1}{N}\sum_{i=0}^{N-1} x'(i)e^{j2\pi\frac{l}{N}i} \\
&= \frac{\sin\pi(l - N\Delta f(R_0 + R_1)/c)}{N\,\sin\pi(l/N - \Delta f(R_0 + R_1)/c)} e^{j2\pi f_0\frac{R_0 + R_1}{c}} e^{j\pi\frac{N-1}{N}(l - N\Delta f(R_0 + R_1)/c)}.
\end{aligned}
\tag{13}
$$

The amplitude is:

$$\left|y_{hrrp1}(l)\right| = \frac{\sin\pi(l - N\Delta f(R_0 + R_1)/c)}{N\,\sin\pi(l/N - \Delta f(R_0 + R_1)/c)}. \tag{14}$$

$\left|y_{hrrp}(l)\right|$ is the HRRP, its mainlobe width is $1/(N\Delta f)$, thus the target range resolution is $c/(2N\Delta f)$, which is equivalent to the range resolution obtained by the signal of $B = N\Delta f$ transmitting bandwidth. The essence of the stepped frequency synthetic wideband signal processing is obtaining the time delay information of the target by utilizing an inverse Fourier transform (IFFT) to a string of sampling values in frequency domain.

When dealing with the measured data, because of the condition $\Delta f < 1/\tau$, the spectrum of each pulse is overlapped, causing the range ambiguity. In order to obtain the real target distance information, we need to select some points from the IFFT results of all sampling points in a certain order, and then synthesize the high resolution range profile according to a certain rule. We employ the backward abandon method to solve the above problem.

The classic abandon method takes out $t_s N\Delta f$ (t_s is the sampling interval, N is the number of frequency points, Δf is the stepped frequency) points spectral line in turn from each group of IFFT results, synthesizes them continuously and abandons others, but it cannot determine the extraction starting point. The backward abandon method applied in the data processing finds the position of the peak value first according to the low resolution envelope feature of echo, and determines the extraction starting point in reverse derivation, then accomplishes the high resolution range profile (HRRP) by means of the classic abandon method.

4   Experiment

4.1   Experiment Design

To meet our need, we build a mainlobe anti-jamming experimental system and design a mainlobe interference suppression experiment. The experimental system includes an S-band radar, a sparse distributed array, a target simulator and a noise interference source. The S-band radar transmits stepped synthetic wideband frequency signal, the pulsewidth is 0.1 μs, the pulse repetition period is 10 μs, the starting frequency of the carrier frequency is 3.3 GHz, the stepped frequency is 5 MHz, the synthetic bandwidth is 320 MHz. The step frequency signal of a frame has 64 pulses and the sampling rate is 100 MHz. The sparse distributed array has one horn antenna for transmitting the signal and four horn antennas for receiving the signal. The aperture of each horn antenna is 0.12 m, for a single antenna, the beamwidth is so large that it reaches 43°. For purpose of reducing the influence of the grating lobe, the receiving antennas are arranged in a non-uniform array [8]. The length of the array is 6 m, the receiving antennas are on the same horizontal line, and their positions are respectively (0.125 m, 2.275 m, 2.575 m, 5.925 m), so the designed array can make the equivalent antenna beamwidth as 0.86°, as we can see, it is much smaller than the beamwidth of a single antenna. The transmitting antenna is located in the middle of the array, facing the target simulator. The target simulator is composed of two horn antennas and it is 40 m straight from the array. One of them is used to receive the radar signal, the other is used to amplify the received signal and send them back. The noise interference source is located 1.2 m from the target simulator, that is, 1.7° off the target. In this case, the interference is in the mainlobe of a single antenna, but inside the sidelobe of the synthetic array. We collect multiple sets of four channel data using a digital collector, and then perform off-line processing and analyze the experimental results. The simulative experiment scene is shown in Fig. 2, the actual experiment scene and the experiment equipment are shown in Fig. 3.

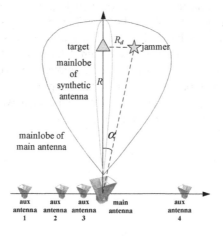

Fig. 2. Simulative experiment scene

a S-band experimental DAR system   b interference source and target simulator

Fig. 3. Actual experiment scene and experiment equipment

4.2 Measured Data Processing

Figure 4 shows the echo data collected. Among them, Fig. 4a is the echo of the target simulator, Fig. 4b is the echo of the target as well as the interference. We can see that the target signal are suppressed seriously by the interference and disappear. According to the Neyman-Person criterion, the detection probability depends on the signal energy to noise ratio, so we can calculate the signal energy to noise ratio to reflect whether the original echo signal is affected by interference. One frame stepped frequency synthetic wideband signal which contains 64 pulses is utilized to process. In general, we use SNR, INR, and SINR to evaluate the suppression result by quantitative analysis. After calculation, the SNR of the original target signal is 39.5 dB, the INR of the interference is 28.9 dB, so the initial SINR is 10.6 dB.

Then we employ the narrowband adaptive processing to each sub-pulse of the four channels collected data, and synthesize the HRRP. The result of the narrowband adaptive processing in time domain is shown in Fig. 5. The result of the synthetic wideband processing in time domain is shown in Fig. 6. As we can see, in two figures, the mainlobe interference is basically suppressed after processed, the target can be clearly distinguished. After processing, we obtain that the output SINR is 36.1 dB, that is, the SINR has increased by 25.5 dB, so the improvement works well. As a consequence, the proposed method in this paper can suppress the mainlobe interference based on the stepped frequency synthetic wideband signal while keeping the target signal energy basically intact and reducing the relative calculation.

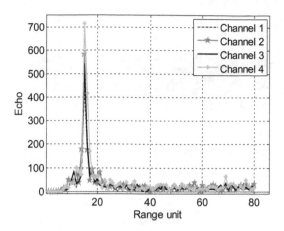

a Original target echo

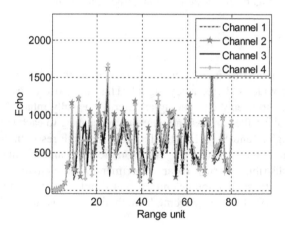

b Original target echo affected by the interference source

Fig. 4. Echo data collected

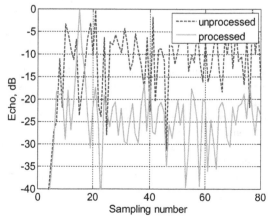

Fig. 5. Narrowband adaptive processing result

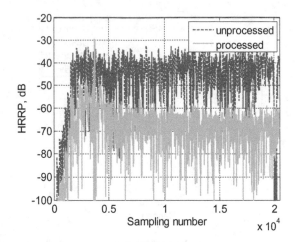

Fig. 6. Synthetic wideband processing result

5 Summary

This paper presents a mainlobe interference suppression method in sparse DAR based on stepped synthetic wideband frequency signal. This method utilizes the equivalent large aperture of DAR to keep the target signal energy basically intact. It contains two steps. Step 1 is employing the narrowband adaptive processing to each sub-pulse of the stepped frequency signal, and Step 2 is synthesizing the high resolution range profile by an inverse Fourier transform (IFFT). Whats more, a mainlobe interference suppression in sparse distributed array radar experiment is implemented by using an S-band radar, a noise interference source and a target simulator. At last, the result of the collected data processed by the presented method confirms the validity of the algorithm.

Acknowledgment. This work was supported by the Chang Jiang Scholars Programme under Grants T2012122, 111 Project of China under Grants B14010. The authors would like to thank Prof. Teng Long, Beijing Institute of Technology, China, for helpful comments and suggestions.

References

1. Vendik, O.G., Kozlov, D.S.: Phased antenna array with a sidelobe cancellation for suppression of jamming. IEEE Antennas Wirel. Propag. Lett. **11**, 648–650 (2012)
2. Qian, J., He, Z.: Mainlobe interference suppression with eigenprojection algorithm and similarity constraints. Electron. Lett. **52**(3), 228–230 (2016)
3. Yu, K.B.: Adaptive digital subarray beamforming and deterministic sum and difference beamforming with jamming cancellation and monopulse ratio preservation. US Patent, 6661366B2, 9 December 2003
4. Yang, X., Yin, P., Zeng, T., Sarkar, T.K.: Applying auxiliary array to suppress mainlobe interference for ground-based radar. IEEE Antennas Wirel. Propag. Lett. **12**, 433–436 (2013)

5. Zhang, H., Luo, J., Chen, X., Liu, Q., Zeng, T.: Fresnel based frequency domain adaptive beamforming for large aperture distributed array radar. In: IEEE International Conference on Signal Processing, pp. 1–5 (2016)
6. Santosh, S., Sahu, O.P., Aggarwal, M.: Different wideband direction of arrival (DOA) estimation methods: an overview. In: Proceedings of 8th WSEAS International Conference on Electronics, Hardware, Wireless and Optical Communication, pp. 159–167. World Scientific and Engineering Academy and Society (WSEAS) (2009)
7. Hung, H., Kaveh, M.: Focussing matrices for coherent signal-subspace processing. IEEE Trans. Acoust. Speech Sig. Process. **36**(8), 1272–1281 (1988)
8. Zeng, T., Yin, P., Liu, Q.: Wideband distributed coherent aperture radar based on stepped frequency signal: theory and experimental results. IET Radar Sonar Navig. **10**(4), 672–688 (2016)

Wideband MIMO Radar Waveform Optimization Based on Dynamic Adjustment of Signal Bandwidth

Yi-shuai Gong[✉], Qun Zhang, Kai-ming Li, and Yi-jun Chen

Information and Navigation College, Air Force Engineering University,
Xi'an 710077, China
13575012196@163.com

Abstract. Considering the need of multi-target imaging, a method about MIMO radar waveform optimization based on dynamic adjustment of signal bandwidth is proposed. At first, the closed-loop feedback between the range profile and the signal bandwidth is established, which can design the required bandwidth of transmit signal in different directions, according to the range profile of targets. And then, considering the request of beampattern and the bandwidth limitation, a waveform optimization model is established and solved. Therefore, the multi-target observation and the dynamic adjustment of the signal bandwidth are accomplished. What's more, satisfactory imaging results are obtained under the least resource consumption. In the end, the simulation has proved the performance of the algorithm in low SNR circumstance.

Keywords: MIMO radar · Cognition · Waveform design · Range profile
Range resolution

1 Introduction

MIMO radar contains multiple antennas at the transmitter and receiver [1–3] and can be divided into distributed MIMO radar [4] and centralized MIMO radar [5]. Each emitter element of centralized MIMO radar can transmit signal independently. Therefore, centralized MIMO radar possesses good waveform diversity gain [5, 6]. In order to design the waveform self-adaptively and improve the radar performance by taking advantage of the prior information and feedback information, cognitive techniques have been introduced to radar system. The most important feature of cognitive radar is the closed-loop feedback. The cognition of the external environment is achieved based on the feedback information, so the exact match between the transmitting signal and the environment is accomplished [7–9].

There have already been some research results about cognitive waveform design based on MIMO radar at home and abroad. And existing cognitive waveform design

Y. Gong—This work was supported by the National Natural Science Foundation of China under Grant 61631019.

principles can be summarized into two aspects: the one is based on the SNR [10–13] and the other is based on the MI [14–17]. However, these algorithms are studied for narrowband signal according to the need of radar tasks like tracking and detection, and the need of imaging task is not considered. Target imaging can provide important target features for identification, so it plays an important role among the radar tasks. To obtain the high resolution range profile, the wideband transmitting signal is required. Thus, the wideband cognitive waveform design focused on imaging task based on MIMO radar is studied in the paper.

As is known to all, the greater the signal bandwidth, the larger the transmitting power. And the larger wear and tear will be caused to the transmitter devices. For imaging task, the bandwidth of transmitting signal determines the range resolution. If the bandwidth of transmitting signal is too large and is enough to distinguish each scatterer of the target in the range direction, the bandwidth resource will be wasted and extra wear and tear will be caused to the transmitter; if the bandwidth of transmitting signal is too small, the aliasing will exist in the range profile. So we should design the bandwidth of transmitting signal synthesized in different target directions cognitively according to the need of task.

In conclusion, a method about MIMO radar waveform optimization based on dynamic adjustment of signal bandwidth is proposed. In the paper, the closed-loop feedback between the range profile and the signal bandwidth is established, which can design the required bandwidth of transmitting signal in different directions; and then, considering the request of beampattern and the bandwidth limitation, a waveform optimization model is established and solved.

2   MIMO Radar Signal Model

Suppose the emitter array of MIMO radar is a uniform array, as shown in Fig. 1, which is consisted of M array elements and the antenna spacing is d. The transmitting signal of the m th array element can be expressed as

$$s_m(t) = x_m(t)e^{j2\pi f_c t}, 0 \leq t \leq T_p \tag{1}$$

where $x_m(t)$ denotes the baseband signal, f_c denotes the carrier frequency, T_p denotes the pulse width. So the transmit signal synthesized at the angle θ can be denoted as

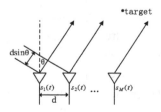

Fig. 1. The diagram of MIMO radar field emitter array

$$s(\theta, t) = \sum_{m=0}^{M-1} x_m(t + \frac{md \sin\theta}{c}) e^{j2\pi f_c(t + \frac{md \sin\theta}{c})}, 0 \le t \le T_p \tag{2}$$

where c denotes the light speed.

In practical application, discrete baseband signal is considered, that is $x_m(n) = x_m(t)|_{t=(n-1)T_s}, n = 1, 2, \cdots, N$. In which, N denotes the number of sub-pulses in a pulse and T_s denotes the pulse width of sub-pulse. So the spectrum expression of discrete baseband signal can be denoted as

$$y_m(l) = \sum_{n=1}^{N} x_m(n) e^{-j\frac{2\pi}{N}(n-1)l}, l = -L/2, -L/2+1, \cdots, L/2 - 1 \tag{3}$$

In which L denotes the number of frequency points. Therefore, at the frequency $f_c + lB/L$ the spectrum of discrete baseband signal transmitted by the whole array is $y(l) = [y_1(l), y_2(l), \cdots, y_M(l)]^T = Xf_l$. In which, $f_l = [1, e^{-j2\pi l/L}, \cdots, e^{-j2\pi(N-1)l/L}]^T$ is the transformation vector of DFT at the l th frequency point, $X = [x_1, x_2, \cdots, x_N]$ is the discrete baseband signal transmitted by the whole array, $x_n = [x_1(n), x_2(n), \cdots, x_M(n)]^T$.

According to the analysis above, at the angle θ the power spectrum of the signal at the frequency $f_c + lB/L$ can be denoted as

$$P_l(\theta) = |a_l^T(\theta) Xf_l|^2 / L \tag{4}$$

in which,

$$a_l(\theta) = [1, e^{j2\pi(f_c + lB/L)\frac{d \sin\theta}{c}}, \cdots, e^{j2\pi(f_c + lB/L)\frac{(M-1)d \sin\theta}{c}}]^T, \\ l = -L/2, -L/2+1, \cdots, -L/2 - 1 \tag{5}$$

denotes the steering vector at the frequency $f_c + lB/L$.

3   Waveform Design Based on Dynamic Adjustment of Signal Bandwidth

During the imaging, if the bandwidth of transmitting signal is too large and is enough to distinguish each scatterer of the target in the range direction, the bandwidth resource will be wasted and extra wear and tear will be caused to the transmitter; if the bandwidth of transmitting signal is too small, the aliasing will exist in the range profile. So we should design the bandwidth of transmitting signal synthesized in different target directions. The detailed process is stated as follows

Step1:   set arbitrary bandwidth values of signals synthesized in the H target directions, that is $\{B_h\}_{h=1}^{H}$ and design the transmitting waveform. Calculate the main lobe areas of these transmitting signals' point spread function (PSF), which can be denoted as $\{S_{0h}\}_{h=1}^{H}$.

Step2: obtain the range profiles of targets in different directions and calculate the areas of all main lobes in the profiles, that is $\{S_{hi_h}\}_{i_h=1}^{I_h}, h = 1, 2, \cdots, H$, where I_h denotes the number of main lobes in range profile of the target in the h th target direction.

Step3: calculate the number of scattering points included in each main lobe, which can be denoted as $\{N_{hi_h}\}_{i_h=1}^{I_h}, h = 1, 2, \cdots, H$. It is easy to know that

$$N_{hi_h} = [S_{hi_h}/S_{0h}], i_h = 1, 2, \cdots, I_h; h = 1, 2, \cdots, H \tag{6}$$

Step4: set $h = 1$. If $\forall i_h \in \{1, 2, \cdots, I_h\}, N_{hi_h} = 1$, we can know that there is no aliasing existing in the range profile of the target in the h th target direction, so we can set $\rho'_h = d_h$, $B'_h = c/(2\rho'_h)$, where ρ'_h is the range resolution, d_h is the closest distance between the two scattering points, B'_h is the bandwidth of the transmitting signal synthesized in this target direction. At the moment, if $h = H$, then the algorithm is finished; otherwise, set $h = h + 1$ and repeat this step. If $\exists i_h \in \{1, 2, \cdots, I_h\}, N_{hi_h} \geq 2$, then carry out the next step.

Step5: in the h th target direction, suppose the aliasing is existing in the $J_h (J_h \leq I_h)$ main lobes of the range profile. According to the Rayleigh criterion, if the minimum synthesis strength of two diffraction spots is the 0.735 times of the maximum strength of an isolated diffraction spot, we can exactly distinguish the two spots. So calculate the bandwidth of these main lobes at the 0.3675 times of the PSF's peak value, which can be denoted as $\{d_{hj_h}\}_{j_h=1}^{J_h}$. What's more, calculate the bandwidth of PSF's main lobe at the 0.3675 times of the peak value, which can be denoted as d_{0h}. Set $\rho'_h = \min_{j_h}\{(d_{hj_h} - d_{0h})/(N_{hj_h} - 1)\}$ and $B'_h = c/(2\rho'_h)$. At the moment, if $h = H$, then set $\{B_h\}_{h=1}^{H} = \{B'_h\}_{h=1}^{H}$ and back to step1; otherwise, set $h = h + 1$ and back to step4.

3.1 Establishment and Solution of Waveform Optimization Model

In the algorithm above, we should optimize the waveform according to the designed signal bandwidth. From the analysis in part 2, we can know that designing the $P_n(\theta_k), k = 1, 2, \cdots, K; n = 1, 2, \cdots, N$ can determine the bandwidth of transmitting signal synthesized in the target directions and the power distribution on the frequency band, where θ_k is the k th discrete azimuth and K is the number of discrete azimuths.

According to the approximation of the designed waveform and desired waveform, the optimization model can be established as follows

$$\min_{\{x_m(l)\}} \quad \sum_{k=1}^{K} \sum_{l=-L/2}^{L/2-1} |P_l(\theta_k) - p_{kl}|^2 \tag{7}$$
$$\text{s.t.} \quad \text{PAR}(x_m) \leq \rho, \quad m = 0, \cdots, M-1$$

in which, p_{kl} denotes the desired power spectrum at the l th frequency point at angle θ_k, ρ denotes the pre-set threshold value of PAR. And the PAR of the transmitting signal of the m th array element can be denoted as

$$\text{PAR}(\boldsymbol{x}_m) = \frac{\max\limits_{n}|x_m(n)|^2}{\frac{1}{N}\sum\limits_{n=0}^{N-1}|x_m(n)|^2} \tag{8}$$

$$\sum_{n=0}^{N-1}|x_m(n)|^2 = N, \quad m = 0,\cdots,M-1 \tag{9}$$

From the analysis above, we can know that the bandwidth values of signals synthesized in the H target directions is $\{B_h\}_{h=1}^{H}$, the total bandwidth of transmitting signals is $B = \sum\limits_{h=1}^{H} B_h$ and the number of frequency points occupied by the transmit signal synthesized in the h th target direction is $N_h = round(B_h L/B)$. Therefore, in the h th target direction, we can get the desired power spectrum by distributing the transmit power on the N_h frequency points according to the actual situation. It is important to note that in order to distinguish the echoes from different target directions, transmitting signals synthesized in different directions should be distributed on the orthogonal frequency band.

For the optimization model above, we can solve it by referring to the solving algorithm in [18]. Through dividing the solving process into two stages, we can get the transmit matrix $\boldsymbol{X}$ in the end.

4 Simulation Experiments

Suppose the emitter array is consisted of ten linearly spaced isotropic emitter array elements, that is $M = 10$ and the inter-element spacing is $d = 0.5 * c/(f_c + B/2)$. The carrier frequency is $f_c = 10\,\text{GHz}$, the number of sub-pulses is $N = 400$, the frequency points number is $L = 400$ and the discrete azimuth number is $K = 181$.

Suppose there is a ISS at $-20°$ and its scatterer model is shown in Figs. 2 and 3.

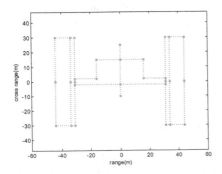

Fig. 2. Scatterer model of the target.

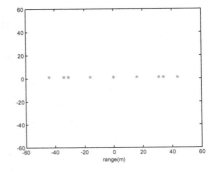

Fig. 3. Scatterer model in the range direction.

Firstly, set arbitrary bandwidth value of the transmitting signal synthesized at $-20°$, that is $B_1 = 30\,\text{MHz}$. The corresponding waveform is designed and is shown in Fig. 4. From the Fig. 4, we can see that parameters of the designed waveform are in accordance with the parameters set before. The PSF of the transmitting signal synthesized at $-20°$ is shown in Fig. 5 and we can get that $d_{01} = 6.8\,\text{m}$, $S_{01} = 4.47$. In low SNR circumstance ($SNR = -10\,\text{dB}$ in the paper), the range profile of the target at $-20°$ is shown in Fig. 6. We can get that the values of $\{S_{1i_1}\}_{i_1=1}^{7}$ are 4.45, 8.98, 4.43, 4.50, 4.59, 8.79, 4.50, so the values of $\{N_{1i_1}\}_{i_1=1}^{7}$ are 1, 2, 1, 1, 1, 2, 1. For the two main lobes that contain aliasing, we can know that the values of $\{d_{1j_1}\}_{j_1=1}^{2}$ are 9.63 m and 9.6 m. So according to the algorithm proposed in the paper, we can make sure the range resolution that can exactly distinguish each scattering point in the range direction is $\rho'_1 = \min_{j_1}\{(d_{1j_1} - d_{01})/(N_{1j_1} - 1)\} = 2.8\,\text{m}$ and the bandwidth of the transmitting signal in this direction is $B'_1 = c/(2\rho'_1) = 54\,\text{MHz}$.

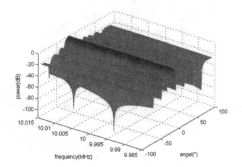

Fig. 4. The designed waveform.

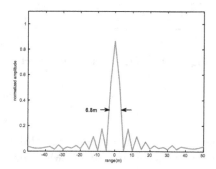

Fig. 5. The PSF of the transmitting signal.

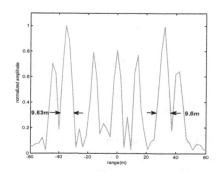

Fig. 6. The range profile of the target.

According to the analysis above, we can know that $B_1 = 54\,\text{MHz}$. The corresponding waveform is designed and is shown in Fig. 7. The PSF of the transmitting signal synthesized at $-20°$ is shown in Fig. 8 and we can get that $S_{01} = 2.75$. In low

SNR circumstance ($SNR = -10\,$dB in the paper), the range profile of the target is shown in Fig. 9. We can get that the values of $\{S_{1i_1}\}_{i_1=1}^{9}$ are 2.97, 2.78, 2.68, 2.72, 2.75, 2.71, 2.62, 2.85, 2.80 and $\{N_{1i_1}\}_{i_1=1}^{9} = 1$. That is to say, each scattering point in the range direction is separated. And from the Fig. 9, we can get the closest distance between the two scattering points is 2.95 m, which is approximated to $\rho'_1 = 2.8\,$m designed by the algorithm in the paper. Therefore, the performance of the algorithm is proved.

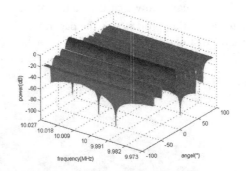

Fig. 7. The designed waveform.

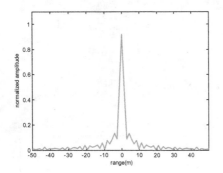

Fig. 8. The PSF of the transmitting signal.

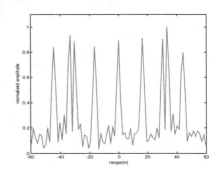

Fig. 9. The range profile of the target.

5 Conclusion

By taking advantage of the good waveform diversity gain of the centralized MIMO radar and the closed-loop feedback of the cognitive radar, a method about MIMO radar waveform optimization based on dynamic adjustment of signal bandwidth is proposed. The simulation results indicate that the method has established the closed-loop feedback between the range profile and the signal bandwidth, which can design the required bandwidth of transmit signal in different directions, according to the range profile of targets. And the simulations have proved the performance of the algorithm in low SNR circumstance in the end.

References

1. Fisher, E., Haimovich, A., Blum, R.S.: MIMO radar: an idea whose time has come. In: Proceedings of IEEE Radar 2004 Conference, PA, pp. 71–78 (2004)
2. Guang, H., Abeysekera, S.S.: Receiver design for range and doppler sidelobe suppression using MIMO and phased-array radar. IEEE Trans. Sig. Process. **61**(6), 1315–1326 (2013)
3. Wang, H.J., Xu, H.B., Lu, M.: Technology and application analysis of MIMO radar. J. Radar Sci. Technol. **7**(4), 245–249 (2009). (in Chinese)
4. Haimovich, A., Blum, R.S., Cimini, L.J.: MIMO radar with widely separated antennas. IEEE Sig. Process. Mag. **25**(1), 116–129 (2008)
5. Li, J., Stoica, P.: MIMO radar with colocated antennas. IEEE Sig. Process. Mag. **24**(5), 106–114 (2007)
6. Stoica, P., Li, J., Xie, Y.: On probing signal design for MIMO radar. IEEE Trans. Sig. Process. **55**(8), 4151–4161 (2007)
7. Haykin, S.: Cognitive radar: a way of the future. IEEE Sig. Process. Mag. **23**(1), 30–40 (2006)
8. Li, X., Fan, M.M., Lu, M.: Research advance on cognitive radar and its key technology. J. Acta Electronica Sinica **40**(9), 1863–1870 (2012). (in Chinese)
9. Jiang, T., Wang, S.L.: Research on the system concept and architecture of cognitive radar. J. Aerospace Electron. Warfare **30**(2), 30–32 (2014). (in Chinese)
10. Wang, S.L., He, Q., He, Z.: LFM-based waveform design for cognitive MIMO radar with constrained bandwidth. EURASIP J. Adv. Sig. Process. **89**(1), 1–9 (2014)
11. Shi, J.N., Jiu, B., Liu, H.W., Wang, S.L.: A beampattern design method for airborne MIMO radar based on prior information. J. Electron. Inf. Technol. **57**(9), 3533–3544 (2009). (in Chinese)
12. Chen, C.Y., Vaidyanathan, P.P.: MIMO radar waveform optimization with prior information of the extended target and clutter. IEEE Trans. Sig. Process. **57**(9), 3533–3544 (2009)
13. Cui, G., Li, H., Rangaswamy, M.: MIMO radar waveform design with constant modulus and similarity constraints. IEEE Trans. Sig. Process. **62**(2), 343–353 (2014)
14. Leshem, A.: Information theoretic adaptive radar waveform design for multiple extended targets. IEEE J. Sel. Topic **1**(1), 42–55 (2007)
15. Yang, Y., Blum, R.S.: Radar waveform design using minimum mean-square error and mutual information. IEEE Workshop Sens. Array Multichannel Process. **2**(4), 234–238 (2006)
16. Yang, Y., Blum, R.S.: Minimax robust MIMO radar waveform design. IEEE J. Sel. Topic **1**(1), 147–155 (2007)
17. Tang, B., Tang, J., Peng, Y.: MIMO radar waveform design in colored noise based on information theory. IEEE Trans. Sig. Process. **58**(9), 4684–4697 (2010)
18. He, H., Petre, S., Li, J.: Wideband MIMO systems: signal design for transmit neampattern synthesis. IEEE Trans. Sig. Process. **59**(2), 618–628 (2011)

Learning Algorithm for Tracking Hypersonic Targets in Near Space

Luyao Cui[✉], Aijun Liu, Changjun Yv, and Taifan Quan

School of Information and Electrical Engineering,
Harbin Institute of Technology, Weihai 264209, China
ilenovoilenovo@163.com

Abstract. With the development of hypersonic vehicles in near space such as X-51A, HTV-2 and so on, tracking for them is becoming a new task and hotspot. In this paper, a learning tracking algorithm is introduced for hypersonic targets, especially for the sliding jump maneuver. Firstly the algorithm uses the Sine model, which makes the tracking model more close to the particular maneuver, next two Sine models different in angular velocity are used into IMM algorithm, and it learns the target tracking error characteristics to adjust the sampling rate adaptively. The algorithm is compared with the single accurate model algorithm and general IMM algorithms with fixed sampling rate. Through simulation experiments it is proved that the algorithm in this paper can improve the tracking accuracy effectively.

Keywords: Learn · Target tracking · Near space · Interacting multiple models
Sampling rate

1 Introduction

Near space is the air space from ground 20–100 km, also known as suborbital space or aerospace transition zone. It is near space where the near space vehicle voyages and completes the specific tasks such as attacking, reconnoitre, communication, early warning, navigation and so on [1]. It has very important military value and significance.

The hypersonic vehicle has high speed, strong maneuver and periodic jumping motion, and its flight process can be simplified into 3 stages: boost section, cruise section and attack section. Sliding jump flight is adopted in the cruise section and this kind of trajectory is not easy to be detected and intercepted with strong penetration capability.

In view of the above characteristics, radar tracking for near space targets is still in the exploratory stage. Based on the relationship between the position estimation value and the acceleration, the literature [2] proposed a modified CS model which can be adjusted adaptively and used it into the IMM algorithm. The literature [3] applied IMM algorithm with CV and CA models in unscented Kalman filter. The algorithms mentioned above are based on the interacting multiple model algorithm. Although the interaction models are different, they adopt the existing maneuvering models which are not close to the sliding jump flight. With the idea of current statistical model, the target angular velocity is corrected in the literature [4], and it was combined with the

© ICST Institute for Computer Sciences, Social Informatics and Telecommunications Engineering 2018
X. Gu et al. (Eds.): MLICOM 2017, Part II, LNICST 227, pp. 206–214, 2018.
https://doi.org/10.1007/978-3-319-73447-7_24

extended Kalman filter, but the maneuvering frequency and maximum acceleration should be set artificially which means poor adaptive ability. The paper [5] establishes a specific target motion model for the jumping maneuver, but it needs speed information and cannot be applied into general phased array radar.

Because of the extremely complex motions of near space targets, it is difficult to establish accurate models [6]. Therefore, this paper introduces the concept of learning algorithm and constructs a learning tracking system, which makes the tracking algorithm adaptive to complex motion situation.

2   Learning Tracking Algorithm

2.1   Framework

The system diagram of this algorithm is as follows (Fig. 1):

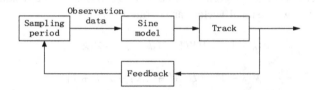

Fig. 1. Learning tracking algorithm framework.

After the system gets the observations in accordance with the corresponding sampling period T, data will be processed in IMM-Kalman filter based on 2 Sine models with different angular velocity, and transmitted to the evaluation system. The evaluation system determines T in the next time according to the target tracking error and adjustment rules.

2.2   Model

At present, the most common movement models for maneuvering targets tracking are Singer model, CS model, Jerk model and corresponding improved model. In the tracking for linear moving targets, these models have good tracking accuracy. But for the non-ballistic trajectory of near space hypersonic targets, particularly the sliding jump maneuver, the former models have low matching degree. This algorithm adopts Sine model [7].

Sine model's state equation is as follows:

$$X(k+1) = F(T, w_0)X(k) + W(k) \tag{1}$$

Where, k represents time; $X = \begin{bmatrix} x & \dot{x} & \ddot{x} & \dddot{x} \end{bmatrix}^T$ represents state vector, including target position, velocity, acceleration and jerk; F is state transition matrix; T is sampling period, and W is Gauss white noise whose covariance is Q.

$$Q(k) = \frac{\sigma_w^2}{\pi} \begin{pmatrix} q_{11} & q_{12} & q_{13} & q_{14} \\ q_{21} & q_{22} & q_{23} & q_{24} \\ q_{31} & q_{32} & q_{33} & q_{34} \\ q_{41} & q_{42} & q_{43} & q_{44} \end{pmatrix} \tag{2}$$

Where, σ_w^2 represents acceleration variance.

Measurement equation is as follows:

$$Z(k) = H(k)X(k) + V(k) \tag{3}$$

In the equation, Z represents measurement vector after unbiased transformation, H is the measurement matrix, and V is Gauss white noise.

2.3 Residual and Norm

The learning method of this algorithm is constructed based on the residual sequence, and the following two residual vectors are defined [8]:

$$V(k+1) = H\hat{X}(k+1|k+1) - Z(k+1) \tag{4}$$

$$\bar{V}(k+1) = H\hat{X}(k+1|k) - Z(k+1) \tag{5}$$

The information represented by the two is different: the residual vector $V(k+1)$ is determined by the filtered value of the corresponding measurement information that has been fused at the $k+1$ moment, and the predicted residual vector $\bar{V}(k+1)$ is determined by the predicted state of the k moment. If the measurement information is reliable, the value of the residual vector indicates the reliability of the $X(k+1|k)$, so the predicted residual vector can reflect the disturbance of the dynamic system better than the residual vector.

Define the norm of the predicted residuals as follows:

$$d(k+1) = \bar{V}^T(k+1)S^{-1}(k+1)\bar{V} \quad (k+1) \tag{6}$$

In the equation, S is the innovation covariance matrix.

2.4 Adjustment for Sampling Period

The norm reflects the tracking effect of the target, so it is considered as the basis for adjusting the sampling period.

Sampling period allocation method: when the target is in the non-maneuvering state, the innovation norm $d(k)$ obeys the $\chi^2(m)$ distribution (m is the observation dimension). Now take $d(k)$ as standard to judge whether the target is maneuvering, and set the false alarm rate of the decision as α, according to the distribution table, we can find the corresponding threshold d_α [9]. The $\alpha(n)$ false alarm rates are selected as the key node, and the corresponding value sequence $d_\alpha(n)$ is obtained by $\chi^2(m)$ table, so that the sequence data can be compared with the sequence value, and the new sampling period can be determined by comparing the results.

Taking node number $N = 3$ as an example, a specific rule is given.

When $d_\alpha(n) < d(k) < d_\alpha(n+1)$,

If $\alpha(n) < 10\%$ we think that the target is likely to be maneuvering, then the maximum data rate is allocated for the target, such as 0.1 s;

If $10\% < \alpha(n) < 90\%$ we consider the accidental flight disturbance or observation outliers to make the norm larger, and then assign a lower data rate for the target, such as 0.2 s;

If $90\% < \alpha(n)$ we think the target is non motorized, then the target data rate is the lowest value, such as 0.5 s.

If the N takes a larger value, the adaptive sampling period tracking algorithm would work better in theory.

In the IMM algorithm, there are many d because of the presence of multiple models. At this point, the d used to decide the sampling interval at the next time is computed by adding products of multiplying the d of each model with the corresponding model probability.

$$d = \sum_{i=1}^{j} d_i * u_i \qquad (7)$$

Where, j is the number of interactive models, u_i is the probability of the i model.

3 Simulation and Analysis

3.1 Simulation Settings

Refering to some basic test data for X-51 released by the U.S. government in May 2013, this paper simplifies the complicated mathematical model [10] (including dynamics model, engine thrust model, aerodynamic model, atmospheric model and so on). According to the primary characteristics of the near space vehicle (including flight height and velocity), an analog trajectory with time length of 300 s is set as follows and its angular velocity is 0.06 rad/s (Fig. 2). In fact, the target does a uniform motion at different speeds in the X and Y axis (for this reason, the following simulation only shows the results in the Y axis), with a sinusoidal motion whose period is 0.06 rad/s in the Z axis. It is assumed that the sampling period of ground-based radar is 0.2 s, the radial distance error is 100 m, the azimuth and pitch angle errors are both 0.1°. The data processing method is an unbiased conversion measurement Kalman algorithm.

3.2 Experiment One

Taking into account that the parameter w of the Sine model is to set artificially in advance, and the aircraft's sliding jump trajectory in the actual situation is not known exactly, so we need to consider the influence on the tracking effect when the angular speed w is set different values. In the experiment we set 3 different angular velocity of

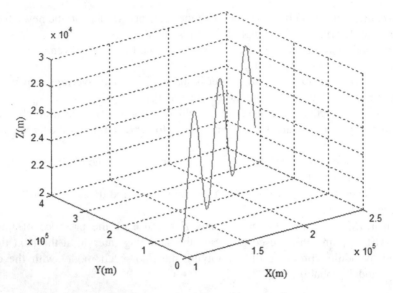

Fig. 2. Trajectory simulation of hypersonic target

0.06 rad/s, 0.05 rad/s, and 0.07 rad/s, among whom 0.06 rad/s matches with the simulated trajectory's angular velocity. And then we use the Kalman filter algorithm to achieve Monte-Carlo simulation for 100 times. The standard examining tracking effect is the position tracking mean square error in the direction of Z axis. The analysis process of the other two axes is similar, no more details.

As can be seen from the Figs. 3 and 4, since the Y axes move at the constant speed, while the Z axis makes sinusoidal acceleration motion, the root mean square curves of the filtering error in the X and Y axis are similar, while that of the Z axis is slightly different. But when different angular velocities are compared, we can find that the error curve when the angular velocity matches is stable and convergent. In time of about first 50 s the other two curves have high coincidence degree with the w = 0.06 rad/s curve, this is because the filter time is not long, the difference is small, then it begins to appear big shock as time goes, the error caused by the mismatch of angular velocity increases and shocks gradually. The mean square error of each axis of the three angular velocities is statistically averaged, as shown in the following Table 1. From this experiment it can be concluded that the Sine model can indeed track high speed targets in sliding jump maneuver with good tracking accuracy, but the premise is the angular velocity set should match with the actual, if there are some errors, tracking will be unstable, the filtering error will appear concussion.

3.3   Experiment Two

It is a good method to make use of several Sine models with different angular speed for interactive tracking under the condition of uncertain target's actual motion parameters. In this experiment, two sine models with different angular velocities w = 0.05 rad/s, and w = 0.07 rad/s are used interactively to track the simulated trajectories of the above w = 0.06 rad/s aircraft.

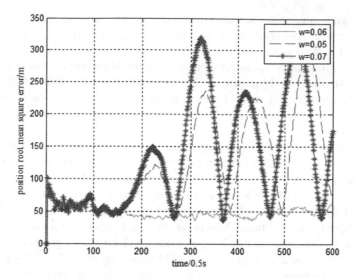

Fig. 3. Position root mean square error in Y axis in different w

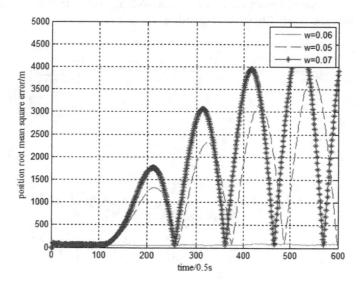

Fig. 4. Position root mean square error in Z axis in different w

Table 1. Statistical average of position root mean error in z axis

w/ (rad/s)	Root mean square error in X/m	Root mean square error in Y/m	Root mean square error in Z/m
0.06	60.2149	63.4617	85.3250
0.05	101.8573	123.0269	1291.1
0.07	104.8638	134.3005	1623.2

The tracking root mean square error is compared between the algorithm with adaptive sampling rate (IMM-AT), and general IMM algorithms whose sampling period are 0.1 s, 0.2 s and 0.5 s.

The filtered root mean square error curve of the IMM algorithm with three different fixed sampling intervals is drawn in Figs. 5 and 6. Overall, although the angular velocity of two Sine models in the interaction differs from the real's, the filtering curve is relatively stable without substantial concussion, and the error is generally much less than single model's error when w = 0.05 rad/s or w = 0.07 rad/s. On the other hand, in either direction axis, the root mean square error decreases as the sampling interval decreases. This shows that, to a certain extent, the filtering results can be improved by reducing the sampling interval. From the statistical error of the following table, when T = 0.5 s, the error of the IMM algorithm on the X and Y axis is less than w = 0.06 single model algorithm, but the filtering effect of the Z axis is not as good as that of the w = 0.06 single model algorithm. This is because the target in the Z axis is accelerated by sinusoidal motion, and the matching of angular velocity has a great influence on its filtering. However, the Z axis error of the IMM algorithm when T = 0.2 s is less than the error from single model algorithm when w = 0.06. So it is possible to reduce the error when the error is large, especially the Z axis error, by changing the sampling interval. The root mean square error of the IMM-AT algorithm in the last line of the Table 2 verifies the feasibility of the algorithm.

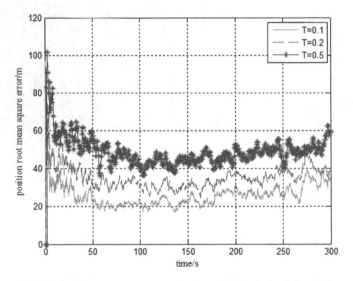

Fig. 5. Position root mean square error in Y axis in different T

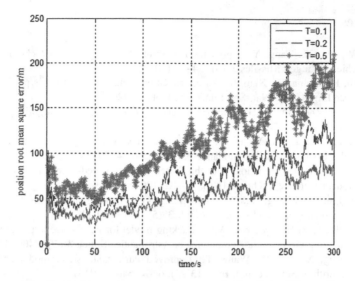

Fig. 6. Position root mean square error in Z axis in different T

Table 2. Statistical average of position root mean error in z axis

Sampling/s	Root mean square error in X/m	Root mean square error in Y/m	Root mean square error in Z/m
0.1	37.2816	27.0823	64.1143
0.2	56.6592	39.7474	96.5491
0.5	68.4965	50.5756	132.8217
IMM-AT	48.2112	34.6849	83.3211

4 Conclusion

Aimed at sliding jump maneuver of near space hypersonic vehicle, an interactive multiple model algorithm based on the Sine model with adaptive sampling rate is proposed. This is a kind of algorithm that can learn and adjust according to the feedback of the system. Compared with the single accurate model algorithm and the IMM algorithm with different fixed sampling rate, it proves the feasibility and practicability of the learning algorithm in this paper.

Acknowledgments. This work was supported by the National Natural Science Foundation of China (No. 61571159).

References

1. Chen, W., Wu, X., Tang, Y.: Application of thrust vectoring control technology in near space vehicle. Winged Missiles J. (5), 64–70 (2013)
2. Li, C., Bi, H., Zhang, B., Xiao, S.: An improved tracking algorithm for hypersonic targets. J. Air Force Eng. Univ. (Nat. Sci. Edn.) **13**(5), 50–54 (2012)
3. Qin, L., Li, J., Zhou, D.: Tracking for near space target based on IMM algorithm. Syst. Eng. Electron. **36**(7), 1243–1249 (2014)
4. Xiao, S., Tan, X., Li, Z., Wang, H.: Near space hypersonic target MCT tracking model. J. Projectiles Rockets Missiles Guidance **33**(1), 185–194 (2013)
5. Cao, Y., Li, Y.: State estimation algorithm based on high speed-acceleration target in near space. Modern Defence Technol. **41**(6), 97–101 (2013)
6. Guo, X., Liu, C., Zhang, Y., Wei, G., Wang, G.: Tracking algorithms for near space hypersonic target. Command Control Simul. **38**(5), 8–12 (2016)
7. Wang, G., Li, J., Zhang, X., Wu, W.: A tracking model for near space hypersonic slippage leap maneuvering target. Acta Aeronautica et Astronautica Sinica **36**(7), 2400–2410 (2015)
8. Liu, Y., Feng, X., Ye, Y., Wang, Y.: Improved current statistical model and adaptive tracking algorithm. Sci. Technol. Eng. **13**(22), 6464–6468 (2013)
9. Shi, L., Wang, X., Xiao, S.: Adaptive data rate tracking of phased array radar based on residue norm. Shipboard Electron. Countermeasure **28**(5), 45–47 (2005)
10. Xiaohua, N., Yiming, X.: Flight trajectory modeling and simulation for target tracking on NSHV. Comput. Simul. **33**(3), 41–46 (2016)

Coherent Integration Algorithm for Weak Maneuvering Target Detection in Passive Radar Using Digital TV Signals

Ying Zhou[✉], Weijie Xia, Jianjiang Zhou, Linlin Huang, and Minling Huang

Laboratory of Radar Imaging and Microwave Photonics,
College of Electronic and Information Engineering, Ministry of Education,
Nanjing University of Aeronautics and Astronautics, Nanjing 211100, China
{nuaazhouying,nuaaxwj,zjjee}@nuaa.edu.cn

Abstract. This paper considers the coherent integration problem of detecting weak maneuvering targets in passive radar using digital television terrestrial broadcasting (DTTB) signals. By dividing the continuous DTTB echoes into multiple segments, the generalized Radon-Fourier transform (GRFT) which was proposed to realize coherent integration of maneuvering targets for pulse Doppler radar can be utilized in DTTB-based passive radar. The GRFT can obtain ideal coherent integration gain but suffers a heavy computational burden. In this paper, a fast implementation algorithm of GRFT using the modified wind driven optimization (MWDO) is proposed. Compared with the existing particle swarm optimization (PSO) method, the proposed method can achieve better detection performance with a similar computational cost in DTTB-based passive radar. Several numerical experiments are also provided to demonstrate the effectiveness of the proposed method.

Keywords: Weak maneuvering target detection · Passive radar
Generalized Radon-Fourier Transform (GRFT)
Wind Driven Optimization (WDO)

1 Introduction

Passive bistatic radar often uses non-cooperative civil radiation sources to detect and locate targets. Compared with the traditional monostatic radar, passive radar has several attractive advantages such as stronger survivability, better anti-jamming ability and potential anti-stealth capacity [1]. Among various illuminators, digital television terrestrial broadcasting (DTTB) signals are better choices for passive radar due to the high power, wide coverage, and higher range resolution.

It is known that pulses integration especially coherent integration can greatly improve the radar detection performance. The traditional coherent integration method for DTTB-based passive radar is to compute the cross-ambiguity function (CAF) [2]. However, the computational burden of CAF is heavy and the integration performance via CAF will be greatly influenced by the range migration (RM) and the Doppler frequency migration (DFM) which are caused by the maneuvering motions of targets

© ICST Institute for Computer Sciences, Social Informatics and Telecommunications Engineering 2018
X. Gu et al. (Eds.): MLICOM 2017, Part II, LNICST 227, pp. 215–224, 2018.
https://doi.org/10.1007/978-3-319-73447-7_25

[3]. To reduce the computational complexity, a signal segmentation method [1] can be utilized. After segmentation, the continuous DTTB signal have equivalent fast time and slow time, which is similar to pulse signal in pulse Doppler radar.

In pulse Doppler radar, the commonly used integration method is moving target detection (MTD) [4], but it will become invalid when RM occurs. Regarding this, Zhang and Zeng [5] have proposed to perform keystone transform (KT) to deal with RM before MTD. However, traditional KT can only correct the first-order RM caused by the velocity of targets. Li et al. [6, 7] have proposed a fast coherent integration method based on adjacent cross correlation function (ACCF) for maneuvering targets. This method can remove the RM and reduce the order of DFM and is free of parameters searching. Unfortunately, ACCF cannot be applied to DTTB-based passive radar because of the pseudo random characteristics of DTTB signals. In recent years, generalized Radon-Fourier transform (GRFT) [8] has been proposed to achieve ideal coherent integration of maneuvering targets via jointly searching in parameter space, but it suffers a heavy computational burden. Through converting the realization of GRFT into an optimization problem, Qian et al. [9] proposed an improved particle swarm optimization (PSO) method to fast implement GRFT.

Although PSO greatly reduces the computational burden of GRFT, it suffers an apparent detection performance loss. For the purpose of improving the detection performance, this paper proposes a fast implementation algorithm of GRFT based on the modified wind driven optimization (MWDO). Compared with PSO, MWDO can achieve better detection performance with similar computational cost in DTTB-based passive radar.

2   Signal Model and Signal Segmentation Method

2.1   Signal Model of Passive Radar

Figure 1 depicts the bistatic passive radar geometry. The baseline runs from the transmitter Tx to the passive radar receiver Rx, and they are separated by the base-length L. Suppose that the target is located at O at the initial time and moves to O' at time t. The distance between the target and the transmitter at the initial time and time t is denoted by R_{T0} and $R_T(t)$ respectively while the distance between the target and the receiver at the initial time and time t is denoted by R_{r0} and $R_r(t)$ respectively. β is the bistatic angle at the initial time and φ denotes the movement direction of the target. The DTTB source transmits the signal $s(t)$. The passive radar receiver collects both a reference signal $x(t)$ via a line-of-sight (LOS) path direct from the illuminator, and a surveillance signal $s_r(t)$ reflected via the target of interest. $s_r(t)$ has a time delay $\tau = R(t)/c$ refers to $x(t)$, where

$$R(t) = R_T(t) + R_r(t) - L \tag{1}$$

The received radar echo can be denoted as

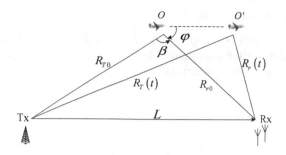

Fig. 1. Sketch map of the bistatic structure of passive radar.

$$s_r(t) = A_e s(t - R(t)/c) \exp(-j2\pi f_c R(t)/c) \tag{2}$$

where c is the speed of light, A_e is the amplitude, and f_c is the carrier frequency.

Assume that the target moving from O to O' is maneuvering. Neglecting the high order components, the instantaneous range $R_m(t)$ between O and O' can be denoted as

$$R_m(t) = v_0 t + \frac{1}{2} a_0 t^2 + \frac{1}{6} g_0 t^3 \tag{3}$$

where v_0, a_0 and g_0 denotes respectively the velocity, acceleration and jerk of the target. From the geometric relationship of Fig. 1, we can obtain that

$$R_T(t) = \sqrt{R_{T0}^2 + R_m^2(t) - 2R_{T0}R_m(t)\cos(\beta + \varphi)} \tag{4}$$

$$R_r(t) = \sqrt{R_{r0}^2 + R_m^2(t) - 2R_{r0}R_m(t)\cos(\varphi)} \tag{5}$$

Then, inserting (4) and (5) into (1) and expanding (1) into Taylor series at $t = 0$, we have

$$R(t) = \alpha_0 - \alpha_1 t - \alpha_2 t^2 - \alpha_3 t^3 \approx R_{T0} + R_{r0} - L - \left[2v_0\cos\left(\varphi + \frac{\beta}{2}\right)\cos\frac{\beta}{2}\right]t$$
$$- \left[a_0\cos\left(\varphi + \frac{\beta}{2}\right)\cos\frac{\beta}{2}\right]t^2 - \left[\frac{1}{3}g_0\cos\left(\varphi + \frac{\beta}{2}\right)\cos\frac{\beta}{2}\right]t^3 \tag{6}$$

Higher order components are ignored. α_0 is the relative initial range and α_1, α_2 and α_3 are the relative motion parameters.

The reference signal $x(t)$ can be simply expressed as a direct path (DP) component from the transmitter and the short delay is neglected for simplicity, i.e.

$$x(t) = A_r s(t) \tag{7}$$

where A_r is the amplitude of the received reference signal. In this paper, it is assumed that the multipath clutter has been preprocessed.

2.2   Signal Segmentation Method

The segmentation method is shown in Fig. 2. First, the number of segments can be determined according to the maximum relative velocity of the target required to be detected by the passive radar system, i.e.

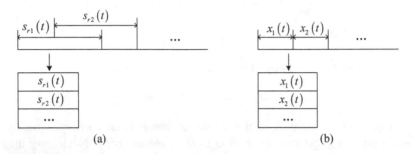

(a)   (b)

Fig. 2. Schematic diagram of signal segmentation method. (a) Segmentation method for echo signal. (b) Segmentation method for reference signal.

$$N = 2v_{\max}T/\lambda \tag{8}$$

where T is the integration time and λ is the wavelength. In this way, the Doppler ambiguity can be avoided. Then the efficient length of each segment of the reference signal is $L_r = L/N$, where L is the total signal length. In order to guarantee the expected detection range, the overlapping segmentation method is utilized for the echo signal. The segment length of echo signal is $L_e = L_r + f_s R_{\max}/c$, and $R_{\max}$ denotes the maximum relative range required to be detected by radar. At last, pad zeros for the segmented reference signal to insure that the length of each segment of reference signal and echo signal is equal.

After segmentation, $T_r = L_r/f_s$ can be considered as the pulse repetition interval. Then the equivalent pulse compression can be calculated as

$$s_{pc}(t_m, \hat{t}) = A's'(\hat{t} - R(t_m)/c) \exp\left(-j\frac{2\pi}{\lambda}R(t_m)\right) \tag{9}$$

where $\hat{t}$ is the fast time, $t_m = mT_r$ $(m = 0, 1, \cdots, N-1)$ is the slow time, $s'(t)$ is the inverse Fourier transform result of $|S(f)|^2$, $S(f)$ stands for the Fourier transform of the transmitted signal $s(t)$, $A' = A_e A_r$, and $R(t_m) = \alpha_0 - \alpha t_m - \alpha_2 t_m^2 - \alpha_3 t_m^3$.

From (9), it's easy to see that the target envelope varies with t_m and the phase is also the cubic function of t_m. The changes of envelope and phase will easily result in RM and DFM. For the purpose of coherently accumulating the target's energy, both the RM and the DFM are required to be compensated [10].

3 Coherent Integration via MWDO

3.1 Definition and Analysis of GRFT

GRFT is a coherent integration algorithm via jointly searching in multi-dimensional parameter space. The definition of GRFT in [8] is given as follows:

Suppose a 2D complex function $f(t_m, \hat{\imath}) \in C$ is defined in the $(t_m, \hat{\imath})$ plane and a parameterized P-dimensional function $\hat{\imath} = \eta(t_m; \hat{\alpha}^P)$ is used for searching a certain time-varied curve in the plane, where $\hat{\alpha}^P = [\hat{\alpha}_0, \hat{\alpha}_1, \cdots, \hat{\alpha}_{P-1}]$. Then GRFT can be defined as

$$G(\hat{\alpha}^P) = \int_{-\infty}^{\infty} f(t_m, \eta(t_m; \hat{\alpha}^P)) \exp(j2\pi\varepsilon\eta(t_m; \hat{\alpha}^P)) dt_m \qquad (10)$$

where ε is a known constant with respect to $\eta(t_m; \hat{\alpha}^P)$.

Let $f(t_m, \hat{\imath}) = s_{pc}(t_m, \hat{\imath})$, then (10) can be rewritten as

$$G(\hat{\alpha}^P) = \int_{-\infty}^{\infty} s_{pc}(t_m, \hat{\tau}(t_m)) \exp(j2\pi f_c \hat{\tau}(t_m)) dt_m \qquad (11)$$

where $\hat{\tau}(t_m) = \frac{1}{c} \sum_{p=0}^{P-1} \hat{\alpha}_p t_m^p$. When the searching values of motion parameters $[\hat{\alpha}_0, \hat{\alpha}_1, \cdots, \hat{\alpha}_{P-1}]$ match with the target's real motion values $[\alpha_0, \alpha_1, \cdots, \alpha_{P-1}]$, the ideal coherent integration gain could be achieved, that is $G(\alpha^P) = NA'$. Then the target can be detected and the motion parameters can be easily obtained by the location of the peak in the parameter space.

In pulse Doppler radar, the blind speed side lobe (BSSL) [11] will appear in GRFT because of limited integration time, Doppler ambiguity, discrete pulse sampling, and finite range resolution, which will cause serious false alarms. In DTTB-based passive radar, the Doppler ambiguity can be avoided by using flexible segmentation method, so the BSSL phenomenon can also be avoided in GRFT.

3.2 Modified Wind Driven Optimization

The model of wind driven optimization (WDO) is based on the definition of trajectories of small air parcels within the earth atmosphere [12]. In WDO, a population of air parcels is distributed throughout a N-dimensional problem space, and the velocity of air parcels is updated in each iteration process based on the equation which is derived from Newton's second law of motion and the ideal gas laws. It is given by

$$U_{new} = (1 - \alpha)U_{cur} - gX_{cur} + \left[RT|1/i - 1|(X_{opt} - X_{cur})\right] + \left(CU_{cur}^{other\ dim}/i\right) \quad (12)$$

where i represents the rankings of the air parcels. Equation (12) demonstrates that the updated velocity U_{new} for the next iteration process is associated with the current velocity U_{cur}, the current position X_{cur}, the optimal position X_{opt} with the highest pressure value that has been found until the current iteration, the current velocity $U_{cur}^{other\ dim}$ which is randomly chosen from other dimensions, and the four coefficients α, g, RT, and C. The position of air parcel can be updated by

$$X_{new} = X_{cur} + U_{new} \tag{13}$$

WDO provides extra degrees of freedom to fine tune in the velocity update equation compared with PSO, which indicates a better optimization capacity. As illustrated in [12], the optimum performance of WDO can be achieved by selecting proper values for the four coefficients, but the optimum values of the WDO coefficients may vary from problem to problem. Considering the problem, we propose the modified WDO (MWDO) to tune the four coefficients in each iteration process by random distributions. The values of coefficients are given by

$$\alpha = RT = g = 0.1 * rand\_L \tag{14}$$

$$C = 2.5 * rand\_U \tag{15}$$

where the random number $rand\_U$ is uniformly distributed between 0 and 1, and the random number $rand\_L$ is subject to Levy distribution [13]. Its probability density function over the domain $x \geq \mu$ is

$$f(x; \mu, \gamma) = \sqrt{\frac{\gamma}{2\pi}} \frac{e^{-\frac{\gamma}{2(x-\mu)}}}{(x-\mu)^{3/2}} \tag{16}$$

where γ is the scale parameter and μ is the location parameter. In this paper, $\mu = 0$ and $\gamma = 0.001$ are selected.

By applying MWDO, the optimization ability of WDO in a noisy environment can be enhanced and at the same time, the difficulty in choosing proper coefficients in WDO can be overcome.

3.3   Fast Implementation of GRFT via MWDO

GRFT can be fast implemented via MWDO. The whole target detection procedure based on MWDO in DTTB-based passive radar is shown in Fig. 3 and the detailed description of the proposed method is given as follows:

Step 1. Specify the basic parameters in MWDO, including the population size S, the maximum number of iteration k_{max}, the dimension of the searching space, the searching range of each parameter, and the restrictions on velocities of air parcels.

Step 2. Initialize air parcels' locations and velocities.

Step 3. Sort air parcels based on their pressure values. In GRFT, pressure value refers to the absolute value of GRFT, denoted by $|G(\mathbf{X})|$.

Step 4. Generate the values of coefficients of MWDO via (14) and (15).

Step 5. Update the velocities and locations of air parcels via (12) and (13).

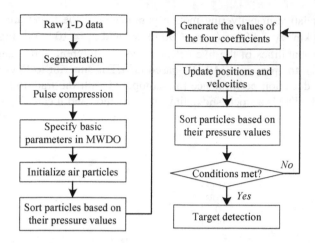

Fig. 3. Flow chart of the target detection method in DTTB-based passive radar.

Step 6. Sort these updated air parcels based on their pressure values and find the current optimal air parcel $\mathbf{X}_{opt}(k)$.

Step 7. Repeat Step 4 to Step 6 until one of the following conditions is met:

(1) $\left|G\left(\mathbf{X}_{opt}(k)\right)\right| > \gamma$ and $k \leq k_{max}$;

(2) $\left|G\left(\mathbf{X}_{opt}(k)\right)\right| \leq \gamma$ and $k > k_{max}$.

The parameter γ is the detection threshold calculated from the preset false alarm probability. When condition 1 is met, the target is detected and when condition 2 is met, the radar system tells that there is no target.

4 Numerical Results

In this section, numerical experiments are provided to demonstrate the effectiveness of the proposed fast implementation method of GRFT. The DTTB-based passive radar parameters are listed in Table 1.

Table 1. Simulation parameters of DTTB-based passive radar.

Signal mode	Bandwidth	Carrier frequency	Integration time
Single-carrier mode	7.56 MHz	674 MHz	0.22 s

4.1 Detection Performance

The detection performances of traditional ergodic-search GRFT, PSO-based GRFT, MWDO-based GRFT, KT, and MTD are investigated via Monte Carlo trials. The false alarm probability is $P_{fa} = 10^{-6}$. The population size $S = 150$ and the maximum number of iteration $k_{max} = 800$ are specified for PSO and MWDO. The relative initial

range and the relative maneuvering motion parameters of the target are given as fol-
lows: $\alpha_0 = 150$ km, $\alpha_1 = 800$ m/s, $\alpha_2 = 90$ m/s^2, and $\alpha_3 = 10$ m/s^3. Figure 4 shows
the detection probabilities of the five detectors versus different SNR values. Figure 4
demonstrates that the proposed MWDO-based GRFT is superior to PSO-based GRFT
but still suffers detection performance loss compared with the traditional GRFT. The
reason is that MWDO is a stochastic optimization method and it cannot jump out of the
convergence to noise peaks each time. The detection performance loss of MWDO is the
cost of the reduced computational complexity.

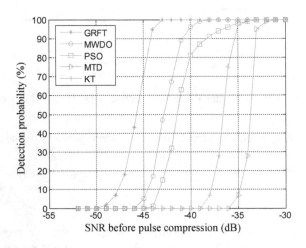

Fig. 4. Detection probability of GRFT, MWDO, PSO, KT, and MTD.

4.2 Computational Cost

Denote the number of range cells, pulses, and searching motion parameters
$\alpha_p (p = 1, 2, 3, \cdots P - 1)$ by M, N, N_p, respectively. Then $\prod\limits_{p=1}^{P-1} NN_p$ searches are needed

and the computational complexity is $O\left(\prod\limits_{p=1}^{P-1} MNN_p\right)$ for the traditional GRFT [14].

While only $k_{\max}$ searches are needed for MWDO and PSO if they are terminated when
the number of iteration reaches $k_{\max}$. In fact, when condition 1 in Step 7 is met, the two
algorithms can be terminated earlier. The running time of the traditional GRFT,
MWDO-based GRFT, and PSO-based GRFT under different motion orders is shown in
Fig. 5. From Fig. 5 we can see that with the increase of the motion order, the time cost
of GRFT grows nearly exponentially while the running time of MWDO and PSO stays
stable. The computational complexity of MWDO is slightly higher than PSO due to the
additional sorting process of air parcels, which is acceptable. It is obvious that when the
motion order equals to 3, the computational complexity of intelligent optimization
algorithms is far less than that of the ergodic-search GRFT, which validates the
physical realizability of the proposed algorithm.

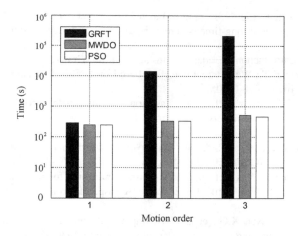

Fig. 5. Computational cost of the ergodic-search GRFT, MWDO, and PSO.

5   Conclusions

This paper deals with the coherent integration problem of the weak maneuvering target in passive radar using DTTB signals. By designing suitable signal segmentation method, GRFT can be applied to achieve ideal integration performance by correcting RM and DFM at the same time in passive radar. Then a fast implementation method for GRFT is proposed to reduce the computational burden, namely MWDO. Compared with the ergodic-search GRFT, MWDO requires much lower computational load, which means it can realize the maneuvering target detection in a much more efficient way. Compared with the existing PSO method, MWDO has better detection perfor-mance with a similar computational complexity. It should be noticed that although MWDO has stronger anti-noise ability, it still suffers some detection performance loss, which is the cost of the reduced computational burden. Finally, several simulation experiments are provided to validate the effectiveness of the proposed method. Future work may further improve the proposed method and extend it to multi-target detection.

Acknowledgments. The work was supported by the National Natural Science Foundation of China (Grant no. 61201366), the Fundamental Research Funds for the Central Universities (Grant no. NS2016040), the Fundamental Research Funds for the Central Universities (Grant no. NJ20150020), and the Priority Academic Program Development of Jiangsu Higher Education Institutions.

References

1. Tao, S., Liu, S.H., et al.: Efficient architecture and hardware implementation of coherent integration processor for digital video broadcast-based passive bistatic radar. IET Radar Sonar Navig. **10**(1), 97–106 (2016)
2. Tao, R., Zhang, W.Q., Chen, E.Q.: Two-stage method for joint time delay and Doppler shift estimation. IET Radar Sonar Navig. **2**(1), 71–77 (2008)

3. Chen, X.L., Guan, J., Liu, N.B., et al.: Maneuvering target detection via Radon-Fractional Fourier transform-based long-time coherent integration. IEEE Trans. Signal Process. **62**(4), 939–953 (2014)
4. Skolnik, M.I.: Introduction to radar system, 3rd edn. Mc-Graw-Hill, New York (2002)
5. Zhang, S.S., Zeng, T.: Weak target detection based on keystone transform. Acta Electron. Sinica. **33**(9), 1675–1678 (2005)
6. Li, X.L., Cui, G.L., Kong, L.J., et al.: Fast non-searching method for maneuvering target detection and motion parameters estimation. IEEE Trans. Signal Process. **64**(9), 2232–2244 (2016)
7. Li, X.L., Cui, G.L., Yi, W.: A fast maneuvering target motion parameters estimation algorithm based on ACCF. IEEE Sig. Process. Lett. **22**(3), 270–274 (2015)
8. Xu, J., Yu, J., Peng, Y.N., et al.: Radon-Fourier transform for radar target detection, I: generalized Doppler filter bank. IEEE Trans. Aerosp. Electron. Syst. **47**(2), 1186–1202 (2011)
9. Qian, L.C., Xu, J., Xia, X.G., et al.: Fast implementation of generalized Radon-Fourier transform for maneuvering radar target detection. Electron. Lett. **48**(22), 1427–1428 (2012)
10. Chen, X.L., Huang, Y., Liu, N.B., et al.: Radon-fractional ambiguity function-based detection method of low-observable maneuvering target. IEEE Trans. Aerosp. Electron. Syst. **51**(2), 815–833 (2015)
11. Xu, J., Yu, J., Peng, Y.N., et al.: Radon-Fourier transform (RFT) for radar target detection (II): blind speed sidelobe suppression. IEEE Trans. Aerosp. Electron. Syst. **47**(4), 2473–2489 (2011)
12. Bayraktar, Z., Komurcu, M., Werner, D.H.: The wind driven optimization technique and its application in electromagnetics. IEEE Trans. Antennas Propag. **61**(5), 2745–2757 (2013)
13. Liang, Y.J., Chen, W.: A survey on computing Levy stable distribution and a new MATLAB toolbox. Sig. Process. **93**(1), 242–251 (2013)
14. Xu, J., Xia, X.G., Peng, S.B., et al.: Radar maneuvering target motion estimation based on generalized Radon-Fourier transform. IEEE Trans. Sig. Process. **60**(12), 6190–6201 (2012)

High-Resolution Sparse Representation of Micro-Doppler Signal in Sparse Fractional Domain

Xiaolong Chen$^{(\boxtimes)}$, Xiaohan Yu, Jian Guan, and You He

Naval Aeronautical University,
Yantai 264001, Shandong, People's Republic of China
cxlcxll209@163.com, guanjian96@tsinghua.org.cn

Abstract. In order to effectively improve radar detection ability of moving target under the conditions of strong clutter and complex motion characteristics, the principle framework of Short-Time sparse Time-Frequency Distribution (ST-TFD) is established combing the advantages of TFD and sparse representation. Then, Short-Time Sparse FRactional Ambiguity Function (ST-SFRAF) method is proposed and applied to radar micro-Doppler (m-D) detection and extraction. It is verified by real radar data that the proposed methods can achieve high-resolution and low complexity TFD of time-varying signal in time-sparse domain, and has the advantages of good time-frequency resolution, anti-clutter, and so on. It can be expected that the proposed methods can provide a novel solution for time-varying signal analysis and radar moving target detection.

Keywords: Sparse representation · Micro-Doppler signal
Sparse time-frequency distribution (STFD)
Short-time sparse fractional ambiguity function (ST-SFRAF)

1 Introduction

Doppler signature extraction and analysis of moving target are quite important for radar target detection and recognition [1]. The traditional Fourier spectrum cannot exhibit time-varying Doppler signature with low spectrum resolution. Recently, the micro-Doppler (m-D) theory has attracted extensive attention worldwide for accurate description of a target's motion [2]. The m-D features reflect the unique dynamic and structural characteristics, which are useful for target recognition and classification. The motion of a marine target is rather complex especially for marine target and maneuvering target [3, 4]. Therefore, how to effectively detect m-D signal is the key step for the following target detection and estimation.

This work was supported in part by the National Natural Science Foundation of China (61501487, 61401495, U1633122, 61471382, 61531020), National Defense Science and Technology Fund (2102014), Young Elite Scientist Sponsorship Program of CAST (YESS20160115) and Special Funds of Taishan Scholars of Shandong.

Time-frequency distributions (TFDs) provide an image of frequency contents as a function of time, which reveals how a signal changes over time. However, the classic TFDs, such as short-time Fourier transform (STFT) or Wigner-Ville distribution (WVD), suffer from the poor time-frequency resolution or cross-terms. Moreover, it is difficult to separate the complex background (clutter) from the weak m-D signal in time domain or frequency domain [5].

In the last decade, sparsity has been proved as a promising tool for a high-resolution solution. Sparse transform is proposed to increase resolution in different transform domains [6], such as the sparse FFT [7, 8] and sparse FRFT (SFRFT) [9], et al. M-D signal can be approximated as sum of frequency-modulated (FM) signals and it can be considered to be sparse in the TF plane [10]. In this paper, the merits of TFD and sparse representation are combined together and a novel method, i.e., short-time sparse fractional ambiguity function (ST-SFRAF) is proposed for high-resolution representation of time-varying m-D signal in the sparse time-frequency domain.

2 Radar M-D Signal Model

Suppose there is a target moving towards radar, and only radial velocity component is considered. Then, the radar line-of-sight (RLOS) distance $r_s(t_m)$ can be modeled as a polynomial function of slow time, i.e.,

$$r_s(t_m) = \sum_i a_i t_m^{i-1} = r_0 - v t_m - \frac{1}{2!} v' t_m^2 - \frac{1}{3!} v'' t_m^3 - \cdots, \quad t_m \in [-T_n/2, T_n/2] \quad (1)$$

where t_m is the slow-time, v is target's velocity and Tn is coherent integration time.

Suppose radar transmits linear frequency modulated (LFM) signal, and after demodulation and pulse compression, the radar returns of a target can be expressed as

$$s_{PC}(t_m) = A_r \text{sinc}\left[B\left(t - \frac{2r_s(t_m)}{c}\right)\right] \exp\left(-j\frac{4\pi r_s(t_m)}{\lambda}\right) \quad (2)$$

where A_r is amplitude, B is the bandwidth of transmitted signal, c represents speed of light, and λ is the wavelength.

Therefore, for the m-D signal, which mostly has the form of nonuniformly translational and rotational motions, can be expressed as a FM signal with fluctuated amplitudes, i.e.,

$$x(t_m) = \sum_{i=1}^{I} a_i(t_m) e^{j\varphi_i(t_m)} \quad (3)$$

where $\varphi(t_m) = 2\pi f_d(t_m) = \sum_k 2\pi a_k t_m^{k-1}$.

In real engineering applications, the m-D signal can be approximated as a LFM signal according to the observation time and integration time. The LFM signal can represents the moving parameters of a target, such as initial velocity and acceleration. For the m-D signal model of (3), its time-frequency distribution (TFD) has the following form.

$$\rho_x(t_m, f) = \sum_{i=1}^{I} a_i^2(t_m) \delta[f - \dot{\varphi}_i(t_m)/2\pi] \tag{4}$$

where $\dot{\varphi}_i(t_m)$ is the estimation of m-D frequency.

3 Principle of STFD and ST-SFRAF

From the above analysis, the m-D signal can be regarded as sum of multiple instantaneous frequency components. In the time-frequency domain, the m-D signal can exhibit an obvious peak at the location of $f = \dot{\varphi}_i(t)$ via sparse representation. And the time-frequency domain $\rho_x(t, f)$ is the sparse representation domain of m-D signal. For example, for an LFM signal, $a_1(t) = 1$, $\dot{\varphi}_1(t) = 2\pi(f_o + at)$.

Any signal can be represented in terms of basis or atoms g [10],

$$\mathbf{x} = \sum_m \alpha_m g_m \tag{5}$$

where m is the number of atoms, and the coefficient α_m denotes the similarity of the signal and the atoms.

It can be found by comparing (9) and (10) that the TFD is a special case of the sparse representation, i.e.,

$$\rho_{\mathbf{x}}(t, f) = \sum_m \alpha_m(t) h(t) g_m(t, f) \tag{6}$$

where $h(t)$ is a window function and $g_m(t, f)$ is the atoms combined with frequency modulated signal.

For the condition without noise, the sparse representation of (11) can be regarded as the optimization problem and solved by l_1-norm minimization,

$$\min \|\rho_x(t, f)\|_1, \text{ s.t. } o\{\rho_x(t, f)\} = b \tag{7}$$

where o is the sparse operator with $K \times N$ dimension. The above equation can be relaxed by the following constraint, i.e.,

$$\min \|\rho_x(t, f)\|_1, \text{ s.t. } \|o\{\rho_x(t, f)\} - b\|_2 \le \varepsilon. \tag{8}$$

When $\varepsilon = 0$, (12) and (13) have the same form. Then the framework of STFD can be defined by the calculation from (11) to (13).

When ρ_x is the Fourier transform (FT) and b is the signal component in the FT domain, the STFD is named as short-time sparse FT (ST-SFT), i.e.,

$$\min \|\mathcal{F}(t,f)\|_1, \text{ s.t. } \|o\{\mathcal{F}(t,f)\} - f\|_2 \le \varepsilon \tag{9}$$

When ρ_x is the fractional ambiguity function (FRAF) and b is the signal component in the FRAF domain, the STFD is named as short-time sparse FRAF (ST-SFRAF),

$$\min \|\mathcal{R}^\alpha(t,f)\|_1, \text{ s.t. } \|o\{\mathcal{R}^\alpha(t,f)\} - f(\alpha, u)\|_2 \le \varepsilon. \tag{10}$$

where $\mathcal{R}^\alpha( )$ is the FRAF operator, $\alpha \in (0, \pi]$ denotes transform angle, $K_\alpha(t, u)$ is the transform kernel.

$$\mathcal{R}^\alpha(\tau, u) = \int_{-\infty}^{\infty} R_x(t, \tau) K_\alpha(t, u) \mathrm{d}t \tag{11}$$

$$K_\alpha(t, u) = \begin{cases} A_\alpha \exp\{j[\frac{1}{2}t^2 \cot \alpha - ut \csc \alpha + \frac{1}{2}u^2 \cot \alpha]\}, & \alpha \ne n\pi \\ \delta[u - (-1)^n t], & \alpha = n\pi \end{cases} \tag{12}$$

where τ is the time delay, $A_\alpha = \sqrt{(1 - j\cot \alpha)/2\pi}$, $R_x(t, \tau)$ is the instantaneous auto-correlation function of $x(t)$,

$$R_x(t, \tau) = x(t + \tau/2)x^*(t - \tau/2) \tag{13}$$

Suppose there is a m-D signal modeled as a QFM signal, i.e.,

$$\begin{aligned} x(t) &= \sigma_0 \exp\left[j4\pi \frac{r_s(t)}{\lambda}\right] = \sigma_0 \exp\left(\sum_{i=0}^{3} j2\pi a_i t^i\right) \\ &= \sigma_0 \exp\left[j2\pi(a_0 + a_1 t + a_2 t^2 + a_3 t^3)\right] \end{aligned} \tag{14}$$

where a_i ($i = 1,2,3$) represents the coefficient of the polynomial of QFM signal.

If the time delay τ is fixed, the relation between $\mathcal{R}^\alpha(\tau, u)$ and $\mathcal{R}^\alpha(t,f)$ is derived as follows,

$$\begin{cases} a_2 = \frac{u}{4\pi\tau} \csc \alpha \\ a_3 = -\frac{1}{12\pi\tau} \cot \alpha \end{cases} \tag{15}$$

And $f(t) = 2\pi(a_1 + 2a_2 t + 3a_3 t^2) = 2\pi(v_0 + \mu t + \frac{1}{2}g t^2)$, where v_0 is the initial velocity, μ is the chirp rate, and g denotes the jerk motion.

Therefore, the proposed STFD and ST-SFRAF are the generalized forms of the classical TFD and FRAF, which indicates promising applications.

4   Sparse Representation of Radar M-D Signal via ST-SFRAF

Flowchart of the ST-SFRAF-based m-D signal extraction method is shown in Fig. 1, which mainly consists of four steps, i.e.,

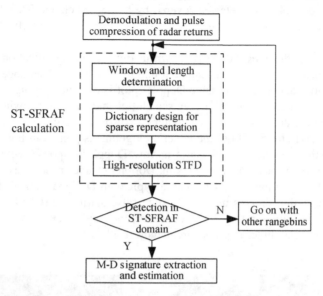

Fig. 1. Observation model of radar and typical micromotion target.

- Perform demodulation and pulse compression of radar returns, which achieves high-resolution in range direction;
- ST-SFRAF, which is the most important procedure, consists of three parts, i.e., window and length determination, dictionary design for sparse representation, and high-resolution STFD;
- Signal detection in ST-SFRAF domain by comparing an adaptive detection threshold;
- M-D signature extraction and estimation.

It should be noted that the choice of dictionary can be determined according to the prior information of target to satisfy the sparsity condition, such as the types of observed target and different sea states. For the micromotion target whose main motion components are the rotation or high mobility, its m-D signal exhibits periodical frequency modulated property. Also, we can use the QFM signal or periodical frequency modulated function as its dictionary.

5 Simulation and Results Analysis

The micromotion of a marine target includes the non-uniform translated motion and three dimension motion, i.e., yaw, pitch, and roll motions. Due to the complex fluctuation of sea surface and motion of target, the m-D signal of a marine target is rather complex and too weak to be detected covered by heavy sea clutter. Therefore, we will employ S-band radar (SSR) dataset with a WaveRider RIB to verify the proposed method.

Descriptions of the SSR dataset is shown in Fig. 2. The specifications of radar as well as the environment parameters can be found in [11]. The dataset under sea state of 4 was chosen for validation. The range-Doppler plot is presented in Fig. 2(b) covering nearly 5 nautical miles. Due to the heavy sea clutter fluctuating downwind, it is rather difficult to separate the target from sea clutter background. Furthermore, high Doppler resolution spectrogram (STFT) of the target's rangebins is plotted in Fig. 3(a1). It can be found that the WaveRider RIB had a narrow Doppler response, with a local disturbance of the sea surface. The time-varying Doppler character indicates a nonuniform motion and Doppler migration, which is a typical m-D signal modeled as a QFM signal. After detection process using a constant false alarm rate (CFAR) detector, the detection result is shown in Fig. 3(a2). However, the true target cannot be figured out due to the heavy sea clutter and poor frequency resolution.

   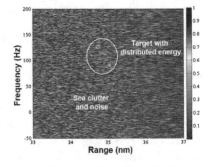

(a) Plan overview of radar deployment site   (b) Range-Doppler analysis

Fig. 2. Description of the S-band radar dataset.

Then, we carry out the ST-SFRAF and compare the detection results with STFT (Fig. 3(b1) and (b2)). The proposed STFD-based method matches up with the micro-motion model better, are more preferable in comparison. In addition, the proposed method has the ability of sea clutter suppression and can accumulate the energy of m-D signal as an obvious peak, which is shown in Fig. 3(b2). Moreover, with the local window, the changes of m-D can be described well. Therefore, the proposed ST-SFRAF method is a good choice for high resolution representation and detection of m-D signal with high-order motion.

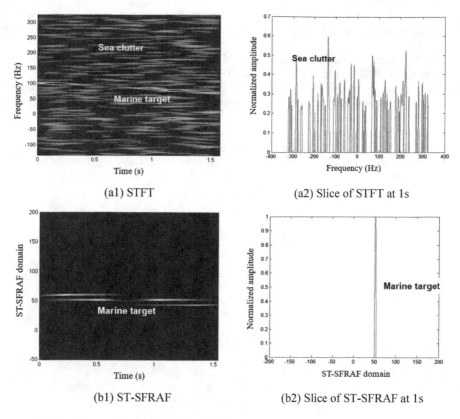

(a1) STFT

(a2) Slice of STFT at 1s

(b1) ST-SFRAF

(b2) Slice of ST-SFRAF at 1s

Fig. 3. Comparisons of STFT and ST-SFRAF based m-D extraction methods.

References

1. Simon, W., Luke, R., Stepjen, B., et al.: Doppler spectra of medium grazing angle sea clutter; part 1: characterisation. IET Radar Sonar Navig. **10**, 24–31 (2016)
2. Chen, V.C., Li, F., Shen-Shyang, H.O., et al.: Micro-Doppler effect in radar: phenomenon, model, and simulation study. IEEE Trans. Aerospace Electron. Syst. **42**, 2–21 (2006)
3. Chen, X., Guan, J., Bao, Z., et al.: Detection and extraction of target with micro-motion in spiky sea clutter via short-time fractional Fourier transform. IEEE Trans. Geosci. Remote Sens. **52**, 1002–1018 (2014)
4. Chen, X., Guan, J., Li, X., et al.: Effective coherent integration method for marine target with micromotion via phase differentiation and Radon-Lv's distribution. IET Radar Sonar Navig. (Special Issue: Micro-Doppler) **9**, 1284–1295 (2015)
5. Guan, J., Chen, X., Huang, Y., et al.: Adaptive fractional Fourier transform-based detection algorithm for moving target in heavy sea clutter. IET Radar Sonar Navig. **6**, 389–401 (2012)
6. Flandrin, P., Borgnat, P.: Time-frequency energy distributions meet compressed sensing. IEEE Trans. Sig. Process. **58**, 2974–2982 (2010)
7. Gholami, A.: Sparse time–frequency decomposition and some applications. IEEE Trans. Geosci. Remote Sens. **51**, 3598–3604 (2013)

8. Gilbert, A.C., Indyk, P., Iwen, M., et al.: Recent developments in the sparse Fourier transform: a compressed Fourier transform for big data. IEEE Sig. Process. Mag. **31**, 91–100 (2014)
9. Liu, S., Shan, T., Tao, R., et al.: Sparse discrete fractional Fourier transform and its applications. IEEE Trans. Sig. Process. **62**, 6582–6595 (2014)
10. Chen, X., Dong, Y., Huang, Y., et al.: Detection of marine target with quadratic modulated frequency micromotion signature via morphological component analysis. In: 2015 3rd International Workshop on Compressed Sensing Theory and Its Applications to Radar, Sonar and Remote Sensing (CoSeRa), Pisa, Italy, pp. 209–213 (2015)
11. Chen, X., Guan, J., Liu, N., He, Y.: Maneuvering target detection via radon-fractional Fourier transform-based long-time coherent integration. IEEE Trans. Sig. Process. **62**, 939–953 (2014)

Estimating of RCS of Ionosphere for High Frequency Surface Wave Radar

Yang Xuguang[1,2], Yu Changjun[3(✉)], Liu Aijun[3], and Wang Linwei[3]

[1] Department of Electronic and Information Engineering,
Harbin Institute of Technology, Harbin 150001, China
[2] Department of Science, Harbin Engineering University, Harbin 150001, China
[3] Department of Information and Electrical Engineering,
Harbin Institute of Technology, Weihai 264209, China
Yuchangjun@hit.edu.cn

Abstract. High Frequency Surface Wave Radar (HFSWR) has been shown to provide enhanced performance in over the horizon detection of targets and sea states remote sensing by the returns of targets and ocean surface. Meanwhile, HFSWR can also receive ionospheric echoes reflected by the ionosphere, which severely affect the radar detection performance. In this paper, the radar cross section (RCS) of ionosphere for HFSWR is estimated, which would help quantify the impact of the ionosphere to radar system and the performance of clutter mitigation techniques. Simulations are provided to illustrate the effect of parameters including radar operating frequency, scale size of irregularities, aspect angle and detection range on the RCS of ionosphere.

Keywords: High Frequency Surface Wave Radar · Ionosphere · RCS

1 Introduction

High Frequency Surface Wave Radar (HFSWR) uses the sea-surface diffraction character of vertically polarized wave which can achieve long ranges detection due to low attenuation over the highly conductive sea surface. Ideally, a perfect conductive plane consisting of sea surface is infinite in coverage area, thus making transmitted wave entirely travel along the sea. However, considering the actual antenna pattern characteristics, poor ground and array error, partial energy is radiated into sky and reflected by ionosphere. Finally the echoes arrived at radar receiver in various paths, interfering target detection severely as ionospheric clutter [1, 2]. The ionospheric clutter primarily restricted the detection performance of HFSWR. Therefore, in order to analyze and simulate the effect of ionosphere on radar system, it is necessary to establish the estimation of radar cross section (RCS) of ionosphere for HFSWR.

It is convinced that the ionospheric clutter of HFSWR mainly occur from coherent scattering between electromagnetic wave and irregularities caused by plasma instabilities. The theory of ionospheric coherent scattering was initially proposed by Booker [3], which demonstrates that the major contribution to the scattered field is given by a spatial spectrum component of electron density fluctuations whose period along the propagation direction, scale size satisfies the Bragg scatter conditions producing

© ICST Institute for Computer Sciences, Social Informatics and Telecommunications Engineering 2018
X. Gu et al. (Eds.): MLICOM 2017, Part II, LNICST 227, pp. 233–239, 2018.
https://doi.org/10.1007/978-3-319-73447-7_27

constructive interference at the refraction point. According to collective scatter theory [4], the backscattered ionospheric echoes come from a large number of ionosphere irregularities inside the Effective Scatter Volume (ESV), which is formed by the intersection of the antenna beam with the ionosphere. The coherent scattering theory has been used in HFSWR to obtained several ionosphere parameters [5]. In this study, we develop the RCS of ionosphere in detail and intensively analyze the effect of each variable on RCS for HFSWR, which would help quantify the impact of the ionosphere to radar system and the performance of clutter mitigation techniques.

In this paper, firstly the generalized radar range equation for distributed target as ionosphere is established. Then the RCS of ionosphere is obtained by coherent scattering theory. Simulations illustrate the effect of each parameter on RCS of ionosphere and indicate the key contributions to the RCS of ionosphere.

2   Modeling RCS of Ionosphere for HFSWR

The classical radar equation for a monostatic HFSWR is defined as

$$P_r = \frac{P_t G_t G_r \lambda^2}{(4\pi)^3 R^4 L_s} \sigma \tag{1}$$

where P_r is the received power; P_t is the transmitted power; G_t is the transmitter antenna gain; G_r is the receiver antenna gain; σ is RCS; λ is the radar wavelength; R is the target range; L_s is the system loss.

2.1   Range Equation for Ionosphere

The ionospheric scatters should be modeled as distributed scattering from a three-dimensional volume rather than a single point scatter. Because of the distributed characteristics and the gain of the antenna varies with (θ, φ), G_t and G_r should be replaced by $G_t(\theta, \varphi)$ and $G_r(\theta, \varphi)$, respectively, that accounts for the effect of antenna power pattern on the power density radiated in a particular direction (θ, φ).

Considering the scattering from an incremental volume dV located at range and angle coordinates (R, θ, φ) (the incremental RCS of volume element is $d\sigma$ square meters), the incremental backscattered power from dV can be expressed as

$$dP_r = \frac{P_t G_t(\theta, \phi) G_r(\theta, \phi) \lambda^2}{(4\pi)^3 R^4 L_s} d\sigma(R, \theta, \phi) \tag{2}$$

Then the total received power is obtained by integrating over all space

$$P_r = \frac{P_t \lambda^2}{(4\pi)^3 L_s} \int_V \frac{G_t(\theta, \phi) G_r(\theta, \phi)}{R^4} d\sigma(R, \theta, \phi) \tag{3}$$

In Eq. (3), the volume of integration V is all of three-dimensional space. However, only scatters within a single resolution cell volume dV contribute significantly to the radar. Therefore, a more appropriate form of the generalized radar range equation can be given by

$$P_r = \frac{P_t \lambda^2}{(4\pi)^3 L_s} \int_{\Delta V(R,\theta,\phi)} \frac{G_t(\theta, \phi) G_r(\theta, \phi)}{R^4} d\sigma(R, \theta, \phi) \qquad (4)$$

where $\Delta V(R, \theta, \phi)$ is the volume of the resolution cell at coordinates (R, θ, ϕ). Suppose the distribution of ionospheric irregularities evenly distributed throughout the volume. We defined η as RCS per cubic meter, or volume reflectivity, then

$$d\sigma = \eta dV \qquad (5)$$

Here η is also the reflectivity of effective scatter volume (ESV) which is formed by the intersection of radar beam with ionosphere. For the antenna having an elliptical beam with azimuth and elevation beam widths θ_3, ϕ_3, the resolution cell volume $\Delta V(R, \theta, \phi)$ can be approximately expressed as

$$\Delta V(R, \theta, \phi) = \frac{\pi}{4} R^2 \Delta R \theta_3 \phi_3 \approx R^2 \Delta R \theta_3 \phi_3 \qquad (6)$$

where ΔR is the range resolution, θ_3, ϕ_3 are the 3 dB beam widths in azimuth and elevation. Thus, the RCS of volume can be obtained:

$$\sigma = R^2 \Delta R \theta_3 \phi_3 \eta \qquad (7)$$

Considering the attenuation of electromagnetic wave propagation in ionosphere and using approximation [6], we can reduce Eq. (3) to the range equation for ionosphere scatters:

$$P_r = \frac{P_t \lambda^2 G_t G_r \Delta R \theta_3 \phi_3 \eta}{(4\pi)^3 R^2 L_s L_p} \qquad (8)$$

2.2   ESV Reflectivity

According the Bragg scatter conditions for monostatic backscatter:

$$\lambda_{irr} = \frac{\lambda_{radar}}{2} \qquad (9)$$

where λ_{irr} is the scale size of ionosphere irregularities, which means the scale size of irregularities between 5–50 m can be observed by HFSWR. For the magnetic plasma in the ionosphere region, irregularities at these scale sizes are highly anisotropic and aligned with the geomagnetic field $\vec{B}$. The reflectivity of ESV depends on the direction, electron density and scale size of the irregularities, etc. which can be expressed as [7]:

$$\eta = f(k, v_d, \phi, \alpha, l, f_{e,i}, \overline{\Delta N_e}, N_e) \tag{10}$$

where k is the radar wave-vector in the medium, v_d is the drift velocity of irregularities, ϕ is the flow angle, i.e. the angle between radar wave-vector and drift velocity, α is the aspect angle i.e. the complement of the angle between $\vec{k}$ and $\vec{B}$, l is the scale length of irregularities, $f_{e,i}$ is the electron and neutral collision frequency, $\overline{\Delta N_e}$ is the average level of the electron density fluctuations, N_e is the electron density of irregularities. Assuming that the magnitude of electron density fluctuations has linearly relationship with the electron density, which also consistent with experimental results [8]. For convenience of discuss, Eq. (10) can be reduced to [9, 10]

$$\eta \propto N_e^2 \exp\{-2k^2(l_\parallel^2 \alpha^2 + l_\perp^2)\} \tag{11}$$

where $l_{\parallel,\perp}$ is the scale size of irregularities along and across the external magnetic field $\vec{B}$, respectively. Equation (10) is based on the assumption that $l_\parallel \gg l_\perp$ and $kl_\parallel \gg 1$ so that η appears peak when $\alpha = 0°$, namely $\vec{k} \perp \vec{B}$ which means the major contribution to the backscattered field is only a small region of ESV.

In summary, our analysis reveals that the backscatter ionospheric clutter of HFSWR should be dominated by the specific ionospheric region in which the wave vector is near perpendicular to the electromagnetic field in simplified situation.

3   Simulations and Analysis

This section presents the results of simulations testing the theory developed in the previous sections. Figure 1 shows the effect of each variable in Eq. (11) on ESV reflectivity. In Fig. 1(a), we choose parameter $l_\parallel = 1000$ m to simulate the ESV reflectivity vary with different frequencies limited to the radar resolution. Figure 1(b) shows the ESV reflectivity vary with different scale size of irregularities. Figure 2 shows ESV reflectivity in three-dimensional with four specific frequencies.

We can see that the ESV reflectivity appears a very strong peak near $\alpha = 0°$ and rapid declines in other incident angles. The higher the frequency is, the more obvious this phenomenon is. Based on the above observation, we can draw a conclusion that the major contribution to the backscattered field is only the region of ionosphere where wave vector is perpendicular to the major axis of field-aligned, regardless of frequency and scale size of irregularities.

We choose different radar operating frequencies to simulate RCS of ionosphere, but they are almost the same. In Fig. 3, the radar frequency is 3 MHz. It is obvious that the RCS of ionosphere do not change with the detection range, only depended on aspect angle. Therefore, the RCS of ionosphere for HFSWR should be dominated by the specific ionospheric region in which the direction of wave vector approaches the normal to the external magnetic field.

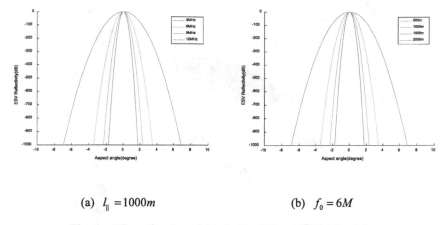

(a) $l_{\parallel} = 1000m$ (b) $f_0 = 6M$

Fig. 1. Effect of each variable in Eq. (11) on ESV reflectivity.

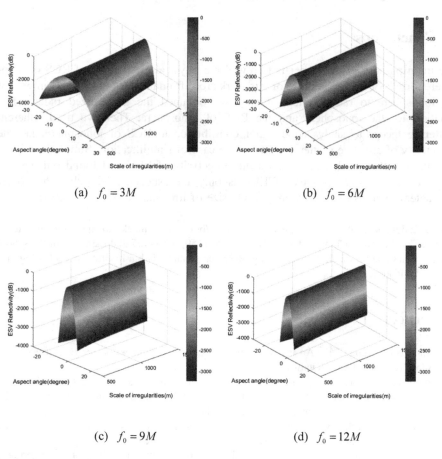

(a) $f_0 = 3M$ (b) $f_0 = 6M$

(c) $f_0 = 9M$ (d) $f_0 = 12M$

Fig. 2. 3D ESV reflectivity varies with different radar operating frequencies, aspect angle and scale size of irregularities along the external magnetic field.

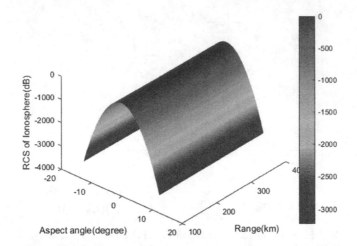

Fig. 3. RCS of ionosphere varies with radar range and aspect angle.

4 Conclusions

The main purpose of this paper is to reveal the physical mechanism of RCS of iono-sphere for HFSWR. The purpose of this work arose from the need of quantify impact of the ionosphere to radar system. Firstly we obtained the generalized radar range equation for the ionosphere and the RCS of ionosphere. Then we used coherent scattering theory to analysis the major contribution to RCS of ionosphere, i.e. the reflectivity of effective scatter volume in the case of simplification. Simulations illus-trate the effect of each parameter on the reflectivity of ESV and found out the key contribution to the reflectivity of ESV is only the aspect angle, rather than other parameters, such as radar frequency, scale size of irregularities or detection range.

Acknowledgments. We would like to express his/her sincere thanks to the National Natural Science Foundation of China under Grant No. 61571159, 61571157 and members of the school of Electronics and Information Engineering, Research Center, Harbin Institute of Technology for technical support.

References

1. Chan, H.C., Hung, E.K.: An investigation in interference suppression for HF surface wave radar. Technical report, Ottawa (1999)
2. Sevgi, L., Ponsford, A., Chan, H.C.: An integrated maritime surveillance system based on high-frequency surface-wave radar, part I: theoretical background and numerical simula-tions. J. IEEE. Antenn. Propag. Mag. **43**(4), 28–43 (2001)
3. Booker, H.G.: A theory of scattering by nonisotropic irregularities with application for radar reflections from aurora. J. Atmos. Terr. Phys. **8**, 2004–2221 (1956)
4. Rytov, S.M., Kravtsov, Y.A., Tatarskii, V.I.: Principles of Statistical Radiophysics. Springer, New York (1988)

5. Xuguang, Y., Changjun, Y., et al.: The vertical ionosphere parameters inversion for high frequency surface wave radar. J. Int. J. Antenn. Propag. **3**, 1–8 (2016)
6. Mark, A.R.: Fundamentals of Radar Signal Processing. New York (2005)
7. Schlegel, K.: Coherent backscatter from ionospheric E-region plasma irregularities. J. Atmos. Solar-Terr. Phys. **58**, 933–941 (1996)
8. Haldoupis, C., Nielsen, E., Schlegel, K.: Dependence of radar auroral scattering cross section on the ambient electron density and the destabilizing electric field. Ann. Geophys. **8**(3), 195–211 (1990)
9. Walker, A.D.M., Greenwald, R.A., Baker, K.B.: Determination of the fluctuation level of ionospheric irregularities from radar backscatter measurements. Radio Sci. **22**, 689–705 (1987)
10. Ponomarenko, P.V., Stmauirice, J.P., et al.: Refractive index effects on the scatter volume location and Doppler velocity estimates of ionospheric HF backscatter echoes. Ann. Geophys. **27**(11), 4207–4219 (2009)

Intelligent Cooperative Communications and Networking

Joint Mode Selection and Beamformer Optimization for Full-Duplex Cellular Systems

Fangni Chen[1,2(✉)], Jingyu Hua[2], Weidang Lu[2],
and Zhongpeng Wang[1]

[1] School of Information and Electronic Engineering,
Zhejiang University of Science and Technology, Hangzhou, China
cfnini@163.com, zhongpengwang@sohu.com
[2] College of Information Engineering, Zhejiang University of Technology,
Hangzhou, China
{eehjy,luweid}@zjut.edu.cn

Abstract. We investigate a novel mode selection scheme for full-duplex (FD) cellular system where the base station (BS) and the user equipments (UEs) are equipped with multiple-input multiple-output (MIMO) antennas. We consider that FD is utilized at the BS, i.e. it enables simultaneous transmission and reception at the same frequency band, while UEs work in the conventional half-duplex (HD) way. Since FD system can not always outperform HD system due to residual self interference (RSI) at the base station, the mode selection is mainly determined by system performance. To address this issue, a joint mode selection and beamformer optimization problem with power constraints is formulated to achieve the maximal weighted sum rate (WSR). On account of the non-convex of original problem, a heuristic algorithm based on decoupling is proposed, which decomposes the original problem into two sub-problems. One is mode selection sub-problem and the other one is mean square error (MSE) minimization sub-problem. By means of simulation, the proposed algorithm shows the ability to choose the mode with greater performance in achievable rate.

Keywords: Full-duplex · Cellular system · Self-interference
Mode selection · WSR

1 Introduction

System rate improvement has become one of the most significant characteristics in 5G cellular communication systems since the great demand for data transmission. Most modern communication systems apply bi-directional communication, which in traditional way needs two different channels for inverse directions, typically using time division duplex (TDD) or frequency division duplex (FDD) technique, to provide isolation between transmission and reception. As we all known, these communication systems utilize half-duplex (HD) technology. Full-duplex (FD) technology can inconceivably increase system throughput and spectral efficiency by enabling fully

© ICST Institute for Computer Sciences, Social Informatics and Telecommunications Engineering 2018
X. Gu et al. (Eds.): MLICOM 2017, Part II, LNICST 227, pp. 243–253, 2018.
https://doi.org/10.1007/978-3-319-73447-7_28

utilizing of both time and frequency resource, which has attracted considerable interest both in industry and academia.

The major obstruction of applying full-duplex technology in real communications is the self-interference (SI) which is generated by simultaneous transmission and reception on the same end. A large amount of research has considered the problem of SI in FD communications by studying various system architectures and self-interference cancellation (SIC) techniques to mitigate SI signal. Generally, SIC techniques can be divided into three types: antenna, analog and digital cancellation. Analog cancellation tries to remove SI before the deteriorated signals are digitized, whereas digital cancellation eliminates the SI after the signals are digitized. Generally one approach alone usually still leaves a majority amount of SI. Recent researches in SIC have made a great progress in reducing SI into a low level. New antenna designs, together with analog and digital cancellation, are applied to eliminate most SI. Digital cancellation in transceiver design was considered in [1] along with taking actual implementation facts of FD systems into account. Moreover, certain experimental results were displayed in [2–4] which can reach 50–80 dB of SI cancellation. A combination of analog and digital cancellation method was proposed in [5], which showed 85 dB cancellation effect over a 20 MHz WLAN channel. Besides the hardware based research, most theoretical works were stemming from array processing technique, that is known as beamforming [6, 7].

However, due to channel estimation errors, the SI cannot be eliminated fully. Hence, the residual self-interference (RSI) remains at a high level, which needs to be cancelled via signal processing at baseband [8]. In other words, RSI cancellation results will dominate that whether the FD system outperforms HD system or not. Therefore, in ideal FD systems, a mode selection method is needed to between FD mode and traditional HD mode. To address this issue, a joint mode selection and beamformer optimization problem is formulated. To find the maximal objective which is the weighted sum data rate, a heuristic algorithm based on decoupling is proposed, which decomposes the original problem into two sub-problems. One is mode selection sub-problem and the other one is weighted mean square error (WMSE) minimization sub-problem.

The remainder of the paper is organized as follows: a multiuser FD MIMO system model and the joint optimization problem are presented in Sect. 2. The specific analysis of the proposed heuristic algorithm is illustrated in Sect. 3. Section 4 provides numerical simulations of overall system performance. Section 5 concludes our work.

2 System Model and Problem Formulation

Consider a multiuser FD MIMO system as depicted in Fig. 1, in which the base station (BS) communicates with K uplink (UL) users and J downlink (DL) users simultaneously. Both the BS and users are equipped with multiple antennas. For simplicity, we assume the same antennas at transmit and receive ends. $\mathbf{H}_k^{UL}$ represents channel from the k-th UL user to BS and $\mathbf{H}_j^{DL}$ represents the channel from BS to the j-th DL user. We assume FD only applied at BS, users work at HD mode because of the hardware

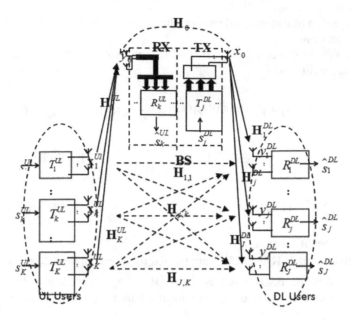

Fig. 1. FD cellular system model

complexity. Thus SI exists only at BS, and SI channel is denoted as $\mathbf{H}_0$. $\mathbf{H}_{j,k}$ denotes the interference channel between UL and DL users.

The signal transmitted by the k-th UL user and the j-th DL user are denoted as $\mathbf{s}_k^{UL}$ and $\mathbf{s}_j^{DL}$, respectively, which are assumed with independent identical distribution and unit power. Denoting the transmit filters for transmit signals as $\mathbf{T}$ and the receive filters for the received data as $\mathbf{R}$. The signal received by the BS and the j-th DL user are denoted as

$$
\begin{aligned}
\mathbf{y}_0 = {}& m[\sum\nolimits_{k=1}^{K} \mathbf{H}_k^{UL}\mathbf{T}_k^{UL}\mathbf{s}_k^{UL} + \sqrt{\eta}\mathbf{H}_0 \sum\nolimits_{j=1}^{J} \mathbf{T}_j^{DL}\mathbf{s}_j^{DL} + \mathbf{n}_0] \\
& + (1-m)[\sum\nolimits_{k=1}^{K} \mathbf{H}_k^{UL}\mathbf{T}_k^{UL}\mathbf{s}_k^{UL} + \mathbf{n}_0]
\end{aligned}
\tag{1}
$$

$$
\mathbf{y}_j^{DL} = \mathbf{H}_j^{DL} \sum\nolimits_{j=1}^{J} \mathbf{T}_j^{DL}\mathbf{s}_j^{DL} + \sum\nolimits_{k=1}^{K} \mathbf{H}_{j,k}\mathbf{T}_k^{UL}\mathbf{s}_k^{UL} + \mathbf{n}_j^{DL}
\tag{2}
$$

where $m \in \{0, 1\}$ is the mode selection parameter. When $m = 1$, FD mode is selected, otherwise HD mode is selected. η is the RSI factor. Meanwhile, $\mathbf{n}_0$ and $\mathbf{n}_j^{DL}$ are additive white Gaussian noise at receivers.

As is shown in (1), the first term contains the inter-user interference; the second term is SI. The second term in (2) is the inter-channel interference. Since FD mode cannot keep outperforming HD mode since RSI exists at the BS, the mode selection parameter m is obviously determined by the performance of the system. Thus, in order to achieve the great performance of this FD MIMO cellular system, we should propose an optimized design of transmit and receive filters to deal with those interference and to maximize system rate.

Since the value of m could only be 0 or 1, the covariance matrices of noise plus interference are written as

$$
\mathbf{C}_k^{UL} = m[\sum_{i=1,k\neq i}^{K} \mathbf{H}_i^{UL}\mathbf{T}_i^{UL}(\mathbf{T}_i^{UL})^H(\mathbf{H}_i^{UL})^H + \sum_{j=1}^{J} \eta \mathbf{H}_0 \mathbf{T}_j^{DL}\mathbf{T}_j^{DL}\mathbf{H}_0^H + \mathbf{I}]
$$
$$
+ (1-m)[\sum_{i=1,k\neq i}^{K} \mathbf{H}_i^{UL}\mathbf{T}_i^{UL}(\mathbf{T}_i^{UL})^H(\mathbf{H}_i^{UL})^H + \mathbf{I}]
$$
(3)

$$
\mathbf{C}_j^{DL} = \sum_{k=1}^{K} \mathbf{H}_{j,k}\mathbf{T}_k^{UL}(\mathbf{T}_k^{UL})^H(\mathbf{H}_{j,k})^H + \sum_{i=1,i\neq j}^{J} \mathbf{H}_i^{DL}\mathbf{T}_i^{DL}\mathbf{T}_i^{DL}\mathbf{H}_i^{DL} + \mathbf{I} \quad (4)
$$

where $\mathbf{I}$ is the identity matrix.

The received signals $\mathbf{R}_k^{UL}$ and $\mathbf{R}_j^{DL}$ are filtered by receiving beamformers. Thus, the estimated signal at the BS is given as $\hat{\mathbf{s}}_k^{UL} = (\mathbf{R}_k^{UL})^H\mathbf{y}_0$. According to [9], the lower bound of the achievable rate of uplink and downlink users under Gaussian signaling are expressed as

$$
I_k^{UL} = \log_2 |\mathbf{I} + \mathbf{H}_k \mathbf{T}_k^{UL}(\mathbf{T}_k^{UL})^H(\mathbf{H}_k^{UL})^H(\mathbf{C}_k^{UL})^{-1}| \tag{5}
$$

$$
I_j^{DL} = \log_2 |\mathbf{I} + \mathbf{H}_j^{DL}\mathbf{T}_j^{DL}(\mathbf{T}_j^{DL})^H(\mathbf{H}_j^{DL})^H(\mathbf{C}_j^{DL})^{-1}| \tag{6}
$$

We try to maximize weighted system sum rate. In general, the rate of uplink and downlink can not be simply added together because they are of different importance. Hence, two weight factors μ_k^{UL} and μ_j^{DL} are introduced here to get system sum rate given by

$$
I = \sum_{k=1}^{K} \mu_k^{UL} I_k^{UL} + \sum_{j=1}^{J} \mu_j^{DL} I_j^{DL} \tag{7}
$$

Therefore, the joint problem with mode selection and beamformer optimization can be formulated as

$$
\max_{m,\mathbf{T},\mathbf{R}} \quad \sum_{k=1}^{K} \mu_k^{UL} I_k^{UL} + \sum_{j=1}^{J} \mu_j^{DL} I_j^{DL}
$$
$$
s.t. \quad tr\{\mathbf{T}_k^{UL}(\mathbf{T}_k^{UL})^H\} \leq P_k
$$
$$
\sum_j tr\{\mathbf{T}_j(\mathbf{T}_j^{DL})^H\} \leq P_T
$$
(8)

where P_k is power constraint for UL user, and P_T denotes the power constraint for BS.

3 Algorithm of Optimization

According to [9], based on the relationship between weighted sum rate (WSR) and weighted minimum mean squared error (WMMSE) problems for FD cellular system, the MMSE receive beamformer applied at BS is expressed as

$$\mathbf{R}_k^{UL} = (\mathbf{T}_k^{UL})^H (\mathbf{H}_k^{UL})^H [\mathbf{H}_k^{UL} \mathbf{T}_k^{UL} (\mathbf{T}_k^{UL})^H (\mathbf{H}_k^{UL})^H + \mathbf{C}_k^{UL}]^{-1} \tag{9}$$

Substitute (9) into $\hat{\mathbf{s}}_k^{UL} = (\mathbf{R}_k^{UL})^H \mathbf{y}_0$ and $\mathbf{E}_k^{UL} = E[(\hat{\mathbf{s}}_k - \mathbf{s}_k)(\hat{\mathbf{s}}_k - \mathbf{s}_k)^H]$, the MSE matrix is written as

$$\mathbf{E}_k^{UL} = [\mathbf{I} - (\mathbf{T}_k^{UL})^H (\mathbf{H}_k^{UL})^H (\mathbf{C}_k^{UL})^{-1} \mathbf{H}_k^{UL} \mathbf{T}_k^{UL}]^{-1} \tag{10}$$

It is obviously that the relationship between achievable rate and MMSE can be denoted as

$$I_k^{UL} = \log_2 |(\mathbf{E}_k^{UL})^{-1}| \tag{11}$$

Similarly, the MMSE bemformer, the MSE matrix and the achievable rate of j-th DL user are as follows,

$$\mathbf{R}_j^{DL} = (\mathbf{T}_j^{DL})^H (\mathbf{H}_j^{DL})^H [\mathbf{H}_j^{DL} \mathbf{T}_j^{DL} (\mathbf{T}_j^{DL})^H (\mathbf{H}_j^{DL})^H + \mathbf{C}_j^{DL}]^{-1} \tag{12}$$

$$\mathbf{E}_j^{DL} = [\mathbf{I} - (\mathbf{T}_j^{DL})^H (\mathbf{H}_j^{DL})^H (\mathbf{C}_j^{DL})^{-1} \mathbf{H}_j^{DL} \mathbf{T}_j^{DL}]^{-1} \tag{13}$$

$$I_j^{DL} = \log_2 |(\mathbf{E}_j^{DL})^{-1}| \tag{14}$$

Now we can formulate the WMMSE problem as

$$\min_{m,\mathbf{T},\mathbf{R}} \quad \sum_{k=1}^{K} tr\{\mathbf{W}_k^{UL} \mathbf{E}_k^{UL}\} + \sum_{j=1}^{J} tr\{\mathbf{W}_j^{DL} \mathbf{E}_j^{DL}\}$$

$$s.t. \quad tr\{\mathbf{T}_k^{UL}(\mathbf{T}_k^{UL})^H\} \le P_k \tag{15}$$

$$\sum_j tr\{\mathbf{T}_j(\mathbf{T}_j^{DL})^H\} \le P_T$$

where $\mathbf{W}_k^{UL}$ and $\mathbf{W}_j^{DL}$ are weight matrix. The WSR and WMMSE problems are equivalent as long as carefully choose weights, which are denoted as

$$\mathbf{W}_k^{UL} = \mu_k^{UL} (\mathbf{E}_k^{UL})^{-1} \Big/ \ln 2 \tag{16}$$

$$\mathbf{W}_j^{DL} = \mu_j^{DL} (\mathbf{E}_j^{DL})^{-1} \Big/ \ln 2 \tag{17}$$

After elaborately choose MSE weights as listed in (16) and (17), the KKT conditions of the WSR and WMMSE problems can be satisfied simultaneously. Therefore the original problem (8) can be settled by solving WMMSE problem (15). Here, we propose a heuristic algorithm by decoupling problem (15) into two sub-problems: beamformer optimization and mode selection.

3.1   Beamformer Optimization

The optimal transmit beamformer $\mathbf{T}_k^{UL}$ of each UL user can be calculated by utilizing the Lagrange method. Then the optimal $\mathbf{T}_k^{UL}$ is expressed as

$$\mathbf{T}_k^{UL} = (\mathbf{X}_k^{UL} + \lambda_k \mathbf{I})^{-1}(\mathbf{H}_k^{UL})^H(\mathbf{R}_k^{UL})^H \mathbf{W}_k^{UL} \tag{18}$$

where $\mathbf{X}_k^{UL} = (\mathbf{H}_k^{UL})^H(\mathbf{R}_k^{UL})^H \mathbf{W}_k \mathbf{R}_k^{UL} \mathbf{H}_k^{UL}$ and λ_k is the Lagrange multiplier, which can be obtained by taking the singular value decomposition of $\mathbf{X}_k = \mathbf{U}_k \mathbf{\Lambda}_k (\mathbf{U}_k)^H$.

Rewrite the power constraint in problem (15) as

$$tr\{\mathbf{T}_k^{UL}(\mathbf{T}_k^{UL})^H\} = \sum_{k=1}^{K} \frac{g_{ki}}{(\lambda_k + \Delta_{ki})^2}$$
$$= P_k \tag{19}$$

where g_{ki} is the i-th diagonal element of $(\mathbf{U}_k)^H(\mathbf{H}_k^{UL})^H(\mathbf{R}_k^{UL})^H \mathbf{W}_k(\mathbf{W}_k)^H \mathbf{R}_k^{UL} \mathbf{H}_k^{UL} \mathbf{U}_k$ and Δ_{ki} denotes the i-th diagonal element of matrix $\mathbf{\Lambda}_k$. After that λ_k is calculated using bisection method.

Similarly, we can obtain close form solutions of the optimal transmit filters $\mathbf{T}_j^{DL}$ under the sum-power constraint as follows

$$\mathbf{T}_j^{DL} = \alpha \overline{\mathbf{T}}_j^{DL} \tag{20}$$

where

$$\alpha = \sqrt{\frac{P_T}{\sum_j tr\{\overline{\mathbf{T}}_j^{DL}(\overline{\mathbf{T}}_j^{DL})^H\}}} \tag{21}$$

and $\overline{\mathbf{T}}_j^{DL}$ is computed as

$$\overline{\mathbf{T}}_j^{DL} = (\mathbf{X}_j + \frac{\sum_k tr\{(\mathbf{R}_j^{DL})^H \mathbf{W}_j^{DL} \mathbf{R}_j^{DL}\}}{P_T})^{-1}(\mathbf{H}_j^{DL})^H(\mathbf{R}_j^{DL})^H \mathbf{W}_j^{DL} \tag{22}$$

where $\mathbf{X}_j = (\mathbf{H}_j^{DL})^H(\mathbf{R}_j^{DL})^H \mathbf{W}_j^{DL} \mathbf{R}_j^{DL} \mathbf{H}_j^{DL}$.

3.2   Mode Selection

Since both in the original WSR problem (8) and equivalent MMSE problem (13), the mode selection parameter m is irrelevant to any of the other variables, m is only determined by the rate performance of different mode. Then, we can compare the system sum rate performance of FD and HD modes and choose m to get the better performance.

3.3   Convergence

Therefore, the optimal solution of original WSR problem (8) can be achieved by solving the equivalent WMMSE problem (13), which can be decoupled into two sub-problems and using the iterative alternating algorithm listed in Table 1.

Table 1. WSR maximum agorithm.

---
1) Set mode selection $m=1$

2) set the iteration number N and start from $n=0$, initialize the transmit filters $\mathbf{T}_k^{UL}$ and $\mathbf{T}_j^{DL}$.

3) $n=n+1$.

4) Calculate the receive filters $\mathbf{R}_i^{UL}$ and $\mathbf{R}_j^{DL}$ using (9) and (12).

5) Calculate the weight matrices $\mathbf{W}_k^{UL}$ and $\mathbf{W}_j^{DL}$ using (16) and (17).

6) Update the transmit filters $\mathbf{T}_k^{UL}$ and $\mathbf{T}_j^{DL}$ using (18) and (20).

7) Repeat step 3) ~ 6) until convergence, or N is reached.

8) Get the achievable rate of FD system using (7).

9) Set mode selection $m=0$.

10) Repeat step 2) ~ 7) until convergence, or N is reached.

11) Get the achievable rate of HD system using (7).

12) Compare the achievable rate of FD scheme with HD scheme, set the mode as the one with higher rate.

---

4   Numerical Simulations

This section is devoted to examine system sum rate performance of the proposed optimization scheme through simulation. For simplicity, we assume the same transmit power constraint.

Figure 2 elaborates the convergence behavior of our algorithm. We can find that the WSR problem converges in a few iterations under different power constraints. We illustrate the achievable sum rate with different numbers of users in Fig. 3. The sum rate of the system increases with the user number, because of the user diversity gain. Figure 4 compares the achievable sum rate under different INR (self-interference noise ratio). It has been seen from the figure that the sum rate of HD mode is constant to INR and the performance of FD mode decreases with INR. When INR is large enough, HD

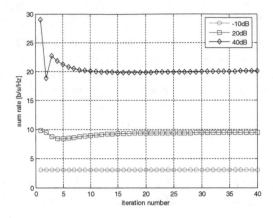

Fig. 2. Convergence behavior of the proposed algorithm

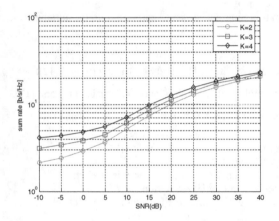

Fig. 3. Achievable rate comparison for different users

system outperform FD system, in other words the advantage of FD system disappears. We can also find in Fig. 4 that the sum rate of FD mode drops below that of HD mode around INR = 0 dB when SNR = 20 dB. Figure 5 gives the performance of the proposed heuristic algorithm. At low-to-mid range of INR, FD mode holds a better performance over HD mode, so the system remains working in FD mode. But when INR increase, sum rate of HD scheme outperforms that of FD scheme, the system will switch to the HD mode. In all, the proposed optimization can provide the freedom to switch between the FD and HD mode then to insure the best performance of the system.

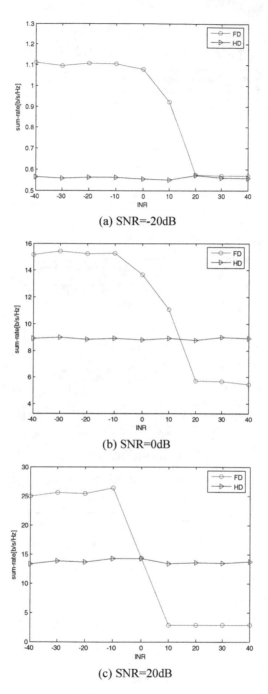

(a) SNR=-20dB

(b) SNR=0dB

(c) SNR=20dB

Fig. 4. Sum-rate comparison for different duplex schemes under different RSI

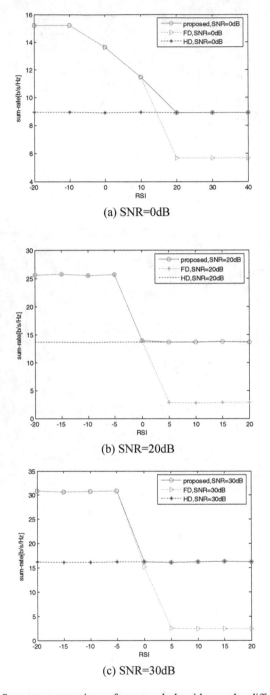

(a) SNR=0dB

(b) SNR=20dB

(c) SNR=30dB

Fig. 5. Sum-rate comparison of proposed algorithm under different RSI

5 Conclusion

In this work, we have considered a full-duplex cellular communication system with the BS transmitting and receiving simultaneously to (from) multiple DL (UL) MSs. The main challenge of such system lies in SI of the BS and will cause the awkward situation that FD mode cannot outperform HD mode. We formulate a joint mode selection and beamformer optimization problem, which has the maximal weighted sum rate as objective and power constraints. Since the non-convex characteristic of the problem, global optimal solution is hard to achieve. Thus a heuristic algorithm based on decoupling is proposed, which decomposes the original problem into two sub-problems. One is mode selection sub-problem and the other one is minimization of weighted sum mean square error sub-problem. Numerical results demonstrate that the proposed algorithm can always choose the mode with greater performance in achievable rate.

Acknowledgments. This work is sponsored by National Natural Science Foundation of China (Grant No. 61601409 and Grant No. 61471322).

References

1. Hua, Y., Liang, P., Ma, Y., Cirik, A.C., Gao, Q.: A method for broadband full-duplex MIMO radio. IEEE Sig. Process. Lett. **12**, 793–796 (2012)
2. Li, S., Murch, R.D.: Full-duplex wireless communication using transmitter output based echo cancellation. In: Proceedings of IEEE Global Communications Conference (GLOBECOM), pp. 1–5 (2011)
3. Choi, J.I., Jain, M., Srinivasan, K., Levis, P., Katti, S.: Achieving single channel, full duplex wireless communication. In: Proceedings of Annual International Conference on Mobile Computer and Network (2010)
4. Duarte, M., Sabharwal, A.: Full-duplex wireless communications using off-the-shelf radios: feasibility and first results. In: Asilomar Conference on Signals, Systems and Computers (ASILOMAR), vol. 45, pp. 1558–1562 (2010)
5. Jain, M., Choi, J.I., Kim, T., Bharadia, D., Seth, S., Srinivasan, K., Levis, P., Katti, S., Sinha, P.: Practical, real-time, full duplex wireless. In: Proceedings of 17th Annual International Conference on Mobile Computing Network, pp. 301–312 (2011)
6. Duarte, M., Dick, C., Sabharwal, A.: Experiment-driven characterization of full-duplex wireless system. IEEE Trans. Wireless Commun. **11**(12), 4296–4307 (2012)
7. Cirik, A.C., Rong, Y., Hua, Y.: Achievable rates of full-duplex MIMO radios in fast fading channels with imperfect channel estimation. IEEE Trans. Sig. Process. **62**(15), 3874–3886 (2014)
8. Cirik, A.C., Wang, R., Hua, Y., Latva-aho, Y.: Weighted sum-rate maximization for full-duplex mimo intereference channels. IEEE Trans. Commun. **63**(3), 801–815 (2015)
9. Christense, S.S., Agarwal, R., De Carvalho, E., Cioffi, J.M.: Weighted sum rate maximization using weighted MMSE for MIMO-BC beamforming design. IEEE Trans. Wireless Commun. **7**(12), 4792–4799 (2008)

Construction of Emergency Communication Network with Multi Constraints Based on Geographic Information

Yuan Feng[1,2], Fu-sheng Dai[1,2(✉)], and Ji Zhou[1,2]

[1] Harbin Institute of Technology, Weihai 264209, China
dfs7113@126.com
[2] Science and Technology on Communication Networks Laboratory,
Shijiazhuang 050081, China

Abstract. Aiming at the problem of deploying the vehicular relay station in the construction of emergency communication network, OpenStreetMap and FME tools are used to construct the electronic map which contains the geographic information such as roads and rivers. A Method for judging the line of sight propagation is also studied. The simulation results show that the proposed algorithm can be more reasonable and applicable to address the vehicle relay station, and can fulfill the requirements of the actual emergency communication link construction better.

Keywords: Emergency communication · Vehicle relay station
Electronic map · Line of sight propagation · Antenna placement

1 Introduction

After large-scale natural disasters, the wired and fixed communication infrastructure in the affected areas is very likely to suffer the serious damage causing the communication interruption. A large number of facts show that existing communication networks are often unable to meet emergency communication needs in the face of sudden natural disasters and public events [1]. Sometimes, due to communication disruption, after the emergency rescue personnel arrived at the scene, they can not communicate well and coordinate the forces of all parties, thus the efficiency of emergency rescue was greatly reduced [2]. Therefore, the establishment of an interconnected, efficient and adaptive emergency communication network can enhance the ability to respond to sudden natural disasters.

In the actual disaster relief process, Relief Commanding Officer will deploy a number of microwave stations and specify the corresponding network topology in order to meet the needs of emergency communication. But between transmitting and receiving microwave stations there are often high mountains, trees and other obstacles. As a result, some of the microwave stations can not communicate normally, the original

Supported by: Science and Technology on Communication Networks Laboratory.

network topology can not be achieved as well. Due to the good mobility and flexibility of the vehicle microwave station [3], it is possible to ensure the proposed network topology by deploying vehicle microwave relay stations.

In the research of vehicle emergency communication, paper [4, 5] analyzes the design and reconstruction of the emergency communication vehicle, but does not study the deployment of communication vehicles in practical application; Paper [6] makes an exploration on addressing vehicle relay stations, but it does not take the factors such as roads and rivers in the actual geographic information into account so the accessibility of the communication vehicle is ignored. Therefore, in order to meet the rapid deployment of emergency communication network [7], we are now striving to find a method to solve the problem of being convenient for the deployment of relay stations under the network topology constraint. This method not only can guarantee the communication requirements of the network topology between the designated microwave stations, but also can combine with the flexibility of the vehicle relay stations, construct the emergency communication network quickly and effectively.

2   Construction of Emergency Communication Network with Multiple Constraints

2.1   Algorithm Idea

In order to construct the emergency communication links, firstly, extract the geographic information such as elevations, roads and rivers in the affected area. Secondly, evaluate the normal communication after giving the microwave stations and the corresponding network topology. Finally, calculate the position of the deployed vehicle relay stations and a series of parameters such as the heights and elevations of the microwave antennas to satisfy the network topology rapidly.

Sometimes, line of sight propagation can not be achieved by the transmitting and receiving station due to the block obstacles such as mountains and forests, so it is necessary to establish microwave relay stations to amplify the signal. In order to meet the requirements of the rapid deployment of the relay stations, the following constraints should be met:

  (i)   The relay stations should be built in places where the terrain is relatively flat and relatively low in altitude;

  (ii) The relay stations should be placed near the road;

  (iii) The relay station should be placed avoided the river;

  (iv) Multiple relay stations should be placed like the word "Z" instead of one on the top of the hill;

Under the above constraints, AHP-TOPSIS (Analytic Hierarchy Process - Technique for Order Preference by Similarity to an Ideal Solution) algorithm is used for addressing vehicle relay stations. The optimal solution is determined by calculating the altitudes and attenuation of every alternative relay stations and measuring the shortest distance from the positive ideal solution (PIS) and the farthest distance from the negative ideal solution (NIS) respectively [8].

2.2   Visualization of Terrain Conditions

In the visual construction of terrain conditions, the Digital Elevation Model (DEM), which is a special case of Digital Terrain Model (DTM), is used where Z axis represents the elevation value of the current position, in other words, it represents the altitude of the current position. Taking E120_N37 as an example, the visualization of the terrain construction steps are as follows:

(i)   Use the DEM with a distance of 1/1200 degree downloaded from geospatial data cloud as the data source. And using the GlobalMapper tool to convert the DEM into the image file [9].

(ii) Use OpenStreetMap to download and extract a variety of terrain information [10].

(iii) Use the FME tool [11] to edit and stratify the map, extract the roads information separately and convert it into Excel or other data types of file containing the latitude and longitude information of roads.

(iv) Extract the rivers information by step two and three. In the end, combine the roads information, rivers information and elevations information of the map.

Based on the visualization of terrain conditions, we not only can see the terrains, roads and rivers directly, but also can extract the elevation of each point and the location of roads and rivers in the electronic map to do operations simply (Figs. 1 and 2).

Fig. 1. Separation and extraction of roads information   **Fig. 2.** Interface of electronic map

2.3   Analysis of Relay Station Deployment

In the construction of microwave communication link, path types are divided into line of sight (LOS) and not line of sight (NLOS) types. The choice of antenna heights affects the attenuation of microwave propagation, so it is necessary to design the antenna heights reasonably. In the project, the determination of the antenna heights is generally setting one end (transmitter or receiver) of the antenna height based on the known conditions firstly, then calculating the height of the other end according to the design requirements.

An algorithm for judging two-point LOS is as follows:

(i) Firstly, set the height range of transmitting and receiving antennas; Secondly, set the height of transmitting antenna h_{ta} from low-to-high in the range and calculate the height of receiving antenna h_{ra}. If the height of transmitting antenna is out of range, it is judged as NLOS, otherwise, go to the next step. In which: $h_{ra} = (2n + 1)\lambda d/4h_{ta}$ ($n = 1, 2, \ldots$).

(ii) If the height of receiving antenna is out of range, increase the initial height of the transmitting antenna, return to step 1, otherwise, go to the next step.

(iii) Calculate the path clearance H_c and the relative clearance P, if condition one and condition two are not satisfied simultaneously, $n = n + 1$, return to step 1, otherwise, go to the next step.

(a) **Condition one**: The minimum clearance $H_{cmin} > 0$; in which $H_{cmin} = \min (H_c)$.

(b) The path clearance H_c is an important parameter to judge whether the antenna can be transmitted as LOS propagation, and it refers to the distance between the obstacle and radio wave. Path clearance: $H_c = [(h_{ta} + H_1)d_2 + (h_{ra} + H_2)d_1]/d - H_3 - d_1d_2/2Ka$ (m); in the formula, H_1, H_2 and H_3 refer to the altitude of the point of transmitting antenna, receiving antenna and the interpolation point; d_1 and d_2 are the distance between the reflection point and the transmitting and receiving antennas respectively; d is the distance between transmitting and receiving antennas; K is the equivalent earth radius factor; a is the actual earth radius.

(c) **Condition two**: Relative clearance $P > 0.577$ (Or $H_c > F_0$). The working point is on the left side of a radiation lobe's maximum value on the P-V curve (making V large enough), and shall be landed in the lower lobe as far as possible [12]. The relative clearance P is the ratio of path clearance H_c to the first Fresnel radius F_1: $P = H_c/F_1$.

(iv) After getting the heights of the transmitting and receiving antenna, judge the path types as follows. If the elevation angle from transmitting antenna of physical field of vision is larger than that of the transmitting antenna to the receiving antenna, the path is tropospheric scatter path, in other words, it's NLOS path. Otherwise it's LOS path. The method to judge the NLOS path is: $\theta_{max} > \theta_{td}$; in which $\theta_{max} = \max(\theta_i)$ ($i = 1, \ldots, n - 1$).

(a) θ_i: The elevation angle of the transmitting antenna to the ith interpolation point: $\theta_i = (h_i - h_{ts})/d_i - 10^3 d/2a_e$ (mrad); In the formula, h_i: The altitude of the i_{th} interpolation point; d_i: The distance between the transmitting antenna and the i_{th} interpolation point; a_e: The median effective earth radius suitable for this path; h_{ts}: The average altitude of transmitting antenna, $h_{ts} = h_0 + h_{ta}$ (m); in which h_0: The altitude of the 0_{th} interpolation point (i.e. the point of the transmitting antenna), h_{ta} is the height of the transmitting antenna.

(b) θ_{td}: The elevation angle of the transmitting antenna to the receiving antenna: $\theta_{td} = (h_{rs} - h_{ts})/d_i - 10^3 d/2a_e$ (mrad); in the formula, h_{rs}: The average altitude of receiving antenna, $h_{rs} = h_n + h_{ra}$ (m), in which h_n: The altitude of the n_{th} interpolation point (i.e. the point of the receiving antenna), h_{ra} is the height of the receiving antenna.

2.4   Link Space Propagation Attenuation Index

The attenuation of the spatial propagation of the link [13] L_f should satisfy: $L_f \leqq [P_t] + [G_t] + [G_r] - [L_t] - [L_r] - [P_r]$; in which: P_t: The transmitted power of the microwave station; P_r: The received power of the microwave station; G_t: Antenna gain of transmitting station; G_r: Antenna gain of receiving station; L_t: Feeder loss; L_r: Branch loss.

The sensitivity of the general receiver is -120 dBm. Assume that a transmitter with a transmit power of 30 W is used, the transmitting and receiving antenna gain are both 20 dB, the feeder and branch loss are both 5 dB. Calculated that L_f is less than or equal to 194.77 dB.

The calculation of L_f can be found in Recommendation ITU-R P.676:

$$L_f = L_{b0}(p) + A_{ht} + A_{hr} (dB). \tag{1}$$

In the formula, $L_{b0}(p)$ is the basic transmission loss given by the LOS model and be predicted 90% of the time that will not be exceeded; A_{ht}, A_{hr} is the corresponding additional loss due to the height in local scatterer–Gain effect.

2.5   AHP-TOPSIS Algorithm with Multiple Constraints

Calculate the Weight of Each Index Using Analytic Hierarchy Process (AHP). In the process of multi-attribute evaluation, different attributes have different importances, the corresponding weight is also different. In some multi-constraint conditions difficult to quantify, AHP gives the method to calculate the weight of each attribute.

(i)   Construct the criterion layer judgment matrix A as shown in Table 1, $C_i{:}C_j = a_{ij}$, The greater the a_{ij}, the higher the importance of C_i than C_j.

Table 1. Judge matrix

	Attenuation (C_1)	Elevation (C_2)	Corner (C_3)	Distance (C_4)	Inclination (C_5)
Attenuation (C_1)	1	2	4	5	7
Elevation (C_2)	1/2	1	2	3	6
Corner (C_3)	1/4	1/2	1	3	4
Distance (C_4)	1/5	1/3	1/3	1	2
Inclination (C_5)	1/7	1/6	1/4	1/2	1

(ii) Carry out the consistency test of the criterion layer matrix that $CR = 0.024 < 0.1$. It can be proved that satisfy the consistency index. In which: $CR = CI/RI$, $CI = (\lambda - n)/(n - 1)$, λ is the largest eigenvalue of the matrix, n is the dimension of the matrix, and RI is the random consistency index.

(iii)   The normalized feature vector corresponding to the largest eigenvalue of the matrix is obtained: w = [0.4563 0.2583 0.1611 0.0785 0.0458]. w is the weight of each attribute.

AHP-TOPSIS Algorithm [14–16]. By combining the TOPSIS method with AHP, the weight calculated by AHP is introduced: $t_{ij} = w_j \cdot b_{ij}$; where: t_{ij} is the weighted specification value of each attribute and b_{ij} is the original value of each attribute. Based on this, construct the PIS and NIS of the problems and the distance between candidate points and the PIS and NIS to calculate the comprehensive evaluation index, then sort all alternatives and get the optimal solution.

Determine the worst alternative: t_{wj} = {[max($t_{ij}|i$ = 1, 2, ...m)| $j \in J_-$], [min($t_{ij}|$ i = 1, 2, ...m)| $j \in J_+$]};

Determine the best alternative: t_{bj} = {[min($t_{ij}|i$ = 1, 2, ...m)| $j \in J_-$], [max($t_{ij}|i$ = 1, 2, ...m)| $j \in J_+$]};

Where:

J_- = {j = 1, 2, ...n| j associated with the criteria having a negative impact};

J_+ = {j = 1, 2, ...n| j associated with the criteria having a positive impact};

Distance between the target alternative and the worst condition:

$$d_{iw} = \sqrt{\sum_{j=1}^{n} (t_{ij} - t_{wj})^2}, i = 1, 2, \cdots, m \tag{2}$$

Distance between the alternative and the best condition:

$$d_{ib} = \sqrt{\sum_{j=1}^{n} (t_{ij} - t_{bj})^2}, i = 1, 2, \cdots, m \tag{3}$$

Comprehensive evaluation index:

$$s_{iw} = d_{iw}/(d_{iw} + d_{ib})(i = 1, \ldots, m) \tag{4}$$

The Specific Steps of the Algorithm

(i)   Given the specified network topology, determine the path types of the microwave stations for communication by the algorithm mentioned in 1.3, if it's LOS, the relay station is not needed, if it's NLOS, go to the next step.

(ii)   Determine the constraints of the relay station addressing range, and limit the range of alternative points: $P = P_c \cap P_r - P_w$. In which: P_c: Set of points in the circle where the center is the midpoint of the two microwave stations, and the diameter is the distance between the two stations; P_r: Set of points less than 10 m on both sides of the road; P_w: Set of points the river passes through. If the point can be transmitted by LOS with any station, then list it as an alternative point.

(iii) Calculate the altitude h of each alternative point, according to formula (1) to calculate the spatial propagation attenuation L_f and other parameters, according to formulas (2)–(4) to calculate the comprehensive evaluation indexes s_{iw} and sort them. The larger the s_{iw}, the better the point.

(iv) Judge whether the optimal relay station and the two microwave stations can transmit along LOS and compare the link attenuation value. If the LOS transmission can not be satisfied or attenuation value is beyond the setting range, go to step 3, using the suboptimal point. If all alternative points can not meet the above conditions, take the optimal point and the NLOS microwave station as transceiver stations, go to step 2 and searching for a second relay station; Otherwise, go to the next step.

(v) Once the communication between the original microwave stations is satisfied, the operation is completed. Output all relay stations' positions, and calculate the antenna height, elevation and other parameters.

3   Experimental Simulation and Program Evaluation

Still take the E120_N37 area as an example, select a number of microwave stations and set the proposed network topology randomly: 1-2, 1-3, 1-4, 2-3.

Set the maximum height of the transmitting and receiving antennas to 20 m, and specify the transmitting antenna height (initial value of 3 m). It is judged by the algorithm that microwave stations 1 and 2, 1 and 3, 2 and 3 can not transmit from each other by LOS. The locations of the vehicle relay stations calculated by the algorithm are shown in Fig. 3 (red hatch fill); the latitudes, longitudes and elevations of the relay stations and microwave stations are shown in Table 2.

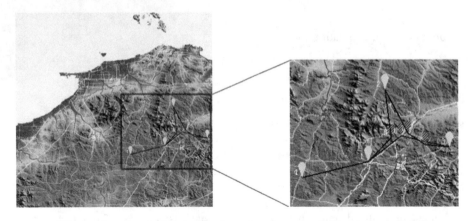

Fig. 3. Emergency link construction of random area (Color figure online)

Table 2. Calculation results

Microwave station number	Longitude/(°)	Latitude/(°)	Elevation/(m)
Microwave station 1	120.75209	37.31874	203
Microwave station 2	120.79625	37.51541	150
Microwave station 3	120.96709	37.35791	223
Microwave station 4	120.57959	37.27541	210
Relay station 5	120.81292	37.38375	126
Relay station 6	120.83875	37.39042	115
Relay station 7	120.85625	37.39708	93
Relay station 8	120.90208	37.36542	122

In order to meet the needs of practical applications, the algorithm finally calculates the antenna heights h_{ta} and h_{ra}, elevation angle θ_{td} and azimuth angle as shown in Table 3.

Table 3. Microwave link

Microwave station number	Antenna height/(m)	Elevation angle/(°)	Azimuth angle /(°)	Attenuation/(dB)
Microwave station 1-5	5.00, 7.75	2.02, −3.03	EbN 46.90, WbS 46.90	117.96
Microwave station 5-2	3.00, 18.97	0.18, −1.83	WbN 82.78, EbS 82.78	125.37
Microwave station 1-6	8.00, 16.18	3.02, −4.26	EbN 39.59, WbS 39.59	120.41
Microwave station 6-3	20.00, 20.00	1.24, 33.08	EbS 14.21, WbN 14.21	172.74
Microwave station 1-4	9.00, 13.93	24.40, −26.19	WbS 14.10, EbN 14.10	123.72
Microwave station 2-7	4.00, 14.18	1.75, −3.34	EbS 63.11, WbN 63.11	129.41
Microwave station 7-8	3.00, 17.65	2.50, −3.10	EbS 34.64, WbN 34.64	116.37
Microwave station 8-3	20.00, 20.00	0.77, 31.94	EbS 6.58, WbN 6.58	161.03

As shown in Fig. 3, the relay stations calculated by the algorithm are selectively distributed near the road but not in the river. The elevation of each relay station is not too high, therefore the fast deployment requirements can be met. It can be seen from Table 3 that the antenna height of each microwave station is within the setting range, and the attenuation value of each link is less than 194.77 dB, which satisfies the general receiver's sensitivity requirement. The calculation of antenna heights, elevation angles and azimuth angles not only proves the feasibility of the algorithm, but also improves the practicability of the algorithm.

4 Conclusion

This paper introduces an emergency communication network construction method combining multi - constraint geographic information, which is used to implement the proposed topology network. Combined with the electronic map, taking into account the actual roads and rivers and other geographic information, the locations of the vehicle relay stations are calculated and simulated under multiple constraints. In addition, the heights and elevations of the transmitting and receiving antennas in the network are also planned. The results show that the method can meet the reachability requirement of vehicle relay stations, and the link attenuation and antenna placement parameters are within reasonable limits and can be effectively used in emergency network construction. In the future work, the algorithm will be combined with spectrum planning and other technologies to allocate the frequency of the constructed communication network.

References

1. Wang, H.: Investigation into the design of emergency communication network and related key technologies. Command Inf. Syst. Technol. (2010)
2. Hao, Y.W., Xiao-Xue, L.I., Zhao, Z., et al.: Summary of public incident emergency integrated space-ground command communication technology. Inf. Technol. (2016)
3. Chang-Mao, X.U., Geng, X.M.: Design of vehicle monitoring system based on WiMAX and satellite communication. Inf. Technol. (2014)
4. Jia, N., Shao, D., Ji, J.: Key technology of modification and system integration of the Shaanxi earthquake emergency communication command vehicle. Technol. Earthq. Disaster Prev. 11(2), 403–411 (2016)
5. Pan, Y.: Research on system integration of emergency communication command vehicle. Telecom. World. (24) (2016)
6. Wang, C., Dai, F., Zou, B.: Construction of emergency microwave communication link using geographic Information. Telecommun. Eng. 57(1), 100–105 (2017)
7. Research and Development Status of Emergency Communication and its Technical Means Analysis. Inf. Commun. Technol. (2011)
8. Lo, C.C., Chen, D.Y., Tsai, C.F., et al.: Service selection based on fuzzy TOPSIS method. In: 2010 IEEE 24th International Conference on Advanced Information Networking and Applications Workshops (WAINA), pp. 367–372. IEEE (2010)
9. Xu, X.: Tactical network planning based on 3D visualization of geographic information. Harbin Institute of Technology, pp. 40–50 (2015)
10. Haklay, M., Weber, P.: Openstreetmap: user-generated street maps. IEEE Pervasive Comput. 7(4), 12–18 (2008)
11. Houzhi, W., Jianping, X.: Building basic terrain database with feature manipulate engine. Urban Geotech. Invest. Surv. 3, 008 (2006)
12. Yang, G.R., Shi, F.Q.: Research of microwave communication antenna selection and optimization method. Electron. Des. Eng. (2009)
13. Zhao, Z.: Planning and design of digital microwave transmission system and transmission solution. Xi'an Electronic and Science University (2014)
14. Yang, H.: Evaluation model of physical fitness of young tennis athletes based on AHP-TOPSIS comprehensive evaluation. Int. J. Appl. Math. Statistics™ 39(9), 188–195 (2013)
15. Xinmin, W., Jianchun, Q., Qinli, Z., et al.: Mining method optimization of Gu Mountain stay ore based on AHP-TOPSIS evaluation model. J. Central South Univ. (Sci. Technol.) 44(3), 1131–1137 (2013)
16. Lin, M.C., Wang, C.C., Chen, M.S., et al.: Using AHP and TOPSIS approaches in customer-driven product design process. Comput. Ind. 59(1), 17–31 (2008)

Design of Turntable Servo Control System Based on Sliding Mode Control Algorithm

Zongjie Bi, Zhaoshuo Tian, Pushuai Shi, and Shiyou Fu[✉]

Information Optoelectronics Research Institute, Harbin Institute of Technology,
Weihai 264209, China
{bizongjie,845331968}@qq.com,
{tianzhaoshuo,fsytzs}@126.com

Abstract. With the development of national defense weaponry and equipment level, higher requirements are put forward for the servo control system. The traditional PID algorithm is difficult to satisfy the target; this paper proposes a sliding mode control algorithm. Firstly, the working principle is analyzed, the DC motor model is established, the sliding mode controller is designed, and the boundary layer method is used to weaken the chattering of sliding mode control, the Stribeck friction model is used at the same time, and the simulation and experimental results is given. The experimental results show that the tracking error of the sliding mode control is 0.36° and the tracking error of the PID control is 0.675° under the same conditions, the results show that the sliding mode control algorithm is better than the PID control algorithm in the robustness and tracking performance.

Keywords: Turntable · Servo system · PID control algorithm
Sliding mode control algorithm

1 Introduction

Nowadays, in the field of aviation, spaceflight, navigation, the world competition for military supremacy is becoming increasingly acute, the performance requirements for the navigation and guidance equipment is improved continuously. As one of the key equipment of the guidance weapon, the turntable also needs higher dynamic performance. The way to improve the control method to improve the tracking accuracy of the turntable has been an urgent problem to be solved [1].

As the motor is often rotated a very small angle when the turntable works, the friction torque, which is often neglected in general motor control, cannot be ignored in the turntable control. So many scholars use various methods to control and compensate the influence of friction torque. Friction is a very complex nonlinear phenomenon, and the traditional control algorithm such as PI control and PID control is not enough to make up for its influence [2]. Li pointed out that although the traditional PID method is simple, well stability algorithm, it is easy to cause the system overshoot or shock [3]. Since the 80s of last century, the research in this field has grown significantly, and many new friction models and friction compensation methods have emerged, and they have been successfully applied to the servo control system [4]. Yan et al. separated the

© ICST Institute for Computer Sciences, Social Informatics and Telecommunications Engineering 2018
X. Gu et al. (Eds.): MLICOM 2017, Part II, LNICST 227, pp. 263–272, 2018.
https://doi.org/10.1007/978-3-319-73447-7_30

friction torque from the load torque and designed an adaptive back stepping controller to achieve the targeted compensation of friction torque [5]. Zhang et al. used the dual observer to observe the changing state of the LuGre friction model aimed at the onboard battery servo control system, and designed an adaptive dynamic compensation algorithm to compensate the nonlinear disturbance of the friction force, and the tracking accuracy is improved [6]. Although the LuGre friction model can describe the dynamic characteristics of the friction force in the servo control system accurately, it is very difficult to measure the parameters of the model as for its high nonlinearity [7]. Yan et al. made a detailed analysis of Coulomb friction model, Stribeck friction model and Lugre friction model, and pointed out that the Lugre model has many parameters and is very difficult to be measured, and the Stribeck friction model is more accurate than the Coulomb friction model and can achieve 90% approximation of the entire friction characteristics [8].

In this paper, a sliding mode switching function and a sliding mode controller are designed, the boundary layer method is used to suppress the chattering in the sliding mode control. The simulation results show that the boundary layer method can restrain the chattering of sliding mode. At the same time, the sliding mode controller is compared with the PID controller and the Stribeck friction model is used. The simulation results show that the sliding mode controller has good tracking performance and robustness. Finally, the turntable servo control device is designed, debugged and analyzed by the LabVIEW PC, and achieved good experimental results.

2   The Working Principle and Design of Sliding Mode Controller

2.1   The Working Principle of Sliding Mode Controller

The schematic diagram of the sliding mode is shown in Fig. 1. It can be seen that the design of sliding mode control system is mainly divided into two parts; one is on the sliding surface movement, also called sliding mode movement, corresponding to the switching function; the other is outside the sliding surface movement, also called reaching movement, corresponding to the sliding mode control rate. Which the sliding surface determines the performance of sliding mode control, influences the robustness of sliding mode control, and the reaching law determines the reaching method from any state to the sliding surface, which influences the rapidity and accessibility of sliding mode control.

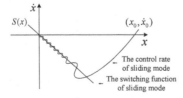

Fig. 1. Schematic diagram of the sliding mode state

Linear sliding surface is the most common sliding surface, and the system has the characteristic of reducing order on the sliding surface. The design of linear sliding surface can be realized by the method of optimal control and pole placement, which is simple and easy to design, and it is widely used in various systems. The linear sliding surface expression is shown in the formula 1, in which $S(x)$ is the sliding surface; C is the sliding mode coefficient; x is the system state.

$$S(x) = C\dot{x} + x \tag{1}$$

2.2 The Design of Sliding Mode Controller

(1) The design of the switching function. The dynamic structure of DC motor under rated excitation is shown in Fig. 2.

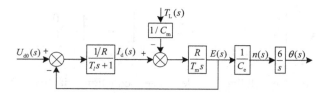

Fig. 2. The dynamic structure of DC motor under rated excitation

According to the model, the relationship between the input voltage and the motor current is shown:

$$[U_{d0}(s) - E(s)] \cdot \frac{1/R}{T_l s + 1} = I_d(s) \tag{2}$$

Through the deformation, taking the position, speed, current as the state variable, the input voltage, load torque as input variables, which can be converted to a state diagram, as shown in Fig. 3.

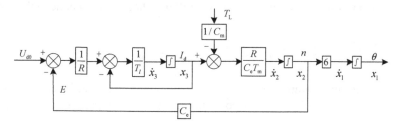

Fig. 3. The state transition diagram of DC motor

If the friction resistance and no-load torque are ignored, the state equation $\dot{\mathbf{x}} = \mathbf{A}\mathbf{x} + \mathbf{B}u$ can be shown in formula 3.

$$
\begin{bmatrix} \dot{x}_1 \\ \dot{x}_2 \\ \dot{x}_3 \end{bmatrix} = \begin{bmatrix} 0 & 6 & 0 \\ 0 & 0 & \frac{R}{C_e T_m} \\ 0 & -\frac{C_e}{L} & -\frac{1}{T_l} \end{bmatrix} \cdot \begin{bmatrix} x_1 \\ x_2 \\ x_3 \end{bmatrix} + \begin{bmatrix} 0 \\ 0 \\ \frac{1}{L} \end{bmatrix} U_{d0}
\tag{3}
$$

Suppose the sliding mode switching function is $\sigma = S_1 x_1 + S_2 x_2 + S_3 x_3$, when the system reaches the switching plane, $\sigma = 0$; $\dot{\sigma} = 0$, the sliding mode equation is shown:

$$
\begin{cases} \dot{x}_1 = (A_{11} - A_{13}S_3^{-1}S_1)x_1 + (A_{12} - A_{13}S_3^{-1}S_2)x_2 \\ \dot{x}_2 = (A_{21} - A_{23}S_3^{-1}S_1)x_1 + (A_{22} - A_{23}S_3^{-1}S_2)x_2 \end{cases}
\tag{4}
$$

Set $K_1 = S_3^{-1}S_1$, $K_2 = S_3^{-1}S_2$, which can be arbitrarily determined by pole placement. Set $S_3 = 1$, and $\mathbf{S} = \begin{bmatrix} K_1 & K_2 & 1 \end{bmatrix}$. Substituting the data, it can be got that

$$
\mathbf{A} = \begin{bmatrix} 0 & 6 & 0 \\ 0 & 0 & 31.609 \\ 0 & -171.429 & -314.286 \end{bmatrix} \quad \mathbf{B} = \begin{bmatrix} 0 \\ 0 \\ 142.857 \end{bmatrix}
\tag{5}
$$

According to the sliding mode state equation, it can be got that $s^2 + 31.609K_2 s + 198.654K_1 = 0$. We assume that the system does not overshoot, assume that the system has two identical real roots $s_{1,2} = -15.805K_2$, and because of the discriminant equals zero we can conclude $K_1 = 1.317K_2^2$, we hope that we can obtain the characteristic as good as the PID regulator in the absence of friction and disturbance. It can be calculated that $K_1 = 0.396$, $K_2 = 0.548$, so the sliding mode switching function is that:

$$
\sigma = 0.396x_1 + 0.548x_2 + x_3
\tag{6}
$$

According to the state equation, it can be written:

$$
\sigma = 0.396x_1 + 0.091\dot{x}_1 + 0.00527\ddot{x}_1
\tag{7}
$$

(2) The design of the sliding mode controller. Choose the exponential reaching law:

$$
\dot{\sigma} = -k\sigma - \eta \operatorname{sgn}(\sigma) \quad (k > 0, \eta > 0)
\tag{8}
$$

According to the definition of sliding mode switching function, it can be seen that $\dot{\sigma} = \mathbf{S}\dot{\mathbf{x}} = \mathbf{S}(\mathbf{A}\mathbf{x} + \mathbf{B}u)$, which is used to form the controller expression:

$$
u = -(\mathbf{SB})^{-1}[\mathbf{SAx} + k\sigma + \eta \operatorname{sgn}(\sigma)]
\tag{9}
$$

Substituting the data, we can obtain that:

$$U_{d0} = -0.007 \times [-169.053x_2 - 296.964x_3 + k\sigma + \eta\mathrm{sgn}(\sigma)] \tag{10}$$

When $k = 20$, it has good reaching speed. Since the sliding mode switching function uses the deviation, the overall jitter is small, so we choose $\eta = 5$. In order to form a contrast with the PID controller, MATLAB is used to simulate the characteristics of the step, given a $36°$ simulation results shown in Fig. 4. It can be seen that the switch function, and the controller output form a high frequency jitter, while the speed, position do a low frequency swing in the steady-state value near the micro amplitude. On the one hand, the rotary inertia of the turntable is too large and the speed is slow; On the other hand, the current feedback is introduced, and the amplitude of the current is small. At the same time, the speed feedback and position feedback are introduced to make the change from current to position smaller and smaller.

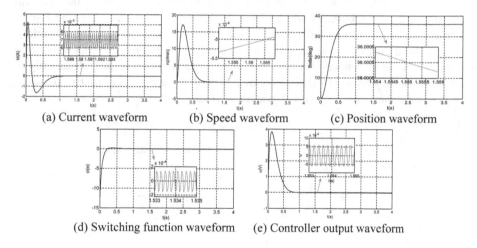

(a) Current waveform   (b) Speed waveform   (c) Position waveform

(d) Switching function waveform   (e) Controller output waveform

Fig. 4. The simulation chart of the step characteristics of sliding mode control

2.3 Boundary Layer Method to Suppress the Chattering of Sliding Mode

In the sliding mode control, the existence of the sign function will cause the chattering of the input control. In order to eliminate the jitter, a thin boundary layer can be set near the sliding mode surface, so that the output can be controlled to the continuous function between the two boundary layers, as shown in Fig. 5.

From the analysis above, it can be shown that the expression of the boundary layer method is actually a symbolic function, as shown in formula 11. When the sliding mode function enters between the boundary layers, the system will be switched from the switching state to the continuous state, that the system can be approximated as the sliding surface.

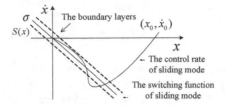

Fig. 5. The boundary layers in sliding mode

$$sat(\sigma) = \begin{cases} \sigma/\phi & |\sigma| < \phi \\ \sigma/|\sigma| & |\sigma| \geq \phi \end{cases} \qquad (11)$$

If the boundary layer is too large, the constraints of system dynamics will be reduced to the sliding surface, and the robustness will be reduced. If the boundary layer is too small, the chattering suppression ability will be reduced to the boundary layer. Take the saturation function instead of the sign function; the system has a small chattering and good robustness when taking the boundary layers, as shown in Fig. 6. Compare Fig. 4 with Fig. 6, the state of the system is fast on the sliding surface $\phi = 0.01$, form the high frequency sliding mode chattering in Fig. 4(d), but the system is very slow to approach, cross, away from the sliding mode switching plane, only to reach the boundary layer will change the direction of movement in Fig. 6(b). It can be seen that the dither frequency of the system is greatly reduced.

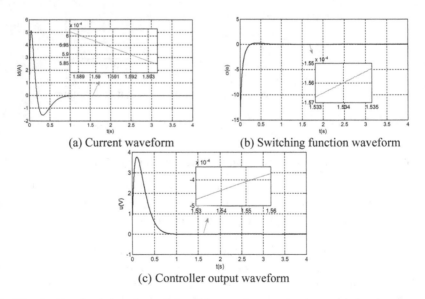

(a) Current waveform   (b) Switching function waveform

(c) Controller output waveform

Fig. 6. The simulation chart of the sliding mode control using saturation function

3   The Performance Analysis of Sliding Mode Controller

3.1   The Tracking Characteristic Analysis

Without considering the friction resistance, the sine wave with the period of 5 s and an amplitude of 36° (Generally, the ship's swing period is not less than 8 s, where the 5 s analysis can be used to cover most of the swing) is simulated by PID controller and sliding mode controller respectively, and the following characteristics are shown in Fig. 7. In Fig. 7 the actual amplitude of PID is given 1, and here magnified 36 times for comparison. Compared with Fig. 7(a) and (b), the tracking performance of the sliding mode controller is much stronger than that of PID controller that is because the sliding mode surface contains the first derivative and the two derivative of the error, which can get the movement trend of control input effectively, so as to produce better following characteristics.

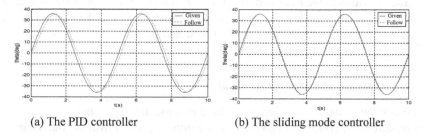

| (a) The PID controller | (b) The sliding mode controller |

Fig. 7. The comparison of tracking characteristics between the PID controller and the sliding mode controller

3.2   The Robustness Analysis

After adding the Stribeck friction to the system, the sketch map of the sliding mode controller is shown in Fig. 8. Compared with Fig. 8 and Fig. 7(b), when the Stribeck friction model is taken into account, the following characteristics of the sliding mode controller are almost unchanged, which shows that the sliding mode controller has good robustness. Parameters of Stribeck friction model in simulation are measured in practice.

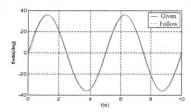

Fig. 8. The tracking characteristics of sliding mode controller with friction

4   The Design and Result Analysis of Turntable Servo Control System

4.1   The Design of Turntable Servo Control System

Combined with the previous analysis, this paper designs the turntable servo control device, including hardware circuit and software PC, etc. Hardware circuit consists with ARM controller as the core, combined with the driver board and other peripheral circuit. The software communicates with the hardware circuit by LabVIEW, and debugs parameters.

The paper choose an absolute PID (non-incremental PID) as the PID regulator, the expression is as follows:

$$uk = ek * Kp + eksum * Ki \tag{12}$$

In order to validate the designed the sliding mode controller, the PID algorithm is compared. The sliding mode controller has no current loop, speed loop and position loop, but it still needs to obtain the current, speed and position. As a result, the current sampling filter, current sampling zero correction program are hold.

4.2   The Experimental Results Analysis

The servo control device is connected to the turntable for debugging. Open the parameter setting interface of LabVIEW host computer, and download the parameters to the lower machine through the serial port. Four working modes are set up respectively, and the results of the four modes are shown in Fig. 9, and it can be calculated that the maximum error is about 0.675°.

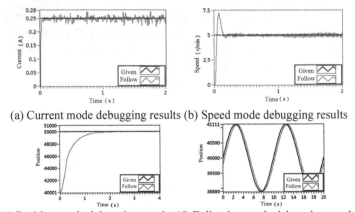

(a) Current mode debugging results (b) Speed mode debugging results

(c) Position mode debugging results (d) Following mode debugging results

Fig. 9. Turntable PID control algorithm debugging results

In the debugging process of sliding mode control algorithm, because of the algorithm own reasons, there exists no elimination of the sliding mode chattering, and the sliding mode controller has no independent current loop and speed loop, so it can only carry on the position debugging and the simulation follow experiment. In the experiment, the first order differential and second order differential make the system oscillate seriously, so omit the second order differential and inhibit the first order differential then choose the sliding mode switching function as shown in formula 13. In the exponential reaching law, in order to guarantee the reachability of the system, it should satisfy $\eta > 0$ in theory, and the position deviation is an integer in the actual system, there will be no decimal tending to zero, so $\eta = 0$ is still suitable for the requirements of accessibility. In order to reduce the current buffeting, accelerate the response speed, and increase the parameter of exponential reaching law, the output expression of sliding mode control is chosen as the formula 14 finally.

$$\sigma(e) = 0.396e + 0.045\dot{e} \tag{13}$$

$$U_{d0} = -0.007 \times [-169.053x_2 - 30x_3 + 200\sigma] \tag{14}$$

The result is obtained in position mode of sliding mode control, as shown in Fig. 10 (a). When reaching the steady state, there exists some chattering, and the results of the simulation following mode is shown in Fig. 10(b), and it can be calculated that the maximum error is about 0.36°.

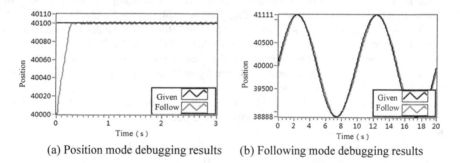

(a) Position mode debugging results   (b) Following mode debugging results

Fig. 10. Turntable sliding mode control algorithm debugging results

Compare Fig. 9(d) with Fig. 10(b), it can be seen that the sliding mode control algorithm has better robustness and tracking performance than the PID control algorithm.

5   Conclusion

In this paper, the sliding mode controller of servo control system is established. Firstly, the working principle is analyzed; the DC motor model is established, the sliding mode controller is designed, the sliding mode switching function is designed by pole placement method, the sliding mode controller is designed with the exponential reaching law, and the boundary layer method is used to weaken the chattering of sliding mode control. At the same time, the simulation model is built in Simulink, and the Stribeck friction is added, and the simulation results show that the sliding mode controller has good tracking performance and robustness. Finally, the turntable servo control system is designed; LabVIEW is used to write the host computer, to control ARM lower machine through the serial port, so as to control the servo motor. The experimental results show that the tracking error of the sliding mode control is 0.36°, and the tracking error of the PID control is as high as 0.675°, which proves that the sliding mode control algorithm has better robustness and tracking performance than the PID control algorithm. However, the sliding mode control algorithm has a large buffeting current, and the way to coordinate these coefficients and reduce the buffeting current is the focus of the next study.

References

1. Songlin, C., Meilin, S., Libin, W.: Disturbance observer-based robust perfect tracking control for flight simulator. Electr. Mach. Control **19**(1), 113–118 (2015)
2. Xiaoping, X., Xuanju, D.: Study on hybrid friction model for motors based on neural network. Comput. Simul. **29**(5), 178–182 (2012)
3. Li, Y.: Design and realization of three axis table. Mod. Electron. Tech. **34**(17), 135–136, 140 (2011)
4. Qiang, L., Er, L.-J., Liu, J.-K.: Overview of characteristics modeling and compensation of nonlinear friction in servo systems. Syst. Eng. Electron. **24**(11), 45–52 (2002)
5. Yan, Y., Rui, L., Tingna, S., et al.: Friction compensation for permanent magnet synchronous motors based on adaptive back-stepping control. Proc. CSEE **33**(33), 76–84 (2013)
6. Zhang, W., Fang, Q.: Adaptive compensation for friction and force ripple in ship-borne gun servo system. In: The 7th World Congress on Intelligent Control and Automation. Chongqing, 25–27 June, pp. 3434–3438 (2008)
7. Zhang, W.: Parameter identification of LuGre friction model in servo system based on improved particle swarm optimization algorithm. In: Chinese Control Conference. Zhangjiajie, 26–31 July, pp. 135–139 (2007)
8. Yan, K., Liu, Y., Dong, Y.: Study on servo system based on model reference adaptive sliding mode control. Comput. Simul. **31**(9), 351–355 (2014)

Joint Power Allocation and Relay Grouping for Large MIMO Relay Network with Successive Relaying Protocol

Hong Peng, Changran Su, Yu Zhang[✉], Linjie Xie, and Weidang Lu

College of Information Engineering, Zhejiang University of Technology,
Hangzhou, China
{ph,yzhang,luweid}@zjut.edu.cn, schangran@163.com,
xielingjie@hotmail.com

Abstract. In this paper, we consider a large relay network with one base station (BS), multiple users and quantities of relays, where the BS and relays are equipped with multiple antennas. Firstly, we propose an amplify-and-forward (AF) transmission scheme with successive relaying protocol for the network. Then both relay grouping and power allocation over multiple data streams at the BS are jointly optimized to further improve the proposed scheme. Numerical results show that the achievable system spectrum efficiency is considerably improved by the proposed optimized relaying scheme.

Keywords: Successive relaying · MIMO · Power allocation · Relay grouping

1 Introduction

Large relay network receives considerable attentions, since the next generation network typically supports a large number of devices which can serve as relays to improve the achievable rate of the network. On the other hand, the technique of multiple-input multiple-output (MIMO) yields great improvements in spectral efficiency through spatial multiplexing, link reliability through space-time coding, and coverage [1, 2] through array gain. Precoding and power allocation over the data streams can further bring performance gain [3, 4].

In conventional relay networks, the source transmits the data frame in the first time slot and the relays forward in the second. It is proved the performance of such one way system with half-duplex protocol will suffer a multiplexing loss (1/2 rate-loss) [5]. Then a new protocol called successive relaying protocol is put forward, in which the relays are divided into two groups to in turns receive and forward the message. Results in [6, 7] have shown that successive relaying protocol performs well in recovering multiplexing loss, so that the achievable rate of network can be markedly improved, especially in large relay networks.

This paper considers a large one-way MIMO relay network in which a BS equipped with M antennas transits messages to M user terminals (each is equipped with single antenna) with the help of quantities of relays. We propose an AF based successive relaying protocol in which each multi-antenna relay is assigned to receive (through

© ICST Institute for Computer Sciences, Social Informatics and Telecommunications Engineering 2018
X. Gu et al. (Eds.): MLICOM 2017, Part II, LNICST 227, pp. 273–282, 2018.
https://doi.org/10.1007/978-3-319-73447-7_31

matched filtering) and forward (through amplify-and-forward scheme) one of the M multiplexed data streams. Furthermore, we jointly consider the power allocation over the M multiplexed data streams at the BS as well as the relay grouping scheme. Numerical results show that the achievable rate of the network can be considerably improved by the proposed joint optimization scheme.

The remaining of this paper is organized as follows. In Sect. 2, we introduce the system model. In Sect. 3, we introduce the improved successive relaying protocol. In Sect. 4, we investigate the impact of joint optimization. Section 5 presents the numerical simulation. We conclude in Sect. 6.

2 System Model

As shown in Fig. 1, we consider a large relay network with one BS (base station), M users and quantities of relays (each equipped with N antennas) which are randomly distributed in a given area. We assume no direct links between BS and users due to long distances and obstacles. We pick K relays out to help transmission. We assume perfect local CSI for each relay and statistic global CSI for BS and each user terminal. Since the considered network consists of a large number of relays, it is very beneficial for the BS and users to avoid the acquisition of the global CSI. However, it's easy to get perfect CSI at each relay with training sequences. The BS which is equipped with M antennas first processes the M data streams with power allocation matrix **P** then transmits the data streams with the help of K relays to M user terminals with successive relaying protocol. The channel for each link experiences independent Rayleigh fading across each time slot.

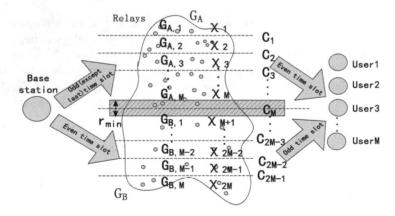

Fig. 1. Successive relaying protocol (when the order of group is in sequential order)

3 Relaying Protocol

As shown in Fig. 1, before transmission, we divide the domain into 2 * M areas denoted as χ_m (m = 1, 2 ,..., 2 * M). We denote C_m (m = 1, 2, ..., 2 * M−1) as the boundary line between area χ_m and area χ_{m+1} (note that χ_1 and χ_{2M} is bounded by the border of whole area). The relays in area χ_1 to χ_M forms G_A, while the relays in area χ_{M+1} to χ_{2M} forms G_B. We set a minimal distance r_{min} between χ_M and χ_{M+1} to avoid a large inter-relay-interference [7]. Then take G_A as an example, the relays in each area χ_m (m = 1, 2, ..., M) help one of the M users, which are denoted as group $G_{A,m}$ if they help the mth user. Note that Fig. 1 shows an example of sequential relay group order where the relays in χ_m and χ_{m+M} (m = 1, 2, ..., M) serve the mth user thus are denoted as $G_{A,m}$ and $G_{B,m}$ respectively. In fact, the boundary of each area and the order of relay groups affect the system performance and need optimization which will be discussed in Sect. 4.

3.1 Successive Relaying Protocol

We assume that a total of $L - 1$ sub-frames are transmitted within L (an odd L is assumed) time slots as a transmission round. Relays in G_A and G_B in turns receive and forward sub-frame from the BS.

As shown in Fig. 1, in the first time slot, the BS carries out power allocation to the original data streams, and then transmits the processed sub-frame to the relays of G_A in the network. The relay k in G_A receives the signal:

$$\mathbf{r}_k^{(1)} = \mathbf{H}_k^{(1)}\mathbf{P}^{(1)}\mathbf{s}^{(1)} + \mathbf{\omega}_k^{(1)}, \ k \in G_A \tag{1}$$

where $\mathbf{s}^{(l)} = [s_1^{(l)} s_2^{(l)} \ldots s_M^{(l)}]^T$ ($\|\mathbf{s}^{(l)}\| = 1$) denotes the original data frame transmitted in l th time slot and $\mathbf{P} = [\mathbf{p}_1\ \mathbf{p}_2 \ldots \mathbf{p}_M]$ ($\mathbf{P}$ is a diagonal matrix) for the $M \times M$ power allocation matrix. Hence $\mathbf{Ps}$ is the transmitted signal from BS. $\mathbf{s}$ and $\mathbf{P}$ satisfies the restriction $\|\mathbf{Ps}\|^2 = P_S$, where P_S is the power constraint at BS. $\mathbf{H}_k^{(l)} = \left[\mathbf{h}_1^{(l)}\ \mathbf{h}_2^{(l)} \ldots \mathbf{h}_k^{(l)} \ldots \mathbf{h}_N^{(l)}\right]^T$ is the $N \times M$ channel coefficient matrix between BS to the relay k in group G_A and each element in $\mathbf{h}_k^{(l)}$ satisfies $CN(0, \theta_k)$ (complex Gaussian distributed i.i.d.). θ_k is the variance of the channel coefficient between BS and relay k which depends on pathloss. $\mathbf{\omega}_k$ is the additive white Gaussian noise (AWGN) sampled at relay k with unit variance.

In the second time slot and the following even time slots l (for $l = 2, 4, \ldots L - 1$) the relays in group G_A forward the received sub-frame to the user terminals. The i th user receives the signals from relays in group G_A:

$$y_i^{(l)} = \sum_{m=1}^{M} \sum_{k \in G_{A,m}} \mathbf{g}_{k,i}^{(l)^H} \mathbf{t}_{A,k}^{(l)} + \mathbf{\omega}_D^{(l)}, \quad i = 1, 2, \ldots, M \tag{2}$$

where $\mathbf{g}_{k,i}^{(l)}$ is the channel coefficient vector from relay k to the i th user, in which the element satisfies $CN(0, \beta_{k,i})$. $\beta_{k,i}$ is the variance of the channel coefficient between the i th user and relay k. $\mathbf{\omega}_D^{(l)}$ is AWGN sampled at i th user with unit variance in the l th time slot. $\mathbf{t}_{A,k}^{(l)}$ denotes the transmitted signal from relay k in group G_A in the l th time slot which satisfies $Ef\left\|\mathbf{t}_{A,k}^{(l)}\right\|^2 = \frac{P_R}{M_A}$, where P_R is the total transmission power constraint of all the relays. M_A denotes the number of relays in group G_A. The generation of $t_{A,k}^{(l)}$ will be discussed in Sect. 3.2.

Meanwhile, the BS transmits new sub-frame to relays in group G_B. The relay k' in group G_B receives:

$$\mathbf{r}_{k'}^{(l)} = \mathbf{H}_{k'}^{(l)} \mathbf{P}^{(l)} \mathbf{s}^{(l)} + \sum_{k \in G_A} \mathbf{F}_{k',k}^{(l)} \mathbf{t}_{A,k}^{(l)} + \boldsymbol{\omega}_{k'}^{(l)}, \quad k' \in G_B \tag{3}$$

where $\mathbf{F}_{k',k}^{(l)}$ denotes the $N \times N$ channel coefficients matrix from relay k' in group G_B to relay k in group G_A in the l th time slot, in which all the entries satisfy $CN(0, \eta_{k',k})$. $\eta_{k',k}$ denotes the variance of channel coefficient between relay k' in group G_B and relay k in group G_A.

In the third time slot and the following odd time slots (for $l = 1, 3, \ldots, L$), relays in group G_B transit signal to the i th user. Meanwhile relay k in group G_A receives the signal from the BS:

$$\mathbf{r}_{k}^{(l)} = \mathbf{H}_{k}^{(l)} \mathbf{P}^{(l)} \mathbf{s}^{(l)} + \sum_{k' \in G_B} \mathbf{F}_{k,k'}^{(l)} \mathbf{t}_{B,k'}^{(l)} + \boldsymbol{\omega}_{k}^{(l)}, \quad k \in G_A \tag{4}$$

where $\mathbf{t}_{B,k'}^{(l)}$ denotes the signal transmitted by relay k' in group G_B in the l th time slot. Meanwhile, The i th user receive the signals from relays in group G_B:

$$y_{i}^{(l)} = \sum_{m=1}^{M} \sum_{k \in G_{B,m}} \mathbf{g}_{k,i}^{(l)^H} \mathbf{t}_{B,k'}^{(l)} + \boldsymbol{\omega}_{D}^{(l)}, k' \in G_B, \; i = 1, 2, \ldots, M \tag{5}$$

In the last time slot L (recall that L is odd), relays in group G_A keep silent, meanwhile the relays in group G_B transmit signal to the user terminals, the situation is similar to (5).

3.2 Amplify-and Forward After Matched Filtering

Recall that we assign each relay groups to serve for one of M users. That's to say, relay group $G_{A,m}$ and relay group $G_{B,m}$ take responsibility to receive and forward the m th user's message. Without loss of generality, we consider relay k in group G_A serves for the n th user. All the relays receive signal with matched filtering. Take the l th (l is even and $l > 2$) time slot as example. According to (4), the relay k in group G_A processes the received signals as follows:

$$\begin{aligned}
\mathbf{t}_{A,k}^{(l)} &= \gamma_k^{(l)} \mathbf{g}_{k,n}^{(l)} \widetilde{\mathbf{h}}_{k,n}^{(l-1)^H} \mathbf{r}_{k}^{(l-1)} \\
&= \gamma_k^{(l)} \mathbf{g}_{k,n}^{(l)} \left(\left\| \widetilde{\mathbf{h}}_{k,n}^{(l-1)} \right\|^2 s_n^{(l-1)} + \sum_{j=1, j \neq n}^{M} \widetilde{\mathbf{h}}_{k,n}^{(l-1)^H} \widetilde{\mathbf{h}}_{k,j}^{(l-1)} s_j^{(l-1)} + \widetilde{\mathbf{h}}_{k,n}^{(l-1)^H} \boldsymbol{\omega}_k^{(l-1)} + \sum_{k' \in G_B} \widetilde{\mathbf{h}}_{k,n}^{(l-1)^H} \mathbf{F}_{k,k'}^{(l-1)} \mathbf{t}_{B,k}^{(l-1)} \right), k \in G_A
\end{aligned}$$

$$\tag{6}$$

where $\tilde{\mathbf{h}}_{k,n} = [\mathbf{h}_1 \mathbf{p}_n \; \mathbf{h}_2 \mathbf{p}_n \; \ldots \; \mathbf{h}_N \mathbf{p}_n]^T$ is equivalent channel coefficient matrix between the BS and relay k. The variance of each element in $\tilde{\mathbf{h}}_{k,n}$ denoted as $\alpha_{k,n}$. Thus we can derive that $\alpha_{k,n} = \mathbf{P}_{1,n}^2 \theta_k + \mathbf{P}_{2,n}^2 \theta_k + \ldots + \mathbf{P}_{Q,n}^2 \theta_k$. The amplifying coefficient $\gamma_k^{(l)}$ of relay k in group G_A can be calculated according to the relay power restriction $Ef \left\| \mathbf{t}_{A,k}^{(l)} \right\|^2 = \frac{\mathbf{P}_R}{M_A}$. The amplifying coefficient $\gamma_k^{(l)}$ in even time slot l is derived as:

$$\gamma_k^{(l)} = \sqrt{\frac{\frac{\mathbf{P}_R}{M_A}}{\frac{1}{M}P_s \sum_{k=1}^N \beta_{k,n} \sum_{k=1}^N 3\alpha_{k,n}^2 + \sum_{j=1,j\neq n}^M \frac{1}{M}P_s \sum_{k=1}^N \beta_{k,n} \sum_{k=1}^N \alpha_{k,n}\alpha_{k,j} + \sum_{k=1}^N \beta_{k,n} \sum_{k=1}^N \alpha_{k,n} + \frac{\mathbf{P}_R}{NM_B} \sum_{k=1}^N \beta_{k,n} \sum_{k=1}^N \alpha_{k,n} \sum_{k'\in G_B}^N \sum_{k=1}^N \eta_{k,k'}}}}, k \in G_A, l = 4, 6 \ldots, L-1 \tag{7}$$

The detailed calculation is similar to the work in [7], which is omitted here. Similarly we can derive the coefficient in the odd and second time slot. Substituting (6) into (2), the received sub-frame at the i th user is given by:

$$y_i^{(l)} = \underbrace{Ef\left(u_{m,k,i}^{(l-1)}\right)s_i^{(l-1)}}_{L_1} + \underbrace{\left(u_{m,k,i}^{(l-1)} - Ef\left(u_{m,k,i}^{(l-1)}\right)\right)s_i^{(l-1)}}_{L_{error}} + \underbrace{u_{m,k,j}^{(l-1)}s_j^{(l-1)}}_{L_2} + \underbrace{v_{m,k}^{(l-1)}\omega_k^{(l-1)}}_{L_3} + \underbrace{v_{m,k}^{(l-1)}\sum_{k'\in G_B}\mathbf{F}_{k,k'}^{(l-1)}\mathbf{t}_{B,k'}^{(l-1)}}_{L_4} + \omega_D^{(l)} \tag{8}$$

where the following notations are used:

$$u_{m,k,i}^{(l-1)} = \sum_{k\in G_{A,i}} \gamma_k^{(l)} \left\|\mathbf{g}_{k,i}^{(l)}\right\|^2 \left\|\tilde{\mathbf{h}}_{k,i}^{(l-1)}\right\|^2 + \sum_{m=1,m\neq i}^M \sum_{k\in G_{A,m}} \gamma_k^{(l)} \mathbf{g}_{k,i}^{(l)H} \mathbf{g}_{k,m}^{(l)} \tilde{\mathbf{h}}_{k,m}^{(l-1)H} \tilde{\mathbf{h}}_{k,i}^{(l-1)}$$

$$u_{m,k,j}^{(l-1)} = \sum_{j=1,j\neq i}^M \left(\sum_{k\in G_{A,i}} \gamma_k^{(l)} \left\|\mathbf{g}_{k,i}^{(l)}\right\|^2 \tilde{\mathbf{h}}_{k,i}^{(l-1)H} \tilde{\mathbf{h}}_{k,j}^{(l-1)} + \sum_{k\in G_{A,j}} \gamma_k^{(l)} \mathbf{g}_{k,i}^{(l)H} \mathbf{g}_{k,j}^{(l)} \left\|\tilde{\mathbf{h}}_{k,j}^{(l-1)}\right\|^2 + \sum_{m=1,m\neq i,j}^M \sum_{k\in G_{A,m}} \gamma_k^{(l)} \mathbf{g}_{k,i}^{(l)H} \mathbf{g}_{k,m}^{(l)} \tilde{\mathbf{h}}_{k,m}^{(l-1)H} \tilde{\mathbf{h}}_{k,j}^{(l-1)} \right)$$

$$v_{m,k}^{(l-1)} = \sum_{k\in G_{A,i}} \gamma_k^{(l)} \left\|\mathbf{g}_{k,i}^{(l)}\right\|^2 \tilde{\mathbf{h}}_{k,i}^{(l-1)H} + \sum_{m=1,m\neq i}^M \sum_{k\in G_{A,m}} \gamma_k^{(l)} \mathbf{g}_{k,i}^{(l)H} \mathbf{g}_{k,m}^{(l)} \tilde{\mathbf{h}}_{k,m}^{(l-1)H} \tag{9}$$

where L_1 is the desired data of the i th user, L_{error} is the interference caused by using the statistical channel information for signal detection and decoding. L_2 is the interference from the other sources and L_3 is the noise from the relays. L_4 is the interference from relay group G_B. It should be noted that in the second time slot, L_4 doesn't exist since relays in group G_B are silent in the first time slot.

Each user terminal applies coherent detection with the statistical channel information. The achievable capacity of the i th user in the even time slot is given by:

$$R_i^{(even)} = \log\left(1 + \frac{Ef|L_1|^2}{\sum_{n=2}^4 Ef|L_n|^2 + Ef|L_{error}|^2 + 1}\right), \quad l = 4, 6, \ldots, L-1 \tag{10}$$

where $Ef|L_n|^2$ (for n = 1, ..., 4) and $Ef|L_{error}|^2$ is calculated as follows:

$$Ef|L_1|^2 = \frac{P_S}{M}\left(\sum_{k\in G_{A,i}}\gamma_k^2\sum_{k=1}^N\beta_{k,i}^2\sum_{k=1}^N\alpha_{k,i}^2 + 2\sum_{k1,k2\in G_{A,i}}\gamma_k^2\sum_{k=1}^N\beta_{k1,i}\sum_{k=1}^N\alpha_{k1,i}\sum_{k=1}^N\beta_{k2,i}\sum_{k=1}^N\alpha_{k2,i}\right)$$

$$Ef|L_{error}|^2 = \frac{P_S}{M}\left(\sum_{k\in G_{A,i}}8\gamma_k^2\sum_{k=1}^N\beta_{k,i}^2\sum_{k=1}^N\alpha_{k,i}^2 + \sum_{m=1,m\neq i}^M\sum_{k\in G_{A,m}}\gamma_k^2\sum_{k=1}^N\beta_{k,i}\beta_{k,m}\sum_{k=1}^N\alpha_{k,i}\alpha_{k,m}\right)$$

$$Ef|L_2|^2 = \frac{P_S}{M}\sum_{j=1,j\neq i}^M\left(\sum_{m=1,m\neq i,j}^M\sum_{k\in G_{A,m}}\gamma_k^2\sum_{k=1}^N\beta_{k,i}\beta_{k,m}\sum_{k=1}^N\alpha_{k,m}\alpha_{k,j} + \sum_{k\in G_{A,i}}\gamma_k^2\sum_{k=1}^N3\beta_{k,i}^2\sum_{k=1}^N\alpha_{k,i}\alpha_{k,j}\right.$$

$$\left.+ \sum_{k\in G_{A,j}}\gamma_k^2\sum_{k=1}^N\beta_{k,i}\beta_{k,j}\sum_{k=1}^N3\alpha_{k,j}^2\right)$$

$$Ef|L_3|^2 = \sum_{m=1,m\neq i}^M\sum_{k\in G_{A,m}}\gamma_k^2\sum_{k=1}^N\beta_{k,i}\beta_{k,m}\sum_{k=1}^N\alpha_{k,m} + \sum_{k_k\in G_{A,i}}\gamma_k^2\sum_{k=1}^N\beta_{k,i}^2\sum_{k=1}^N\alpha_{k,i}$$

$$Ef|L_4|^2 = \sum_{k\in G_{A,i}}\gamma_k^2\frac{P_R}{NM_B}\sum_{k=1}^N3\beta_{k,i}^2\sum_{k=1}^N\alpha_{k,i}\sum_{k'\in G_B}\sum_{k'=1}^N\eta_{k,k'}$$

$$+ \sum_{m=1,m\neq i}^M\sum_{k\in G_{A,m}}\gamma_k^2\frac{P_R}{NM_B}\sum_{k=1}^N\beta_{k,i}\beta_{k,m}\sum_{k=1}^N\alpha_{k,m}\sum_{k'\in G_B}\sum_{k'=1}^N\eta_{k,k'} \tag{11}$$

The detailed calculation of $Ef|L_n|^2$ (for n = 1, ..., 5) and $Ef|L_{error}|^2$ is similar to [7]. Similarly we can derive the i th user's achievable rate in the second time slot and odd time slots denoted by $R_i^{(odd)}$ and $R_i^{(2)}$. The detailed expression is omitted here. We assume the channel varies in different time slot but the variance of channel coefficient is stable from time to time. Thus, we can derive the sum achievable rate of the network as follows:

$$R_{sum} = \frac{1}{L}\sum_{i=1}^M\left(\frac{L-1}{2}R_i^{(odd)} + \frac{L-3}{2}R_i^{(even)} + R_i^{(2)}\right) \tag{12}$$

4 Joint Optimization

In this section, we consider a joint optimization on power allocation matrix **P** and relay grouping to maximize the achievable sum rate of the network. Relay grouping includes the order of relay groups and the boundary line between different relay group (as shown in Fig. 1). The flowchart of the joint optimization is shown in Fig. 2. For the inner loop of the algorithm, for each fixed order of relay groups, we in turns optimize the power allocation matrix **P** and the boundary line with differential evolution scheme (DE). The inner loop stops when a pre-set iteration time is reached. Then for the outer loop, we exhaustively search any possible order of relay groups and do the joint optimization (i.e., the inner loop). The algorithm stops when all the orders of relay groups are traversed and the best one to maximize the achievable rate is chosen.

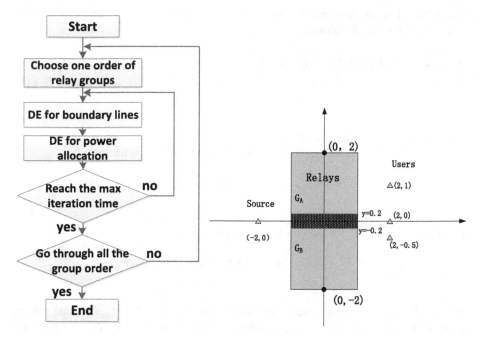

Fig. 2. Flowchart of joint optimization.   **Fig. 3.** The simulation scenario.

4.1 Optimization for the Order of Relay Groups

The order of relay groups affects the network rate by two factors: 1. inter-relay interference 2. large scale fading. We use exhaustive method to perform optimization on order of relay groups. We traverse all the relay group sort and then select the best one to maximize the achievable sum rate. Although exhaustive method can traverse all possible situations, the complexity of optimization will be quite high. One can design heuristic methods based on fairness principle to ensure that there is a balance between the interference and distance between the transmitter/user and the relay. We do not discuss heuristic methods here due to limited space.

4.2 Optimization for the Boundary Lines Between Relay Groups and Power Allocation

For the sake of simplicity, we denote the diagonal elements of power allocation matrix as $\tilde{\mathbf{P}} = \begin{bmatrix} P'_1, & P'_2, \ldots, P'_M \end{bmatrix}$ and the boundary line matrix as $[C_1, \ldots C_M, \ldots C_{2M-1}]$ (recall that C_m (m = 1, 2, ..., 2 * M−1) is the boundary line between area χ_m and area χ_{m+1}). The group model is shown in Fig. 1.

First we optimize the boundary line. We determine the max iteration number of optimization and generate D ($D = 20 * M$) initial solution candidates which meet the system constraints. We denote each solution candidate as $C_{i,G}$, where G is for the generation and i for the candidate number. The element in each candidate is defined as

$C_{j,i,G}$, where j is the element number. The first element in i th candidate in first generation is formed as follows:

$$C_{1,i,0} = rand(0,1) \cdot (C_j^{(U)} - C_j^{(L)}) + C_j^{(L)}, \quad (i = 1,2\ldots,D, j = 1,2,\ldots,2M-1)$$
(13)

where $C_j^{(U)}$ and $C_j^{(L)}$ represent the upper bound and the lower bound of boundary line.

Similarly we can get all the element in $C_{i,0}$ and then we can have all the candidate in first generation. Next we generate the mutation of the first generation by:

$$V_{i,G+1} = C_{r1,G} + F \cdot (C_{r2,G} - C_{r3,G})$$
(14)

where $r1$, $r2$, $r3$ is different to each other. $F = F_0 \cdot 2^\lambda$, $\lambda = e^{1-\frac{G_m}{G_m+1-G}}$, $F_0 \in (0,0.5)$. Then we get the crossover candidate $U_{i,G+1}$ by:

$$U_{ji,G+1} = \begin{cases} V_{ji,G+1} & \text{if rand}(0,1) \le 0.9 \text{ or } j = randperm(i) \\ C_{ji,G} & else \end{cases}$$
(15)

where randperm (i) denotes random number between 1 and 2M−1. The next step is selection. We generate the new generation by choose better candidate to max the achievable rate between $C_{ji,G}$ and $U_{ji,G+1}$:

$$C_{i,G+1} = \begin{cases} U_{i,G+1}, & \text{if } f(U_{i,G+1}) > f(C_{i,G}) \\ C_{i,G}, & else \end{cases}$$
(16)

If the round of iteration reaches the max times, the new generation will be regarded as the optimal boundary line and then the optimization on boundary comes to an end. Otherwise, the new solution will be taken as initial solution of the next generation and the optimization continues.

Power allocation is similar to the method of optimizing the relay boundary line.

5   Numerical Simulation

In this section, we examine the performance of the proposed AF successive relaying protocol. As for the simulation scenario, we consider the network depicted in Fig. 3, in which with a BS on (−2,0) and three user terminals (M = 3) on (2,1), (2,0) and (2, −0.5). K relays are randomly and independently distributed in a bounded domain. The domain is a rectangle region whose vertices are (1,2), (1,−2), (−1,2) and (−1−2). The minimal distance r_{min} is set to 0.2 and for DE, F = 0.5, $G_m = 5$. The variance of channel coefficient is denoted as $1/d^3$ where d is the distance between two nodes. The power constraints on BS and all the relays are set to 100 and 50, respectively. We examine the performances of joint optimization given in Sect. 4 when the relay antenna number is fixed to N = 8 in Fig. 4 (a) and the relay number is fixed to K = 800 in Fig. 4 (b), respectively.

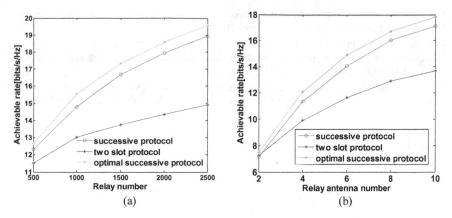

Fig. 4. Achievable sum rate over (a) different relay number; (b) different relay antenna number.

As shown in the two figures, we can see both the achievable rates with successive protocol and with two-slot protocol increase as the relay number and antenna number increase. It is observed that the rate with successive relaying protocol scales quickly than with two-slot protocol. And the performance of the successive relaying protocol is considerably improved due to the joint power allocation and relay grouping optimization.

6   Conclusion

This paper investigates the joint optimization on power allocation and relay grouping in relay network with successive relaying protocol. We consider a scenario where a base station transfers data to the user terminals through multiple relays. Each relay works in amplify-and-forward scheme. We find that the achievable rate of the system can be markedly improved by jointly optimizing the relay grouping and the power allocation matrix **P** with DE.

Acknowledgement. This work was supported by National Natural Science Foundation of China (No. 61401391) and Zhejiang Provincial Natural Science Foundation of China under Grant No. LY17F010014.

References

1. Chiurtu, N., Rimoldi, B., Telatar, E.: On the capacity of multi-antenna Gaussian channels. Eur. Trans. Telecommun. **10**(6), 585–595 (1999)
2. Bolcskei, H., Nabar, R.U., Oyman, O., Paulraj, A.J.: Capacity scaling laws in mimo relay networks. IEEE Trans. Wirel. Commun. **5**(6), 1433–1444 (2006)
3. Lozano, A., Tulino, A.M., Verdu, S.: Optimum power allocation for parallel Gaussian channels with arbitrary input distributions. IEEE Trans. Inf. Theory **52**(7), 3033–3051 (2006)

4. Vojcic, B.R., Jang, W.M.: Transmitter precoding in synchronous multiuser communications. IEEE Trans. Commun. **46**(10), 1346–1355 (1998)
5. Gastpar, M., Vetterli, M.: On the capacity of wireless networks: the relay case. In: Proceedings of Joint Conference of the IEEE Computer and Communications Societies, vol. 3, pp. 1577–1586 (2002)
6. Fan, Y., Wang, C., Thompson, J., et al.: Recovering multiplexing loss through successive relaying using repetition coding. IEEE Trans. Wirel. Commun. **6**(12), 4484–4493 (2007)
7. Zhang, Y., Zhang, Z., Ping, L., Chen, X.: Capacity scaling of relay networks with successive relaying. In: Proceedings of IEEE International Symposium on Information Theory, pp. 176–180 (2015)

The Second Round

Generation of Low Power SSIC Sequences

Bei Cao[1(✉)] and Yongsheng Wang[2]

[1] Electronic Engineering School,
Heilongjiang University, Harbin 150080, China
caobei@hlju.edu.cn
[2] Microelectronic Center, Harbin Institute of Technology, Harbin 150000, China

Abstract. Single input change (SIC) sequence for VLSI testing has been researched because of effectiveness to more test fault models and low power consumption testing. It is the high fault coverage in deterministic built-in self-test (BIST) with low test cost and short test application time. The sequential single input change (SSIC) sequence used in deterministic BIST is presented in this paper for decreasing the dynamic power, reducing test application time and increasing fault coverage. The selection of seed vectors is the significant technique in deterministic BIST. The critical features of SSIC sequence are proposed for selecting seed vectors. The SSIC sequence generator is designed. The simulation results using benchmark circuits show that the SSIC sequences can increase fault coverage and decrease application time than random SIC sequences. SSIC sequence also has low dynamic power consumption.

Keywords: Single input change sequence · BIST · Low power testing
Fault coverage

1 Introduction

BIST technique have been widely improved and applied to reduce the cost and to solve testing problems of complex chips. In BIST, the test methods frequently used are exhaustive testing, pseudorandom testing and deterministic testing. A great number of test vectors are generated to assure high testing fault coverage in the exhaustive and pseudorandom schemes. The patterns based on fault model are generated by automatic test pattern generation (ATPG) software in the deterministic BIST. The high fault coverage and optimized application times make it a more attractive testing strategy.

Test pattern generator (TPG) is a very important hardware in BIST. Some main design objectives should be satisfied, such as improving fault coverage, reducing test time, decreasing power consumption, and so on. The single stuck-at fault is the classic fault model in VLSI testing technique. At present, more defecting types would appear in advanced CMOS technology. And effective fault models and testing methods should be considered to avoid chip failure. The power consumption during the chip testing could be higher than that in normal model [1]. Chips under testing may be damaged because of high test power dissipation. Researching and designing to generate the test sequences with low power consumption, high fault coverage and low hardware cost has become a significant topic to VLSI testing.

© ICST Institute for Computer Sciences, Social Informatics and Telecommunications Engineering 2018
X. Gu et al. (Eds.): MLICOM 2017, Part II, LNICST 227, pp. 285–293, 2018.
https://doi.org/10.1007/978-3-319-73447-7_32

The SIC sequences are more effective than the multiple input change (MIC) sequences for some fault types, which is researched in depth and proved in the previous work [2, 3]. The SIC sequences can be used to meet the above testing objectives as an effective BIST scheme [2–7]. Research and application on SIC sequence has become an important topic [3–6]. The SIC sequence generator is significant design in BIST. Design criteria about the sequence generator is proposed by David, which must be satisfied to generate RSIC sequences [5]. SIC generator and seed generating algorithm were presented [6, 7]. Normally, RSIC TPG used in BIST mainly consists of two key parts, such as pseudorandom sequence source circuit and decoder circuit. Linear feedback shift register (LFSR) can generate pseudorandom sequences, which is used to control the variable bits in RSIC generator. RSIC sequences must have enough test length for achieving high fault coverage. How to select seed vectors is also a key technique [6].

SSIC sequence and its properties used in deterministic BIST are proposed to solve problems of RSIC in this paper. Applying the properties of SSIC sequences, a novel seed vector selection algorithm is proposed. The value in the input change bits is changed sequentially in the proposed SSIC sequence. The counter can be used as pseudorandom source circuit instead of the LFSR. The SSIC TPG is easier to implement with low hardware cost. The simulation results used benchmark circuits ISCAS'85 show that the proposed SSIC TPG and algorithm of seed vectors selection are effective than RSIC sequences. The SIC sequences can be used in low dynamic power testing because of low switching activity (SA).

2   Theory Research of SIC Sequence

2.1   Theories of SIC Sequence Generation

Normally, values in some bits are not the same between successive testing vectors, which are called as MIC sequence. Only one bit can be changed for successive test sequence pairs, named SIC test sequences. It is firstly defined as follows. Let S is a test sequence,

$$S = V(1)V(2)...V(i)...V(L) \tag{1}$$

n-bits and L successive test vector $V(i) = \{v_n \, v_{n-1}....v_1\}$ constitute sequences S. For any $i > 1$, $V(i)$ is not the same as $V(i-1)$ in only one bit. The current change bit and the previous change bit are not repeated in the sequence loop. The principle of SIC generation is shown as Fig. 1.

LFSR based on the primitive polynomial can generate M-sequences, which is used commonly as pseudo-random pattern source. The code transition circuit is another important component. At any time t, $R(t) = r_1(t) \, r_2(t)...r_m(t)$ as the m-bit binary code can be generated in LFSR. It is mapped to a decimal value $d(t)$, and $1 \leq d(t) \leq n$. The $R(t)$ is transformed to $d(t)$, which map the $d(t)$ bit in $V(t-1)$ as a changing bit. The value of $d(t)$ bit is transformed in the code transition circuit. The $V(t)$ of the SIC sequences can be obtained from SIC generator.

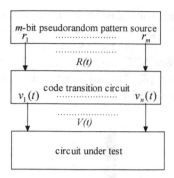

Fig. 1. Generation principle of SIC sequences.

The algebraic models of SIC sequences are shown as Eqs. (2)–(8). Initially, $R(t)$ is generated as a binary value in pseudorandom source circuit LFSR. The input changing bit $d(t)$ is a decimal value, which is converted from $R(t)$ using the code transition circuit.

$$R(t) = r_1(t)r_2(t)...r_m(t) \tag{2}$$

$$d(t) = \sum_{j=1}^{m} 2^{r_j(t)} \tag{3}$$

$$V(t) = v_n(t)v_{n-1}(t)....v_i(t)....v_1(t) \tag{4}$$

For example, if $d(t) = i$,

$$V(t+1) = v_n(t+1)....v_i(t+1)....v_1(t+1) = v_n(t)....\overline{v_i(t)}....v_1(t) \tag{5}$$

The above formula (2) and (5) are expressed as (6).

$$V(t+1) = V(t) \otimes 2^{d(t)-1} \tag{6}$$

The symbol "$\otimes$" is exclusive or operation. Using the above expressions, The SIC sequences can be generated if $V(0)$ is given as the seed vector. Obviously, the cycle is $2n$ for a SIC sequence set based an n-bits seed vector. The length of LFSR m can be determined from seed vector bits n, which is shown as (7) and (8).

$$2^m \geq n \tag{7}$$

$$m \geq \log_2 n = \lceil \log_2 n \rceil \tag{8}$$

Here, the symbol $\lceil x \rceil$ is ceiling function. Ceiling operation for x means that arbitrary real number x is the smallest integer, and not less than x. The SIC sequences can be described and generated using algebraic model (2)–(8).

The SA in the circuit under test can be reduced effectively using SIC sequences because only one value is changed between successive testing vectors. An experiment about the SA used benchmark circuits ISCAS'85 was performed. It is the comparison of power consumption between MIC sequences and SIC sequences. We obtained the MIC sequences using Atlantic [8]. The SA means the dynamic power consumption. The experimental results are shown as Fig. 2.

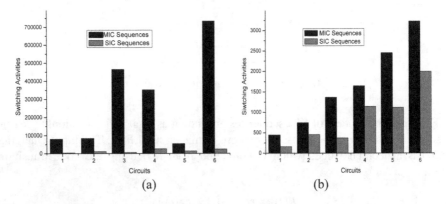

Fig. 2. Comparison of power total SA (a) and peak SA (b) for SIC and MIC sequences.

The SIC sequences are obtained according to the random seed vectors in the experiment. The amounts of SIC and MIC sequences are the same. The simulation results demonstrate that the SIC sequences can significantly reduce SA relative to the MIC sequences. It means the dynamic power consumption is decreased during test using SIC sequences. The X-axis refers to the experimental circuit. The Y-axis indicates the numbers of SA.

2.2   Research of SSIC Generation

The changing bit of SIC sequence is controlled by a pseudo-random source circuit. LFSR based the primitive polynomial is commonly used. The SIC test sequences are applied to deterministic BIST in this paper. The changing bits control is better suited to a counter instead. Here, the sequential single input change (SSIC) sequence is proposed. Suppose $V(0) = \{v_1\ v_2....v_i....v_n\}$ to be a SSIC vector, n represents the number of bits, where $v_i \in \{0, 1\}$. Each vector bit is inverted sequentially in the given n-bit test vector according to the clock. The SSIC vector is produced sequentially until the original seed vector appears. The definition and instance of SSIC sequence are shown in Fig. 3. The value in the first bit is active. Then the value of the second bit is changed at next clock, in turn. Obviously, only one bit is mapped and changed between the neighboring clocks. The $2n$ SSIC sequences are generated by a seed vector, which are referred to as segment, such as $S = \{v(1)...v(n), v(n+1),...v(2n)\}$. The clock cycle of each SSIC segment is $2n$, also be seen as a testing subset. The seed vectors are obtained using the proposed algorithm.

The size of segment will be $2n \times n$ if it is generated by an n-bit seed vector. SSIC segment can be partitioned into eight sub-segments in Fig. 3(b), which are signed respectively. S_i' and S_i'' are named neighboring sub-segment. A neighboring sub-segment

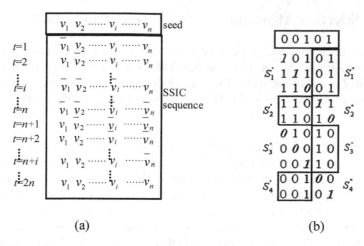

(a)   (b)

Fig. 3. Definition of the SSIC test sequence (a) and an instance of segment (b)

is considered as a subset of SSIC segment. The size of each sub-segment is (n/2) × (n/2) if n is even. The size of sub-segment has several cases while n is odd. Concretely, the size of sub-segment are $[(n + 1)/2) \times (n + 1)/2]$ for S_1' and S_3', $[(n - 1)/2) \times (n + 1)/2]$ for S_2' and S_4', $[(n + 1)/2) \times (n - 1)/2]$ for S_1'' and S_3'', $[(n - 1)/2) \times (n-1)/2]$ for S_2'' and S_4'', respectively. The parts are called head-segment if they include S_i'. Similarly, the parts including S_i'' are tail-segment. Both of head-segment and tail-segment are n in all. It is defined as a deterministic sub-segment if it has the same sub-vector in a sub-segment. Otherwise, it is named as transformable sub-segment. The deterministic sub-segments are S_1'', S_2', S_3'', S_4' in Fig. 3(b), respectively. The other sub-segments are transformable. Some properties of SSIC sequence are described as follows.

Property 1: SSIC segment $S = \{v(1)... v(n), v(n + 1), ... v(2n)\}$ generated by an n-bits seed vector, if $v(i)$ and $v(j)$ are complementary, here $i, j \in \{1, ...n, ...2n\}$, i is not equal to j, then $|i - j| = n$.

Property 2: Deterministic sub-segment S_1'' and S_3'', S_2'' and S_4' are complementary, respectively.

Property 3: Each vector can be considered two sub-vectors which belong to neighboring sub-segment. One sub-vector is in the deterministic sub-segment, and the other is in the transformable sub-segment.

Property 4: There is a changing bit between successive vectors in deterministic sub-segment or transformable sub-segment.

Property 5: The difference between successive vectors for SSIC sequence can be expressed. $|v(i) - v(i - 1)| = 2^{n-i}$ if $i \leq n$, and $|v(i) - v(i - 1)| = 2^{2n-i}$ if $n < i \leq 2n$.

The SSIC seed vectors can be obtained from ATPG deterministic test patterns according to seed selection algorithm based on the above definitions and properties. Corresponding SSIC generator can be designed easily.

3 Seed Selection Algorithm and SSIC Generator Design

The previous definitions and properties can be used in seed vectors selection based on correlative characteristic of the test sequence. The testing vectors are correlative if they have appeared in a SSIC segment. They can be defined isolated vectors if the vector is not correlative with any ones in ATPG deterministic test set. A weight value is defined based on correlative characteristic of vectors, which is used to select and optimize the seed vectors.

The proportion of don't care bits "X" in ATPG deterministic test sets are high. In most cases, the don't care bits may be able to exceed 90% [9]. How to map don't care bits is key technique instead of random filling. The number of seed vectors can be optimized if mapping in terms of primary vector is used. The each vector is regarded as a primary vector one by one. "X" of other vectors is substituted by the corresponding value according to the primary vector. The weight based correlative characteristic is calculated between the primary vectors and other ones after "X" filling. An anticipant weight value matrix of two-dimension is built to indicate the correlative characteristic among testing vectors.

The key to seed vectors selection algorithm is to build the anticipant weight value matrix. The SSIC properties are the principle of correlative characteristic in this paper. The anticipant weight value "$ANT_{i,j}$" is defined according to vector i and j:

$$ANT_{i,j} = \lambda * (c_i + c_j) \tag{9}$$

Here, λ is a precedence parameter of correlative characteristic. It has precedence when Property 1 is satisfied for both vector i and vector j. It is $\lambda > 1$, and $\lambda = 1$ for other correlative property. c_i and c_j denote that the numbers of vectors is same for their sub-segment. The more original vectors may be included into an SSIC segment if the high anticipant weight vector is selected as a seed vector. It is good to optimize the seed vectors. Algorithm of anticipant weight value matrix is shown as follows.

```
Algorithm 1: Anticipant Weight Value ANT()
    Initialize the parameter λ;
    Partition the front sub-segment and the tail sub-
    segment in terms of n;
    for (i=1 to m) //m is the number of ATPG sequences;
        Calculating cᵢ according to mapping principle of
        primary vector;
    end for
    for (i=1 to m-1)
        for (i=i+1 to m)
        Judging the correlative characteristic;
        Computing anticipant weight about i and j;
        end for
    end for
    Analysis and return solutions;
```

The pseudo-code of the SSIC seed vectors selection is depicted in Algorithm 2.

```
Algorithm 2: Seed Vectors Selection
   Loading the deterministic test sequence set;
   Initializing the sign variable flag;
   Partition the front sub-segment and the tail sub-
segment according to n;
   Calling function ANT();
   while flag=1
   The vector i and j are selected to constitute the
SSIC segment if ANT_{i,j} is high;
   The seed vector is determined according the current
SSIC segment;
   Deleting the vectors included in the current SSIC
segment from test sets;
   Mapping don't care bits in SSIC segment according to
corresponding vectors;
   Revising signs of anticipant weight value matrix and
original test sequences;
   Judging the variable flag;
      If flag=1; vectors are not treated; return and
continue to call ANT();
      Else continue to the next step;
      If there are isolated vectors, return and
continue to call ISO_V();
      Else end if;
   end while
   Calling function ISO_V( ); //optimize seed vector
for the isolated vectors;
   Statistic the seed vectors:
   Print the solutions;
```

There is no direct correlation characteristic between the isolated vectors and other vectors. And it may be treated as seed vector. Vector will be first selected as an initial vector if the proportion of don't care bits 'X' is low in this paper.

The hardware structure to generate SSIC sequences is similar to SIC generator. Two pseudorandom source circuits and code transition circuit are designed. However

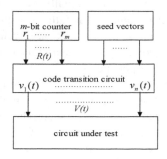

Fig. 4. Generator of SSIC sequences

an m-bit counter is used to generate changing bits. The counter is more suitable for generating SSIC than LFSR. The bits m of the counter can be computed according to n-bit value. It is shown as function (8) (Fig. 4).

4   Experimental Results and Conclusions

The simulations were performed to verify the proposed SSIC seed vector selection algorithm using benchmark circuits ISCAS'85. The algorithm is designed based on MATLAB. The deterministic test sequences are generated from the Atlantic ATPG [8].

The simulation results are obtained to generate the proposed SSIC sequences in Table 1. The number of input ports and seed vectors are shown in the second and third column respectively. The SA of SSIC sequences are given to analyze the dynamic power consumption. The total power and peak power based the SA are shown in the fourth and fifth columns respectively.

Table 1. Simulation results of SSIC test sequences generation

Benchmark circuits	Input (n)	Number of seeds	Switching activity for SSIC sequences	
			Total SA	Peak SA
c432	36	16	6750	89
c499	41	55	900	8
c1355	60	107	26218	47
c6288	41	49	580987	2492
c1908	33	136	469537	742
c3540	233	153	813214	1415
c5315	50	158	1795938	1763
c880	178	68	88478	301
c2670	32	119	631794	958
c7552	207	249	3643206	3063

The proposed scheme compared to the RSIC generation technique, which is 10-bit RSIC seed selection circuits in the Table 2 [6]. The test length represents the number of SIC vectors. These vectors are generated gradually by the seed vectors. Seed vectors play an important role in determining the length of testing. SFC means the single stuck-at fault coverage. The proposed SSIC sequences generation scheme can obtain high fault coverage. It is the advantage of deterministic BIST. The test length can reduce effectively for fewer input port numbers.

Low power testing in BIST is now becoming focus of both academic and industry communities. The novel SSIC test sequence is proposed in this paper. The algorithm of seed vector selection is presented using SSIC the correlative characteristic. As a result of SA, 80% of the total power consumption in the CMOS circuit is caused by SA. The SSIC test sequences can reduce effectively the SA and decrease test application time. Test costs have also been effectively reduced based on the deterministic BIST.

Table 2. Experimental results comparison

Benchmark circuits	Input (n)	Proposed		Reference [6]	
		Test length	SFC (%)	Test length	SFC (%)
c432	36	1152	99.24	9216	98.70
c499	41	4510	98.95	5248	99.50
c880	60	8160	100.00	15360	92.03
c1355	41	8774	99.49	10496	97.56
c1908	33	8976	99.52	8448	97.15
c2670	233	55454	95.74	28224	75.68
c3540	50	15300	96.00	12800	87.20
c5315	178	40448	98.90	23784	88.55
c6288	32	3136	99.56	8192	98.08
c7552	207	103086	98.27	52992	80.68

References

1. Zorian, Y.: A distributed BIST control scheme for complex VLSI devices. In: Proceedings of 11th IEEE VLSI Test Symposium, Los Alamitos, California, pp. 4–9 (1993)
2. Virazel, A., David, R., Girard, P., Landrault, C., Pravossoudovitch, S.: Delay fault testing: choosing between random SIC and random MIC test sequences. J. Electron. Test.: Theory App. **17**, 233–241 (2001)
3. Li, X., Cheung, Y.S.: High-level BIST synthesis for delay testing. In: International Symposium Defect and Fault Tolerance in VLSI Systems, pp. 2–4. November 1998
4. David, R., Girard, P., Landrault, C., Pravossoudovitch, S., Virazel, A.: On using efficient test sequence for BIST. In: Proceedings of the 20th IEEE VLSI Test Symposium, pp. 145–150 (2002)
5. David, R., Girard, P., Landrault, C., Pravossoudovitch, S., Virazel, A.: On hardware generation of random single input change test sequences. In: Proceedings of European Test Workshop, pp. 117–123 (2001)
6. Lei, S.C., Hou, X.Y., Shao, Z.B., Liang, F.: A class of SIC circuits: theory and application in BIST design. IEEE Trans. Circuits Syst.-II **55**, 161–165 (2008)
7. Voyiatzis, I., Haniotakis, T., Halatsis, C.: Algorithm for the generation of SIC pairs and its implementation in a BIST environment. IEE-Proc.-Circuits Devices Syst. **153**, 427–432 (2006)
8. Lee, H.K., Ha, D.S.: On the generation of test patterns for combinational circuits. Technical report, Department of Electrical Engineering, Virginia Polytechnic Institute and State University, pp. 12–93
9. Lee, J., Touba, N.A.: LFSR reseeding scheme achieving low power dissipation during test. IEEE Trans. Comput.-Aided Des. **26**, 396–401 (2007)

Intrusion Detection with Tree-Based Data Mining Classification Techniques by Using KDD

Mirza Khudadad[(✉)] and Zhiqiu Huang

College of Computer Science and Technology,
Nanjing University of Aeronautics and Astronautics,
Nanjing 210016, Jiangsu, China
mirza_khudadad@hotmail.com, zqhuang@nuaa.edu.cn

Abstract. In the recent time a huge number of public and commercial service is used through internet so that the vulnerabilities of current security systems have become the most important issue in the society and threats from hackers have also increased. Many researchers feel intrusion detection systems can be a fundamental line of defense. Intrusion Detection System (IDS) is used against network attacks for protecting computer networks. On another hand, data mining techniques can also contribute to intrusion detection. The intrusion detection has two fundamental classes, Anomaly based and Misuse based. One of the biggest problem with the anomaly base intrusion detection is detecting a high numbers of false alarms. In this paper a solution is provided to increase the attack recognition rate and a minimal false alarm generation is achieved with the study of different Tree-based data mining techniques. KDD cup dataset is used for research purpose by using WEKA tool.

Keywords: Data mining · Intrusion detection system · Decision Tree J48
Hoeffding Tree · Rep Tree · Random Forest · Random Tree · KDD dataset

1 Introduction

With the passage of time, internet security is gaining a huge importance in the recent times. Data security has been suffering from numerous groups of attacks which are emerging as hazardous for trust of user and organization's repute now. So it's a need of time to propose the most effective and accurate detecting model for network data protection. The intrusion detection (ID) on computer networks, is a form of security management systems and hence intrusion detection system is implemented for knowing about computer attacks by examining different logs and records of data. The key role of a network IDS is a passive as it only works by gathering, identifying, logging and alerting IDS systems. It uses different attempts to identify intrusions that misuses as well as abuses the computer network system by malicious users in addition with some IDS monitors only a single computer while others have ability to monitor several connected computers on a network. There are two types of attacks as network based and host based. In host based an attack attempts to access a restricted service or resource from a single computer. While network based attack restricts legitimate users

X. Gu et al. (Eds.): MLICOM 2017, Part II, LNICST 227, pp. 294–303, 2018.
https://doi.org/10.1007/978-3-319-73447-7_33

from accessing several services of network by capturing network resources and its services as this can be achieved by sending a large number of network traffics. In network based attack, network traffic detection can be analyzed from the intrusion encounter by leading to two subcategories of anomaly inquiry systems. The 1st one is described with specification and set of rules. The 2nd one is based on learning and training the normal behavioral system. So like IDS, it is usually used for rule base intrusion detection in which rules are written manually for identification of known attacks. Other type is behavior based IDS and the benefit of this approach is to identify attempts, to exploit new and unforeseen vulnerabilities. One of the major problems of anomaly based IDS is detection of high false alarm and here in this paper this issue is solved by applying the different data mining Tree based algorithms as well as by finding the most appropriate algorithm that could give the best results on comparing to other algorithms.

2 Literature Survey

Anderson (1980) [1], 1st time presented his ideas related to IDS in his technical report as he accomplished the computer audit transformable mechanism and became able to provide a list of risks and warnings for techniques of computer safety. This discovery provided analytical way of applicability on user's behavior for disclosing those intruders who had an illegal system access. Therefore, in 1987 Dorothy gave the paradigm on intrusion recognition as Denning and Neumann both were the starters of intrusion exploration domain. With this they found the framework of intrusion-detection expert system and that was called IDES (Intrusion Detection Expert System) [2] as it was originated in 1985's paper of requirements and model on IDES – a real-time intrusion detection system [3]. Hoge and Austin provided a detailed investigation on anomaly disclosure by the help of machine learning and numerical processes [4]. Both of them recommended a study of latest operations for exceptional detections. Moreover Markou and Singh [5] granted a wide range of inspections for intrusion detection by employing ANN as well as arithmetical structure. Patcha and Park [6] further extended the research of various anomaly techniques concerning cyber intrusion detection. A lot of books and research materials were again observed for intrusion and irregularities of observation (Hawkins 1980, Barnett, Lewis 1994, Bakar, et al.) [7–9] and various anomaly detection systems are like NIDES (Next generation Intrusion Detection Expert System) [10], ALAD (Application Layer Anomaly Detector) [11] and PHAD (Packet Header Anomaly Detector) [12] for generating mathematical proven shape to an ordinary network data flow with warning generation technique was discovered on finding deviation in a normal model. After all, many of them used network packet header's feature extraction as ALAD and NIDES used the source, TCP connection state, port address and destination IP.

Zhang et al. [13] showed network survey related to techniques and methods of anomaly detection. Peng et al. (2007) [14] made exhaustive survey of techniques for detecting DoS and distributed DoS attacks. Wu and Banzhaf [15] analyzed the main methods of CI, including soft computing, swarm intelligence, artificial immune systems, evolutionary computation, fuzzy systems along with artificial neural networks.

Dong et al. [15] conferred the mechanism in accordance to them and proved to be a more credible on its comparison to Markov and K. mean Graph-based Sequence Learning Algorithm (GSLA) included construction, normal profile data pre-processing in addition with session marking. Within GSLA, an average figure was created by a session-learning lineup and it was defined to determine an anomaly period. Udzir [16] invented a Signature-Based Anomaly Detection Scheme (SADS) that could be enforced to study packet header behavior patterns with more precisely and promptly. Integrating data mining classifiers such as Naive Bayes and Random Forest could also be utilized in decreasing fake bugs for shortening the time of processing too. As a part of analysts likewise preferred the concept, selection of features to recognize intrusion. Liu et al. [17] described feature selection as a useful way for dimension downsizing injunction with a compulsory step in effectual data mining applications and its direct advantages include: sample building with better clear models, making data mining efficient and helping in preparing clear understandable data. Harbola [18] also used featured adoption procedure to advance accuracy. Its main aim was to deliver the broad conclusion of feature selection design for NSL-KDD intrusion identification dataset.

3   Intrusion Detection System

Intrusion can be said as an illegal attempt to get access to any network or system. The system regarding intrusion detection is developed to expose this kind of mistrustful activity on a network or device. The IDS examines hardware, software or a union of both to check the network flow for the hunt of intrusions. An intrusion detection system (IDS) reviews entire out going, in coming network activity and identifies doubtful patterns.

3.1   Type of IDS

Intrusion detection system can also be subcategorized under two main divisions as Host-based Intrusion Detection System (HIDS) and Network-based Intrusion Detection System (NIDS).

3.1.1   Host-Based Intrusion Detection System

Host based intrusion detection (HIDS) defines the detection of intrusion which happens to a single host system. It is an application of a software which is installed on a system for the sake of its protection against intruders. HIDS is an operating system dependent so need some prior outlining ahead of its execution by having a capability of buffer overflow for attack's examination.

3.1.2   Network-Based Intrusion Detection System

Thus, network-based intrusion detection system (NIDS) has concern with network traffic control to secure a system from threats from network-based intrusion. All inbound packets and searches for any suspicious patterns are processed by NIDS. It is operating system independent and it appoints advanced protection to deal with denial of service (DoS) attacks.

3.2   Type of Attacks Detected by IDS

Four categories of IDS detected attacks (Table 1).

Table 1. IDS Detected Attacks

Denial of Service (DoS): Attack or an attempt which makes a network resource inaccessible to its expected legal users such as services suspension of a host connected to the internet
User to Root (U2R): Attack where an attacker attempts to get an unauthorized access of a targeted system
Remote to User Attack (R2L): Where an attacker tries to control a remote machine by guessing its password
Probing Attack (Probe): Where an attacker examines the machine to get useful information

4   KddCup'99 Dataset

For research objective the standard sets of data were published in KDD CUP 1999 [19]. IDS used it to assess various feature selection methods. This set of data has 41 features and 42nd feature shows the connection as 'Normal' or an attack nature. Here 4 main forms (DoS, Probe, R2L and U2R) cover this set of data which has altogether 24 kinds of attacks that have already been discussed.

Most of the datasets were repeated out of 5 million instances as just 10% KddCup'99 dataset was tried for training and verification of a suggested framework. There were 494021 instances in 10% of KddCup'99 dataset so 396743 instances were assumed to be in any one type of attack and remaining 97278 instances were declared as 'Normal' instances.

4.1   Preprocessing

In recommended model to reduce the performance evaluation complexity of 42nd feature of KddCup'99 dataset is defined in five leading sections in the pre-processing class labelled module. These labels i.e. DoS, Probe, R2L, U2R and Normal are considered as five subclasses which are formed in an action of pre-processing.

4.2   Splitting into Test and Train Dataset

The training and testing sets are two autonomous sets of the given data so testing set contains 44% of the dataset and other 66% of the data is assigned to training set. The derived model of accuracy is determined by the testing set as advised framework is concluded by the training set. After dividing it into two sets training set has 326054 instances and testing sets have 167967 instances.

4.3   Four Distinct Types of Attacks Used in Experimental Dataset

Categories of Attacks & Associated Tags (Table 2).

Table 2. Attack Categories & Associated Tags

Type	Attacks
DoS	udpstorm, teardrop, smurf, processtable, pod, neptune, mailbomb, land, back, apache
PROBE	satan, saint, portsweep, nmap, mscan, ipsweep
U2R	xterm, sqlattack, ps, rootkit, perl, loadmodule, buffer_overflow
R2L	multihop, imap, guess_password, ftp_write

Samples of KDD'99 Intrusion Detection Datasets (Table 3).

Table 3. Intrusion Detection Datasets Samples

Type	Train	Test
DoS	391458	229853
PROBE	4107	4166
U2R	1126	16347
R2L	52	70
NORMAL	97278	60591

5 Results and Experiment

We performed the experiment with KDD cup dataset by using 10% [20] train and test dataset (using WEKA).

5.1 Experiment Setup

Experiment performed under following hardware and software.

- Hardware: Intel core i5, 1.8 GHz processor with 4 GB Ram.
- Software: Microsoft Windows 10, WEKA 3.7.

5.2 Using Train Dataset

Experiment performed under the above mentioned hardware and software system specifications (Tables 4, 5, 6 and 7).

Table 4. Classifiers & Instances using Train Dataset

Classifiers	Classified Instances	
	Correctly	Incorrectly
Hoeffding Tree	99.472	0.527
J48	99.963	0.036
Random Forest	**99.983**	**0.017**
Random Tree	99.963	0.036
RepTree	99.950	0.496

Table 5. Classifiers & DoS, PROBE Class Attacks using Train Dataset

Classifiers	DoS		PROBE	
	Correct	False +V	Correct	False +V
Hoeffding Tree	390637	821	2987	1120
J48	391435	23	4076	31
Random Forest	**391455**	**3**	**4079**	**26**
Random Tree	391442	16	4071	36
Rep Tree	391420	38	4012	95

Table 6. Classifiers & R2L, U2R Class Attacks using Train Dataset

Classifiers	R2L		U2R	
	Correct	False +V	Correct	False +V
Hoeffding Tree	711	415	13	39
J48	1076	50	25	27
Random Forest	**1105**	**21**	**36**	**16**
Random Tree	1091	35	36	16
Rep Tree	1099	27	25	48

Table 7. Classifiers & Normal Class Attacks using Train Dataset

Classifiers	Normal	
	Correct	False +V
Hoeffding Tree	97069	209
J48	97229	39
Random Forest	**97262**	**16**
Random Tree	97202	76
Rep Tree	97220	58

5.3   Using Test Dataset

See Tables 8, 9, 10, and 11.

Table 8. Classifiers & Instances using Test Dataset

Classifiers	Classified Instances	
	Correctly	Incorrectly
Hoeffding Tree	97.0501	2.9499
J48	98.0416	1.9584
Random Forest	**98.0818**	**1.9182**
Random Tree	98.0371	1.9629
RepTree	98.0262	1.9738

Table 9. Classifiers & DoS, PROBE Class Attacks using Test Dataset

Classifiers	DoS		PROBE	
	Correct	False +V	Correct	False +V
Hoeffding Tree	229407	446	3792	374
J48	229825	28	4098	68
Random Forest	**229835**	**18**	**4122**	**44**
Random Tree	229823	30	4099	67
Rep Tree	229817	36	4071	95

Table 10. Classifiers & R2L, U2R Class Attacks using Test Dataset

Classifiers	R2L		U2R	
	Correct	False +V	Correct	False +V
Hoeffding Tree	12923	3424	52	18
J48	13518	2829	32	38
Random Forest	**13553**	**2794**	**52**	**18**
Random Tree	13540	2807	49	21
Rep Tree	13458	2889	50	20

Table 11. Classifiers & Normal Class Attacks using Test Dataset

Classifiers	Normal	
	Correct	False +V
Hoeffding Tree	55678	4913
J48	57463	3128
Random Forest	**57499**	**3092**
Random Tree	57411	3180
Rep Tree	57492	3099

6   Result and Analysis

Percentage of results using Test Set.

The above table shows the results of test dataset that proves J48 classifier performs well in U2R, R2L and Normal categories (Fig. 1). In DoS and PROBE, Random Forest (RF) has a minor difference (Table 12).

Percentage of result using Train set.

In the above table it is analyzed that more than 90% attack detection is done by all classifiers in DoS, PORBE as well as in R2L but the Normal category has more than 99% of attack detection results as only in U2R attack its ratio is less than 75% and it's just because of having fewer attacks in training dataset (Fig 2). By comparing to other classifiers it is proven Random Forest performs slightly better in DoS, U2R, R2L but J48 works better only in PROBE (Table 13).

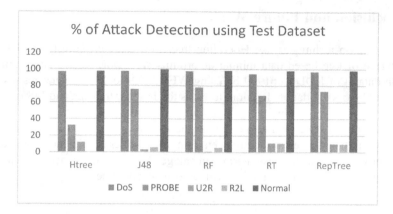

Fig. 1. Attack Detection Analysis with Test Dataset

Table 12. % of Results using Test Set

	DoS	PROBE	U2R	R2L	Normal
Htree	96.67048	32.35717715	11.84210526	0.012354	97.2884657
J48	97.31785	75.42006721	3.070175439	5.843474	99.485089
RF	**97.42401**	**77.98847816**	0.877192982	5.49756	98.3034344
RT	94.3342	68.45895343	10.96491228	10.71098	98.3298401
RepTree	96.97676	73.45175228	10.0877193	9.691766	98.2456719

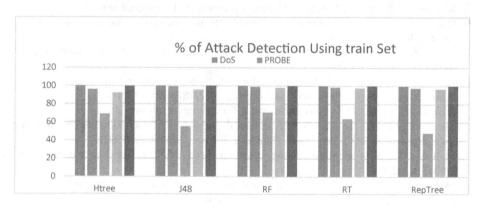

Fig. 2. Attack Detection Analysis with Train Dataset

Table 13. % of Results using Train Set

	DoS	PROBE	U2R	R2L	Normal
Htree	99.97140515	96.03117	68.9655172	92.26667	99.66706
J48	99.99493896	99.36693	55.1724138	95.82222	99.96172
RF	**99.9994939**	99.0017	**70.6896552**	**98.04444**	**99.97685**
RT	99.9936737	98.56343	63.7931034	97.77778	99.93412
RepTree	99.99114319	97.68688	48.2758621	96.88889	99.95638

7 Conclusion and Future Work

The classification techniques like Hoeffding tree, J48, Random Forest, Random Tree and RepTree of tree based data mining algorithms were practiced to study intrusion detection dataset of KDD Cup1999 by using WEKA 3.9 tool. In general results show using 10 fold cross validation, Random forest is the best for train set and J48 is the best for test dataset by considering their comparative classification accuracy.

Achieving high detection rate along with the lowest false alarm ratio is the biggest challenge to intrusion detection so not even a single classifier is efficient enough to give high veracity of decreasing false alarm percentage. Finally, to improve overall attack detection performance two or more classifiers can be combined.

References

1. https://www.sans.org/reading-room/whitepapers/detection/history-evolution-intrusion-detection344
2. Denning, D.E.: An intrusion-detection model. IEEE Trans. Softw. Eng. **SE-13**(2), 222–232 (1987)
3. Denning, D.E., Neumann, P.E.: Requirements and model for IDES-A real-time intrusion detection system. Technical report, Computer Science Laboratory, SRI International, Menlo Park, CA, USA (1985)
4. Hodge, V.J., Austin, J.: A survey of outlier detection methodologies. J. Artif. Intell. Rev. **22**, 85–126 (2004)
5. Markou, M., Singh, S.: Novelty detection: a review-part 1: statistical approaches
6. Patcha, A., Park, J.: An overview of anomaly detection techniques. Existing solutions and latest technological trends
7. Bakar, Z., Mohemad, R., Ahmad, A., Deris, M.: A comparative study for outlier detection techniques in data mining
8. Hawkins, D.: Identification of Outliers. Monographs on Applied Probability and Statistics. Springer, Heidelberg (1980). https://doi.org/10.1007/978-94-015-3994-4
9. Barnett, V., Lewis, T.: Outliers in Statistical Data. Wiley, Hoboken (1994)
10. Javits, H., Valdes, A.: "The NIDES statistical component" Description and justification. Technical report, SRI International, Computer Science Laboratory (1993)
11. Mahoney, M.: Network traffic anomaly detection based on packet bytes. In: Proceedings of ACMSAC (2003)
12. Mahoney, M., Chan, P.K.: Learning non stationary models of normal network traffic for detecting novel attacks. In: Proceedings of SIGKDD (2002)
13. Zhang, W., Yang, Q., Geng, Y.: A survey of anomaly detection methods in networks. In: Proceedings of International Symposium on Computer Network and Multimedia Technology, pp. 1–3, January 2009
14. Wu, S.X., Banzhaf, W.: The use of computational intelligence in intrusion detection systems: a review (2010)
15. Dong, Y., Hsu, S., Rajput, S., Wu, B.: Experimental analysis of application level intrusion detection algorithms. Int. J. Secur. Netw. **5**, 198–205 (2010)
16. Yassin, W., Udzir, N., Abdullah, A.: Signature-based anomaly intrusion detection using integrated data mining classifiers. In: International Symposium on Biometrics and Security Technologies (ISBAST) (2014)

17. Liu, H., Motoda, H., Setiono, R.: Feature selection: an ever evolving frontier in data mining (2010)
18. Harbola, A., Harbola, J.: Improved intrusion detection in DDOS applying feature selection using rank & score of attributes in KDD-99 data set (2014)
19. Tavallaee, M., Baghe, E.: A detailed analysis of the KDD cup 99 data set (2009)
20. http://kdd.ics.uci.edu/databases/kddcup99/kddcup99.html2

Night Time Image Enhancement by Improved Nonlinear Model

Yao Zhang, Chenxu Wang[✉], Xinsheng Wang, Jing Wang,
and Le Man

Information and Electrical Engineering School,
Harbin Institute of Technology, Harbin, China
{yzhang, xswang}@hit.edu.cn,
{wangchenxu, express}@hitwh.edu.cn,
dolphinmanle@hotmail.com

Abstract. Low light or poor shooting angle and other issues often make the camera to take night time images and affect the naked-eye observation or computer identification, so it is important to enhance the lightness of night time image. Although the existing non-linear luminance enhancement method can improve the brightness of the low light area, the excessive promotion led to high light area distortion. Based on the existing image luminance processing algorithm, we proposed an adaptive night time image improving method in the basis of nonlinear brightness enhancement model is proposed to process the segmentations of image brightness by using the logarithmic function. The segmentation threshold is determined by the Otsu, and the adjustment factor of the backlight region in the transfer function is calculated from the area ratio of the backlight area. The conclusion comes from the simulation. The method involves improving the image quality and ensuring that the entire picture is natural without distortion. In the meanwhile, the processing speed is not much slower compared with the existing processing algorithms.

Keywords: Night time images · Brightness · Adaptive Nonlinearity Model
Otsu Threshold

1 Introduction

The camera adjusts the degree of sensitivity through the sensor chip. Therefore, when the camera lens is shooting in front of the light source, the sensor chip to detect the subject of the reflected light is weak and its sensitive to the surrounding light source reflects the light is strong. After imaging, the main body of the image brightness is low and the same as ambient brightness under the night condition. It is difficult to obtain the effective information from the picture and affect the extraction of information. The four pictures in Fig. 1 are photographed in the night low light environment. There is a significant darkness in brightness in the picture. The main area brightness is too low to affect identification of the details information. Therefore, it is necessary to restore the night image.

The enhancement of night images should be conducive to visual observation and accurate identification of the computer. We need to enhance the brightness of the

© ICST Institute for Computer Sciences, Social Informatics and Telecommunications Engineering 2018
X. Gu et al. (Eds.): MLICOM 2017, Part II, LNICST 227, pp. 304–315, 2018.
https://doi.org/10.1007/978-3-319-73447-7_34

(a) night school yard image   (b) night road image

(c) night building image   (d) night people image

Fig. 1. Low light night-time image

low-light area of the night image and try to keep the brightness of the high-brightness area unchanged. The picture should not be distorted after restoration.

In the image processing area, many researchers have been explored the methods to change the image brightness. In [4], the traffic image is adjusted according to the time variation, which is convenient for vehicle detection and license plate recognition. In [5], the relationship between the histogram and the brightness is explored and it is found that the histogram of the image brightness suitable for human eye observation should be evenly distributed. In [6], brightness adjustment is achieved from the histogram of the equalization. In [7, 8], the image is adjusted by brightness and wavelet transformation. The brightness of the original image is changed by the wavelet transformation so that to improve the readability of the image. In [9], the color image is enhanced by the non-linear Retinex illumination reflection model, which improves the local contrast of the image. In [10], a method of uneven brightness images based on theory of homomorphic filtering is proposed. This method suppresses the low frequency component and enhances the high frequency component. In [11], the brightness of the backlit image is segmented linearly processed, and it is proved that the brightness processed in the HSI space is more effective than in the histogram equalization method, the homomorphic filtering and the retinex theory. In [12], using the logarithmic function in the HSI space model to adjust the brightness of the image, which improves the image quality. In [13], utilize the adaptive Gamma Correction model is used to adjust the image brightness in the HSI space model to improve the contrast. In [14], the power function of different parameters is used to adjust the brightness in the HSI space model to improve the influence of illumination unevenness on the image information acquisition.

Generally speaking, the enhancement of night images should be conducive to the rapid observation of the naked eye and the computer. Based on the literature [11–14], we choose to process the brightness in the spatial domain.

2 Prior Adjustment Model

The color of image pixels can be represented by a vector in the RGB color space, as shown in Fig. 2(a), it can also be represented by a vector in the HSI color space, as shown in Fig. 2(b). In the HSI color space, H represents the hue, S is saturation and I means the intensity. The night time condition is strongly affect the brightness of the image, while smaller influence on the shade of the image. At the same time, the luminance component we has nothing to do with the color information of the image and can be dealt with individually in the HSI model, so we choose to process the image in the HSI model.

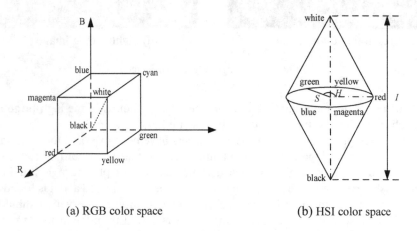

(a) RGB color space   (b) HSI color space

Fig. 2. Color space representation

The formula for converting each pixel color from RGB to HSI model in the image is:

$$H = \begin{cases} \theta & B \leq G \\ 360 - \theta & B > G \end{cases} \tag{1}$$

$$S = 1 - \frac{3}{(R+G+B)}[\min(R, G, B)] \tag{2}$$

$$I = \frac{1}{3}(R+G+B) \tag{3}$$

Hypothesis that the values of R, G, and B are normalized to the interval [0, 1], then the values of S and I are [0, 1], the value of H is [0, 360], and the values of θ are:

$$\theta = \arccos \frac{\frac{1}{2}[(R-G)+(R-B)]}{[(R-G)^2 + (R-B)(G-B)]^{1/2}} \qquad (4)$$

The transformation makes the luminance component, we can be carried out separately in the subsequent algorithm processing, which greatly simplifies the computation. In the low light image, assume that the luminance of the pixel normalized at the coordinates (x, y) is $f_n(x, y)$, and the adjusted luminance is $g_n(x, y)$. The values of $f_n(x, y)$, $g_n(x, y)$ are [0, 1] (the larger the value represents the higher the brightness). The low light recovery process can be regarded as passing the normalized image luminance $f_n(x, y)$ through a transformation function T_r, which is:

$$g_n(x, y) = Tr[f_n(x, y)] \qquad (5)$$

In order to facilitate the narrative, in the night image that needs to be enhanced, we refer to the region with low brightness under the low light condition, which is called the dark region, and the region with high brightness under the condition of strong light source is called well-light region. To restore the night image, the brightness of the dark area needs to be increased and the brightness of the original well-light area stays stable.

2.1 Piecewise Linear Regulation

The relationship between the brightness of piecewise linear adjustment is:

$$g(x, y) = \begin{cases} k_1 \times f_n(x, y) + b_1 & f_n(x, y) \leq \tau \\ k_2 \times f_n(x, y) + b_2 & f_n(x, y) > \tau \end{cases} \qquad (6)$$

Result of brightness adjustment can be changed by modified values of k_1, k_2, b_1, b_2 and τ in the equation. When $k_1 = 8/3$, $k_2 = 2/7$, $b_1 = 0$, $b_2 = 5/7$, $\tau = 0.3$, the recovery results are shown in the following figure.

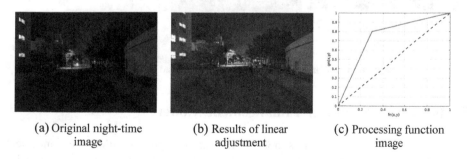

| (a) Original night-time image | (b) Results of linear adjustment | (c) Processing function image |

Fig. 3. Comparison of piecewise linear adjustment results

It can be concluded from Fig. 3 that the segmented model improves the dark portion, but the processing is ineffective and the distortion of the junction is present. Distortion is caused by the non-smoothness of the function segment. If you want to get better processing in the dark part, the brightness of non-backlight part will rise rapidly, it will also cause distortion. It is clear that the processing of the night image by the piecewise linear model does not fully meet the demand of people.

2.2   Logarithmic Regulation

Literature [12, 14] adopted logarithmic function and power functions with different parameters to adjust brightness. Based on the requirements for backlighting image brightness processing, the logarithmic function [12] is used to improve the adjustment to the high-brightness area, the equation is:

$$g_n(x, y) = C \times \log_2[D \times f_n(x, y) + 1] \tag{7}$$

Taking D as the adjustment coefficient, it is used to change the brightness of transformation function to improve performance. The value of C is as follows:

$$C = \frac{1}{\log_2(D + 1)} \tag{8}$$

Choosing D = 20, the result of backlight processing on Fig. 1(a) is shown in Fig. 4. Even though this result is much better than the one of linear regulation, there are still distortion existed in high-brightness area.

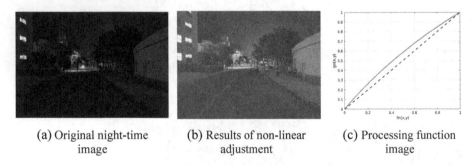

| (a) Original night-time image | (b) Results of non-linear adjustment | (c) Processing function image |

Fig. 4. Comparison of piecewise non-linear adjustment results

3   Improved Nonlinear Enhancement Model

Processing of well-light area is not ideal, even though logarithmic enhancement adjustment model can improve dark area well. So we proposed an adaptively piecewise method by power function, instead of logarithmic function, which would adjust brightness of dark area rapidly and slowly in well-light area. Adjustment formula is,

$$g_n(x, y) = C_i \cdot f_n(x, y)^{\frac{1}{a}} \qquad (9)$$

where, a is a constant.

Night time image has very low light in dark place, after transfer to gray image, the luminance of most pixel centered on 0–30. According to Fig. 5, Power function can rise the brightness rapidly in low light area than other function. Inversely, in well-luminance area, adjustment function should be serial and convergent gradually, then selected apposite adjustment coefficient to improve brightness.

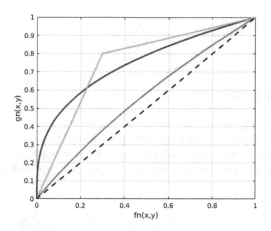

Fig. 5. Three adjustment functions. The blue is power function, the red is logarithmic function and the green is piecewise linear function. It shows the gradient of power function is the largest when $f_n(x,y)$ range from 0 to 0.2, and rises slowly during 0.3 to 1.0. (Color figure online)

3.1   Threshold Selection

We divide the luminance in two parts, threshold T belongs 0 to 1, and define that $f_n(x, y) \leq$ T is low light area, and $f_n(x, y) \geq$ T is high light area. The Selection of T can distinguish the low light area and high light area effectively. So we decided computing T by Otsu Threshold Algorithm, steps as follows: Setting night time image has M × N pixels, {0, 1/L, 2/L, ..., (L − 1)/L} means that levels of luminance are L, n_i represents the number of pixels in i lightness, therefore title pixel numbers of night time image is MN = $n_0 + n_1 + ... + n_{L-1}$. Hypothesis threshold T (0 < T < (L − 1)/ L) classifies lightness of image into two parts, low luminance area C_1 and high luminance area C_2, $p_i = n_i/MN$ is the percentage of pixels with lightness level i. Then threshold T can get the maximum of σ_B^2, which is the variance in different parts.

$$\sigma_B^2(T) = \frac{[m_I P_1(T) - m(T)]^2}{P_1(T)[1 - P_1(T)]} \qquad (10)$$

In (10), $P_1(T)$ is the probability that pixels can be divided into C_1, $m(T)$ represents accumulative mean value to level T, m_I means the average luminance of the whole image.

$$P_1(T) = \sum_{i=0}^{T} p_i \tag{11}$$

$$m(T) = \sum_{i=0}^{T} ip_i \tag{12}$$

$$m_I = \sum_{i=0}^{L-1} ip_i \tag{13}$$

3.2   Coefficient Selection

When adjustment by logarithmic function, it just partly be enhanced if D is appointed a random positive constant, and not effective to the image take by dark place. There is still a large space for lightness improving unexpected, when $f_n(x, y)$ is larger. So we proposed a new piecewise function based on nonlinear power function. $g_n(x, y)$ is defined as:

$$g_n(x,y) = \begin{cases} C_1 \times f_n(x,y)^{\frac{1}{D_1}} & 0 \leq f_n(x,y) \leq T \\ C_2 \times f_n(x,y)^{\frac{1}{D_2}} + A & T \leq f_n(x,y) \leq 1 \end{cases} \tag{14}$$

$$C_i = \begin{cases} 1 & i = 1 \\ 1 - A & i = 2 \end{cases} \tag{15}$$

There, threshold T will be achieved by computing Ostus threshold segment method. D_i is the adjustment coefficient in i section (i = 1, 2). When $f_n(x,y) \leq T$, select D_1 as adjustment coefficient; $f_n(x,y) \leq T$, D_2 is better. We expected an adjustment coefficient that D_i is a serial function of $f_n(x, y)$, if $f_n(x,y) \leq T$, D_1 is large; if $f_n(x,y) \leq T$, D_2 will be smaller gradually, and the transfer function will converge to $g_n(x, y) = f_n(x, y)$. In other words, high light area would keep its luminance or be improved little. Follow the requirements, formula of D_i is:

$$D_i = \begin{cases} C \times A & f_n(x,y) \leq T \\ \frac{1}{\lg_T[(C_1 T^{(1/CA)} - A)/C_2]} & f_n(x,y) \geq T \end{cases} \tag{16}$$

A is a positive real, when A is larger, the luminance of $f_n(x,y) \leq T$ improved higher. According to experiments, A is not the larger the better. If it's too large, will result in the lightness of low light area improved excessively and artifacts. We hope that when the area of low light region bigger than high light, the luminance of

$f_n(x, y) \leq T$ rises more; the area of low light region smaller than high light, the luminance of $f_n(x, y) \leq T$ rises little. So we select A as:

$$A = k \times \sqrt{\frac{n_{[f_n(x,y) \leq T]}}{MN}} \qquad (17)$$

where k is a positive constant, and $n_{[f_n(x,y) \leq T]}$ stands for pixel numbers when $f_n(x, y) \leq T$.

3.3   Compute Procedure

Base on the theory before, the processing of enhancing night-time image lightness summarized in Table 1.

Table 1. Processing of luminance enhancement

Algorithm1 Process of enhancement
1. Read original night-time image I;
2. Statistic the pixel width and height of image I;
3. Transfer I from RGB space to HSI space;
4. Compute threshold T and ratio A;
5. Select adjust coefficient D_i;
6. Adjust the lightness according to the transfer relationship;
7. Achieve the enhancement image I'.

4   Result and Discussion

4.1   Enhancement Result

This paper proposes improved algorithm on a computer of memory of 8G (model for DDR RME510H38C6T-400), frequency of 3.4 GHz and 64 bit Linux operating system, simulating and calculating the original night image in Fig. 6(a)–(d) to get the result through process of 2.3. The recovered images with improved nonlinear adjustment method of this paper are illustrated in Fig. 6(a')–(d'). Get the Fig. 6(a'')–(d'') compared with the proposed method of [12].

We can effectively enhance the original image brightness in the dark part of the details with the method described in this article, and the improved adjustment method of this paper changes less on the well-light part and causes no distortion in compared with the traditional method of nonlinear inverse processing method described in this article. In Fig. 6, compare with the results of [12], ours can enhance the brightness obviously and successfully avoid distortion caused by excessive improvement. From Fig. 6(a) and (b), trees beside the street are difficult to identify because of lowlight condition, we can clearly recognize the details of the tree and the road in (a') and (b'). Our results keep luminance of the well-light area in (a) and (b), compared with (a'') and (b'') computed by [12],which light brightness is too high to cause distortion.

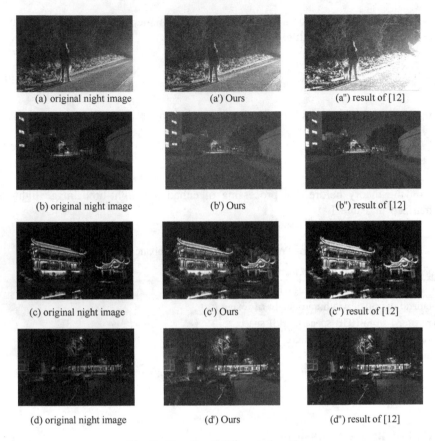

(a) original night image   (a') Ours   (a") result of [12]

(b) original night image   (b') Ours   (b") result of [12]

(c) original night image   (c') Ours   (c") result of [12]

(d) original night image   (d') Ours   (d") result of [12]

Fig. 6. Results of different algorithms

Two buildings details in (c) are hard to distinguish, power function algorithm can observe the texture of the wall and the stone in (c'). In the Fig. 6(c") which results of [12], the building's top is too bright and little details left. Cars and trees in Fig. 6(d) are difficult to distinguish because of darkness, our method recover the details of cars and trees in Fig. 6(d'). Especially we can restore the information of the sky, but (d") only provide the shape of the car in front of the image.

4.2   Judgment Criteria

The steps of processing are measured in length in the experiment environment described in Sect. 3.1, and the intensity of the image normalization is calculated to get Tables 2 and 3.

We find that the running time of the program is related to the size of the image, namely pixel value (M × N). The larger M × N, the longer processing time. The improved method will slow the traditional method of [12] on the processing speed,

Table 2. Statistic time of processing.

Pic	Pixel num	Time of us (s)	Time of [12] (s)
(a)	442 * 299	4.465262	3.307465
(b)	1148 * 858	13.44732	3.442836
(c)	700 * 465	4.223594	3.352265
(d)	690 * 388	8.889232	3.418154

which is mainly due to the improvement to piecewise nonlinear adjustment of brightness, rather than the whole nonlinear adjustment, but in general, the improved method has higher operation efficiency and satisfactory processing speed, which mainly depends on that this paper only uses the I component of HSI model for low light processing, rather than the three color components of the RGB model.

Make new statistics of brightness, and compared to the number of pixels before, Table 3 shows the result.

Table 3. Comparison of luminance threshold after processing and before.

Normalization luminance	0–0.3	0.3–0.7	0.7–1	Numbers of total pixel
(a) Original night image	0.9013	0	0.0987	422 * 299
(a') Ours	0.3824	0.5289	0.0887	
(b) Original night image	0.9915	0	0.0085	1148 * 858
(b') Ours	0.0091	0.98	0.0109	
(c) Original night image	0.9538	0	0.0462	700 * 465
(c') Ours	0.7271	0.2063	0.0666	
(d) Original night image	0.9964	0	0.0036	690 * 388
(d') Ours	0.8554	0.1184	0.0262	

From the above table, the paper can be concluded that there is a widespread phenomenon in the original night image: there is a huge difference between the brightness of the background and the main part. The background is mainly in high brightness (0.7–1) and the main part mainly in the low light (0–0.3). There is basically no pixels in the range of 0.3–0.7. Backlight processing mainly transfers the pixels of the lower area to middle brightness area by nonlinear transformation, which can be proved from the processed data. Table 2 shows that proportion of pixels with the improved method is closer to the original image than traditional methods in the range of 0.7–1. The improved method mainly adjusts the image pixel brightness by transferring the 0–0.3 area to the 0.3–0.7 area, and high brightness area (0.7–1) changes little, meanwhile the traditional method of [12] changes a lot in the high brightness area. In addition, the more even the brightness distribution is, the broader, the better the quality of the image is in theory, which can also be found from data processing. The processing of this paper is conducive to a better resolution.

5 Conclusion

In order to improve the night image to make it better for naked eye and computer identification, an improved method for nonlinear brightness improving model is put forward in this paper. Get segmentation threshold T with Otsu threshold segmentation method and the well-light area brightness improving coefficient by calculating the ratio of backlighting area to total pixels. Improve brightness of night image by piecewise method. The enhanced image can clearly get the details of the original dark area after processing.

Acknowledgments. This work was partially supported by the NSF project of Shandong province in China with granted No. ZR2014FM023, and Research and Innovation Fund project of Harbin Institute of Technology with granted No. HIT.NSRIF.2016108.

References

1. Gan, B., Wei, Y.C., Zhang, R.: Automatic white balance algorithm for CMOS image sensor chip. LCD Disp. **26**(2), 224–228 (2011)
2. Guo, H.N.: Research on the key technology of color digital camera imaging system. Graduate University of Chinese Academy of Sciences, Xi'an Institute of Optics and Fine Mechanics (2014)
3. Chen, C.N., Deng, H.Q., Wang, J.H.: Research on automatic exposure algorithm based on iris control. Sens. Micro Syst. **30**(11), 46–48 (2011)
4. Liu, C., Zheng, H., Li, X.: Traffic image enhancement processing based on adaptive luminance reference drift. J. Wuhan Univ. (Inf. Sci. Ed.) **40**(10), 1381–1385 (2015)
5. Graham, D., Schwarz, B., Chatterjee, A., et al.: Preference for luminance histogram regularities in natural scenes. Vis. Res. **120**, 11–21 (2016)
6. Santhi, K., Wahida, B.: Contrast enhancement using brightness preserving histogram plateau limit technique. Int. J. Eng. Technol. **6**(3), 1447–1453 (2014)
7. Yang, J., Zhao, Z.M.: Research on remote sensing image fusion method based on IHS transform and brightness adjustment. Comput. Appl. **24**(4), 195–197 (2007)
8. Zhang, H.: A novel enhancement algorithm for low-illumination images. In: 6th International Congress on Image and Signal Processing, pp. 240–244. IEEE Press (2013)
9. Zhang, X.F., Zhao, L.: Image enhancement algorithm based on improved. Retin. J. Nanjing Univ. Sci. Technol. (Nat. Sci. Ed.) **40**(1), 24–28 (2016)
10. Liu, Y., Jia, X.F., Tian, Z.J.: An image processing method based on the principle of the image of the light in the underground mine. Min. Autom. **39**(1), 9–12 (2013)
11. Kang, G., Huang, J., Li, D., et al.: A novel algorithm for uneven illumination image enhancement. In: 2012 Second International Conference on Instrumentation, Measurement, Computer, Communication and Control, pp. 831–833 (2012)
12. Wang, S., Zheng, J., Hu, H.: Naturalness preserved enhancement algorithm for non-uniform illumination images. IEEE Trans. Image Process. **22**(9), 3538–3548 (2013)
13. Shin, Y., Jeong, S., Lee, S.: Efficient naturalness restoration for non-uniform illmination images. IET Image Proc. **9**(8), 662–671 (2015)
14. Yun, H., Wu, Z., Wang, G., et al.: A novel enhancement algorithm combined with improved fuzzy set theory for low illumination images. Math. Probl. Eng. **20**(16), 1–9 (2016)

15. Gonzalez, R.C.: Digital Image Processing, 3rd edn, pp. 257–262. Pearson Prentice Hall, New Jersey (2008)
16. Gao, Y.P.: Research and implementation of image enhancement method. Huazhong University of Science and Technology, Wuhan (2008)
17. Susrama, I.G., Purnama, K.E., Purnomo, M.H.: Automated analysis of human sperm number and concentration (oligospermia) using otsu threshold method and labelling. Mater. Sci. Eng. **105**(1), 012038–012048 (2016)

Research on Non-contact Heart Rate Detection Algorithm

Chenguang He[1,2(✉)], Yuwei Cui[1], and Shouming Wei[1,2]

[1] Communication Research Center, Harbin Institute of Technology,
Harbin, China
{hechenguang, weishouming}@hit.edu.cn,
15866632753@163.com
[2] Key Laboratory of Police Wireless Digital Communication,
Ministry of Public Security, People's Republic of China, Harbin, China

Abstract. The heart rate is one of the important characteristic of human health. Fast and convenient heart rate measurement has become one aspect of daily life. The non-contact measurement method of heart rate gathers information of face via color video camera, analyzes the change of displacement of the surface of the skin and body color, then uses the methods such as filtering, spectrum analyze and peak detection to analysis the heart rate quantitatively. What's more, we study a non-contact method to detect the implementation of the heart rate based on the video acquisition, image processing and signal processing technology. We have done a thorough study of the implementation framework of the non-contact measurement of heart rate.

Keywords: Photoplethysmography · Non-contact
Independent component analysis

1 Introduction

Heart rate is a very important parameter in the diagnosis of today's medical treatment. Non-contact heart rate measurements have also attracted increasing attention, especially for newborns and the elderly, whose skin is very fragile and traditional contact heart rate measurements may make them feel uncomfortable. In addition to providing a non-contact way to measure heart rate, the method can also be used to monitor subtle changes in heartbeat for long periods of time as other basis for clinical diagnosis. This method of heart rate monitoring can be widely recognized by using the camera to collect face information, which non-contact to measure the heart rate, instead of contacting with skin.

In this article, we use the heartbeat cycle caused by the delicate changes in the head color to extract the information of heart rate. With blood flowing through the abdominal aorta and neck arteries to the head, the head will produce cyclical changes in color.

© ICST Institute for Computer Sciences, Social Informatics and Telecommunications Engineering 2018
X. Gu et al. (Eds.): MLICOM 2017, Part II, LNICST 227, pp. 316–325, 2018.
https://doi.org/10.1007/978-3-319-73447-7_35

2 Relate Works

2.1 Photo-Plethysmo-Graphy

Photo-plethysmo-graphy (PPG) is a non-invasive photo detection device that detects blood volume changes by means of optoelectronic devices. Hemoglobin is different for red and infrared light absorption, so we can measure hemoglobin in the blood by measuring the degree of weakening of each light reflected or transmitted by blood [1]. At present, the market of PPG sensors are usually more cost-effective LED and red photodetector with the use. In addition, it is also important to select photodetectors whose spectral characteristics match the light source. [2] PPG signal acquisition system is as follows (Fig. 1):

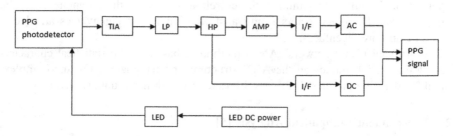

Fig. 1. PPG signal acquisition

2.2 Existing Detection Program [3]

General contact heart rate testing equipment is expensive, and the user is not convenient to carry. So people began to explore non-contact detection of heart rate. At present, the non-contact methods for determining heart rate are laser Doppler, Doppler radar, biological radar, thermal imaging and so on.

3 Algorithm Principle

This paper presents a method of non-contact heart rate testing. The method uses a camera to collect color images of the face and analyzes the changes in human skin color. And then use filtering, spectral analysis, peak detection and other methods in signal processing to analyze the heart rate characteristics. Compared with the existing PPG detection technology, the detection method uses a conventional digital camera as a detector, rather than using a photodiode. While the light source required by the method is only normal ambient light.

The main research algorithms are: face detection, independent component analysis, peak detection and so on.

3.1 Face Detection [4]

Face detection as the first stage of face recognition system, is recognized by most experts. Face detection methods are method based on the face gray model, method based on the feature space and method based on the neural network.

The detection method based on the face gray scale model is: First extract the geometry, gray level, the skin lines and other characteristics of the face. And then check whether the results extracted above are consistent with the prior knowledge of the face.

Based on the feature space method, the face region image is transformed into a feature space. And then it is divided into "human face" and "non-human face" two types of models according to its distribution in the feature space. Principal Component Analysis (PCA) is a commonly used method. It is orthogonal according to the statistical properties of the image to eliminate the correlation between the components of the original vector. The eigenvectors from transformation whose eigenvalues are decremented in turn are eigenfaces.

The artificial neural network (ANN) method is based on the statistical characteristics of the model implicit in the ANN structure and parameters. For the complex, difficult to describe the model, the ANN-based approach has a unique advantage.

3.2 Independent Component Analysis [5]

Independent Component Analysis (ICA) is a statistical and computational technology. It is used to reveal hidden components in random variables, measured data and signal. For a multivariate observation data usually given in the form of a large number of sample databases, ICA defines a generation model. This model assumes that the observed variable is a linear or non-linear blend of some unknown intrinsic variables. And not only the intrinsic variables are unknown, but the system that achieves the mix is also unknown. We also assume that those intrinsic variables are non-Gaussian and independent of each other and call them an independent component of the observed data. These independent components (also known as sources or factors) can be found by ICA.

In order to give the strict definition of ICA, we can use the "hidden variable" statistical model. We can assume that random variables $x1, \cdots, xn$, are observed, these variables are linearly combined by the other random variables $s1, \ldots, sn$. In this model, we also need to assume that the variable si is statistically independent of each other.

What is mentioned above is the model of ICA. Since this model shows how we see the data from si, we refer to this model as the generation model. Among them, si as an independent component, cannot be directly observed by us, so we call it "hidden variable". In this model, the only thing we can know is that the random variables $x1, \ldots, xn$. So, when we do independent component analysis we cannot ignore the commonly used assumptions. So that we can only use our observed variables to get all the unknown.

3.3   Peak Detection [6]

As shown in Fig. 2, P1 and P2 is the peak that we want to detect. We have to pre-set the amount of rise and fall. The core of the peak detection algorithm is: the peak point is the maximum value of the waveforms we studied, which has the rising and down-ward quantities. We must first determine a gate value, which is to give up some smaller voltage change caused by noise. For the voltage below the gate voltage, we set it directly to 0 and the voltage higher than the gate voltage, we can retain its original data. Finally, we start to check one by one to find all the qualifying data, and that is the peak we want.

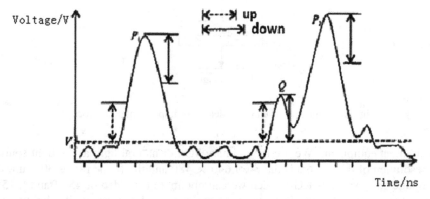

Fig. 2. Peak detection diagram

4   System Framework

Non-contact heart rate detection implementation process is shown in Fig. 3. The algorithm steps are: first in the natural light, use a video camera to collect information of a face; the face detection algorithm is used to extract the faces from each frame of the image. Then, we will separate each frame face image and generate R, G, B three-channel image. We can use the mean of all the pixels in each image as the eigenvalues of each channel and signals XR (t), XG (t) and XB (t) are used to represent the signals generated by the three channels. Next, we make independent component analysis of the three signals after standardization, so that three new signals YA (t), YB (t) and YC (t) independently of each other are obtained. Then, we use correlation analysis, filtering, and peak detection to obtain the heartbeat frequency (sub/min).

4.1   Image Acquisition

By the PPG measurement principle, video acquisition is an important step in the detection of heart beat frequency. The light that is reflected and scattered by the incident light through the skin, blood vessels, muscles and other tissues need to be recorded and the optical signal is converted into an electrical signal [2]. The camera is the most convenient photoelectric conversion device, which is our preferred

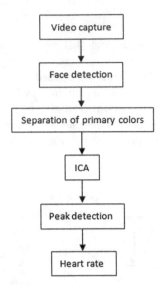

Fig. 3. Non-contact heart rate detection implementation process

measurement equipment. We use the ordinary light or natural light as the light source; The resolution of the camera is the pixel 640 × 480 and the frame rate is 30 frames/s; The image color space is RGB; Then we can obtain a face video of 450 frames, 15 s. We use the other measuring instruments to measure the heart rate while shooting the video. The measuring device is shown in Fig. 4:

Fig. 4. Non - contact heart rate measurement device

In the video capture, to reduce noise, there are four main points to note. (1) Try to shoot in good light conditions. The more the light is, the more the change in the color of the face is. (2) Turn off the camera's white balance performance. The camera automatically detects the environment and adjusts the color with white balance, which can destroy useful color information. (3) People in the video shooting time should not be too much action. The action will provide artifacts, which will cause the noise in the extracted signal. (4) When video has been captured, in order to prevent the camera just started will affect the color extraction, we need to intercept the middle of 15 s to analyze. We then turn the video into a frame format, and continue to the following analysis.

4.2 Face Detection

As the video in this paper requires the participants' action range cannot be too large, and the participants are almost completely static, so the video is only composed of a large number of static image sequences. Through the analysis of each face detection algorithm, we use the face detection algorithm is based on skin color characteristics of human detection technology. This kind of face detection algorithm is relatively simple, and the video collected in this article is only a person's head, so it is easier and more accurate to achieve.

As the light changes will also affect the effect of face detection, so before the face detection, we need light compensation for the image. Histogram equalization is the simplest method of lighting compensation. It can eliminate the effects caused by the changes in lighting conditions. Although this method has poor effect on face image processing under extreme light conditions such as high light and all black, before the face detection, we use the histogram equalization method to carry out its light compensation considering that the algorithm generally requires better lighting conditions, extreme light conditions do not occur.

When a face detection for each frame is successful, the image should be saved on the computer for the primitive PPG signal.

4.3 Separation of Primary Colors

When a face detection for each frame is successful, the image should be saved on the computer for the primitive PPG signal.

We detect the face, and then we split the color signal in order to get R, G, B channel color components and save it as a three-dimensional matrix. Taking the pixel mean of the face image as our sample value, we can get three consecutive channels with heart rate information for 15 s. Three-channel sampling signal is shown in Fig. 5:

Details show that in the study of human blood cells to absorb light capacity, we found that blood cells absorb green light or yellow light ability is stronger than other colors of light. So we can conclude that the green waveform is most correlated with heart rate information in the above three waveform signals.

4.4 Independent Component Analysis

Since the heart rate signal is usually mixed with a variety of physiological signals such as respiratory waves, we cannot obtain the source signal of heart rate through priori knowledge, and we can estimate the source signal only through the observation data. Therefore, separating the source signal from the mixed observation signal is a typical blind source signal separation problem. So we use the ICA algorithm to divide the above three channels of the initial signal into three independent source signal.

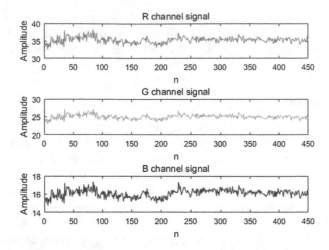

Fig. 5. Three-channel sampling signal (Color figure online)

First of all, the above three signals should be standardized, mean 0, variance of 1. Standardized signal is shown in Fig. 6. Then we use the ICA algorithm to remove the noise, and we will get three independent source signal. The three independent source signal is shown in Fig. 7. Since the three signals are disordered, it is not possible to determine which of the three separate signals corresponds to the signal in the mixed signal before separation. So we need to use the correlation analysis method to screen out the most relevant signal with the heart beat. Select a signal that is most relevant to the green signal for the next analysis. In order to find the independent source signal most relevant to the green channel signal, we need to calculate the correlation coefficient between the three independent source signals and the green signal separately,

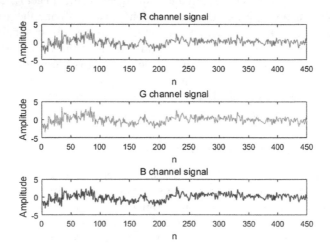

Fig. 6. Standardized signal (Color figure online)

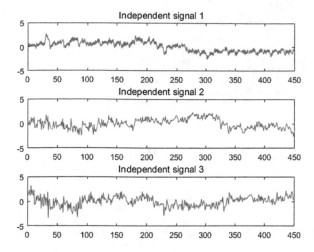

Fig. 7. The three independent source signal (Color figure online)

which requires the correlation function corrcoef in Matlab. The correlation between the three signals and the green signal is 0.4749, 0.3260 and 0.9400. So the green signal is most relevant to the third signal.

4.5 Signal Processing

The collected heart rate signal also contains some high-frequency noise, making the signal "glitch", which requires us to use some signal processing methods to filter out. Studies have shown that a normal adult's resting pulse rate [0.75, 2] HZ, so it can be filtered using 5-point moving average filter, and then using a band pass [0.75, 5] HZ Butterworth filter. The signal processing results are as follows (Figs. 8 and 9):

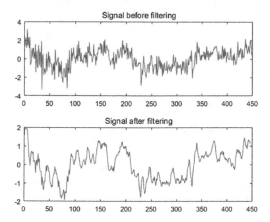

Fig. 8. Comparison of signal before and after the first filter

324   C. He et al.

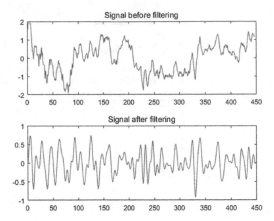

Fig. 9. Comparison of signal before and after the second filter

Peak detection of the above signals which has been subjected to the necessary filtering and calculate the average of the time interval between each peak. We use the peak detection algorithm to measure the heartbeat interval time so as to get the maximum peak frequency f. Heart rate calculation method: HR = 60 * f. The signal processing results is shown in Fig. 10. The heart rate is 96 times/min.

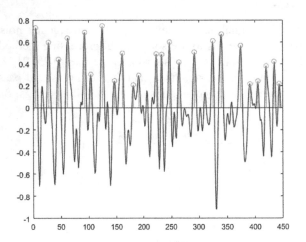

Fig. 10. Peak detection processing results

Acknowledgment. This work was supported by the National Science and Technology Major Specific Projects of China (Grant No. 2015ZX03004002-004) and the Fundamental Research Funds for the Central Universities (Grant No. HIT. NSRIF. 201616).

References

1. Peng, F., Wang, W., Liu, H.: Development of a reflective PPG signal sensor. In: 7th International Conference on BioMedical Engineering and Informatics (BMEI 2014) (2014)
2. Verkruysse, W., Svaasand, L.O., Nelson, J.S.: Remote plethysmographic imaging using ambient light. Opt. Express 16(26), 21434–21445 (2008)
3. Chia, M.Y., Leong, S.W., Sim, C.K., et al.: Through-wall UWB radar operating within FCC's mask for sensing heart beat and breathing rate. In: IEEE European Microwave Conference, vol. 3, no. 14 (2005)
4. Naruniec, J.: Discrete area filters in accurate detection of faces and facial features. Image Vis. Comput. 32(12), 979–993 (2014)
5. Comon, P.: Independent component analysis, a new concept. Sig. Process. 36(3), 287–314 (1994)
6. Li, X., Gao, Q., Oin, S.: A low-power high-frequency CMOS peak detector. Chin. J. Semicond. 27(10), 1707–1710 (2006)

Lorentzian Norm Based Super-Resolution Reconstruction of Brain MRI Image

Dongxing Bao[1,2], Xiaoming Li[3], and Jin Li[1(✉)]

[1] College of Automation, Harbin Engineering University, Harbin 150001, China
lijin@hrbeu.edu.cn
[2] School of Electronic Engineering,
Heilongjiang University, Harbin 150080, China
[3] Department of Microelectronics Science and Technology,
Harbin Institute of Technology, Harbin 150001, China
eastarbox@163.com

Abstract. Nowadays, SRR (super resolution image reconstruction) technology is a very effective method in improving spatial resolution of images and obtaining high-definition images. The SRR approach is an image late processing method that does not require any improvement in the hardware of the imaging system. In the SRR reconstruction model, it is the key point of the research to choose a proper cost function to achieve good reconstruction effect. In this paper, based on a lot of research, Lorenzian norm is employed as the error term, Tikhonov regularization is employed as the regularization term in the reconstruction model, and iteration method is employed in the process of SRR. In this way, the outliers and image edge preserving problems in SRR reconstruction process can be effectively solved and a good reconstruction effect can be achieved. A low resolution MRI brain image sequence with motion blur and several noises are used to test the SRR reconstruction algorithm in this paper and the reconstruction results of SRR reconstruction algorithm based on L2 norm are also be used for comparison and analysis. Results from experiments show that the SRR algorithm in this paper has better practicability and effectiveness.

Keywords: MRI image · Super resolution image reconstruction
Lorentzian norm · Regularization · Iteration

1 Introduction

In order to achieve a good visual effect, people always want to get clear images with high quality. In the current CCD imaging systems, for increasing image's spatial resolution by improving performance and structure of the imaging system often results in additional expenditure and noise. In addition, LR images can only be obtained in some image acquisition processes. In order to get HR images, super resolution image reconstruction (SRR) technology has become an effective method in image later processing process.

Super resolution image reconstruction technology refers to the process of image processing: from low resolution image sequences to reproduce one high resolution images. This technique can reconstruct one high resolution images by collecting

X. Gu et al. (Eds.): MLICOM 2017, Part II, LNICST 227, pp. 326–332, 2018.
https://doi.org/10.1007/978-3-319-73447-7_36

additional information between sub pixels of low resolution image sequence taken from the same scene. By this method, the limitations of the intrinsic frequency of the imaging process can be overcome. Earlier work on super resolution image reconstruction was done by Tsai and Huang [1] in 1984, which is a SRR method of single-image in frequency-domain using DFT. Then, a serious of frequency domain super-resolution reconstruction method based on discrete-cosine-transform (DCT) [2], wavelet-transform [3] is presented. Because the frequency domain reconstruction effect is not ideal, in recent years, the research area has moved to the spatial domain. The typical spatial super-resolution image reconstruction model includes: IBP method [4], non-uniform- interpolation method [5], MAP method [6], ML method [7], POCS method [8], mixed-MAP/POCS method [9], and adaptive-filtering method [10], etc. Based on these algorithms, combining reconstruction and registration algorithm [11], multi-spectral and color image SRR algorithm [12], compressed sensing reconstruction algorithm [13], and Example-based SRR algorithm have also been proposed [14].

In this paper, the SRR algorithm based on Lorenzian norm [15] is introduced, and is applied to the reconstruction of low resolution MRI brain image sequence. Results from experiments show that the proposed algorithm is more efficient than that of L_2 norm based SRR algorithm in solving the outliers and edge preserving problems in super-resolution reconstruction process.

The structure of this paper includes: Sect. 2 introduces basic observation-model of HR image. Section 3 gives the SR image reconstruction algorithm based on Lorenzian norm and Tikhonov regularization. Section 4 gives the reconstruction results of two reconstruction methods based on a series of low resolution MRI brain images. Section 5 gives the conclusion of this paper.

2 Image Observation Model

The process to get low resolution image from high resolution image includes down sampling, blurring, warping, and noise addition. The image-observation-model [9] is

$$y_k = DBM_k x + n_k, \quad k = 1, 2, \ldots, P \tag{1}$$

Where x represents the initial HR image, the size of it is $L_1 N_1 \times L_2 N_2$, L_1 represents the horizontal direction down sampling factor, and L_2 represents the vertical direction down sampling factor. y_k is low-resolution-image sequence with the size of $N_1 \times N_2$. M_k represents motion matrix with moving, rotation, zoom motion and the size of it is $L_1 N_1 L_2 N_2 \times L_1 N_1 L_2 N_2$, B represents the blur matrix and the size of it is $L_1 N_1 L_2 N_2 \times L_1 N_1 L_2 N_2$, D represents sampling matrix, the size of it is $N_1 N_2 \times L_1 N_1 L_2 N_2$, n_k represents Gauss white noise, the size of it is $N_1 N_2 \times 1$.

Formula (1) can also be expressed as

$$y_k = H_k x + n_k, \quad k = 1, 2, \ldots, P \tag{2}$$

where $H_K = DBM_K$ can be regarded as a composite degenerate operator.

3   SR Image Reconstruction Algorithm

The image reconstruction process of SR is estimating one HR image from LR image sequence taken from same scene using complementary information between sub-pixels. Super resolution image reconstruction is ill-posed-inverse-process, and reconstruction model is very sensitive. Small noise and error can lead to serious distortion of the reconstructed-image.

The key problem of reconstruct HR image from LR image-sequence is to get a proper cost function. From formulas (1) and (2) we get

$$\hat{x} = argmin\left[\sum_k \rho(y_k - H_k x) + \alpha R(x)\right] \tag{3}$$

Where x is the initial HR image, $\hat{x}$ is the reconstructed SRR image, y_k is LR image sequence, $\rho(\bullet)$ is error estimation term (fidelity of the solution), $R(x)$ is the regularization term (smoothness of the solution), α is regularization-parameter (control the trade-off between ρ and $R(x)$).

3.1   Error Estimate Term

At present, the error-estimation-term used in SRR is the error estimate [6] based on the Lp norm. If the value of P is 1, it becomes the L_1 norm, and when the value of P is 2, it becomes the L_2 norm. A common problem with these methods is the over smoothing and edge ringing effects of reconstructed images.

The Lorenzian norm and its influence function are defined as

$$\rho_{LOR}(x) = \log\left[1 + \frac{1}{2}\left(\frac{x}{T}\right)^2\right] \tag{4}$$

$$\rho'_{LOR}(x) = \frac{2x}{2T^2 + x^2} \tag{5}$$

The Lorenzian norm is used as error estimation term, which concentrates the advantages of L_1 norm and L_2 norm, and can effectively suppress ringing and noise effect, especially salt & pepper noise.

$$\hat{x} = argmin\left[\sum_k \rho_{LOR}(y_k - H_k x) + \alpha R(x)\right] \tag{6}$$

where T is a soft threshold, when $x \leq T$, it is the L_2 norm, and when $x > T$, it is saturated. Therefore, only those values that are not greater than T are valid (Fig. 1).

3.2   Regularization Term

The regularization-term in the super-resolution-image-reconstruction model can restrict the solution space and improve the solution's stability by introducing a pri-knowledge.

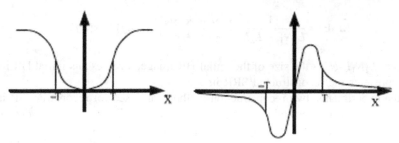

(a) Lorentzian norm function   (b) Lorentzian norm influence function

Fig. 1. Lorentzian norm and influence function.

The regularization method used in this paper is the effective and commonly used Tikhonov regularization.

$$\hat{x} = argmin \left[\sum_k \rho_{LOR}(y_k - H_k x) + \alpha \|Cx\|_2^2 \right] \tag{7}$$

where C is a two-dimensional Laplacian operator. α is a regularization parameter that adjusts the ratio between the regularization and the error estimate term. If the value of alpha is too large, the solution will deviate from the real solution, and if the alpha value is too small, the solution will lead to instability. Therefore, the determination of an appropriate alpha value is a key factor in achieving better reconstruction effectiveness.

3.3   Iteration Reconstruction Method

In this paper, iterative reconstruction method is employed for the realization of SRR algorithm.

$$x_{n+1} = x_n + \lambda \left[\sum_k (H_k^T y - (H_k^T H_k + \alpha(x_k)C^T C)x_k) \right] \tag{8}$$

Where λ means iteration step value.

4   Experiment

In this paper, the low-resolution MRI brain image sequence is used to test the SR image-reconstruction algorithm. Meanwhile, the SRR algorithm based on L_2 norm is also used for comparison of the reconstruction effect.

PSNR and RMSE are used for evaluating the performance of the reconstruction methods quantitatively.

$$PSNR = 10log_{10} \left(\frac{255^2}{MSE} \right) \tag{10}$$

$$\text{MSE} = \frac{1}{L_1 N_1 \times L_2 N_2} \sum_{i=1}^{L_1 N_1} \sum_{j=1}^{L_2 N_2} (\hat{x}(i,j) - x(i,j))^2 \tag{11}$$

Where $L_1 N_1 L_2 N_2$ is the size of the initial HR image, $\mathbf{x}$ represents initial HR image, and $\hat{x}$ represents the reconstructed SRR image.

In the experiments, two reconstruction methods are used for reconstruct SR image from LR image sequences and two types of noises is added. LR image sequence in the experiment is taken from the original HR MRI brain image (see Fig. 2) by global motion (assuming the motion parameters are known), *3 × 3* Gauss kernel blur, the factor of 2 down sampling of the horizontal direction and vertical direction, and the addition of two different types of noise (Gauss noise, salt & pepper noise), see Fig. 3. Based on the two reconstruction methods, the results of super resolution image reconstruction for different noise cases are shown in Figs. 4 and 5.

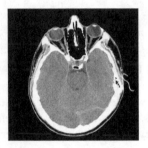

Fig. 2. Initial MRI brain image.

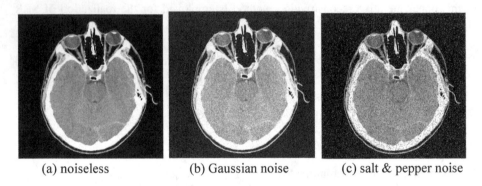

(a) noiseless   (b) Gaussian noise   (c) salt & pepper noise

Fig. 3. LR images with different type of noise.

The results from experiments show that the reconstruction effect of the super resolution image reconstruction method in this paper is better than that of based on the L_2 norm in the objective and subjective aspects. The reconstructed HR image with the algorithm in this paper has better visual and edge preservation effect. The reconstruction results show that this paper's algorithm can keep better robustness and adaptability in different kinds of noise, especially for the case of salt & pepper noise.

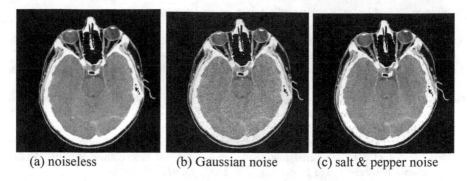

(a) noiseless   (b) Gaussian noise   (c) salt & pepper noise

Fig. 4. Reconstructed results for different type of noise by L_2 norm SRR.

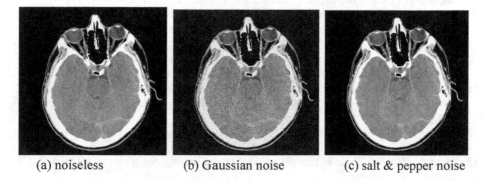

(a) noiseless   (b) Gaussian noise   (c) salt & pepper noise

Fig. 5. Reconstructed results for different type of noise by Lorentzian norm SRR.

5 Conclusion

In order to solve the edge preserving and outliers problem in SR image reconstruction, the reconstruction algorithm based on Tikhonov regularization, Lorenzian error norm, and iterative method is employed. The results of the experiments show that the low resolution MRI brain images with different noise conditions are well reconstructed and the robustness and adaptability of this algorithm is better compared to L2 norm based reconstruction algorithm–not just remove the noise of different types, and also has better edge preserving effect. However, this method has the problem of large computation and slow processing speed. The work of next step is to improve the algorithm by considering adaptive regularization in the motion estimation model.

References

1. Tsai, R.Y., Huang, T.S.: Multi-frame image restoration and registration. Adv. Comput. Vis. Image Process. **1**(2), 317–339 (1984)
2. Rhee, S., Kang, M.G.: Discrete cosine transform based regularized high-resolution image reconstruction algorithm. Opt. Eng. **38**(8), 1348–1356 (1999)

3. Nguyen, N., Milanfar, P.: A wavelet-based interpolation restoration method for superresolution. Circ. Syst. Sig. Process. **19**(4), 321–338 (2000)

4. Irani, M., Peleg, S.: Improving resolution by image registration. CVGIP: Graph. Models Image Process. **53**(3), 231–239 (1991)

5. Ur, H., Gross, D.: Improved resolution from subpixel shifted pictures. CVGIP: Graph. Models Image Process. **54**(2), 181–186 (1992)

6. Hardie, R.C., Barnard, K.J., Armstrong, E.E.: Joint MAP registration and high-resolution image estimation using a sequence of undersampled images. IEEE Trans. Image Process. **6**(12), 1621–1633 (1997)

7. Tom, B.C., Katsaggelos, A.K.: Reconstruction of a high resolution image from multiple-degraded misregistered low resolution images. In: Proceedings of SPIE, Visual Communications and Image Processing, vol. 2308, pp. 971–981 (1994)

8. Patti, A.J., Sezan, M.I., Tekalp, A.M.: High-resolution image reconstruction from a low-resolution image sequence in the presence of time-varying motion blur. In: IEEE International Conference Image Processing (ICIP 1994), vol. 1, pp. 343–347 (1994)

9. Elad, M., Feuer, A.: Restoration of a single superresolution image from several blurred, noisy, and undersampled measured images. IEEE Trans. Image Process. **6**(12), 1646–1658 (1997)

10. Elad, M., Feuer, A.: Superresolution restoration of an image sequence: adaptive filtering approach. IEEE Trans. Image Process. **8**(3), 387–395 (1999)

11. Woods, N.A., Galatsanos, N.P., Katsaggelos, A.K.: Stochastic methods for joint registration, restoration, and interpolation of multiple undersampled images. IEEE Trans. Image Process. **15**(1), 201–213 (2006)

12. Farsiu, S., Elad, M., Milanfar, P.: Multiframe demosaicing and super-resolution of color images. IEEE Trans. Image Process. **15**(1), 141–159 (2006)

13. Tsaig, Y., Donoho, D.L.: Extensions of compressed sensing. Sig. Process. **86**(3), 549–571 (2006)

14. Yang, J., Lin, Z., Cohen, S.: Fast image super-resolution based on in-place example regression. In: Computer Vision Foundation (2013)

15. Patanavijit, V., Jitapunkul, S.: A Lorentzian stochastic estimation for a robust iterative multiframe super-resolution reconstruction with Lorentzian-Tikhonov regularization. EURASIP J. Adv. Sig. Process. **2007**, 1–21 (2007)

A Virtual Channel Allocation Algorithm for NoC

Dongxing Bao[1], Xiaoming Li[2(✉)], Yizong Xin[3], Jiuru Yang[1],
Xiangshi Ren[4], Fangfa Fu[2], and Cheng Liu[2]

[1] School of Electronic Engineering, Heilongjiang University,
Harbin 150080, China
[2] Department of Microelectronics Science and Technology,
Harbin Institute of Technology, Harbin 150001, China
lixiaoming@hit.edu.cn
[3] School of Information Engineering, Shenyang University of Technology,
Shenyang 110870, China
[4] School of Information, Kochi University of Technology,
Kochi 780-8520, Japan
eastarbox@163.com

Abstract. Virtual channel (VC) flow control proves to be an alternative way to promote network performance, but uniform VC allocation in the network may be at the cost of chip area and power consumption. We propose a novel VC number allocation algorithm customizing the VCs in network based on the characteristic of the target application. Given the characteristic of target application and total VC number budget, the block probability for each port of nodes in the network can be obtained with an analytical model. Then VCs are added to the port with the highest block probability one by one. The simulation results indicate that the proposed algorithm reduces buffer consumption by 14.58%–51.04% under diverse traffic patterns and VC depth, while keeping similar network performance.

Keywords: VC allocation · Block probability · Network-on-chip

1 Introduction

SoC designs are confronted with various challenges caused by the increasing complexity of the designs [1]. The on-chip communication bandwidth requirement is growing rapidly, and simultaneously the interconnect delay exceeds the average on-chip clock period [2]. Network-on-chip (NoC) which replaces bus with network to implement the communication among processing elements (PE) has been proposed [3, 4], and becomes one of the most promising on-chip interconnection architectures [5]. NoC is composed of Network Interface (NI), Router, and Link basically. Compared with traditional on-chip bus, NoC has many advantages—reusability, scalability, parallelism, etc., which satisfies future SoC interconnection requirements [3–5].

The benefits of NoC are attractive, but attaining their full potential will present lots of challenges among which power consumption stands out as one of the most critical

© ICST Institute for Computer Sciences, Social Informatics and Telecommunications Engineering 2018
X. Gu et al. (Eds.): MLICOM 2017, Part II, LNICST 227, pp. 333–342, 2018.
https://doi.org/10.1007/978-3-319-73447-7_37

challenges [5]. Since router is one of the kernel components of NoC and it has significant influence on both the performance and power consumption of NoC [6], we mainly focus on it in this paper. A typical virtual channel router structure is shown in Fig. 1. It is composed of Routing Computation (RC), VC Allocator (VA), Switch Allocator (SA), VC, crossbar, and Mux as well as Demux. Among the five parts of router, VC has prominent effect on router. However, VC takes up most of the power and area consumption of router [7], especially more than sixty percent of the static power consumption [8, 9]. On the other hand, VC number and capacity determines the router performance with specific router architecture. With more VCs and larger capacity, data in the network will be able to forward to the destination node more fluently, while under the opposite situation, the network are prone to get blocked and saturated. To get out of such a dilemma, the researchers proposed many strategies from diverse points of view. The authors of [10, 11] introduce power gating to shut down idle VCs. Although power gating can reduce the system static power consumption, it needs additional technology support. What's worse, the static power saving will decrease greatly under heavier workload. The authors of [12, 13] propose dynamic buffer allocation strategy adjusting the VC number or depth based on network status. The strategy can be effective in diverse traffic; however, the designs are usually complex and result in additional hardware consumption. Therefore little power saving can be achieved when the data width is not very large. It is tough to find out a general method to make compromise on performance and power consumption.

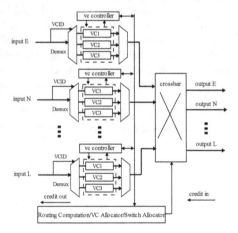

Fig. 1. A general virtual channel router architecture.

NoC design typically aims at certain specific application, thus the NoC architecture can be customized to specific application to obtain the best design trade-offs [14]. Taking this matter into consideration, Hu and Marculescu work out an analytical performance model for NoC, and then proposed a buffer capacity allocation algorithm based on the performance model [7]. According to the algorithm, the buffer with the highest full probability is assigned larger buffer capacity. However, such an allocation algorithm is limited to router with single buffer channel. Consequently, when it comes to higher throughput requirements application, router based on VC is necessary and the algorithm will be not available. To remedy this situation, Huang et al. [15] develop a VC planning algorithm. The algorithm only adds VCs to channels which present the highest bandwidth usage. Although the algorithm presents prominent power savings when the VC is deep, it doesn't work well when the VC is shallow. In fact, the probability due to feedback of VCs in the next router can't be ignored, especially when the VCs are shallow. In this paper, a novel VC number allocation algorithm is proposed. Taking both arbitration contention and VC feedback probability into account, we add VCs to port with the highest block probability.

2 Buffer Utilization Characteristic for NoC

To get a better view of VC utilization characteristic in NoC, we make a stat. of VC utilization under hotspot traffic with a cycle accurate SystemC simulator. X-Y routing algorithm is adopted in a 4 × 4 2D Mesh NoC. And there are three four-flit-VCs in each input port of the router. Average injection rate is 0.3 flit/node/cycle and the hotspot locates in (2, 2). The simulation begins with a warm-up period of 100000 cycles. Then performance data is collected 100000 cycles later. Figure 2-(a) shows the buffer utilization in different ports of different nodes. It is obviously that the buffer utilization of different nodes differs notably. Even buffer utilization in the same node varies significantly. The lowest buffer utilization in the network is 0.0053, while the highest is 0.427 and it is 80 times higher than the lowest! Figure 2-(b) indicates the buffer utilization under uniform traffic. It is amazing that buffer utilization differs greatly even under uniform traffic. The highest buffer utilization is 0.0562, which is about 8 times higher than the lowest.

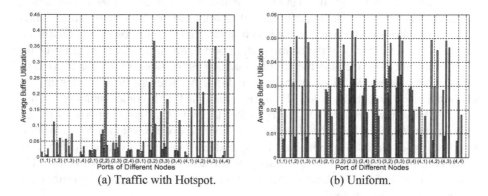

(a) Traffic with Hotspot.   (b) Uniform.

Fig. 2. VC utilization of different ports in each node.

The simulation results illustrate that unbalance of buffer utilization exits in diverse traffic patterns including uniform traffic. The main reason is 2D Mesh topology as well as X-Y deterministic routing. In fact, the application characteristic, routing algorithm, topology etc. have notable effect on buffer utilization in network. Therefore, unbalanced buffer utilization in NoC is usual. As buffer utilization varies across the network, with uniform VC allocation, VCs in some ports might be idle and wasted, while VCs in some other ports might be insufficient and a mass of data might be blocked. Hence customizing the VCs configuration in NoC based on the application characteristic will decrease buffer consumption through reducing superfluous VCs and alleviate block by adding VCs. At the same time, the network performance can be maintained or even improved.

3   Static Virtual Channel Number Allocation

3.1   Basic Idea

To fully utilize the limited VCs in the network and satisfy the performance requirements with the least VCs, VCs are allocated across the network based on needs of the ports. But the problem is how to define the needs of ports in the network. To make the problem clear, we explain how the data is transmitted in a router first. Router receives and stores data injected from the input ports. When the data in the VCs gets through the Mux, and there are available VCs in the next router, it sends request to VA. With the grant of VA, it still needs to make sure that the assigned VC is not full before the data sends request to SA for the output port. With the grant of SA, the data will be sent to crossbar and then leaves from the output port. All the data that fails to request or be granted by VA or SA is stored in VCs of current router. In other words, all the data that is blocked will be stored. The higher the block probability is, the more data needs to be stored and the worse the performance is. Therefore alleviating the block probability will be one of the possible ways to improve the network performance.

The root of block is limited bandwidth of the link and limited buffer capacity of the router. Generally speaking, the bandwidth of the link is fixed. Under this situation, especially when the link bandwidth of the link is sufficient, we have to turn to the buffer capacity. Buffer is used to smooth the injection rate and the ejection rate of the router. Increasing buffer capacity of the corresponding port in the next router will alleviate the block probability and increase the ejection rate. As buffer capacity is limited, we only increase VCs where the block probability is high. As a result, there are fewer VCs where the block probability is low. However, when the link becomes saturated, adding VC will bring few benefits. On the opposite, the hardware consumption increases. So VC number in each port will be limited. Therefore we develop a VC allocation algorithm based on block probability. Compared with uniform VC configuration, the buffer consumption is reduced significantly, while achieving similar performance. The analytical model of the blocking probability and VC number allocation algorithm will be described in detail below.

3.2   Problem Formulation

For convenience, the notations used in analysis are listed in Table 1. And the problem of VC number allocation can be formulated as follow.

Table 1. Parameter notion.

Parameter	Description
S	Total VC number budget
$\lambda_{x,y}$	PE injection rate of node (x,y)
$P_{x',y'}^{x',y'}$	The probability that node (x,y) sends data to node (x',y')
R	Routing function
D	VC depth
U	Port number of the router
$v_{x,y,j}$	VC number of input port j in node (x,y) , $j \in \{E,N,W,S,L\}$
$\lambda_{x,y,j}$	Injection rate of input port j in node (x,y) , $j \in \{E,N,W,S,L\}$
$\lambda_{x,y,j,k}$	Flit transmission rate of node (x,y) that injects from input port j in and ejects from output port k, $j \in \{E,N,W,S,L\}$, $k \in \{E,N,W,S,L\}$
$\mu_{x,y,j}$	Service rate of input port j in node (x,y), $j \in \{E,N,W,S,L\}$
$\rho_{x,y,j}$	Traffic intensity of input port j in node (x,y), $j \in \{E,N,W,S,L\}$
$P_{input\_block\_x,y}$	Block probability of input port j in node (x,y) , $j \in \{E,N,W,S,L\}$
$P_{block\_x,y,k}$	Block probability of corresponding output port in previous node of input port k in node (x,y) , $k \in \{E,N,W,S,L\}$
$P_{ARB\_con\_x,y,k}$	Arbitration contention probability of output port k in node (x,y) , $k \in \{E,N,W,S,L\}$
$P_{ARB\_con\_x,y,k}$	Arbitration contention probability of n flits requesting for output port k in node (x,y), $k \in \{E,N,W,S,L\}$, $n \in \{0,1,2,3,4,5\}$
$P_{VC\_full\_con\_x}$	VC full probability of input port k in node (x,y) , $k \in \{E,N,W,S,L\}$

Assume:

PE injects packet with a Poisson distribution.

Given:

Total VC number budget, S
Application communication characteristic, $\lambda_{x,y}$ and $P_{x,y}^{x',y'}$
Routing algorithm, R
Virtual channel depth, D

Determine:

VC configuration $v_{x,y,j}$
Which minimizes average network latency Lat

$$\text{Min}(Lat) \quad \text{s.t.} \quad \sum_{\forall x}\sum_{\forall y}\sum_{\forall j} v_{x,y,j} \leq S \tag{1}$$

3.3 Block Probability Analysis

For convenience, single VC is configured in each input port. $\forall x, \forall y, j \in \{N, E, S, W, L\}$, $v_{x,y,j} = 1$. With previous analysis, it is natural that the block probability is consist of two aspects—arbitration probability including VA and SA and VC feedback probability. Therefore $P_{block\_x,y,k}$ can be derived:

$$P_{block\_x,y,k} = 1 - \left(1 - P_{ARB\_con\_x',y',k'}\right) \times \left(1 - P_{VC\_full\_con\_x,y,k}\right) \tag{2}$$

Node (x', y') indicates the node that connects with input port k in node (x, y), and k' is corresponding output port in node (x', y').

When more than two flits request for the same output port k, there is an arbitration contention. Then the arbitration contention probability is:

$$P_{ARB\_con\_x,y,k} = \sum_{n=2}^{U} P_{ARB\_con\_x,y,k,n} \tag{3}$$

$$\begin{aligned} P_{ARB\_con\_x,y,k,n} = &\left(1 - \lambda_{x,y,E,k}\right) \times \cdots \times \left(1 - \lambda_{x,y,j,k}\right) \\ &\times \underbrace{\lambda_{x,y,j+1,k} \times \cdots \times \lambda_{x,y,j+n,k}}_{n} \\ &\times \left(1 - \lambda_{x,y,j+n+1,k}\right) \times \cdots \times \left(1 - \lambda_{x,y,L,k}\right) \end{aligned} \tag{4}$$

$$\lambda_{x,y,j} = \sum_{k \in \{N,E,S,W,L\}} \lambda_{x,y,j,k} \tag{5}$$

$$\lambda_{x,y,j,k} = \sum_{\forall x_s,y_s} \sum_{\forall x_d,y_d} R(x_s, y_s, x_d, y_d, x, y, j, k) \times \lambda_{x_s,y_s} \tag{6}$$

$R(x_s, y_s, x_d, y_d, x, y, j, k)$ indicates the routing algorithm. When there is data transmitted from source node (x_s, y_s) to destination node (x_d, y_d), and the data is injected from input port j of node (x, y) and leaves from output k of node (x, y), R returns 1, or else it returns 0.

The full probability of VC can be calculated with M/M/1/K queuing model.

$$P_{VC\_full\_con\_x,y,k} = \frac{1 - \rho_{x',y',k'}^{D}}{\left(1 - \rho_{x',y',k'}\right)^{D+1}} \tag{7}$$

Node (x', y') is the node that corresponds to output port k of node (x, y), and k' is the corresponding input port of node (x', y').

Without block, the service rate is 1. Thus the service rate of the queue can be approximated:

$$\mu_{x,y,j} = 1 - P_{input\_block\_x,y,j} \tag{8}$$

$$P_{input\_block\_x,y,j} = \sum_{k=1}^{N} P_{x,y,j,k} \times P_{output\_block\_x,y,j,k} \tag{9}$$

$$P_{output\_block\_x,y,j,k} = \sum_{i \in \{N,E,S,W,L\}, i \neq j} \lambda_{x,y,i,k} \tag{10}$$

$$P_{x,y,j,k} = \frac{\lambda_{x,y,j,k}}{\sum\limits_{i \in \{N,E,S,W,L\}} \lambda_{x,y,i,k}} \tag{11}$$

Then the traffic intensity of the queue is:

$$\rho_{x,y,j} = \lambda_{x,y,j} / \mu_{x,y,j} \tag{12}$$

When there are multiple VCs in ports of the router, as an output port won't be blocked before all the VCs are blocked. Therefore, $P_{block\_x,y,k}$ can be approximated:

$$P_{block\_x,y,k} = \left(1 - \left(1 - P_{VA\_con\_x',y',k'}\right) \times \left(1 - P_{VC\_full\_con\_x,y,k}\right)\right)^{V_{x,y,k}} \tag{13}$$

Node (x', y') indicates the node that connects with input port k in node (x, y), and k' is corresponding output port in node (x', y').

3.4   VC Number Allocation Algorithm

As shown in Fig. 3, an effective greedy algorithm based on the aforementioned block probability model is proposed.

Given the design parameters (topology, routing algorithm and so on) and Communication Task Graph (CTG), the network scale and traffic characteristic can be acquired with mapping. At the same time, VC budget can be derived from power budget of the target application with NoC power model. Then the VC number allocation begins. First of all, the number of VCs in each port is initialized to one. Then the block probability of each output port can be calculated to find out the port with the highest block probability. If the VC number in the corresponding input port is equal to the upper VC limit max_vc, set the block probability zero and search for the next candidate. Or else, add a VC to the input port, and decrease by one from the total VC budget. Iteration restarts as long as the VC budget is still available. When the process stops, the VC configuration is derived.

max_vc is greatly influenced by the topology, packet length, traffic characteristic, VC number and depth, routing algorithm and son on, so it is almost impossible to determine with an analytical model. With specific simulation environment, we add VC uniformly. When the performance won't be improved notably, the VC number in each port is max_vc. max_vc used in this paper is four.

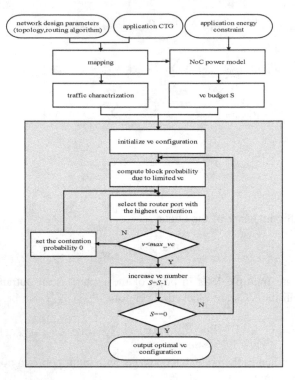

Fig. 3. VC allocation algorithm flowchart.

4   Simulation and Analysis

The simulation environment is based on a cycle-accurate, flit-level SystemC simulator.

During simulation, the data packets are yielded by a Poisson process at a definite traffic rate from the source PEs. 10000 packets are injected into each node and all the performance is abstracted after 100000 warm-up cycles. Detailed simulation condition is listed in Table 2. Besides, V0-NoC, V1-NoC and V2-NoC respectively indicate NoC

Table 2.   Experiment condition.

Topology	2D mesh
Network scale	4 × 4
Temporal distribution	Poisson
Packet length	8
VC depth	4, 8, 16
Flit width	64 bit
Routing algorithm	X-Y deterministic routing
Arbitration algorithm	Round Robin
Flow control	Worm-hole

with uniform VC allocation, NoC with VC allocation algorithm proposed in [15] and NoC with VC allocation algorithm proposed in this paper.

Tables 3, 4 and 5 exhibit the average network latency when the VC depth is 4, 8, 16 respectively under diver traffic. It indicates that the system benefits from customizing VC configuration with both allocation algorithms under almost all the traffic patterns. Buffer consumption can be reduced by 14.58%–51.04% under diverse traffic patterns and VC depth, while keeping similar network performance. However, Compared with the algorithm proposed in [15], the algorithm developed in this paper achieves 4.17%–42.71% more buffer savings when the VC depth is 4. And it still performs better basically when the VC depth is 8. While when the VC depth is 16, the two algorithms acquire similar buffer savings. The reason for this is that the algorithm proposed in [15] doesn't take VC depth into consideration. In fact, when the VC is shallow, the block probability due to feedback of VC has notable influence on network performance. When the VC gets larger, the feedback probability can be ignored, therefore the two algorithms perform similar.

Table 3. NoC performance when VC depth is 4.

Evaluation metrics	Uniform distribution			Hotspot in the center			Hotspot in the edge			Hotspot in the corner		
	$V0$-NoC	$V1$-NoC	$V2$-NoC	$V0$-NoC	$V1$-NoC	$V2$-NoC	$V0$-NoC	$V1$-NoC	$V2$-NoC	$V0$-NoC	$V1$-NoC	$V2$-NoC
Average latency	247.5	239.3	220.1	289.6	294.9	278.3	332.5	334.2	328.7	176.5	169.8	179.6
VC number	192	192	110	192	128	100	192	112	104	192	144	120

Table 4. NoC performance when VC depth is 8.

Evaluation metrics	Uniform distribution			Hotspot in the center			Hotspot in the edge			Hotspot in the corner		
	$V0$-NoC	$V1$-NoC	$V2$-NoC	$V0$-NoC	$V1$-NoC	$V2$-NoC	$V0$-NoC	$V1$-NoC	$V2$-NoC	$V0$-NoC	$V1$-NoC	$V2$-NoC
Average latency	152.7	149.1	168.9	213.5	231.1	221.2	249.4	214.8	224.1	240.4	236.3	223.9
VC number	192	188	164	192	114	94	192	112	108	192	112	112

Table 5. NoC performance when VC depth is 16.

Evaluation metrics	Uniform distribution			Hotspot in the center			Hotspot in the edge			Hotspot in the corner		
	$V0$-NoC	$V1$-NoC	$V2$-NoC	$V0$-NoC	$V1$-NoC	$V2$-NoC	$V0$-NoC	$V1$-NoC	$V2$-NoC	$V0$-NoC	$V1$-NoC	$V2$-NoC
Average latency	224.7	229.5	252.1	239.4	233.7	257.9	343.8	310.3	334.7	277.6	252.9	274.6
VC number	192	128	132	192	96	96	192	96	96	192	100	108

Acknowledgment. This work has been supported by the Research Funds of Education Department of Heilongjiang Province, Grant No. 12531518.

References

1. Ho, R., Mai, K., Horowitz, M.: The future of wires. Proc. IEEE **89**(4), 490–504 (2001)
2. Dally, W.J., Towles, B.: Route packets, not wires: on-chip interconnection networks. In: The 38th Design Automation Conference, pp. 684–689 (2001)
3. Benini, L., De Micheli, G.: Networks on chips: a new SoC paradigm. IEEE Trans. Comput. **35**(1), 70–78 (2002)
4. Guerrier, P., Greiner, A.: A generic architecture for on-chip packet-switched interconnections. In: Design Automation and Test in Europe (DATE 2000), pp. 250–256 (2000)
5. Bjerregaard, T., Mahadevan, S.: A survey of research and practices of network-on-chip. ACM Comput. Surv. **38**(3), 1–51 (2006)
6. Kim, J., Nicopoulos, C., Park, D., et al.: A gracefully degrading and energy-efficient modular router architecture for on-chip networks. In: The 33rd International Symposium on Computer Architecture (ISCA 2006), pp. 4–15 (2006)
7. Hu, J., Marculescu, R.: Application-specific buffer space allocation for networks-on-chip router design. In: The IEEE/ACM International Conference on Computer Aided Design (ICCAD), pp. 354–361 (2004)
8. Nicopoulos, C.A., Park, D., Kim, J., et al.: VichaR: a dynamic virtual channel regulator for network-on-chip routers. In: The 39th Annual IEEE/ACM International Symposium on Microarchitecture, pp. 333–344 (2006)
9. Chen, X., Peh, L.-S.: Leakage power modeling and optimization in interconnection networks. In: The International Symposium on Low Power Electronics and Design, pp. 90–95 (2003)
10. Matsutani, H., Koibuchi, M., Wang, D., Amano, H.: Run-time power gating of on-chip routers using look-ahead routing. In: Design Automation Conference (ASPDAC), pp. 55–60 (2008)
11. Matsutani, H., Koibuchi, M., Wang, D., Amano, H.: Adding slow-slient virtual channels for low-power on-chip networks. In: The 2nd IEEE International Symposium on Networks-On-Chip, pp. 23–32 (2008)
12. Ding, J., Bhuyan, L.N.: Evaluation of multi-queue buffered multistage interconnection networks under uniform and non-uniform traffic patterns. Int. J. Syst. Sci. **28**(11), 1115–1128 (1997)
13. Ni, N., Pirvu, M., Bhuyan, L.: Circular buffered switch design with wormhole routing and virtual channels. In: Computer Design: VLSI in Computers and Processors, pp. 466–473 (1998)
14. Bolotin, E., Cidon, I., Ginosar, R., Kolodny, A.: QNoC: QoS architecture and design process for network on chip. Spec. Issue Netw. Chip J. Syst. Architect. **50**(2–3), 105–128 (2004)
15. Huang, T., Ogras, U.Y., Marculescu, R.: Virtual channels planning for networks-on-chip. In: Proceedings of the 8th International on Quality Electronic Design (ISQED), pp. 879–884 (2007)

A Two-Layered Game Approach Based Relay's Source Selection and Power Control for Wireless Cooperative Networks

Yanguo Zhou[1]([✉]), Hailin Zhang[1], Ruirui Chen[1], and Tao Zhou[2]

[1] Xidian University, Xi'an 710071, China
ygzhou@stu.xidian.edu.cn
[2] CETC No. 38 Research Institute, Hefei 230088, China

Abstract. Cooperative relay communication has become a promising technology to extend the network coverage and enhance the system performance. To avoid the interference among the relays assisted the same source and maximize the relay utility in multisource multirelay networks, we propose the two-layered game based distributed algorithm, which jointly considers power control and the relay's source selection. Power control and relay's source selection are formulated as a general non-cooperative game and an evolutionary game, respectively. By using the alternate iterations between the non-cooperative game and the evolutionary game, the proposed distributed algorithm can effectively suppress the interference and choose the optimal source. Simulation results are presented to analyze the performance of the proposed distributed algorithm.

Keywords: Power control · Relay's source selection
Evolutionary game · Two-layered game · Distributed algorithm

1 Introduction

Cooperative relay communication has become an emerging transmitting strategy to extend the network coverage and enhance the system performance [1, 2]. The goal of cooperative transmission in wireless networks is to increase transmission diversity at less transmission power. The power control and relay's selection have attracted much research attention. Many papers have focused on cooperative communication for wireless networks over the past decade. In [3], the authors propose a relay-ordering based scheme, which can dynamically select relay and adjust power allocation based on the SNR and channel condition. The authors in [4] analyze the relay selection problem: when to cooperate and whom to cooperate with. By using a game approach, the authors of [5] study the distributed relay selection in randomized cooperation. Power control with a pricing is discussed in [6, 7]. In [8], the authors investigate distributed relay selection and power control for cooperative communication networks, which consists of one

© ICST Institute for Computer Sciences, Social Informatics and Telecommunications Engineering 2018
X. Gu et al. (Eds.): MLICOM 2017, Part II, LNICST 227, pp. 343–350, 2018.
https://doi.org/10.1007/978-3-319-73447-7_38

source and multiple relays. Evolutionary game [9] is a useful tool to address the relay's selection problem in changeable environment. The authors in [10] propose an energy-aware dynamic cooperative partner selection for relay-assisted cellular networks, and the evolutionary game theory is first introduced to resolve the dynamic cooperative partner-selection problem with incomplete private information.

Different from the existing literatures that focus on the source's selection of relays, we concentrate on relay's selection of sources in multi-relay and multi-source networks. Because the relays occupy the frequency resource, they should select optimal source and determine their own transmit power, which can effectively suppress the interference and choose the optimal source. Therefore, for this multi-relay and multi-source networks, there are two main questions:

(1) Among all source nodes, which is the optimal source node for relay nodes?
(2) Once the optimal source node is selected, how the relay node determines the transmit power?

As an answer to these two questions, we present the two-layered game based distributed algorithm, which jointly considers the relays' source selection and power control. The proposed distributed algorithm can effectively suppress the interference and choose the optimal source.

2 System Model

We consider a cooperative relay networks, which consists of source node $s \in \mathcal{S} \triangleq \{1, ..., S\}$, destination $d \in \mathcal{D} \triangleq \{1, ..., D\}$, and relay node $r \in \mathcal{R} \triangleq \{1, ..., N\}$. Furthermore, it is assumed that each relay node can only select one source to help with its feasible transmit power P_r and S is equal to D. Therefore, there are S source-to-destination pairs in the cooperative relay networks.

We can denote the path gain between node i and node j by $G_{i,j}$. σ^2 represents the variance of additive white Gaussian noise (AWGN) at each node, which is assumed to be constant. As in [11], we employ the AF protocol in this paper. The SNR with relay's help at node d can be expressed as

$$\gamma_{s,r,d} = \frac{P_s P_r G_{s,r} G_{r,d}}{\sigma^2 (P_s G_{s,r} + P_r G_{r,d} + \sigma^2)}, \tag{1}$$

where P_s is the transmit power of source node s.

It is assumed that the maximal-ratio combining (MRC) detector is applied to node d. Then, we can get the combined rate as follows:

$$R_{s,r,d} = log_2(1 + \gamma_{s,d} + \sum_{i \in L_s} \gamma_{s,i,d}), \tag{2}$$

where $\gamma_{s,d} = \frac{P_s G_{s,d}}{\sigma^2}$ is the SNR of the direct link of source s, and L_s denotes the set of relay nodes that assist the source s.

We design a relay's utility function based on its contribution to source's rate. We adopt the similar Sharply method used in coalition game to guarantee fairness among relay nodes. Thus, relay node r's utility function can be expressed as

$$u'_r = \alpha_s(R_{s,r,d} - R_{s,-r,d}),$$ (3)

where α_s denotes relay node's gain per unit rate at the MRC output from source node s, and $R_{s,-r,d}$ represents the source s's transmission rate without relay node r's help.

Substituting Eq. (2) into (3), we can get

$$u'_r = \alpha_s log_2(1 + \frac{\gamma_{s,r,d}}{1 + \gamma_{s,d} + \sum_{i \in L_s, i \neq r} \gamma_{s,i,d}}).$$ (4)

It can be observed that relay node r's utility is dependent on not only its own transmit power P_r, but also other relay nodes' selection and transmit power.

Each relay node's utility is a monotonically increasing function of its own transmit power. Therefore, each relay node has the incentive to transmit signal with its maximal transmit power, which results in the energy inefficiency. It is necessary to add a cost function with respect to transmit power, and then the relay node r's payoff, or net utility function can be written as follows:

$$u_r = \alpha_s log_2(1 + \frac{\gamma_{s,r,d}}{1 + \gamma_{s,d} + \sum_{i \in L_s, i \neq r} \gamma_{s,i,d}}) - c_r P_r,$$ (5)

where c_r is relay r's cost per unit transmit power.

3   Problem Formulation

A. *Relay's power control*

The power control optimization problem can be formulated as a non-cooperative game, which is expressed as

$$\begin{aligned} \max \quad & u_r \quad \forall r \\ \text{s.t. } & 0 \leq P_r \leq \bar{P}_r, \end{aligned}$$ (6)

where $\bar{P}_r$ is the power upper bound for relay node r.

(1) Existence of the Equilibrium for the power control game:
By using the payoff function's concavity, we will proof the existence of Nash Equilibrium (NE) for power control game.

Theorem 1: A NE exists in game $G = [\mathcal{R}, P(r), u_r]$, if for all $r \in \mathcal{R}$

(1). $P(r)$ is a non-empty, convex and compact subset of some Euclidean space.
(2). u_r is continuous and quasi-concave in P_r.

Proof: For any $r \in \mathcal{R}$, each relay r has a strategy space of the transmit power for helping the selected source. For any $P_r \in P(r) = [0, \bar{P}_r]$, it is easy to proof that relay r's power space $P(r)$ is non-empty and compact. By utilizing the definition of the convex set, given any $p1, p2 \in P(r)$ and any $\epsilon \in [0, 1]$, we have $0 \leq \epsilon p1 \leq \epsilon \bar{P}_r$ and $0 \leq (1 - \epsilon)p2 \leq (1 - \epsilon)\bar{P}_r$. Based on the above two in equations, we can get $0 \leq \epsilon p1 + (1 - \epsilon)p2 \leq \bar{P}_r$. Thus, the power space $P(r)$ is convex.

Then, we will show that the payoff function u_r is concave with respect to P_r. We can get the payoff function u_r's second-order derivation

$$\frac{\partial^2 u_r}{\partial^2 P_r} = -\frac{\alpha_s}{\ln 2} \frac{P_s G_{s,r} G_{r,d} T + \sigma^2 T^2 \frac{\partial \gamma_{r,s,d}}{\partial P_r}}{(\Gamma'_{-r} + \gamma_{s,r,d})\sigma^2 T^2 + P_s P_r G_{s,r} G_{r,d} T}, \tag{7}$$

where T is a positive value defined in Eq. (10). Then, we can derive the first-order derivation of $\gamma_{s,r,d}$ as

$$\frac{\partial \gamma_{s,r,d}}{\partial P_r} = \frac{P_s G_{s,r} G_{r,d}(P_s G_{s,r} + \sigma^2)}{\sigma^2 T^2}, \tag{8}$$

which is a positive value.

Therefore, we can draw a conclusion that the payoff function of relay node r is concave. Theorem 1 follows.

(2) The optimal P_r^*:

Taking the derivative of Eq. (5), we can get

$$\frac{\partial u_r}{\partial P_r} = \frac{\alpha_s}{\ln 2} \frac{1}{1 + \gamma_{s,d} + \Gamma_{-r} + \gamma_{s,r,d}} \frac{\partial \gamma_{s,r,d}}{\partial P_r} - c_r, \tag{9}$$

where $\Gamma_{-r} = \sum_{i \in L_s, i \neq r} \gamma_{s,i,d}$.

Substituting Eq. (8) into (9), we can get

$$\frac{\partial u_r}{\partial P_r} = \frac{\alpha_s}{\ln 2} \frac{P_s G_{s,r} G_{r,d}(P_s G_{s,r} + \sigma^2)}{(\Gamma'_{-r} + \gamma_{s,r,d})\sigma^2 T^2 + P_s P_r G_{s,r} G_{r,d} T} - c_r, \tag{10}$$

where $T = P_s G_{s,r} + P_r G_{r,d} + \sigma^2$ and $\Gamma'_{-r} = 1 + \gamma_{s,d} + \Gamma_{-r}$.

Let Eq. (10) be zero, we can find that the equation can be rewritten as one quadratic function with respect to relay node r's power P_r, which satisfies the following expression

$$AP_r^2 + BP_r + C = 0, \tag{11}$$

where

$$A = G_{r,d}^2(P_s G_{s,r} + \sigma^2 \Gamma'_{-r}), \tag{12}$$

$$B = (P_s G_{s,r} + \sigma^2)(P_s G_{s,r} G_{r,d} + 2\sigma^2 G_{r,d}\Gamma'_{-r}), \tag{13}$$

and

$$C = \sigma^2 \Gamma'_{-r}(P_s G_{s,r} + \sigma^2)^2 - \frac{\alpha_s}{c_r \ln 2} P_s G_{s,r} G_{r,d}(P_s G_{s,r} + \sigma^2). \tag{14}$$

According to this function's properties, the necessary condition for the existence of one positive solution is $C < 0$. Then, we define relay's revenue-to-cost-ratio (RCR) as $\rho_{s,r}$, which should satisfy the following requirement

$$\rho_{s,r} > \rho_{s,r}^0, \tag{15}$$

where $\rho_{s,r} = \frac{\alpha_s}{c_r}$ and $\rho_{s,r}^0 = \frac{\ln 2\sigma^2 \Gamma_{-r}'(P_s G_{s,r}+\sigma^2)}{P_s G_{s,r} G_{r,d}}$. This means that if $\rho_{s,r}$ is smaller than the threshold $\rho_{s,r}^0$, the relay node r will not help source node s.

Solving this quadratic function (11), we can get

$$\hat{P}_r = \frac{\sqrt{B^2 - 4AC} - B}{2A}. \tag{16}$$

Under relay's power constraint, the optimal power P_r^* is determined by

$$P_r^* = \begin{cases} 0, & \rho_{s,r} \leq \rho_{s,r}^0; \\ \hat{P}_r, & \hat{P}_r \leq \bar{P}_r; \\ \bar{P}_r, & \hat{P}_r > \bar{P}_r. \end{cases} \tag{17}$$

B. Relay's source selection

Note that the payoff may be different for relay node r if it selects different source node s to help, even it transmits at the same power. Thus, to get a maximal payoff, the relays have the incentive to select the best source node.

Then, we can formulate this problem as an evolutionary game. Let n_s denote the number of relay nodes selecting source node s, and $N = \sum_{s=1}^{S} n_s$. The proportion of relay nodes selecting the strategy s can be denoted by $x_s = n_s/N$. The replicator dynamics of relay's selection game can be defined as

$$\frac{\partial x_s(t)}{\partial t} = \dot{x}_s(t) = \delta x_s(t)(u_s - \bar{u}), \tag{18}$$

where δ controls the evolution speed, and

$$u_s = \frac{\sum_{i \in L_s} u_i}{n_s} \tag{19}$$

and then

$$\bar{u} = \sum_{s=1}^{S} x_s u_s. \tag{20}$$

With the evolution of all relay nodes, the evolutionary game will converge to the stable evolutionary strategy (ESS) which can be determined by solving such set of equations

$$\dot{x}_s = 0, \qquad \forall s. \tag{21}$$

C. Two-layered game's distributed algorithm

We can combine the non-cooperative game and evolutionary game into one two-layered game. By using the alternate iterations between the non-cooperative game of power control and the evolutionary game of source selection, the proposed distributed algorithm can effectively suppress the interference and choose the optimal source.

The distributed algorithm is described as follows:

(1) Initial: For each relay, the transmit power and source are randomly chosen.
(2) Power control game begins:
(3) Each player adopts the optimal power according to Eq. (17) at time t.
   if $\max_{r \in \mathcal{R}} \| P_r^*(t) - P_r^*(t+1) \| > \varepsilon$, then
   Let $t = t + 1$ and return to step (3).
   Else, go to step (4).
(4) Power control game ends.
(5) Relay's selection game begins:
(6) The relays begin source selections according to Eqs. (19) and (20),
   if $u_s < \bar{u}$, then
   if $rand() < \| \frac{\bar{u} - u_s}{\bar{u}} \|$,
   Give up the strategy s and choose the strategy k, where $k = \arg\max_{i \in \mathcal{S}} u_i$,
   and return to step (6).
   Else if $u_s = \bar{u}$ $\forall s$, then go to step (7).
(7) Source selection game ends.
(8) Judge whether it comes the NE of the whole two-layered game.
(9) If $\max_{r \in \mathcal{R}} \| P_r^*(t) - P_r^*(t+1) \| > \varepsilon$,
   Return to step (2), and repeat this process.
   Else, go to step (10).
(10) This two-layered game ends.

4   Simulation Results and Analysis

In this section, simulation results are presented to evaluate the proposed algorithm. In this simulation, all basic parameters are set as follows: $N = 100$, $S = D = 2$, $\alpha_s = 20$, $\bar{P}_s = 1$ $\forall s$, $G_{s,d} = 1$ $\forall (s, d)$, $\sigma^2 = 1$, $G_{s,r} = 1$ $\forall (s, r)$, $G_{r,d} = 1$ $\forall r, d$, and $c_r = 0.1$ $\forall r$.

A. *source's direct channel parameter $G_{s,d}$ impact*

We consider two sources' direct links with $G_{s,d} = 1$ and $G_{s,d} = 4$. From Fig. 1, it can be observed that each relay's payoff is same after certain iterations under different $G_{s,d}$. However, the number of relay nodes helping source 1 and 2 is different. Thus, source node's direct link condition has the effect on source selection, but has no impact on relay node's payoff. Furthermore, we can see that the worse the source node's direct link condition is, the larger the probability that the relay nodes select this source node.

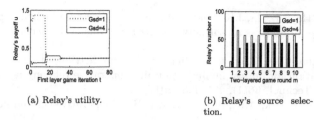

(a) Relay's utility.

(b) Relay's source selection.

Fig. 1. Source's direct link's $G_{s,d}$ impact

B. *relay's channel parameter $G_{s,r}$ impact*

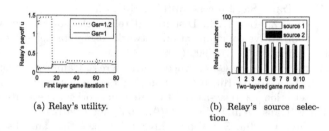

(a) Relay's utility.

(b) Relay's source selection.

Fig. 2. Relay's channel condition's $G_{s,r}$ impact

We set $G_{s,r} = 1.2, r = 1, ..., 50$ (group 1) and $G_{s,r} = 1, r = 51, ..., 100$ (group 2) to analyze its impact. From Fig. 2, we can see that the payoff of relay node from group 1 is higher than that of relay node from group 2. Furthermore, when the two-layered game reach the NE, there are about 50 relays helping source 1 and 2, respectively. Therefore, relay node's channel condition affects the relay node's payoff but not the source selection. Furthermore, we find that a better channel condition of relay node will result in a higher payoff.

5   Conclusions

In this paper, we propose a two-layered game approach based a distributed algorithm for relay's source selection and power control in multi-source and multi-relay networks. Simulation results demonstrate that the worse the source node's direct link condition is, the larger the probability that the relay nodes select this source node, and relay node with better channel conditions can get a higher payoff as compared with other relays.

References

1. Wang, C.L., Chen, J.Y.: Power allocation and relay selection for AF cooperative relay systems with imperfect channel estimation. IEEE Trans. Veh. Technol. **65**(9), 7809–7813 (2016)

2. Yang, Q.Q., He, S.B., Li, J.K., Chen, J.M., Sun, Y.X.: Energy-efficient probabilistic area coverage in wireless sensor networks. IEEE Trans. Veh. Technol. **64**(1), 367–377 (2015)
3. Liu, L.Y., Hua, C.Q., Chen, C.L., Guan, X.P.: Semidistributed relay selection and power allocation for outage minimization in cooperative relaying networks. IEEE Trans. Veh. Technol. **66**(1), 295–305 (2017)
4. Ibrahim, A.S., Sadek, A.K., Su, W., Liu, K.R.: Cooperative communications with relay-selection: when to cooperate and whom to cooperate with? IEEE Trans. Wirel. Commun. **7**(7), 2814–2826 (2008)
5. Sergi, S., Vitetta, G.M.: A game theoretical approach to distributed relay selection in randomized cooperation. IEEE Trans. Wirel. Commun. **9**(8), 2611–2621 (2010)
6. Saraydar, C.U., Mandayam, N.B., Goodman, D.J.: Efficient power control via pricing in wireless data networks. IEEE Trans. Commun. **50**(2), 291–303 (2002)
7. Ren, S., Van der Schaar, M.: Pricing and distributed power control in wireless relay networks. IEEE Trans. Sig. Process. **59**(6), 2913–2926 (2011)
8. Wang, B.B., Han, Z., Liu, K.R.: Distributed relay selection and power control for multiuser cooperative communication networks using stackelberg game. IEEE Trans. Mob. Comput. **8**(7), 975–990 (2009)
9. Weibull, J.W.: Evolutionary Game Theory. MIT Press, Cambridge (1997)
10. Wu, D., Zhou, L., Cai, Y., Hu, R.Q., Qian, Y.: Energy-aware dynamic cooperative strategy selection for relay-assisted cellular networks: an evolutionary game approach. IEEE Trans. Veh. Technol. **63**(9), 4659–4669 (2014)
11. Zhong, W., Chen, G., Jin, S., Wong, K.K.: Relay selection and discrete power control for cognitive relay networks via potential game. IEEE Trans. Sig. Process. **62**(20), 5411–5424 (2014)

A Novel Method of Flight Target Altitude Attributes Identification for HFSWR

Shuai Shao, Changjun Yu[✉], and Kongrui Zhao

School of Information and Electrical Engineering,
Harbin Institute of Technology, Weihai 264209, China
yuchangjun@hit.edu.cn

Abstract. Recently, flight target altitude estimation using high frequency surface wave radar (HFSWR) gains popularity. In practical flight target early warning applications, the most concerned characteristics of the targets are generally the high/low altitude attribute and the line-of-sight/over-the-horizon. For HFSWR, the target altitude attribute identification is somewhat more meaningful and available than the accurate altitude estimation. In this paper, a novel method, which is based on the propagation attenuation of the vertically polarized wave at different altitude intervals, is proposed to identify target altitude attribute in HFSWR. The method continuously identify the target altitude attributes and evaluate the credibility of altitude attributes identification. Practical trials demonstrate that the flight target altitude attribute is quickly identified using a small amount of data, and meanwhile the credibility is superior to 0.9.

Keywords: High frequency surface wave radar
Altitude attribute identification · Propagation attenuation

1 Introduction

High frequency surface wave radar (HFSWR), which transmits vertical polarized radio waves along the sea surface, is able to detect flight targets for hundreds of kilometers away [1–4]. The radar has been applied by the maritime surveillance departments to combat sea smuggling, to control maritime traffic and to protect exclusive economic zone [5–7]. HFSWR takes the advantage of the diffraction propagation of the radio wave to detect the over-the-horizon flight targets, while the radar can also be employed to detect the high-altitude line-of-sight target due to the relatively wide vertical beam. However, the signal and data processing methods utilized in traditional HFSWR provide only the distance, velocity and orientation information of the targets, i.e. the altitude information of the flight target is unavailable. Therefore, HFSWR is fails to identify the target altitude attribute, and unable to judge whether it is a high altitude target or a low altitude target. As pointed out in [8], HFSWR cannot immediately distinguish between targets that are at different altitude in the same range over the horizon.

In order to identify the high/low altitude attribute of the flight target, the target altitude can be accurately estimated by the traditional method. However, HFSWR is currently using slope and azimuth information to estimate the altitude of high-altitude

© ICST Institute for Computer Sciences, Social Informatics and Telecommunications Engineering 2018
X. Gu et al. (Eds.): MLICOM 2017, Part II, LNICST 227, pp. 351–360, 2018.
https://doi.org/10.1007/978-3-319-73447-7_39

targets, these methods cannot be applied to low-altitude flight target altitude estimates. In [9], a real-time estimation method of altitude and radar cross section (RCS) of target using echo is proposed. However, this method is a multi-solution problem at altitude estimation resulting in highly estimated error and low credibility. Although many improved algorithms are proposed based on the above methods, there is still no fundamental solution to the highly estimated multiresolution problem [10–12] and cannot be applied to HFSWR practical systems so far. From the point of view of engineering application, HFSWR flight target altitude estimation is still in the exploratory stage. In the HFSWR marine flight target early warning applications, whether the target is a high/low altitude flight and line-of-sight/over-the-horizon is mostly concerned. It is more practical to quickly and directly identify the flight target as a high/low altitude attribute, line-of-sight/over-the-horizon attribute, that is to obtain the flight target altitude attribute more than the specific flight altitude of the accurate estimation, and it is easier to realize on the actual HFSWR system.

Based on the above engineering design, this paper focuses on solving the HFSWR flight target high/low altitude attribute, line-of-sight/over-the-horizon attribute identification issue. According to the different propagation attenuation characteristics of the vertically polarized waves in the range of high and low altitude that will be introduced in Sect. 2, a target altitude attribute identification algorithm is proposed without estimating the specific flight altitude of the target in Sect. 3. This method is able to identify the target altitude attribute, and calculate the credibility of altitude attribute identification. Furthermore, in Sect. 4, the algorithm is verified by the in situ data. A brief conclusion is given in Sect. 5.

2   HFSWR Propagation Attenuation

According to the monostatic HFSWR equation, the power of the received signal can be expressed as

$$P_r = P_t G_t \frac{1}{l_b^2(R,h)} \frac{\sigma}{(\lambda^2/4\pi)} G_r \tag{1}$$

where P_r is the received target echo; P_t is the transmitting station signal transmission power; G_t is the transmit antenna gain; G_r is the receive antenna gain; σ is the target RCS; h is the target altitude; R is the distance between the target and the radar observation station; $l_b(\bullet)$ is the surface wave propagation attenuation used by the International Telecommunication Union (ITU), which is a function of the target flight altitude h and the distance R from the target to the observation station; λ is operating wavelength of radar.

The HFSWR Eq. (1) takes the logarithm, and decibel representation is

$$P_r(dB) = -20 \lg l_b(R,h) + 10 \lg \sigma + 10 \lg c \tag{2}$$

where $C = 10 \lg c$, $\zeta_b(R,h) = 10 \lg l_b(R,h)$ and $\Psi = 10 \lg \sigma$. Hence (2) can be expressed as

$$P_r(dB) = -2\zeta_b^r(R, h) + \Psi + C \tag{3}$$

In (3), it is assumed that the radar system parameters are constant, and C is also known. The target echo is regarded as a known constant, and the target RCS and the wave propagation attenuation have a linear constraint relationship. In addition, the wave propagation attenuation is a function of the target distance and flight altitude. Therefore, to achieve the target flight altitude attribute identification, it is necessary to analyze the propagation attenuation of the vertically polarized wave propagating at different altitude.

In the high frequency band, the Rotheram model takes into account the atmospheric refraction index and expatiates the propagation decay model in detail. The propagation decay curve is adopted by the ITU as radio wave propagation attenuation standard in 10 kHz–30 MHz [13, 14]. Therefore, based on the unique advantage of the Rotheram propagation attenuation model, the Rotheram propagation attenuation model is used to calculate propagation decay curves at different altitude and distances.

For radar operates in 11.2 MHz, the altitude of transmitting station is 20 m, and the range of distance between radar station and target is 30 km–140 km, the low- and high-altitude propagation decay curve is shown in Figs. 1 and 2, respectively. As shown in Fig. 1, the attenuation decreases gradually with the increasing altitude in the low altitude region. When the flight altitude is lower than 2 km, the attenuation at different altitude is different, and the altitude change 0.5 km can cause the deviation of 2 dB. In Fig. 2, the propagation attenuation difference at different altitude is getting less. It can be seen that the difference in propagation attenuation in the high-altitude region is not obvious. Therefore, the different propagation attenuation of the vertical polarization wave propagation attenuation in the different space regions provides the possibility of identifying the target altitude attribute.

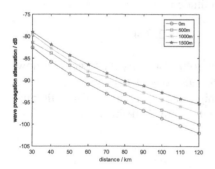 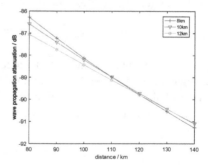

Fig. 1. Low-altitude propagation attenuation   **Fig. 2.** High-altitude propagation attenuation

3 Altitude Attribute Identification Algorithm

The purpose of this paper is to directly identify the altitude attribute of the flight target without estimating the specific flight target altitude, and to improve the estimating performance of goal threat in HFSWR.

Line-of-sight/over-the-horizon of the target is related to the target distance and flight altitude. In order to simplify line-of-sight/over-the-horizon attribute identification problem complexity, the target high/low altitude flight status is identified before identifying the altitude attribute, then the high/low altitude flight status is used to identify line-of-sight/over-the-horizon attribute of the target. Therefore, the altitude attribute of the flight target is divided into four categories: high-altitude and line-of-sight, high-altitude and over-the-horizon, low-altitude and line-of-sight, low-altitude and over-the-horizon.

In order to make full use of the propagation attenuation characteristics of vertically polarized waves in different altitude intervals, the target echo correction is needed in the altitude attribute identification algorithm.

In the low-altitude region, the attenuation of the surface wave caused by seawater is large. Therefore, it is assumed that the height region of 0–2 km is a low-altitude area. The altitude of the 0–2 km range is divided into four altitude sub-intervals, the altitude division nodes are respectively $h_0 = 0$ km, $h_1 = 0.5$ km, $h_2 = 1$ km, $h_3 = 1.5$ km, $h_4 = 2$ km. The propagation attenuation on the ith altitude sub-interval is approximated by the propagation attenuation on the node altitude h_i. That is

$$\zeta_b(R, h_{i-1} < h < h_i) \approx \zeta_b(R, h_i) \quad i = 1, 2, 3, 4 \tag{4}$$

The target altitude is higher in the high altitude region, and the influence of the flight altitude on the attenuation of the radio wave propagation is very small, and the influence of the altitude on the target echo can be neglected. Thus, the propagation attenuation at the altitude of the $h_H = 10$ km is used instead of the propagation attenuation at any altitude in the high altitude region. That is

$$\zeta_b(R, h) \approx \zeta_b(R, h_H = 10\,\text{km}) \tag{5}$$

Thus, the target echo corresponding to each altitude node is

$$P_r(dB) = -2\zeta_b(R, h_i) + \Psi + C \quad i = 1, 2, 3, 4, H \tag{6}$$

In this paper, we use the multi-model algorithm to first identify the target high/low altitude flight state. Independent filtering models are constructed on each altitude sub-interval of the low altitude region and the high altitude region. In the filtering model of the ith altitude sub-interval, the target state vector is defined as

$$\mathbf{X}_k^i = \left[\Psi_k, \dot{\Psi}_k\right]^T \tag{7}$$

where Ψ_k is the RCS size of the target relative to the station at k, and $\dot{\Psi}$ is the target RCS rate of change at k. It can be seen from (7) that the target state vector does not contain unknown altitude information and contains only RCS information, thus avoiding the multi-solution problem of state estimation. The target state equation of the ith filter model is defined as

$$\mathbf{X}_k^i = \mathbf{F}\mathbf{X}_{k-1}^i + \mathbf{v}_{k-1} \tag{8}$$

where $\mathbf{F} \in \mathbf{R}^{2 \times 2}$ is the state transition matrix, $\mathbf{v}_{k-1}$ is the white Gaussian process noise with mean of 0 and variance of $\mathbf{Q}_{k-1}^i$.

The target echo is used as the observation value of each filter model, and the observation equation is defined as

$$P_r(dB) = -2\zeta_b(R, h_i) + \Psi_k + C + \omega_k \tag{9}$$

where ω_k is the white Gaussian observation noise with mean of 0 and variance of R_k.

A set of multi-models filters can be established using the filtering model on all altitude sub- intervals of the low-altitude region and the high-altitude region. This set of multi-models filters is defined as follows

$$\begin{cases} \mathbf{X}_k^i = \mathbf{F}\mathbf{X}_{k-1}^i + \mathbf{v}_{k-1} \\ P_r(dB) = -2\zeta_b(R, h_i) + \Psi_k + C + \omega_k \end{cases} \quad i = 1, 2, 3, 4, H \tag{10}$$

In the high/low altitude flight state identification, the Kalman filter algorithm is used to calculate the predicted value $\hat{Z}_{k/k-1}^i$, the state $\hat{X}_{k/k}^i$ and the covariance $P_{k/k}^i$ of the ith filter model at k . $\hat{Z}_{k/k-1}^i$ is used to calculate the confidence level of the high/low altitude flight state. At the time of $k+1$, the ith filter model is initialized with $\hat{X}_{k/k}^i$ and $P_{k/k}^i$. The target high/low altitude flight status identification process is shown in Fig. 3.

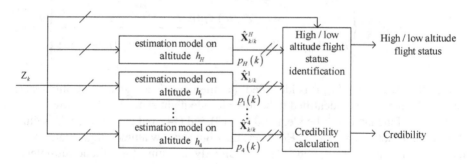

Fig. 3. High/low altitude flight status identification flow chart

The input information Z_k is the target echo value; the model on the altitude h_i is the state filtering model defined by (10). The high/low altitude flight status identification and confidence calculation module input information is estimated value $\hat{X}_{k/k}^i$ of the state filter model and the likelihood function $p_i(k)$ of the filtering model. For the ith filter model, likelihood value of the observed value Z_k is

$$p(Z_k/h_i) = \frac{1}{\sqrt{2\pi|\mathbf{S}_k^i|}} \exp\left\{-\frac{1}{2}\Delta\hat{Z}_{k/k-1}^i{}^T\mathbf{S}_k^{i-1}\Delta\hat{Z}_{k/k-1}^i\right\} \tag{11}$$

where $\mathbf{S}_k^i$ is the new covariance matrix of ith filtering model at time k; $\Delta\hat{Z}_{k/k-1}^i$ is the new information of ith filter model at time k, defined as

$$\Delta\hat{Z}_{k/k-1}^i = Z_k^i - \hat{Z}_{k/k-1}^i \tag{12}$$

The confidence values of high/low altitude flight states are defined by the likelihood function given by (11) as follows:

(1) High altitude flight state confidence value

$$
\begin{aligned}
p(D_1(k)) &= p(h_H(k)) \\
&= \frac{p(Z_k/h_H) \cdot p(h_H(k-1))}{p(Z_k/h_H) \cdot p(h_H(k-1)) + \sum_{j=1}^{4} p(Z_k/h_j) \cdot p(h_j(k-1))}
\end{aligned} \tag{13}
$$

(2) Low altitude flight state confidence value

$$
\begin{aligned}
p(D_2(k)) &= \max_{i=1,2,3,4} \{p(h_i(k))\} \\
&= \max_{i=1,2,3,4} \left\{ \frac{p(Z_k/h_i) \cdot p(h_i(k-1))}{p(Z_k/h_H) \cdot p(h_H(k-1)) + \sum_{j=1}^{4} p(Z_k/h_j) \cdot p(h_j(k-1))} \right\}
\end{aligned} \tag{14}
$$

If $p(D_1(k)) > p(D_2(k))$, it is identified that the target is a high altitude flight state. Conversely, the target is identified to be low altitude flight state. The high/low altitude flight states of the target can be identified by (13) and (14), but the target flight altitude information is not given directly. However, the high and low altitude flight states of the identification defined by (13) and (14) can indirectly determine the altitude sub-interval of the target.

Therefore, the altitude attribute is defined by the high/low altitude flight state and the line of sight/over-the-horizon, as follows

(1) Assuming $p(D_1(k)) > p(D_2(k))$ and $R(km) < 4.2\sqrt{h_H(m)}$, then the target is the high-altitude line-of-sight attribute
(2) Assuming $p(D_1(k)) > p(D_2(k))$ and $R(km) > 4.2\sqrt{h_H(m)}$, then the target is the high-altitude and over-the-horizon attribute
(3) Assuming $p(D_1(k)) < p(D_2(k))$ and $R(km) < 4.2\sqrt{h_l(m)}$, where $l = \arg\max_{i=1,2,3,4}\{p(h_i(k))\}$, then the target is the low-altitude and line-of-sight attribute

(4) Assuming $p(D_1(k)) < p(D_2(k))$ and $R(km) > 4.2\sqrt{h_l(m)}$, where $l = \underset{i=1,2,3,4}{\arg\max}$ $\{p(h_i(k))\}$, then the target is the low-altitude and over-the-horizon attribute.

When the target satisfies the altitude attribute criterion (1) or (2), the altitude attribute credibility value is defined as $p(D_1(k))$ (Fig. 4).

When the target satisfies the altitude attribute criterion (3) or (4), the altitude attribute credibility value is defined as $p(D_2(k))$.

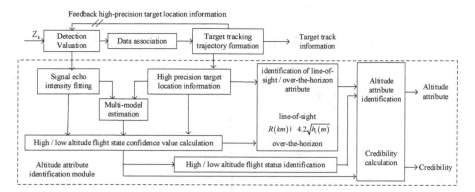

Fig. 4. Frame of flight target altitude attribute identification algorithm for HFSWR

4 Practical Trials Validation

This section uses Weihai high frequency surface wave radar station experimental data to analyze the performance of the altitude attribute identification algorithm. HFSWR operating frequency is 11.2 MHz, the transmission power is 1 kw, the sampling period is 10 s. The target distance observation error is 1 km, and the target echo observation error is 1 dB.

(1) The track of the first batch flight targets is shown in Fig. 5. The target flight height is 200 m, and the azimuth angle of the radar station is 14° and the distance between the target and the observation station is 23.2 km–59.5 km. Figure 6 shows that after four sampling points, the target low altitude flight state reliability value is close to 1, and the high altitude flight state reliability value is close to 0. Therefore, the target can be judged as a low-altitude flight target.

(2) The second batch of aircraft target track is shown in Fig. 7, the aircraft target flight direction suspected of Japan, South Korea direction. Figure 8 shows that the result of the altitude estimation matches with the flight altitude of the international civil aviation aircraft. The target heading speed is 921.6 km/h and also conforms to the international flight speed.

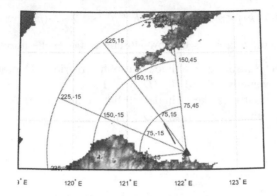

Fig. 5. Target relative to the observation station track

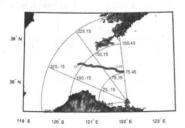

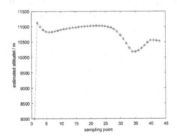

a) low-altitude flight state credibility   b) high-altitude flight state credibility

Fig. 6. High/low-altitude flight state credibility

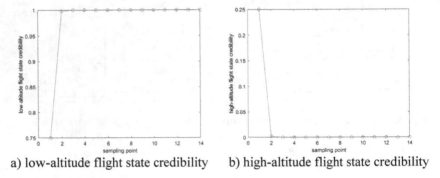

Fig. 7. Target track   **Fig. 8.** Estimated altitude results

The high and low altitude flight states values shown in Fig. 9 indicate that the target is at high altitude and the high altitude flight state reliability is more than 0.95. In the calculation of the high-altitude flight state confidence value shown in Fig. 9(a), $p(h_H)$ is more than 0.95. The target is within the high altitude range defined herein, and its

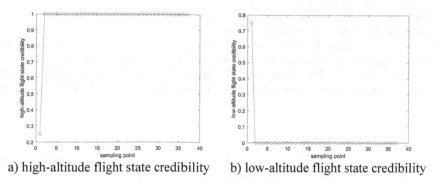

a) high-altitude flight state credibility   b) low-altitude flight state credibility

Fig. 9. High/low-altitude flight state credibility

altitude is replaced by $h_H = 10$ km, and the target distance is about 75 km–160 km. According to the line-of-sight and over-the-horizon attribute judgment criterion, the target distance and the altitude always meet $R(km) < 4.2\sqrt{h_H(m)}$, the target is the line-of-sight target. In summary, the target attribute is the high-altitude line-of-sight attribute. As can be seen from the altitude attribute confidence value, the high-altitude flight state confidence value shown in Fig. 9(a) is also the altitude attribute identification confidence value.

5   Conclusion

Based on the different propagation attenuation characteristics of vertically polarized waves in high-altitude and low-altitude regions, this paper proposed an algorithm of flight target altitude attribute identification and target altitude attribute identification credibility calculation, and defined an altitude attribute identification criteria. The algorithm used the target high/low altitude flight status information and target distance information to determine the target line-of-sight and over-the-horizon attributes. The practical trials showed that the proposed algorithm identified the line-of-sight and over-the-horizon attributes of the flight target, in the meanwhile, identified the high/low altitude flight status of the flight target. The correctness of the target altitude attribute identification is 0.9 or more.

Acknowledgments. The authors would like to thank the support of National Natural Science Foundation projects 61171188 and 61571159 for the project.

References

1. Anderson, S.J.: Optimizing HF radar siting for surveillance and remote sensing in the strait of Malacca. IEEE Trans. Geosci. Remote Sens. **51**(3), 1805–1816 (2013)
2. Xie, J., Sun, M., Ji, Z.: First-order ocean surface cross section for shipborne HFSWR. Electron. Lett. **49**(16), 1025–1026 (2013)

3. Zhou, H., Wen, B., Wu, S.: Ionospheric clutter suppression in HFSWR using multilayer crossed-loop antennas. IEEE Geosci. Remote Sens. Lett. **11**(2), 429–433 (2013)
4. Grosdidier, S., Forget, P., Barbin, Y., et al.: HF bistatic ocean doppler spectra: simulation versus experimentation. IEEE Trans. Geosci. Remote Sens. **52**(4), 2138–2148 (2014)
5. Bruno, L., Braca, P., Horstmann, J., et al.: Experimental evaluation of the range-doppler coupling on HF surface wave radars. IEEE Geosci. Remote Sens. Lett. **10**(4), 850–854 (2013)
6. Sathyan, T., Chin, T.J., Arulampalam, S., et al.: A multiple hypothesis tracker for multitarget tracking with multiple simultaneous measurements. IEEE J. Sel. Topics Signal Process. **7**(3), 448–460 (2013)
7. Abramovich, Y.I., Frazer, G.J., Johnson, B.A.: Principles of mode-selective MIMO OTHR. J. IEEE Trans. Aerosp. Electr. Syst. **49**(3), 1839–1868 (2013)
8. Skolnik, M.: Introduction to Radar Systems, 3rd edn, pp. 392–393. Publishing House of Electronics Industry, Beijing (2007). (Trans. by, Q.S. Zhuo)
9. Howland, P.E., Clutterbuck, C.F.: Estimation of target altitude in HF surface wave radar. In: Seventh International Conference on Hf Radio Systems and Techniques, pp. 296–300. IET (1997)
10. Zhang, S., Jin, Y.G., Yu, C.J., et al.: HPEKF algorithm of target altitude estimation initializing in HF surface wave radar. J. Harbin Inst. Technol. **39**(5), 725–729 (2007)
11. Gai, M.J., Xiao, Y., You, H., et al.: An approach to tracking a 3D-target with 2D-radar. In: IEEE International Radar Conference, pp. 763–768. IEEE (2005)
12. Guo, R.J., Yuan, Y.S., Quan, T.F.: Study of anti-weak aerial target tracking for high frequency surface wave radar. J. Acta Electron. Sin. **16**(2), 1586–1589 (2005)
13. Rotheram, S.: Ground-wave propagation. Part 1: theory for short distances. IEE Proc. F – Commun. Radar Signal Process. **128**(5), 275–284 (1981)
14. Rotheram, S.: Ground-wave propagation. Part 2: theory for medium and long distances and reference propagation curves. IEE Proc. **128**(5), 285–295 (1981)

A Minimum Spanning Tree Clustering Algorithm Inspired by P System

Xiaojuan Guo[✉] and Xiyu Liu

School of Management Science and Engineering, Shandong Normal University,
Jinan, China
guoxiaojuan@stu.sdnu.edu.cn

Abstract. In recent years, urbanization development in Shandong Province is rapidly and turns into a transition period. The main research work in this paper focused on the following aspects: In the first place, we introduce a new method called Membrane Computing in computing which is abstracted from living cells. Then we modify the traditional tissue-like P systems, and the object is viewed as control signal to conduct the rules execution flow. What is more, we summarize a P system model according to tissue-like P System to implement Minimum Spanning Tree (MST) algorithm. On the basis of this, we use the new MST algorithm based P system model to research differences of urbanization development in Shandong Province and solve the realistic problems of the seventeen cities' urbanization level. Finally, we give our advice for Urbanization development such as tax, science and technology plan, finance and insurance, land policy and so on.

Keywords: Urbanization development · Membrane computing
Minimum Spanning Tree algorithm

1 Introduction

1.1 Urbanization

Urbanization is the most significant change in contemporary human society. Urbanization is a "population-economy-space" three-dimensional integration process. Its internal coordination is the key to sustainable urban development. Based on the retrospective analysis of the existing about the quality of urbanization, this paper starts from the economic urbanization, population urbanization, space urbanization three dimensions and its related relation, and establishes the evaluation system of urbanization.

This article selects the data of 2013, and combines P system with MST-based clustering together. Then use the membrane in P system to achieve the whole process of cluster computing. The research results show that the urbanization level of Shandong province has rapidly developed in recent years. Urban population is still leading into the early stages of development in a period of rapid urbanization. However, such cities as Liaocheng and Heze which are in the west of Shandong Province, there is still a large gap compared with the eastern cities. Finally, from the scientific planning and

© ICST Institute for Computer Sciences, Social Informatics and Telecommunications Engineering 2018
X. Gu et al. (Eds.): MLICOM 2017, Part II, LNICST 227, pp. 361–370, 2018.
https://doi.org/10.1007/978-3-319-73447-7_40

population development, economic development, urban space in Shandong Province using four aspects proposed "the population- economy-space" the coordinated development of the related countermeasures. We expect to offer some useful evidence in the smooth implementation of the new urbanization development through the research.

1.2   Membrane Computing

Membrane computing is a new branch of natural computing. As a hot cross-discipline, it includes computer science, mathematics, biology and artificial intelligence, etc. It was initiated by Păun in 1998, inspired from the structure and the function of biological cells. So, we call it P system sometimes. P system have the characteristics of distribution and highly parallelism, thus have high efficiency. It shows a huge development potential [7].

P system is mainly used to summarize models of computation motivated of a living cell. There are different biochemical reactions in tissues or biological cells. On the basis of these, there are three main types of P system: Cell-like P System, Tissue-like P System and Neural-like P System. As you can see, they are abstracted from cells, tissues and the nervous system respectively. Due to the parallelism, the research in this area developed very fast in the theoretical direction as well as in the direction of applications. Membrane computing has been applied to economics, linguistics, biological modeling, cryptography, computer graphics, and other fields [8].

2   Background

2.1   Significance of Urbanization Research

Shandong Province is a large coastal economic province and there are more than 9600 million people. For the past few years, people's living standards continue to improve. And as we can see, Shandong plays a more and more important role in eastern coastal of our country. This paper starts from three dimensions-population, economic and space. Then build a "population-economy-space" urbanization integrated measure index by P system to analyze the differential development of urbanization in Shandong Province. This can help us know more about the problems in urbanization development [3].

2.2   Progress of Urbanization Research

At present, urbanization is a more systematic and comprehensive research at home and abroad. Urbanization refers to the historical process of human production and life style turn into a modern way from the form of rural. The main performance is the increasing people in cities as well as the process of continuous development and improvement of the city.

Shimou Yao and Dadao Lu proposed the urbanization development strategy of China in a comprehensive and scientific way [4]. Linchuang Fang and Deli Wang have come up with a new method to evaluate the quality of urbanization development which called three-dimensional spherical model. And the model covers 12 economic efficiency indexes from three aspects: the quality of economic development of urbanization, social urbanization development quality and the protection quality of space urbanization. The model is based on Delphi AHP model in order to assign weights related indicators [5]. In the research of urbanization developments, some scholars have focused on the process of urbanization in two areas. Fenggui Chen options two points-the urbanization of population and the land urbanization to measure the level of urbanization in China. According to the research, they proposed that spatial pattern of population urbanization and land urbanization coordinated development has such features as overall low, stage disparities and regional differentiation distinctive [6]. This paper is from a "population-economy-space" three dimensional integration way. The related research is fewer.

3   Approaches

3.1   Tissue-like P System

This paper mainly research Tissue-like P System. Tissue-like P System is an important expansion of the cell-like membrane system. Tissue-like P System includes three basic elements: membrane structure, rules and objects. Membranes divide the whole system into different regions. Rules and objects exist in regions. The outermost membrane is called skin membrane. Basic membrane refers to that there are no membranes in it (Fig. 1).

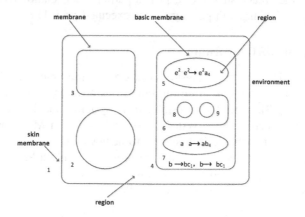

Fig. 1. The structure of P system

Tissue-like P System refers to that many cells are placed freely in the same environment. Both cells and the environment can contain objects. Transport rules are used for communication, not only between cells but also between cells and the environment [9, 10].

3.2   The Membrane Structure of P System

When calculating, the membrane structure of P systems with active membranes changes with the rules. P system can generate space of exponential growth in linear operation steps. It is very useful to solve computationally hard problems in a feasible time frame [12].

In general, P system m is as follows:

$$\Pi = (V, O, H, \quad \mu, w_1, \ldots, w_m, R_1, \ldots, R_m, i_0). \tag{1}$$

Where:

O is an alphabet. It's elements are called objects;

μ is a membrane structure of degree m, each membrane has a corresponding label

H = {1, 2, ..., m} is the label set of $\prod$;

$W_i(i = 1, 2, \ldots, m)$ is the multiset of objects in membrane i;

$R_i(i = 1, 2, \ldots, m)$ is the evolution rules of membrane i

The basic evolution rule is a pair (u, v) in the form of (u $\rightarrow$ v), where u is a string over V and v = v' or v = v'δ where v' is a string over $\{a_{here}, a_{out}, a_{in} \mid a \in V, 1 \leq j \leq m\}$, and δ is a special symbol not in V. When there is δ in a rule, the membrane will be dissolved after performing the rule. r is promoters or inhibitors and r = r' or r = $\neg$r'. One rule can execute only the promoters r' appear and one rule can stop only the inhibitors appear. What is more, the radius of the rule u $\rightarrow$ v refers to the length of u. R is the finite set of the evolution rules. Each R_i is associated with the region i over the membrane structure μ. ρi is a partial order relation over R_i which is called precedence relation. High priority rule is executed prior [11].

3.3   P System for MST Algorithm

The parallel computing feature of P systems can significantly improve the performance of the algorithm. The MST clustering algorithm has advantages in finding irregular boundary clusters [13]. And the constructed P system model can make use to accomplish better clustering. So P system was combined with MST-based clustering together. And use the membrane in P system to achieve the whole process of cluster computing. The rewrite, transport rules in membrane can build a MST. Therefore, we can divide the spanning tree, and obtain k clusters [14, 15].

The form expressions of P system are as follows:

$$\Pi = (O, \sigma_0, \sigma_1, \sigma_2, \cdots \sigma_n, \sigma_{n+1}, ch, c_0, \rho)$$

Where

$$O = (\delta_{11}, a_1, a_2, \ldots a_n, \alpha_1, \chi_1, \xi_1, T_0, \varphi, \Phi_1)$$

$$Ch = \{\{0, 1\}, \{0, 2\}, \{0, 3\} \ldots \{0, n\}, \{0, n+1\}, \{n+1, 1\}, \{n+1, 2\} \ldots \{n+1, n\}, \{n+1, c_0\},$$

$$\sigma_0 = (\omega_0, 0, R_0)$$

$$r_1' = \left\{ A_{i_1 j_1} A_{i_2 j_2} \ldots A_{i_{n-p} j_{n-p}} \rightarrow A_{i_1 j_1} A_{i_2 j_2} \ldots A_{i_p j_p} U_{i_1 j_1}^{w_{i_1 j_1}} U_{i_2 j_2}^{w_{i_2 j_2}} \ldots U_{i_{n-p} j_{n-p}}^{w_{i_{n-p} j_{n-p}}} \right\}$$

$$\left| 1 \le u, v, i_s, j_s, p \le n \right.$$

$$r_2' = \left\{ \delta_{u,v} U_{i_s j_s}^0 \rightarrow \delta_{u+1,i_s} \left(W_{u,i_s j_s}^{w_{i_s j_s}} \right)_{in_{n+1}} \left(V_{u+1,i_s} \right)_{in_{1,2,\ldots n}} \middle| 1 \le i_s, j_s, v \le n, 1 \le u \le n-1 \right\}$$

$$r_3' = \left\{ U_{i_1 j_1}^{w_{i_1 j_1}} U_{i_2 j_2}^{w_{i_2 j_2}} \ldots U_{i_{n-p} j_{n-p}}^{w_{i_{n-p} j_{n-p}}} \rightarrow U_{i_2 j_2}^{w_{i_1 j_1}-1} U_{i_2 j_2}^{w_{i_2 j_2}-1} \ldots U_{i_{n-p} j_{n-p}}^{w_{i_{n-p} j_{n-p}}-1} \middle| 1 \le i_s, j_s, p \le n \right\}$$

$$r_4' = \left\{ \delta_{n,j_n} \rightarrow \eta_{in_{n+1}} \right\}$$

$\bullet \sigma_i = \left(w_{i,0}, R_i \right) (1 \le i \le n)$

$w_{i,0} = a_i, V_{1,1}$

$R_i (1 \le i \le n)$:

$$r_1 = \left\{ a_i, V_{s,i} \rightarrow V_{s,i} \middle| 1 \le i, s \le n \right\}$$

$$r_{1+p} = \left\{ a_i, V_{1 j_1} V_{2 j_2} \ldots V_{p j_p} \rightarrow a_i, V_{1 j_1} V_{2 j_2} \ldots V_{p j_p} U_{i,j_1}^{w_{ij_1}} U_{i,j_2}^{w_{ij_2}} \ldots U_{i,j_p}^{w_{ij_p}} \middle| 1 \le i, j_p \le n \right\}$$

$$r_{2+p} = \left\{ a_i, U_{i,j_s}^0 \rightarrow a_i \left(A_{i,j_s} \right)_{in_0} \middle| 1 \le i, s, j_s \le n \right\} U \left\{ U_{i,j_1}^{w_{ij_1}} U_{i,j_2}^{w_{ij_2}} \ldots U_{i,j_p}^{w_{ij_p}} \rightarrow \lambda \middle| 1 \le i, j_p \le n \right\}$$

$$r_{3+p} = \left\{ U_{i,j_1}^{w_{ij_1}} U_{i,j_2}^{w_{ij_2}} \ldots U_{i,j_p}^{w_{ij_p}} \rightarrow U_{i,j_1}^{w_{ij_1}-1} U_{i,j_2}^{w_{ij_2}-1} \ldots U_{i,j_p}^{w_{ij_p}-1} \middle| 1 \le i, j_p \le n \right\}$$

$$r_4 = \left\{ V_{1 j_1} V_{2 j_2} \ldots V_{n,j_n} \rightarrow \lambda \right\}$$

$\bullet \sigma_{n+1} = \left(w_{n+1,0}, R_{n+1} \right)$

$w_{n+1,0} = \alpha_0, \chi_0, \xi_1, T_0, \phi_1, \varphi$

R_{n+1}:

$$r_{1+n+1} = \left\{ \eta W_{1,i_1 j_1}^{w_1} W_{2,i_2 j_2}^{w_2} \ldots W_{n-1,i_{n-1} j_{n-1}}^{w_{n-1}} \rightarrow \eta W_{1,i_1 j_1}^{w_1} W_{2,i_2 j_2}^{w_2} \ldots W_{n-1,i_{n-1} j_{n-1}}^{w_{n-1}} W^\varpi \middle| 1 \le i_s, j_s \le n \right\}$$

$$r_{2+n+1} = \left\{ \xi_s W_{s,i_s j_s}^{w_s} W^\varpi \rightarrow \xi_{s+1} W_{s,i_s j_s}^{w_s} W^\varpi Q_s^{w_s - \varpi} \middle| 1 \le i_s, j_s \le n, 1 \le s \le n-1 \right\}$$

$$U \left\{ W_{s,i_s j_s}^{w_s} Q_s^{w_s} T_t \rightarrow T_{t+1,i_s j_s} \middle| w_s' > 0 \right\}$$

$$r_{3+n+1} = \left\{ T_t \rightarrow \mu \middle| t > k-1 \right\} U \left\{ T_t \rightarrow v \middle| t < k-1 \right\} U \left\{ T_t \rightarrow \theta \middle| t = k-1 \right\}$$

$$r_{4+n+1} = \left\{ v \chi_c W_{h,i_h j_h}^0 \rightarrow v \chi_{c+1} T_{t+1,i_h j_h} \middle| c \le k-1-t \right\}$$

$$r_{5+n+1} = \left\{ v W_{1,i_1 j_1}^{w_1} W_{2,i_2 j_2}^{w_2} \ldots W_{n-1,i_{n-1} j_{n-1}}^{w_{n-1}} \rightarrow v W_{1.i_1 j_1}^{w_1 - M} W_{2,i_2 j_2}^{w_2 - M} \ldots W_{n-1,i_{n-1} j_{n-1}}^{w_{n-1} - M} \right\}$$

$$r_{6+n+1} = \left\{ v W_{1,i_1 j_1}^{w_1'} W_{2,i_2 j_2}^{w_2'} \ldots W_{n-1,i_{n-1} j_{n-1}}^{w_{n-1}} \rightarrow v W_{1.i_1 j_1}^{w_1' + 1} W_{2,i_2 j_2}^{w_2' + 1} \ldots W_{n-1,i_{n-1} j_{n-1}}^{w_{n-1} - M} \right\}$$

$$r_{7+n+1} = \left\{ \mu \alpha_f \omega W_{q,i_q j_q} \rightarrow \mu \alpha_{f+1} \omega b_{f+1,i_q} b_{f+1 j_q} \middle| 1 \le f, i_q, i_q \le n \right\}$$

$$r_{8+n+1} = \left\{ \phi_q b_{q,j_1} b_{q j_2} b_{q j_3} \ldots \rightarrow \phi_q b_{q j_1} b_{q j_2} b_{q j_3} \ldots U_{j_1 j_2}^{w_{j_1 j_2}} U_{j_1 j_3}^{w_{j_1 j_3}} \ldots \middle| 1 \le q, j_s \le n \right\}$$

$$r_{9+n+1} = \left\{ \phi_q U_{j_1 j_2}^{w_{j_1 j_2}} U_{j_1 j_3}^{w_{j_1 j_3}} \ldots \rightarrow \phi_q U_{j_1 j_2}^{w_{j_1 j_2}} U_{j_1 j_3}^{w_{j_1 j_3}} \ldots U_{j_1}^{w_{j_1}} \middle| 1 \le j_s \le n \right\}$$

$$r_{10+n+1} = \left\{ \phi_q U_{j_s}^0 b_{q j_s} \rightarrow \phi_{q+1} \alpha_{j_s} \middle| 1 \le j_s \le n \right\} U \left\{ \varphi \alpha_{j_s} \rightarrow V_{1 j_s} \middle| 1 \le j_s \le n \right\}$$

$$r_{11+n+1} = \left\{ \phi_q U_{j_1}^{w_{j_1}} U_{j_2}^{w_{j_2}} \ldots \rightarrow \phi_q U_{j_1}^{w_{j_1}-1} U_{j_2}^{w_{j_2}-1} \ldots \right\}$$

$$r_{12+n+1} = \left\{ V_{1,j_s} a_{j_2} \ldots a_{j_p} \to \left(V_{1,j_s} \right)_{in_{j_s} j_1 j_2 \ldots j_p} \left(a_{j_2} \right)_{in_{j_2}} \right\}$$
$$\bigcup \{ \eta Q \to \lambda \}$$
$$r_{13+n+1} = \left\{ \phi \omega W_{q,i_q j_q} \to \left(\omega a_{i_q} a_{j_q} \right)_{in_{c0}} \Big| 1 \le q, i_q, j_q \le n \right\}$$
$$\rho = \{ r_1' > r_2' > r_3' > r_4' > \} \bigcup \{ r_i > r_j | 1 \le i \le j \le 6 \} \bigcup \{ r_{i+n+1} > r_{j+n+1} | 1 \le i \le j \le 12 \}$$

3.4   Operational Process in P System

After the start of the operation in the P system, limited by the initial multiple set and the regular set of the membrane, rule r_1 is executed first. This rule operates on objects a_i and $V_{s,i}$ that are contained in the membrane at the same time. When both are present, it means that object a_i in the membrane has been added to the node in MST. In order to avoid repeating object a_i added into MST, keeping object $V_{s,i}$ only. Then, the loop variable p controls rule r_{1+p} to start working. The objects $U_{i,j1}^{\omega_{ij1}} U_{i,j2}^{\omega_{ij2}} \ldots U_{i,jp}^{\omega_{ijp}}$ represent the distance between nodes. And $U_{i,js}^{\omega_{ijs}} (1 \le s \le p)$ indicates the distance between a_i and V_{s,j_s} is ω_{ij}, then rule r_{3+p} is looped until object $U_{i,js}^0$ appears, indicating that the distance between object a_i and node V_{s,j_s} is minimal. Copy the object a_i, one of which remains in the membrane i, the other is rewritten as A_{i,j_s} into the membrane 0,while the remaining object $U_{i,j}^{\omega_{ij}}$ is cleared.

When all the objects $A_{i,j_s} (n - p, 1 \le i, j_s \le n)$ enter into the membrane 0, rules are excited. Rule r_1' represents the distance between a_i and $V_{s,j_s} - U_{i,js}^{\omega_{ijs}}$, then rule $r_2' r_3'$ are looped until object $U_{i,js}^0$ appears. The distance can be the weight of the newly added edge. The object a_{i_s} becomes the new node V_{u+1,i_s}, and enter into the membrane $\sigma_i (1 \le i \le n)$.

Subsequently, the rule set in the membrane n + 1 will cluster the generated MST hierarchically.

4   Case Study

4.1   Data

In this article, we use the data of urbanization index in 2013 (Table 1). The meaning of the data in the table is as follows: PU2013 refers to the population urbanization rate in 2013. EU2013 refers to the economy urbanization rate in 2013. SU2013 refers to the spatial urbanization rate in 2013. U2013 refers to the comprehensive urbanization rate in 2013. Pe refers to the rate of population and economy urbanization development in 2013. Ps refers to the rate of population and spatial urbanization development in 2013. Es refers to the rate of economy and spatial urbanization development in 2013.

Table 1. The data of urbanization index in 2013

Number	City	Data				
		PU2013	EU2013	SU2013	U2013	Data object
1	Qingdao	8	9	6	8	(8, 9, 6, 8)
2	Jinan	8	9	5	7	(8, 9, 5, 7)
3	Zibo	7	7	6	7	(7, 7,6 , 7)
4	Dongying	6	8	8	7	(6, 8, 8, 7)
5	Weihai	6	7	9	8	(6, 7, 9, 8)
6	Yantai	5	7	7	6	(5, 7, 7, 6)
7	Taian	6	6	6	6	(6, 6, 6, 6)
8	Weifang	5	6	5	5	(5, 6, 5, 5)
9	Zaozhuang	5	5	6	5	(5, 5, 6, 5)
10	Jining	5	5	6	5	(5, 5, 6, 5)
11	Linyi	5	5	4	4	(5, 5, 4, 4)
12	Laiwu	5	5	8	6	(5, 5, 8, 6)
13	Binzhou	4	6	6	5	(4, 6, 6, 5)
14	Liaocheng	4	5	5	5	(4, 5, 5, 5)
15	Rizhao	4	5	6	5	(4, 5, 6, 5)
16	Dezhou	4	5	8	6	(4, 5, 8, 6)
17	Heze	4	4	3	4	(4, 4, 3, 4)

4.2 Computing

4.2.1 Clustering Process

$$D_{17,17} = \begin{pmatrix}
00 & 02 & 06 & 10 & 17 & 18 & 17 & 28 & 34 & 34 & 45 & 33 & 34 & 42 & 41 & 40 & 66 \\
02 & 00 & 06 & 14 & 25 & 16 & 15 & 22 & 30 & 30 & 35 & 35 & 30 & 36 & 37 & 42 & 54 \\
06 & 06 & 00 & 06 & 11 & 06 & 03 & 10 & 12 & 12 & 21 & 13 & 14 & 18 & 17 & 18 & 36 \\
10 & 14 & 06 & 00 & 03 & 04 & 09 & 18 & 18 & 18 & 35 & 11 & 16 & 26 & 21 & 14 & 54 \\
17 & 25 & 11 & 03 & 00 & 09 & 14 & 27 & 23 & 23 & 44 & 10 & 23 & 33 & 26 & 13 & 65 \\
18 & 16 & 06 & 04 & 09 & 00 & 03 & 06 & 06 & 06 & 17 & 05 & 04 & 10 & 07 & 06 & 30 \\
17 & 15 & 03 & 09 & 14 & 03 & 00 & 03 & 03 & 03 & 10 & 06 & 05 & 07 & 06 & 09 & 21 \\
28 & 22 & 10 & 18 & 27 & 06 & 03 & 00 & 02 & 02 & 03 & 11 & 02 & 02 & 03 & 12 & 10 \\
34 & 30 & 12 & 18 & 23 & 06 & 03 & 02 & 00 & 00 & 05 & 05 & 02 & 02 & 01 & 06 & 12 \\
34 & 30 & 12 & 18 & 23 & 06 & 03 & 02 & 00 & 00 & 05 & 05 & 02 & 02 & 01 & 06 & 12 \\
45 & 35 & 21 & 35 & 44 & 17 & 10 & 03 & 05 & 05 & 00 & 20 & 07 & 03 & 06 & 21 & 03 \\
33 & 35 & 13 & 11 & 10 & 05 & 06 & 11 & 05 & 05 & 20 & 00 & 07 & 11 & 06 & 01 & 31 \\
34 & 30 & 14 & 16 & 23 & 04 & 05 & 02 & 02 & 02 & 07 & 07 & 00 & 02 & 01 & 06 & 14 \\
42 & 36 & 18 & 26 & 33 & 10 & 07 & 02 & 02 & 02 & 03 & 11 & 02 & 00 & 01 & 10 & 06 \\
41 & 37 & 17 & 21 & 26 & 07 & 06 & 03 & 01 & 01 & 06 & 06 & 01 & 01 & 00 & 05 & 11 \\
40 & 42 & 18 & 14 & 13 & 06 & 09 & 12 & 06 & 06 & 21 & 01 & 06 & 10 & 05 & 00 & 30 \\
66 & 54 & 36 & 54 & 65 & 30 & 21 & 10 & 12 & 12 & 03 & 31 & 14 & 06 & 11 & 30 & 00
\end{pmatrix}$$

Cities are represented by the object $a_i(1 \leq i \leq 17)$, and then calculate the dissimilarity matrix of the data object $D_{17,17}$.

The initial state of the P system performs evolutionary communication rules, and the MST containing the respective nodes are generated. Then calculate the mean of the weights of the edges, and the weights are removed beyond the mean. Sub-tree is formed, and the new MST is constructed on the representative node inside each sub-tree, until the number of sub-trees is equal to the number of cluster clusters.

By implementing the corresponding rules, the MST containing all the objects (nodes) is constructed, and its visualization is shown in the following Fig. 2.

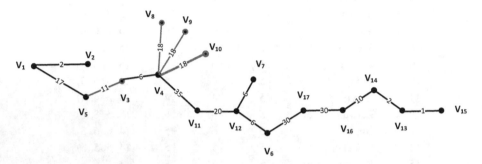

Fig. 2. The MST including all nodes

In the analysis of the operation of the clustering process in the P system, it is known that the minimum spanning tree is generated iteratively. Calculate the average of the weights in the MST, and then cut off the edges that exceed the mean, we can eventually get clustering results.

4.2.2   Results
After the calculated by P system combined with the MST algorithm, we can know that the average degree of urbanization development is 0.5309. At the same time, we get a conclusion that the cities in Shandong Province can be divided into four categories: high level of coordinated development (1, 2), middle level of coordinated development

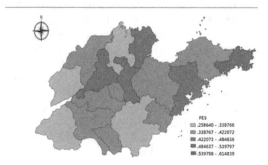

Fig. 3. The spatial differentiation of population-economy-space urbanization of Shandong province of 2013

(3, 4, 5), middle low level of coordinated development (6, 7, 8, 9, 10, 11, 12), low level of coordinated development (13, 14, 15, 16, 17). The results show in the following Fig. 3 [14]. From the result, we can know the urbanization development level for each city.

5   Discussions and Suggestions

5.1   Discussions

The pace of urbanization in Shandong Province is faster overall. As we can see, all of the population, economic, and space urbanization have a more significant development. Among them, the urbanization base on population is gradually turning into a kind of economy and space leading urbanization development. Since 2013, the level of economic urbanization is similar as space urbanization development, slightly higher than the population urbanization. Population - economy - space urbanization development is coordinated highly. And according to previous studies, this state is conducive to urbanization positive development.

We also found that, in the high level urbanization areas, the economic urbanization plays a very important role. It is a significant driving force for the development of urbanization. And in the lower level of coordinated development areas, spatial urbanization is dominant, which may be related to the local governments because of the dependents on land and finance policies. Objectively, the way of building infrastructure, creates a more favorable development for future of the region [16].

5.2   Suggestions

Measures should be taken to make population, resources and environment integrated and coordinated development. The city's development is inseparable from the support of population, resources and environment. From the perspective throughout Shandong Province, there are many problems such as enormous population pressure, the lack of resources, environmental pollution and other issues. We must start from the regional level to co-ordinate the development of the various problems and promote urban development.

Strengthen investment in education, and improve the quality of the population. Then there will be a huge capital and human resources which turned from the force adult population resources. Thus the urban economy will be better. Finally, the urban employment must increase on this occasion.

Only the development of urban economy can provide the power of improving employment and the welfare of urban residents. Actively develop the urban economy through capital investment, technological innovation, accelerate the growth of industrial scale. And then focus on improving the proportion of urban services, the development of new formats, new hot hatch, and gradually increase the proportion of tertiary industry.

The use of urban land should adjust to the size of population. And the reasonable land targets should be formulated. Then draw the urban land red line.

Acknowledgments. This work was supported by the Natural Science Foundation of China (No. 61472231). Natural Science Foundation of China (No. 61502283). Natural Science Foundation of China (No. 61640201).

References

1. Chan, K.W.: Cities with Invisible Walls: Reinterpreting Urbanization in Post-1949 China. Oxford University Press, Hong Kong (1994)
2. Davis, K.: The urbanization of the human population. In: Scott, W. (ed.) Perspectives on Population: An Introduction to Concepts and Issues, vol. 213, no. 3, pp. 40–53 (1965)
3. Armstrong, W., McGee, T.G.: Theatres of Accumulation: Studies in Asian and Latin American Urbanization. Cambridge University Press, London (1985)
4. Song, J., Pan, Z.: Shandong Province Urbanization Development Report 2013, pp. 37–42. Huanghe Press, Jinan (2013)
5. Fang, C., Wang, D.: Integrated measurement and enhanced the quality of the development path of China's urbanization. Geograph. Res. **11**, 1931–1946 (2011)
6. Chen, F., Zhang, H., Qitao, W.U.: Chinese population urbanization and coordinated development of urbanization. Hum. Geograph. **5**, 53–58 (2010)
7. Gheorghe, M., Paun, G., Perez-Jimenez, M.J., et al.: Research frontiers of membrane computing: open problems and research topics. Int. J. Found. Comput. Sci. **24**(5), 547–623 (2013)
8. Frisco, P., Gheorghe, M., Perez-Jimenez, M.J.: Applications of membrane Computing in Systems and Synthetic Biology. Emergence, Complexity and Computation. Springer, Heidelberg (2014). https://doi.org/10.1007/978-3-319-03191-0
9. Pan, L., Pérez-Jiménez, M.J.: Computational complexity of tissue-like P systems. J. Complex. **26**(3), 296–315 (2010)
10. Zhang, G., Cheng, J., Gheorghe, M., Meng, Q.: A hybrid approach based on differential evolution and tissue membrane systems for solving constrained manufacturing parameter optimization problems. Appl. Soft Comput. **2013**, 1528–1542 (2013)
11. Paun, G., Rozenberg, G., Salomaa, A.: Membrane Computing. Oxford University Press, New York (2010). pp. 282–301
12. Marc, G.A., Daniel, M., Alfonso, R.P., Petr, S.: A P system and a constructive membrane-inspired DNA algorithm for solving the Maximum Clique Problem. BioSystems **90**(3), 687–697 (2007)
13. Zhao, Y., Liu, X., Li, X.: The improved hierarchical clustering algorithm by a P system with active membranes. WSEAS Trans. Comput. **12**(1), 8–17 (2013)
14. Grygorash, O., Zhou, Y., Jorgensen, Z.: Minimum spanning tree based clustering algorithms. **14**(2), 73–81 (2006)
15. Li, Q.: EC Tissue-like P System Based Clustering Problem Research. Shandong Normal University (2016)
16. Baodi, G., Chenxin, W., Xuegang, C.: The Study of population-economy-space perspective of space-time evolution of urbanization in Shandong province. Econ. Geograph. **36**(5), 79–84 (2016)

Transfer Learning Method for Convolutional Neural Network in Automatic Modulation Classification

Yu Xu[1], Dezhi Li[1], Zhenyong Wang[1,2(✉)], Gongliang Liu[1], and Haibo Lv[1]

[1] School of Electronics and Information Engineering,
Harbin Institute of Technology, Harbin, Heilongjiang, China
{xu_yu,lidezhi,ZYWang,liugl,elitelv}@hit.edu.cn
[2] Shenzhen Academy of Aerospace Technology, Shenzhen, Guangdong, China

Abstract. Automatic modulation classification (AMC) plays an important role in many fields to identify the modulation type of signals, in which the deep learning methods have shown attractive potential development. In our research, we introduce convolutional neural network (CNN) to recognize the modulation of the input signal. We used real signal data generated by instruments as dataset for training and testing. Based on analysis of the unstable training problem of CNN for weak signals recognition with low SNR, a transfer learning method is proposed. Experiments results show that the proposed transfer learning method can locate better initial values for CNN training and converge to a good result. According to the recognition accuracy performance analysis, The CNN with the proposed transfer learning method has higher average classification accuracy and is more compatible for unstable training problem.

Keywords: Modulation classification · Convolutional neural network
Transfer learning method

1 Introduction

Automatic modulation classification is aiming to detect the modulation type of received signals in order to recover signals by demodulation. The dominant approach of signal modulation recognition can be categorized as likelihood-based (LB) methods and feature-based (FB) methods [1]. Many neural networks have been applied to the automatic modulation classification, which have shown better performances than the traditional LB methods and FB methods [2–6]. In the former research on a deep learning architecture based on convolutional neural network for modulation classification of wireless signals, it is found that the same programs get different results under the same experiment conditions. Even sometime the result is terrible. The phenomenon is defined as Unstable Training Problem in our paper, which comes out in training process with the random seed. Because the same initializer is involved at the beginning of training process, it is important to focus on the robustness of modulation classification based on CNN against noise in training process.

© ICST Institute for Computer Sciences, Social Informatics and Telecommunications Engineering 2018
X. Gu et al. (Eds.): MLICOM 2017, Part II, LNICST 227, pp. 371–380, 2018.
https://doi.org/10.1007/978-3-319-73447-7_41

In former experiments under conditions of various SNR, the modulation classification method based on CNN shows fairly good recognition performances for SNR ≥ 0 dB wireless signals, in which the unstable training problem is rare. As the SNR of wireless signals drops, the unstable training problem is becoming obvious and it is hard to carry on training process of the CNN. The reason of the unstable training problem is regarded as infeasible robustness of the neural network to noise-like dataset [7]. For the Unstable Training Problem, if the SNR is very low, the features of modulation are influenced by noise and are hard to be extracted. The modulation classification method based on CNN will encounter numerical difficulties and we can't get a satisfied performance, because the signal dataset cannot provide a good estimation of gradient to training.

Transfer learning method refers to the situation where some learned knowledge is transferred to improve generalization in another setting. The objective is to inherit extracted information from advantage of data in the first setting, so as to help learning process or even making predictions directly in the second setting. The motivation is that the same representation may be useful in both settings.

The main idea of this paper is to investigate transfer learning to solve the unstable training problem in training process of a stacked convolutional neural network of deep learning architecture for modulation classification of wireless signals automatically. The rest of the paper is organized as follows. In Sect. 2, based on analysis of Stochastic Gradient Descent and initialization problem of training process of CNN, the transfer learning is investigated. Based on real sampled data of wireless signals, an improved CNN architecture is trained and proposed with transfer learning in Sect. 3. In Sect. 4, according to the experiment results, the effect of transfer learning to solve unstable training problem is analyzed in term of recognition accuracy in various SNR conditions. Finally, conclusions are drawn in Sect. 5.

2   Training Process Based on Transfer Learning

2.1   Stochastic Gradient Descent

Nearly all of deep learning is powered by important Stochastic Gradient Descent (SGD) algorithm. Stochastic Gradient Descent is typical and preferred to training process for neural networks. One row of data is inputted into the network at a time. The network activates neurons forward to produce an output value finally. Then the output value is compared to the expected output value to generate an error value. The error is backward propagated through the network, in which the weights of layer are updated one after another, according to the contributed amount to the error. The process is repeated for all of the examples in the training data to get a trained network of the intended goal.

The weights in the network can be updated from the calculated errors for each training example, which can result in fast but also chaotic changes to the network. On the other hand, the errors can be saved up across all of the training examples and the network can be updated at the end.

The cost function used by a machine learning algorithm often decomposes as a sum over training examples of some per-example loss function. For example, the negative conditional log-likelihood of the training data can be written as

$$J(\theta) = E_{x,y \sim p_{data}} L(x, y, \theta) = \frac{1}{m} \sum_{i=1}^{m} L(x^{(i)}, y^{(i)}, \theta) \tag{1}$$

where L is the per-example loss:

$$L(x, y, \theta) = -\log p(y \mid x; \theta) \tag{2}$$

For these additive cost functions, gradient descent requires computing

$$\nabla_\theta J(\theta) = \frac{1}{m} \sum_{i=1}^{m} \nabla_\theta L(x^{(i)}, y^{(i)}, \theta) \tag{3}$$

Considering the computational cost, we use a small set of samples to approximately estimate the true gradient. Specifically, on each step of the algorithm, we can sample a minibatch of examples $B = \{x^{(1)}, \ldots, x^{(m')}\}$ drawn uniformly from the training set. The minibatch size m' is typically chosen to be a relatively small number of examples, ranging from 1 to a few hundred.

Based on examples from the mini-batch B, The estimate of the gradient is formed as

$$g = \frac{1}{m'} \nabla_\theta \sum_{i=1}^{m'} L(x^{(i)}, y^{(i)}, \theta) \tag{4}$$

The stochastic gradient descent follows the estimated gradient downhill:

$$\theta \leftarrow \theta - \varepsilon g \tag{5}$$

where ε is the learning rate.

2.2   Initialization Problem of Training Process

Training algorithms for deep learning models are usually iterative in nature and thus require us to specify some initial point from which to begin the iterations. However, training deep models is a sufficiently difficult task that most algorithms strongly affected by the choice of initialization. The initial point can determine whether the algorithm converges with some initial points begin so unstable that the algorithm encounters numerical difficulties and fails. When learning does converge, the initial point can determine how quickly learning converges and whether it converges to a point with high or low cost.

Different task have different solution space, but they are similar in some extents. Neural network training is non-deterministic, and converges to a different function every time it is run. As can be seen from the Fig. 1, the training process may encounter many numerical difficulties like local maximum or shoulder location. The state when we stop training not only depends on the optimization algorithm. The initial values where we start iteration also have a great impact on the result. A bad initial value can result in numerical difficulties.

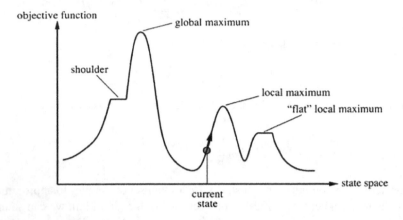

Fig. 1. One-dimensional solution space state illustration

Moreover, when training our neural network, it is possible that training initializes the model in a location which is surrounded by areas where the cost function varies so much from one sample point to another that mini-batches give only a very noisy estimate of the gradient, or region surrounded by areas where the Hessian matrix is so poorly conditioned that gradient descent methods must use very small steps. It slow down the training by requiring lower learning rates and careful parameter initialization, and makes it hard to train models.

Another related method is greedy layer-wise unsupervised pre-training. This greedy learning procedure could be used to find a good initialization for a joint learning procedure over all the layers [8]. In the context of a supervised learning task, it can be viewed as regularization and a form of parameter initialization.

Unsupervised pre-training takes the parameters into a region that would otherwise be inaccessible and it brings much success. Neural networks that receive unsupervised pre-training consistently halt in the same region of function space, while neural networks without pre-training consistently halt in another region. The region where pre-trained networks arrive is smaller, suggesting that pre-training reduces the variance of the estimation process, which can in turn reduce the risk of severe over-fitting [9].

2.3   Transfer Learning Method

Transfer learning refers to the situation where what has been learned in one setting P_1 is exploited to improve generalization in another setting P_2. In transfer learning, the learner must perform two or more different tasks, but we assume that many of the factors that explain the variations in P_1 are relevant to the variations that need to be captured for learning P_2. Using the same representation in both settings allows the representation to benefit from the training data that is available for both tasks.

A brief example of transfer learning is show in Fig. 2. In most case, one task is easy to fulfill while another is hard due to the low quality of dataset. We can use transfer learning through sharing weight between the two learning process. Sometimes what is shared among the different tasks is not the input but the output. In cases like these, it makes more sense to share the upper layers of the neural network, as illustrated in Fig. 3. The transfer learning may help to learn representations that are useful to quickly generalize.

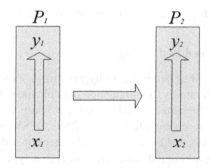

Fig. 2. An example of transfer learning

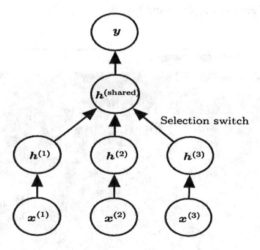

Fig. 3. An example of transfer learning sharing the output

3 The CNN for Modulation Classification

To meet the requirements of modulation classification, our network architectures are mainly inspired by ALEXNET [10], as shown in Fig. 4.

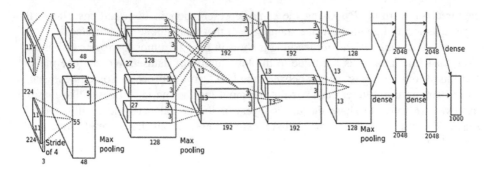

Fig. 4. The architecture of ALEXNET

3.1 Signals Data Sampled and Process

Because digital modulation has better immunity performances to interference, which is mostly discussed in the literatures for modulation classification. Here, it is assumed that there is a single carrier-transmitted signal in additive white Gaussian noise (AWGN) channel. The modulation types include 2ASK, BPSK, QPSK, 8PSK and 16QAM.

The signal data are produced by vector signal generator SMU200A. The sampling rate is 1 GHz. All the signal data of different modulation types have the same carrier frequency of 100 MHz and bandwidth of 25 MHz. Every sample has 2000 raw points and there are 25000 samples in total, 5000 samples for each modulation type. The only preprocess is to rescale the amplitude to the range of −2 V to 2 V. The spectrum map of sampled BPSK signal is shown in the Fig. 5.

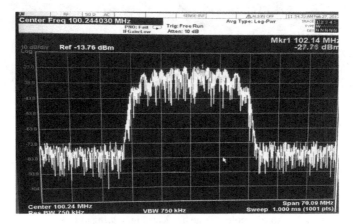

Fig. 5. The spectrum map of BPSK signal

For most classification and regression process, there is still possibility to get results even with small random noise added to the input. However, neural networks are proved not robust to noise [7]. One way to improve the robustness of neural networks is simply to do training process with input random noise data. So in training procedure to improve the robustness, training data of same SNR are included, which are also used to test the performance of proposed method in different SNR conditions.

When the network layers are not deep, it is not likely to encounter the problems like vanishing/exploding gradients. The principle of maximum likelihood is taken as the cost function, which means the cross-entropy between the training data and the prediction of the model is regarded as the cost function. The weights are initialized with Gaussian distribution initializers, which have zero means and unit variances. The SGD is involved with a mini-batch size of 256. The weight decay is 0.0001 and the momentum is 0.9. The learning rate starts from 0.1. When there are errors plateaus occur, the learning rate descends at rate of 10 times.

As for the testing process, it is typically to use a simple separation of the same sampled data into training and testing datasets. In experiments, 80% data of the sampled signal is assigned to training dataset and 20% data of the sampled signal is assigned to testing dataset. Finally when the training is halt, we get the accuracy through inputting the testing datasets and statistical the accuracy.

3.2 The CNN Architecture

It is found that the removal of the fully-connected layers of ALEXNET will reduce the amount of weight parameters and get little impact of the recognition accuracy performance. In this paper, the large kernel size is designed for better performances and acceptable complexity. Moreover, after investigating the deep neural network with more than 30 layers, it is found there are over-fitting problems. It is possible to apply a shallow neural network to compete modulation recognition for signals with reasonable SNR.

Based on the analysis above, the number of input neuron is set to 2000, which means every sample has 2000 raw points. The CNN is proposed with 3 convolutional layers, and each convolutional layer is followed by a max pooling layer. At the end of the CNN network, a 5-way fully-connected layer with softmax is used to output the probability of 5 kinds of signal modulations classification. The convolutional layers have filter kernels with length of 40. 64 filter kernels are used in both the input layer and the second layer. For the third layer, the filter kernels are increased to length of 128. The max pooling layers perform down-sampling with stride of 2 and pool width of 3 to get overlapping pooling. We do not use the any regularization like dropout. So, the CNN consists of 4 weighted layers, as shown in Fig. 6.

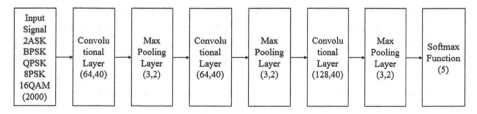

Fig. 6. The CNN Structure

4 Experiments and Results Analysis

We initialize the weights with the same initializers to explore the performance of the proposed neural network architecture in different SNR conditions and encounter the unstable training problem. We take the experiment with the SNR ranks −1 to −3 as an example to describe this phenomenon. The result of three times in different SNR conditions is list in Table 1, we report 'failed' when the accuracy is lower than 40%.

Table 1. The accuracy comparison under various SNR conditions

SNR	The 1st experiment	The 2nd experiment	The 3rd experiment
−1 dB	99.86%	99.44%	99.50%
−2 dB	failed	97.31%	92.10%
−3 dB	92.08%	failed	94.45%

As can be seen in Table 1, when the SNR is high, the experiment works well and the proposed CNN gets satisfied recognize accuracy at approximate 100%. We contribute the reason for this good result to the simple architecture of shallow network. The solution space is not very complicate. The dataset can provide a good estimation of gradient to update the parameter so the initial point does not matter. An approximate global maximum point can be achieved. As the drop of the SNR, the model encounters the problem which we called unstable training. In this case, we think that the mini-batches give only a very noisy estimate of the gradient and it easy to fall into a local minimum point which blocks the training. The algorithm cannot calculate a right direction to move which contribute to a failure. The results fluctuated severely and a method based on transfer learning is proposed in the following.

We apply the weights trained in the high SNR condition as the initial weights when we training the model in the low SNR conditions, which is a kind of transfer learning. We got the convergent point in high SNR condition and the gradient become small. There are two tasks which have a same target to recognize the modulation type of the signal but have the different input. To some extent one task has a more clear input while the input of another task can be seen as a more polluted signal suffer from AWGN channel. Our experiment results show that the unstable training problem is well addressed in this setting. Besides, we also get a lift in the performance of accuracy.

We evaluate our method based on transfer learning by using the pretraining initial weights and the results is show in Fig. 7. The line 1 is the performance of the original method using Gaussian distribution random initializers without pretraining. Due to the unstable training problem, we run the program 5 times and choose the best result as the final result. We first trains the model in 0 dB and it exists no difficult to get a satisfied recognize accuracy approximate 100%. We save the weights as the initial weights when we experiment the performance in other low SNR conditions and the result is show in line 2. It is obvious that we obtain the accuracy gains from this method. We argue that the initial weights bring the network the simple capacity to recognize the true modulation type of the signal data and that is otherwise hard to access. We use the weights based on iterative SNR to explore the performance of the neural network in line 3. For example, we initial the weights trained in the SNR of −1 dB when we train the model in the SNR of −2 dB and recursively. Somehow surprisingly, the results are improved by healthy margins and report in Fig. 7. In our opinion, the initial weights can not only have the ability to recognize the modulation type but also extract features which is covered by noise simply. So this method can lift the performance of the proposed neural network architecture to recognize the modulation type of signal a lot.

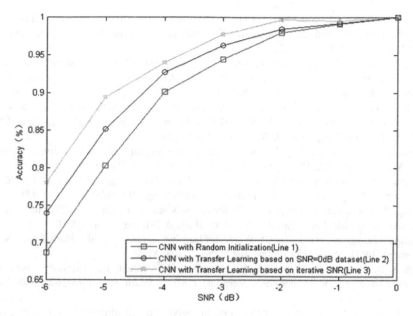

Fig. 7. Recognition accuracy comparison

5   Conclusion

The aim of our experiment is to design a method to fulfill the task of recognizing the modulation of input signal. We try to use stacked convolutional neural network to recognize the modulation of the input signal and we also get a good performance. We found that it is easily to encounter numerical difficulties when the SNR is low which is called unstable training is this paper. This motivates us to propose a transfer learning method to solve this problem. The unstable training problem is well addressed in this setting and we manage to obtain accuracy gains from this method.

Acknowledgement. This work was supported by National Natural Science Foundation of China. (No. 61601147, No. 61571316, No. 61371100) and the Fundamental Research Funds for the Central Universities (Grant No. HIT. MKSTISP. 2016013).

References

1. Hazza, A., Shoaib, M., Alshebeili, S.A., Fahad, A.: An overview of feature-based methods for digital modulation classification. In: 2013 1st International Conference on Communications, Signal Processing and their Applications, pp. 1–6. IEEE Press, New York (2013)
2. Zhu, X., Fujii, T.: A modulation classification method in cognitive radios system using stacked denoising sparse autoencoder. In: 2017 IEEE Radio and Wireless Symposium, pp. 218–220. IEEE Press, New York (2017)
3. Dai, A., Zhang, H., Sun, H.: Automatic modulation classification using stacked sparse auto-encoders. In: 13th IEEE International Conference on Signal Processing, pp. 248–252. IEEE Press, New York (2017)
4. Mendis, G.J., Wei, J., Madanayake, A.: Deep learning-based automated modulation classification for cognitive radio. In: 2016 IEEE International Conference on Communication Systems, pp. 1–6. IEEE Press, New York (2016)
5. O'Shea, T.J., Corgan, J., Clancy, T.C.: Convolutional radio modulation recognition networks. In: Jayne, C., Iliadis, L. (eds.) EANN 2016. CCIS, vol. 629, pp. 213–226. Springer, Cham (2016). https://doi.org/10.1007/978-3-319-44188-7_16
6. Fu, J., Zhao, C., Li, B., Peng, X.: Deep learning based digital signal modulation recognition. In: Mu, J., Liang, Q., Wang, W., Zhang, B., Pi, Y. (eds.) The Proceedings of the Third International Conference on Communications, Signal Processing, and Systems. LNEE, vol. 322, pp. 955–964. Springer, Cham (2015). https://doi.org/10.1007/978-3-319-08991-1_100
7. Tang, Y., Eliasmith, C.: Deep networks for robust visual recognition. In: 27th International Conference on Machine Learning, pp. 1055–1062. ACM, New York (2010)
8. Hinton, G.E., Osindero, S., Teh, Y.W.: A fast learning algorithm for deep belief nets. Neural Comput. **18**(7), 1527–1554 (2006). IEEE Press, New York
9. Erhan, D., Bengio, Y., Courville, A., Manzagol, P., Vincent, P., Bengio, S.: Why does unsupervised pre-training help deep learning? J. Mach. Learn. Res. **11**(3), 625–660 (2010). ACM, New York
10. Krizhevsky, A., Sutskever, I., Hinton, G.E.: ImageNet classification with deep convolutional neural networks. In: 2012 26th Annual Conference on Neural Information Processing Systems, vol. 25, no. 2, pp. 1097–1105. ACM, New York (2012)

Pulse Compression Analysis for OFDM-Based Radar-Radio Systems

Xuanxuan Tian[1(✉)], Tingting Zhang[1], Qinyu Zhang[1], Hongguang Xu[1],
and Zhaohui Song[2]

[1] Shenzhen, Harbin Institute of Technology, Shenzhen 518055, China
tianxuanxuan2008@163.com, {zhangtt,zqy,xhg}@hit.edu.cn
[2] East China Normal University, Shanghai 200062, China
zhsong@ce.ecnu.edu.cn

Abstract. Orthogonal frequency division multiplexing (OFDM) radar
has been studied in the last years for its suitability to combine simultaneous radar-radio (RadCom) operations. There exists the problem of low
data rate and high range sidelobes in an OFDM-based RadCom System
using the classic pulse compression processing. To solve the problem, a
signal model in which monopulse is composed of multi-OFDM symbols is
presented. The analysis of pulse compression processing through ambiguity function is presented, where the effects of Doppler and random phase
codes on pulse compression are discussed in detail. Theoretical analysis
and simulation results show that the presented method can obviously
alleviate the effects of the random phase codes on range performance of
OFDM signals, while keeps high data rate.

Keywords: OFDM · Radar-radio · Pulse compression
Ambiguity function

1 Introduction

The joint operation of radar-radio (RadCom) systems using one common waveform, have recently been studied to integrate wireless communications and sensing within a single transceiver platform [1]. The study on RadCom systems is
mainly to improve the spectrum efficiency and cost effectiveness. A typical application area is the intelligent transportation networks which require the ability
of inter-vehicle communication as well as reliable environment sensing.

Orthogonal frequency division multiplexing (OFDM) is a widely adopted
modulation format for communications. Due to the wide bandwidth of the
adopted waveform, it can be used for high range resolution radar [2,3], and dual
use of communication and radar functions in a single platform [4,5]. Due to their
advantages on high spectral efficiency, thumbtack-liked ambiguity function, good
Doppler tolerance [6], flexible waveform structure and easy implementations [7],
OFDM signals are attractive to both academic and industrial researchers.

© ICST Institute for Computer Sciences, Social Informatics and Telecommunications Engineering 2018
X. Gu et al. (Eds.): MLICOM 2017, Part II, LNICST 227, pp. 381–390, 2018.
https://doi.org/10.1007/978-3-319-73447-7_42

When considering the range processing approaches in OFDM-based Rad-Com systems, a modulation symbol-based processing technique that estimates the range of a target at short range was presented in [1]. It completely removed the influence of the communication data, and the achieved range resolution was generally in the order of 1 m. A classical correlation-based processing was presented in a Ultra Wideband OFDM system [4], where one subcarrier carried 1 bit data, resulting in a low data rate and high range sidelobes. A subspace projection method based on the compensated communication information was appeared in [8], in which the transmitted radar pulses were consisted of multi-OFDM symbols to improve the data rate, that leaded to high computational complexity. A non-linear least squares approach using weighted OFDM modulation was presented in [9], which also had a low data rate. A novel OFDM radar signal processing scheme which retrieved range information was derived in [10], in which the priori knowledge of the target position was required. A subspace-based algorithm based on rotation invariance to obtain range profile of a target was developed in [11], which suffered from a high computational burden. In conventional pulsed radar systems, each pulse only transmit one single OFDM symbol, which generally leads to the problems including range ambiguity and low transmission data rate.

In views of the above, an OFDM waveform with random phase modulation that transmits monopulse consisting of multi-OFDM symbols is presented to improve data rate, and the analysis of the pulse compression is presented to improve range resolution. The paper is organized as follows. The signal model of OFDM signals is given in Sect. 2. The analysis of pulse compression using ambiguity function is presented in Sect. 3. The simulation results are given in Sect. 4. Conclusion of the paper is given in Sect. 5.

2   Signal Model

2.1   Transmitted Signal

We consider a monostatic radar transmitting monopulse which is composed of multi-OFDM symbols, each symbol consists of transmitted data modulated onto a set of orthogonal subcarriers. Then the complex envelope of OFDM radar can be represented as [12]

$$x(t) = \sum_{m=0}^{M-1} \sum_{n=0}^{N-1} d_{m,n} e^{j2\pi f_n t} \text{rect}\left(\frac{t - mT_s}{T_s}\right) \tag{1}$$

where N is the number of subcarriers, M is the number of symbols, T_s is the OFDM symbol duration, $d_{m,n} = e^{j\varphi_{m,n}}$ denotes the communication data on the nth subcarrier of the mth symbol, which is transmitted using m-ary phase shift keying (m-PSK) modulation schemes, and $\text{rect}\left(\frac{t}{T_s}\right)$ is a rectangular window of duration T_s.

Interference between individual subcarriers is avoided based on the following condition given by

$$f_n = n\Delta f = \frac{n}{T_s} \quad n = 0, \ldots, N-1 \tag{2}$$

2.2   Pulse Compression Processing

Pulse compression is performed to achieve range (delay) estimation using a matched filter whose impulse response is equal to $H(t) = x^*(-t)$, where $*$ denotes the complex conjugate. The matched filter output can be expressed as

$$MF = \int_{-\infty}^{\infty} x(t)x^*(t-\tau)dt \tag{3}$$

Where τ is the relative time delay.

The Doppler shift caused by the movement of the target is also taken into consideration. The received signal can be expressed as a delayed version of the transmitted signal multiplied by a complex exponential that represents the Doppler shift. Hence, the equivalence of the pulse compression processing output to the ambiguity function expression is used to assess the radar performance of OFDM signals [13], which can be expressed as

$$\chi(\tau, \upsilon) = \int_{-\infty}^{\infty} x(t)x^*(t-\tau)e^{j2\pi\upsilon t}dt \tag{4}$$

where υ is the relative Doppler shift.

3   Analysis of Pulse Compression Processing

In this section, we discuss performances of the pulse compression processing based on the ambiguity function. We mainly focus on the effect of Doppler and random phase codes on pulse compression.

3.1   Mathematical Expression of Ambiguity Function

Firstly, we give the mathematical expression of the ambiguity function for the OFDM signal. Substituting (1) into (4), we obtain

$$
\begin{aligned}
\chi(\tau, \upsilon) = \sum_{m=0}^{M-1}\sum_{n=0}^{N-1}\sum_{p=0}^{M-1}\sum_{q=0}^{N-1} d_{m,n}d_{p,q}^* e^{j2\pi q\Delta f\tau} \\
\times \int_{0}^{MT_s} e^{j2\pi((n-q)\Delta f+\upsilon)t}\operatorname{rect}\left(\frac{t-mT_s}{T_s}\right)\operatorname{rect}\left(\frac{t-pT_s-\tau}{T_s}\right)dt
\end{aligned}
\tag{5}
$$

Assuming $\lfloor \frac{\tau}{T_s} \rfloor = i$, where i is an integer. Setting $\tau' = \tau - iT_s$ and $\tau'' = \tau - (i+1)T_s$. Substituting τ' and τ'' into (5), we can get

$$\chi(\tau, \upsilon) = \sum_{p=0}^{M-1-i} \chi_1(\tau', \upsilon) + \sum_{p=1}^{M-1-i} \chi_2(\tau'', \upsilon) \tag{6}$$

where

$$\chi_1(\tau', \upsilon) = (T_s - \tau') \sum_{p=0}^{M-1-i} \sum_{n=0}^{N-1} \sum_{q=0}^{N-1} d_{p+i,n} d_{p,q}^*$$
$$\times e^{j2\pi \frac{(n+q)\Delta f \tau'}{2}} e^{j2\pi \frac{n-q}{2}} e^{j2\pi \upsilon \frac{(2(p+i)+1)T_s + \tau'}{2}} \tag{7}$$
$$\times \mathrm{sinc}\left\{((n-q)\Delta f + \upsilon)(T_s - \tau')\right\}$$

$$\chi_2(\tau'', \upsilon) = (T_s + \tau'') \sum_{p=1}^{M-1-i} \sum_{n=0}^{N-1} \sum_{q=0}^{N-1} d_{p+i,n} d_{p-1}^*,$$
$$\times e^{j2\pi \frac{(n+q)\Delta f \tau''}{2}} e^{j2\pi \frac{n+q}{2}} e^{j2\pi \upsilon \frac{(2(p+i)+1)T_s + \tau''}{2}} \tag{8}$$
$$\times \mathrm{sinc}\left\{((n-q)\Delta f + \upsilon)(T_s + \tau'')\right\}$$

and $\mathrm{sinc}(x) = \sin(\pi x)/(\pi x)$.

3.2   Pulse Compression Loss

The pulse compression loss due to Doppler has been analyzed for one single OFDM symbol case in [6], where the compression loss indicates the loss at the output of the matched filter as compared to the zero Doppler case. To limit the compression loss lower than 1dB, it has shown that the Doppler shift should not exceed $\Delta f / 4$. Herein, we are interested in the compression loss for the case of monopulse containing M OFDM symbols. Hence, we can give an expression for the compression loss (L_{pc}) due to Doppler as

$$L_{pc}[\mathrm{dB}] = 20 \lg |\chi(0, 0)| - 20 \lg |\chi(0, \upsilon)| \tag{9}$$

Let $\eta = \frac{\upsilon}{\Delta f}$ be the normalized Doppler shift obtained through dividing the Doppler shift by the subcarrier separation. In order to reduce the effect of the random phase codes in (9), we run 100 Monte carlo simulations, and the mean value of $L_{pc}[\mathrm{dB}]$ at different η is shown in Fig. 1.

As show in Fig. 1, it can be seen that compression loss increases as η rises. The marker shows that the 1dB compression loss occurs at $\upsilon \approx \frac{\Delta f}{4M}$. This observation complies with the result given in [6] for one single OFDM symbol case. Indeed, an equivalent monpulse containing multi-OFDM symbols would be obtained when the subcarrier spacing is dropped to $\frac{\Delta f}{M}$.

From the above analysis, if we want to set a maximum allowable compression loss of 1dB, the maximum target velocity can be given as $V_{\max} = \frac{cB}{8NMf_c}$, where B is the system bandwidth and f_c is carrier frequency.

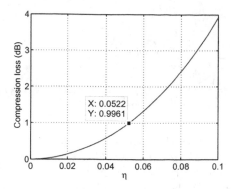

Fig. 1. Compression loss as a function of the normalized Doppler shift for $N = 16$ subcarriers, $M = 5$ OFDM symbols, the symbol duration $T_s = 0.1\,\mu\text{s}$

3.3   Effect of Random Phase Codes on Range Performance

The pulse compression precessing to achieve the range profile of a target, results in high sidelobes for transmitting random phase codes. Therefore, the effect of random phase codes on the range ambiguity function is analyzed as follows.

Substituting $\upsilon = 0$ in (6), we can obtain the range ambiguity function of the OFDM signal

$$\chi(\tau,0) = \sum_{p=0}^{M-1-i} \chi_1(\tau',0) + \sum_{p=1}^{M-1-i} \chi_2(\tau'',0) \tag{10}$$

where

$$\chi_1(\tau',0) = (T_s - \tau') \sum_{p=0}^{M-1-i} \sum_{n=0}^{N-1} \sum_{q=0}^{N-1} d_{p+i,n} d_{p,q}^*$$
$$\times\, e^{j2\pi \frac{(n-q)\Delta f(\tau'+T_s)}{2}} e^{j2\pi q \Delta f \tau'} \beta_1 \tag{11}$$

$$\chi_2(\tau'',0) = (T_s + \tau'') \sum_{p=1}^{M-1-i} \sum_{n=0}^{M-1} \sum_{q=0}^{N-1} d_{p+i,n} d_{p-1,q}^*$$
$$\times\, e^{j2\pi \frac{(n-q)\Delta f(\tau''+T_s)}{2}} e^{j2\pi q \Delta f \tau''} \beta_2 \tag{12}$$

and

$$\beta_1 = \operatorname{sinc}\{(n-q)\Delta f(T_s - \tau')\} \tag{13}$$
$$\beta_2 = \operatorname{sinc}\{(n-q)\Delta f(T_s + \tau'')\} \tag{14}$$

From (11) and (12), we get that β_1 and β_2 have great effects on performance of range ambiguity function.

Firstly, in (13), we get the term $0 < \Delta f(T_s - \tau') < 1$, giving an integer N_1, the values of β_1 are located in the mainlobe of sinc function when $|n - q| < N_1$. Hence, (11) can be approximated as

$$\chi_1(\tau', 0) \approx (T_s - \tau')$$

$$\times \left\{ \sum_{k=-N_1+1}^{0} \sum_{q=-k}^{N-1} d_{p+i,q+k} d_{p,q}^* e^{j2\pi \frac{k\Delta f(\tau'+T_s)}{2}} e^{j2\pi q \Delta f \tau'} \right. \tag{15}$$

$$\left. + \sum_{k=1}^{N_1-1} \sum_{q=0}^{N-1-k} d_{p+i,q+k} d_{p,q}^* e^{j2\pi \frac{k\Delta f(\tau'+T_s)}{2}} e^{j2\pi q \Delta f \tau'} \right\}$$

The expression in (15) shows that, in order to improve the range resolution, phase codes on the pth and $(p+i)$th OFDM symbols has a better aperiodic cross-correlation function (CCF) for $|k| < N_1$.

Secondly, in (14), we get the term $0 < \Delta f(T_s + \tau'') = \Delta f \tau' < 1$. Then, the values of β_2 are located in the mainlobe of sinc function when $|n - q| < N_2$, where N_2 is an integer. Hence, (12) can be approximated as

$$\chi_2(\tau'', 0) \approx (T_s + \tau'')$$

$$\times \left\{ \sum_{k=-N_2+1}^{0} \sum_{q=-k}^{N-1} d_{p+i,q+k} d_{p-1,q}^* e^{j2\pi \frac{k\Delta f(\tau''+T_s)}{2}} e^{j2\pi q \Delta f \tau''} \right. \tag{16}$$

$$\left. + \sum_{k=1}^{N_2-1} \sum_{q=0}^{N-1-k} d_{p+i,q+k} d_{p-1,q}^* e^{j2\pi \frac{k\Delta f(\tau''+T_s)}{2}} e^{j2\pi q \Delta f \tau''} \right\}$$

The expression in (16) shows that the phase codes on the pth and $(p+i+1)$th OFDM symbols has a better aperiodic CCF for $|k| < N_2$ to improve range resolution. Besides, the more N_1, the less N_2. For $i = 0$, we get that phase codes of each OFDM symbol has the aperiodic auto-correlation function (ACF) to improve range resolution.

Finally, we consider a special case of $\tau = iT_s$, (10) can be changed as

$$\chi(iT_s, 0) = T_s \sum_{p=0}^{M-1-i} \sum_{n=0}^{N-1} \sum_{q=0}^{N-1} d_{p+i,n} d_{p,q}^* (-1)^{n-q} \text{sinc}(n-q) \tag{17}$$

From (17), $\chi(iT_s, 0) = 0$ when $n \neq q$. Hence, (17) can be rewritten as

$$\chi(iT_s, 0) = T_s \sum_{p=0}^{M-1-i} \sum_{n=0}^{N-1} d_{p+i,n} d_{p,n}^* \tag{18}$$

which only depends on the phase codes. If we take the expected value of $\chi(iT_s, 0)$ only have the minimum value for $0 < i < M-1$, then the phase codes of different OFDM symbols should be orthogonal.

From the above analysis, we can get that in order to reduce the effect of transmitted data on the radar performance, the phase codes must possess excellent aperiodic ACF and CCF.

4   Simulations Results

4.1   Ambiguity Function Analysis

From the above analysis, we can select the phase codes with excellent aperiodic ACF and CCF to improve radar performance. Hence, we introduce two phase coding to investigate the performance of ambiguity function of the OFDM signal in this simulation. The first phase codes is constructed based on Walsh matrix using genetic algorithm (GA) for optimization presented in [14], the second is based on the consecutive ordered cyclic shift of m-sequence.

The signal parameters are designed as follows: the carrier frequency $f_c = 5.9\,\text{GHz}$, number of subcarriers $N = 32$, number of symbols $M = 16$, symbol duration $T_s = 0.1\,\mu\text{s}$. We construct a Walsh matrix of size $N \times N$ and m-sequence of length N, and the transmitted data of length M is randomly generated. We limit the volume computations of ambiguity function over a region $\Re = \{0 \leq \tau \leq MT_s, |v| \leq 1/T_s\}$. The ambiguity diagram of the OFDM signals based on the two phase codes are shown in Figs. 2 and 3, respectively.

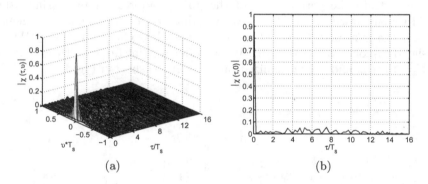

(a)   (b)

Fig. 2. Ambiguity diagram of OFDM signal using phase codes based on Walsh matrix using GA for optimization (a) ambiguity function (b) range ambiguity function

As shown in Figs. 2 and 3, the ambiguity function of Fig. 2(a) presents a thumbtack-type in both delay and Doppler domains, while of the Fig. 3(a) has a high sidelobes in all domains. In Fig. 2(b), the sidelobes reduction of range ambiguity function has been improved evidently. Besides, $\chi(\tau, 0) = 0$ when the delay is integral multiple of symbol duration. We run 100 Monte carlo simulations, and the mean value of peak sidelobe (PSL) in Fig. 2(b) and Fig. 3(b) are $-26.47\,\text{dB}$ and $-12.84\,\text{dB}$, respectively.

From the above, we can get that the OFDM signal using the first phase codes provides a better radar performance. This is because, the phase codes has a better aperiodic ACF and CCF, and keeps strict orthogonality, which has been shown in [14]. While, m-sequence has a better aperiodic ACF, but a worse CCF, because the periodic characteristic of m-sequence results in a peak at a certain shift.

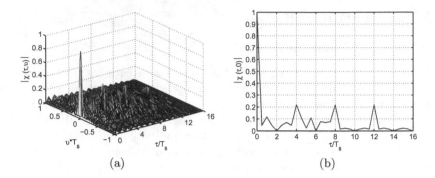

(a)   (b)

Fig. 3. Ambiguity diagram of OFDM signal using phase codes based on the consecutive ordered cyclic shift of m-sequence (a) ambiguity function (b) range ambiguity function

4.2   Range Profile

We demonstrate the performance of the pulse compression processing using OFDM signals based on the the above two phase codes. The signal parameters setting is the same as before, adding in additive white Gaussian noise (AWGN) and signal-to-noise (SNR) is 10 dB. We consider a point target with $R = 100$ m and $V = 10$ m/s, and the normalized range profile is show in Fig. 4.

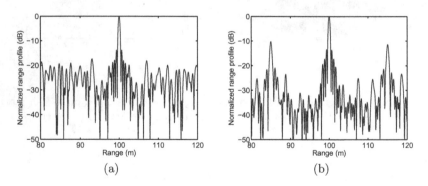

(a)   (b)

Fig. 4. Normalized range profile of a point target with $R = 100$ m and $V = 10$ m/s for OFDM signal using the two phases codes (a) Walsh matrix using GA for optimization (b) the consecutive ordered cyclic shift of m-sequence

It can be seen that in Fig. 4, the OFDM signal using the first phase codes has better sidelobes characteristics in range profile, this observation complies with the result of ambiguity function analysis. The simulation results show that the phase codes which possess a better auto and cross correlation properties can improve the range resolution.

5   Conclusion

In this paper, the analysis of pulse compression processing in an OFDM-based radar-radio system is presented. The monopulse signal is composed of mult-OFDM symbols with random phase modulation, results in a high data rate. The analysis of the algorithm based on ambiguity function is presented. From theoretical analysis and simulation results, we can get that: (i) an expression of pulse compression loss due to Doppler is given, which is a function of the Doppler frequency and symbol number. In order to limit the compression loss, setting a limit to the allowed target velocity is needed. (ii) The phase codes which possess excellent aperiodic auto and cross correlation properties can improve range resolution. If the priori knowledge of the transmitted data is known, we can use pre-coding method that makes phase codes has a better correlation properties to both improve the range performance and data rate.

Acknowledgment. This paper was supported by the Natural Science Foundation of China (NSFC) under Grant No. 91638204 and the Natural Science Foundation of Shenzhen under Grant No. JCYJ20160531192013063.

References

1. Sturm, C., Wiesbeck, W.: Waveform design and signal processing aspects for fusion of wireless communications and radar sensing. Proc. IEEE **99**, 1236–1259 (2011)
2. Levanon, N.: Multifrequency complementary phase-coded radar signal. IEE Proc. Radar Sonar Navig. **147**, 276–284 (2000)
3. Huo, K., Deng, B., Liu, Y., Jiang, W., Mao, J.: High resolution range profile analysis based on multicarrier phase-coded waveforms of OFDM radar. J. Syst. Eng. Electron. **22**, 421–427 (2011)
4. Garmatyuk, D., Schuerger, J., Morton, Y.T., Binns, K., Durbin, M., Kimani, J.: Feasibility study of a multi-carrier dual-use imaging radar and communication system. In: European Radar Conference, Munich, pp. 194–197. IEEE Press (2007)
5. Donnet, B.J., Longstaff, I.D.: Combining MIMO radar with OFDM communications. In: European Radar Conference, Manchester, pp. 37–40. IEEE Press (2006)
6. Franken, G.E., Nikookar, H., Van, G.P.: Doppler tolerance of OFDM-coded radar signals. In: European Radar Conference, Manchester, pp. 108–111. IEEE Press (2006)
7. Huo, K., Zhao, J.: The development and prospect of the new OFDM radar. J. Electron. Inf. Technol. **37**, 2776–2789 (2015)
8. Liu, Y., Liao, G., Yang, Z., Xu, J.: A super-resolution design method for integration of OFDM radar and communication. J. Electr. Syst. Inf. Technol. **02**, 425–433 (2016)
9. Turlapaty, A., Jin, Y., Xu, Y.: Range and velocity estimation of radar targets by weighted OFDM modulation. In: IEEE Radar Conference, Cincimnati, pp. 1358–1362. IEEE Press (2014)
10. Lellouch, G., Mishra, A., Inggs, M.: Impact of Doppler modulation on the range and Doppler processing in OFDM radar. In: IEEE Radar Conference, Cincimnati, pp. 1–4. IEEE Press (2014)

11. Gu, J.F., Moghaddasi, J., Wu, K.: Delay and Doppler shift estimation for OFDM-based radar-radio (RadCom) system. In: 2015 IEEE International Wireless Symposium, Shenzhen, pp. 1–4. IEEE Press (2015)
12. Yang, X., Song, Z., Lu, Z., Fu, Q.: A novel range-Doppler imaging algorithm with OFDM radar. J. Chin. Aeronaut. **29**, 492–501 (2016)
13. Tigrek, R., Heij, D., Genderen, V.: OFDM signals as the radar waveform to solve Doppler ambiguity. J. IEEE AES **48**, 130–143 (2012)
14. Ying, S., He, Z., Liu, H., Li, J., Gao, S.: Binary orthogonal code design for MIMO radar systems. In: International Symposium on Intelligent Signal Processing and Communication Systems, Chengdu, pp. 1–4. IEEE Press (2010)

Implementation of Video Abstract Algorithm Based on CUDA

Hui Li[(✉)], Zhigang Gai, Enxiao Liu, Shousheng Liu, Yingying Gai,
Lin Cao, and Heng Li

Institute of Oceanographic Instrumentation, Shandong Academy of Science,
Qingdao 266001, China
lihuihuidou@163.com

Abstract. The dynamic video abstract is an important part of video content analysis. Firstly, the objective of motion is analyzed, and the objective of the movement is extracted. Then, the moving trajectory of each target is analyzed, and different targets are spliced into a common background scene, and they are combined in some way. The algorithm uses Gaussian mixture model and particle filter to do a large number of calculations to achieve the background modeling and the detection of moving object. With the increase of image resolution, the computing increased significantly. To improve the real-time performance of the algorithm, a video abstract algorithm based on CUDA is proposed in this paper. Through the data analysis and parallel mining of the algorithm, time-consuming modules of the calculation, such as Histogram equalization, Gaussian mixture model, particle filter, were implemented in GPU by using massively parallel processing threads to improve the efficiency. The experimental results show that the algorithm can improve the calculation speed significantly in NVIDIA Tesla K20 and CUDA7.5.

Keywords: Video abstract · Gaussian mixture model · Particle filter
GPU · CUDA · Parallel computing

1 Introduction

The video abstract is a technique that generalizes the main content of the original video. It is also called video synthesis. With the increasing demand for video data processing and the increasing amount of video data, we need to set up a digest for a long video to quickly browse to make better use of it. By using the video abstract technology, we can not only use words in our content-based video retrieval, but also make full use of audio and video information [1]. Video abstract technology solves the problem that how to present video data effectively and fast access. It uses video content analysis to reduce the video storage, classification and indexing, and improve the efficiency, availability and accessibility of the video. It is the development of video analysis technology that based on content.

The generation of the video abstract uses the Gaussian mixture model and particle filtering to perform a large number of operations to achieve the background modeling and motion target detection tracking. Because of the large computational complexity

© ICST Institute for Computer Sciences, Social Informatics and Telecommunications Engineering 2018
X. Gu et al. (Eds.): MLICOM 2017, Part II, LNICST 227, pp. 391–401, 2018.
https://doi.org/10.1007/978-3-319-73447-7_43

and long processing time of Histogram equalization, such as Gauss mixture model and particle filter, it is difficult to apply in real-time video processing with higher real-time requirements [2]. Therefore, the processing time of the algorithm must be effectively reduced to meet more real-time applications.

In recent years, GPU (Graphics Processing Unit) has been applied to large-scale parallel computing and floating point calculation, and its multi-thread and multi-core processors are especially suitable for data parallel computing. CUDA architecture, that uses SIMT (single-instruction-thread, multi-thread) model, is a software platform that can be used to implement fine-grained parallelism. Developing CUDA programs becomes more flexible and efficient because of their easy programmability when accelerating image processing in program-level parallelism. This paper presents a video abstract algorithm based on GPU CUDA, which exploits a large number of parallel threads and heterogeneous memory hierarchy of GPU to improve the execution efficiency.

2 Gauss Mixture Model and Particle Filter

2.1 Gauss Mixture Model

Gaussian mixture Model is a classical adaptive background extraction method presented by Stauffer et al. [3]. It is a kind of method based on background modeling, and it constructs each pixel according to the distribution of each pixel in the time domain of the color distribution model in the video, in order to reach the purpose of background modeling. The Gaussian mixture Model is a weighted sum of finite Gauss functions, which can describe the multimodal state of pixels, and it is suitable for accurate modeling of complex backgrounds such as light gradients and tree swaying.

By looking for a random sample spread in state space to approximate the probability density function, replace the integral operation with the sample mean, and obtains the state minimum variance distribution. The core idea is that through the random state particles extracted from the posterior probability to express the distribution. It is a kind of sequential importance sampling method. It is often used background subtraction method to extract the moving object when the camera fixed. Subtract the current image from background image that previously obtained, if the pixel exceeds a certain threshold, the pixel is identified as the target region; otherwise that is the background area.

The estimation algorithm of single Gauss background model is suitable for indoor environment and outdoor environment which is not very complicated.

The first step is initializing the background image. The average gray value μ_0 of each pixel and the variance σ_0^2 of the pixel gradation in the video sequence image $f(x, y)$ are calculated for a period of time. The initial background image of B_0 with Gauss distribution is composed of μ_0 and σ_0^2. As shown in formulas (1) (2).

$$\mu_0(x, y) = \frac{1}{T} \sum_{i=0}^{T=1} f_i(x, y) \tag{1}$$

$$\sigma_0^2(x,y) = \frac{1}{T}\sum_{i=0}^{T=1}[f_i(x,y) - \mu_0(x,y)]^2 \tag{2}$$

The second step is to update the background image. If the scene changes, the background model needs to respond to these changes. The algorithm updates the background model by using the real-time information provided by the video sequence, where $F_t(x,y)$ represents the real-time image at time t, $B_{t-1}(x,y)$ represents the background image at time t − 1, as shown in formula (3).

$$B_t(x,y) = (1-\rho)\cdot B_{t-1}(x,y) + \rho\cdot F_t(x,y) \tag{3}$$

The background update rate ρ is a constant that reflects the update speed of the current image to the background. Since the influence of the moving target on the background is not taken into account, the pixel on the moving target is also involved in the updating of the background image, resulting in an error in the updated background and the actual background. Thus, Koller et al. improved the algorithm by updating pixels that were labeled as background areas. As shown in formula (4), respectively indicate that $B_t(x,y)$ is judged as background or foreground.

$$B_t(x,y) = \begin{cases} (1-\rho)\cdot B_{t-1}(x,y) + \rho\cdot F_t(x,y) \\ B_{t-1}(x,y) \end{cases} \tag{4}$$

In video surveillance systems, surveillance cameras are generally fixed. If the background is completely stationary, each pixel in the background image can be described by a Gauss model [4]. But in reality, the background is not absolute static, such as the branches swing, or a pixel in the background image at a certain moment may be the sky, may be leaves, may also be branches; each state of the color value of the pixel is different. Therefore, a Gauss model can not reflect the actual background. So, the Gauss mixture distribution is used to describe the background model. The Gauss distribution, which is used to describe the color of each pixel, is K, and K is determined by the computational power and the available memory of the computer, and it generally takes between three and five. The distribution of the currently observed pixel values is as formula (5) shows.

$$P(X_i) = \sum_{i=1}^{k}\omega_{i,t}*\eta\left(X_i,\mu_{i,t},\Sigma_{i,t}\right) \tag{5}$$

$\omega_{i,t}$ is an estimate of the weight of a Gaussian model at time t, $\mu_{i,t}$ is the mean of a Gaussian model at time t, and $\Sigma_{i,t}$ is the covariance matrix of a Gaussian model at time t. η is a Gaussian probability density function as shown in formula (6).

$$\eta(X_t,\mu,\Sigma) = \frac{1}{(2\pi)^{\frac{n}{2}}|\Sigma|^{\frac{1}{2}}}e^{-\frac{1}{2}(X_t-\mu_t)^T\Sigma^{-1}(X_t-\mu_t)} \tag{6}$$

The covariance matrix is assumed to be as follows.

$$\Sigma_{k,t} = \sigma_k^2 I \tag{7}$$

At time t, the weight $\omega_{k,t}$ of the K distribution is updated as follows.

$$\omega_{k,t} = (1 - \alpha)\omega_{k,t-1} + \alpha(M_{k,t}) \tag{8}$$

In the formula, α is the learning rate, the matching model $M_{k,t}$ is 1, and the remaining mismatch model is 0. For the mismatched model, the model parameters are unchanged, and the matching parameters in the matched model are updated as follows.

$$\mu_t = (1 - \rho)\mu_{t-1} + \rho X_t \tag{9}$$

$$\sigma_t^2 = (1 - \rho)\sigma_{t-1}^2 + \rho(X_t - \mu_t)^{\mathrm{T}}(X_t - \mu_t) \tag{10}$$

$$\rho = \alpha\eta(X_t|\mu_k, \sigma_k) \tag{11}$$

Each Gaussian distribution is arranged in order of priority, the former B as the background model, and B is defined as follows.

$$B = \arg\min_b \left(\sum_{k=1}^{b} \omega_k > T \right) \tag{12}$$

T is a pre-defined threshold, which can actually reflect the minimum proportion of the data in the background to the total data.

2.2   Particle Filter

In this paper, we use the sequential importance particle filter algorithm, which uses the weighted sum of a series of random samples to represent the required posterior probability density, obtains the estimated value of the state, realizes the tracking of the moving target and obtains the target trajectory [5].

In the Monte Carlo simulation method which based on importance sampling, it is necessary to recalculate the importance weight of the whole state sequence by estimating the posterior filtering probability and using all the observed data. Sequential importance sampling is the basis of particle filtering, which applies the sequential analysis method in statistics to the Monte Carlo method, so as to realize the recursive estimation of the probability density of the posterior filter [6]. Assume that the importance probability density function $q(x_{0:k}|y_{1:k})$ can be decomposed by the following formula.

$$q(x_{0:k}|y_{1:k}) = q(x_{0:k-1}|y_{1:k-1})q(x_k|x_{0:k-1}, y_{1:k}) \tag{13}$$

Set the system state is a Markov process, and individual observations are independent in a given system state, there are,

$$p(x_{0:k}) = p(x_0) \prod_{i=1}^{k} p(x_i|x_{i-1}) \tag{14}$$

$$p(y_{1:k}|x_{1:k}) = \prod_{i=1}^{k} p(y_i|x_i) \tag{15}$$

The recursive form of the posterior probability density function can be expressed as the following formula.

$$\begin{aligned}
p(x_{0:k}|Y_k) &= \frac{p(y_k|x_{0:k}, Y_{k-1})p(x_{0:k}|Y_{k-1})}{p(y_k|Y_{k-1})} \\
&= \frac{p(y_k|x_{0:k}, Y_{k-1})p(x_k|x_{0:k-1}, Y_{k-1})p(x_{0:k-1}|Y_{k-1})}{p(y_k|Y_{k-1})} \\
&= \frac{p(y_k|x_k)p(x_k|x_{k-1})p(x_{0:k-1}|Y_{k-1})}{p(y_k|Y_{k-1})}
\end{aligned} \tag{16}$$

The recursive form of particle weights $w_k^{(i)}$ can be expressed as formula (17).

$$\begin{aligned}
\omega_k^{(i)} &\propto \frac{p\left(x_{0:k}^{(i)}|Y_k\right)}{q\left(x_{0:k}^{(i)}|Y_k\right)} = \frac{p\left(y_k|x_k^{(i)}\right)p\left(x_k^{(i)}|x_{k-1}^{(i)}\right)p\left(x_{0:k-1}^{(i)}|Y_{k-1}\right)}{q\left(x_k^{(i)}|x_{0:k-1}^{(i)}, Y_k\right)q\left(x_{0:k-1}^{(i)}|Y_{k-1}\right)} \\
&= \omega_{k-1}^{(i)} \frac{p\left(y_k|x_k^{(i)}\right)p\left(x_k^{(i)}|x_{k-1}^{(i)}\right)}{q\left(x_k^{(i)}|x_{0:k-1}^{(i)}, Y_k\right)}
\end{aligned} \tag{17}$$

In general, it is necessary to normalize the weight of the particle, as formula (18).

$$\varpi_k^{(i)} = \frac{\omega_k^{(i)}}{\sum_{i=1}^{N} \omega_k^{(i)}} \tag{18}$$

The sequential importance sampling algorithm generates the sampled particles from the importance probability density function, and obtains the corresponding weights with the arrival of the measured values. Finally, the posterior filtering probability density is described in the form of particle weighting sum, and then get the state estimate.

3   CUDA Architecture

CUDA (Compute Unified Device Architecture) is a general parallel computing architecture introduced by NVIDIA [7], and the architecture can dramatically improve computational performance by using GPU.

There are many SMs (Streaming Multiprocessor) in a GPU in the hardware architecture of GPU CUDA, these similar to the CPU core, and a SM is equipped with a number of SPs (Streaming Processor). SP, namely CUDA core, is the basic processing unit of CUDA, and the specific instructions and tasks are handled in the SP. GPU parallel computing, that is, the parallel processing of multiple SP.

GPU threads are organized in a grid and each grid contains a number of thread blocks [8]. The thread is the basic execution unit in CUDA, a number of threads forms a thread block and the thread block can be a one dimensional, two-dimensional or three-dimensional structure. Many threads in the same thread block have the same instruction address, which not only can execute in parallel, but also can realize the communication among the blocks through the shared memory and the barrier. The CUDA memory access model is shown in Fig. 1.

CUDA code applies to both the host processor (CPU), but also applies for the device processor (GPU) [9]. The host processor is responsible for deriving a multi-thread task (CUDA called a kernel program) that runs on a GPU device processor. When using CUDA programming, the program is divided into two parts, host side and device side. Host side is executed on the CPU part, and it is the serial code. Device side is executed on the GPU part, and it is the parallel code. Program in device side is also called "kernel", and the grid is composed of all threads generated by kernel [10]. In CUDA, host and device have different memory spaces. When these tasks have

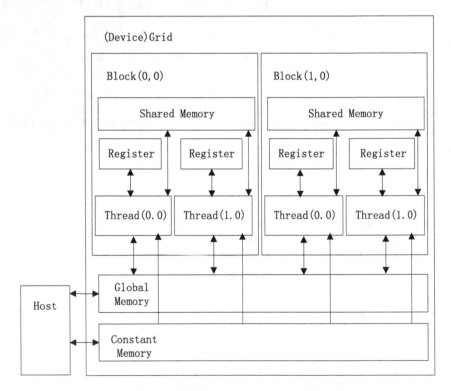

Fig. 1. CUDA memory access model

enough parallelism, with the increase of SM in GPU, the computing speed of the program will be increased. Figure 2 shows the CUDA thread model.

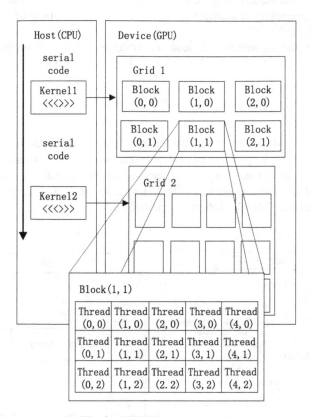

Fig. 2. CUDA program model

4 Realization of Video Abstract Based on CUDA

The R, G and B color components of the image are calculated respectively by the video abstract algorithm when processing the input image. That is, data calculation is independent of each other, so it can take full advantage of SIMT characteristics of CUDA for high-performance parallel processing.

The program based on the CUDA architecture is executed in collaboration in the host side and the device side. In the CUDA programming of MSR algorithm, it should increase the data parallel as much as possible, and reduce the data copy between the host side and the device side, to maximize the advantages of GPU computing. In this paper, the host side is used to realize the reading of the input image, the memory allocation and recovery, and the data transmission between the host and the device. The rest of the implementation process of the algorithm are executed at the device side, mainly Gauss mixture model, erosion, dilation, histogram and particle filter.

In order to achieve higher efficiency of the instruction stream, the algorithm allocates a processing thread for each pixel and uses the shared memory to store convolution operator. Since the size of the CUDA warp is 32, so the number of threads in the thread block is preferably a multiple of 32 to take full advantage of the computing power of each thread.

In this paper, the algorithm is divided according to the size of 64 threads of each thread block according to the two-dimensional allocation method:

```
dim3 blockSize, gridSize
blockSize.x = 8
blockSize.y = 8.
```

When the size and dimensions of the thread block are determined, the number of thread blocks in the thread grid can be determined according to the size of the image. In order to avoid the error caused by the processing of the boundary of the image, the determination of the dimensions of the thread grid in the X and Y directions of the algorithm is determined by the following method:

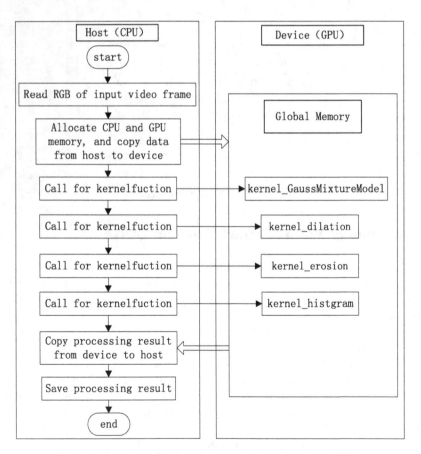

Fig. 3. Flowchart of video abstract algorithm based on CUDA

gridSize.x = (ImageWidth + blockSize.x − 1)/blockSize.x;
gridSize.y = (ImageHeight + blockSize.y − 1)/blockSize.y;

In the case of the histogram equalization, the thread grid in the X, Y, Z direction of the dimension is determined by the following method,

gridSize.x = (Hx[0] * 2 * 2 + blockSize.x − 1)/blockSize.x
gridSize.y = (Hy[0] * 2 * 2 + blockSize.y − 1)/blockSize.y
gridSize.z = N.

Hx and Hy are the size of the filter window, and N is the number of particles. The execution process of the whole algorithm is shown in Fig. 3.

5 Experimental Simulations and Analysis

This algorithm uses NVIDIA Tesla K20 and CUDA7.5 for performance testing, in which the CPU of 2.66 GHz, 2.67 GHz Core Duo. The NVIDIA Tesla K20 has 2496 SPs, and the processing power of single precision is 3524GFLOPS. In this experiment, video frame image with a resolution of 640×360 was selected for performance testing. Finally, the speed of the algorithm in CPU and GPU are compared.

In the CPU algorithm, the basic time that detects a new target of a frame by the first is 180 ms, the filtering time is n times of 15 ms, and the n is the number of filtering. Background modeling frames and tracking multiple frames of detected targets are about 60 ms and 100 ms. For a total of 60 frames, for example, the average frame time is 350 ms, and the core processing time is 150 ms.

In the CUDA algorithm, the basic time that detects a new target of a frame by the first is 80 ms, the filtering time is n times of 15 ms, and the n is the number of filtering. The marker area pixel mu is significantly optimized, the time drops from 25 ms to 1 ms, and the time of the target contour rectangle is extracted from 90 ms to 7 ms. Background modeling frames and tracking multiple frames of detected targets are stabilized to 40 ms and 80 ms. Take a total of 60 frames, for example, the average frame time is 300 ms, and the core processing time is 100 ms.

In the CPU algorithm, statistical histogram algorithm need N dynamic particle multiple iterations. Each iteration takes 20 ms, and each particle filter needs multiple iterations, so it is an obvious bottleneck. After porting the algorithm to GPU, the iteration time fell from 20 ms to 5 ms, and the performance increased by four times.

Figure 4(a) is the background image, Fig. 4(b)(c) is two different goals at the different time in the same scene, Fig. 4(d) sets the two goals in the same frame to form a video abstract.

The experimental results show that the total calculation speed of the video abstract algorithm based on CUDA proposed in this paper is obviously improved compared with the CPU implementation. And the result of the target detection is relatively accurate, the target can be tracked continuously, the formation of the abstract video can effectively save the original video information.

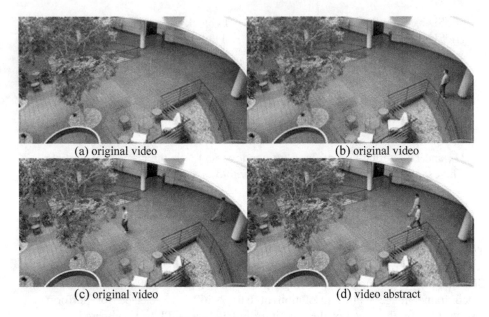

(a) original video   (b) original video

(c) original video   (d) video abstract

Fig. 4. Video abstract result

6 Conclusions

The significant characteristic of video abstract is browsing all moving targets in the video for several hours in a few minutes. Browse video abstract can greatly shorten the time to view the original video, so it can improve the efficiency and accuracy of artificial recognition. However, the complexity of computing has seriously affected in its actual applicability, especially for high-definition video. Based on the CUDA architecture, this paper proposes a video abstract algorithm based on CUDA. The experimental results show that the processing speed is significantly higher than that of the CPU algorithm, and the real-time performance of the algorithm is better.

Acknowledgments. This work was supported by the Natural Science Foundation of Shandong Province, Grant No. ZR2015YL020.

References

1. Wang, J., Jiang, X., Sun, T.: Summary of video abstract technology. J. Image Graph. **19**(12), 1685–1695 (2014)
2. Tian, H., Ding, S., Yu, C., Zhou, L.: Research on video abstract technology based on target detection and tracking. Comput. Sci. **43**(11), 297–312 (2016)
3. Hua, Y., Liu, W.: Improved Gauss mixture model for moving target detection. J. Comput. Appl. **34**(2), 580–584 (2014)
4. Li, B., Yang, G.: Adaptive foreground extraction of Gauss mixture model. J. Image Graph. **18**(12), 1620–1627 (2013)

5. Li, T., Fan, H., Sun, S.: Particle filter theory and method and its application in multi-target tracking. Acta Autom. Sin. **41**(12), 1981–2002 (2015)
6. Wang, F., Lu, M., Zhao, Q.: Particle filter algorithm. Chin. J. Comput. **37**(8), 1679–1694 (2014)
7. CUDA parallel computing platform [EB/OL]. http://www.nvidia.cn/object/cuda-cn.html
8. Cook, S.: CUDA parallel programming: guide for GPU programming. In: Su, T., Li, D. (eds.) Translated Version.1, pp. 191–200. Mechanical Industry Press, Beijing (2014)
9. Jian, L., Wang, C., Liu, Y., et al.: Parallel data mining techniques on Graphics Processing Unit with Compute Unified Device Architecture (CUDA). J. Supercomput. **64**(3), 942–967 (2013)
10. Yang, N.Z., Zhu, Y., Pu, Y.: Parallel image processing based on CUDA. In: 2008 International Conference on Computer Science and Software Engineering, ICCSSE 2008. IEEE Computer Society, California, pp. 198–201 (2008)

Realization of Traffic Video Surveillance on DM3730 Chip

Xin Zhang[✉] and Hang Dong

College of Electronics and Information Engineering,
Tongji University, Dianxin Building, Jiading District, Shanghai, China
{mic_zhangxin, dh}@tongji.edu.cn

Abstract. A general method for traffic video surveillance task involves foreground detecting and moving objects' tracking. The Gaussian mixture model is generally used in detecting foreground and the Kalman filter is used in multi-objects tracking. This paper has implemented a multi-objects tracking system using DM3730 development board as the hardware platform, which is powerful at image processing and analysis. This paper will adopt an Open Computer Vision library (OpenCV) to efficiently implement the overall system. The OpenCV library with a large amount of optimized algorithms in computer vision and machine learning will facilitate the realization of the system. The testing results demonstrate the effectiveness of the system through tracking of vehicles.

Keywords: Multi-objects tracking · DM3730 · OpenCV

1 Introduction

With the urgent demand of constructing a smart city and intelligent transportation, the techniques of traffic video surveillance have been significantly developed and widely used. Especially, we require a sound and excellent digital video surveillance system in the areas where traffic profile is heavy and complicated [1].

An effective approach was proposed for real-time tracking in [2]. The Gaussian mixture model (GMM) was used to distinguish the moving objects. Then the Kalman filter was used to keep track of moving objects in image sequences [2, 3]. This paper has realized the tracking scheme in hardware and can follow and keep track of the moving objects in traffic video correctly.

Initially, a sequence of images is obtained using V4L2 to drive camera to capture images [4]. V4L2 is the application programming interface (API) for video capturing in Linux system which offers unified interfaces for application. Then, this paper has applied GMM in detecting foreground of image sequences [2] and Kalman filter in keeping track of each moving object [6].

The rest of the paper will be organized as follows: In Sect. 2, the hardware platform based on embedded Linux system, where the overall scheme was implemented, will be discussed firstly. In Sect. 3, the flowchart of the scheme proposed in [2] will be explicitly explained. In Sect. 4, the testing results of the realized system will be shown. In Sect. 5, we will conclude the important procedures of the system.

© ICST Institute for Computer Sciences, Social Informatics and Telecommunications Engineering 2018
X. Gu et al. (Eds.): MLICOM 2017, Part II, LNICST 227, pp. 402–409, 2018.
https://doi.org/10.1007/978-3-319-73447-7_44

2 Hardware Platform Based on Embedded Linux System

2.1 Hardware Platform

In order to solve the real-time tracking problem for multi-objects, we need a set of processing and controlling system with high speed performance, low power consumption, high speed data I/O, large storage capability and high reliability. The programmable ARM + DSP engine allows multiple signal processing tasks and its video processor is suitable for video processing tasks [4]. Therefore, this paper will use the DM3730 circuit as the hardware platform to implement the tracking scheme.

The Application Processor module (AP module) of DM3730 is a powerful circuit. AP module integrates an ARM Cortex A8 core, a powerful TI C64x + DSP core, a POWERVR SGX graphic accelerator, and a TI TPS65950. The AP Module functional block diagram is shown in Fig. 1 [4].

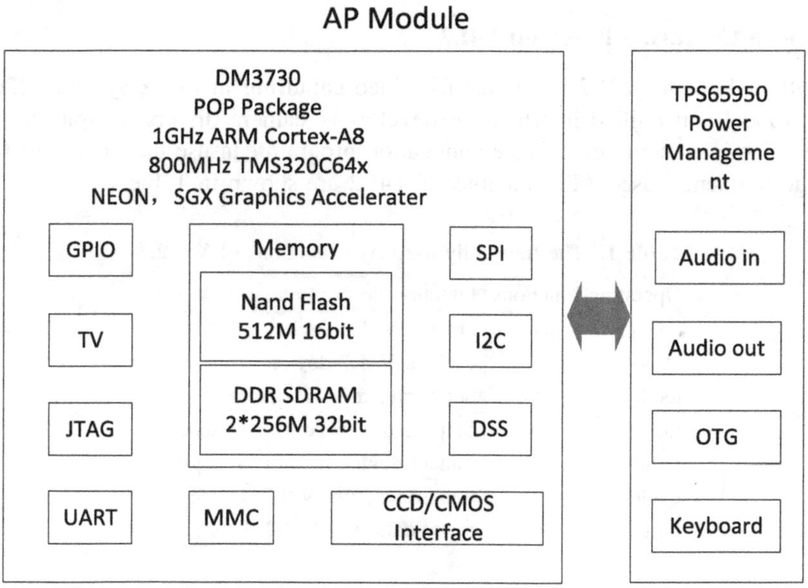

AP Module

Fig. 1. AP module functional block diagram [4].

2.2 Cross-Compiling for OpenCV Library

OpenCV is an open source computer vision and machine learning software library with more than 2500 optimized algorithms [6]. Since the OpenCV can be run and transplanted on different platforms, this paper will use OpenCV library to implement the tracking scheme. Therefore, we need to cross-compile the OpenCV Library and transplant the compiled files to the kernel of DM3730 so that the optimized algorithms in computer vision can work on the hardware system.

3　The Implementation Scheme

The implementation scheme of the multi-objects detecting and tracking system involves following steps: video capturing, objects detecting, and multi-objects tracking. Initially, the system will capture image sequences using V4L2. Afterwards, GMM will be adopted to detect moving objects. Ultimately, the Kalman filter will be used to keep track of individual moving object. The complete diagram of the implementation scheme is shown in Fig. 2.

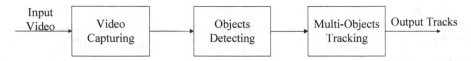

Fig. 2. Implementation scheme diagram.

3.1　Video Capturing Based on V4L2

As mentioned above, V4L2 is an API for video capturing in Linux system, offering explicit model and unified interface for developing camera drivers. Despite the differences among camera devices, the application program can use the same API function. The frequently used API functions of V4L2 are shown in Table 1.

Table 1. The frequently used API functions of V4L2.

Operating functions	Function description
open()	Open a V4L2 device
close()	Close a V4L2 device
ioctl()	Set parameters for device
mmap()	Map kernel space to user space
munmap()	Cancel device memory mapping
read()	Read data from V4L2 device
write()	Write data into V4L2 device

The flowchart of video capturing is shown in Fig. 3.

The principal steps of video capturing are as follows:

(1) Open the camera device and get file descriptor of device. The application can open the video device under blocking mode or non-blocking mode.
(2) Check the functions of the camera device such as video capturing and stream collecting.
(3) Set format of image sequences. The application can set image format manually as MJPEG format, BMP format or YUV format.
(4) Reserve buffer area and use mmap function to map memory to the user space.
(5) Start capturing video and wait for the driver to put images to the user space so as to capture images successively.
(6) Stop capturing video and shut the device.

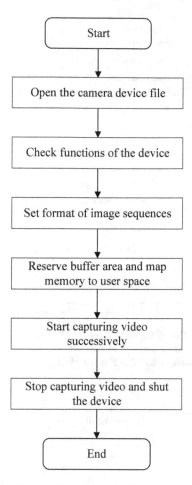

Fig. 3. The flowchart of video capturing.

3.2 Objects Detecting Using GMM

The objects detecting module has been implemented using GMM to model each individual pixel. The parameters of background Gaussian distributions will be updated to improve the adaptability of the background changes. The flowchart of objects detecting algorithm is shown in Fig. 4.

The objects detecting module will model individual pixel of each image with K Gaussian distributions [2]. Then the difference between the pixel and the mean value will be checked if it is within 2.5 times of standard deviation in order to determine whether the pixel belongs to background or not. Afterwards, the weights of all Gaussian distributions will be updated respectively. If none of the Gaussian distributions match with the pixel value, the distribution with least probability will be substituted by current pixel value.

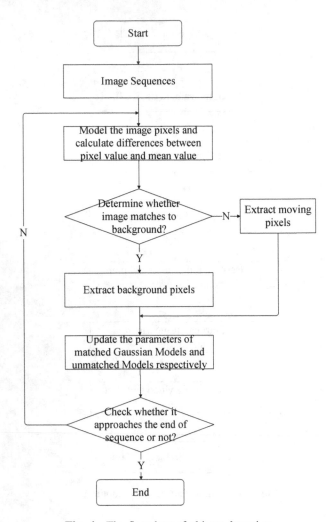

Fig. 4. The flowchart of objects detecting.

3.3   Multi-objects Tracking Using Kalman Filter

After successfully extracting foreground and updating background using GMM, we need to keep track of moving objects in image sequences. Once moving objects detected, a Kalman Filter will be assigned to keep track of moving objects. Multi-objects tracking scheme will be implemented using online multi-objects tracking method for maintaining sets of Kalman filters [2]. The flowchart of the implementation scheme is shown in Fig. 5.

The location of each moving object will be recorded and updated in a vector only if the maximum SIFT feature is greater than threshold value [5]. The moving object will be compared with five predicted locations. If none of the locations matches with the threshold value, it means that the moving object has disappeared.

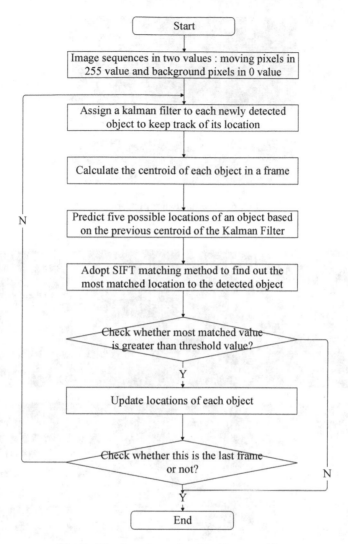

Fig. 5. The flowchart of multi-objects tracking.

4 Testing Results

After applying GMM for image sequences in Sect. 3, moving pixels have been detected from video clips. In this section, we will display the hardware platform in Fig. 6 and some testing results in real scenes such as crossroads in Figs. 7 and 8.

There are four tracks of vehicles in the video shown in Fig. 7 and two tracks of pedestrians in Fig. 8.

These four pictures show the tracks existing in video clips. Figure 7(a) shows that a vehicle is driving vertically first and then turning left. Figure 7(b) shows that a vehicle

Fig. 6. The hardware platform.

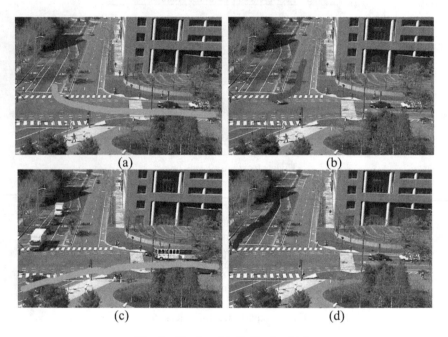

Fig. 7. Tracks of individual vehicle.

is making a turnaround. Figure 7(c) shows that a vehicle is turning right. Figure 7(d) shows that a vehicle changes its lane to the rightmost one preparing to turn right.

The two pictures in Fig. 8 show the tracks of pedestrians in video clips. Figure 8(a) shows that a person is walking across the zebra crossing and Fig. 8(b) shows that a person is walking along the road and turns right.

(a)   (b)

Fig. 8. Motions of individual pedestrian.

5 Conclusions

We have used DM3730 as hardware platform and OpenCV to implement the real-time tracking method proposed in [2]. The procedures of using V4L2 to drive camera capture image sequence, GMM to extract foreground, and Kalman Filter to keep track of moving objects have been explicitly explained. The multi-objects tracking results are presented using the realized system with DM3730 hardware platform.

References

1. Wang, X., Ma, X., Grimson, W.E.L.: Unsupervised activity perception in crowded and complicated scenes using hierarchical bayesian models. TPAMI **31**(3), 539–555 (2009)
2. Stauffer, C., Grimson, W.E.L.: Adaptive background mixture models for real-time tracking. In: Proceedings of IEEE CVPR, pp. 246–252, June 1999
3. Faragher, R.: Understanding the basis of the Kalman filter via a simple and intuitive derivation. IEEE Sig. Process. Mag. **29**(5), 128–132 (2012)
4. Varfolomieiev, A., Lysenko, O.: An improved algorithm of median flow for visual object tracking and its implementation on TI OMAP. In: Proceedings of EDERC, pp. 261–265, September 2012
5. Sakai, Y., Oda, T., Ikeda, M., Barolli, L.: An object tracking system based on SIFT and SURF feature extraction methods. In: INWC, pp. 561–565, September 2015
6. Li, D., Liang, B., Zhang, W.: Real-time moving vehicle detection, tracking, and counting system implemented with OpenCV. In: Proceedings of IEEE ICIST, pp. 631–634, April 2014

Fertilization Forecasting Algorithm Based on Improved BP Neural Network

Tong Xue[1,2] and Yong Liu[1(✉)]

[1] School of Electronics Engineering,
Heilongjiang University, Harbin 150080, China
1995020@hlju.edu.cn, xtong940213@163.com
[2] School of Electronics and Information Engineering,
Harbin Institute of Technology, Harbin 150080, China

Abstract. In this paper, we consider a fertilization forecast algorithm based on improved BP neural network. By analyzing traditional single fertilization forecast algorithm, we find that they are too simple, lack of network training and cannot take into account the impact of different nutrients. Then, we consider an improved BP neural network algorithm, which is based on the Lagrangian multiplier method to optimize the BP neural network and nutrient balance method by weighted combination algorithm. The simulation results show that the improved method can accurately guide the amount of fertilizer, only a small amount of learning data.

Keywords: Fertilization forecast · BP neural network
Nutrient balance method · Weighted combination method

1 Introduction

In recent years, excessive use of chemical fertilizers caused a lot of waste of fertilizer and irreversible damage to our environment [1]. At present, our government has realized that the important of precision fertilization in increasing yield and protecting ecology [2]. With the application of big data in the field of agriculture, the research of fertilization forecasting algorithm becomes a research focus.

The current solution for fertilization forecasting is based on linear or single variable [3]. However, both of these solutions exist interaction. In [4], Wang et al. using the improved BP neural network algorithm to predict the amount of fertilizer, the K-means clustering is used to optimize the weight of the neural network to be integrated by the Lagrangian multiplier method.

In this paper, we consider an improved BP algorithm. Firstly, calculate the predictive value of BP neural network and nutrient balance method respectively. Then, we utilize weighted combination method based on prediction error square minimum. Taking into account the interaction between fertilizers and increasing the factors of light time and rainfall. In the case of less learning samples, more accurate fertilization predictions can be made.

© ICST Institute for Computer Sciences, Social Informatics and Telecommunications Engineering 2018
X. Gu et al. (Eds.): MLICOM 2017, Part II, LNICST 227, pp. 410–417, 2018.
https://doi.org/10.1007/978-3-319-73447-7_45

The rest of the paper is organized as follows. In Sect. 2, we provide system model for fertilizer forecast. We provide a single forecast algorithm model, including BP neural network and nutrient balance method in Sect. 3. Section 4 provides the improved algorithm model. We utilize weighted combination method based on prediction error square minimum. In Sect. 5, we show the performance of our algorithm by simulation.

2   System Model and Problem Formulation

The factors that affect crop yields are not only nitrogen, phosphorus and kalium, but also light time, chlorophyll content, precipitation, water content in different depths, soil conductivity. These factors exist complex interaction rather than linear. Problem model, as shown in Fig. 1. Note that N, P and K represent the content of nitrogen, phosphorous and potassium, W represents the water content in different depths. SC and CC represents soil conductivity and chlorophyll content, L represents light time. FN, FP, FK and FW represent the fertilization forecast value of nitrogen, phosphorous, kalium and water. In this paper, we should research an algorithm to find the relationship between soil parameters and fertilization. The purpose of our algorithm is that could calculate the amount of water that should be irrigated when light time hadn't achieve the best.

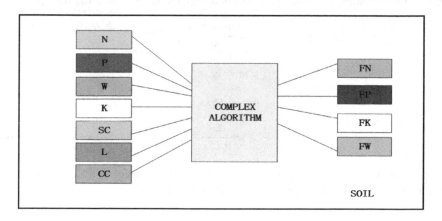

Fig. 1. Problem mode

Our problem formulation deals with complex relationship between soil parameters and fertilization. We propose an improved algorithm for BP neural network algorithm, which is based on the Lagrangian multiplier method to optimize two kinds of single prediction algorithms by using weighted combination method to reduce the prediction error of fertilization lowest. Figure 2 shows the improved algorithm model. The key to solving this problem is to determine the weights of the coefficients l_1 and l_2.

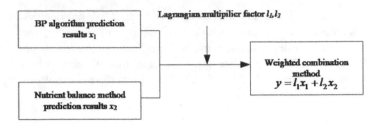

Fig. 2. The improved BP neural network algorithm model

3 Single Forecast Algorithm

3.1 Nutrient Balance Method

The nutrient balance method proposed by Truog in 1960s. The nutrient balance method is used to estimate the amount of fertilizer according to the difference between target yield and soil supply [5]. The formula for the amount of fertilizer is (1)–(4). In the formula, y is the amount of fertilizer, m is the amount of fertilizer required for the soil, g is the amount of fertilizer required for the soil, k is the amount of fertilizer required for crop units, z is the target yield, λ is the effective nutrient correction coefficient for soil, x is the soil nutrient value, μ is the nutrient content in the fertilizer, η is the fertilizer utilization, q is the amount of the element absorbed by the lack of nutrient area, k is based on the statistical analysis of agricultural experts to determine the data [6].

$$y = \frac{m - g}{\mu\eta} \tag{1}$$

$$m = kz \tag{2}$$

$$g = 0.15\lambda x \tag{3}$$

$$\lambda = \frac{q}{0.15x} \tag{4}$$

However, the method requires a large number of parameters to be calculated. It is difficult to effective management of fertilization parameters.

3.2 BP Neural Network Algorithm

The BP algorithm was proposed by D. Rumerlhart and J. McCelland in the mid-1980s [7]. BP algorithm is divided into learning and forecasting two parts. Figure 3 is the neural network learning part of the schematic diagram.

Firstly, we put given data of the test group into input layer parameters, put forecast data of the test group into output layer (tutor vectors). Then, input layer parameters pass through the hidden layer of complex calculated, the results will be given to the output. Compared with tutor vectors, we put error feedback to hidden layer. Last, the hidden layer of neurons to adjust. BP neural network consider the influence between fertilizes

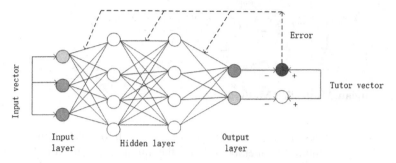

Fig. 3. The neural network learning part of the schematic diagram

and raining. But BP neural network algorithm has disadvantage of slow convergence, the number of hidden layer nodes is difficult to determine and different value has different neural network.

4 Improved Algorithm Model

4.1 Weighted Combination Method

Weighted combination method is an evaluation function method, which is based on the importance of each goal to give it corresponding weighted coefficient, and then find the solution method of multi-objective programming for linear combination [8].

Suppose that a set of observations for a given object is $x_t(t = 1,2,...,N)$. It exists m kinds of single prediction methods. Assume that the predicted value of the ith single prediction method is $x_{it}(i = 1,2,...,m)$. $e_{it} = x_t - x_{it}$ is predicts error of ith single prediction. $l_i(i = 1,2,...,m)$ is weighted coefficient of ith single predicted method, $\sum_{i=1}^{m} l_i = 1$.

Weighted combination predicted model is (5) and its predictive value is y_t. Formula (6) and (7) are respectively the prediction error and the prediction error squared sum. In it, e_t is prediction error, J is prediction error squared sum.

$$y_t = \sum_{j=1}^{m} l_i x_{it} = l_1 x_{1t} + l_2 x_{2t} + \ldots + l_m x_{mt} \tag{5}$$

$$e_t = x_t - y_t = \sum_{i=1}^{m} l_i e_{it} \tag{6}$$

$$J = \sum_{t=1}^{N} e_t^2 = \sum_{t=1}^{N} \sum_{i=1}^{m} \sum_{j=1}^{m} l_i l_j e_{it} e_{jt} \tag{7}$$

Therefore, the solution of the optimal weight of the weighted combination forecast is the solution of the formula under the objective of the sum of the squares of errors. In this paper, the improved algorithm involves two kinds of single prediction algorithms (BP neural network algorithm, nutrient balance method). Formula reduced to (8) can be solved the value of l_1 and l_2.

$$\begin{cases} min\, J = \sum_{i=1}^{N} e_t^2 = \sum_{t=1}^{N} \sum_{i=1}^{2} \sum_{j=1}^{2} l_i l_j e_{it} e_{jt} \\ \sum_{i=1}^{2} l_i = 1 \end{cases} \qquad (8)$$

4.2   Lagrangian Multiplier Method

The lagrangian multiplier method is a method of solving the extreme value of a function whose variables are limited by one or several conditions [9]. In this paper, we use the Lagrangian multiplier method to find the minimum value of the function $J = \sum_{i=1}^{N} e_t^2 = \sum_{t=1}^{N} \sum_{i=1}^{2} \sum_{j=1}^{2} l_i l_j e_{it} e_{jt}$ when the condition $\sum_{i=1}^{2} l_i - 1 = 0$ is satisfied.

$$\begin{cases} min\, J = L^T E L \\ R^T L = 1 \end{cases} \qquad (9)$$

$$L = L^T E L + \lambda (R^T L - 1) = 0 \qquad (10)$$

$$L^* = \frac{E^{-1} R}{R^T E^{-1} R} \qquad (11)$$

$$J^* = \frac{1}{R^T E^{-1} R} \qquad (12)$$

In order to simplify the calculation, let $L = (l_1, l_2)^T$, $R = (1,1)^T$, $E_i = (e_{i1}, e_{i2}, \ldots, e_{iN})^T$. L is the column vector of the Lagrangian multiplier weighting factor. E_i is the column vector of predicted error of ith predictive algorithm. Let $E_{ij} = E_i^T E_j (i = 1,2, j = 1,2)$, $E = (E_{ij})_{(2 \times 2)}$. (8) can be reduced to (9). (10) is Lagrangian multiplier formula. L is derived and set to zero. The optimal solution L^* and the optimal objective function J^* is the simultaneous solution equations.

5   Simulation Results

This paper uses MATLAB 2014b version for simulation [10]. Table 1 is part of the standard data measured over years of testing. Among them, columns 1 to 10 are data for monitoring in the soil, columns 11 to 14 are the best fertilizer application amounts.

The optimum nitrogen fertilizers, phosphate fertilizers and potash fertilizers were compared with those of 30 groups before and after the improvement. The accuracy of the fertilization was improved before and after the improvement. Figure 4 is a comparison of the prediction accuracy of the improved and pre-improved fertilization.

In Fig. 4, it indicates the difference between BP neural network and improved BP neural network algorithm. Figure 4(a) compares the prediction error of nitrogen fertilizer. Sample 18 to 28, improved algorithm prediction results are similar to early algorithm. However, the prediction error of Nitrogen is 4.2% lower than the BP algorithm. The peak error from 43 down to 24. Figure 4(b) compares the prediction

Table 1. Part of the standard data measured over years of testing

No.	N (mg kg⁻¹)	P (mg kg⁻¹)	K (mg kg⁻¹)	Yield (kg)	Light time (h)	Water content in 10 cm	Water content in 20 cm	Water content in 30 cm	Rainfal l (mm)	Chloro- phyll content	FW (kg hm⁻²)	FN (kg hm⁻²)	FP (kg hm⁻²)	FK (kg hm⁻²)
1	101.5	9.12	199	7713	9.9	53.43	49.99	37.67	55.78	3.34	27.89	160	20	35
2	92.79	11.56	186	7760	9.99	46.74	43.3	30.98	49.09	2.94	24.54	160	20	37
3	109.6	10.1	191	8361	10.9	46.6	42.12	29.8	48.95	2.93	24.47	160	20	40
4	107.42	14.8	193	8038	10.01	43.26	39.86	27.54	45.61	2.73	22.08	158	14	35
5	99.02	15.78	196	7078	10.23	44.57	41.13	28.81	46.92	2.81	23.46	158	14	35
6	107.73	17.26	203	9092	9.9	46.37	42.93	30.61	48.72	2.92	24.46	178	14	40
7	104.3	20.98	202	9192	9.78	45.51	42.07	29.75	47.86	2.87	23.36	170	14	40
8	199.27	15.98	199	10508	10.13	47.65	44.21	31.89	50	3.21	25	195	24	63
9	146.96	16.38	210	8741	10.21	47.78	44.34	32.02	50.13	3.02	25.06	179	24	42
10	146.96	21.56	239	8502	9.89	39.74	36.3	23.98	42.09	3.31	21.04	168	20	35
11	145.72	13.14	188	9070	11.01	52.74	49.3	36.98	55.09	2.94	0	189	28	48
12	118.94	7.56	192	7383	10.34	46.65	43.12	30.89	49	2.93	24.5	155	28	39
13	127.66	7.16	181	9304	9.99	46.54	43.21	30.8	48.89	3.06	24.44	189	26	45
14	129.53	6.56	173	8510	11.01	48.7	45.28	32.96	51.05	2.64	25.52	152	27	47
15	141.05	9.61	176	6985	9.57	41.68	38.24	25.92	44.03	2.49	22.01	147	21	37
16	94.34	12.16	187	6332	11.2	39.23	35.79	23.47	41.58	2.81	20.79	156	18	30
17	94.96	14.12	205	6419	10.23	44.57	41.13	28.81	46.92	2.92	23.79	156	18	29
18	99.01	14.42	183	8464	9.9	46.37	42.93	30.61	48.72	2.87	23.46	176	18	40
19	98.71	17.16	199	7696	9.99	45.51	42.07	29.75	47.86	2.43	0	170	18	40
20	110.54	15.3	193	8440	10.9	43.67	40.23	27.91	46.02	1.92	23.93	165	21	37

error of Phosphate fertilizer. The prediction error of Phosphate is 8.3% lower than the BP algorithm. Figure 5 compares the prediction error of Kalium fertilizer. Among all samples, the improved algorithm errors are under 8 and 13% lower than the BP algorithm.

Figures 4 and 5 compares the prediction error of nitrogen fertilizer, phosphate fertilizer and potash fertilizer respectively. The solid line represents the prediction error of the BP algorithm, and the dotted line represents the prediction error of the improved

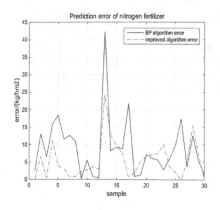

a. Comparison of prediction error for Nitrogen

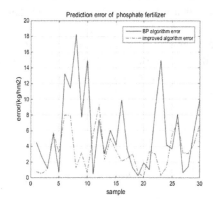

b. Comparison of prediction error for Phosphate

Fig. 4. Comparison of prediction error before and after algorithm improved

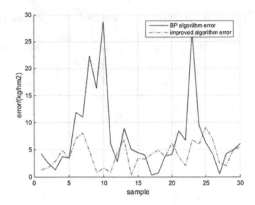

Fig. 5. Comparison of prediction error for Kalium

algorithm. The error comparison standard comes from the actual amount of fertilizer applied from Table 1. The actual amount of fertilizer is a comprehensive consideration of the factors that affect the fertilization of the standard fertilization yield. It can be seen that the improved algorithm is less error-prone than the BP algorithm and is closer to the actual fertilizer. The prediction error is 7% lower than the BP algorithm.

6 Conclusion

In this paper, the advantages and disadvantages of various fertilization forecast methods are compared. Aiming at the shortcomings of BP neural network which requires a large number of learning samples, we proposes a method to improve BP algorithm by weighted combination method. That is, the use of less sample learning data, to carry out agricultural precision fertilizer guidance. It is difficult to see that the accuracy of the optimization algorithm proposed in this paper is improved by 7% through the analysis of MATLAB software programming results. Another breakthrough is that we could calculate the amount of water when light time hadn't achieve the best.

Due to limited time, there are still many shortcomings in this paper. For example, the fertilization cost cannot be taken into account in the fertilization forecasting algorithm, only one crop of maize is predicted, the test sample is small and the variety is single.

References

1. Zhu, M.: Study on the effect of precision agriculture technology in Chinese agricultural development. J. Anhui Agric. Sci. **36**(25), 11126–11128 (2008)
2. Zhao, C.: Strategy thinking on precision agriculture of China. Agric. Netw. Inf. **4**, 5–8 (2010)

3. Yang, Y., Ran, C., Liu, W.: Algorithm of fertilization knowledge model based on fuzzy-neural network. In: IEEE International Conference on Intelligent Computing and Intelligent Systems, pp. 40–43. IEEE (2010)

4. Wang, H.C., Song, F., Wen, F.W.: An improved BP algorithm and its application. Adv. Mater. Res. **765–767**, 489–492 (2013)

5. HU, S., Dai, Y., Yao, M.Y., et al.: Application of soil nutrient balance method on corn fertilization recommended. Inner Mong. Agric. Sci. Technol. (2007)

6. Han, F., LI, L., Peng, Z., et al.: Indica hybrid rice recommended fertilization parameter based on nutrient balance method in guizhou. Guizhou Agric. Sci. (2014)

7. Ding, S., Su, C., Yu, J.: An optimizing BP neural network algorithm based on genetic algorithm. Kluwer Academic Publishers (2011)

8. Zhang, H.W., Peng, L., Yan, X.Q.: Study on optimal weighted combination method of air quality mid-long term prediction. J. Tianjin Inst. Text. Sci. Technol. (2005)

9. Ilanko, S., Monterrubio, L.E., Mochida, Y., et al.: Lagrangian multiplier method. In: The Rayleigh-Ritz Method for Structural Analysis, pp. 33–37. Wiley, Hoboken (2014)

10. Zhao, Z., Xin, H., Ren, Y., et al.: Application and comparison of BP neural network algorithm in MATLAB. In: International Conference on Measuring Technology and Mechatronics Automation, pp. 590–593. IEEE Computer Society (2010)

Green Resource Allocation in Intelligent Software Defined NOMA Networks

Baobao Wang[1,2], Haijun Zhang[2](✉), Keping Long[2], Gongliang Liu[3],
and Xuebin Li[1]

[1] Beijing University of Chemical Technology, Beijing, China
eebaobaowang@gmail.com
[2] Beijing Engineering and Technology Research Center for Convergence Networks,
University of Science and Technology Beijing, Beijing, China
haijunzhang@ieee.org
[3] Harbin Institute of Technology, Weihai, China
liugl@hit.edu.cn

Abstract. Non-orthogonal multiple access (NOMA) with successive interference cancellation (SIC) is a promising technique for fifth generation wireless communications. In NOMA, multiple users can access the same frequency-time resource simultaneously and multi-user signals can be separated successfully with SIC. In this paper, with recent advances in software-defined networking (SDN), an architecture of SDN-NOMA network was proposed and the SDN controller has a global view of the network. We aim to investigate the resource allocation algorithms for the virtual resource blocks (VRB) assignment and power allocation for the downlink SDN-NOMA network. Different from the existing works, here, energy efficient dynamic power allocation in SDN-NOMA networks is investigated with the constraints of QoS requirement and power consumption. The simulation results confirm that the proposed scheme of SDN-NOMA system yields much better sum rate and energy efficiency performance than the conventional orthogonal frequency division multiple access scheme.

Keywords: Energy efficient · NOMA · SDN · Resource allocation

1 Introduction

With the explosive growth of smart mobile devices and the increasing demands for high spectral efficiency in recent years, orthogonal channel access in orthogonal frequency division multiple access (OFDMA) is becoming a limiting factor of spectrum efficiency since each subchannel can only be utilized by at most one user in each time slot [1]. Then, non-orthogonal multiple access (NOMA) has been envisioned as a promising technique to relieve the heavy burden of overloaded traffic in base station (BS) [2]. The improvement in spectral efficiency of NOMA network is significant by allowing multiple users to share the same subchannel in power domain [3]. The capacity region which achieved in NOMA

© ICST Institute for Computer Sciences, Social Informatics and Telecommunications Engineering 2018
X. Gu et al. (Eds.): MLICOM 2017, Part II, LNICST 227, pp. 418–427, 2018.
https://doi.org/10.1007/978-3-319-73447-7_46

is significantly outperforms the orthogonal multiple access schemes by power domain multiplexing at the transmitter and SIC at the receivers [4].

As a key technology in the 5G mobile communication, inter-user interference over each subchannel will be created when multiple users sharing the same subchannel [5]. As a multi-user detection technique, SIC can be applied at the end-user receivers to decode the received signals [6]. The outage performance of NOMA was evaluated in [7], while in [8], the authors investigated the system sum-rate of multiuser NOMA single-carrier systems as well as proposing a sub-optimal power allocation and presenting a precoder design. A low-complexity suboptimal algorithm with power proportional factors determination for sub-channel multiplexed users was investigated in [9]. By considering imperfect CSI, energy efficiency improvement for a downlink NOMA single-cell network is investigated and an iterative algorithm for user scheduling and power allocation is proposed in [10].

Software-defined networking (SDN) is proposed by Stanford University and has been regarded as a promising network platform which enables the adoption of new technologies and dynamic reconfiguration large scale complex networks [11]. By means of standardized interfaces (e.g., OpenFlow), independent devices of varies vendors can be fast control by the SDN controller [12]. The authors in [13] studied SDN information-centric cellular network virtualization with D2D communication and the subscribers from different mobile virtual network operators can share the virtualized contents. In order to reduce the emission of global greenhouse gas to protect our environment, the research of maximizing the system energy efficiency has been highly attractive [14]. However, most of the existing works considered resource allocation of energy efficiency using SDN only in OFDMA systems. To the best of the authors' knowledge, energy efficient resource allocation for SDN-NOMA networks has not been studied in previous works.

In this paper, we investigate the virtual resource blocks and power allocation respectively in a downlink SDN-NOMA network by considering energy efficiency, quality of service (QoS) requirements, power limits. Based on the novel energy efficient NOMA network optimization framework that we developed, we design a VRB assignment algorithm based on matching theory and a power allocation algorithm with multiple constraints.

2   SDN-NOMA System Model

We consider the downlink of a SDN-based resource sharing system of NOMA network. In the SDN framework, the control plane and the data plane are separated which eases resource management and network optimization. In the data plane, the distributed small cell base stations (SCBSs) which operated by the same or different network operators (service providers) provide data services to the users with different applications. All the transmitters are equipped with a single antenna. The users are uniformly distributed in the coverage of the base stations (BSs). As the high deployed density, the coverage areas of the heterogeneous BSs are overlapped seriously. For the control plane, the SDN controller has a global view of the network, including the traffic demands of users, available wireless resource and the channel status information. As the information of traffic demands arrived, the SDN controller design a resource allocation strategy between users and SCBSs with virtual resource blocks (VRBs).

In SDN-NOMA network, one user can receive signals from the BS through arbitrary VRB and one VRB can be allocated to multiple users at the same time. Since the user j on VRB n causes interference to the other users on the same VRB, each user j adopts SIC after receiving the superposed signals to demodulate the target message. The interference signals caused by user j whose channel gain is better than user u cannot be decoded and will be treated as noise this is because user u with higher channel gain can only decode the signals of user i with worse channel gain. Then, when the transmitted power of user u of SCBS k over VRB n is $p_{k,n}^u$, after SIC, the interference for user u caused by other users of the same SCBS k on the same VRB n is given by

$$\widetilde{I}_{k,n}^u = \sum_{s \in \{U_k | g_{k,n}^s > g_{k,n}^u\}} a_{k,n}^s p_{k,n}^s g_{k,n}^u \tag{1}$$

where $g_{k,n}^u$ is the channel gain from small cell k of user u on VRB n, U_k is the set of users of SCBS k. $a_{k,n}^u = 1$ means that user u is allocated to the VRB n of SCBS k and $\sigma_n{}^2$ is the noise variance. Modeling this residual interference as additional AWGN, the received SINR of small cell user $u \in \mathcal{U} = \{1, 2, ..., U\}$ in SCBS k on the nth VRB is given by

$$\gamma_{k,n}^u = \frac{a_{k,n}^u p_{k,n}^u g_{k,n}^u}{I_{k,n}^u + \widetilde{I}_{k,n}^u + \sigma^2} \tag{2}$$

where $I_{k,n}^u$ is the interference caused by other SCBSs to user u in SCBS k on VRB n, which is given by

$$I_{k,n}^u = \sum_{l \neq k}^K b_{l.k} \sum_{s \in U_l} a_{l,n}^s p_{l,n}^s g_{l,k,n}^s \tag{3}$$

where $g_{l,k,n}^s$ is the channel gain from small cell l of user s to small cell k on VRB n. $b_{l.k} \in [0, 1]$ is the interference parameters between the SCBSs l and k. $b_{l.k} = 0$ denote the two BSs are operated by different operators and applying different licensed spectrum for direct transmission, otherwise, $b_{l.k} = 1$.

3   Resource Allocation for Energy Efficient Optimization

In this section, the VRB assignment is investigated in the NOMA network and the optimization problem for energy efficient is solved with the constraints of QoS requirements of users and power consumption of BSs.

3.1   Resource Blocks Matching

We assume that all the users can transmit on the VRB n of SCBS k arbitrarily in a SDN-NOMA system. Considering the complexity of decoding and the fairness of users, each VRB can only be allocated to at most D_n users and each user can only occupy at most one VRB of one SCBS. The dynamic matching between the users and the VRBs of SCBSs is considered as a two-sided matching process between the set of $\mathcal{U}$ users and the set of $\mathcal{N}$ VRBs of SCBSs. User u is matched with VRB n of SCBSs k if $a_{k,n,u} = 1$. Based on the channel state information, we assume user u prefers channel n_1 of SCBS k_1 over n_2 of SCBS k_2 if and only if $g_{k_1,n_1,u} > g_{k_2,n_2,u}$. Then, the preference lists of the users can be denoted by

$$\mathrm{Pr}ef\_U = [\mathrm{Pr}ef\_U(1), ..., \mathrm{Pr}ef\_U(u), ... \mathrm{Pr}ef\_U(U)]^T \qquad (4)$$

where $\mathrm{Pr}ef\_U(u)$ is the preference list of user u which is in the descending order of channel gains of VRBs of SCBSs. We propose a suboptimal matching algorithm for VRB allocation as follows.

Algorithm 1. Suboptimal Matching Algorithm for VRB Allocation

---

1: Initialize the matched list $S_{k,n}$ and S_u to denote the number of users matched with VRB n ($\forall n \in \{1, 2, ..., N\}$) of SCBS k ($\forall n \in \{1, 2, ..., K\}$) and the number of VRBs of SCBSs matched with user u ($\forall n \in \{1, 2, ..., U\}$), respectively;

2: Initialize preference lists $\mathrm{Pr}ef\_U(u)$ for all the users according to channel state information;

3: Initialize the set of not matched users $S_{U\_F}(u)$ to denote users who have not been matched with a VRB of a SCBS;

4: **while** $S_{U\_F}(u) \neq \phi$ **do**

5:    **for** $u = 1$ to U **do**

6:       **if** $S_u < 1$ **then**

7:          User u sends a matching request to its most preferred VRB $\widehat{n}$ of SCBS $\widehat{k}$ according to $\mathrm{Pr}ef\_U(u)$;

8:       **if** $S_{\widehat{k},\widehat{n}} < D_n$ **then**

9:          Set $a_{\widehat{k},\widehat{n},u} = 1$, $S_u = S_u + 1$ and $S_{\widehat{k},\widehat{n}} = S_{\widehat{k},\widehat{n}} + 1$;

10:       **else if** $S_{\widehat{k},\widehat{n}} = D_n$ **then**

11:          Find the minimum channel gain of users $g_{\widehat{k},\widehat{n},\widehat{u}}$ on channel $\widehat{n}$ of SCBS $\widehat{k}$ and compare it with $g_{\widehat{k},\widehat{n},u}$;

12:          **if** $g_{\widehat{k},\widehat{n},\widehat{u}} < g_{\widehat{k},\widehat{n},u}$ **then**

13:             Set $a_{\widehat{k},\widehat{n},u} = 1$, $a_{\widehat{k},\widehat{n},\widehat{u}} = 0$, $S_u = S_u + 1$, and $S_{\widehat{u}} = S_{\widehat{u}} - 1$;

14:          **else**

15:             Remove VRB $\widehat{n}$ of SCBS $\widehat{k}$ from the $\mathrm{Pr}ef\_U(u)$ and find the next $(\widehat{k}, \widehat{n})$ of user u according to $\mathrm{Pr}ef\_U(u)$.

16:          **end if**

17:       **end if**

18:       **end if**

19:    **end for**

20: **end while**

3.2 Total Capacity and Power Consumption

We denote the total bandwidth of VRBs with each SCBS as $\mathcal{B}$. Using the Shannon's capacity formula, we can write the capacity of user $u \in \mathcal{U} = \{1, 2, ..., U\}$ in SCBS k on the nth VRB as

$$r_{k,n}^u = \frac{B}{N} \log_2(1 + \gamma_{k,n}^u). \tag{5}$$

The capacity of user u can be written as

$$r^u = \sum_{k=1}^{K} \sum_{n=1}^{N} r_{k,n}^u, \forall u \in \mathcal{U}. \tag{6}$$

The total capacity of all the users of the BS is

$$R_{tot} = \sum_{u=1}^{U} r^u. \tag{7}$$

In order to specify the QoS of users, we let R^u be the QoS requirement in terms of minimum capacity of user u which is thus given as

$$C1 : r^u \geq R^u, \forall u \in \mathcal{U}. \tag{8}$$

Denote by p_k and P_{tot} the transmit power of SCBS k and the total power consumption of the BSs respectively, which can be written as

$$p_k = \sum_{u \in U_k} \sum_{n=1}^{N} p_{k,n}^u, \forall k \in \mathcal{K}. \tag{9}$$

and

$$P_{tot} = \sum_{k=1}^{K} (p_k + p_C^k) \tag{10}$$

where p_C^k accounts for the circuit power consumption of SCBS k. The power constraints of SCBS k is denoted by P_k, which can be given by

$$C2 : p_k \leq P_k, \forall k \in \mathcal{K}. \tag{11}$$

Let EE denote the energy efficient which is the ratio of the total data capacity to the corresponding total power consumption. It is given as

$$EE = \frac{R_{tot}}{P_{tot}}. \tag{12}$$

3.3   Optimization Problem Formulation

In this subsection, when considering all constraints, the utility function is expressed as

$$\max EE = \frac{R_{tot}}{P_{tot}}$$
$$s.t. C1, C2$$
$$C3 : \sum_{k=1}^{K} \sum_{n=1}^{N} a_{k,n}^{u} \leq 1, \forall u \in \mathcal{U} \qquad (13)$$
$$C4 : \sum_{u=1}^{U} a_{k,n}^{u} \leq D_n, \forall k \in \mathcal{K}, u \in \mathcal{U}$$

where the constraint $C1$ ensures the QoS of users; $C2$ is the maximum transmit power of SCBS k; $C3$ denote that user u is allocated at most one VRB of SCBSs; and $C4$ ensures one VRB of each SCBS can be allocated to at most D_n users.

4   Solution of the Optimization Problem

In this section, we introduce a transformation of objective function (14) which is a non-convex function. We focus on the equivalent objective function with the constrains above.

4.1   Equivalent Objective Function

We define the optimal energy efficient EE^{opt} as

$$EE^{opt} = \frac{R_{tot}(p^*)}{P_{tot}(p^*)} = \max \frac{R_{tot}(p)}{P_{tot}(p)} \qquad (14)$$

where p^* denotes the optimal power allocation that yields EE^{opt}. We introduce Theorem 1 as follows.

Theorem 1 (Ghoussoub-Preiss). *The optimal energy efficient EE^{opt} can be reached if and only if*

$$\max R_{tot}(p) - EE^{opt} P_{tot}(p) = R_{tot}(p^*) - EE^{opt} P_{tot}(p^*) = 0$$
$$for R_{tot}(p) \geq 0, P_{tot}(p) \geq 0 \qquad (15)$$

□

Proof: The proof of the theorem is omitted due to space limitations. A similar detailed proof can be found in [15]. Then, in the rest of this paper, we can only focus on the function $R_{tot}(p) - EE^{opt} P_{tot}(p)$ which is a non-convex mixed integer programming problem.

4.2   Iterative Algorithm for Power Allocation

According to Theorem 1, the (non-convex) optimization problem (15) can be rewritten in the more tractable form

$$\max_{p} R_{tot}(p) - \eta_{EE} P_{tot}(p) \atop s.t. C1, C2 \tag{16}$$

where the definition of η_{EE} is as shown in Algorithm 2. It is the ratio of the data capacity to the corresponding total power consumption in each iteration of the main loop. The above proposed approach based on KKT condition for solving the EE optimization problem in (17) can be summarized in Algorithm 2.

Algorithm 2. Iterative Power Allocation Algorithm

1: Initialize the $a_{k,n}^u$ using suboptimal Algorithm 1;
2: Initialize $p_{k,n}^u$ using equal power allocation;
3: Initialize the maximum number of iterations $L_{\max}$ and the maximum tolerance δ;
4: Set current maximum value of energy efficiency $\eta_{EE} = \frac{R_{tot}}{P_{tot}}$ and iteration index $l = 0$;
5: **repeat**
6:    Obtain the allocation policies of power $\hat{p}_{k,n}^u$ in the current iteration according to (34);
7:    Calculate the value of $\hat{R}_{tot}$ and $\hat{P}_{tot}$ by solving (7) and (10);
8:    **if** $\hat{R}_{tot} - \eta_{EE}\hat{P}_{tot} \prec \delta$ **then**
9:       Convergence=1
10:      obtain $p_{k,n}^{*u} = \hat{p}_{k,n}^u$ and $EE^{opt} = \frac{\hat{R}_{tot}}{\hat{P}_{tot}}$.
11:    **else**
12:      Convergence=0
13:      set $\eta_{EE} = \frac{\hat{R}_{tot}}{\hat{P}_{tot}}$ and $l = l + 1$.
14:    **end if**
15:    Update Lagrangian multipliers of λ, β by solving (35);
16: **until** Convergence or certain stopping criteria is met

---

Let $\omega_{k,n}^u = a_{k,n}^u p_{k,n}^u, \forall u \in \mathcal{U}, n \in \mathcal{N}, k \in \mathcal{K}$; then we can rewrite the SINR of user u in SCBS k on VRB n as

$$\gamma_{k,n}^u = 1 + \frac{\omega_{k,n}^u g_{k,n}^u}{\sum\limits_{l \neq k}^{K} b_{l,k} \sum\limits_{s \in U_l} \omega_{l,n}^s g_{l,k,n}^s + \sum\limits_{s \in \left\{ U_k | g_{k,n}^s > g_{k,n}^u \right\}} \omega_{k,n}^s g_{k,n}^u + \sigma^2} \tag{17}$$

To satisfy the series of constraints, the Lagrange function of the problem (17) can be expressed as

$$F(\lambda, \beta, p) = \max L(\lambda, \beta, p)$$

$$= R_{tot}(p) - \eta_{EE} P_{tot}(p) + \sum_{u=1}^{U} \lambda_u \left(\sum_{k=1}^{K} \sum_{n=1}^{N} r_{k,n}^u - R^u \right) + \sum_{k=1}^{K} \beta_k \left(P_k - \sum_{u \in U_k} \sum_{n=1}^{N} p_{k,n}^u \right)$$

$$= \sum_{u=1}^{U} \left[\left(\frac{B}{N} + \lambda_u \right) \sum_{k=1}^{K} \sum_{n=1}^{N} \log_2(1 + \frac{\omega_{k,n}^u g_{k,n}^u}{\sum\limits_{l \neq k}^{K} b_{l,k} \sum\limits_{s \in U_l} \omega_{l,n}^s g_{l,k,n}^s + \sum\limits_{s \in \left\{ U_k | g_{k,n}^s > g_{k,n}^u \right\}} \omega_{k,n}^s g_{k,n}^u + \sigma^2}) \right] \cdot$$

$$- \sum_{k=1}^{K} \left[(\eta_{EE} + \beta_k) \sum_{u=1}^{U} \sum_{n=1}^{N} \omega_{k,n}^u \right] - \left(\sum_{u=1}^{U} \lambda_u R^u - \eta_{EE} \sum_{k=1}^{K} P_C + \sum_{k=1}^{K} \beta_k P_k \right)$$

$$(18)$$

where λ, β are the Lagrange multiplier vectors for the constraints in (17). Taking the first order derivation of $F(\lambda, \beta)$ with respect to $\omega_{k,n}^u$, we can get the optimal power allocation as

$$p_{k,n}^{u*} = \frac{\omega_{k,n}^{u*}}{a_{k,n}^u} = \frac{\frac{B}{N} + \lambda_u}{\ln 2 (\eta_{EE} + \beta_k)} - \frac{\sum\limits_{l \neq k}^{K} b_{l,k} \sum\limits_{s \in U_l} \omega_{l,n}^s g_{l,k,n}^s + \sum\limits_{s \in \left\{ U_k | g_{k,n}^s > g_{k,n}^u \right\}} \omega_{k,n}^s g_{k,n}^u + \sigma^2}{g_{k,n}^u}.$$

$$(19)$$

Based on the subgradient method [16], the master dual problem in (17) can be solved by

$$\lambda_u^{l+1} = \left[\lambda_u^l - \varepsilon_\lambda^l \left(\sum_{k=1}^{K} \sum_{n=1}^{N} r_{k,n}^u - R^u \right) \right]^+, \forall u \in \mathcal{U}$$

$$\beta_k^{l+1} = \left[\beta_k^l - \varepsilon_\beta^l \left(P_k - \sum_{u \in U_k} \sum_{n=1}^{N} p_{k,n}^u \right) \right]^+, \forall k \in \mathcal{K}$$

$$(20)$$

5   Simulation Results and Discussions

In this section, simulation results are given to evaluate the performance of the proposed algorithms. For the simulation, the number of SCBS is $K = 5$. The maximum transmit power and circuit power consumption of each SCBS is set as 3 $Watt$ and 0.5 $Watt$ respectively. The maximum of users can be allocated to each VRB n of SCBS k is $D_n = 2$. The QoS requirement of each user is $R_u = 3$ bps/Hz. The number of VRB is depend on the number of users and they are nearly full matched in the SDN-NOMA system.

In Fig. 1, the performance of EE is evaluated versus the number of users with different D_n which is maximum number of matched users of each VRB. It is shown that, with the increase of users, the value of EE decreases. And for the same value of user number, the larger value of D_n leads to larger value of energy efficient. This is because a larger D_n leads to more selection of users and bigger bandwidth of each VRB. And it is shown that the energy efficient in NOMA is better than the average EE in OFDMA.

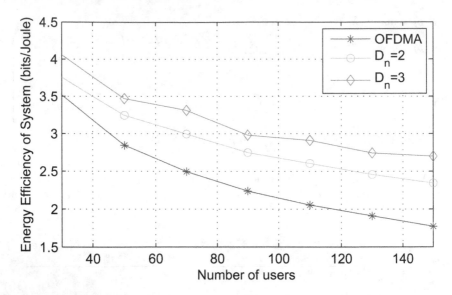

Fig. 1. Energy efficient performance versus user number with different D_n.

6   Conclusions

We investigated the dynamic resource allocation in downlink SDN-NOMA networks. We developed a framework in NOMA network by means of SDN technology. We considered the energy efficient of the network as optimization function. We proposed a suboptimal VRB assignment algorithm based on the two-side matching method. By considering minimum QoS requirement and maximum power constraint, we formulated the power allocation as a mixed integer programming problem as the considered problem was transformed into an equivalent problem with a tractable iterative solution. The mathematical analysis and simulation results demonstrated that the effectiveness of the proposed algorithms.

Acknowledgements. This work is supported by the National Natural Science Foundation of China (61471025, 61771044), the Young Elite Scientist Sponsorship Program by CAST (2016QNRC001), Research Foundation of Ministry of Education of China & China Mobile (MCM2018-1-8), Beijing Municipal Natural Science Foundation (L172025), and the Fundamental Research Funds for the Central Universities (FRF-GF-17-A6, etc.).

References

1. Ng, D.W.K., Lo, E.S., Schober, R.: Energy-efficient resource allocation in multi-cell OFDMA systems with limited backhaul capacity. IEEE Trans. Wirel. Commun. **11**(10), 3618–3631 (2012)
2. Ding, Z., Adachi, F., Poor, H.V.: The application of MIMO to non-orthogonal multiple access. IEEE Trans. Wirel. Commun. **15**(11), 537–552 (2016)

3. Wei, Z., Yuan, J., Ng, D.W.K., Elkashlan, M., Ding, Z.: A survey of downlink non-orthogonal multiple access for 5G wireless communication networks. ZTE Commun. **14**, 17–26 (2016)

4. Jindal, N., Vishwanath, S., Goldsmith, A.: On the duality of Gaussian multiple-access and broadcast channels. IEEE Trans. Inf. Theory **50**(5), 768–783 (2004)

5. Ding, Z., Peng, M., Poor, H.V.: Cooperative non-orthogonal multiple access in 5G systems. IEEE Commun. Lett. **19**(8), 1462–1465 (2015)

6. Higuchi, K., Benjebbour, A.: Non-orthogonal multiple access (NOMA) with successive interference cancellation for future radio access. IEICE Trans. Commun. **98**(3), 403–414 (2015)

7. Ding, Z., Yang, Z., Fan, P., Poor, H.: On the performance of non-orthogonal multiple access in 5G systems with randomly deployed users. IEEE Signal Process. Lett. **21**(12), 1501–1505 (2014)

8. Hanif, M.F., Ding, Z., Ratnarajah, T., Karagiannidis, G.K.: A minorization-maximization method for optimizing sum rate in the downlink of non-orthogonal multiple access systems. IEEE Trans. Signal Process. **64**(1), 76–88 (2016)

9. Fang, F., Zhang, H., Cheng, J., Leung, V.C.M.: Energy-efficient resource allocation for downlink non-orthogonal multiple access network. IEEE Trans. Commun. **64**(9), 3722–3732 (2016)

10. Fang, F., Zhang, H., Cheng, J., Roy, S., Leung, V.C.M.: Energy-efficient resource scheduling for NOMA systems with imperfect channel state information. IEEE J. Sel. Areas Commun. (2017 accepted)

11. Chin, W.H., Fan, Z., Haines, R.: Emerging technologies and research challenges for 5G wireless networks. IEEE Wirel. Commun. **21**(2), 106–112 (2014)

12. Hu, F., Hao, Q., Bao, K.: A survey on software-defined network and openflow: from concept to implementation. IEEE Commun. Surv. Tutor. **16**(4), 2181–2206 (2014)

13. Wang, K., Li, H., Yu, F.R., Wei, W.: Virtual resource allocation in software-defined information-centric cellular networks with device-to-device communications and imperfect CSI. IEEE Trans. Veh. Technol. **65**(12), 10011–10021 (2016)

14. Zhang, H., Huang, S., Jiang, C., Long, K., Leung, V.C.M., Vincent Poor, H.: Energy efficient user association and power allocation in millimeter wave based ultra dense networks with energy harvesting base stations. IEEE J. Sel. Areas Commun. **35**, 1936–1947 (2017 accepted)

15. Dinkelbach, W.: On nonlinear fractional programming. Manag. Sci. **13**, 492–498 (1967). http://www.jstor.org/stable/2627691

16. Boyd, S., Vandenberghe, L.: Convex Optimization. Cambridge University Press, Cambridge (2004)

An Algorithm for Chaotic Masking and Its Blind Extraction of Image Information in Positive Definite System

Xinwu Chen, Yaqin Xie, Erfu Wang[⊠], and Danyang Qin

Key Laboratory of Electronics Engineering College, Heilongjiang University,
Xuefu Road 74, Harbin 150080, China
Cxw808@qq.com, 648427372@qq.com, efwang_612@163.com,
qindanyang@hlju.edu.cn

Abstract. According to the renewable and the noise-like characteristic of chaotic signal, the effective frequency band and the energy band of image information are used to carry out the chaotic masking transmission, so as to achieve the security transmission of image information. Chen chaos is selected as the carrier to carry out the chaotic masking transmission for the image information of the two time-frequency aliasing under the positive definite transmission model, and the blind extraction algorithm is used to restore it in the receiver. The influence of additive noise source on the extraction effect is analyzed, and a secure transmission method of image information under chaotic masking is proposed in this paper.

Keywords: Image information · Positive definite system
Masking transmission · Blind extraction · Chen chaos

1 Introduction

As one of the popular multimedia forms in today's society, digital image has been widely used in politics, economy, national defense and education. In some relatively special areas, such as military, commercial, digital image has a high confidentiality requirements [1, 2]. Since 1990, many researchers have made many kinds of image encryption algorithms by using the spatio-temporal property and visual perception of images [3]. Banerjee and Barrera use something similar to chaos to achieve encryption by improving and transforming chaos [4, 5]. Chaotic signal is the description of complex and irregular motion in a deterministic system. The chaotic masking technology uses the chaotic signals with statistical characteristics to hide the useful signals, so that the useful signal and the chaotic signal can be superimposed to achieve the communication security effect [6–8]. Blind source separation (BSS) is a subject developed in the middle and late 80s of last century, which can recover the target source signal from the observed aliasing signal, just using the statistical characteristics of the source signal, even the input signal and channel parameters are unknown. In recent years, blind source separation (BSS) technology has been widely used in wireless communications, biomedical engineering, speech processing and image processing, etc. [9, 10]. On the basis of this, we combine the image information and the chaotic signal, and propose a method to cover the image information by using the chaotic signal and extract the image information through the blind source separation technique in the determined model, so as to achieve the effect of the secure communication.

2 The Mathematical Model of Blind Source Separation and Chaos Signal

2.1 The Mathematical Model

Positive definite hybrid system model is the system model which assuming that the source are independent and the number is n, and at the receiving end using n receive antennas to receive n signals. The mathematical model of the positive definite hybrid blind source separation system as shown in Fig. 1.

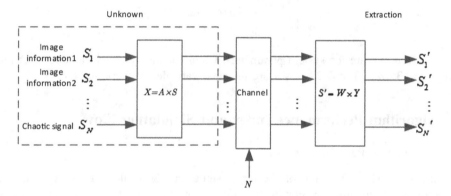

Fig. 1. Mathematical model of positive definite blind source separation

Given the vector quantity of original signal $S = [s_1(t), s_2(t), \cdots, s_N(t)]^T$, which means the number of unknown original signal is N. In order to transmit the signal in secrecy, one of vector quantity is chosen to as a chaotic signal, then the image information is hided in the chaotic signal effectively, then realize the secret transmission. A is an unknown channel hybrid matrix of order $N \times N$, which generated by system randomly. $N = [n_1(t), n_2(t), \cdots, n_N(t)]^T$ is the additive white gaussian noise of the channel. It can conclude that the vector formulation of the positive definite hybrid system observed signal is shown as follow:

$$Y = A \times S + N. \tag{1}$$

The key step of positive definite hybrid system for blind source separation is to solve the separation matrix W. $S' = [s_1'(t), s_2'(t), \cdots, s_N'(t)]^T$ is the original signal estimated from the observed signal. Through the matrix W, the target signals S' can be extracted from the observed signal Y, the output of the separation system or the extracted vector expression is

$$S' = W \times Y = W \times A \times S + W \times N. \tag{2}$$

ICA is the common method for blind signal processing. This paper adopts the algorithm for blind source separation to get the separation matrix W, due to the FastICA algorithm has good convergence, the short training time and small dependence on learning step factor.

2.2   Chaotic Signal

This paper based on chaotic signal to do the research of target signal blind extraction, so the Chen chaotic system is selected. The dynamic expression of Chen chaotic system [11] is given.

$$\begin{cases} \frac{dx}{dt} = a(y - x) \\ \frac{dy}{dt} = (c - a)x - xz + cy \cdot \\ \frac{dz}{dt} = xy - bz \end{cases} \tag{3}$$

Where a, b, c are the system parameters. Chen chaotic system in a state of chaos when $a = 35, b = 3, c = 28$. x, y, z are the state variables of the system.

3   Algorithm Performance Index and Simulation Flow

3.1   Algorithm Performance Index

For the successful separation of the target signal can be evaluated by two aspects, qualitative and quantitative. For image information, qualitative analysis can visually contrast the image information before and after blind source separation so as to obtain an intuitive evaluation [12]. Quantitative analysis can evaluate the performance of the algorithm objectively through the performance evaluation function, the similarity coefficient [13] is the most commonly used evaluation criterion.

3.2   Simulation Flow

The detailed implementation steps and algorithm flow chart are given. The chaotic signal is used as the background to judge the validity and universality of the algorithm. The algorithm flow diagram is shown in Fig. 2.

Implementation steps:

Step 1: Select gray scale pictures from the standard test picture library and convert it from a two-dimensional image to one dimensional array data, making the one-dimensional array data into binary array data.

Step 2: Simulate the unknownness of the channel, randomly generate the mixed matrix. The observed signal is obtained after the source signal have passed by the

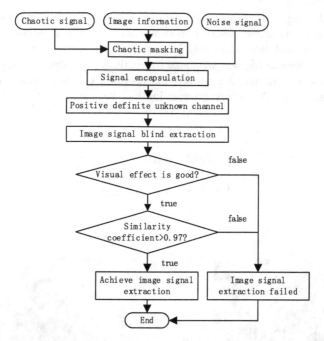

Fig. 2. Flow chart of positive definite blind source separation algorithm

hybrid matrix, then the observation signal is observed to see if the image information has been hidden by chaotic signals and can not be distinguished by human eyes.

Step 3: Use the FastICA algorithm to do blind source separation for the observed signal, and extract the target signal from it.

Step 4: Observe the image information before and after blind source separation through the visual system and view the similarity coefficients. If the extracted image information can be clearly recognized by the human eye, and the similarity coefficient is more than 0.97, the separation is considered to be successful.

Because this paper is based on the mathematical model of positive definite mixed system to realize blind source separation, the algorithm simulation process randomly generates a full rank square matrix.

4 Simulation Experiment and Performance Analysis

4.1 Blind Separation of Two Image Signals Without Noise

Select two gray scale pictures from the standard test picture library shown as Figs. 3 and 4 256 × 256 and convert it from a two-dimensional image to one dimensional array data, making the one-dimensional array data into binary array data. Then encapsulate it with Chen chaotic signals. A 3 × 3 matrix is generated randomly through the system, making into aliasing with encapsulated data to obtain three way observation signals. Then convert the data of the observation signal into a decimalization date and turn it into a two-dimensional date. The image information is shown in Figs. 5, 6 and 7. And then the matrix after aliasing was separated by FastICA algorithm to can get estimated value of each source signal. We convert the resulting estimates into a decimal and two-dimensional date. The image information can be shown in Figs. 8 and 9 (The image information after separating from source signal is displayed here).

The random generation of the hybrid matrix for this experiment is

$$A = \begin{bmatrix} 0.8694 & 0.1014 & 0.2086 \\ 0.4122 & 0.7794 & 0.8096 \\ 0.1678 & 0.1066 & 0.2961 \end{bmatrix}$$

Fig. 3. Image information of first source signal

Fig. 4. Image information of second source signal

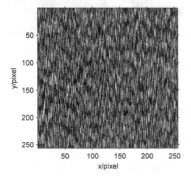

Fig. 5. Image information of the first observation signal in noise free model

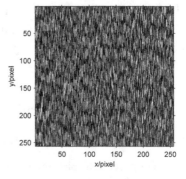

Fig. 6. Image information of the second observation signal in noise free model

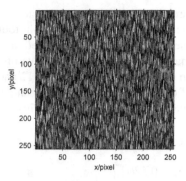

Fig. 7. Image information of the third observation signal in noise free model

Fig. 8. Image information of the first extracting signal in noise free model

Fig. 9. Image information of the second extracting signal in noise free model

According to Figs. 5, 6 and 7 we can clearly find that the Image information reconstructed by observed signal could not be identified which shows that the image signals are obscured by Chen chaotic signals and cannot be recognized by human eyes. By comparing Fig. 3 with Fig. 8 and Fig. 4 with Fig. 9, we can clearly find that the similarity between the two images is high and almost no difference, and the image information can be easily seen with human vision. By calculation, the similarity coefficient between Figs. 3 and 8 is 0.9999, and the similarity coefficient between Figs. 4 and 9 is 0.9999. In summary, it can be concluded that the image information of the source signal is well separated, and the simulation has also achieved the desired results.

4.2 Blind Separation of Two Images with Superimposed Noise

We select two gray scale pictures from the standard test picture library, as shown in Figs. 3 and 4, and convert it from a two-dimensional image to one dimensional array data, then making the one-dimensional array data into binary array data. A Gaussian white noise is randomly generated by the system, and then the Gaussian white noise, the binary array data and the Chen chaotic signal are encapsulated. A 4×4 matrix is randomly generated by the system and mixed with the encapsulated data to obtain four channel observation signals. The data of the observation signal is converted into decimal and then the four channel image information which made by converting one-dimensional data into two-dimensional data can be shown in Figs. 10, 11, 12 and 13. And then the matrix after aliasing was separated by FastICA algorithm, we can get the estimated value of the source signal. Then the image information shown in Figs. 14 and 15 can be obtained by repeating the above steps.

The random generation of the hybrid matrix for this experiment is

$$A = \begin{bmatrix} 0.3935 & 0.5669 & 0.8033 & 0.5702 \\ 0.0788 & 0.8792 & 0.0240 & 0.4017 \\ 0.2789 & 0.7586 & 0.7554 & 0.9707 \\ 0.4431 & 0.4590 & 0.4078 & 0.1747 \end{bmatrix}$$

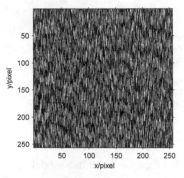

Fig. 10. Image information of the first observation signal in noise model

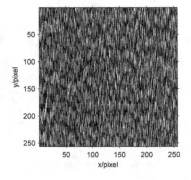

Fig. 11. Image information of the second observation signal in noise model

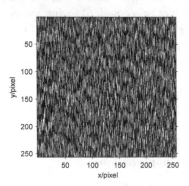

Fig. 12. Image information of the third observation signal in noise model

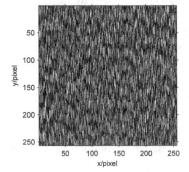

Fig. 13. Image information of the fourth observation signal in noise model

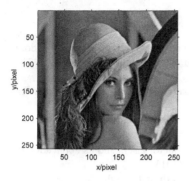

Fig. 14. Image information of the first extracting signal in noise model

Fig. 15. Image information of the second extracting signal in noise model

In Figs. 10, 11, 12 and 13 observations can be found that the image information can't be identified only by the human eye. It shows that the image signal is covered well by the Chen chaos signal, which is not recognized by the human eye. Through the comparison between Figs. 3 and 14 and Figs. 4 and 15, it can be clearly seen that the extracted image information has a high similarity with the image information of the source signal, which shows that the content of the image information can be easily found. By calculation, the similarity coefficient between Figs. 3 and 14 is 0.9999, and the similarity coefficient between Figs. 4 and 15 is 0.9999. In summary, it can be basically concluded that the image information of the source signal is well separated, and the validity of the algorithm is also verified.

5   Conclusion

The secure communication transmission technology based on chaotic signals is widely used in various information security fields. Considering the importance of image information for secure transmission of the signal, this paper proposes that the signal of image information can be masked by Chen chaotic signal. After the channel transmission of determined system, the image information is extracted by blind extraction. The simulation results show that the method can obscure the image information and can extract the image information well. Even in the case of white Gaussian noise (WGN), better experimental results can be obtained, and the validity is verified as well. That will prepare for the secrecy and blind separation of the image information under the under-determined background.

Acknowledgments. This work was supported by the National Natural Science Foundation of China (grant 61571181), Postdoctoral Research Foundation of Heilongjiang Province (grant LBH-Q14136), and Graduate Student Innovation Research Project Fundation of Heilongjiang University (grant YJSCX2017-148HLJU).

References

1. Vinod, P.: A robust and secure chaotic standard map based pseudorandom permutation-substitution scheme for image encryption. Opt. Commun. **284**(19), 4331–4339 (2011)
2. Arroyo, D.: Comment on image encryption with chaotically coupled chaotic maps. Physica **239**(12), 1002–1006 (2010)
3. Pan, T.G., Li, D.Y.: A bit transformation image encryption algorithm based on chaotic map. Electr. Mach. Control **17**(10), 97–100 (2013)
4. Banerjee, S.: Synchronization of spatiotemporal semi-conductor lasers and its application in color image encryption. Opt. Commun. **12**(9), 234–236 (2011)
5. Barrera, J.F., Rueda, E., Rios, C.: Experimental opto-digital synthesis of encrypted sub-samples of an image to improve its decoded quality. Opt. Commun. **284**(19), 4350–4355 (2011)
6. Ren, H.P., Baptista, M.S., Grebogi, C.: Wireless communication with chaos. Phys. Rev. Lett. **110**(18), 4101–4105 (2013)
7. Lou, R., Wang, Y.L.: Finite-time stochastic combination synchronization of three different chaotic systems and its application in secure communication. Chaos **22**(2), 023109 (2012)
8. Sun, J.W., Shen, Y., Yin, Q.: Compound synchronization of four memristor chaotic oscillator systems and secure communication. Chaos **23**(1), 013140 (2013)
9. Christoph, A., Robert, L., Markus, R.: RFID reader receivers for physical layer collision recovery. IEEE Trans. Commun. **58**(11), 3526–3537 (2010)
10. He, F.T., Zhang, M., Bai, K.: Image encryption method based on laser speckle and Henon mapping. Infrared Laser Eng. **04**, 275–279 (2016)
11. Chen, G.R., Ueta, T.: Yet another chaotic attractor. Int. J. Bifurc. Chaos **9**(7), 1465–1466 (1999)
12. Ma, J.C., Niu, Y.L., Chen, H.Y.: Blind Singal Processing. National Defense Industry Press, Beijing (2006)
13. Abolghasemi, V., Ferdowsi, S., Sanei, S.: Blind separation of image sources via adaptive dictionary learning. IEEE Trans. Image Process. **21**(6), 2921–2930 (2012)

Instruction Detection in SCADA/Modbus Network Based on Machine Learning

Haicheng Qu[1], Jitao Qin[1(✉)], Wanjun Liu[1], and Hao Chen[2]

[1] Institute of Software, Liaoning Technical University, Huludao 125105, China
quhaicheng@lntu.edu.cn, lgc_qinjitao@sina.com,
liuwanjun39@163.com
[2] Department of Information Engineering, Harbin Institute of Technology,
Harbin 150001, China
hit_hao@hit.edu.cn

Abstract. Cyber security threats of industrial control system have become increasingly sophisticated and complex. In the related intrusion detection, there is a problem that intrusion detection based on network communication behavior cannot fully find out the potential intrusion. The Machine Learning is applied to seek out the abnormal of industrial network. First of all, the supervised learning methods, such as Decision Tree, K-Nearest Neighbors, SVM and so on, were adopted to deal with SCADA network dataset and related discriminated features. Next, an anomaly detection model is built using One-Class classification method, and the effect of the One-Class Classification method in the SCADA network dataset is analyzed from the recall rate, the accuracy rate, the false positive rate and the false negative rate. It is shown that the anomaly detection model constructed by the One-Class Support Vector Machine (OCSVM) method has high accuracy, and the Decision Tree method can commendably detect the intrusion behavior.

Keywords: Cyber security · Intrusion detection · Supervised learning
OCSVM

1 Introduction

1.1 Survey of Industrial Network Intrusion Detection

At present, most of the key infrastructure and industrial systems, such as oil and gas pipelines, water treatment systems, reservoir valve control, power grids and nuclear power plants, are all controlled by the Supervisory Control and Data Acquisition system (SCADA) [1]. These systems allow remote monitoring and remote access and control for geographically dispersed facilities, enabling operators in these facilities to monitor and control the entire system in real time. Traditionally, this control network is completely isolated in the application environment.

However, with the development of industrial control systems and traditional computer networks, industrial control networks have become fully open or semi-open networks in order to facilitate the control of industrial processes and the combination of industrial control networks and Internet networks. As the traditional industrial control

© ICST Institute for Computer Sciences, Social Informatics and Telecommunications Engineering 2018
X. Gu et al. (Eds.): MLICOM 2017, Part II, LNICST 227, pp. 437–454, 2018.
https://doi.org/10.1007/978-3-319-73447-7_48

system is based on physical isolation, the main focus on data transmission real-time and accuracy, did not take into account the aspects of Cyber security, and lacking of appropriate protective measures. So in recent years for industrial control equipment, more and more attacks, especially in 2010, the outbreak of the complex malware Stuxnet virus, exposed the industrial network there are major flaws. In view of this, industrial safety research is of great significance. The intrusion detection technology as a Cyber security protection of the first step in industrial Cyber security has a very important sense.

Network intrusion detection, through the network data and behavior patterns, determine whether the Cyber security system is valid. Its purpose is to identify intruders, identify intrusion, and monitor successful security breakthroughs, and provide important security information. In fact, there is no essential difference between the industrial network and the traditional computer network; they check the network or system for violations of security policies and signs of attacks by collecting and analyzing network behavior, security logs, audit data, information available on other networks [2, 3], and information about key points in the computer system.

Industrial network intrusion is related to the structure of industrial control system. The current industrial control system [1] in the specific deployment usually involves the following network: enterprise office network (enterprise network or office network), process control and monitoring network (monitoring network), field control system.

Office network: According to the data of the monitoring network, the managers manage the enterprises and make the decision. Through the industrial management system for enterprise planning production, storage management, production scheduling and other processes, the managers conduct a unified deployment.

Monitoring network: The operator monitors and controls the field running equipment through the SCADA system.

Field control system: It includes distributed control system (DCS), programmable logic controller (PLC), and remote terminal unit (RTU). In these systems, the staff on the field device performs logical control, data sampling, instruction execution and other operations.

1.2   Advances in Related Fields

The study of industrial network intrusion detection does not have a mature theoretical system so far. Therefore, most of the researches on intrusion detection with industrial network are based on the traditional Internet network intrusion detection method.

In the paper [4], the intrusion detection method, combined with SCADA network and traditional intrusion detection, complete the industrial intrusion detection task; it also discusses the attack patterns of industrial network attackers and the vulnerability of industrial networks. The method of Kernel entropy [5] is used to ensure that the original data information loss is minimized in the process of dimensionality reduction, and then the intrusion detection model is constructed by artificial immune method, which avoids the high-dimensional space and the immune algorithm on the lack of data coverage shortcomings. However, the artificial immune algorithm cannot be detected for variant attacks in industrial networks. [6] It studies the function code characteristics in the Modbus/TCP protocol. Using the depth packet analysis technique, the function code in the protocol is parsed, and then the pattern matching method is used to match the rules to judge the abnormality or normal. It is ideal to use intrusion detection rules in real-time aspect, and could detect some of the attacks, but only the use of functional code analysis is not comprehensive enough.

Machine Learning and Deep Learning in recent years for the development of network intrusion detection technology provides a new impetus. [7] It is a combination of stratified misuse detection and anomaly detection combined with intrusion detection. The algorithm uses C4.5 to construct the misuse detection model, divide the normal training data into multiple subsets, and then use the subset data to create multiple OCSVM models. The process not only improves the detection accuracy, but also reduces the training and testing time. However, ignores the possible relevance of the subset. In this paper [8], the approach of isolating forest is put forward in view of the fact that the number of abnormal samples is small and the majority of the data are isolated. It constructs the isolation tree, divides the data space by the isolation tree, and judges the abnormality according to the path length of the tree structure. The method has the characteristics of low computational cost, fast operation speed, high detection accuracy of most abnormal points, and has been widely used in the field of abnormal network identification, factory production process abnormal judgment and financial data field.

In paper [9], PLS (Partial Least Squares) and CVM (Core Vector Machine) were adopted to construct the intrusion detection model in order to address the feature selection and large sample data. Experiments show that this method has high accuracy, low false alarm and false negative rate and high real - time performance compared with intrusion detection using SVM method. The SVM algorithm is combined with D-S evidence theory [10]. Similar to the method of ensemble learning, a number of SVM classifiers with different differences are combined by D-S evidence theory to obtain the final classification result. In paper [11], the PSO automatically finds the parameters that adapt to the SVM algorithm in a specific industrial control network, which improves the classification accuracy of SVM algorithm. Before, the dataset can be reduced dimension by KPCA method to improve the training speed of the classifier.

In recent research, Intrusion detection in industrial control network focus on ICS security schema which is mainly upon the traditional active defense solution. However, the ICS security schema could not be used to effectively forecast and control under the condition of high real-time and resource constraints. Therefore, in recent years, industrial network intrusion detection is the hotspot in this field. Machine learning and Data mining technology is able to find hidden attributes in the data. The machine learning method is applied to intrusion detection which is the trend of intrusion detection technology development in recent years.

This paper begins with the following sections. The first section introduces the industrial network and intrusion detection, and explains the research status of industrial network intrusion detection. In the second section, the principle of Machine Learning and One-class classification is expounded in detail. The third section is the experiment on the SCADA dataset. The final section is the experimental conclusion.

2 The Application of Machine Learning in Intrusion Detection

Machine learning algorithm [12], from the data itself, uses statistical laws and mathematical knowledge to dig out the information contained in the data. The traditional machine learning algorithm solves the problem of data classification, regression, and clustering and association rule learning and so on. In recent years, machine learning has achieved great success in text classification, natural language processing, machine translation, situational awareness, and image processing and computer vision. This also stimulates the development of machine learning methods to other areas.

2.1 Overview of Traditional Machine Learning Methods

In the SCADA dataset, intrusion detection can be seen as a multi-class approach in nature, and there are many mature machine learning algorithms in completing the classification task. In the following, we mainly from The Decision Tree, Logistic Regression, K-Nearest Neighbor and other algorithms to analyze the industrial network data.

(a) Logistic Regression
    Logistic regression can be used as a regression algorithm, but also as a classification algorithm, which is a linear regression. It is a process that deals with a regression or classification problem, establishes a cost function, then solves the optimal model parameters by optimizing the method, and then tests to verify that the model we are solving is good or bad. The advantage is that it can be a linearly separable data set to construct a good linear model, and fast, easy to understand; of course, for non-linear data, will not complete the classification task.

(b) K-Nearest Neighbor
    K-Nearest Neighbor is one of the traditional classification algorithms, and it is also one of the simplest classification algorithms. The idea of this method is that in the feature space, if the majority of K samples in the vicinity of a sample (that is, the nearest neighbor in the feature space) belong to the same category, the sample also belongs to this category. In the SCADA network data set, the normal data set has such a characteristic that the distribution of normal data sets is relatively concentrated. Using K-Nearest Neighbor algorithm to analyze SCADA network data set should be able to get a good classification effect.

(c) The Decision Tree
    The Decision Tree algorithm is one of the data mining algorithms, with strong intuition. It is a typical classification method, the first data processing, and then uses the induction algorithm to generate the relevant rules, and finally use the decision to analyze the new data. On the other hand, the decision tree is an algorithm that classifies data according to rules. For SCADA Cyber security datasets, there is a clear correlation between some intrusion and rules, and the decision tree can mine the relevant rules and store them.

(d) Support Vector Machine (SVM)

Support vector machine algorithm is one of the best machine learning algorithms to solve small sample, non-linear and high dimensional data classification, and has the best classification effect and generalization ability. But for the large sample data, there is a long calculation time and low real-time performance. So in the actual production, using SVM algorithm is relatively small. But as one of the best classification methods, SVM algorithm can show a good classification effect on SCADA network dataset.

(e) Random Forest (RF)

Random forest is a kind of integration method, which integrates and evaluates the classification result of multiple weak classifiers, and finally obtains the whole classification effect. The random forest algorithm was proven to have a faster training speed and a higher accuracy rate in a variety of classification cases. Therefore, applying this method to the SCADA Cyber security datasets can improve the classification accuracy of a single classifier.

These approaches aim at helping the traditional IDS in detecting malicious activities and cyber-attacks threatening the critical infrastructures.

2.2 Anomaly Detection Algorithm Based on One-Class Classification

In the traditional intrusion detection, mainly divided into abnormal detection and misuse detection two categories. The anomaly detection is to establish a model for normal data, through which the intrusion event can be identified, but the method cannot accurately identify the specific category of intrusion; Misuse detection is to build a classification model for a variety of intrusion behavior, this way can detect the known intrusion category, and the higher accuracy; However, if there is a new type of intrusion, the algorithm will not be able to identify the intrusion. Misuse detection model training requires known intrusion data, belonging to the scope of supervision learning. And the anomaly detection comes from the normal data model, which belongs to the unsupervised learning category.

One-class classifiers learn the normal behavior modes of the studied system [13], and determine decision rules that accept as many normal samples as possible, and detect most of the outliers; through this classifier, the dataset is divided into parts that are similar to the model and portions that differ from the model. The single classification method belongs to unsupervised classification method, no need to label, only need to ensure that the training classifier data to meet the normal dataset requirements. From the detection method, the single classification method is one of the abnormal detection methods.

In the process of using traditional supervised learning methods, the linear indivisibility, which is the characteristic of this SCADA network dataset, is solved by using the kernel function method for the majority of machine learning algorithms. This method maps the data to a higher dimension space (Reproducing Kernel Hilbert Space) where the data can be linearly segmented. The data mapping process cannot be shown, so the use of a function conversion calculation. In this paper, the kernel function is Gaussian kernel function (also known as RBF function), as shown in formula (1).

$$k(x_i, x_j) = \exp\left(-\frac{\|x_i - x_j\|_2^2}{2\sigma^2}\right) \tag{1}$$

This chapter analyzes the classification effect of the One-Class classification the One-Class classification method based on kernel function, the One-Class classification method based on KPCA and the One Class Support Vector Machine (OCSVM).

(a) The One-Class classification based on Kernel function [13, 14]
   In this method, the decision function in this approach is based on the Euclidean distance in the feature space between the samples and the center of the hyper sphere. Let c_n be the center of the data in the feature space estimated using all available training samples. And $c_n = (1/n)\sum_{i=0}^{n} \phi(x)$. The expression of the squared distance between any sample $\phi(x)$ and the center c_n can is given as follows:

$$\|\phi(x) - \phi(x_0)\|_H^2 = k(x, x) - \frac{2}{n}\sum_{i=1}^{n} k(x, x_i) + \frac{1}{n^2}\sum_{i,j=1}^{n} k(x_i, x_j) \tag{2}$$

In this measure, after assessing the distance between all training samples and the estimation center, use the estimated threshold to evaluate the calculated sample distance. If the distance is farther than a predetermined threshold, the data would be treated as an outlier point. The above algorithm needs to estimate the threshold to evaluate. However, if the threshold is not appropriate, the classification effect will be reduced and performances become terrible.

(b) One-Class Support Vector Machine (OCSVM)
   OCSVM [15] is an extension of traditional SVM in unsupervised learning. The algorithm aim to construct a hyper plane which can classify the normal sample set as much as possible. The model constructs a decision function based on the hyper plane to determine which side of each data is in the hyper plane. Figure 1. Two - dimensional Case of OCSVM Method displays the situation in the classification method in two-dimensional space. Based on the principle of separating the origin from the normal data as much as possible, the algorithm constructs the quadratic convex optimization function, such as formula (3).

$$\min_{\omega, \rho, \xi} \frac{1}{2}\|\omega\|_H^2 + \frac{1}{vn}\sum_{i=1}^{n} \xi_i - \rho \tag{3}$$

$$s.t. \langle \omega, \phi(x_i)\rangle_H \geq \rho - \xi_i, \xi_i \geq 0 (i = 1, \ldots \ldots, n)$$

Where the slack variables $\xi_i \geq 0$ penalize the excluded samples and the tunable parameter v represents an upper bound on the fraction of outliers. By solving the problem of nonlinear programming, the parameters ω and the parameter ρ are solved. And build the decision function on the sample:

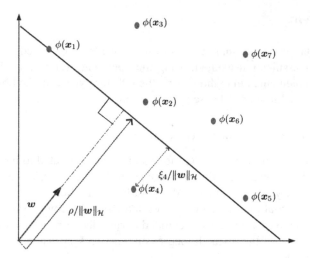

Fig. 1. Two - dimensional Case of OCSVM Method

$$f(x) = \langle \omega, \phi(x_i) \rangle_H - \rho \tag{4}$$

When $f(x) \geq 0$, the data become the normal sample; otherwise, the sample belongs to the outliers between the origin and the hyper plane.

(c) Based on KPCA One-Class Classification Method [13, 14, 16]

The KPCA is a nonlinear extension of the PCA (principal component analysis method) in a Kernel-defined feature space. KPCA extracts the subspace from the maximum variance of the data and performs dimension reduction and denoising by projecting the sample into the subspace. In the use of KPCA as anomaly detection, it introduces a new method of measurement that the data can be sorted by One-Class method. The use of KPCA classification method want to avoid the impact of noise in the data, but the calculation may be very large; this is a drawback of the algorithm. The measure is as shown in (5).

$$p(x) = \|\phi(x) - \phi(x_0)\|_H^2 - \|W\phi(x) - W\phi(x_0)\|_H^2 \tag{5}$$

where

$$f_l(x) = \sum_{i=1}^{n} \alpha_i^l \left[k(x, x_i) - \frac{1}{n} \sum_{r=1}^{n} k(x_i, x_r) - \frac{1}{n} \sum_{r=1}^{n} k(x, x_r) + \frac{1}{n^2} \sum_{r,s=1}^{n} k(x_r, x_s) \right]$$

Likewise, after using the above method to evaluate the distance between all training samples and the estimation center, the calculated sample distance is evaluated using the estimated threshold. If the distance is greater than a predetermined threshold, the sample is treated as an outlier. Such as the Sample One-Class Classification, it is critical to the KPCA Classification that the threshold setting.

3 Experiment

The experimental process is mainly used to introduce the supervised learning method and the single classification method, using the operating system for windows 7; the experiment is implemented in python, using the IDE for pyCharm; the library files used include: numpy, scikit-learn 0.18, scipy and so on.

3.1 Industrial Control Cyber Security Datasets

At present, there is no uniform standard for public datasets related to industrial control Cyber security. First, because of the industrial control Cyber security research has been developed in recent years, the industry does not have a unified dataset; second, due to the variety of industrial production processes and industrial configuration networks, it is inconvenient to have a unified data set that describes the prevailing industrial control Cyber security. Most of the research focuses on a network intrusion under a particular process of production.

Next, we introduce two of the most used industrial control Cyber security datasets: gas pipeline real dataset and storage tank dataset. The dataset includes network traffic, process control, and process measurement functions from a set of 28 attacks on two industrial control systems using the MODBUS application layer protocol. It can easily and effectively compare SCADA intrusion detection solutions.

SCADA Dataset Attack Types
The dataset apply the same type of attack [17], regardless of the normal type, a total of four major categories of 8 sub-class attacks, which contain reconnaissance attacks (RA), denial of service attacks (DOS), malicious function command injection (MFCI), malicious parameter command injection attacks (MPCI), malicious state command injection (MSCI) attacks, complex malicious response injection (CMRI) attacks, and original malicious response injection (NMRI) attacks. The following describes the contents of these attacks.

- The NMRI attack injects the response packet into the network, but lacks some information about the process being controlled and monitored; therefore some of the injected content may be invalid.
- The CMRI attacks are more complex than NMRI. Because they need to understand the physical processes of industrial control, try to mask the real state of the research process and influence the system's feedback control loops.
- The MSCI convey a malicious command to a remote field device to change the state of the physical process, driving the system from the security state to the critical state.
- The MPCI changes the controller parameter set points for sensors, actuators, and programmable logic controllers.
- The MFCI is used to affect the communication of the client server by modifying the command function field of the sent message.
- The DOS attacks try to stop the normal operation of the physical system and are designed to send the transmission speed faster than the processing speed, or by

sending an incorrect packet to change the industrial control system. This causes the operating system of the running program or target device to crash.

- The RA collects information about the control system network and builds network architecture to identify device features such as manufacturer, model, supported network protocols, and system address/memory mapping. The information collected can be used for other attacks.

The Content of SCADA Datasets

SCADA network datasets [13, 17, 18] organization has two parts: network traffic characteristics and effective content characteristics; the network traffic characteristics are related to SCADA network communications, and the effective content characteristics are related to the specific industrial control process. In the effective content characteristics, it includes the system of measured values, key system operating status parameters, system mode and other key information. One of the most important is the measured value attribute.

(a) Gas pipeline real dataset
   The gas pipeline dataset contains key data for the natural gas pipeline control process, which contains 26 features. In the gas pipeline dataset, the core attribute is the pressure in the gas pipeline. After the study and analysis, the gas pipeline, there are three normal modes:

   - The first mode is a relatively low pressure near 0.1 PSI.
   - The second mode keeps the pressure near 10 PSI (between 9 and 11 PSI).
   - The third mode maintains a pressure of about 20 PSI (between about 18 and 22 PSI).

   In these three modes, the gas pipeline operates in normal condition, and most of the intrusion attacks are distributed around these normal datasets.
(b) Storage tank dataset
   The reservoir dataset simulates the state of the liquid in the tank: When the liquid is located in the tank between the high and low alert position, the system is normal; when the highest alert or below the minimum alert bit, the system gives the corresponding alarm. The dataset contains 23 attribute values; some core attributes are the current water level measurement, the highest alert water level and the minimum warning level. In the storage tank system, the operator can change the corresponding system mode to change the maximum alert water level and the minimum warning level, so the attribute in the system mode is also the focus of attention in this research.

3.2   Result Analysis

The Classification of Supervise Learning Methods

Using the machine learning algorithm such as Decision tree, K-Nearest Neighbor and SVM to deal with two SCADA Cyber security datasets, the results of the classification of each method are shown in Table 1. Gas pipeline real dataset classification results and Table 2. Storage tank dataset classification results. In the evaluation of intrusion

Table 1. Gas pipeline real dataset classification results

		Logistic	KNN	DT	SVM	RF
Accuracy rate		65.41%	98.63%	98.66%	98.38%	98.77%
Recall	Normal	99.66%	99.42%	99.10%	99.45%	99.24%
	NMRI	90.88%	90.98%	92.87%	94.28%	92.44%
	CMRI	0.00%	99.85%	99.64%	98.40%	99.65%
	MSCI	0.00%	82.35%	93.22%	94.88%	94.88%
	MPCI	0.00%	98.05%	96.39%	97.43%	97.04%
	MFCI	0.00%	72.95%	93.37%	80.98%	95.46%
	DOS	0.00%	88.79%	93.03%	75.56%	90.80%
	RA	0.00%	99.19%	100.00%	99.43%	100.00%
Precision	Normal	96.85%	98.56%	98.85%	98.52%	98.87%
	NMRI	90.82%	97.44%	94.55%	88.34%	95.48%
	CMRI	0.00%	99.03%	99.23%	99.37%	99.03%
	MSCI	0.00%	96.99%	92.75%	97.38%	97.36%
	MPCI	0.00%	97.46%	97.12%	97.45%	97.56%
	MFCI	0.00%	100.00%	97.27%	100.00%	99.09%
	DOS	0.00%	99.63%	97.66%	99.86%	99.17%
	RA	0.00%	99.96%	100.00%	100.00%	100.00%

Table 2. Storage tank dataset classification results

		Logistic	KNN	DT	SVM	RF
Accuracy rate		67.20%	96.23%	98.24%	95.66%	97.08%
Recall	Normal	91.60%	97.15%	98.88%	95.85%	97.83%
	NMRI	0.00%	97.06%	97.57%	96.59%	97.23%
	CMRI	0.00%	73.00%	85.19%	82.25%	78.09%
	MSCI	0.00%	95.47%	95.42%	95.36%	95.68%
	MPCI	0.00%	96.81%	98.18%	98.42%	98.40%
	MFCI	0.00%	95.30%	100.00%	94.70%	99.55%
	DOS	0.00%	93.62%	99.19%	85.04%	98.46%
	RA	4.61%	99.98%	100.00%	99.50%	100.00%
Precision	Normal	72.06%	98.56%	98.89%	98.53%	98.32%
	NMRI	0.00%	97.44%	96.79%	98.49%	97.29%
	CMRI	0.00%	99.03%	85.19%	59.44%	72.65%
	MSCI	0.00%	96.99%	95.42%	96.95%	96.48%
	MPCI	0.00%	97.46%	98.18%	86.24%	98.98%
	MFCI	0.00%	100.00%	100.00%	100.00%	100.00%
	DOS	0.00%	99.63%	99.35%	99.34%	99.34%
	RA	4.62%	99.96%	100.00%	100.00%	100.00%

detection dataset classification effect, the use of three indicators: accuracy, precision rate and recall rate. From the above three evaluation indicators, it can be roughly described the classification effect of the classifier. In this experiment, the grid search method is used to find the optimal parameters of each classifier. The result is not only unique, but also can get the best classification effect.

According to the classification effect of these kinds of machine learning methods, there are some conclusions:

(1) The accuracy of the Logistic Regression is the lowest of the comparison algorithm (65.41% in gas data, 67.20% in water data), it can be seen that the dataset is linear inseparable. But the normal data of the recall and precision are relatively high. Through the study of the classification of the data set (gas pipeline dataset), the algorithm does not separate the normal data according to the case of confounding matrix; Since most of the attack types are close enough to the normal data set, the linear model can only identify attacks that differ greatly from the normal dataset. In short, the dataset is linear inseparable; only the non-linear classification method can solve the problem.

(2) K-Nearest Neighbor, as a method based on distance measurement, in the gas and water data sets, has achieved very good results (98.63% and 96.23% respectively). And in each attack category of recall and precision, it also has a relatively high ratio. Essentially, by computing the "similarity" on the dataset, K-Nearest Neighbor identifies K samples with the most recent "similarity" as the same category.

Using KNN classifier in the SCADA dataset and the results description that: Normal datasets are usually aggregated extensively, while exception datasets are mostly distributed at the boundaries of normal datasets. Using distance classification can separate part of the attack behavior and normal behavior. Although the overall classification of the classifier is better, but the classification rate of individual attack is still relatively low. Through the analysis of the confusion matrix, it is found that some attack categories are missing, and these attacks may be difficult to distinguish from the normal data set, resulting in being classified as normal data. KNN has a good classification effect,it shows that by calculating the distance between the samples or similarity, based on the similarity and distance comparison, you can sort out most of the attacks.

However, there are some problems with the use of the KNN method in the SCADA network datasets:

- The dimensions of the two datasets in the sample are simple. If the data collected in other industrial control networks has a high dimension, the calculation cost of KNN will be very large. It can be considered that using some dimensionality reduction ways to reduce the cost of KNN model calculations; At present, the mainstream PCA, LDA dimensionality reduction method is essentially linear dimensionality, and it is necessary to find a non-linear dimensionality reduction method to reflect the distribution of data; Dimension reduction process often leads to loss of information in the original space. Therefore, the appropriate dimensionality reduction method also needs to keep the distance between the data in the original data space as much as possible; in this way, the results in the new dimension space will be close to the results in the original dimension space.

- Although KNN are good enough for both datasets, the invasive data in different industrial control processes is different, KNN effect may be different, and even be unable to detect.

Nonetheless, KNN's performance on SCADA datasets shows that methods based on distance metrics and similarity metrics are viable in intrusion detection, but the computational cost is related to the data form and may be required when the cost is high with some distributed computing framework.

(3) The accuracy of the Decision Tree classification algorithm in the two types of datasets is 98.66% (gas dataset) and 98.24% (water dataset). The Decision Tree also has a high percentage of recall and precision rate. Decision tree is a mining and storage rules of the structure, the data show that there is a certain correlation between the data set and the intrusion category, or there are rules related to the feature in the intrusion. Using the decision tree algorithm to establish the rules and the pattern matching, finally in the two datasets, can get a high accuracy. However, in the decision tree, each of its branch nodes is a feature; there is no relevant way to consider the impact of multiple related characteristics on the classification results.

In the SCADA dataset used, since the industrial control process in the dataset is simple compared with the real industrial control process, the rules contained in it are relatively simple, and the decision tree can effectively classify the dataset. In the traditional IT network intrusion detection, the use of regular pattern matching is also used in the intrusion detection process.

(4) In the result of the classifier processing, the effect of SVM on nonlinear separable data sets is obvious and Ensemble learning on data classification results as same as SVM. The Ensemble learning is fast and the training cost is small, and it is equally feasible to classify the evaluation results by integrating multiple classifiers. As a result of the advantages of the method, in the reality of the classification task, Ensemble learning becomes more popular.

(5) As shown in Fig. 2. Comparison of Multiple Machine Learning Algorithms for Gas Dataset And Fig. 3. Comparison of Multiple Machine Learning Algorithms for Water Dataset, the gas dataset, for example, for a certain attack (MFCI, MSCI), KNN and SVM on the category of detection precision rate is low; Water dataset, for CMRI attacks, both the recall rate or precision rate, the ratio is relatively low. From the figure reflects the situation can be seen, different industrial processes focus on different attacks, the more critical attacks are more difficult to detect out.

The Decision trees, K-Nearest Neighbors, SVM, and Random Forest methods have achieved the desired results in both gas and water datasets. The above machine learning algorithm automatically establishes the classification model, and classifies the normal data and the abnormal data from the dataset. But the above machine learning method is Supervise Learning, which means that the establishment of intrusion detection model

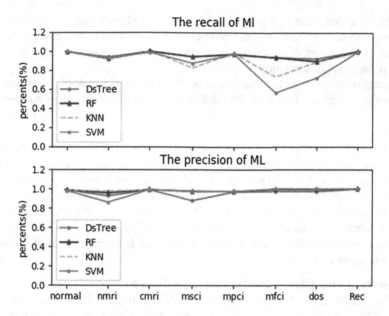

Fig. 2. Comparison of multiple machine learning algorithms for gas dataset

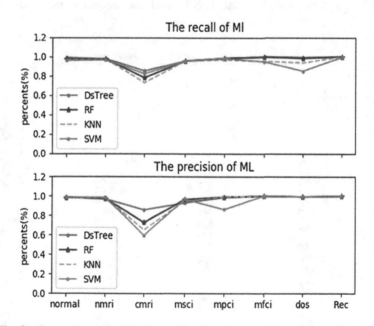

Fig. 3. Comparison of multiple machine learning algorithms for water dataset

on the premise that there is a large dataset of data, and each data intrusion category should be labeled. Otherwise, the above-mentioned algorithms cannot be used. Obtaining a calibrated data set is costly and almost infeasible, so the use of the algorithm has a lot of limitations.

In addition, the above classification, whether it is a multi-classification process or two classification process, there is little difference between the data item number in the different categories. However, if the number of data in each of these data sets is very different, for most of the supervised learning methods, there is a problem that the classifier is not adequately trained, which will seriously influence the classification results. In the real industrial control network, usually hundreds of normal data mixed with a few abnormal data; Normal data and abnormal data is seriously unbalanced, as for the use of supervised learning classification method, although the accuracy rate is high, the intrusion detection process used less. In short, the real problem leads to the traditional supervised classification method is not feasible in the real world. The use of appropriate unsupervised or semi-supervised approach is the main task of building an intrusion detection model.

The Results of One-Class Classification Experiments

In the One-Class Classification method, OCSVM, simple One-Class classification method, KPCA-based One-Class Classification method comparison results shown in Figs. 3 and 4. According to the figure, the use of OCSVM, whether in the false positive rate (FPR) and false negative rate (FNR) and the accuracy rate, has a better

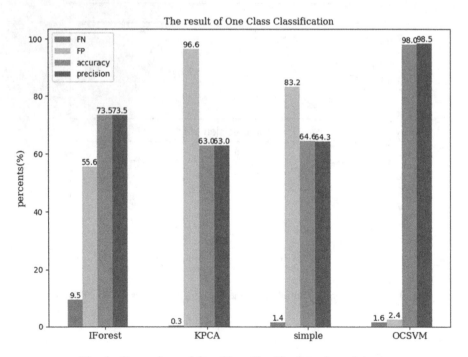

Fig. 4. Comparison of One-Class Classification of gas datasets

performance results. And this conclusion applies to two SCADA datasets in the sample. If you want to get better results, you need to adjust the algorithm's learning rate and kernel function parameters.

The results of the KPCA classification method and the simple One-Class Classification method have poor results in the false negative rate (FNR). After analysis, the threshold is not appropriate to lead to poor classification results. Solving the above problems can deal with introducing a penalty function; or use traditional supervised learning methods, such as decision tree algorithms, to learn a variety of attacks on the model

In addition, there is a lot of computing process in KPCA and Kernel method of One-Class Classification, resulting in relatively high operating costs. Although the One-Class Support Vector Machine (OCSVM) also needs to calculate the kernel matrix, the existing OCSVM algorithm introduces a sparse method to find the support vector associated with the hyper-plane. Therefore, for the same size of the dataset, OCSVM computing costs are reduced.

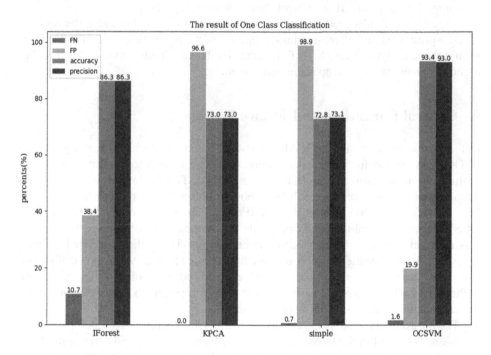

Fig. 5. Comparison of One-Class Classification of water datasets

Moreover, In Figs. 3 and 4, the comparison of the results of the algorithm application of the isolated forest (IForest) was added. The IForest algorithm [8] is used to mine anomaly data, such as attack detection and traffic anomaly analysis in Cyber security, and financial institutions are used to exploit fraud. The algorithm requires very low memory requirements and is fast and its time complexity is linear. It can handle high-dimensional data and large data, and can also be used as online anomaly detection. The algorithm is the most commonly used anomaly detection algorithm. The accuracy of the algorithm is 73.51%, the precision rate is 73.46%, the false negative rate (FP) is 55.62%, and the false positive rate (FN) is 9.49% (see the gas dataset result of IForest method). Compared with the OCSVM algorithm (the precision rate is 98.54%, the accuracy rate is 98.04%, the false negative rate is 2.40% and the false positive rate is 1.60%). The result is worse than the OCSVM algorithm. IForest is the integration of a number of randomly created isolation tree, the role of the tree is to continue to divide the data space, if the data tree where the number of layers, it is considered abnormal. The algorithm is the integration of a number of randomly created isolation tree, the role of the tree is to continue to divide the data space, if the data tree where the number of layers is shallow, and it is considered abnormal. It is also based on a distance measurement of the conversion, but the method does not use all the data, there may be errors; additionally, for industrial control intrusion, most of the structural form and the normal data is very close, the use of isolation tree space may not be accurate enough to determine. However, if you want to conduct online intrusion detection, the use of fast IForest algorithm is also appropriate.

The different results produced by the same algorithm in the gas and water datasets reveal a phenomenon: Different industrial control of the production process is different, even if the same type of attack, its focus is also different. Choosing the right algorithm requires manual testing, comparison and screening.

4 General Conclusion and Future Works

In the Instruction Detection in SCADA Network based on Machine Learning, the use of OCSVM method for abnormal detection can get a high detection rate, effectively limiting the false alarm rate and false negative rate; The limitations of a One-Class method based on a kernel approach lie in how to obtain the appropriate threshold and how to reduce the computational cost; IForest's application effect is not high in OCSVM, but it has real-time and can handle the characteristics of large-scale data, and it is appropriate to use this method in online learning. Using the supervised learning algorithm, especially the decision tree method, you can quickly learn, establish and store the learned intrusion rules, to achieve the purpose of multi-classification. Although the effect of KNN's use of distance metrics is similar to that of decision trees, the computational cost of KNN limits its use.

The intrusion in the industrial control network is different from the Internet network intrusion. The threat of the former focuses on the defects of using industrial control and the defects of industrial hardware, rather than looking for the defects of network communication. It is feasible to use machine learning and data mining to find the relationship between normal and abnormal.

In the course of the experiment, the use of One-Class Classification method for intrusion detection can only detect the existence of abnormal, and cannot find abnormal categories. From the experimental purpose and results analysis, the use of unsupervised learning for intrusion detection has limitations, applying the semi-supervised approach to the intrusion detection model is an improved aspect.

Acknowledgment. This paper uses the dataset for the intrusion detection and evaluation of industrial control systems proposed by the Key Infrastructure Protection Center of Mississippi State University in 2014. The author would like to thank T. Morris to create and share this dataset.

In addition, this work was supported in part by the general project of scientific research of the Education Department of Liaoning Province under grants L2015216 and other foundations under grants FJ1603, 20160092T.

References

1. Knowles, W., Prince, D., Hutchison, D., et al.: A survey of cyber security management in industrial control systems. Int. J. Crit. Infrastruct. Prot. **9**, 52–80 (2015)
2. Shang, W., An, P., Wan, M., et al.: Research and development overview of intrusion detection technology in industrial control system. Appl. Res. Comput. **34**(2), 328–333, 342 (2017)
3. Yang, A., Sun, L., Wang, X., et al.: Intrusion detection techniques for industrial control systems. J. Comput. Res. Dev. **53**(9), 2039–2054 (2016)
4. Bartman, T., Kraft, J.: An introduction to applying network intrusion detection for industrial control systems. In: AISTech 2016, The Iron & Steel Technology Conference and Exposition, 16–19 May 2016
5. Luo, Y., Chen, W.: On a network anomaly detection method based on kernel entropy component analysis and artificial immune. J. Southwest China Normal Univ. (Nat. Sci. Ed.) **41**(6), 119–124 (2016)
6. Wan, M., Shang, W., Zeng, P., Zhao, J.: Modbus/TCP communication control method based on deep function code inspection. Inf. Control **45**(2), 248–256 (2016)
7. Ayres, E., Nkem, J.N., Wall, D.H., et al.: A novel hybrid intrusion detection method integrating anomaly detection with misuse detection. **41**(4), 1690–1700 (2014). Pergamon Press, Inc
8. Liu, F.T., Ting, K.M., Zhou, Z.H.: Isolation-based anomaly detection. Acm Trans. Knowl. Disc. Data **6**(1), 1–39 (2012)
9. Wu, L., Li, S., Gan, X., et al.: Network anomaly intrusion detection CVM model based on PLS feature extraction. Control Decis. **32**(4), 755–758 (2017)
10. Li, H., Liu, Y.: A new kind of SVM intrusion detection strategy for integration. Comput. Eng. Appl. **48**(4), 87–90 (2012)
11. Wang, H., Yang, Z., Yan, B., Chen, D.: Application of fusion PCA and PSO-SVM method in industrial control intrusion detection. Bull. Sci. Technol. **33**(1), 80–85 (2017)
12. Zhou, Z.H.: Machine Learning. Tsinghua University Press, Beijing (2016)
13. Nader, P.: One-class classification for cyber intrusion detection in industrial systems. IEEE Trans. Industr. Inf. **10**(4), 2308–2317 (2015)
14. Nader, P., Honeine, P., Beauseroy, P.: The role of one-class classification in detecting cyberattacks in critical infrastructures. In: Panayiotou, C.G.G., Ellinas, G., Kyriakides, E., Polycarpou, M.M.M. (eds.) CRITIS 2014. LNCS, vol. 8985, pp. 244–255. Springer, Cham (2016). https://doi.org/10.1007/978-3-319-31664-2_25
15. Shang, W., Li, L., Wan, M., Zeng, P.: Intrusion detection algorithm based on optimized one-class support vector machine for industrial control system. Inf. Control **44**(6), 678–684 (2015)

16. Hoffmann, H.: Kernel PCA for novelty detection. Pattern Recognit. **40**(3), 863–874 (2007)
17. Morris, T., Gao, W.: Industrial control system traffic data sets for intrusion detection research. In: Butts, J., Shenoi, S. (eds.) ICCIP 2014. IFIP Advances in Information and Communication Technology, pp. 66–78. Springer, Heidelberg (2014). https://doi.org/10. 1007/978-3-662-45355-1_5
18. Shirazi, S.N., Gouglidis, A., Syeda, K.N., Simpson, S., Mauthe, A., Stephanakis, I.M., Hutchison, D.: Evaluation of anomaly detection techniques for SCADA communication resilience. In: Resilience Week (RWS) 2016, pp. 140–145. IEEE (2016)

A Joint Source-Channel Error Protection Transmission Scheme Based on Compressed Sensing for Space Image Transmission

Dongqing Li, Junxin Luo, Tiantian Zhang, Shaohua Wu$^{(\boxtimes)}$, and Qinyu Zhang

Shenzhen Graduate School, Harbin Institute of Technology, Harbin, China
{lidongqing,luojunxin,zhangtiantian}@stu.hit.edu.cn,
{hitwush,zqy}@hit.edu.cn

Abstract. High reliable and efficient image transmission is of primary significance for the space image transmission systems. However, typical image compression techniques have the characteristics of high encoding complexity and limited resiliency to channel errors. And the typical channel decoding strategy is simply discarding the error data block. All of this results in the potential loss of the transmission performance. Due to the low encoding complexity and error-tolerance ability of the compressed sensing (CS), to improve the image transmission performance, this paper proposes a joint source-channel error protection transmission scheme based on CS for space image transmission. Meanwhile, we evaluate the performance of different CS reconstruction algorithms under the two schemes and solve the optimal decoding strategy under different conditions. Simulation results show that the proposed scheme can achieve a better performance than the typical transmission scheme that the error data block is simply discarded in the bottom layer.

Keywords: Compressed sensing · Error-tolerance
Space image transmission · Deep Learning

1 Introduction

The typical image compression techniques, such as joint photographic experts group (JPEG), JPEG2000, set partitioning in hierarchical trees (SPIHT) [1,2], have characteristics of high compression efficiency. However, a critical problem with these techniques is that they have high encoding complexity and limited resiliency to channel errors [3]. The compressed sensing (CS) is known for its advantages including the high compression efficiency, the low encoding complexity, and the error-tolerance ability [4]. Consequently, more and more applications

D. Li, J. Luo and T. Zhang—These authors contributed equally to this work.
This research has been sponsored in part by the National Natural Science Foundation of China (Grant nos. 61371102, 61001092, 61201144 and 91638204) and the Natural Science Foundation of Guangdong Province (Grant no. 2015A030310343).

© ICST Institute for Computer Sciences, Social Informatics and Telecommunications Engineering 2018
X. Gu et al. (Eds.): MLICOM 2017, Part II, LNICST 227, pp. 455–462, 2018.
https://doi.org/10.1007/978-3-319-73447-7_49

use the CS for image compression in the application layer. Ref. [5] proposes a cross-layer framework for high-efficient deep space image transmission, the CS image compression and the Spinal code is incorporated in the framework to jointly work with the LTP [6]. And we usually assume that the bottom layer has perfectly corrected the bit errors and the received compression values have no bit error. However, in the space network which is characterized by high error rate [7], it is impossible to completely eliminate the bit errors from the bottom-layer to the application layer. Therefore, it is inevitable that the received data has a portion of the error bits after channel coding. To ensure the data passed to the upper layer is all correct, the typical channel decoding strategy is simply discarding the error data blocks which can not pass the cyclic redundancy check (CRC) check [8]. Although this way guarantees that the data passed to the application layer is all correct, but it also imposes the burden of the error protection in the bottom layer, and increases the number of feedback indirectly, leading to the loss of the transmission performance.

Due to the limited resiliency to channel errors in the application layer and limited ability of error protection in the bottom layer, typical image transmission schemes cannot cope with the above challenges. In this paper, to improve the image transmission performance, we aim to propose a joint source-channel error protection transmission scheme based on CS. Different from the scheme proposed in [5], the proposed scheme in this paper allows a portion of the error blocks that meet the certain condition to be passed to the application layer for the CS reconstruction, this also causes that there are the error CS compression values in the image reconstruction. Moreover, we expect to take advantage of the CS error-tolerance ability to further improve the image performance. Meanwhile, the performance of various CS reconstruction algorithms are investigated, and we select the optimal CS reconstruction algorithm for the proposed scheme. Simulations are carried out for performance evaluation. Results show that the proposed image transmission scheme can improve the image performance compared with the typical scheme.

The main contributions of the paper are summarized as follows:

- We propose a joint source-channel error protection transmission scheme based on CS. And the proposed scheme shows a performance improvement compared with the existing typical scheme.
- We evaluate the performance of different CS reconstruction algorithms when adopted in the two schemes, and then the optimal decoding strategy under different conditions are indicated.

The remainder of this paper is organized as follows. In Sect. 2, the model of image transmission system is introduced. The Sect. 3 presents the proposed scheme. The performance analysis through the simulation results is introduced in Sect. 4. Finally, we conclude this paper in Sect. 5.

2   System Model

In this section, we present the model of image transmission in deep space communications and and introduce the basics of CS.

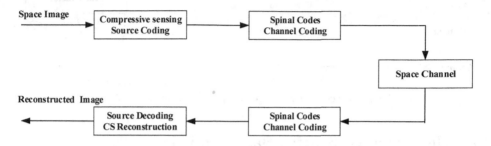

Fig. 1. The space image transmission system model.

2.1   Space Image Transmission System Model

As illustrated in Fig. 1, the image transmission in deep space communications [9] typically involves the modules including the source coding module, the channel coding module, space channel module, channel decoding module and source decoding module. In the process of image compression, the source coding module firstly performs the CS image compression [10], and then we adopt the Spinal codes as the channel coding technique for error protection. After being transmitted through the space channels, the images received are channel decoded and CS reconstructed at the receiver module.

In the module of channel coding, the Spinal code [11] is a rateless code which has been proved to be capacity-achieving over both additive white gaussian noise (AWGN) and binary symmetric channel (BSC). Different from other typical codes, Spinal code employs a nonlinear hash function as the coding kernel, and the Spinal symbols encoded are sent pass-by-pass. In the module of channel, the Earth-Mars communication scenario and the Gilbert-Elliot channel model for Ka-band transmission [12] are used for case study.

2.2   The Basics of CS

For the basic process of CS image compression and reconstruction, the process is shown in Fig. 2, the image signal X of size N is said to be sparse in the domain Ψ, if its transform coefficients α $(\alpha = \Psi x)$ are mostly zeros or close to zeros. The signal X is measured by taking M $(M \leq N)$ measurements from linear combinations of the element vectors through a linear measurement operator Φ. The CS reconstruction of image signal X from y is formulated as the following constrained optimization problem:

$$\min_{\alpha} \|\alpha\|_0 \ s.t. \ y = \Phi x = \Phi \Psi^{-1} \alpha = A\alpha, \tag{1}$$

where Φ denotes the measurement matrix, and A represents projection matrix.

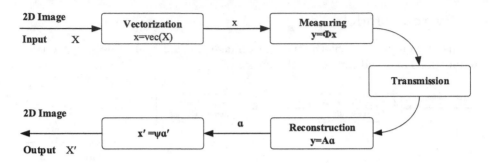

Fig. 2. The process of CS image compression and reconstruction.

3   The Proposed Scheme Based on CS

In this section, we present the framework of the proposed scheme based on CS.

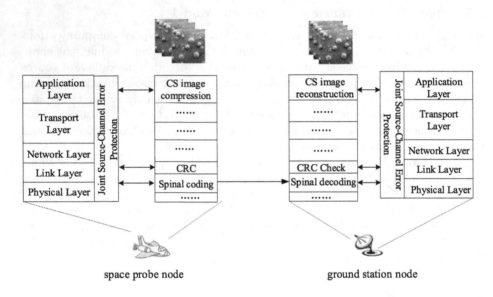

Fig. 3. The framework of the proposed scheme based on CS.

As illustrated in Fig. 3, the node of space probe firstly performs the CS image compression. By the global projection operation, all the CS compression values are equally important, which means that each compression value carries the global information of the whole image. In case of partial loss of compression values (e.g., packet loss of lower layers), the receiver may also reconstructs the image through the CS reconstruction algorithm. Therefore, we can do erasure correcting coding at the same time by generating some redundant compression values. After a cluster of compressed values are generated by the CS image compression and CS erasure coding modules, they are sent to the lower layers for cyclic redundancy check (CRC) encoding. After that, the bitstreams are encoded by the Spinal code in the physical layer and then the Spinal symbols are sent to the ground station node. On receiving the Spinal symbols, the receiver conducts decoding sequentially, and take CRC check on each decoded block. Meanwhile, the parameter of the bit error rate (BER) that after channel coding is calculated, and the indexes of failed decoding blocks are saved.

Different from the decoding strategy adopted in [5], the proposed scheme adopts the decoding strategy that allows a portion of the error blocks which meet the certain condition to be passed to the application layer for the CS reconstruction. We expect to take advantage of the CS error-tolerance ability to achieve the joint source-channel error protection and further improve the image performance. To derive the detailed decoding strategy, we investigate the performance effect of the relevant parameters in different CS reconstruction algorithm. The performance evaluation is shown in next section.

4 Performance Evaluation

In this section, we introduce three advanced CS reconstruction algorithms which are respectively the BM3D-AMP [13], TVAL3 and ReconNet algorithms [14]. Furthermore, we make performance comparison for the proposed scheme that adopts the error-tolerance strategy and the typical scheme that adopts the error-discard strategy among the three CS reconstruction algorithms.

Firstly, we briefly introduce the three CS reconstruction algorithms. BM3D-AMP algorithm is capable of high-performance reconstruction. We use BM3D denoiser since it gives a good trade-off between time complexity and reconstruction quality. TVAL3 algorithm performs excellent when solving a class of equality-constrained non-smooth optimization problems. The algorithm effectively combines an alternating direction technique with a nonmonotone line search to minimize the augmented Lagrangian function at each iteration. And the ReconNet reconstruction algorithm which based on the fully connected neural network (CNN), its intermediate reconstruction is fed into an off-the-shelf denoiser to obtain the final reconstructed image.

Next, we conduct a series of simulation experiments and make performance comparisons. Figure 4 illustrates the performance comparison of TVAL3, BM3D-AMP, and ReconNet (Deep Learning) algorithms under the two transmission schemes when the CS compression ratio is 0.04. It can be seen that when the CS compression rate is very low, the three algorithms perform better under error-tolerance transmission scheme. In the case of a very low CS compression ratio, we can obtain a limited number of compression values, and the effect of the amount of compression values on the reconstruction performance is greater than the error in the compression values. To a certain extent, even if the compression values return to the application layer remain some errors, it can also guarantee the image reconstruction performance. But if we choose the error-discard transmission scheme, the return values will be further reduced, which has a much

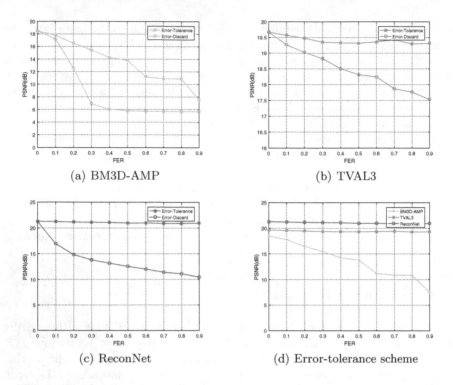

(a) BM3D-AMP (b) TVAL3

(c) ReconNet (d) Error-tolerance scheme

Fig. 4. CS reconstruction performance comparison (compression ratio = 0.04).

greater effect on the reconstruction performance than the errors. With the frame error rate (FER) goes up, the advantage of error-tolerance transmission scheme increases, and the PSNR improvement of the Deep Learning reconstruction algorithm can reach about 11 dB. Figure 4 also shows the performance comparison of the three algorithms under the error-tolerance transmission scheme. The results show that, in this kind of transmission scheme, Deep Learning has a certain advantage compared with the other two reconstruction algorithms.

Figure 5 illustrates the performance comparison of the three CS reconstruction algorithms when the CS compression ratio is 0.25. It can be seen from the figure that there is an intersection between the performance curves of the two schemes. When FER is less than the intersection value, the error-dicard transmission scheme is better in PSNR, and when the FER goes up, we should choose the other scheme to guarantee the reconstruction performance. To some extend, we can obtain more compression values under this compression ratio. When the FER is low, the performance of typical error-dicard transmission scheme is better the error-tolerance scheme. Figure 5 also shows the performance comparison of the three algorithms under the error-tolerance transmission scheme. The results show that, in this kind of transmission scheme, BM3D-AMP has a certain advantage compared with the other two reconstruction algorithms. Meanwhile, when the compression rate increases gradually, the intersection of the two per-

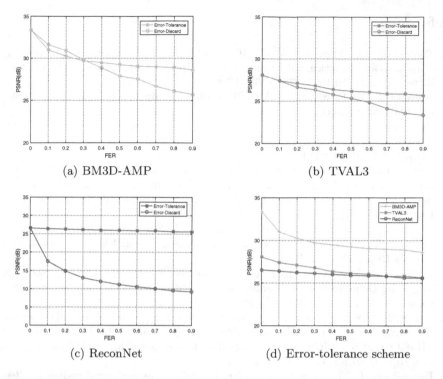

(a) BM3D-AMP

(b) TVAL3

(c) ReconNet

(d) Error-tolerance scheme

Fig. 5. CS reconstruction performance comparison (compression ratio = 0.25).

formance curves moves in the direction of increasing FER, which shows that as the compression ratio increases, the influence of the return compression values number on the reconstruction performance is gradually reduced. Only when the FER reaches a certain value, the performance advantage of the error-tolerance will be revealed.

5   Conclusion

In order to improve the image transmission performance, this paper proposes a joint source-channel error protection transmission scheme based on CS for space image transmission. Meanwhile, we evaluate the performance of different CS reconstruction algorithms under the two schemes and solve the optimal decoding strategy under different conditions. Simulation results show that the proposed scheme that adopts the error-tolerance strategy and reconstructs with Recon-Net algorithm can achieve a better performance than that typical transmission scheme in the case of a very low CS compression ratio. When the compression ratio increases gradually and the FER is in low range, the typical error-discard scheme that reconstruct with BM3D-AMP algorithm performs better. When the FER increases to a certain threshold, we should turn to the error-tolerance transmission scheme to obtain high image performance.

References

1. Taubman, D.S., Marcellin, M.W.: JPEG2000: Image Compression Fundamentals, Standards and Practice, vol. 11, no. 2, p. 286. Springer International, Berlin (2002). https://doi.org/10.1007/978-1-4615-0799-4
2. Wheeler, F.W., Pearlman, W.A.: SPIHT image compression without lists. vol. 4, pp. 2047–2050 (2000)
3. Pudlewski, S., Prasanna, A., Melodia, T.: Compressed-sensing-enabled video streaming for wireless multimedia sensor networks. IEEE Trans. Mob. Comput. **11**(6), 1060–1072 (2012)
4. Lampe, L.: Bursty impulse noise detection by compressed sensing. pp. 29–34 (2011)
5. Luo, J., Wu, S., Xu, S., Zhang, Q.: A cross-layer image transmission scheme for deep space exploration. In: IEEE 86th Vehicular Technology Conference (VTC Fall), pp. 1–5. IEEE (2017)
6. Wang, R., Burleigh, S.C., Parikh, P., Lin, C.-J., Sun, B.: Licklider transmission protocol (LTP)-based DTN for cislunar communications. IEEE/ACM Trans. Netw. (TON) **19**(2), 359–368 (2011)
7. Burleigh, S., Hooke, A., Torgerson, L., Fall, K., Cerf, V., Durst, B., Scott, K., Weiss, H.: Delay-tolerant networking: an approach to interplanetary internet. IEEE Commun. Mag. **41**(6), 128–136 (2003)
8. Zheng, H., Song, Z., Zhang, S., Chai, S., Shao, L.: A CRC-aided LDPC erasure decoding algorithm for SEUs correcting in small satellites. In: Huang, X.-L. (ed.) MLICOM 2016. LNICST, vol. 183, pp. 35–43. Springer, Cham (2017). https://doi.org/10.1007/978-3-319-52730-7_4
9. Bursalioglu, O.Y., Caire, G., Divsalar, D.: Joint source-channel coding for deep-space image transmission using rateless codes. IEEE Trans. Commun. **61**(8), 3448–3461 (2013)
10. Donoho, D.L.: Compressed sensing. IEEE Trans. Inf. Theory **52**(4), 1289–1306 (2006)
11. Perry, J., Balakrishnan, H., Shah, D.: Rateless spinal codes. In: Proceedings of 10th ACM Workshop on Hot Topics in Networks, p. 6. ACM (2011)
12. Sung, I., Gao, J.L.: CFDP Performance over Weather-dependent Ka-Band Channel. Jet Propulsion Laboratory, National Aeronautics and Space Administration, Pasadena (2006)
13. Metzler, C.A., Maleki, A., Baraniuk, R.G.: BM3D-AMP: a new image recovery algorithm based on BM3D denoising. In: 2015 IEEE International Conference on Image Processing (ICIP), pp. 3116–3120. IEEE (2015)
14. Kulkarni, K., Lohit, S., Turaga, P., Kerviche, R., Ashok, A.: ReconNet: noniterative reconstruction of images from compressively sensed random measurements. arXiv preprint arXiv:1601.06892 (2016)

Local Density Estimation Based on Velocity and Acceleration Aware in Vehicular Ad-Hoc Networks

Xiao Luo[1(✉)], Xinhong Wang[1], Ping Wang[1], Fuqiang Liu[1,2], and Nguyen Ngoc Van[3]

[1] College of Electronic and Information Engineering,
Tongji University, Shanghai, China
18817514236@163.com, wang_xinhong@163.com,
{pwang, liufuqiang}@tongji.edu.cn
[2] College of Design and Innovation, Tongji University, Shanghai, China
[3] College of Electronics and Telecommunications,
Hanoi University of Science and Technology, Hanoi, Vietnam
van.nguyenngoc@hust.edu.vn

Abstract. In vehicular ad-hoc networks (VANET), node density is constantly changing in both time and space. Well communication quality depends on the nodes density. Knowing the density of the vehicle communication system is very important for achieving better wireless communication performance. In recent years, many researchers have proposed a resource allocation scheme based on vehicle density. Therefore, in this paper, we introduced an acceleration aware density estimation (VAADE) algorithm to map the relationship between vehicle density and resource requirements. In VAADE, a car estimates the density of the driving road according to its own velocity and acceleration in real time. VAADE is accurate because it employs both velocity and acceleration, which are sufficient for density estimation. The simulation results indicate that the proposed algorithm can map the relationship between the communication resource demands and the acceleration.

Keywords: Density estimation · Velocity and Acceleration Aware
Resource demands

1 Introduction

VANET as a promising Intelligent Transportation System (ITS) technology aims to realize a highly reliable and low latency communication. An effective resource allocation scheme can effectively improve resource utilization while reducing the likelihood of transmission collisions. To this end, the researchers proposed a dynamic allocation of resources scheme, such as based on vehicle density of one lane. Other applications, such as traffic status monitoring, routing and distribution of data, also use the information which is provided by density estimation to make the decision.

As an essential metric, traffic density is used in many traffic information systems and also affects the performance of vehicular networks such as capacity, routing

© ICST Institute for Computer Sciences, Social Informatics and Telecommunications Engineering 2018
X. Gu et al. (Eds.): MLICOM 2017, Part II, LNICST 227, pp. 463–471, 2018.
https://doi.org/10.1007/978-3-319-73447-7_50

efficiency, delay, and robustness. The commonly used vehicle density estimation scheme is designed for Infrastructure-Based Traffic Information Systems [1] (IBTIS). However, these mechanisms are of low reliability, limited coverage, and require high deployment and maintenance costs. The most important is that it can't calculate density estimate in real time. As for Infrastructure-Based density estimation algorithms are not enough for the highly dynamic and scalable environment of VANET system. The infrastructure-Free Traffic Information System [2] (IFTIS) was designed to provide vehicles with an estimate of traffic density on urban roads. Thanks to most vehicles now are equipped with built-in wireless communication capabilities, vehicle density can be measured more accurate in real-time [3].

In this paper, the classical density estimation is introduced and simulated. As an improvement, we proposed a local and real-time density estimation algorithm that requires the vehicle to track its own speed and acceleration pattern, because of the strong correlation between these two metrics and road state.

The rest of the paper is organized as follows. In Sect. 2, the relevant topics in traffic theory are introduced. The traffic simulation environment is given in Sect. 3. Explain and simulate the classical Artimy's method for local density estimation in Sect. 4. Then we proposed Velocity and Acceleration Aware Density Estimation (VAADE) in Sect. 5. Finally, Sect. 6 gives some conclusions.

2   Introduction to Traffic-Flow Theory

There are three main quantities in traffic-flow theories: density, flow, and speed [7]. The density k is the amount of vehicles per unit distance that pass a detector, expressed in vehicles per kilometer per lane (veh/km/lane). The flow f means the number of vehicles that pass an observer per unit time, presented in vehicles per hour per lane (veh/h/lane). The speed u equals to the distance that a vehicle travel per unit time, expressed in kilometers per hour (km/h). The relationship among the three quantities is like

$$f = u \times k. \tag{1}$$

Several theories attempt to define the relationships among these three variables in (1), but no one completely done. The following is a brief introduction to the principles most relevant to the scope of this paper.

Car-following models describe the speed-density relationship that is suitable for a dense single lane traffic where overtaking is not permitted and assume that each driver responds in a particular way to the stimulation of the front or rear vehicle. On the other hand, this model do not apply in free-flow case where no communication like broadcast occurs.

In Pipes proposed car-following model, it assumes that drivers maintain a certain distance with neighboring vehicles. Given the relation of the following

$$u = \lambda \left(\frac{1}{k} - \frac{1}{k_{jam}} \right), \tag{2}$$

where λ represents the vehicle interaction sensitivity, and k_{jam} is the maximum traffic density of vehicle when the road congest.

3 Traffic Simulation Environment

'Simulation of Urban Mobility' (SUMO) is designed to produce realistic traffic patterns and handle large road networks as a highly portable, microscopic and continuous road traffic simulation package. The car movement pattern in SUMO is developed by Krauß, which is a space-continuous and time-discrete car-following model [5]. Traffic assignment in SUMO employs the DUA-approach [6].

The traffic simulation environment we used is shown in Fig. 1. According to SUMO's configuration, vehicles travel in a two-lane road where overtaking is allowed.

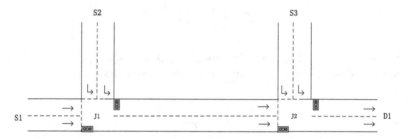

Fig. 1. The simulation environment

There are three sources S1, S2 and S3, one destination D1, obviously two T-Junctions J1 and J2. Define the maximum speed of each lane as 15 m/s (equal to 54 km/h). The junction J1 and J2 are both set with traffic light, while traffic light in J2 always be in red state, which causes an increase in vehicle density until the traffic jam happened.

4 Local Density Estimation

In this section, we deduce a relationship for local density estimate according to the car-following model, the NaSch-S2S model and the two-fluid model. It will be proven that cars' own movement pattern can be used to estimate the local vehicle density.

4.1 Density Estimation

As mentioned earlier, car-following models suggests some relationship between the average velocity and density like Eq. (2). According to that, the average velocity can be expressed as a function of density

$$u = u(k). \tag{3}$$

Two-fluid theory relates the fraction of vehicles that are stopped in traffic f_s to the average speed of all vehicles [7]

$$u = u_{max}(1 - f_s)^{\eta + 1},$$

(4)

where η indicates the service quality of vehicular network, u_{max} equals to the allowed maximum velocity on the road.

According to the definition of f_s, it can be obtain by the total vehicle numbers N and the stopped vehicles numbers N_s, which can be obtained by an external observer

$$f_s = N_s/N$$

(5)

From (2), we get the normalized vehicle density k' is

$$k' = \left(\frac{u'}{\lambda'} + 1\right)^{-1},$$

(6)

where $k' = k/k_{jam}$, $u' = u/u_{max}$ and $\lambda' = \lambda/(u_{max} k_{jam})$, respectively.

According to (4) and (5), the normalized average vehicles' speed is

$$u' = \left(1 - \frac{N_s}{N}\right)^{\eta + 1}$$

(7)

Substituting (7) into (6), finally estimated density K is shown as following

$$K = \left[\frac{(1 - N_s/N)^{\eta + 1}}{\lambda'} + 1\right]^{-1}$$

(8)

4.2   Evaluation of Local Density Estimation

Simulation using the vehicle network mentioned earlier to determine whether (8) can provide a reasonable density estimate of various traffic conditions. In the simulation, we calculate f_s and K in each time step. Due to vehicle density variable in spaces and time, the density measurement over the whole road segment does not reflect the local traffic conditions experienced by vehicles. Therefore, we only estimate density of vehicles between J1 and J2 with length of 1000 m. All the parameters in the simulation scenario are summarized in Table 1.

In order to show the accuracy of the density estimation, comparison chart between estimate density K and actual density k is shown below.

Figure 2 shows that (8) performs well in density estimation, but the K-k relation deviates from a straight line at the free-flow range (k < 1/5). Within that range, (8) has a constant value about 0.18, because of $N_s = 0$. In other word, (8) do better in congested traffic condition while not applicable in free-flow condition.

Table 1. Simulation parameters

Parameter	Font size and style
Simulation time	520 s
u_{max}	15 m/s
λ	0.5557
η	0

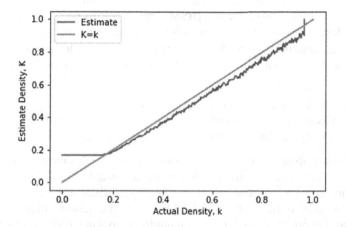

Fig. 2. Density estimate K versus actual density k

5 Velocity and Accelerate Aware Density Estimation

In the previous section we learned that (8) was not suitable for free-flow traffic condition, only in relation to the number of vehicles and cannot reflect the vehicle's communication needs. Therefore, an algorithm for estimating vehicle density using speed and acceleration is proposed.

In this paper, we defined D_s as density indicator of one road used for dynamic resource allocation. It is clear that resource required of vehicle communication are not only decided by the number of cars, but also with regard to the interaction frequency between cars.

5.1 Density Estimate

Mobility model of each individual vehicle are affected by the change of traffic flow. That means the mobility model is an excellent flow indicator used to estimate the density of neighboring vehicles. Two examples are given to illustrate this issue.

a. In free-flow network, vehicles tend to travel at reference velocity with little deviation of velocity and acceleration. In this case, drivers are more likely to keep a constant speed unless some emergencies are recognized.

b. For dense network, travel pattern of some vehicle has to change frequently. A driver tries to increase speed, while others restrict it. That means velocity and acceleration are easily change in a short time.

In this section, Velocity and Accelerate Aware Density Estimation (VAADE) is introduced. The estimate is done separately in each node and no more information from other vehicles are required.

Obtain vehicle's movement pattern information is the key of VAADE algorithm. For example, when a vehicle is at high speed, conclusion can be drawn that the density is low and only Basic Safe Message (BSM) are needed to be send. In other words, frequently changes in acceleration demonstrate a denser network, maybe a traffic accident is happened with too many event-triggered messages to broadcast. In view of the velocity and acceleration information of a car, four cases can be defined as follow:

(A) Higher velocity, lower acceleration
(B) Higher velocity, higher acceleration
(C) Lower velocity, lower acceleration
(D) Lower velocity, higher acceleration

Case A often occurs in free-flow situation where vehicles move at high constant speed and the variations in acceleration is approximately zero. Case B generally happens when emergency situations is detected by a driver. Case C means driver is moving freely. Due to the driver's personal behavior, the network may be sparse, and may be dense but not congested. Case D more likely to show a dense network, where vehicle is restricted by other's movement.

According to the discussion above, the high acceleration derivative usually indicates of many vehicles nearby or some emergency occurs. In the other word, the derivative of acceleration has a direct relationship with the density of the lane.

$$D_\mathrm{s} \propto \left| \frac{da}{dt} \right| \qquad (9)$$

where a represents acceleration.

A high speed indicates a free-flow network. Thus D_s should be inversely proportional to velocity, so (9) can be modified to

$$D_\mathrm{s} \propto \frac{1}{u} \left| \frac{da}{dt} \right|. \qquad (10)$$

Both (9) and (10) provide a simple and useful means of density estimate. Base on the concept above, we defines a formula to indicate density of one road

$$D_s = \begin{cases} \frac{|a|}{\alpha u_i + (1-\alpha)u_{i-1}} & 1 \le i \le n, u_i \ne 0 \\ 1 & u_i = 0 \end{cases}. \qquad (11)$$

where i equals to the time value of each time step. The value of a presents the acceleration at time i, while u means the value of speed. A parameter α is introduced to indicate acceleration or deceleration.

$$\alpha = \begin{cases} 0 & decelerate \\ 1 & accelerate \end{cases}. \tag{12}$$

5.2   Evaluation of VAAED

Simulation under the network mentioned above to demonstrate whether Eq. (11) performed well in both free-flow and congested traffic condition, especially whether it can well reflect the communication resource needs. In the simulation, we calculate D_s of each car on the lane between J1 and J2 in each time step, the take the average to represent the road state. The system parameters in the simulation scenario are summarized in Table 2.

From Fig. 3, we can easily obtain the relationship between velocity, acceleration and D_s. Vehicles travel at approximately the maximum speed, while acceleration is

Table 2. Simulation parameters

Parameter	Value
Simulation time	520 s
Time step	1 s

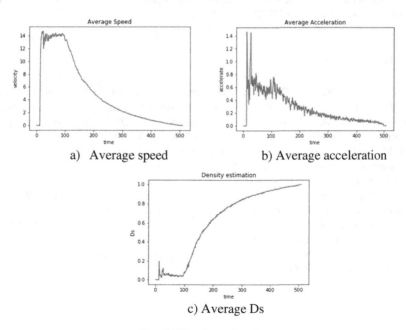

a) Average speed   b) Average acceleration

c) Average Ds

Fig. 3. Density estimation

maintained at around 0.6 during time 20 and time 100, and DS is steady in value 0.05. This presents a sparse network with less interactive. As time goes on, road between J1 and J2 is getting denser, as more and more cars come to here without one left. During time 100 and 200, the speed and acceleration rapidly decreased, resulting in a sharp increase in D_s. Large acceleration deviation means frequent interaction between vehicles, which requires more resource to broadcast or unicast. Finally, the road is in a fully congested state with Ds equals to 1.

6 Conclusion

In this paper, we first analysis a classical density estimate algorithm, which is based on its movement pattern. Many VANET protocols, which are depends on traffic conditions can use this estimate to configure parameters. The simulation results show that the algorithm is more accurate when the vehicles are stopped, but fails when the vehicle is running normally.

Velocity and Accelerate Density Estimation (VAADE) was introduced as an estimation technique which only depend on self-information. VAADE can be employed for vehicular dynamic resource allocation based on density estimation, due to the full use of the relationship between acceleration deviation and communication resource demands. According to the simulation result, it was proved that VAADE performed well under free-flow and congested traffic condition.

A future study will involve a performance analysis of vehicular system using dynamic resource allocation based on VADDE.

Acknowledgement. This work was supported by the National Science and Technology Major Project of MIIT under Grant 2015ZX03002009-003.

References

1. Barrachina, J., Garrido, P., Fogue, M., Martinez, F.J., Cano, J.-C., Calafate, C.T., Manzoni, P.: I-VDE: a novel approach to estimate vehicular density by using vehicular networks. In: Cichoń, J., Gębala, M., Klonowski, M. (eds.) ADHOC-NOW 2013. LNCS, vol. 7960, pp. 63–74. Springer, Heidelberg (2013). https://doi.org/10.1007/978-3-642-39247-4_6
2. Jerbi, M., Senouci, S.M., Rasheed, T., et al.: An infrastructure-free traffic information system for vehicular networks. In: Vehicular Technology Conference, 2007, VTC-2007, pp. 2086–2090. IEEE, Fall 2007
3. Mao, R., Mao, G.: Road traffic density estimation in vehicular networks. In: IEEE Wireless Communications and Networking Conference, pp. 4653–4658. IEEE (2013)
4. Darwish, T., AbuBakar, K.: Traffic density estimation in vehicular ad hoc networks: a review. Ad Hoc Netw. Part A **24**, 337–351 (2015). ISSN 1570-8705
5. Kai, N., Wagner, P., Woesler, R.: Still flowing: approaches to traffic flow and traffic jam modeling. Oper. Res. **51**(5), 681–710 (2003)

6. Santi, P., Blough, D.M.: An evaluation of connectivity in mobile wireless ad hoc networks. In: Proceedings of International Conference on Dependable Systems and Networks, DSN 2002, pp. 89–98. IEEE (2002)
7. Artimy, M.: Local density estimation and dynamic transmission-range assignment in vehicular ad hoc, networks. IEEE Trans. Intell. Transp. Syst. **8**(3), 400–412 (2007)
8. Shirani, R., Hendessi, F., Gulliver, T.A.: Store-carry-forward message dissemination in vehicular ad-hoc networks with local density estimation. In: Vehicular Technology Conference, pp. 1–6. IEEE, Fall 2009

Research on Millimeter Wave Communication Interference Suppression of UAV Based on Beam Optimization

Weizhi Zhong[✉], Lei Xu, Xiaoyi Lu, and Lei Wang

College of Astronautics, Nanjing University of Aeronautics and Astronautics,
Nanjing 210000, People's Republic of China
zhongwz@nuaa.edu.cn, 742426820@qq.com

Abstract. To support high data rate urgent, millimeter-wave (mmWave) UAV is considered and the beam forming technology which can further improve the mmWave communication performance is adopted. In the scene of mmWave communications for UAV group, the interference signal from other UAV and the reflected signal from the airframe can cause the communication quality to decrease. Therefore, it is very important to study the beam anti-interference performance based on the beam optimization. In this paper, a spatial interference channel model is established for UAV groups, and the expression of signal to interference plus noise ratio (SINR) depended on codebook design and direction of arrival (DOA) is obtained. Based on this, the performance of the beam interference suppression based on codebook optimization is simulated and the results show that the proposed optimization method can effectively suppress the interference and improve the system performance.

Keywords: UAV · Millimeter wave · Beamforming · Anti-interference

1 Introduction

Unmanned aerial vehicles (UAVs) have received increasing attention in the past decade [1, 2], thanks to potential applications in reconnaissance, firefighting, aerial photo, remote sensing, disaster rescue, and others. With the increasingly mature of UAV technology, UAV group combat model has become a new trend, and the concept of UAV group in the field of defense and civilian has caused more and more attention. However, real-time image transmission, spectrum sensing, heterogeneous data fusion and other technologies employed in UAVs require large bandwidth support. For this reason, large bandwidth is quite needed in the communication of UAVs.

Millimeter wave's can significantly improve system capacity as abundant frequency spectrum resource exists in the mmWave frequency band [3]. The wavelength of mmWave is very small, which makes the antenna array can be concentrated in a very

---

L. Xu—Foundation of Graduate Innovation Center in NUAA (kfjj20171501) supported by "the Fundamental Research Funds for the Central Universities".

X. Gu et al. (Eds.): MLICOM 2017, Part II, LNICST 227, pp. 472–481, 2018.
https://doi.org/10.1007/978-3-319-73447-7_51

compact space, and because of this, the application of large-scale antenna arrays on UAVs is possible. Therefore, UAV group communication based on the bandwidth of mmWave gradually attracted the attention of researchers [2]. However, when considering mmWave communication, an immediate concern is the extremely high propagation loss, since Friis' transmission law states that the free space omnidirectional path loss grows with the square of the carrier frequency. Fortunately, the small wavelength of mmWave signals also enables greater antenna gain for the same physical antenna size [4]. In addition, the Doppler effect as a result of UAV movement may not be catastrophic when high gain directional transmission is used [5]. For these reasons, mmWave UAV communications needs to be realized by large-scale array antenna.

For UAV group internal communication, the performance is affected by the more serious interference, mainly from signal send by other UAVs and the phenomenon of signal reflections and scattering [3, 6]. As a result, the degree of the interference is closely related to the relative position of UAV and the density of the UAV groups. In the past, there have been few studies on mmWave UAV communications, especially for beamforming interference suppression and real-time beam matching. Therefore, in this paper, for the UAV group communication environment, the interference characteristics are analyzed, the spatial interference channel model is established, and according to these, the SINR associated with the codebook and the direction of the DOA is obtained. Hence, the interference suppression based on codebook optimization is simulated and analyzed, which is the basis for the improving of beam optimization algorithm.

2 Interference Channel Model in UAV Group Environment

2.1 UAV Communication Scene

A typical UAV cellular network is shown in Fig. 1, where the base station (BS) is mounted on a flying UAV in the air, and mobile stations (MS) are distributed at low altitude or on the ground. The UAV group contains two kinds of communication links, one is responsible for UAV control and state information transmission, and the amount

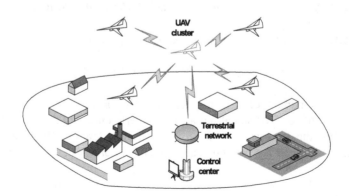

Fig. 1. UAV communication scenario

of data transmitted on this link is small. The other one is the information transmission link, which plays a major role in the mission implementation. On this link, large video monitoring traffic data from many camera sensors need to be collected and sent to other UAVs. Therefore, mmWave technology is mainly used in the second link. For information transmission link, when the commander establishes a contact with a UAV, the multipath reflection of the transmitted information and the information from other UAVs become the source of interference. Then, according to the specific position of the UAV, the interference model is modeled and the transmission channel coefficient is determined, and based on this the SINR is achieved.

2.2   The Interference Model of UAV Group

Let the signal of interest as $d(t)$, the arrival direction of it is θ_d, and the signal of unexpected can be expressed as $i_j(t), j = 1, 2, \ldots, J$, these undesired signals are regarded as interference. The noise on each channel is the additive white Gaussian noise (AWGN), with mean equal to 0 and the variance of σ^2. Under the above conditions, the received signal of the specified UAV can be described as follow

$$
\begin{aligned}
y(t) &= w^H x(t) \\
&= w^H \left[h_d d(t) w_d + \sum_{j=1}^{J} h_j i_j(t) w_j + n(t) \right]
\end{aligned}
\tag{1}
$$

Where $n(t)$ is the AWGN with mean 0 and variance σ^2, w is the receiver beam weight vector, and w_x denotes beam weight vector of the transmitter. h_d is the channel state parameter of the desired signal, h_j is the channel state parameter of the interfering signal, both can be expressed as

$$
\begin{cases}
h_d = \lambda_d a(\theta_{Ad}) [a(\theta_{Dd})]^H \\
h_j = \lambda_j a(\theta_{Aj}) [a(\theta_{Dj})]^H
\end{cases}
\tag{2}
$$

Where λ_x $(x \in \{d, j\})$ represents the channel amplitude, θ_{Ax} and θ_{Dx} are the angles of transmit (AOA) and the direction of arrival (DOA) of the desired signal and the interference, respectively.

$a(\theta)$ denotes the array response, which can be expressed as

$$
a(\theta) = [1, \quad e^{-j\frac{2\pi}{\lambda}d \sin\theta}, \cdots e^{-j\frac{2\pi}{\lambda}d(M-1)\sin\theta}]
\tag{3}
$$

Where M is the number of elements. As shown in formula (1), the received signal contains not only the desired signal but also the interference and the noise from other UAVs. Therefore, the expression of the SINR is very important for the measurement of the interference, and can lay the foundation for the future design of the interference suppression scheme.

According to the received signal expression in formula (1), the average received power of the N samples of the received signal can be described as

$$P(\omega) = \frac{1}{N}\sum_{t=1}^{N}|y(t)|^2$$
$$= \frac{1}{N}|w^H h_d w_d|^2 \sum_{t=1}^{N}|d(t)|^2 + \frac{1}{N}\sum_{j=1}^{J}|w^H h_j w_j|^2 \sum_{t=1}^{N}|i_j(t)|^2 + \|w^H\|^2 \frac{1}{N}\sum_{t=1}^{N}n(t).$$

(4)

Therefore, according to formula (4), the SINR can be expressed as

$$SINR = \frac{\frac{1}{N}|w^H h_d w_d|^2 \sum_{t=1}^{N}|d(t)|^2}{\frac{1}{N}\sum_{j=1}^{J}|w^H h_j w_j|^2 \sum_{t=1}^{N}|i_j(t)|^2 + \|w^H\|^2 \frac{1}{N}\sum_{t-1}^{N}n(t)}.$$

(5)

As shown in Eq. (5), the value of SINR depends on the noise and interference. When the noise value is constant, the interference item determines the value of SINR. The number of disturbances is related to the weight of the beam design and the number of interference. Meanwhile, the numerical value of interference depends on the quantity and density of the UAVs, and weight w_m depends on the codebook design. Therefore, optimizing the codebook is critical to the interference suppression.

3   Uniform Linear Array Beam Optimization for mmWave

There are three kinds of millimeter-wave beam optimization methods. The first one is loading-window designing method, that is, changing the amplitude without adjust the direction, and achieving the side lobe suppression by amplitude-weighted. The second one is based on the optimization of the codebook design, that is, through the codebook design [8], to obtain better beam characteristics and array gain. The third one is window function based codebook design, that is, fusion window function and codebook design to improve the performance of the interference reduction.

3.1   Beam Optimization Based on Window Function

In this paper, the uniform linear array (ULA) is adopted. The structure of the antenna is shown in Fig. 2.

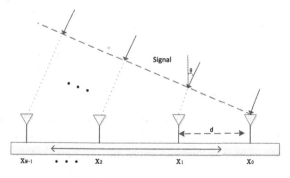

Fig. 2. Structure of the ULA

x_m stands for antenna array element, and θ represents the AOA [6], the time delay of the m-th element is expressed as follow

$$\tau_m(\theta) = -(x_m \sin \theta)/c, m = 0 : M - 1. \tag{6}$$

The beam response can be described as

$$p(\theta) = w^H \alpha(\theta) = \sum_{m=0}^{M-1} w_m^* e^{-jw\tau_m(\theta)} = \sum_{m=0}^{M-1} w_m^* e^{j\frac{2\pi}{\lambda}md \sin \theta}. \tag{7}$$

Where w^H is the weight vector, which can be a window function, or a codebook design, and this is the focus of the paper. $\alpha(\theta)$ is the array response.

Window function optimization is to suppress the side lobes by the design of the weight vector w^H, which is only associated with amplitude changing. Common window functions have many different window types, such as binomial weighting function, Hamming weighting function, Hanning window function and Blackman window function. The optimization results of the window function is shown in Fig. 3. The comparison between the Chebyshev window and the uniform window is shown in Fig. 3(a), and the simulation results of the Hanning window and the uniform window is shown in Fig. 3(b). Through the window function optimization, the sidelobes can be effectively inhibited and the main lobe gain is improved. The simulation results also show that, the Chebyshev window and the Hanning window make the main lobe width changed.

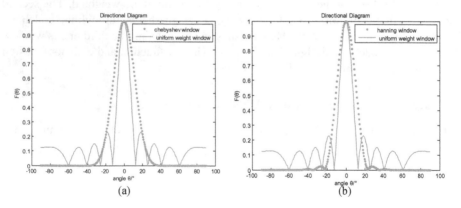

Fig. 3. Direction diagram with various windows

3.2   Beam Optimization Based on Codebook Design

The optimization of normalized weight vectors is an important part of codebook design. codebook $\mathbf{W} = [\mathbf{w}_1, \ldots, \mathbf{w}_K] \in \mathbf{C}^{M \times K}$ is consisted of K beamforming vectors $\mathbf{w}_m$, which produced by phase shifter, and $\mathbf{w}_m = [w_1, \ldots, w_M]^T \in \mathbf{C}^M$. Every element in the matrix is expressed as

$$w_m = e^{j\varphi_m}, \varphi_m \in \left\{0, 2\pi/2^B, \ldots, 2\pi(2^B - 1)/2^B\right\}. \tag{8}$$

In formula (8), B can be any integer, and the two codebook designs mentioned below are based on the change in B.

Taking the design of the beam codebook in the IEEE802.11.3c standard as an example, in which the beam vectors are given by column vectors of the following matrix

$$w(m, k) = f^{ix}\left(\frac{m \times \mathrm{mod}(k + (K/2), K)}{K/4}\right) \tag{9}$$
$$m = 0 : M - 1; \ k = 0 : K - 1;$$

Where M is the number of elements, and K denotes the number of beams. The function fix() returns the biggest integer which is smaller or equal to its value. M = mod(x,y) is defined as $x - n_1 y$, where n_1 is the nearest integer less or equal to x/y. The essence of the 3C codebook is that it composes of four complex numbers with a phase interval of 90°. To meet the low power consumption and complexity requirements, the codebook changes the phase shift without adjusting the amplitude, and its beam pattern is shown in Fig. 4(a).

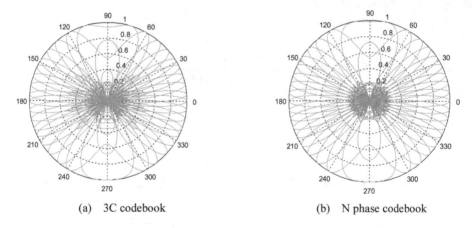

(a) 3C codebook   (b) N phase codebook

Fig. 4. Normalized polar coordinate beam pattern

This paper also introduces an improved N-phase codebook design scheme [4], which is an extension of the 3C codebook. Compared with the 3C codebook, the phase interval between the N-phase codebook weights is further reduced, the beam is finer and the sidelobe gain can be further suppressed. The N-phase beam codebook can be expressed as follow

$$w(m, k) = e^{\frac{2\pi}{N}j f^{ix}\left(\frac{m \times \mathrm{mod}(k + (K/2), K)}{K/N}\right)} \tag{10}$$
$$m = 0 : M - 1; k = 0 : K - 1$$

N represents the number of phases. Figure 4(b) shows the beam pattern generated by the N-phase codebook when N = 8.

The simulation results show that the beam phase adjustment can be done by codebook design, while the sidelobe interference of N phase codebook is significantly smaller than that of 3C codebook, and the performance can be improved remarkably. In [8], the design principle of complex codebook is introduced systematically, and the codebook scheme for surface antenna is also proposed. It is proved that the codebook design is one of the most important idea to solve the beamforming problem in future development [9].

3.3   Codebook Design Based on Window Function

Figure 5 is the beam pattern of 3C codebook and N phase codebook after the windowing. Figure 5(a) is the beam pattern of 3C codebook with Chebyshev window, and Fig. 5(b) is beam pattern of N phase codebook with Chebyshev window. Figure 5(c) is the beam pattern of 3C codebook with Hanning window, and Fig. 5(d) is the N phase codebook with Hanning window. Combined with Fig. 3 it is not difficult to find that, the codebook design with the window function can not only change the beam direction, but also further inhibit the sidelobes. Certainly, it needs further analysis to determine the specific performance changes.

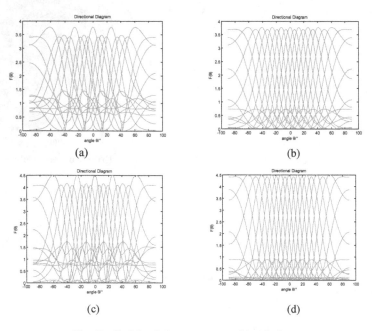

(a)   (b)

(c)   (d)

Fig. 5. Codebook beam pattern with windows

4   Interference Suppression of UAV Group Based on Beam Optimization

Based on the above expression of SINR and the beam optimal design schemes, in this section, the interference suppression method for UAV group communication based on beam optimization is simulated and discussed.

As shown in Eq. (5), the SINR is related to the weight vector w_m, and when the noise is constant, the interference can be effectively suppressed by optimizing the weight of the codebook. As shown in Sect. 3, the codebook design based on window function has better interference suppression effect compared to the simple loading-window and codebook design. Therefore, based on the derived SINR expression, the interference suppression performance of various codebook optimization schemes can be simulated and analyzed.

The simulation conditions are as follows. Assuming that other UAVs are randomly determined by the Poisson distribution around the command machine, the communication channel does not consider the attenuation and other factors, and only the existence of AWGN is taken into account. The interference mainly comes from other UAV communication signal, and the interference signal power setting is the same. The signal-to-noise ratio (SNR) is set to a certain value, and the anti-interference performance of the system under different beam optimization schemes is studied by increasing the number of UAV interfering devices from 1 to 50. The simulation parameters are shown in Table 1.

Table 1. Communication parameters in UAV group

Signal frequency	60 GHz
Signal transmission rate	100M bit/s
Bandwidth of the signal	1.08G
Channel condition	Gaussian channel with SNR = 10 dB
Relative rate between UAVs	0 m/s
Location distribution of UAVs	Poisson distribution
Type of antenna	Transmitter-no directional antenna; Receiver-antenna array

It is known in expression (5) that the SINR decreases as the interference increases. The number of disturbances is closely related to the density of the UAVs group and the number of interference. The interference power depends on the transmission power and the distance between the UAVs. When the number of disturbances and interference power is constant, the SINR of the received signal can be influenced by the optimized design of the beam.

As shown in the Fig. 6(a), the interference suppression performance of the windowless N-phase codebook is better than that of the 3C codebook without window. As the N-phase codebook is designed with more phase values, then better beam pattern can be obtained and the shortage of the 3C codebook is overcame. N-phase codebook with any window has the better performance than both N-phase codebook without window

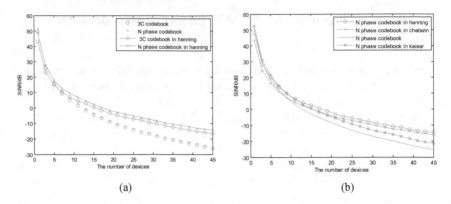

Fig. 6. SINR for various beam designs

and 3C codebook with the same window. It happens as the improving of the side-lobe suppression enhances the anti-interference performance [4]. As shown in Fig. 6(b), among the all optimization schemes, N-phase codebook based on Hanning window has the best interference suppression ability.

5 Conclusion

UAVs group communication based on millimeter-wave is now widely concerned by researchers. However, the interference among the UAVs has significant influence on system performance. Therefore, focusing on the millimeter-wave UAVs communication, this paper establishes the spatial interference channel model of the UAVs group, obtains the SINR expression based on the codebook and the direction of the DOA, and then several typical optimization schemes is proposed. Simulation results show that, the proposed optimal scheme can further depress the interference and effectively improve the communication performance.

References

1. Yong, Z., Zhang, R., Teng, J.L.: Wireless communications with unmanned aerial vehicles: opportunities and challenges. IEEE Commun. Mag. **54**(5), 36–42 (2016)
2. Xiao, Z.Y., Xia, P., Xia, X.G.: Enabling UAV cellular with millimeter-wave communication: potentials and approaches. IEEE Commun. Mag. **54**(5), 66–73 (2016)
3. Roh, W., Seol, J.Y.: Millimeter-wave beamforming as an enabling technology for 5G cellular communications: theoretical feasibility and prototype results. IEEE Commun. Mag. **52**(2), 106–113 (2014)
4. Zou, W.X., Cui, Z., Li, B.: Beamforming codebook design and performance evaluation for 60 GHz wireless communication. In: IEEE International Symposium on Communications and Information Technologies, pp. 30–35. IEEE Press, Hangzhou (2011)

5. Vutha, V., Heath, R.-W.: Basic relationship between channel coherence time and beamwidth in vehicular channels. In: IEEE Vehicular Technology Conference, pp. 1–5. IEEE Press, Boston (2015)
6. Hansen, R.-C.: Phased Array Antennas, 2nd edn. Wiley, Hoboken (2009)
7. Jin, S., Zhang, X.L., Qi, Z.: A statistical model for the UAV communication channel. Acta Aeronautica Et Astronautica Sinica **25**(1), 62–65 (2004)
8. Song, J.H., Choi, J., Love, D.-J.: Common codebook millimeter wave beam design: designing beams for both sounding and communication with uniform planar arrays. IEEE Trans. Commun. **65**(4), 1859–1872 (2017)
9. Noh, S., Zoltowski, M.-D, Love, D.-J.: Multi-resolution codebook and adaptive beamforming sequence design for millimeter wave beam alignment. IEEE Trans. Wirel. Commun. 1 (2017)

Global Dynamic One-Step-Prediction Resource Allocation Strategy for Space Stereo Multi-layer Data Asymmetric Scale-Free Network

Weihao Xie[✉], Zhigang Gai, Enxiao Liu, and Dingfeng Yu

Institute of Oceanographic Instrumentation, Shandong Academy of Science,
Qingdao 266000, China
bangongxinxiang@126.com

Abstract. Many real communication networks possess space stereo multi-layer structure and the data transmitted in these networks is asymmetric. As the network resource is limited and resource allocation scheme is one of the most effective ways to promote the network performance, it is of great interest to explore a resource allocation strategy that can highly utilize the network resource and further improve the network capacity. In this light, the global dynamic one-step-prediction resource allocation (GDORA) strategy for the space stereo multi-layer data asymmetric scale-free network under the established directly proportional network framework is introduced in this work. Compared with the node degree and node betweenness resource allocation strategies, the GDORA scheme can achieve much higher network capacity and promote the network performance effectively.

Keywords: Capacity · Multi-layer network · Scale-free · Resource allocation

1 Introduction

The researches related to the complex network [1–3] have opened a new way to explore the traffic dynamics for the real communication networks. Recently, an interesting way to promote the network performance has been drawn more attention by researchers, which can be classified as network resource allocation strategy. In continuous flow level, a capacity distribution scheme is introduced in [4], including flow rate adjustment and network capacity rearrangement. However, in many real communication networks, such as self-organization sensor networks, the data transmission is in the form of packet and restricting the flow generation rate may influence the process of data collection and transmitting. A capacity allocation scheme by utilizing the node degree is presented in [5], and it was applied to the shortest path routing and local routing strategies. Meanwhile, as the betweenness can comprehensively describe the situation of packet delivery of nodes in the network, in [6], the resource allocation method based on the node betweenness is proposed. And also, another traffic resource allocation scheme grounded on the node betweenness is introduced in [7], and it proved that the shortest path routing scheme can bring the improvement for the network capacity.

© ICST Institute for Computer Sciences, Social Informatics and Telecommunications Engineering 2018
X. Gu et al. (Eds.): MLICOM 2017, Part II, LNICST 227, pp. 482–489, 2018.
https://doi.org/10.1007/978-3-319-73447-7_52

However, in the real communication networks, such as self-organized wireless sensor network, the sensors are distributed to the observation area randomly and the data generated by sensors is not uniform, the hot region is the interested area, which means that many nodes may deploy in the hot region, and these nodes will generate much more proportion of packets created by the network and deliver more packets to the sink node than the other nodes located in the disinterested region. The network is in the form of asymmetric data network. As the link from sensor nodes to their sink node is one-one correspondence, there are limited links between sensor nodes in the hot region and their sink node. It is obvious that by using the resource allocation scheme based on the node degree, these sink nodes may become bottleneck nodes easily. On the other hand, when utilizing the resource allocation scheme based on the node betweenness, after the selection of the source node, the nodes on its routing path to the destination will be considered in the model, and the resource for nodes will be pre-allocated before the packets arrived and the packets that go through one node cannot arrive at the same time, which means that some allocated resource is wasted.

At the same time, many real communication networks are self-organized and space stereo multi-layer [8]. Meanwhile, as the observation area usually consists of interested region and disinterested region, the data transmission in the network is asymmetric. Therefore, it is of great interest to explore a resource allocation scheme that can further improve the network capacity for the data asymmetric space stereo multi-layer network. Actually, no matter what kind of resource allocation method is used, its essence is how to deal with the packets accumulated in the nodes reasonably. Thus, starting from this view of point, in this paper, the global dynamic one-step-prediction resource allocation (GDORA) scheme is introduced to further improve the network performance.

2 Traffic Model

As many real communication networks are self-organized and stereo multi-layer in space, the space stereo multi-layer network structure described in [8] is used in this work, where the traffic model of space stereo multi-layer data asymmetric network is made up of three layers: upper layer, lower layer and inter-layer, and as the coverage of each node in the net is finite, the upper layer and lower layer are parted into several districts, source nodes in the lower layer will deliver the information to their destination nodes located in the upper layer through the corresponding inter-layer based on the given routing strategy. As the particularity of scale-free network, the data congestion appears easily in this kind network and many researchers spend a lot of energy on improving the scale-free network capacity. Similar to the properties of real communication networks, it easily can be seen that the nodes in the upper layer not only establish links to the nodes in the upper layer, but also set up links to the lower layer. Accordingly, the nodes in the upper layer will possess more possibilities to be congestion nodes. So, this work will mainly focus on the resource allocation scheme for the nodes in the scale-free upper layer. Meanwhile, for the nodes in the real network is usually self-organized, they may be deployed in the form of Peer-to-Peer or hierarchical [9, 10], then, this work further expands the study of space stereo multi-layer network on the resource allocation schemes, and investigates two kinds of network topologies for space stereo multi-layer data asymmetric scale-free network: (I) upper layer is Hierarchical, inter-layer is Hierarchical and lower layer is Peer-to-Peer. (II) upper layer is Hierarchical, inter-layer is Peer-to-Peer and lower layer is Peer-to-Peer. Without loss of generality, this work uses the BA model [11] to generate the hierarchical network based on the node degree K, and uses the ER model [12, 13] to generate the Peer-to-Peer network connecting two of them randomly with N nodes, until the conditions are satisfied. The shortest path routing strategy [7] is used in this work.

To evaluate the performances of introduced resource allocation scheme, in this work, the order parameter [7, 13, 14] is used

$$\eta(R) = \lim_{t \to \infty} \frac{\langle \Delta N_p \rangle}{R \Delta t} \qquad (1)$$

where $\Delta N_p = N_p(t + \Delta t) - N_p(t)$ is the packets that stay in the network during time width Δt, $N_p(t)$ is the total number of packets in the network at time step t, $\langle \rangle$ means the average. When there is no congestion, the network is in the free step and $\eta(R)$ is around 0. With the increase of packet generation R created by the network, the network will be in the congestion step and $\eta(R)$ is obviously larger than zero. Therefore, the critical packet generation value R that makes the $\eta(R)$ around 0 can be used to evaluate the network capacity.

3 Global Dynamic One-Step-Prediction Resource Allocation (GDORA) Strategy

When the network works, it will generate R new packets and deliver them from source nodes to the destination nodes in each time step based on the given routing path. As the observation area could be interested region or disinterested region, network is data asymmetric space stereo multi-layer network. That is, the generation and distribution of R new packets on nodes in the lower layer are not uniform. Nodes in the lower layer located in the hot region may generate more part of R newly generated packets. As the network resource is limited, this work assumes that the total packets handling ability of the network is H and the handling ability of each node is H_i. When the new packets generated at time $t - 1$, they will reach to its next hop node according to the routing strategy at time t, then, the global dynamic one-step-prediction resource allocation strategy for the nodes located in the upper layer can be denoted as

$$H_i(t) = \frac{P_{bi}(t)}{\sum\limits_{j=1}^{N} P_{gj}(t - 1)} H \qquad (2)$$

where $P_{bi}(t)$ is the number of packets accumulated in the buffer of node i in the upper layer at time step t, and $\sum\limits_{j=1}^{N} P_{gj}(t - 1)$ is the sum of generated packets of N nodes in the lower layer at time step $t - 1$.

To realize the global dynamic one-step-prediction resource allocation scheme, the number of packets $P_{bi}(t)$ will include the number of packets $B_{vi}(t)$ that will be delivered to the node i in the upper layer network and the number of packets $B_{ri}(t)$ that cannot be delivered to its next hop node for the limitation of delivery ability. Accordingly, the number of packets $P_{bi}(t)$ that used on resource allocation can be expressed as

$$P_{bi}(t) = B_{vi}(t) + B_{ri}(t) \tag{3}$$

From the global dynamic one-step-prediction resource allocation strategy, it can be seen that if there are more packets accumulated in nodes, there will be more resource allocated to them.

4 Simulations and Discussions

As mentioned before, nodes deployed in the interested region may generate more proportion packets generated by the network. This work assumes that the nodes in the lower layer which are the neighbors of nodes with larger node degree in the upper layer generate more part of R newly created packets. Under this directly proportional situation, the performances of GDORA, node degree and node betweenness resource allocation strategies are investigated. To realize the positive proportional environment, the following scheme is used:

(i)   Sort the sequence for the nodes in the upper layer based on the number of links.
(ii) Let those upper layer top *Packet_scale_percent* percent nodes' neighbor in the lower layer generate more part of R newly created packets.

To realize the step (ii), the parameter *Packet_scale* is used to promote the packet generation probability for these upper layer top *Packet_scale_percent* percent nodes' neighbor located in the lower layer.

In this work, the upper layer and the lower layer are assumed to be divided into 4 square districts, and each district is unit length. Both the network sizes in the upper layer and lower layer are N and these nodes are distributed randomly. The topology average is executed to evaluate $\eta(R)$. The resource allocation is proportional to the node degree for node degree resource allocation scheme. The total packets handling ability of the network H is equal to the network size N. The *Packet_scale* = 1.5, *Packet_scale_percent* = 30% and the network size $N = 300$. The average degree of upper layer is 7 and the average degree of inter-layer is 4.

Figure 1 shows the order parameter $\eta(R)$ vs R for the node degree, node betweenness and GDORA resource allocation strategies, where the constructions of upper layer and inter-layer are both hierarchical. It can be seen that the performance of $\eta(R)$ is node degree resource allocation strategy < node betweenness resource allocation strategy < GDORA resource allocation strategy. Under the directly proportional situation, the nodes in the hot region will generate more part of R newly created packets to their destination nodes. Along with the growth of the newly created packets R by network, the number of generated packets may larger than the established links and the number of accumulated packets may exceed the node's processing ability casily for

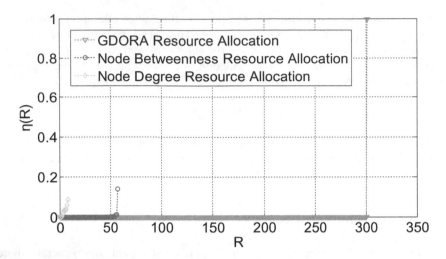

Fig. 1. The order parameter $\eta(R)$ vs R under different resource allocation strategies. The upper layer and inter-layer are both hierarchical.

node degree resource allocation strategy. Then, the nodes in the upper layer cannot resist the influence of data asymmetric generation, and the congestion will easily occur in the network, so the network capacity is low. For the node betweenness resource allocation scheme, if more packets go through one node, more network resource will be assigned to this node. Then, under the directly proportional circumstance, with the growth of the newly created packets R by network, nodes will obtain reasonable network resource to handle the network congestion. However, as mentioned before, the packets that go through one node cannot arrive at the same time, some network resource is wasted. Different from the two former strategies, the GDORA scheme gets the highest network performance. For the GDORA strategy, the packet handling ability of one node is based on the number of packets accumulated in this node. The whole network resource will be distributed proportionally to the accumulated number of packets that need to be handled in one node. Consequently, the network capacity is further improved.

Figure 2 gives the order parameter $\eta(R)$ vs R for three kinds of resource allocation strategies. The network structure of upper layer is hierarchical and the inter-layer is Peer-to-Peer. From Fig. 2, it can be seen that the performance tendency of $\eta(R)$ is still node degree resource allocation strategy < node betweenness resource allocation strategy < GDORA resource allocation strategy. When the inter-layer network framework is Peer-to-Peer, the distribution of network structure is homogenous corresponding to the hierarchical network structure. Subjecting to the restriction of node degree allocation scheme, in the Peer-to-Peer inter-layer network frame, the packet processing ability assigned to node is still very low, thus, the network capacity is poor. Corresponding to the node degree resource allocation scheme, even though the distribution of network links in the Peer-to-Peer inter-layer network structure is more uniform, however, based on the properties of node betweenness, the node betweenness

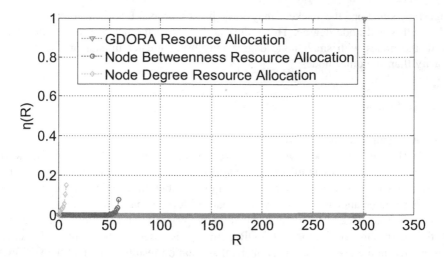

Fig. 2. The order parameter $\eta(R)$ vs R under different resource allocation strategies. The upper layer is hierarchical and the inter-layer is Peer-to-Peer.

resource allocation strategy still perform better than node degree resource allocation strategy. From Fig. 2, it can be seen that the GDORA scheme still gets the highest network performance. This result profits from the features of GDORA strategy, where the network resource allocation essence is the number of packets that one node needs to be handled rather than the packets routing path or the number of links.

For the congestion is also an interesting characteristic for the network, then, the packet probability distribution $P(K)$ vs node degree K is investigated for GDORA strategy when the network is in the congestion phase under two kinds of network frames. From Fig. 3(a) and (b), it can be found that for different node degree K, the distribution of packet probability $P(K)$ is asymmetric, and when the network is in the

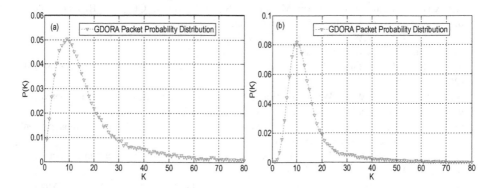

Fig. 3. The packet probability distribution $P(K)$ vs node degree K in the congested network for the GDORA scheme. (a) The upper layer and inter-layer are both hierarchical. (b) The upper layer is hierarchical, and inter-layer is Peer-to-Peer.

congestion situation, the packets may have higher probability to accumulate in the nodes with small node degree. This indicates that when the network congestion happened, the nodes with small node degree may bring greater impact on the network capacity than the other nodes.

5 Conclusion

Many real communication networks are space stereo multi-layer and how to improve the network capacity has been widely studied. As the reasonable utilization of network resource is one of the most effective ways to promote the network performance, the resource allocation schemes have been drawn more attention recently. In this paper, the GDORA resource allocation strategy is introduced for the space stereo multi-layer data asymmetric scale-free network and the directly proportional circumstance is established. The resource allocation of GDORA strategy is based on the number of packets accumulated in the node's buffer. Numerical simulation results show that the GDORA strategy reaches much high network capacity compared with the node degree and node betweenness resource allocation strategies. As the network resource allocation is important on promoting the network performance, such insights might be useful on investigating the real communication networks in the future.

Acknowledgments. This research was supported by the Youth Science Funds of Shandong Academy of Sciences, China (2014QN032), the Natural Science Foundation of Shandong Province (ZR2015YL020), the Special Fund for Marine Public Welfare Scientific Research (201505031), Qingdao Entrepreneurship and Innovation Leading Talent Project (13-CX-23, 13-CX-24).

References

1. Zhang, X., Chen, B.Z.: Study on node importance evaluation of the high-speed passenger traffic complex network based on the structural hole theory. Open Phys. **15**, 1–11 (2017)
2. Hu, X.B., Gheorghe, A.V., Leeson, M.S., Leng, S., Bourgeois, J., Qu, X.B.: Risk and safety of complex network systems. Math. Probl. Eng. 1–3 (2016)
3. Cai, K.Q., Tang, Y.W., Zhang, X.J., Guan, X.M.: An improved genetic algorithm with dynamic topology. Chin. Phys. B **25**, 128904 (2016)
4. Xia, Y.X., Hill, D.: Optimal capacity distribution on complex networks. EPL **89**, 58004 (2010)
5. Yang, H.X., Wang, W.X., Wu, Z.X., Wang, B.H.: Traffic dynamics in scale-free networks with limited packet-delivering capacity. Phys. A **387**, 6857–6862 (2008)
6. Gong, X.F., Kun, L., Lai, C.-H.: Optimal resource allocation for efficient transport on complex networks. EPL **83**, 28001 (2008)
7. Ling, X., Hu, M.B., Long, J.C., Ding, J.X., Shi, Q.: Traffic resource allocation for complex networks. Chin. Phys. B **22**, 018904 (2013)
8. Xie, W.H., Zhou, B., Liu, E.X., Lu, W.D., Zhou, T.: Global forward-predicting dynamic routing for traffic concurrency space stereo multi-layer scale-free network. Chin. Phys. B **24**, 098903 (2015)

9. Abidoye, A.P., Azeez, N.A., Adesina, A.O., Agbele, K.K.: UDCA: energy optimization in wireless sensor networks using uniform distributed clustering algorithms. Res. J. Inf. Technol. **3**, 191–200 (2011)
10. Monica, Sharma, A.K.: Comparative study of energy consumption for wireless sensor networks based on random and grid deployment strategies. Int. J. Comput. Appl. **6**, 28–35 (2010)
11. Barabási, A.L., Albert, R.: Emergence of scaling in random networks. Science **286**, 509–512 (1999)
12. Erdős, P., Rényi, A.: On the evolution of random graphs. Publ. Math. Inst. Hung. Acad. Sci. **5**, 17–61 (1960)
13. Zhuo, Y., Peng, Y.F., Liu, C., Liu, Y.K., Long, K.P.: Traffic dynamics on layered complex networks. Phys. A **390**, 2401–2407 (2011)
14. Arenas, A., Díaz-Guilera, A., Guimerá, R.: Communication in networks with hierarchical branching. Phys. Rev. Lett. **86**, 3196–3199 (2001)

Machine Learning Based Key Performance Index Prediction Methods in Internet of Industry

Haowei Li[1], Liming Zheng[1], Yue Wu[2(✉)], and Gang Wang[1]

[1] Communication Research Center, Harbin Institute of Technology, Harbin 150080, China
lihwl0@qq.com, {zheng, gwang51}@hit.edu.cn
[2] Management School, Harbin Institute of Technology, Harbin 150080, China
wuy@hit.edu.cn

Abstract. The Internet of industry (IoI) has been well advanced in modem factory accompanying with increasing application of sensor network. The industry intelligent is just basing on techniques of IoI and industry data analysis and predication. In this paper, both the training process, in which the modeling between the input of environment and technological parameters and the output of key performance index (KPI) is built, and the functional process, where the model built in training process and current is used for KPI predication. Both multivariable linear regression and nonlinear BP neural network model are employed and verified with authentic data set.

Keywords: Internet of industry · Industry intelligent · Machine learning
Neural network · Predication

1 Introduction

The Internet of industry driven by the wireless sensor network and industry data analysis are promoting the progress of the modern industry [1]. The modern industry with Internet of things (IOT) supported, which is the use of IOT, machines and other production facilities can be accessed to the internet by industrial enterprises to build a cyber-physical systems (CPS). Therefore, the real-time data information can be perceived, transmitted and processed intelligently, so as to achieve the real-time monitoring, early warning of the production process, optimal allocation of production resources and intelligent management.

The IOT has been greatly developed along with the integration of China's industrialization and information. IOT has various forms. According to the information acquisition, transmission, processing and dimension of utilization, the IOT can be divided into four layers: perceptual recognition layer, network transport layer, data intermediate layer and integrated application layer [2]. Among which, the data intermediate layer is responsible for data aggregation, management and intelligent analysis. The IOT has the characteristics of high real-time, large amount of data, heterogeneous

© ICST Institute for Computer Sciences, Social Informatics and Telecommunications Engineering 2018
X. Gu et al. (Eds.): MLICOM 2017, Part II, LNICST 227, pp. 490–497, 2018.
https://doi.org/10.1007/978-3-319-73447-7_53

data sources etc. Internet data is one of the most important sources of big data and IOI data processing is the core of industrial intelligence systems.

In different industries, especially the Internet, the data is getting larger and larger. The traditional way is almost impossible to effectively find patterns to improve productivity today, only computers can be used to complete many complex missions. Machine learning can automatically learn programs from data. As a result, this rising discipline has become more and more important. It has been widely used in web search, spam filtering, recommendation systems, advertising, credit evaluation, fraud detection, stock trading and drug design and data mining etc. According to a recent report by the McKinsey Global Institute, machine learning (also known as data mining or predictive analysis) will drive the next round of innovation [3, 4]. This paper explores the application of machine learning methods in the prediction of IOI.

2   Predictive Modeling Method

2.1   Multivariable Linear Regression Model

Regression analysis was put forward by Galton in the late nineteenth century. The simplest method is linear regression, which is a regression analysis of the relationship between one or more independent variables and dependent variables, using least squares function of linear regression equation. Linear regression with only one independent variable is called simple linear regression. However, in practice a variable is usually affected by many factors, simple linear regression is not enough to achieve the purpose of solving problems. Multivariable linear regression modeling (MLRM) is a model with more than one independent variable. The general expression of MLRM is as follows:

$$Y = \beta_0 + \beta_1 x_1 + \beta_2 x_2 + \ldots + \beta_p x_p + \varepsilon, \ \varepsilon \sim N(0, \sigma^2). \tag{1}$$

Where, $x_1, x_2, \ldots, x_p (p \geq 2)$ are the value of independent variables. Y is dependent variable, $\beta_1, \beta_2, \ldots, \beta_p$ are model coefficients and ε is random error.

If conduct n observations, the data collected by the n groups of samples is $x_{i1}, x_{i2}, \ldots x_{ip}, Y_i \ (i = 0, 1, \ldots, n, n > p)$ can be expressed in the form of matrix as follows:

$$\mathbf{Y} = \begin{bmatrix} Y_1 \\ Y_2 \\ \vdots \\ Y_n \end{bmatrix}, \mathbf{X} = \begin{bmatrix} 1 & x_{11} & \ldots & x_{1p} \\ 1 & x_{21} & \ldots & x_{2p} \\ \vdots & \vdots & & \vdots \\ 1 & x_{n1} & \cdots & x_{np} \end{bmatrix}, \boldsymbol{\beta} = \begin{bmatrix} \beta_0 \\ \beta_1 \\ \vdots \\ \beta_p \end{bmatrix}, \boldsymbol{\varepsilon} = \begin{bmatrix} \varepsilon_0 \\ \varepsilon_1 \\ \vdots \\ \varepsilon_p \end{bmatrix}. \tag{2}$$

Where, $Y = X\beta + \varepsilon$ is called linear regression data model, X is the design matrix and ε is the error vector which meets the random conditions.

The propose of linear regression is to find the mean square error of linear function on $x_1, x_2, \ldots, x_p$:

$$E(Y) = \beta_0 + \beta_1 x_1 + \beta_2 x_2 + \ldots + \beta_p x_p. \tag{3}$$

Where, $Q(\beta) = \|Y - X\beta\|^2$ is minimum unbiased estimator, that is, the regression equation:

$$\hat{Y} = \hat{\beta}_0 + \hat{\beta}_1 x_1 + \hat{\beta}_2 x_2 + \ldots + \hat{\beta}_p x_p. \tag{4}$$

The least squares estimation of β is defined as $\hat{\beta} = (X^T X)^{-1} X^T Y$, through which the unbiased estimator of Y can be obtained.

2.2   Nonlinear BP Neural Network Model

In late 80s, the error back-propagation algorithm (BP algorithm) [6] and its application in artificial neural network learning process had greatly promoted the development of machine learning, and led the development of statistical machine learning model trend until now. Researchers found that with back-propagation algorithm, the artificial neural network model can automatically correct its parameters in the training process, making neural network model fit the training data to a greater degree. Using a large number of training samples, the neural network can be trained to learn statistical rules to predict unknown events. This kind of machine learning model based on statistical rules shows great superiority in many aspects, compared with the previous methods based on artificial rules. Although during this period, artificial neural network can also be referred to as multilayer perceptron, but in fact it is a shallow model, which contains only a layer of hidden nodes.

BP neural network has three layers: input layer, hidden layer and output layer. One topology of an ordinary BP neural network is shown in the following figure:

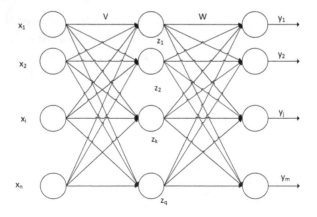

Fig. 1. Topological structure of BP neural network.

The learning process of a BP neural network can be represented by Fig. 1. The process consists of forward propagation of input data and back propagation of error.

The direction of forward propagation is from the input layer through the hidden layer to the output layer. Forward propagation processes data layer by layer, the state of each layer of neurons only affects the next layer of neurons. Then at the output layer the neurons compare the actual output with the desired output, if the result does not match, the deviation between the actual output and the desired output is calculated, which will be transmitted back. When the deviation is returned to the input layer, the weights and thresholds of each neuron in the hidden layer are modified so as to minimize the deviation.

v_{ki} is the weight between the input layer and the hidden layer, w_{jk} is the weight between the hidden layer and the output layer, f_1 is the transfer function of the hidden layer and f_2 is the transfer function of the output layer. Then the output of the hidden layer and layer node can be defined as:

$$z_k = f_1(\sum_{i=0}^{n} v_{ki}x_i), \; k = 1, 2, \ldots, q. \tag{5}$$

$$y_j = f_2(\sum_{k=0}^{q} w_{jk}z_k), \; j = 1, 2, \ldots, m. \tag{6}$$

The number of learning samples $x_1, x_2, \ldots, x_p$ is p. Assuming the actual output of the l sample is y_j^l, expected output is t_j^l. Then the deviation between the actual output and the expected output of the l sample is:

$$E_l = \frac{1}{2}\sum_{j=1}^{m} (t_j^l - y_j^l)^2. \tag{7}$$

The global deviation produced by p samples is:

$$E = \sum_{l=1}^{p} E_l = \frac{1}{2}\sum_{l=1}^{p}\sum_{j=1}^{m} (t_j^l - y_j^l)^2. \tag{8}$$

The change of weight:

$$\Delta w_{jk} = -\eta \frac{\partial E}{\partial w_{jk}} = -\eta \frac{\partial}{\partial w_{jk}}(\sum_{l=1}^{p} E_l) = \sum_{l=1}^{p}(-\eta \frac{\partial E_l}{\partial w_{jk}}), \eta \in (0, 1). \tag{9}$$

Where, η is the learning rate, which needs to be chosen properly. The system will be unstable if η is too large. η being too small will lead to long training time and slow convergence. η is generally chosen between 0.01 and 0.8.

Deviation signal is defined as:

$$\delta_{lj} = -\frac{\partial E_l}{\partial S_j} = -\frac{\partial E_l}{\partial y_j}\frac{\partial y_l}{\partial S_j}. \tag{10}$$

Where, S_j is the net output of summation unit of output layer of neurons.

$$\frac{\partial E_l}{\partial y_j} = \frac{\partial}{\partial y_j} \left[\frac{1}{2}\sum_{j=1}^{m}(t_j^l - y_j^l)^2\right] = \sum_{j=1}^{m}(y_j^l - t_j^l). \tag{11}$$

$$\frac{\partial y_l}{\partial S_j} = f_2'(S_j). \tag{12}$$

From to Eqs. (10)–(12):

$$\delta_{lj} = \sum_{j=1}^{m}(t_j^l - y_j^l) f_2'(S_j). \tag{13}$$

Also:

$$\frac{\partial E}{\partial w_{jk}} = \frac{\partial E}{\partial S_j}\frac{\partial S_j}{\partial w_{jk}}. \tag{14}$$

Then:

$$\frac{\partial E}{\partial w_{jk}} = -\delta_{lj}z_k = -\sum_{j=1}^{m}(t_j^l - y_j^l) f_2'(S_j)z_k. \tag{15}$$

From Eq. (9) and Eq. (15), it can be seen that the weight of the output layer is changed:

$$\Delta w_{jk} = \sum_{l=1}^{p}\left(-\eta\frac{\partial E}{\partial w_{jk}}\right) = \eta\sum_{l=1}^{p}\sum_{j=1}^{m}(t_j^l - y_j^l) f_2'(S_j)z_k. \tag{16}$$

Similarly, the change of hidden layer weights:

$$\Delta v_{ki} = \eta\sum_{l=1}^{p}\sum_{j=1}^{m}(t_j^l - y_j^l) f_2'(S_j)w_{jk}f_1'(S_k)x_i. \tag{17}$$

The purpose of building the whole network is achieved by changing the weights of each neuron in the hidden layer.

3   Performance Simulation

In this paper, we used a set of 7 input 2 output food IOI data. Input is 7 performance indicators collected by the IOI sensor, which is: temperature, humidity, drying time, the original ratio, processing time of raw materials and other industrial and environmental parameters. The output value y_1 is the water content of the product, y_2 is nutritional content and data set size is 5000. Multiple linear regression model and BP neural network model were used to analyze the data. Fitting model is used to the prediction test of data and the mean square error (MSE) is used to evaluate the performance of the two different models. 3725 data is used for model learning and 1225 data is for verification.

Figure 2 is the result of the model training process using multiple linear regression method. The ordinate is the key index value and the abscissa is data record index for the validation of data set, where the blue line is the true value, the red line is the fitting output value. It can be seen that the fitting values of y1 and y2 converge to the true values except for very few peak values.

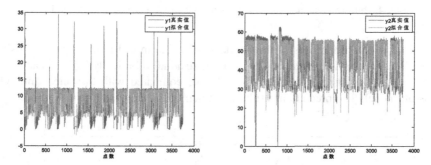

Fig. 2. Fitting value and real value of y1, y2 in Multivariable linear regression model (Color figure online)

Figure 3 shows the results of the validation using a multiple linear regression model in the workflow. The ordinate is the residuals of the predicted and true values of the key indicators and the abscissa is data record index for the validation of data set. It can be seen that the residual is basically 0, but the residual value is larger on more discrete points, which affects the overall prediction performance.

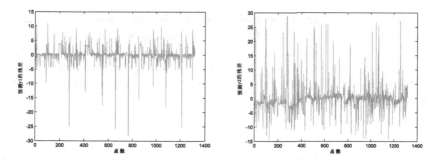

Fig. 3. Residual error between predicted and real values in multivariate linear regression model

Figure 4 shows the output result of the model training process using BP neural network. It can be seen that under the conditions of nonlinear model, the fitting values of y1 and y2 also converge to the true values in addition to very few peak values.

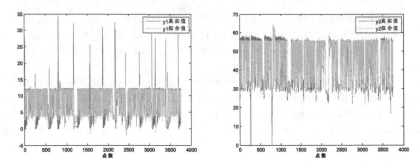

Fig. 4. Fitting value and real value of y1, y2 in BP neural network model

Figure 5 shows the results of the application of the model training process using multiple linear regression. It can be seen that the residual is basically 0. The peak value whose residual is larger is significantly reduced, compared with the linear multiple regression model. The prediction results are much better than the linear method.

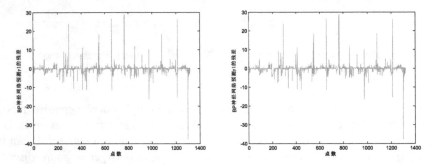

Fig. 5. Residual error between predicted and real values in BP neural network model

Table 1 shows the quantitative comparison of the mean square error between multiple linear regression model and BP neural network model during the training and working stage. It can be seen that the nonlinear BP neural network model can achieve better mean square error performance both in the training and working stage. The neural network model is improved by 43% and 37% respectively compared with linear model, especially the output value y2.

Table 1. The comparison of multiple linear regression model and BP neural network model.

MSE (y1/y2)	Multiple linear regression mode	BP neural network model
Training stage	10.0/20.5	7.5/11.1
Working stage	9.9/23.1	9.3/14.5

4   Conclusion

This paper discusses the application of machine learning methods in IOI. The multiple linear regression model and the nonlinear BP neural network model are introduced. The application of the two models above in the prediction of key performance indicators in IOI is given. At last, the model is validated by the real production environment data. The quantitative comparison of the mean square error of the linear method and the nonlinear method is given. Through the analysis and simulation, it is proved that the nonlinear BP neural network model can greatly improve the performance compared with the linear multiple regression.

Acknowledgement. This work was supported by the National Natural Science Foundation of China under Grant No. 61401120.

References

1. Wang, X.: Made in China 2015: from an industrial country to an industrial power. Internet Things Technol. **5**(5), 3–4 (2015)
2. Liu, Y.: Introduction to Internet of Things. Science Press, Beijing (2013)
3. Conway, D., White, J.: Machine Learning for Hackers. O'Reilly Media Inc., Newton (2012)
4. Domingos, P.: A few useful things to know about machine learning. Commun. ACM **55**(10), 78–87 (2012)
5. Bao, Y.: Data Analysis Tutorial. Tsinghua University Press, Beijing (2011)
6. Hecht-Nielsen, R.: Theory of the back propagation neural network. In: International Joint Conference on Neural Networks, IJCNN, pp. 593–605. IEEE (1989)

An Auction-Gaming Based Routing Model for LEO Satellite Networks

Ligang Cong[✉], Huamin Yang, Yanghui Wang, and Xiaoqiang Di

School of Computer Science and Technology,
Changchun University of Science and Technology, Changchun 130022, China
clg_cust@126.com, dixiaoqiang@126.com,
{yhm,wyh}@cust.edu.cn

Abstract. Characteristics of LEO satellite networks, like dynamically changed topological structures, limited on-board resources, and longer communication delay, have brought new challenges to the construction of satellite networks. By analyzing existing routing models for satellite networks, this paper proposes an auction-gaming-based routing model for LEO satellite networks, based on the DTN protocol and against such characteristics. By making use of an auction model, it takes space propagation loss, residual storage space of a node, and routing hop counts as important bases for routing selection. Analysis shows that besides the routing function, this model also plays an active role in avoiding "selfish" satellite nodes, as well as in relieving network congestion.

Keywords: Auction gaming · LEO satellite networks · Routing model

1 Introduction

LEO satellite networks have been taken seriously due to their unique advantages. However, their existing characteristics, such as dynamically changed topological structures, limited node resources, and longer communication delay, have brought about many problems to be solved during construction of such networks, and routing is just a highlighted one of these problems.

The routing technology is critical to the network construction. Some proposals were given to solve the problem. Chang et al. [1] advanced a routing algorithm based on the finite-state automation (FSA), which shielded the dynamic nature of topological structures to simplify the computation, but resulted in poor adaptation to emergent situations of networks, as well as in bigger demand for on-board storage resources. Ercetin et al. [2] put forward a probabilistic routing protocol (PRP), which reduced the number of times of call interruption and routing redefinition due to routing switching, but increased the call blocking rate and the probability of network congestion. Lee and Kang [3] proposed a hierarchical QoS routing protocol (HQRP), which reduced call

Supported by the National High-tech R&D Program of China (2015AA015701); Supported by Foundation of Jilin Educational Committee (JJKH20170628KJ); Supported by Science and Technology Development Project of Jilin Province (20150312030ZX).

© ICST Institute for Computer Sciences, Social Informatics and Telecommunications Engineering 2018
X. Gu et al. (Eds.): MLICOM 2017, Part II, LNICST 227, pp. 498–508, 2018.
https://doi.org/10.1007/978-3-319-73447-7_54

interruption through optimization of the switching process and considered optimization of channel resources, but increased network overhead and lowered the whole network efficiency. Taleb [4] proposed an explicit load balancing routing algorithm (ELB), with which routing was selected under the condition that the load of the next link was known, and when links were congested, other satellites would be informed to lower the sending speed to reduce network congestion. However, this algorithm would fail in the case of severe congestion. Besides above methods, typical satellite routing algorithms also include ALBR [5], DRA [6], CEAARS [7], etc.

It is hard to tell which one of the above algorithms is more advantageous, because each has a different emphasis, as well as its own characteristics in different application environment. This paper proposes an auction-gaming-based routing model for LEO satellite networks, based on the DTN protocol. By fully using periodicity of topological structures of LEO satellite networks, this model divides dynamically changed topological structures into relatively static time slots and then introduces auction gaming into such time slots to solve routing problems of LEO satellite networks. Meanwhile, it avoids selfish nodes in networks to the greatest extent, and also prevents network congestion due to excessive resource consumption of individual nodes.

2 Definition of the System Model

2.1 Topological Structures of LEO Networks

Different from computer networks on the ground, LEO satellite networks have movable nodes, resulting in changeable topological structures. However, satellites move strictly along defined orbits, producing periodical and predictable changes in relevant topological structures. Therefore, during the research on routing of satellite networks, relevant strategies are generally adopted to shield the dynamic nature of such topological structures, and abstract static models are used instead for research. At present, relevant strategies mainly include the virtual topology strategy [8], virtual node strategy [6] and division of coverage domains [9]. This paper adopts the virtual topology strategy, which discretizes the dynamic topological relationship of satellite network nodes, and divides a complete running cycle of a satellite network into several time slots $[t_0,t_1]$, $[t_1,t_2]$, $[t_2,t_3]$, $[t_3,t_4]$, ..., $[t_n,t_{n-1}]$. The topology of a satellite network is considered to be fixed in each time slot, and it only changes at time nodes of t_1, t_2, t_3 ... t_n.

Satellite nodes in a network store not only their own status information, but also status information of adjacent satellite nodes related to the routing. Such status information includes communication distances, residual node storage space, node hop counts to the destination, etc., which is stored in satellite nodes as tables. These tables will change periodically as the topological structure of the satellite network changes. By taking the satellite node of v_1 as an example, Table 1 shows some status information of its adjacent satellite nodes, within the time slot of t.

Table 1. Information table of a satellite node

Adjacent satellite nodes	Communication distance (Unit: km)	Hop counts through this neighbor node to the target	Satellite storage space (Unit: MB)
v2	d2	h2	m2
v3	d3	h3	m3
v4	d4	h4	m4

2.2   Definition of the Routing Problem

The key part of this research is to set up a reliable and highly efficient spatial routing path by designing an incentive mechanism to boost cooperation between nodes. The LEO satellite network studied by this paper is based on DTN, and the basic store-and forward routing mode is adopted. Therefore, the routing problem can be converted into a problem to find the proper store-and-forward nodes.

As shown in Fig. 1, in a LEO satellite network, multiple paths are available for selection when a node generates data and needs to send them to the destination. The first step for path selection is to select the suitable node for data forwarding among multiple neighbor nodes, with a process similar to the item auction in real life. Therefore, it is possible to abstract the selection of a forwarding node as an auction gaming process [12, 13], in which the data source node is considered as a buyer of forwarding services, while its neighbor nodes are considered as sellers of such services. As shown in Fig. 2, in general cases, multiple forwarding nodes will be used before data can be sent to the destination, and therefore auctions will be repeated for many times. Every time an auction is finished, except the data-forwarding node, other nodes will not participate in the next auction, and this data-forwarding node will turn from the seller into a buyer in the new auction, which will repeat until the destination node is reached.

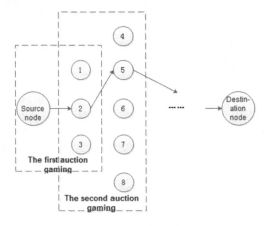

Fig. 1. Schematic drawing of data auction

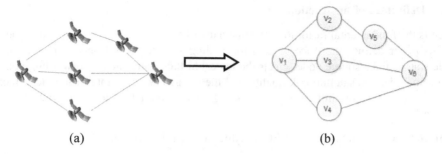

(a)   (b)

Fig. 2. Sketch of local satellite network connection

3   Definition of the Routing Auction-Gaming Model

As mentioned above, the routing problem is abstracted as a data auction process. In this section, gain rules related to such auctions are defined, and gain models of both the source and the forwarding nodes are described.

3.1   Definition of Gain Rules

In a routing auction model, a data-sending node is considered as a buyer, while its neighboring nodes that have participated in an auction before are considered as sellers. Such sellers provide the buyer with data forwarding services, and the buyer determines the forwarding node by selecting the best among various service prices offered by these sellers. The destination node will provide expense compensation for nodes involved in data transmission. During data forwarding, the forwarding success rate is introduced to avoid selfish nodes. The higher the success rate, the higher the gains. On the contrary, the lower the success rate, the lower the gains. Detailed gain rules of relevant nodes are listed as follows:

(1) During the whole routing process in a LEO satellite network, involved nodes can be classified into three types: data source nodes, forwarding nodes and destination nodes;
(2) If a satellite node doesn't belong to any one of three types mentioned in (1), its gain is 0;
(3) For a source node, its gain comes from the compensation provided by a destination node;
(4) For a forwarding node, its gain can be divided into two parts, which are gains obtained during two gaming processes of data reception and transmission respectively;
(5) For a destination node, it has no gain, and it only pays for services of other nodes;
(6) Deduction of relevant costs is needed to get final gains of a source and a forwarding node.

3.2   Definition of an Auction Bid

Price is the fundamental factor to determine a data-forwarding node. The auction model in this paper defines the price of data forwarding services based on link quality and node status, and a source node selects the lowest bid to determine the forwarding node. A bid includes the satellite link quality and the data-forwarding rate of a node, which are two critical points influencing the routing auction model. Relevant definitions are shown below:

Definition 1: link quality of a LEO satellite network is represented as:

$$r_{ij}(t) = \frac{L_{ij}(t)}{100} + h_j(t) + \frac{m_{ip}}{m_j(t)} \tag{1}$$

where $L_{ij}(t) = 32.44 + 20\log d_{ij}(t) + 20\log f_i$ means the spatial propagation loss produced during data transmission from the satellite node of v_i to satellite node of v_j at the time oft; $d_{ij}(t)$ refers to the distance between nodes of v_i and v_j at the time of t $h_j(t)$ means the hop counts that the node of v_i needs at the time of t to reach the destination node while through the node of v_j, and its value depends on the scale of the LEO satellite network; $m_j(t)$ means the residual storage space of v_j at the time of t; m_{ip} means volume of data that needs to be transmitted. The bigger the value of $r_{ij}(t)$ is, the poorer the link quality is. On the contrary, the smaller this value is, the better the link quality is.

Definition 2: the data forwarding rate is defined as:

$$s_i(t) = \frac{p_{is}(t)}{p_{ir}(t)}, \tag{2}$$

where $p_{is}(t)$ means the sum total of data packages sent by the satellite node of v_i up to the time of t; $p_{ir}(t)$ means the sum total of data packages received or generated by the satellite node of v_i up to the time of t.

According to above definitions, a bid for forwarding services, which is composed of the satellite link quality and the data-forwarding rate, can be represented as:

$$c_{ij}(t) = \frac{r_{ij}(t)}{s_j(t)}, \tag{3}$$

which means the routing service price provided by the node j, at the time of t, for the node i. The price is in direct proportion to the link quality, while it is in inverse proportion to the data forwarding rate.

The network studied in this paper is based on the DTN protocol, with basic routing mode of "store – carry – forward". If node storage space is 0 or smaller than data to be received, routing can't be done. Therefore, neighboring nodes that don't have enough storage space to meet requirements of data reception will not participate in bidding.

After all neighboring nodes place their bids, the data source node will select the node with the lowest price for data forwarding, and at this time, the expense that the data sending node needs to pay is:

$$o_{ik}(t) = \min c_{ik}(t) \quad k \in N_i, \tag{4}$$

where N_i is the set of neighboring nodes of the node i. The selected node will trade with the price of $o_i(t)$.

3.3   Gain Model for Source Nodes

A source node generates data, and then completes data transmission once. It plays as a routing buyer in the auction model. Suppose that every time the source node sends units data, the destination node will give corresponding compensation. Then, the sending node uses such compensation to pay for forwarding expenses and meanwhile obtains certain gains. The compensation is represented by g. For simplicity, suppose that the cost of data generation and transmission of a source node is 0, and therefore the gain function of the source node, i, is:

$$u_i(t) = g \bullet m_{ip} - o_i(t) \, k \in N_i, \tag{5}$$

where m_{ip} means the data volume sent by the source node; $g \bullet m_{ip}$ means the total compensation obtained from the destination node. If $g \bullet m_{ip} < = o_i(t)$, the source node has a negative gain, and at this moment it will refuse to send data as there is no incentive. Therefore, a destination node must provide suitable compensation: higher prices for key source nodes and lower prices for subordinate source nodes. In addition, as the data forwarding rate is introduced, the source node will improve the success rate as much as possible in order to obtain more gains. It can be said that this mechanism not only improves network routing efficiency, reduces network loads and relieves network congestion, but also avoids selfishness of satellite nodes.

3.4   Gain Model for Forwarding Nodes

Suppose the node of v_j is selected for data forwarding and v_j is not a destination node. Thus, its gains include two parts. The first part is the forwarding expenses paid by its prior node, when the node serves as a seller. The second part is the compensation obtained during a new auction, when the node serves as a source node, a buyer.

(1)   Gains of a forwarding node as a seller

The forwarding node of v_j will be paid for data reception, with a price of $c_{ij}(t)$. Besides, the received data will take up certain storage space of the node, which means the cost of the forwarding node. Therefore, the gain function can be represented as:

$$u_{j1}(t) = c_{ij}(t) - \frac{m_{jr}}{m_j(t)}, \tag{6}$$

where m_{jr} is the received data volume, and $m_j(t)$ is the residual storage space of the node before it receives the data packages.

(2) Gains of a forwarding node as a buyer

When the forwarding node, v_j, sends data, it becomes the buyer for forwarding services in a new auction. This new auction has the same process as the last one, except that the prior node v_i is not involved any more. Therefore, the gain function for node v_j as a buyer can be represented as:

$$u_{j2}(t) = g \bullet m_{jp} - o_j(t), \tag{7}$$

where $o_j(t)$ means the trade price between node v_j and its neighboring nodes during the second gaming process; m_{jp} is the volume of data packages to be sent. Therefore, the total gain of node v_j in routing is the sum of gains obtained during data receiving and forwarding processes, which can be expressed as:

$$u_j(t) = u_{j1}(t) + u_{j2}(t) \tag{8}$$

4 Analysis of the Routing Model

According to formulas defined in Sect. 3, major factors that influence satellite node gains during the routing process include free-space propagation loss of electromagnetic waves, node storage space, and path hop counts. Values of the three factors will directly influence gains of spatial nodes, and further influence selection of routing nodes. This section focuses on relationships between the three factors and node gains as well as routing selection.

As shown in Fig. 2, a local part of a LEO satellite network in a time slot of t is taken for analysis, which is abstracted as an undirected graph shown in Fig. 2(b). In this graph, v_1, v_2, v_3, v_4, v_5 and v_6 are six satellite nodes, among which v_1 is a source node and v_6 is a destination node. The line between any two nodes means an available communication link between the two satellites, and two nodes without a line in between can't communicate with each other directly. When the node of v_1 generates data and needs to send such data to the destination node of v_6, its neighboring nodes will participate in auction gaming. Hop counts of v_1, through v_2, v_3 and v_4, to the destination are 2, 1 and 1 respectively. Suppose that the data volume of the source node is 100 MB, and the compensation that the destination node has to pay for transmission of 100 MB data is g. Then, influences of spatial propagation loss, hop counts and residual storage space on node gains and routing can be studied based on conditions mentioned above.

4.1 Analysis of Node Bids

Suppose that the change interval of spatial propagation loss is [100, 500] that the change interval of residual node space is [1, 9], and that satellite nodes have two data forwarding rates of 70% and 90% respectively. Thus, changes in bids of v_2, v_3 and v_4 can be shown in Figs. 3 and 4.

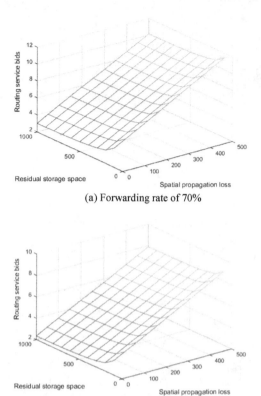

(a) Forwarding rate of 70%

(b) Forwarding rate of 90%

Fig. 3. Bid changes of v_2

From the Fig. 3, bids of the node v_2 increase as the spatial propagation loss increases, while decrease as the residual storage space increases. Under the same conditions, the higher the data forwarding rate is, the lower the bids are.

As nodes of v_3 and v_4 have the same hop counts, they will have consistent changes in bids for routing services. From the Fig. 4, under the condition of the same hop counts from a node to the destination, the bigger the residual space of a node is and the smaller the free-space propagation loss is, the lower the bid of a node is, and otherwise the higher the bid is. Compared with the Fig. 3, it can be seen that under the same conditions, the bigger the hop counts, the higher the bids.

4.2 Analysis of Node Gains and the Routing Process

Suppose that nodes of v_2, v_3, v_4 and v_5 in the network model have status parameters shown in Table 2, and that receiving data volume equals to sending data volume during the data transmission between nodes. Then, gains of nodes can be analyzed through a simple simulation of routing selection.

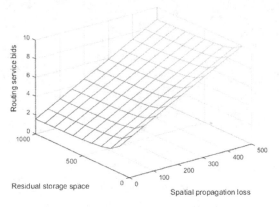

(a) Forwarding rate of 70%

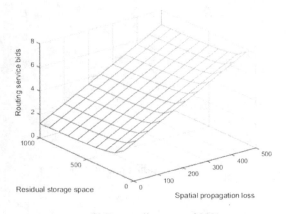

(b) Forwarding rate of 90%

Fig. 4. Bid changes of v_3 and v_4

Table 2. Scene parameter table for data analysis

Node parameter	Free-space propagation loss	Residual storage space	Hop counts to the destination	Data forwarding rate
v_2	220	400	2	80%
v_3	270	500	1	80%
v_4	170	400	1	90%
v_5	170	300	1	80%

As mentioned above, there are three paths from the source node to the destination: $v_1 \rightarrow v_2 \rightarrow v_3 \rightarrow v_4 \rightarrow v_5 \rightarrow v_6$ and $v_1 \rightarrow v_4 \rightarrow v_6$. After comparison of node gains, obtained through above formulas, under the three conditions, the selected path is

$v_1 \rightarrow v_4 \rightarrow v_6$. See Table 3 for details. The selection of routing is converted into a game to find the cost-optimal forwarding services. By comparison, the node v_1 selects the node with the lowest bid for data forwarding. Lower bids mean better forwarding services, which refer to lower spatial propagation loss, more residual storage space, and few number of times of forwarding. It can be concluded that the source node can find a suitable data forwarding path after repeated gaming.

Table 3. Gains of nodes in different paths

Node gain path	v_1	v_2	v_3	v_4	v_5
$v_1 \rightarrow v_2 \rightarrow v_5 \rightarrow v_6$	g − 5.563	g + 1.521	0	0	g + 3.459
$v_1 \rightarrow v_3 \rightarrow v_6$	g − 4.875	0	g + 4.675	0	0
$v_1 \rightarrow v_4 \rightarrow v_6$	g − 3.278	0	0	g + 3.028	0

5   Conclusions

This paper solves the routing problem in a LEO satellite network by introducing an auction-gaming model, converts the routing selection into a process to find forwarding services with the lowest price, and introduces four important parameters related to network service quality, including spatial propagation loss, residual storage space of nodes, data forwarding hop counts, and data forwarding rate of satellite nodes, into the decision-making process for neighboring node bidding so as to determine relations between various parameters and forwarding service bids through model analysis. In addition, routing selection is done and gains of various nodes are analyzed through this model. Theoretically, this model can avoid selfish nodes in a network, and meanwhile it can also prevent nodes with inadequate space from forwarding data, effectively relieving congestion of the network.

In future work, comparative analysis between this model and other routing models for satellite networks will be conducted through network simulation tools. Moreover, this model will be further improved so as to fully exert its advantages in solving routing problems, reliving network congestion, and enhancing network efficiency.

References

1. Chang, H.S., Kim, B.W., Lee, C.G.: FSA-based link assignment and routing in low-earth orbit satellite networks. IEEE Trans. Veh. Technol. **47**(3), 1037–1048 (1998)
2. Ercetin, O., Krishnamurthy, S., Dao, S., Tassiulas, L.: Provision of guaranteed services in broadband LEO satellite networks. Comput. Netw. **39**(1), 61–77 (2002)
3. Lee, J., Kang, S.: Satellite over satellite (SOS) network: a novel architecture for satellite network. In: Proceedings of the IEEE INFOCOM. IEEE, Piscataway, pp. 315–321 (2000)
4. Tarik, T., Daisuke, M., Jamalipour, A.: Explicit load balancing technique for NGEO satellite IP networks with on-board processing capabilities. IEEE/ACM Trans. Netw. **17**(1), 281–293 (2009)

5. Rao, Y., Wang, R.C.: Agent-based load balancing routing for LEO satellite networks. Comput. Netw. **54**(17), 3187–3195 (2010)
6. Ekici, E., Akyildiz, I.F., Bender, M.D.: A distributed routing algorithm for datagram traffic in LEO satellite networks. IEEE/ACM Trans. Netw. **9**(2), 137–147 (2001)
7. Cao, J.H., Stefanovic, M.: Cross entropy accelerated ant routing in satellite networks. In: Proceedings of the American Control Conference (ACC). IEEE, Piscataway, pp. 5080–5087 (2010)
8. Werner, M.: A dynamic routing concept for ATM-based satellite personal communication networks. IEEE J. Sel. Areas Commun. **15**(8), 1636–1648 (1997)
9. Hashimoto, Y.: Design of IP-based routing in a LEO satellite network. In: Proceedings of the 3rd International Workshop on Satellite-Based Information Services. ACM, New York, pp. 81–88 (1998)
10. Lu, Y., Zhao, Y.J., Sun, F.C., Li, H.B., Ni, G.Q., Wang, D.J.: Routing techniques on satellite networks. J. Softw. **25**(5), 1085–1100 (2014)
11. Xi, Y., Yeh, E.M.: Pricing, competition, and routing for selfish and strategic nodes in multi-hop relay networks. In: Proceedings of IEEE INFOCOM 2008. IEEE, Phoenix, pp. 2137–2145 (2008)
12. Ng, S.-K., Seah, W.K.: Game-theoretic model for collaborative protocols in selfish, tariff-free, multihop wireless networks. In: Proceeding of IEEE INFOCOM 2008. IEEE, Phoenix, pp. 762–770 (2008)
13. Keränen, A., Ott, J., Kärkkäinen, T.: The ONE simulator for DTN protocol evaluation. In: 2nd International Conference on Simulation Tools and Techniques, SIMUTools 2009, Rome, March 2009
14. Vahdat, A., Becker, D.: Epidemic routing for partially connected ad hoc networks. Technical report CS-200006, Duke University (2000)

Parameters Estimation of Precession Cone Target Based on Micro-Doppler Spectrum

MingFeng Wang, AiJun Liu[✉], LinWei Wang, and ChangJun Yu

School of Information and Electrical Engineering,
Harbin Institute of Technology, Harbin 264209, China
mylaj@hitwh.edu.cn

Abstract. The micro-Doppler (m-D) provides valuable information for the motion parameters extraction and the target recognition of space targets. To address the issue of estimating the motion parameters of precession warhead targets, a new method based on the m-D spectrum of the top and the bottom of the cone is proposed in this paper. In this method, the m-D features of the cone target are firstly extracted by calculating the first-order moments of the time-frequency distribution of the echo signal. Then, the motion parameters of the target are roughly estimated by the Fourier transformation of the m-D curve. Based on the rough estimation, the search method is employed to estimate the motion parameters of the cone target precisely. The validity of the proposed method is verified by the analysis data.

Keywords: Procession cone target · micro-Doppler features · Search method Precession parameters estimation

1 Introduction

Space target recognition is a key part of ballistic missile defense system. From launch to landing, the flight phase of the ballistic missile includes boost stage, middle section, and reentry stage. In the boost phase and reentry stage, the target flying time is short, and the missile defense system must complete target identification in a short time to implement effective interception. There is still no reliable solution to this problem. While the middle section is the longest flight time of the missile, and the space environment is relatively simple. Therefore, the current research of ballistic missile identification mainly focuses on the middle section [1]. In order to improve the survivability of missile and interfere with the work of missile defense system, the ballistic missile will take penetration measures such as releasing decoys and electromagnetic interference. In addition, at the end of the boost stage, the warheads and the propeller rockets will produce some debris, including booster rockets, mother cabins, etc. Thus, the target group in the middle section of the trajectory includes warhead targets, debris, bait and false targets, which fly at roughly at the same speed to form a diffuse threat band. The task of identifying the target in the middle target is to determine the position of the warhead target from the target group.

Micro-motion feature are often used to identify warhead targets. In order to ensure the reentry angle of attack, the warhead target is usually oriented by spin in the middle

© ICST Institute for Computer Sciences, Social Informatics and Telecommunications Engineering 2018
X. Gu et al. (Eds.): MLICOM 2017, Part II, LNICST 227, pp. 509–517, 2018.
https://doi.org/10.1007/978-3-319-73447-7_55

flight. When a spinning warhead target is disturbed, such as the release of the decoy or the separation of the projectile and rocket, certain precession or nutation occurs. However, the non-attitude control systems such as bait, decoy and debris usually do not have regular micro-motion features. Because the micro-motion features of warhead target are of great value to distinguish warhead and decoy. Therefore, the extraction of target micro-motion features from radar echoes and the estimation of micro-motion parameters have received extensive attention in the radar community [2–4]. The main tasks can be divided into two categories: the first is to extract target micro-motion features from wideband radar echoes, and the other is to extract target micro-motion features from narrowband radar echoes. Although the theory and method of the target precession parameters based on wideband radar echo are more studied, the technologies of narrowband radar system are more mature. The m-D spectrum of the target [5] can be obtained by narrow band radar, so it is of great practical significance to study target precession parameter estimation algorithm based on m-D spectrum.

2   Radar Echo Signal Model of Precession Cone Target

Radar observation of the precession of the cone-shaped target is shown in Fig. 1. Establish reference coordinate system O-XYZ: take the target centroid as the origin, and take the cone precession axis as the Z axis, and the cone top direction is the Z axis forward. Define the Y-axis and the initial time cone symmetry axis coplanar, and perpendicular to the Z axis. The X axis is determined by the right hand criterion. The angle between the target symmetry axis and the Z axis is the precession angle θ. The target is spinning at an angular velocity wr, and simultaneously coning at an angular velocity wc. The azimuth of the radar line of sight in the reference coordinate system is v. α is the mean angle of view, which represents the angle between the radar line of sight and the Z axis of the precession axis.

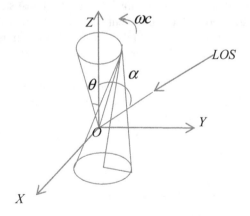

Fig. 1. The cone-shaped target model

As defined by the coordinate system, the unit vector of the precession axis in the reference coordinate system is: $\vec{e} = [0 \quad 0 \quad 1]^T$, the unit vector of radar sight in the reference coordinate system is: $\vec{n} = [\sin\alpha\cos v \quad \sin\alpha\sin v \quad -\cos v]^T$. Precession can be divided into two components, the rotation of a symmetrical axis and the rotation of the precession axis. Under the radar observation, the radial distance variation of P at any point of the precession cone target is investigated.

The position of P in target body coordinate system is $\vec{r}_0 = [x \quad y \quad z]^T$, and P in the reference coordinate position is $\vec{r}_1 = [X \quad Y \quad Z]^T$. Because of the precession of the target body, the coordinate transformation from the ontology coordinate system to the reference coordinate system is composed of three parts: the initial transformation matrix, the spinning transformation matrix and the coning transformation matrix. The initial conversion transformation matrix refers to the conversion of the target initial position to the reference coordinate system. As defined by the coordinate system, the reference coordinate system is obtained by the θ angles around the X axis from the initial time ontology coordinate system. The initial transformation matrix can be expressed as follows.

$$R_{int} = \begin{bmatrix} 1 & 0 & 0 \\ 0 & \cos\theta & \sin\theta \\ 0 & -\sin\theta & \cos\theta \end{bmatrix}. \tag{1}$$

At time t, the rotation matrix caused by the cone rotation can be represented as

$$R_c(t) = \exp(\hat{w}\,t). \tag{2}$$

where $\hat{w} = wc\,\hat{e}$ and $\hat{e}$ is the skew symmetric matrix formed by the unit vector $\vec{e}$ of the precession axis. According to the Rodrigues equation, the cone rotation transformation matrix (2) can be simplified as

$$R_c(t) = I + \hat{e}\sin wct + \hat{e}^2(1 - \cos wct) = \begin{bmatrix} \cos wct & -\sin wct & 0 \\ \sin wct & \cos wct & 0 \\ 0 & 0 & 1 \end{bmatrix}. \tag{3}$$

Similar to the coning transformation matrix, the rotation matrix of the target spins about the symmetry axis can be expressed as

$$R_s(t) = I + \hat{u}\sin wrt + \hat{u}^2(1 - \cos wrt). \tag{4}$$

where $\hat{u}$ is the skew symmetric matrix formed by unit direction vector $\vec{u}$ of the spin axis, the spin axis is the target symmetry axis. In the target body coordinate system: $\vec{u} = [0 \quad 0 \quad 1]^T$. Combining (4), the spin transition matrix can be obtained

$$R_s(t) = \begin{bmatrix} \cos wrt & -\sin wrt & 0 \\ \sin wrt & \cos wrt & 0 \\ 0 & 0 & 1 \end{bmatrix}. \tag{5}$$

Then the position of P in the reference coordinate system is

$$\vec{r}(t) = R_C(t) \bullet R_{init} \bullet R_s(t) \bullet \vec{r}_0. \tag{6}$$

Therefore, the radial distance from the radar to P is

$$\vec{r}(t) = R_0 + [R_C(t) \bullet R_{init} \bullet R_s(t) \bullet \vec{r}_0]^T \bullet \vec{n}. \tag{7}$$

Assuming that the scattering characteristics of the target can be represented by N equivalent scattering centers. Considering that the scattering center is an isotropic echo model, and σ_n is the scattering intensity of the nth scattering center. The fundamental frequency form of the forward target radar echo can be expressed as

$$s(t) = \sum_{n=1}^{N} \sigma_n \exp\left\{ j2\pi f_0 \frac{2r_n(t)}{c} \right\}. \tag{8}$$

According to the definition of m-D, the electron micrograph of the nth scattering center of the precession target is

$$f_{mD}^n = \frac{1}{2\pi} \frac{d\varphi(t)}{dt} = 2\frac{f_0}{c} \left[\frac{d}{dt} r_n(t) \right]. \tag{9}$$

3 Precession Parameter Estimation

3.1 Initial Value Estimation of Precession Parameters

It can be seen from the above, the radar baseband echo signal of the precession target is

$$s(t) = \sum_{n=1}^{N} \sigma_n \exp\left\{ j2\pi f_0 \frac{2r_n(t)}{c} \right\}. \tag{10}$$

Then the time-frequency analysis is done with short time Fourier transform (STFT):

$$|S(t,f)| = \sum_{n=1}^{N} |S_n(t,f)|^2 + 2 \sum_{a,b=1,a\neq b}^{N} |S_a(t,f)||S_b(t,f)| \cos(Kr_a(t) - Kr_b(t)). \tag{11}$$

$$S_n(t,f) = 2\Delta\tau\sigma_n \exp(-jKr_n(t)) \exp(-j2\pi ft) \sin c\left[2\pi\Delta\tau\left(f - f_{mD}^n(t)\right)\right]. \tag{12}$$

where $K = 4\pi f_0/\lambda$, $2\Delta\tau$ is the width of the window function for STFT [6]. According to [7, 8], the instantaneous frequency of the signal is the first-order moments of the time-frequency distribution:

$$f(t) = \frac{\int f |s(t,f)|^2 df}{\int |s(t,f)|^2 df}.$$ (13)

$$f(t) = \frac{\int f |s(t,f)|^2 df}{\int |s(t,f)|^2 df} = \frac{1}{|A|^2} \left(4\Delta\tau^2 A A_k^2 \sum_{n=1}^{N} f_{mD}^n(t) \right).$$ (14)

The instantaneous frequency of the target is equal to the linear superposition of the m-D frequency of the scattering points of the target. Through the spectral analysis of $f(t)$, we can get wr, wc, $wr + wc$. According to the prior knowledge of the space cone target, there is $wr + wc > wr > wc$, so the initial value of the spinning angular velocity and the coning angular velocity of the target can be determined as $\widehat{wr1}$, $\widehat{wc1}$. At this point, the accuracy of the estimated spinning frequency and coning spin frequency is limited by resolution, and the frequency resolution of the time-frequency plane is

$$\Delta f = 1/T.$$ (15)

where T is the accumulation time.

3.2 Optimal Value Estimation of Precession Parameters by Search Method

Based on the initial values, radar parameters and the observation time of the target, the maximum estimation error is determined as Δwc and Δwr. Suppose that $\widehat{wc} \in \left[\widehat{wc1} - \Delta wc, \widehat{wc1} + \Delta wc \right]$, $\widehat{wr} \in \left[\widehat{wr1} - \Delta wr, \widehat{wr1} + \Delta wr \right]$, and $\hat{\theta} \in [0, 90°]$. For any point P (x, y, z) on the target, the distance of the point and the echo signal can be obtained according to (7) and (8) respectively. Then the mean square error (MSE) of the echo signal and the real echo signal under this search parameters is calculated. When the estimate is consistent with the true value, the MSE reaches the minimum; otherwise, the MSE will increase. Therefore, the optimal estimation parameters can be determined according to the MSE of the estimated value and the true value $\widehat{wr1}$, $\widehat{wc1}$, and θ.

4 Simulations

The simulation circumstance is set up as follows: the radar frequency $f_0 = 10$ GHz. For the cone target, it is 2 m high, the bottom radius is 0.2 m, the distance between the center of mass and the center of the base is 0.4 m, the spin frequency is 3 Hz, the coning frequency is 1 Hz, and the precession angle $\theta = 18°$. The azimuth angle of the radar line of sight in the reference coordinate system $\alpha = 50°$, and the mean angle of view $v = 270°$. The precession parameters of the cone target are estimated by using the cone vertex P1 (0, 0, 1.6 m) and the bottom edge scattering point P2 (0, −0.2 m, −0.4 m). The radar sampling frequency is 1 kHz, the signal accumulation time is 2 s, and the Gaussian white noise is added to the echo, and SNR = 10 dB.

(1) Comparison of the calculated m-D spectra and the m-D spectra obtained by STFT.

The m-D spectrum of the precession target obtained by the simulation in Fig. 2 is basically consistent with the calculated m-D derived by the ideal formula. Thus, the correctness of the precession model can be explained, which lays a good theoretical foundation for the extraction of the following precession parameters.

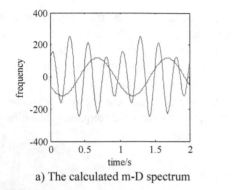
a) The calculated m-D spectrum

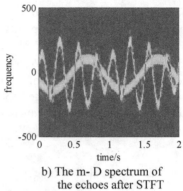
b) The m- D spectrum of
the echoes after STFT

Fig. 2. The calculated m-D spectrum

(2) The first-order moment method is used to estimate the instantaneous frequency of signals and to estimate the spinning and coning frequencies by Fourier transform roughly.

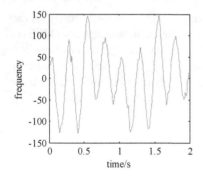

Fig. 3. Estimation of instantaneous
frequency

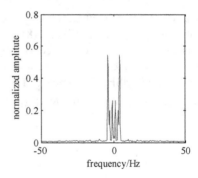

Fig. 4. A rough estimation of spinning
frequency and coning frequency

Figure 3 shows the instantaneous frequency of the signals. The three amplitude maximum are selected. The above theory shows that they correspond to the spinning frequency, coning frequency and the sum of the two frequencies respectively. According to a priori knowledge of the spatial cone target, the spinning frequency and the coning frequency is greater than the spinning frequency, and the spinning frequency is greater than the coning frequency. Figure 5 is obtained by partial amplification of Fig. 4. Therefore, the spinning frequency 3 Hz and the coning frequency 1 Hz can be estimated roughly.

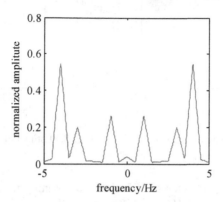

Fig. 5. The amplification of Fig. 4

(3) Accurate estimation of precession parameters by search method.

When the signal accumulation time is 2 s, the frequency estimation error is 0.5 Hz. The spinning frequency is searched in the range of 0.5 to 1.5 Hz based on the above-mentioned rough estimation of the spinning frequency and the coning frequency, and the spinning frequency is searched in the range of 2.5 to 3.5 Hz. The precession is searched in the range of 0–90°. The frequency step is 0.05 Hz, and the precession angle step is 1°.

As can be seen from Figs. 6, 7 and 8, the minimum of the MSE of the estimate and the true values is obtained at the spinning frequency of 3 Hz. Therefore, the spinning frequency of the cone target can be accurately estimated to be 3 Hz, which is exactly

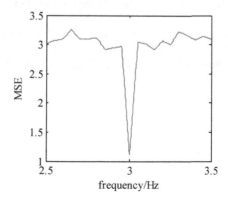

Fig. 6. Estimation of spinning frequency

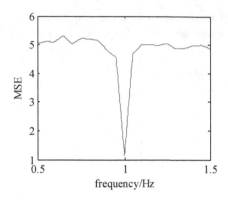

Fig. 7. Estimation of coning frequency

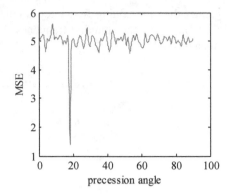

Fig. 8. Estimation of precession angle

the same as the model parameter set. Similarly, the coning frequency and precession angle of the cone target are 1 Hz and 18° respectively.

In general, the spinning frequency, coning frequency and precession angle estimated by the search method are exactly the same as those set in the model. The method provided in this paper can be effectively used in estimating the parameters of precession cone target.

5   Conclusion

In middle section of flight phase, for the common warhead with cone top and cone bottom, only the cone top scattering center and an equivalent scattering center on the cone bottom can be visible. A new method for estimating the precession parameters of a cone target based on the m-D spectrum of two scattering centers is proposed. The specific expressions of the m-D spectrum of the target cone top and the cone bottom scattering center of the precession cone are theoretically analyzed and deduced, and then a new method for estimating the parameters of the target precession is designed. Finally, the validity of the proposed method is verified by the simulation data.

Acknowledgments. This project is sponsored by the National Marine Technology Program for Public Welfare (No. 201505002), the National Natural Science Foundation of China (No. 61571157) and the Subject Guide Fund of Harbin Institute of Technology at Weihai (No. WH20150111).

References

1. Lin, J.: Technique of target recognition for ballistic missile. J. Modern Radar **30**(2), 1–5 (2008)
2. Wang, T., Wang, X.S., Chang, Y.L., et al.: Estimation of precession parameters and generation of ISAR images of ballistic; missile targets. J. IEEE Trans. Aerosp. Electron. Syst. **46**(4), 1983–1995 (2010)
3. Yao, H.Y., Sun, W.F., Ma, X.Y.: Precession and structure parameters estimation of cone-cylinder target bases on the HRRPs. J. Electron. Inf. Technol. **35**(3), 537–544 (2013)
4. Tian, S.R., Jiang, Y.H., Guo, R.J., et al.: Ballistic target micro-Doppler feature extraction method based on the time-frequency analysis. J. Modern Radar **34**(1), 40–43 (2012)
5. Chen, V.C., Li, F.Y., Ho, S.S., et al.: Micro-doppler effect in radar: phenomenon, model, and simulation study. J. IEEE Trans. Aerosp. Electron. Syst. **42**(1), 2–21 (2006)
6. Djurović, I., Popović-Bugarin, V., Simeunović, M.: The STFT-based estimator of micro-doppler parameters. J. IEEE Trans. Aerosp. Electron. Syst. **53**(3), 1273–1283 (2017)
7. Lovell, B.C., Williamson, R.C., et al.: The relationship between instantaneous frequency and time-frequency representations. J. IEEE Trans. Signal Process. **41**(3), 1458–1461 (1993)
8. Chen, V.C., Ling, H.: Time-Frequency Transforms for Radar Imaging and Signal Analysis. Artech House Inc., Boston (2001)

Automated Flowering Time Prediction Using Data Mining and Machine Learning

Runxuan Li[1], Yu Sun[2(⊠)], and Qingquan Sun[3]

[1] The Baylor School, Chattanooga, TN 37405, USA
runxuan.lil983548012@gmail.com
[2] Department of Computer Science, California State Polytechnic University,
Pomona, Pomona, CA 91768, USA
yusun@cpp.edu
[3] School of Computer Science and Engineering, California State University,
San Bernardino, San Bernardino, CA 92407, USA
qsun@csusb.edu

Abstract. This paper presents a solution for the predictions of flowering times concerning specific types of flowers. Since flower blooms are necessarily related to the local environment, the predictions (in months), are yielded by using machine learning to train a model considering the various environmental factors as variables. The environmental factors, which are temperature, precipitation, and the length of day, contribute to the chronological order of flowering periods. The predictions are accurate to a fraction of a month, and it can applied to control the flowering times by changing the values of the variables. The result provides an example of how data mining and machine learning presents itself to be a useful tool in the agricultural or environmental field.

Keywords: Flowering time · Machine learning · Data mining

1 Introduction

Understanding the patterns of nature and making use of it is a topic that is both practical and fascinating in the modern era. Not until the year 1996 did the American scientists applied the technology of genetic engineering and put the products into mass production. By studying and engineering a specific crop or plant, people understand the traits of living plants. Plants, just like humans, respond to a variety of environmental changes; the results of the responds are expressed directly on the exterior part of the plant through the accelerating or tardiness of the growth of leaves, the chronological delay or outstrip of flower blooms, or the time of the last stage of fruit maturity.

Flowers, tend to show more stability than those that are incapable of flowering in terms of the cycle that plants follow. Flowering plants rigidly follows the cycle of seed, germination, growth, reproduction, pollination, and seed spreading. The ultimate goal of any flowering plant is to reproduce fertile offsprings, and by flowering, those plants become capable of receiving or giving pollen to itself or other flowers in the same species [4]. After pollination, the flowers fall down from the plant, and the seed that carries the next generation replace the part where the flowers were. The seeds

© ICST Institute for Computer Sciences, Social Informatics and Telecommunications Engineering 2018
X. Gu et al. (Eds.): MLICOM 2017, Part II, LNICST 227, pp. 518–527, 2018.
https://doi.org/10.1007/978-3-319-73447-7_56

eventually grows into the prosperity of the original plant while the original plant goes on through the cycle of life once again.

The context that this paper focuses on is the flowering month of specific flowers. Every plant that goes through the process mentioned above have a flowering period, and in which the plant form the process of reproduction through seed spreading, and this period lasts from 1 to 6 months depending on the plant discussed. Despite so, the flowering month mentioned in this project is concerned with the average month of the year between the month that it starts flowering and the time it falls. For example, if the dahlia flower starts blooming in January and fall in March, the flowering month is set to be February (Fig. 1).

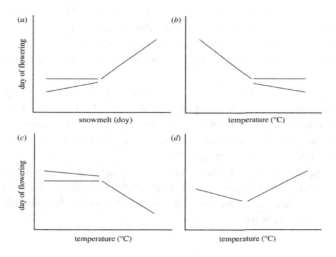

Fig. 1. Flowering time and temperature

Plants in nature take in a lot of different influences, and the time that it flowers can vary directly or implicitly determined by these influential factors. Wind, interference of insects or animals, and even the quality of air can affect the growth of a plant; the determination of which factors are the foremost of all that influence significantly to the flowering month of a plant can be a challenging problem. After making observations on the ten different types of flowers in different climatic environments that this research is based upon, a consensus is reached: the flowering time of the year for plants is extremely dependent on various factors: temperature, precipitation, and sunshine (length of day). These are the major independent variables in terms of the flowering time. The same observation also eliminated the effect of wind along with other factors due to their inconsequential effect that it would not change the flowering process by more than half a month. Finally, a conclusion is drawn that the major independent factors are the temperature, precipitation, and the length of day.

But of course, the effect of these factors contribute quite differently on distinct types of flowers. The effect exerted by temperature on cherry blossom might have a far more significant effect on the flowering month than it exerts on frangipani. It is indeterminant that if one factor exert a more significant influence than the other one. Furthermore, the impact of the same variable on two distinct flower types can have astonishingly distinct effects. For example, the lack of watering for sunflower might not be a big thing while iris definitely can not withstand a dry environment.

Due to the fact that the influence of each factor is different as mentioned in the previous paragraph, the amount of influence they can exert is believed to be a constant, and this constant, or fixed amount of influence is somewhat similar to the coefficient of a variable in a function. This suggests that people can look at the month of flowering of a plant as a function of several variables: type of flower, temperature, precipitation, and length of day. Furthermore, a rough model can be build based on these variables; this is viable, and more importantly, practical. Because researchers can use the model to estimate the month of flowering if they input the four variables that are requisite in terms of yielding a result. Nevertheless, since this model contains four separate variables, it is not a viable way to figure out the relations through manual calculations. Also, the correlations between the separate variables can yield a unique effect on the final result.

In this paper, we present a complete approach to model the flowering time using both data mining and machine learning techniques. A hybrid system (i.e., mobile and web) has been built to expose the prediction functionality to end users.

The rest of the paper is organized as follows: In Sect. 2 we explain the 3 major challenges that occurred in predicting the flowering month; Sect. 3 provides the solutions to solve for these problems with technical details; Sect. 4 demonstrates the experiments conducted to improve the accuracy of the prediction; Sect. 5 presents the related work, while Sect. 6 summarizes the project by giving a conclusion and providing future work directions.

2 Challenges

2.1 Challenge 1: The Diversity of Data Factors

As mentioned in Sect. 1, different types of flowers tend to bloom at different times in distinctive locations. For example, the flowering month of Cherry Blossom in Fuzhou Fujian, China in the year 2016 is promptly at April, but the flowering month for the same type of flower in Matsumae Hokkaido, Japan is around May [REF]. The location differences contribute to these distinct factors. In 2016, Fuzhou had a yearly average temperature of 69.25 Fahrenheit, a monthly average precipitation rate of 4.63 in., and an average length of day of 13 h. In the same year, Matsumae had different factors: temperature at 47.92 F, precipitation at 0.5 in., and the length of day at 12.25 h. Thus, the first challenge here is how to package these data factors in a way that leads to an effective prediction model.

2.2 Challenge 2: The Inefficiency of Processing Data Manually

Based on some of the flowering data factors mentioned above, it is a common misconception that the higher the temperature, bigger the precipitation, and the longer the length of day, the cherry blossom would bloom earlier. However, the problem often involves a large number of data, and it is time-consuming and error-prone to dig into the data and decide the effect of each manually.

Furthermore, the multi-dimensions of the data makes an infeasible task to accurately model manually. In the traditional way of manually doing this problem, researcher have to build 10 models of flowers in terms of the variables x, y, z, and this suggests that each model has to contain 3 separate equations of these three variables. In this case, the traditional method of manually working our way through is excluded from the solution methods. An alternative way of processing data needs to be found.

2.3   Challenge 3: The Unpredictable Variance of Factors Weight

Another similar challenge concerning the factors is that it is hard to understand the weight of each factors in terms of the impact to the flowering time. Apparently some of the factors weight less than others due to the fact that some flowers can blossom even in extreme environment. In general flowering time researches, researchers tend to directly look at the data and decide on the trend that flowers follow, but if the research becomes specific and needs accurate data for the month of flowering, the general analysis would not be very useful.

2.4   Challenge 4: The Difficulty of Selecting the Appropriate Training Model

After figuring out how we can solve the previous challenges, the question becomes what is the most accurate model that the predictions can be based upon. In other words, what type of regression should the research data be fitted in. Since the weight of factors represent the coefficients of the variables, the model represent the general equation which the data take form in. In this case, the data can be fit into various models, such as exponential model or linear model. The challenge is to acquire a model which yield the most accurate results.

3   Solution

In order to provide a solid solution that everyone can have access to, we have developed a machine learning approach to predict the flowering time based on a number of factors. The solution has been implemented in both a web-and a mobile-based application.

3.1   Data Model and Collection

As mentioned in the introduction, the task of modeling and dealing with data would be put upon machine learning and data mining. The process of this project is designed to be as the following:

(1) Gather the flowering information needed
(2) Change the information into data points

(3) Choose an accurate algorithm for the prediction
(4) Algorithm and back-end implementation
(5) Front-end development for both mobile and web

The method of the collection of data is similar to researching about the climate of a specific region. But gathering the information is a little more complicated. In order to accomplish step 1 in the procedure, research is one inevitable step. The information section contains the time when one type of flower blossom in one specific area, and by searching the temperature, precipitation and length of day in one year in that area, one data point is obtained. Then, the process is repeated over again, this time finding a new location in which the flower blossoms.

The hidden difficulty appears to be the first step of finding a place that have one type of flower. For some flowers, such as cherry blossom, is easy to extract information due to the fact that a lot of places (Washington DC., Hokkaido, etc.) held cherry blossom festivals. These festivals often have websites which tells the tourists when the cherry blossom tend to bloom and when they would fall. The following step is to get the information of the previous year in which the flower blossom. For example, Fig. 2 shows the cole flower in Fuzhou, Fujian China blossom in March in the year 2016.

Table 1

flower type	month	temp(F)	precipitation(in)	length of day(h)
primrose 1	3.3, 3, 2, 1, 2.5, 4	65.83, 69.25, 59.67, 65.58, 67.3, 69.1	0.97, 4.63, 2.9, 0, 1.7, 3.2	12.15, 13, 12.15, 13.25, 12.8, 13.2
tulip 2	4, 3, 6, 2, 1.5	68.58, 69.25, 50.3, 70.1, 70.3	0, 4.63, 2.14, 3.1, 4.5	13.25, 13, 12.7, 13.2, 13.23
dahlia 3	9, 8.5, 8, 7, 10	55.25, 60.08, 62.3, 63.4, 52.5	3.75, 1.39, 2.1, 3.62, 1.28	12.23, 12.18, 12.12, 13.23, 12.01
sunflower 4	10, 8, 6.5, 9, 7	50.67, 56.83, 68.17,52.7, 65.8	3.5, 2.93, 5.06, 2.7, 4.87	12.18, 12.23, 12.45,12.19, 12.65
cole 5	3, 4, 4.5, 6, 2.5,	69.25, 68.58, 59.67, 57.3, 70	4.63, 0, 2.9, 2.48, 3.63	13, 13.25, 12.15, 12.84, 13
cherry blossom 6	3, 5, 4, 2, 5.5	69.25, 47.92, 61.42, 70.23, 46.23	4.63, 0, 3.48, 4.72, 0,	13, 12.25, 12.17, 13.1, 12.13
iris 7	3, 6, 4, 1, 3.5	64.58, 59.67, 62.7, 70.43, 63.4	0, 2.9, 2.65, 3.23, 2.56	13.25, 12.15, 13.2, 13.3, 13.18
magnolia 8	3.5, 2.5, 1, 2, 4,	69.25, 68.58, 59.67, 63.17, 70.16	4.63, 0, 2.9, 1.8, 2.67	13, 13.25, 12.15, 12.07, 13.4
frangipani 9	8.5, 9, 5, 7, 6	62.25, 61.58, 69.67, 67.2, 68.37,	2.9, 0, 4.63, 3.24, 4.23	13.25, 12.25, 13.4, 13.32, 13.39
jasmin 10	8, 4, 6, 5, 7	69.25, 68.14, 64.2, 66.38, 68.69	4.63, 3.73, 3.38, 3.47, 2.96	13, 13.25, 12.98, 12.83, 13.3

Fig. 2. The data table for all flowers and factors

In this case, we went to the weather website containing the previous monthly average temperature, sum of precipitation, and average length of day; we extracted these data from April 2015 to March 2016 and averaged them in order to get exactly three numbers representing the three factors. After doing that, we put the data into a table ready for edit in order to export to the python program.

3.2   Machine Learning

Generally speaking, machine learning is a method of analyzing data and making predictions with auxiliary programs like Java, Matlab, C, etc. The program that we used in the research is Python. Unlike manually operating with a pen and paper, machine learning already have written programs for various types of algorithms, and the only job we are doing is to figure out which algorithm yield a result that is the closest to the precise flowering time.

The Python library has numerous algorithms that is provided by programmers, so it is really convenient to use. In the current edition of Python, to use the algorithms that the Python Community provided, programmers can type in the order "import", which represent the importation of a long written program and running it on the user's Python program. This is an easy and solid way to model the data, and furthermore, it save us time to try more than one or two algorithms in order to determine which one can make the prediction that is closest to the precise precise result.

In addition, we believe the issue around the question "At what conditions would a flower blossom in a specific month?" is worth researching upon. So we started a new group of codes based on the predictions of the old one. Given the the flowering month and the type of flower, the program would provide the user with the information concerning the three factors.

3.3   Web Service

After the completion of the program concerning the algorithm of the prediction, the file is working only locally. So the next task is to upload the program onto the web and let everyone with internet have excess to it. we bought a domain recently, so we uploaded the converted front end file to one of the sub-domains: http://flower.runxuanli.com. The client was developed using one side language: HTML, since it can work on any browser.

The webpage contains four boxes:

(1)   The flower type (labeled in numbers)
(2)   The monthly average temperature for one year
(3)   One year of precipitation
(4)   Average length of day in one year

After clicking the submit button when the data are typed in, another web page will pop up stating your predicted month. The month is expressed accurate to the hundredth place, which can be converted to days by multiplying 30 or 31 depending on the month. The flowering time is accurate to one hundredth of a month, and the result of the conversion is generally in the form of month plus days (Fig. 3).

3.4   Mobile App

The last step of the project is the development of a mobile app for the users to have a more easy access to the application. Some changes on the program were made in order to adapt the requirements of the mobile app. The basic preview of it is quite similar with front end web page; the user is asked to fill in the four boxes and hit submit (Fig. 4).

The challenges in the previous section is more or less addressed and solved for in this section. The research of gathering the data was made into a table and later applied in the Python Program for machine learning. Also, the deficiency of manual operation

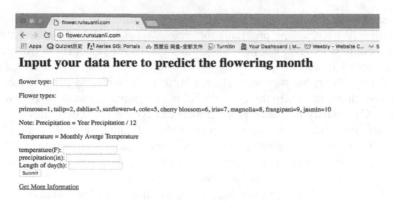

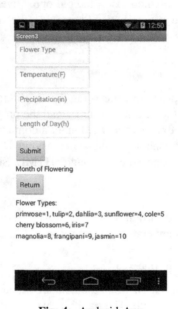

Fig. 3. Overview of the webpage

Fig. 4. Android App

and the problem concerning the weight of the factors is resolved by the powerful machine learning. Lastly, by various tentative approaches, the model which the data are fitted into is determined. Therefore, all of the major problems in the research are solved.

4   Experiments

In this section, we verify the accuracy of the algorithm that is currently in use. In addition, the verification also includes the experiments conducted using the variables other than the temperature, precipitation and length of day. Based on the result, we either verify that the algorithm in use is the most precise or change and improve the algorithm.

4.1   Experiment 1: The Accuracy of the Overall Prediction

The following experiments 2 and 3 will test the accuracy of the model in use in terms of algorithms and the factors chosen. However, the foremost auxiliary experiment that experiment 2 and 3 are persistently using but not mentioning the way to conduct it is the experiment that proves the model is accurate to what extent. When doing any kind of verifying, it is important to match the predicted result to the actual result. This method of experimenting is to take a number of data point that is one less than the number of data points that you obtained. After training the data points and fitting them into a model, try predicting by using the variables in the last data point. In this way, the result of the prediction can be compared with the result of the actual situation.

After doing the experiments 2 and 3, experiment 1 is always applied, and the result will be described in the following experiments.

4.2   Experiment 2: The Accuracy When Using Different Machine Learning Algorithms

Often the hardest part of solving a machine learning problem is finding the right estimator for the job. Different estimators are better suited for different types of data and different problems. And by far, there are too many models for the classical guess and check method. Therefore, we have to manually exclude some of the algorithms from our list.

There are two major groups of algorithms designated for machine learning: regression and classification. After providing data, the regression algorithm yields specific numbers as the result. This works similar as a function: when you input the "x value", the function gives you the "y value". In the classification algorithm, however, the computer groups the datas into clusters and designate which general cluster belongs to which group. For example, 3 apple trees have the following tree trunk lengths: 3 m, 3.5 m, and 3.6 m; Cherry trees have the following tree trunk length: 1 m, 1.2 m, and 1.3 m. If given a tree with the tree trunk length of 1.4 m, which tree is it? The classification algorithm would first group the datas together and tell you that the tree is a cherry tree. However, if you represent the apple tree with the number 1 and cherry tree with the number 2 and use one kind of regression to solve for the type of tree, the computer would not tell you what kind of tree it is, but would give an ambiguous answer like 2.3. And since we are operating the data to get a month, accurate to a hundredth of a month, regression will be our first choice.

However, by far the experiment had only solved half of the problem by eliminating one group of algorithms. We still have numerous algorithms in the regression group to choose from. After researching about the relationship between temperature and flowering, we found out that the flowering month corresponds to the temperature in the form of a parabola [2]. So we experimented on the even polynomials, and it turns out that the secondary polynomial gives the answer that is the most precise (Fig. 5).

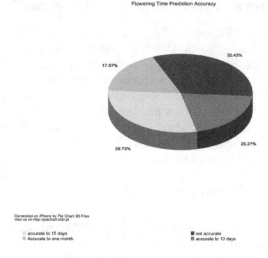

Flowering Time Prediction Accuracy

Fig. 5. Accuracy of prediction

4.3   Experiment 3: The Accuracy When Using Different Sets of Factors

Experiment 3 conducts an experiment that decides which factors should be added or subtracted that are used in coming up with the result. Like mentioned in the introductory section, temperature, precipitation, and length of day are not the only factors determining flower blooming; therefore, we decided to take two other factors: wind speed and humidity. We consider these two factors to be the most influential on the prediction and put them into the data set for the prediction.

It turns out that due to the erratic behavior of the wind speed, a discrepancy occurs in the prediction with the two factors and without the factors. And using the method described in experiment 1 of leaving out a data point to test the two methods, the one without adding the two factors appears to be the closest to the actual flowering time.

5   Related Work

There had been many studies concerning the reasons of flower bloom [1, 3, 5]. Most of them are focusing on the genetic part of the flowering process. Furthermore, these researches often focus only on one flower and how variety of influences tend to change the normal flowering time. This approach is tremendously useful for mass agricultural studies related to the biological field. However, these studies does not provide a solid reference for individual gardening practice since flowers as a genre of decorative plants, can be controlled in a more practically of watering and controlling the temperature.

6 Conclusion and Future Work

In conclusion, this project has derived information from more than 50 data points, using one machine learning based algorithm model to make predictions of flowering time. The practicability of machine learning applied on gardening practice is the foremost objective of this project. With a website and a mobile app, the practical achievement of the research is made accessible and tangible to the audience using the product.

In the long term, we hope to develop or get the permission to use a flower recognition app on the cellphone to correlate with the present project. If that app is developed, we will write a code using the Python Program to extract the information in terms of temperature, precipitation, and length of day in the specific region that the flower is spotted and taken a picture of. Then the data points will be added onto the original data sets and make the predictions more transparent and precise.

References

1. An, H., et al.: CONSTANS acts in the phloem to regulate a systemic signal that induces photoperiodic flowering of Arabidopsis. Development **131**, 3615–3626 (2004)
2. Shull, C.A.: Temperature and flowering. Bot. Gaz. **78**(2), 244–245 (1924)
3. Fornara, F., de Montaigu, A., Coupland, G.: SnapShot: control of flowering in Arabidopsis. Cell **141**, 550.e1 (2010)
4. Zeevaart, J.A.D.: Physiology of flower formation. Annu. Rev. Plant Physiol. **27**, 321–348 (1976)
5. Wellmer, F., Riechmann, J.L.: Gene networks controlling the initiation of flower development. Trends Genet. **26**, 519–527 (2010)
6. Iler, A.M., Høye, T.T., Inouye, D.W., Schmidt, N.M.: Nonlinear flowering responses to climate: are species approaching their limits of phenological change?
7. Ausubel, F.M., Brent, R., Kingston, R.E., Moore, D.D., Seidman, J.G., Smith, J.A., Struhl, K.: Current Protocols in Molecular Biology. Wiley, New York (1995)
8. Blazquez, M.A., Ahn, J.H., Weigel, D.: A thermosensory pathway controlling flowering time in Arabidopsis thaliana. Nat. Genet. **33**, 168–171 (2003)
9. Hutvagner, G., McLachlan, J., Pasquinelli, A.E., Balint, E., Tuschl, T., Zamore, P.D.: A cellular function for the RNA-interference enzyme Dicer in the maturation of the let-7 small temporal RNA. Science **293**, 834–838 (2001)
10. Hutvagner, G., Zamore, P.D.: A microRNA in a multiple-turnover RNAi enzyme complex. Science **297**, 2056–2060 (2002)
11. Kawasaki, H., Taira, K.: Hes1 is a target of microRNA-23 during retinoic-acid-induced differentiation of NT2 cells. Nature **423**, 838–842 (2003)
12. Olsen, P.H., Ambros, V.: The lin-4 regulatory RNA controls developmental timing in Caenorhabditis elegans by blocking LIN-14 protein synthesis after the initiation of translation. Dev. Biol. **216**, 671–680 (1999)
13. Tang, G., Reinhart, B.J., Bartel, D.P., Zamore, P.D.: A biochemical framework for RNA silencing in plants. Genes Dev. **17**, 49–63 (2003)
14. Xu, P., Vernooy, S.Y., Guo, M., Hay, B.A.: The Drosophila microRNA Mir-14 suppresses cell death and is required for normal fat metabolism. Curr. Biol. **13**, 790–795 (2003)

Spatial Crowdsourcing-Based Sensor Node Localization in Internet of Things Environment

Yongliang Sun[1,2]($\boxtimes$), Yejun Sun[1], and Kanglian Zhao[2]

[1] School of Computer Science and Technology,
Nanjing Tech University, Nanjing, China
syl_peter@163.com
[2] School of Electronic Science and Engineering, Nanjing University, Nanjing, China

Abstract. With the development of mobile computing, sensor technology and wireless communications, Internet of Things (IoT) has been one of the research hotspots in recent years. Because sensor node localization plays an important role in IoT, we propose a spatial crowdsourcing-based sensor node localization method in this paper. Based on the concept of spatial crowdsourcing, anchor nodes are assigned to new locations according to node location relationship for localization performance improvement. Then, unknown nodes are upgraded to be anchor nodes. Finally, localization coordinates are calculated with DV-Hop method. Simulation results prove that our proposed localization method outperforms DV-Hop method.

Keywords: IoT · Spatial crowdsourcing · Localization
Node upgradation

1 Introduction

Internet of Things (IoT) can be defined as a network of Internet-connected objects and is able to exchange data with sensors [1]. Based on Internet technology, IoT is developed as an extension and expansion of Internet, through which clients and objects are connected. Therefore, information acquisition and fusion have been the key technologies in IoT. Meanwhile, perceptions, recognition and other functions are mainly finished by sensor nodes, so the sensing layer of IoT that consists of sensor nodes is a necessary component [2,3].

In most scenarios, location information of sensor nodes is needed and makes the collected data meaningful. Therefore, sensor node localization plays an important role in IoT. Generally, localization methods can be divided into two classes: range-based and range-free localization methods. So far, many localization methods have been proposed for sensor node localization such as trilateration method, DV-Hop method and centroid method [4,5]. Meanwhile, machine learning and intelligent optimization algorithms are also applied for localization performance improvement [5–7].

© ICST Institute for Computer Sciences, Social Informatics and Telecommunications Engineering 2018
X. Gu et al. (Eds.): MLICOM 2017, Part II, LNICST 227, pp. 528–536, 2018.
https://doi.org/10.1007/978-3-319-73447-7_57

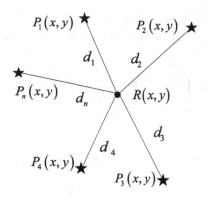

Fig. 1. Maximum likelihood method.

Recently, crowdsourcing has been an emerging concept. Crowdsourcing is the process of getting work or funding from a crowd of people online. The development of mobile computing and sensor technology has enhanced the capability of crowdsourcing [8]. As one of the crowdsourcing technologies, spatial crowdsourcing opens up a new mechanism for spatial tasks. These tasks are assigned according to workers' locations [9]. Based on the concept of spatial crowdsourcing, we try to apply spatial crowdsourcing to sensor node localization in order to achieve a better localization performance.

In this paper, we use a small number of anchor nodes to locate unknown nodes. In particular, we focus on the application of spatial crowdsourcing for sensor node localization in IoT and the influence of the anchor node locations on localization accuracy. In addition, unknown nodes are located and can also be upgraded to be new anchor nodes. Through simulation, we analyze the performance of our proposed localization method. Our proposed method is effective in reducing localization errors of sensor nodes in IoT.

The remainder of this paper is organized as follows: we review the related works in Sect. 2. The proposed localization method is described in detail in Sect. 3. The simulation results and analyses are given in Sect. 4. Finally, Sect. 5 concludes this paper.

2   Related Works

2.1   Maximum Likelihood Method

Maximum likelihood method is developed from trilateration method. Although trilateration method is simple, when the intersection of three circles cannot meet at one point, it is difficult to obtain accurate localization coordinates [5]. With multiple anchor nodes, we exploit maximum likelihood method in this paper. Through solving localization equations, we can get the location coordinates of an unknown node. Assume the distances between an unknown node $R(x, y)$ and nearby anchor nodes $P_1(x_1, y_1), P_2(x_2, y_2), \cdots, P_n(x_n, y_n)$ are $d_1, d_2, \cdots, d_n$, respectively. The adopted maximum likelihood localization method is shown in Fig. 1. According to the measured distances between nodes, the localization equations can be given by:

$$\begin{cases} (x - x_1)^2 + (y - y_1)^2 = d_1^2 \\ (x - x_2)^2 + (y - y_2)^2 = d_2^2 \\ \cdots \\ (x - x_n)^2 + (y - y_n)^2 = d_n^2 \end{cases} \tag{1}$$

Then the equations are solved and location coordinates can be denoted by:

$$X = \left(A^\mathrm{T} A\right)^{-1} A^\mathrm{T} B \tag{2}$$

where $X = \begin{pmatrix} x \\ y \end{pmatrix}$; $B = \begin{bmatrix} x_1^2 - x_n^2 + y_1^2 - y_n^2 + d_n^2 - d_1^2 \\ \vdots \\ x_{n-1}^2 - x_n^2 + y_{n-1}^2 - y_n^2 + d_n^2 - d_{n-1}^2 \end{bmatrix}$;

$A = \begin{bmatrix} 2(x_1 - x_n) & \cdots & 2(y_1 - y_n) \\ \vdots & \ddots & \vdots \\ 2(x_{n-1} - x_n) & \cdots & 2(y_{n-1} - y_n) \end{bmatrix}$. Therefore, the location coordinates

of unknown node $R(x, y)$ can be estimated.

2.2   DV-Hop Localization Method

DV-Hop method is considered as a distributed localization method with high localization accuracy [10]. First, this method needs to know the number of hops and distances between nodes, then the target node can be located. The method is divided into three steps as follows:

Step 1: Each anchor node carries location data, with which hop number can be estimated. Assume the communication radius is r and distance between nodes is d, then the hop number is estimated. As shown in Fig. 2, if r is larger than d, one hop is needed. If r is smaller than d, two hops are needed.

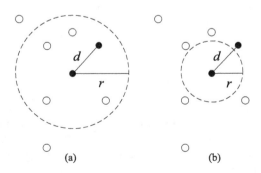

Fig. 2. Calculation of hop number with different r: (a) r is larger than d, (b) r is smaller than d.

Step 2: Through communications among these nodes, the distances between anchor nodes can be calculated, which are also obtained by other nodes. Then the average hop distance can be calculated by:

$$\bar{d} = \frac{\sum\limits_{j \neq i} \sqrt{(x_i - x_j)^2 + (y_i - y_j)^2}}{\sum\limits_{j \neq i} h_j} \tag{3}$$

where (x_j, y_j) represent the coordinates of anchor node j; (x_i, y_i) represent the coordinates of anchor node i; h_j represents the hop number of anchor node j to anchor node i; $\bar{d}$ is the mean hop distance.

Step 3: When the distance information is available to other nodes, the maximum likelihood method mentioned above is performed to calculate the final localization coordinates. In this paper, localization methods are compared with mean error, which can be calculated as follows:

$$e = \frac{\sum\limits_{i=1}^{N} \sqrt{(X_i - x_i)^2 + (Y_i - y_i)^2}}{N} \tag{4}$$

where (x_i, y_i) are the localization coordinates of node i; (X_i, Y_i) are the real coordinates of node i; e is the mean error.

2.3   Influence of Anchor Node Location on Localization Performance

Because if the coverage area of each anchor node is too large, the node resource will be wasted [11]. Thus, we need to adjust the locations of anchor nodes to enlarge the coverage area without overlap and also improve localization performance. When anchor nodes have the same radius, the ideal location relationship is that the intersect point is at the center of the triangle as shown in Fig. 3. At this time, the circle covers the larger area and better localization performance can be achieved [12]. In this paper, we applied spatial crowdsourcing to

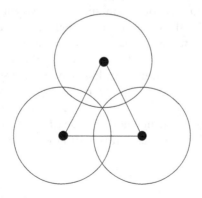

Fig. 3. Node location relationship.

sensor node localization. The locations of anchor nodes are adapted by spatial crowdsourcing to improve localization accuracy.

3   Proposed Localization Method

In this paper, we proposed a spatial crowdsourcing-based sensor node localization method that mainly has four steps: node movement, node selection, node upgradation, and DV-Hop localization. The flow chart of the proposed method is shown in Fig. 4.

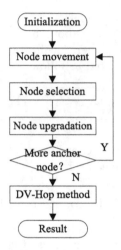

Fig. 4. Flow chart of the proposed method.

Assume the initial set of unknown nodes is $\boldsymbol{R} = \{R_i\,(x_i, y_i)\,|i = 1, 2, \cdots, N\}$ and the initial set of original anchor nodes is $\boldsymbol{P} = \{P_i\,(x_i, y_i)\,|i = 1, 2, \cdots, M\}$, in the beginning, anchor node $P_i(x_i, y_i), i \in \{1, 2, \cdots, M\}$ moves from location (x_i, y_i) to location (x'_i, y'_i) based on spatial crowdsourcing in order to compute a more accurate localization result. Then an unknown node is selected and upgraded to be a new anchor node. So the new set of anchor nodes can be denoted as $\boldsymbol{P'} = \{P_1\,(x_1, y_1), P_2\,(x_2, y_2), \cdots, P_M\,(x_M, y_M), R_i\,(x_i, y_i)\}$. In this paper, the node with minimum localization error is selected and upgraded. Although this selection method is not very practical, how to select nodes for upgradation is not concentrated in this paper. If more nodes are needed to be upgraded, then the original anchor nodes in set $\boldsymbol{P}$ move again based on spatial crowdsourcing. If not, then localization coordinates are calculated with DV-Hop method.

4   Experimental Results and Analyses

4.1   Experimental Setup

In this paper, we first set the node distribution area and randomly distribute the nodes. The node distribution area is a square area with dimensions of 100 m × 100 m. We let the numbers of anchor nodes and unknown nodes be 10 and 90, respectively, and the communication radius be 50 m. In this scenario, the mean error of sensor node localization with DV-Hop method is 34.51 m. The initial distribution of all the nodes is shown in Fig. 5.

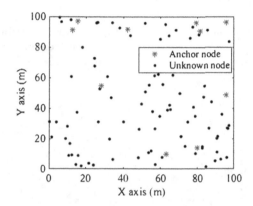

Fig. 5. Node initial distribution.

4.2   Localization Results with Anchor Nodes at Different Locations

As shown in Figs. 6 and 7, a simple example of node location influence on localization performance is given. We generate four nodes randomly. Three of them are anchor nodes and the other one is an unknown node. At first, the localization error is 16.53 m. One anchor node moves to a new location based on spatial crowdsourcing. Then the distribution of the anchor nodes approximates to the location relationship shown in Fig. 3. At this time, the localization error is reduced to 0.82 m. In practical, the possible area where the unknown nodes are deployed can be known, with which anchor nodes can move to better locations for localization.

4.3   Node Upgradation

Because upgrading unknown nodes to be anchor nodes can improve localization performance, we first deploy 3 original anchor nodes and move the original anchor nodes to better locations for localization, then we upgrade an unknown node to be a new anchor node one time. As mentioned before, we select the unknown node with minimum localization error for simplicity and then upgrade the node.

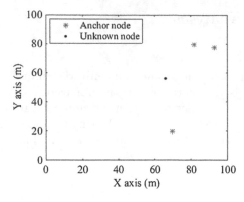

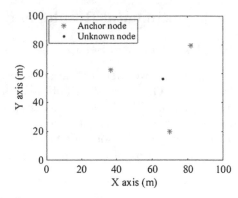

Fig. 6. Initial distribution of three anchor nodes.

Fig. 7. Node distribution after node movement based on spatial crowd-sourcing.

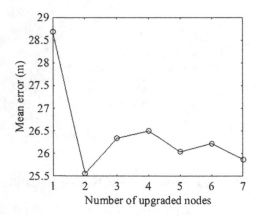

Fig. 8. Mean errors with different numbers of upgraded nodes.

Finally, localization coordinates are computed with DV-Hop method. In this paper, a total of 7 nodes are upgraded in turn and the mean errors with different numbers of upgraded anchor nodes are shown in Fig. 8.

In this paper, a total of 7 unknown nodes are upgraded to be anchor nodes. With the growth of anchor node number, the mean error first decreases sharply and reaches the minimum error. Then the mean error fluctuates, but it has a downward trend. As shown in Fig. 8, with three original anchor nodes, the minimum mean error is achieved when two unknown nodes are upgraded. The fluctuation is probably caused by random distribution of nodes. The mean errors with different numbers of anchor nodes are shown in Table 1. The simulation results show that our proposed method has a better localization performance with 10 anchor nodes than basic DV-Hop method whose mean error is 34.51 m.

Table 1. Mean errors with different numbers of anchor nodes

Anchor node number	4	5	6	7	8	9	10
Mean error (m)	28.68	25.56	26.35	26.50	26.04	26.22	25.87

5 Conclusion

In this paper, we study maximum likelihood method, DV-Hop method and influence of anchor node locations on localization performance in detail and also investigate the application of spatial crowdsourcing in sensor node localization. Then we proposed a spatial crowdsourcing-based sensor node localization method in IoT. Based on spatial crowdsourcing, anchor nodes move to new locations according to node location relationship for localization performance improvement. Then unknown nodes are upgraded as new anchor nodes and localization coordinates are computed by DV-Hop method. Simulation results show that our proposed localization method is able to achieve a better localization performance.

Acknowledgment. The authors gratefully thank the referees for the constructive and insightful comments. This work was supported by the National Natural Science Foundation of China under Grant No. 61701223, the Natural Science Foundation of Jiangsu Province under Grant No. BK20171023, and the Natural Science Foundation of the Jiangsu Higher Education Institutions of China under Grant No. 16KJB510014.

References

1. Perera, C., Zaslavsky, A., Christen, P., Georgakopoulos, D.: Context aware computing for the internet of things: a survey. IEEE Commun. Surv. Tutorials **16**(1), 414–454 (2014)
2. Zanella, A., Bui, N., Castellani, A., Vangelista, L., Zorzi, M.: Internet of things for smart cities. IEEE Internet Things J. **1**(1), 22–32 (2014)
3. Xu, L.D., He, W., Li, S.C.: Internet of things in industries: a survey. IEEE Trans. Industr. Inform. **10**(4), 2233–2243 (2014)
4. Sun, Y.L., Meng, W.X., Li, C., Zhao, N., Zhao, K.L., Zhang, N.T.: Human localization using multi-source heterogeneous data in indoor environments. IEEE Access **5**, 812–822 (2017)
5. Han, G.J., Jiang, J.F., Zhang, C.Y., Duong, T.Q., Guizani, M., Karagiannidis, G.K.: A survey on mobile anchor node assisted localization in wireless sensor networks. IEEE Commun. Surv. Tutorials **18**(3), 2220–2243 (2016)
6. Sun, Y.L., Xu, Y.B.: Error estimation method for matrix correlation-based Wi-Fi indoor localization. KSII Trans. Internet Inf. Syst. **7**(11), 2657–2675 (2013)
7. Li, S.C., Wang, X.H., Zhao, S.S., Wang, J., Li, L.: Local semidefinite programming-based node localization system for wireless sensor network applications. IEEE Syst. J. **8**(3), 879–888 (2014)
8. Ma, H.D., Zhao, D., Yuan, P.Y.: Opportunities in mobile crowd sensing. IEEE Commun. Mag. **52**(8), 29–35 (2014)
9. To, H., Shahabi, C., Kazemi, L.: A server-assigned spatial crowdsourcing framework. ACM Trans. Spatial Algorithms Syst. 1(1), 21–28 (2015)

10. Zheng, J., Wu, C., Chu, H., et al.: An improved DV-Hop localization algorithm. In: 2010 IEEE International Conference on PIC, vol. 1, pp. 469–471 (2010)
11. Guo, J., Jafarkhani, H.: Sensor deployment with limited communication range in homogeneous and heterogeneous wireless sensor networks. IEEE Trans. Wirel. Commun. **15**(10), 6771–6784 (2016)
12. Xiang, M.T., Sun, L.H., Li, L.H.: Survey on the connectivity and coverage in wireless sensor networks. In: 2011 International Conference on Wireless Communications, Networking and Mobile Computing, vol. 7, pp. 1–4 (2011)

Influence of Inter-channel Error Distribution on Mismatch in Time-Interleaved Pipelined A/D Converter

Yongsheng Wang[✉], Chen Yin, and Xunzhi Zhou

Micro-electronic Department, Harbin Institute of Technology,
92 West Dazhi Street, Nangang District, Harbin, China
{yswang,yinchen}@hit.edn.cn

Abstract. Influence of channel error distribution on inter-channel mismatches of pipelined time-interleaved A/D converters (TIADCs) is discussed in this paper. TIADC systems can increase the maximum sample rate, but the mismatch between the channels significantly reduce the systems' performance. This paper analyzes the mismatch in frequency domain, and discusses the influence of amplitude distribution of the inter-channel errors on the mismatch. Finally comes to a conclusion that when the error of one channel is equal to the median of the two adjacent channel errors, them is match of the overall TIADC system is minimal. According to simulation results, it can instruct a way to reduce the mismatch of TIADCs.

Keywords: Time-Interleaved ADC · Offset mismatch · Gain mismatch
Time sampling mismatch · Channel error distribution

1 Introduction

ADC's accuracy and speed directly restrict the performance of the communication system, such as the software radio [1], the intelligent communication, the intelligent positioning and navigation [2] etc. In order to pursue both high resolution and high speed, the time-interleaved ADC (TIADC) is widely used. However, channel mismatches in this structure such as offset mismatch, gain mismatch and time sampling mismatch which caused by circuit structure asymmetry and process deviation significantly reduce the system performance [3]. While Inter-channel mismatch of TIADC has been analyzed by behavioral modeling [4], and the influence of offset error, gain error and time sampling deviation on mismatches has been researched in [5–7], they have only analyzed the effect of errors within each channel on mismatches. Spurs produced by channel mismatch in output signal spectrum have been investigated in [8], however, they have only discussed the relationship between the spurs amplitude and the error within each channel.

In this paper, the inter-channel mismatch is analyzed in frequency domain and the results of the analysis indicate that not only the errors within each channel determine the frequency and amplitude of the spurs in output spectrum, but also the amplitude distribution of the inter-channel errors affects the magnitude of the spurs. The

© ICST Institute for Computer Sciences, Social Informatics and Telecommunications Engineering 2018
X. Gu et al. (Eds.): MLICOM 2017, Part II, LNICST 227, pp. 537–545, 2018.
https://doi.org/10.1007/978-3-319-73447-7_58

remainder of the paper is organized as followers. Section 2 introduces a modeling of TIADC and analyzes the inter-channel mismatch in frequency domain. Section 3 analyzes the influence of inter-channel error samplitude distribution on mismatches. Section 4 gives the simulation results and Sect. 5 concludes the paper.

2 Modeling of TIADC Mismatches

2.1 Modeling of Multi-channel TIADC

Several channel ADCs with high resolution but relatively slower sample rateconvert the input signal parallel in TIADC [3]. Figure 1 shows the model of a typical TIADC system.

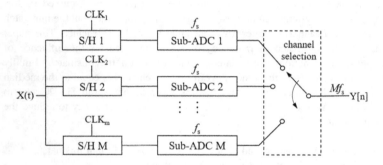

Fig. 1. Model of a typical TIADC system

When there are M channels and the time interval between adjacent channels is T_s, the sampling period of each sub-channel ADC is MT_s, and the sampling time of the m-th sub-channel ADC is $t_m = nMT_s + mT_s$, $n = 0, 1, 2 \ldots$; $m = 0, 1, 2 \ldots M - 1$. The discrete sampling sequence of each ideal sub-channel ADC can be obtained as follows [9],

$$\begin{cases} y_0 = [x(mMT_s)] \\ y_1 = [x(mMT_s + T_s)] \\ \quad \vdots \\ y_k = [x(mMT_s + kT_s)] \qquad m = 0, 1, 2, \ldots; k = 0, 1, 2, \ldots, M - 1 \quad (1) \\ \quad \vdots \\ y_{M-1} = [x(mMT_s + (M - 1)T_s)] \end{cases}$$

2.2 Mismatches in Frequency Domain

Assume that the offset error, gain error and sampling time deviation in each channel are $os_0, os_1, os_2, \ldots os_{M-1}$, $g_0, g_1, g_2, \ldots g_{M-1}$ and $\Delta t_0, \Delta t_1, \Delta t_2, \ldots \Delta t_{M-1}$. Therefore, the discrete sampling sequence of each sub-channel ADC can be obtained as follows,

$$
\begin{cases}
y_0 = [g_0 x(mMT_s + \Delta t_0) + os_0] \\
y_1 = [g_1 x(mMT_s + T_s + \Delta t_1) + os_1] \\
\quad \vdots \\
y_k = [g_k x(mMT_s + kT_s + \Delta t_k) + os_k] \\
\quad \vdots \\
y_{M-1} = [g_{M-1} x(mMT_s + (M-1)T_s + \Delta t_{M-1}) + os_{M-1}]
\end{cases}
\qquad m = 0, 1, 2, \ldots; k = 0, 1, 2, \ldots, M-1
$$

$$(2)$$

The above equation scan be seen as a sampling pulse sequence $p_g(t)$ sample the input signal $x(t + \Delta t_m)$, which deviate Δt_m with the ideal input signal $x(t)$. Where the sampling pulse sequence of the *k-th* channel is

$$
p_g(t) = \sum_{m=0}^{M-1} g_m \sum_{k=-\infty}^{+\infty} \delta(t - kMT_s - mT_s)
\tag{3}
$$

Its Fourier transform is

$$
P_g(j\omega) = 2\pi \sum_{m=-\infty}^{+\infty} C_{m,k} \delta\left(\omega - m\frac{\omega_s}{M}\right)
\tag{4}
$$

In the above equation,

$$
\begin{aligned}
C_{m,k} &= \frac{1}{MT_s} \int_{-MT_s/2}^{MT_s/2} p_k(t) e^{-j\frac{2\pi m}{MT_s}t} dt \\
&= \frac{1}{MT_s} \sum_{m=0}^{M-1} g_m \int_{-MT_s/2}^{MT_s/2} \sum_{n=-\infty}^{+\infty} \delta(t - nMT_s - kT_s) e^{-j\frac{2\pi m}{MT_s}t} dt \\
&= \frac{1}{MT_s} \sum_{m=0}^{M-1} g_m e^{-jkm\frac{2\pi}{M}}
\end{aligned}
\tag{5}
$$

According to the convolution theorem, the sampling output signal containing the gain mismatch and the sampling time mismatch is

$$
\begin{aligned}
Y_{g,t}(j\omega) &= \frac{1}{2\pi} FT[x(t + \Delta t_m)] * P_g(j\omega) \\
&= \frac{1}{2\pi} \left[X(j\omega) e^{j\omega \Delta t_m} \right] * P_g(j\omega) \\
&= \frac{1}{T_s} \sum_{k=-\infty}^{+\infty} \left[\left(\frac{1}{M} \sum_{m=0}^{M-1} g_m e^{-jkm\frac{2\pi}{M}} e^{j\left(\omega - k\frac{\omega_s}{M}\right)\Delta t_m} \right) \cdot X\left(\omega - k\frac{\omega_s}{M}\right) \right]
\end{aligned}
\tag{6}
$$

Since each channel samples the input signal as MT_s for the cycle, so the offset error can be expressed as

$$o(t) = \sum_{m=0}^{M-1} \sum_{n=-\infty}^{+\infty} os_m \cdot \delta(t - nMT - mT_s) \tag{7}$$

The Fourier transform of the above equation is

$$O(\omega) = \frac{2\pi}{T_s} \sum_{k=-\infty}^{+\infty} \left[\frac{1}{M} \sum_{m=0}^{M-1} os_m e^{-jkm\frac{2\pi}{M}} \cdot \delta\left(\omega - k\frac{\omega_s}{M}\right) \right] \tag{8}$$

According to the linear nature of Fourier transform, we can get the sampling signal spectrum that contains three kinds of mismatches as below

$$Y(j\omega) = \frac{1}{T_s} \sum_{k=-\infty}^{+\infty} \left(\frac{1}{M} \sum_{m=0}^{M-1} g_m e^{-jkm\frac{2\pi}{M}} e^{j\left(\omega - k\frac{\omega_s}{M}\right)\Delta t_m} \right) X\left(j\left(\omega - k\frac{\omega_s}{M}\right)\right)$$
$$+ \frac{2\pi}{T_s} \sum_{k=-\infty}^{+\infty} \left(\frac{1}{M} \sum_{m=0}^{M-1} os_m e^{-jkm\frac{2\pi}{M}} \delta\left(\omega - k\frac{\omega_s}{M}\right) \right) \tag{9}$$

Where we set

$$A(k) = \frac{1}{M} \sum_{m=0}^{M-1} g_m e^{-jkm\frac{2\pi}{M}} e^{j\left(\omega - k\frac{\omega_s}{M}\right)\Delta t_m} \tag{10}$$

$$B(k) = \frac{1}{M} \sum_{m=0}^{M-1} os_m e^{-jkm\frac{2\pi}{M}} \tag{11}$$

Equation (8) indicates that when there are M channels, the frequency of the spurs generated by the gain error and the sampling time deviation in the TIADC is located at $\omega = |\pm\omega_{in} + k\omega_s/M|$, $(k = 1, 2, \ldots M - 1)$ and the frequency of the spurs generated by the offset error is located at $\omega = k\omega_s/M$, $(k = 1, 2, \ldots M - 1)$. When there are three kinds of mismatches, the SINAD (Signal to noise and distortion ratio) is

$$SINAD = 10 \log_{10} \left(\frac{P_{signal}}{P_{noise} + P_{HD}} \right)$$
$$= 10 \log_{10} \left(\frac{A(0)^2}{\sum_{k=1}^{M-1} A(k)^2 + \sum_{k=0}^{M-1} B(k)^2} \right) \tag{12}$$

3   Inter-channel Error Distribution

Equation (8) shows the amplitude of spurs is related to the coefficients $A(k)$ and $B(k)$. $A(k)$ and $B(k)$ can be regarded as the offset error, gain error and sampling time deviation of each sub-channel equidistant distribute in the unit circle $e^{-jk2\pi}$ and then accumulate. So the amplitude distribution of the errors between the channels will affect the coefficients $A(k)$ and $B(k)$. Next, a four-channel ADC will be used as an example to discuss the influence of the amplitude distribution of the offset error, the gain error and the sampling time deviation on the coefficients $A(k)$ and $B(k)$.

Equation (10) indicates that the magnitude of the offset error affects only the coefficient $B(k)$. When the number of channels $M = 4$, by Nyquist sampling theorem there should be $k\omega_s/M \le \omega_s/2$ in Eq. (10), therefore $k \le 2$. When $k = 0$, there should be $\omega = 0$ to make $\delta(\omega - k\omega_s/M) \ne 0$, it is expressed as a frequency independent of the DC component in the output spectrum, so needn't consider it. Then substitute $k = 1$ and $k = 2$ into Eq. (10), we can get

$$
\begin{aligned}
B(1) &= \frac{1}{4}\left(os_0 + os_1 e^{-j\frac{\pi}{2}} + os_2 e^{-j\pi} + os_3 e^{-j\frac{3}{2}\pi}\right) \\
&= \frac{1}{4}[os_0 - os_2 + j(os_1 - os_3)]
\end{aligned}
\tag{13}
$$

$$
\begin{aligned}
B(2) &= \frac{1}{4}\left(os_0 + os_1 e^{-j\pi} + os_2 e^{-j2\pi} + os_3 e^{-j3\pi}\right) \\
&= \frac{1}{4}(os_0 - os_1 + os_2 - os_3)
\end{aligned}
\tag{14}
$$

Since the mismatch between channels is caused by the relative error between the channels, the 0th channel is regarded as the standard channel, that is to make the 0th channel as a reference, therefore $os_0 = 0$. So the errors $os_k (k = 1, 2, 3)$ present in the remaining channels refer to the relative error between the k-th channel and the standard channel, rather than the absolute error relative to the ideal case.

Equation (11) indicates that the effect of spurious mismatches on SINAD is determined by the square sum of the spurious coefficient $B(k)$. Therefore, for the four-channel ADC there is

$$
\begin{aligned}
B(1)^2 + B(2)^2 &= \frac{1}{16}\left[(-os_2 + (os_1 - os_3))^2 + (os_2 - (os_1 + os_3))^2\right] \\
&= \frac{1}{8}\left(os_1^2 + os_2^2 + os_3^2 - 2os_1 os_2\right)
\end{aligned}
\tag{15}
$$

Since the first channel and the third channel have a phase difference of π, and are symmetrically distributed at the center of the second channel, it is assumed that $|os_1| = |os_3|$, so the Eq. (14) becomes

$$B(1)^2 + B(2)^2 = \frac{1}{8}\left(2os_1^2 - 2os_1os_2 + os_2^2\right) \tag{16}$$

In the same way, for gain error and sampling time deviation, there are

$$A(1)^2 + A(2)^2 = \frac{1}{8}\left(2g_1^2 - 2g_1g_2 + g_2^2\right) \tag{17}$$

$$A(1)^2 + A(2)^2 = \frac{1}{8}\left(2e^{2j\omega_{in}\Delta t_1} - 2e^{j\omega_{in}(\Delta t_1 + \Delta t_2)} + e^{2j\omega_{in}\Delta t_2}\right) \tag{18}$$

So when $|os_1| = |os_3| = \frac{1}{2}|os_2|$, $|g_1| = |g_3| = \frac{1}{2}|g_2|$ and $\left|e^{j\omega_{in}\Delta t_1}\right| = \left|e^{j\omega_{in}\Delta t_3}\right| = \frac{1}{2}\left|e^{j\omega_{in}\Delta t_2}\right|$, the above Eqs. (15)–(17) respectively has a minimum $\frac{1}{16}|os_2|^2$, $\frac{1}{16}|g_2|^2$ and $\frac{1}{16}\left|e^{j\omega_{in}\Delta t_2}\right|^2$.

Therefore, it can be concluded that for the multi-channel ADC, when the absolute amplitude of the error in the k-th channel is the intermediate value of the absolute amplitude of the error in the $k - 1th$ channel and the $k + 1th$ channel, the spurs generated by the mismatch has the least effect on the SINAD of the whole ADC system, so that the ADC has the largest ENOB (Effective number of bits).

4 Simulation Results

In this section a four-channel 12bits ADC will be used as an example to simulate and verify the conclusion. The 0th channel of the ADC is regarded as a standard channel. That is to make the 0th channel as a reference with no mismatch error in it. The errors in the remaining channels refer to the relative error to the 0th channel, rather than the absolute error relative to the ideal case.

In the following simulation, 0.5% of the offset error, 10 dB gain error and 200ps sampling time deviation are added in the second channel, by changing the magnitude of the error in the first and third channels to verify the influence of the error amplitude distribution on the mismatch. The input signal frequency $\omega_{in} = 12.5488\,\text{MHz}$. According to the analysis in the Sect. 3, we assume that the errors in the 1st and 3rd channels are the same.

When the 1st and 3rd channel does not exist any error, the output signal spectrum is shown in Fig. 2. The amplitude of the spurs produced by offset mismatch at $\omega_s/4$ and $\omega_s/2$ are -52.64 dB and -67.69 dB respectively. The amplitude of the spurs produced by gain mismatch and time sampling mismatch at $\pm\omega_{in} + \omega_s/4$ and $\omega_s/2 - \omega_{in}$ are -48.72 dB, -48.23 dB and -49.04 dB respectively. The SINAD of the whole TIADCsystem is 42.7923 dB and the ENOB is 6.8153 bits.

When the error of the 1st and 3rd channel is the half of the error of the 2nd channel, that is 0.25% of the offset error, 5 dB gain error and 100ps sampling time deviation are added in the 1st and 3rd channels, the output signal spectrum is shown in Fig. 3. The amplitude of the spurs produced by offset mismatch at $\omega_s/4$ and $\omega_s/2$ are -52.64 dB and -83.11 dB respectively. The amplitude of the spurs produced by gain mismatch and time sampling mismatch at $\pm\omega_{in} + \omega_s/4$ and $\omega_s/2 - \omega_{in}$ are -48.72 dB,

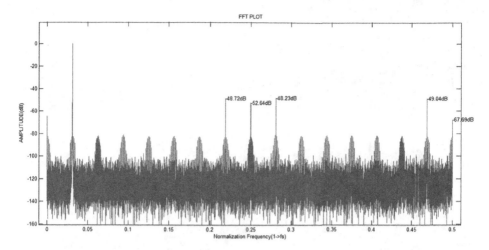

Fig. 2. Output signal spectrum without error in the 1st and 3rd channels

−48.24 dB and −80.08 dB respectively. The SINAD of the whole TIADC system is 44.2959 dB and the ENOB is 7.0651 bits.

When the error of the 1st and 3rd channel is the same as the error of the 2nd channel, that is 0.5% of the offset error, 10 dB gain error and 200ps sampling time deviation are added in the 1st and 3rd channels, the output signal spectrum is shown in Fig. 4. The amplitude of the spurs produced by offset mismatch at $\omega_s/4$ and $\omega_s/2$ are −52.64 dB and −67.71 dB respectively. The amplitude of the spurs produced by gain mismatch and time sampling mismatch at $\pm\omega_{in} + \omega_s/4$ and $\omega_s/2 - \omega_{in}$ are −48.73 dB, −48.24 dB and −49.06 dB respectively. The SINAD of the whole TIADC system is 42.7345 dB and the ENOB is 6.8057 bits.

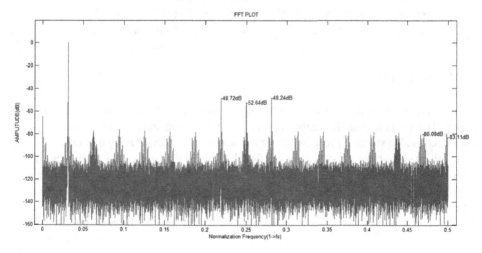

Fig. 3. Output signal spectrum under conditions that the 1st and 3rd channels' error is half of the 2nd channel

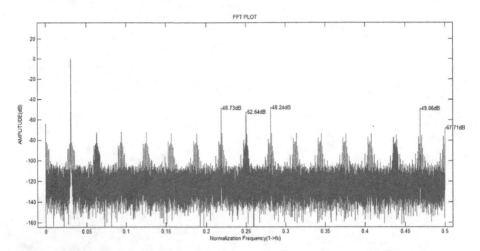

Fig. 4. Output signal spectrum under conditions that the 1st and 3rd channels' error is same as the 2nd channel

From simulation results, it is indicated that when the error of the 1st and 3rd channel is the half of the error of the 2nd channel, the amplitudes of the spurs which frequency at $\omega = \omega_s/2$ decreases almost 15 dB and that at $\omega = \omega_s/2 - \omega_{in}$ decreases almost 30 dB. The comparison of the results under three difference cases is shown in the Table 1.

Table 1. Comparison of results under three cases

	SINAD	ENOB	$\omega = \omega_s/2$	$\omega = \omega_s/2 - \omega_{in}$
No error	42.79 dB	6.8153	−67.69 dB	−49.04 dB
Half of the 2nd channel	44.30 dB	7.0651	−83.11 dB	−80.08 dB
Same as the 2nd channel	42.73 dB	6.8057	−67.71 dB	−49.06 dB

5 Conclusion

Three kinds of inter-channel mismatches in the frequency domain are analyzed in this paper. The influence of the amplitude distribution of the inter-channel errors on the mismatch is also studied. From results of the theoretical analysis and simulation results, it is indicated that not only the errors of each channel determine the frequency of the spurs which produced by mismatches in the output spectrum, but also the amplitude distribution of the inter-channel errors affects the magnitude of the spurs. Especially when the error of the 1st and 3rd channel is the half of the error of the 2nd channel, the amplitudes of part of the spurs decrease almost 15 dB and 30 dB respectively.

References

1. Ferrari, P., Flammini, A., Sisinni, E.: New architecture for a wireless smart sensor based on a software-defined radio. IEEE Trans. Instrum. Meas. **60**(6), 2133–2141 (2011)
2. Kristoffersen, S., Hoel, K.V., Thingsrud, Ø., Kalveland, E.B.: Digital coherent processing to enhance moving targets detection in a navigation radar. In: 2014 International Radar Conference, Lille, pp. 1–6 (2014)
3. Pereira, J.M.D., Girao, P.M.B.S., Serra, A.M.C.: An FFT-based method to evaluate and compensate gain and offset errors of interleaved ADC systems. IEEE Trans. Instrum. Meas. **53**(2), 423–430 (2004)
4. Jridi, M., Monnerie, G., Bossuet, L., Dallet, D.: Two time-interleaved ADC channel structure: analysis and modeling. In: Proceedings of 2006 IEEE Instrumentation and Measurement Technology Conference, Sorrento, pp. 781–785 (2006)
5. Huynh, V.T.D., Noels, N., Steendam, H.: Effect of offset mismatch in time-interleaved ADC circuits on OFDM-BER performance. IEEE Trans. Circuits Syst. I: Regul. Pap. **PP**(99), 1–12
6. Yin, Y., Yang, G., Chen, H.: A novel gain error background calibration algorithm for time-interleaved ADCs. In: 2014 International Conference on Anti-Counterfeiting, Security and Identification (ASID), Macao, pp. 1–4 (2014)
7. Zhang, Y., Zhu, X., Chen, C., Ye, F., Ren, J.: A sample-time error calibration technique in time-interleaved ADCs with correlation-based detection and voltage-controlled compensation. In: 2012 IEEE Asia Pacific Conference on Circuits and Systems, Kaohsiung, pp. 128–131 (2012)
8. Leger, G., Peralias, E.J., Rueda, A., Huertas, J.L.: Impact of random channel mismatch on the SNR and SFDR of time-interleaved ADCs. IEEE Trans. Circuits Syst. I Regul. Pap. **51**(1), 140–150 (2004)
9. Vogel, C., Kubin, G.: Analysis and compensation of nonlinearity mismatches in time-interleaved ADC arrays. In: 2004 IEEE International Symposium on Circuits and Systems, (IEEE Cat. No. 04CH37512), vol. 1, pp. I-593–6 (2004)

Distributed Joint Channel-Slot Selection for Multi-UAV Networks: A Game-Theoretic Learning Approach

Jiaxin Chen[1(✉)], Yuhua Xu[2], Yuli Zhang[2], and Qihui Wu[1]

[1] Nanjing University of Aeronautics and Astronautics, Nanjing 211106, China
{chenjiaxin0507,wuqihui2014}@sina.com
[2] PLA University of Science and Technology, Nanjing 210007, China
yuhuaenator@gmail.com, yulipkueecs08@126.com

Abstract. Unmanned aerial vehicle (UAV) has found promising applications in both military and civilian domains worldwide. In this article, we investigate the problem of distributed opportunistic spectrum access under the consideration of channel-slot selection simultaneously in multi-UAV networks from a game-theoretic perspective, and take into account the distinctive features of the multi-UAV network. We formulate the distributed joint channel-slot selection problem as a weighted interference minimization game. We prove that the formulated game is an exact potential game, and then use the distributed stochastic learning automata based joint channel and time slot selection algorithm to achieve the pure-strategy Nash equilibrium. The algorithm does not need information exchange among UAVs in the network which is more suitable for dynamic and practical enviroment. The simulation results demonstrate the effectiveness of the algorithm.

Keywords: Multi-UAV network · Joint channel-slot selection
Weighted interference minimization game
Potential game · Stochastic learning automata

1 Introduction

Unmanned aerial vehicle (UAV) has found promising applications in military areas and holds an important position in complex tactical offensive/defensive missions and natural security, such as surveillance and reconnaissance [1,2], information collection, etc. Meanwhile, its broad potential applications in the civilian domain have drawn great attention all over the world. It can be applied

This work was supported in part by the Natural Science Foundation for Distinguished Young Scholars of Jiangsu Province under Grant BK20160034, in part by the National Science Foundation of China under Grant 61631020, Grant 61671473, and Grant 61401508, and in part by the Open Research Foundation of Science and Technology on Communication Networks Laboratory.

© ICST Institute for Computer Sciences, Social Informatics and Telecommunications Engineering 2018
X. Gu et al. (Eds.): MLICOM 2017, Part II, LNICST 227, pp. 546–557, 2018.
https://doi.org/10.1007/978-3-319-73447-7_59

in many fields such as source seeking [3], target detection and localization [4], disaster sensing [5], communication coverage expansion [6].

With the development of technology, the multi-UAV network has been attached much attention to accomplish complex and dangerous tasks. The task of how to allocate scarce spectrum resource and mitigate the interference among the UAVs should be first addressed. Fortunately, opportunistic spectrum access (OSA) has been regarded as an efficient technology to deal with the spectrum shortage problem. Amount of research on OSA, e.g., [7–9], validates its effectiveness, therefore the solution can be applied in multi-UAV networks.

However, most existing research about OSA technology only studies either the channel resource or time slot resource. The limited spectrum resources can not meet the communication demands of large-scale multi-UAV network in the future, it is desirable to use time resource reasonably [10]. Therefore, the joint channel-slot selection scheme is one of the most powerful methods to solve the issues discussed above. Meanwhile, compared with the OSA systems in [7–9], there are several distinctive features of the multi-UAV network: (1) UAVs in the same cluster tend to choose the same channel when they have enough time slot resource; (2) considering the spatial locations of UAV clusters, the utility of the cluster is only affected by its nearby clusters, namely its neighbors; and (3) the experienced interference of UAV n can be divided into intra-cluster and inter-cluster interference, which represent the interference among UAVs belonging to the same cluster as UAV n and the neighboring clusters respectively.

The main contributions of this article are summarized as follows:

(1) We investigate the joint channel-slot selections of UAVs. Moreover, we distinguish intra-cluster and inter-cluster interference by formulating this problem as a weighted interference minimization game. The game is an exact potential game with at least one pure-strategy Nash equilibrium. Futhermore, this solution can minimize the aggregate interference level.

(2) In the distributed stochastic learning automata based joint channel and time slot selection algorithm, we consider the random payoff with the distinctive feature of multi-UAV network, e.g., UAVs in the same cluster choose the same channel when the slot resource is enough to suppress interference.

The remainder of this article is organized as follows. Section 2 discusses the system model and problem formulation. In Sect. 3, we formulate the weighted interference minimization game model and present theorem for the existence of NE. Then we use SLA based algorithm to achieve the optimum. Finally, simulation results for verifying the proposed game model are discussed in Sect. 4 while Sect. 5 contains the conclusion of this article plus some open issues for further work.

2   System Model and Problem Formulation

2.1   System Model

Consider a multi-UAV network involving N UAVs which belong to Q clusters. There are M channels and T time slots available for UAVs in each cluster.

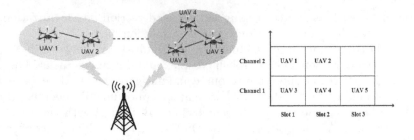

Fig. 1. Corresponding interference graph of the multi-UAV network example, where the dotted lines represent the interference between two UAV clusters while the solid lines mean the interference among the UAVs in the same cluster.

Denote UAV set and cluster set as $\mathcal{N} = \{1, 2, ..., N\}$ and $S_{\mathcal{Q}} = \{S_1, S_2, ..., S_{\mathcal{Q}}\}$ respectively; moreover, the set of the available channel is $\mathcal{M} = \{1, 2, ..., M\}$. Similarly, the time slot set is denoted as $\mathcal{T} = \{1, 2, ..., T\}$. Suppose that the UAVs in the same cluster affect each other due to the connectivity inside the UAV cluster. Meanwhile, when the distance between two clusters is far enough, they will not cause mutual interference when choosing the same channel at the same time. That is, the communication of any cluster only directly affects the neighboring clusters. Therefore, for an arbitrary UAV n, the interference can be divided into intra-cluster and inter-cluster interference level. Motivated by these observations, we define the set of UAVs which are located in the same cluster with UAV n as $U_n = \{i \in S_q, i \neq n\}$. Similarly, we denote the neighboring UAV cluster set of UAV cluster S_q as J_{S_q}, i.e., $J_{S_q} = \{S_k \in S_{\mathcal{Q}} : d_{S_q S_k} < d_0\}$; moreover the set of UAVs in the J_{S_q} can be defined as $J_n = \{j \in S_k : S_k \in J_{S_q}\}$. An example topology of multi-UAV network is illustrated in Fig. 1.

2.2 Problem Formulation

Suppose that all channels and time slots are available for multi-UAV network. The interference emerges when two or more UAVs select the same channel to communicate at the same time. Let $a_n = (c_n, t_n)$ be the channel and slot chosen by UAV n, where $c_n \in \mathcal{M}, t_n \in \mathcal{T}$. The intra-cluster and inter-cluster interference level are defined as follows.

$$s_{n(in)} = \sum_{i \in U_n} f(a_n, a_i) \tag{1}$$

$$s_{n(out)} = \sum_{i \in J_n} f(a_n, a_i). \tag{2}$$

where $f(a_n, a_i)$ is the function defined as:

$$f(a_n, a_i) = \begin{cases} 1, & c_n = c_i \quad and \quad t_n = t_i \\ 0, & others. \end{cases} \tag{3}$$

Note that $s_{n(in)}$ and $s_{n(out)}$ are in different positions, we consider the weighted interference level as $s_n = \alpha s_{n(in)} + (1-\alpha)s_{n(out)}$, where α is weight satisfies $0 < \alpha < 1$. Then we have:

$$s_n = \alpha \sum_{i \in U_n} f(a_n, a_i) + (1-\alpha) \sum_{i \in J_n} f(a_n, a_i). \tag{4}$$

The weight α is designed to balance the tradeoff between $s_{n(in)}$ and $s_{n(out)}$. Obviously, the influence of the intra-cluster interference is more serious than the other one. Therefore, we usually have $0.5 < \alpha < 1$.

The individual interference will be minimized if the number of UAVs using the same channel resource to communicate at the same time decreases. Therefore, in order to guarantee communication quality, we need to find an optimal combination of the joint channe-slot selections to minimize the aggregate interference level of all UAVs in the multi-UAV network, namely:

$$P1 : a \in \min \sum_{n \in \mathcal{N}} s_n. \tag{5}$$

3 Weighted Interference Minimization Game and Distributed Learning Algorithm

3.1 Weighted Interference Minimization Game Model

We formulate the problem of joint channel-slot selection for multi-UAV network mentioned above as a non-cooperative game, which is denoted as $\mathcal{F} = \{\mathcal{N}, \{\mathcal{A}_n\}_{n \in \mathcal{N}}, \{u_n\}_{n \in \mathcal{N}}\}$. In this game, $\mathcal{N} = \{1, 2, ..., N\}$ is a set of UAVs, which are regarded as the players in this game. $\mathcal{A}_n$ is a set of available actions for UAV n, and u_n is the utility function of UAV n. For presentation, the action space of UAV n is $\mathcal{A}_n = \{c_1, c_2, ..., c_M\} \otimes \{t_1, t_2, ..., t_T\}$, where "$\otimes$" is the Cartesian product. $u_n(a_n, a_{-n})$ is regarded as the utility function of the game, where $a_n = (c_n, t_n)$ is the action of UAV n, and $a_{-n} = (c_{-n}, t_{-n})$ represents the action profile of all UAVs excluding UAV n. Since the analysis of the interference mentioned before, the utility of any UAV n is influenced by its own action and the action profile of UAVs in U_n and J_n [8]. Therefore, we can define the set $B_n = U_n \cup J_n$, and then the utility function of UAV n can be expressed as $u_n(a_n, a_{B_n})$.

Note that in order to guarantee the communication connectivity and individual performance, each UAV expects to experience a lower interference level. Thus, we design the utility function as follows:

$$u_n(a_n, a_{B_n}) = -s_n. \tag{6}$$

where s_n represents the weighted interference level of UAV n which is specified by (4). Therefore, the ultimate goal of the proposed game is to maximize the utility function for each UAV, namely:

$$\max_{a_n \in \mathcal{A}_n} u_n(a_n, a_{B_n}), \forall n \in \mathcal{N}. \tag{7}$$

3.2   Analysis of Nash Equilibrium

Nash equilibrium (NE) [11] is the well-known stable solution in game model. Exact potential game (EPG) [11] is one of the most attractive potential games with several perfect features. For a game, it is an EPG if the change in the utility of an arbitrary player because of its own selection deviation leads to exactly the same in the potential function. The most important and excellent properties of EPG are: (1) every EPG has at least one pure-strategy NE, (2) the NE is the solution that can optimize the problem. We study the existence of NE for the weighted interference minimization game and the following theorem provides characterization of the formulated game.

Theorem 1. *The weighted interference minimization game $\mathcal{F}$ is an EPG with at least one pure-strategy NE. The solution can minimize the aggregate interference level of the multi-UAV network.*

Proof. Motivated by [8], we can obtain the following potential function:

$$\phi(a_n, a_{-n}) = -\frac{1}{2} \sum_{n \in \mathcal{N}} s_n(a_1, a_2, ...a_N)$$
$$= \underbrace{-\frac{1}{2}\alpha \sum_{n \in \mathcal{N}} \sum_{i \in U_n} f(a_n, a_i)}_{\phi 1(a_n, a_{-n})} \underbrace{-\frac{1}{2}\beta \sum_{n \in \mathcal{N}} \sum_{i \in J_n} f(a_n, a_i)}_{\phi 2(a_n, a_{-n})}. \tag{8}$$

Then, we define $\mathcal{I}_n(a_n, a_{U_n})$ as the set of UAVs in U_n using the same channel to communicate at the same time slot with UAV n, i.e.

$$\mathcal{I}_n(a_n, a_{U_n}) = \{i \in U_n : a_i = a_n\} \tag{9}$$

where U_n is the set of UAVs located in the same cluster with UAV n. Then the notation $|\mathcal{I}_n(a_n, a_{U_n})|$ means the number of UAVs in $\mathcal{I}_n(a_n, a_{U_n})$. Similarly, $\mathcal{H}_n(a_n, a_{J_n})$ can be defined as follows:

$$\mathcal{H}_n(a_n, a_{J_n}) = \{i \in J_n : a_i = a_n\}. \tag{10}$$

Accordingly, the utility function can be given as follows:

$$u_n(a_n, a_{B_n}) = \underbrace{-\alpha\left|\mathcal{I}_n(a_n, a_{U_n})\right|}_{u1_n(a_n, a_{B_n})} \underbrace{-\beta\left|\mathcal{H}_n(a_n, a_{J_n})\right|}_{u2_n(a_n, a_{B_n})}. \tag{11}$$

Note that the mathematical forms of the intra-cluster and inter-cluster interference are similar, for the sake of simplicity, we only give the proof of intra-cluster interference.

It is assumed that an arbitrary UAV n in the network changes its joint channel-slot selection from $a_n = (c_n, t_n)$ to $a_n^* = (c_n^*, t_n^*)$ while others keep their selections unchanged. The change in utility function $u1_n(a_n, a_{B_n})$ is $\Delta u1_n$:

$$\Delta u1_n = u_n(a_n^*, a_{B_n}) - u1_n(a_n, a_{B_n}) = \alpha[|\mathcal{I}_n(a_n, a_{U_n})| - |\mathcal{I}_n(a_n^*, a_{U_n})|]. \tag{12}$$

Then we discuss the change in $\phi 1(a_n, a_{-n})$ due to the unilateral joint channel-slot selection change of UAV n is $\Delta \phi 1$:

$$\Delta \phi 1 = \frac{1}{2} \alpha \{ |\mathcal{I}_n(a_n, a_{U_n})| - |\mathcal{I}_n(a_n^*, a_{U_n})| + \sum_{k \in \mathcal{I}_n(a_n, a_{U_n})} [|\mathcal{I}_k(a_k, a_{U_k})| - |\mathcal{I}_k(a_k, a_{U_k}^*)|]$$
$$+ \sum_{k \in \mathcal{I}_n(a_n^*, a_{U_n})} [|\mathcal{I}_k(a_k, a_{U_k})| - |\mathcal{I}_k(a_k, a_{U_k}^*)|] + \sum_{k \in \mathcal{I}, k \neq n} [|\mathcal{I}_k(a_k, a_{U_k})| - |\mathcal{I}_k(a_k^*, a_{U_k})|] \} \cdot$$
$$(13)$$

In (13), we define $\mathcal{I} = \mathcal{N} \backslash \{ \mathcal{I}_n(a_n, a_{U_n}) \cup \mathcal{I}_n(a_n^*, a_{U_n}) \}$. It means that $\mathcal{I}_n(a_n, a_{U_n})$ and $\mathcal{I}_n(a_n^*, a_{U_n})$ are excluded from $\mathcal{N}$. Since the selection of UAV n only affects the UAVs in U_n, the following equations hold:

$$|\mathcal{I}_k(a_k, a_{U_k})| - |\mathcal{I}_k(a_k, a_{U_k}^*)| = 1, \forall k \in \mathcal{I}_n(a_n, a_{U_n}) \tag{14}$$

$$|\mathcal{I}_k(a_k, a_{U_k})| - |\mathcal{I}_k(a_k, a_{U_k}^*)| = 1, \forall k \in \mathcal{I}_n(a_n^*, a_{U_n}) \tag{15}$$

$$|\mathcal{I}_k(a_k, a_{U_k})| - |\mathcal{I}_k(a_k^*, a_{U_k})| = 0, \quad \forall k \in \mathcal{I}, k \neq n. \tag{16}$$

The detailed proof of inter-cluster interference is omitted here to avoid unnecessary repetition. According to the equations above, we can easily have:

$$u_n(a_n^*, a_{B_n}) - u_n(a_n, a_{B_n}) = \phi(a_n^*, a_{-n}) - \phi(a_n, a_{-n}). \tag{17}$$

The Eq. (17) satisfies the definition of EPG [12]. Due to the attractive features of EPG, Theorem 1 is proved. □

3.3 Distributed Stochastic Learning Automata Based Algorithm

The distributed algorithm without information exchange is needed with the aim of achieving the NE more practically. We use a distributed SLA based algorithm which is proposed in [7]. In this algorithm, each UAV selects its channel and time slot in accordance with its mixed strategy, and then updates its mixed strategy according to certain rules in (18) which is related to the received random payoff. The algorithm in detail is given later and the asymptotic behavior of the algorithm is given and proved in [7] (Theorem 6).

The received payoff function can affect the selections of UAVs and influence the performance of the learning algorithm. In order to develop comprehensive random payoff and make full use of the unique feature of the multi-UAV network, we consider the received random payoff from two aspects. On the one hand, each UAV wants to mitigate the experienced interference, which motivates us to develop the random payoff as the decreasing function of the interference level. On the other hand, when an arbitrary UAV chooses the same channel with the UAVs in the same cluster at different time slots, it can get reward value.

According to the analysis above, we design the following random payoff received by UAV n:

$$r_n(k) = D - \varepsilon \cdot s_n + \eta \sum_{i \in U_n} g(a_n, a_i). \tag{20}$$

Algorithm 1. The Distributed SLA Based Joint Channel and Time Slot Selection Algorithm

---

Initialization: set $k = 1$ and initialize each UAV's joint channel and time slot selection probability vector to $q_{nm}(k) = \frac{1}{MT}, \forall n \in \mathcal{N}, m \in \mathcal{A}_n$.
Loop $k = 1, 2, ...$
1: Each UAV n randomly selects its action $a_n(k) = (c_n(k), t_n(k))$ in accordance with its current selection probability vector $\mathbf{q}_n(k)$.
2: Each UAV uses selected actions to communicate and then receives a random payoff $r_n(k)$ characterized by (22).
3: According to the received random payoff, each UAV follows the following rules to update their probability vector:

$$\begin{aligned} q_{nm}(k+1) &= q_{nm}(k) + \sigma \tilde{r}_n(k)(1 - q_{nm}(k)), & m = a_n(k) \\ q_{nm}(k+1) &= q_{nm}(k) - \sigma \tilde{r}_n(k)q_{nm}(k), & m \neq a_n(k) \end{aligned} \qquad (18)$$

where σ is the learning step size satisfies $0 < \sigma < 1$ and $\tilde{r}_n(k)$ is the following normalized received payoff:

$$\tilde{r}_n(k) = r_n(k)/r_{\max}. \qquad (19)$$

where $r_{\max} = D + \eta \cdot (T - 1)$ is the interference-free and reward-full payoff, T is the number of time slots.
End Loop

---

where $D > 0$ is a predefined constant so that the received payoff remains positive, ε and η are weights, s_n is the weighted interference level and $g(\cdot)$ is the function defined as follows:

$$g(a_n, a_i) = \begin{cases} 1, & c_n = c_i \quad and \quad t_n \neq t_i \\ 0, & others. \end{cases} \qquad (21)$$

In (20), the purpose of the proposed weights ε and η are to balance the experienced interference and received reward. The function $g(\cdot)$ means the number of UAVs in the same cluster with UAV n which choose the same channel but the different time slots compared with UAV n. However, the predefined positive constant D affects the convergence of the algorithm if D is too large. On the contrary, if D is too small, the received random payoff will be negative. Thus we modify:

$$r_n(k) = \max\{r_n(k), 0\}. \qquad (22)$$

4   Simulation Results and Discussion

We conduct the simulation from three aspects: the influence of weight α, convergence behavior and performance evaluation so as to demonstrate the effectiveness of the SLA based algorithm and the formulated game model. All UAVs located in a $1000\,\mathrm{m} \times 500\,\mathrm{m}$ rectangle region. To distinguish the neighboring UAV clusters, we set the distance as $150\,\mathrm{m}$. There are $M = 2$ channels and $T = 2$ time slots. In order to reduce the interference among UAVs and increase the probability for UAVs located in the same cluster to choose the same channels, we choose $\varepsilon = 0.7$ and $\eta = 0.3$. The learning step size is $\sigma = 0.15$ and the predefined constant $D = 1.8$.

4.1 The Influence of Weight α

The weight α is designed to measure the importance of intra-cluster interference. A larger value for the weight α will increase the significance of intra-cluster interference. Figure 2 shows the variation trend of the two kinds of interference when α ranges from 0 to 1. There is an upward trend in the inter-cluster interference when α increases from 0 to 1. That means smaller α leads to lower inter-cluster interference level. When $\alpha = 0$, that means we only consider the inter-cluster interference no matter how high the intra-cluster interference is and vice versa. We choose $\alpha = 0.7$ in this simulation.

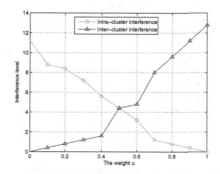

Fig. 2. The interference level comparison with different weight α.

4.2 Convergence Behavior

Figure 3 illustrates a considered multi-UAV network topology where the neighboring UAV cluster sets vary from cluster to cluster. For example, the neighboring UAV cluster set of the 4 clusters are $J_{S_1} = \{2\}$, $J_{S_2} = \{1, 3, 4\}$, $J_{S_3} = \{2, 4\}$ and $J_{S_4} = \{2, 3\}$ respectively.

The joint channel and slot selection probabilities of UAV cluster S_1 is presented in Fig. 4. At the beginning, UAV 1 and UAV 2 choose actions randomly with equal probabilities. As the algorithm iterates, they finally converge to different selections. Moreover, Table 1 shows the selections of all UAVs. We can summarize that each UAV select the same channel but different slots due to the reward when there are only two UAVs in the same cluster. When the number of UAV becomes larger, other UAVs select the other channel because the intra-cluster interference is more serious. The results validate the effectiveness of the payoff function.

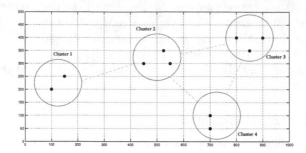

Fig. 3. An example topology of the multi-UAV network with 10 UAVs and 4 clusters lcoated in the rectangle region. The small solid black dots represent the UAVs and the large dashed blue circles mean the UAV clusters. The red dotted lines represent the existence of interference between the two clusters. (Color figure online)

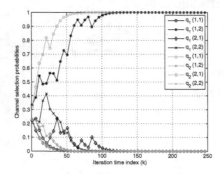

Fig. 4. The convergence of the SLA based algorithm of UAV cluster S_1

Table 1. Joint channel and slot selections of UAVs

UAV cluster	UAV	Channel selection	Slot selection
S_1	No. 1	1	2
	No. 2	1	1
S_2	No. 3	2	1
	No. 4	1	1
	No. 5	2	2
S_3	No. 6	2	1
	No. 7	1	1
	No. 8	1	2
S_4	No. 9	2	2
	No. 10	2	1

4.3   Performance Evaluation

First, we compare the aggregate interference level in different scenarios. We consider the multi-UAV network involving 2 channels, 2 slots and the number of UAVs increasing from 8 to 14 located in each cluster randomly. For comparison, we develop 4 methods: random selection, best NE, worst NE, and the SLA based algorithm. The results shown in Fig. 5 can be listed as follows: (i) when the number of the UAVs becomes larger, the aggregate interference level becomes higher; (ii) the learning solution is almost the same as the best NE because the learning solution asymptotically achieves global optimum.

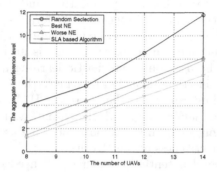

Fig. 5. The aggregate interference level when varying the number of UAVs. The number of channels and slots are $M = 2$ and $T = 2$ respectively.

Second, we compare the aggregate interference level in different numbers of available channels. We consider 5 approaches: optimal, random selection, best NE, worst NE, and the SLA based algorithm. Figure 6 shows the comparison among the 5 methods in terms of the aggregate interference level by increasing the channels from 1 to 4. Some significant results can be obtained from the

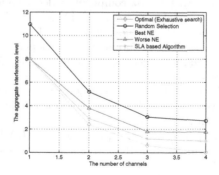

Fig. 6. The aggregate interference level when varying the number of channels. The simulation scenario is given in Fig. 3. The number of slots is $T = 2$.

Fig. 6: (i) with the increase of the number of channels, the aggregate interference level becomes lower; (ii) the best NE can obtain the best performance which is the same as the optimal one (exhaustive search), and the learning solution is very close to them; (iii) when the number of channel is 4, it means there are 8 selections for each UAV, the system can fulfill the demand of the UAVs.

5   Conclusion

In this article, we investigated the problem of distributed opportunistic spectrum access under the consideration of channel-slot selection simultaneously in multi-UAV network from a game-theoretic perspective, and took into account the distinctive features of the multi-UAV network. We formulated the joint channel-slot selection problem as a weighted interference minimization game. We proved that the weighted interference minimization game is an exact potential game with, and then used the distributed stochastic learning automata based joint channel and time slot selection algorithm to achieve the Nash equilibrium. The algorithm did not need information exchange among UAVs in the network which was more suitable for dynamic and practical enviroment. The simulation results showed that the learning solution was almost the same as the optimal solution which validated the effectiveness of the algorithm.

There are still several potential research issues needed to be studied. For instance, the ground station can allocate different numbers of time slots to different UAV clusters dynamically due to its load. Moreover, we can consider the business requirements for different UAVs and the formation of the UAV clusters. The resaerch of these factors will continue in the future.

References

1. Scherer, J., Rinner, B.: Persistent multi-UAV surveillance with energy and communication constraints. In: 2016 IEEE International Conference on Automation Science and Engineering (CASE), pp. 1225–1230. IEEE, Piscataway (2016)
2. Bhaskaranand, M., Gibson, JD.: Low complexity video encoding and high complexity decoding for UAV reconnaissance and surveillance. In: 15th IEEE International Symposium on Multimedia (ISM), pp. 163–170. IEEE Press, New York (2013)
3. Han, J., Chen, Y.: Multiple UAV formations for cooperative source seeking and contour mapping of a radiative signal field. J. Intell. Robot. Syst. **74**(1–2), 323–332 (2014). Springer, Dordrecht
4. Minaeian, S., Liu, J., Son, YJ.: Vision-based target detection and localization via a team of cooperative UAV and UGVs. IEEE Trans. Syst. Man Cybern. **46**(7), 1005–1016 (2016). IEEE, Piscataway
5. Luo, C.B., Nightingale, J., Asemota, E., Grecos, C.: A UAV-cloud system for disaster sensing applications. In: 81st IEEE Vehicular Technology Conference (VTC Spring), pp. 1–5. IEEE Press, New York (2015)
6. Koulali, S., Sabir, E., Taleb, T., Azizi, M.: A green strategic activity scheduling for UAV networks: a sub-modular game perspective. IEEE Commun. Mag. **54**(5), 58–64 (2016). IEEE, Piscataway

7. Xu, Y.H., Wang, J.L., Wu, Q.H., Anpalagan, A., Yao, Y.D.: Opportunistic spectrum access in unknown dynamic environment: a game-theoretic stochastic learning solution. IEEE Trans. Wirel. Commun. **11**(4), 1380–1391 (2012). IEEE, Piscataway
8. Xu, Y.H., Wang, J.L., Wu, Q.H., Anpalagan, A., Yao, Y.D.: Opportunistic spectrum access in cognitive radio networks: global optimization using local interaction games. IEEE J. Sel. Topics Sig. Process. **6**(2), 180–194 (2012). IEEE, Piscataway
9. Wu, Q.H., Xu, Y.H., Wang, J.L., Shen, L., Zheng, J.C., Anpalagan, A.: Distributed channel selection in time-varying radio environment: interference mitigation game with uncoupled stochastic learning. IEEE Trans. Veh. Technol. **62**(9), 4524–4538 (2013). IEEE, Piscataway
10. Wang, H.C., Wang, J.L., Wang, C.C., Wang, L., Ren, J., Cheng, F.Y.: Joint frequency and time resource partitioning for OFDM-based small cell networks. Wirel. Netw. https://doi.org/10.1007/s11276-016-1429-2. (Published Online)
11. Monderer, D., Shapley, L.S.: Potential games. Games Econ. Behav. **14**, 124–143 (1996)

Ship Detection in SAR Using Extreme Learning Machine

Liyong Ma$^{(\boxtimes)}$, Lidan Tang, Wei Xie, and Shuhao Cai

School of Information and Electrical Engineering,
Harbin Institute of Technology, Weihai 264209, China
maly@hitwh.edu.cn

Abstract. Ship detection is an important issue in many aspects, vessel traffic services, fishery management and rescue. Synthetic aperture radar (SAR) can produce real high resolution images with relatively small aperture in sea surfaces. A novel method employing extreme learning machine is proposed to detect ship in SAR. After the image preprocessing, some features including entropy, contrast, energy, correlation and inverse difference moment are selected as features for ship detection. The experimental results demonstrate that the proposed ship detection method based on extreme learning machine is more efficient than other learning-based methods with prior performance of accuracy, time consumed and ROC.

Keywords: Ship recognition · Extreme learning machine
Synthetic aperture radar (SAR)

1 Introduction

Ship detection is an important issue in many aspects, vessel traffic services, fishery management and rescue. Traditional ship detection method such as patrol ships or aircrafts are costly and limited by many circumstances, coverage area and weather condition. Particularly, because of many air cash in recent years, ship detection has become more and more important for ship monitoring and ship searching to save people in time.

Synthetic aperture radar (SAR) can produce images of objects, such as landscapes and sea surfaces. SAR is usually mounted on mobile platforms such as aircrafts. The movement of platform can acquire a lager synthetic antenna and provide better azimuth resolution. Generally speaking, the larger aperture is, the higher image of resolution it will be, no matter the aperture is physical or synthetic. For these reason, SAR can produce a real high resolution image with relatively small aperture. There are many other advantages for us to use SAR images. SAR images can be obtained in many circumstances, regardless of whether it is during day or night, rain or snow. SAR system can be so useful when optical tools can not be used.

© ICST Institute for Computer Sciences, Social Informatics and Telecommunications Engineering 2018
X. Gu et al. (Eds.): MLICOM 2017, Part II, LNICST 227, pp. 558–568, 2018.
https://doi.org/10.1007/978-3-319-73447-7_60

SAR has been widely used for ship detection. A K-means clustering and land masking method was reported on a novel method in coastal regions of SAR images in [1]. A morphological component analysis method was developed in [2] to achieve satisfactory results in complex background SAR images. A new technique using color and texture from spaceborne optical images as a complementary to SAR-based images was employed in [3].

Some ship detection methods using SAR based on common machine learning algorithms were also reported. Neural network based method was used in SAR to acquire better results in rough water and false alarm rates in [4]. Texture features from SAR image to discriminates speckle noise from ship was also reported in [5]. A method based on support vector machines (SVM) combined with grid optimization was employed for false alarm removal in [6], and tensor based approaches were also reported in [7,8]. There are some papers that use deep learning in SAR for ship detection [9], they present a high network configuration used for ship discrimination.

Extreme learning machine (ELM) is a machine learning algorithm with simple optimization parameters, fast speed and good generalization performance [10–12]. It has been widely used in many applications of image processing and machine vision [13–15]. In comparison with SVM, ELM has a simple implementation and requires less optimization works. Meanwhile, ELM has better learning performance with fast speed for its better generalization ability while SVM can just achieve sub-optimal solutions with higher computational complexity. In this paper, we perform ship recognition in SAR employing ELM method. One of the main contributions of this paper is that an efficient ship recognition method employing ELM for SAR is proposed.

2   Extreme Learning Machine

ELM algorithm includes two steps. The first step is data mapping where input data are mapped into the hidden layer employing random feature mapping or kernel learning approach. The second step is output. The final output can be obtained by multiplying the middle results with their corresponding weights. Different from the traditional learning process of three-layer neural networks where all the parameters are tuned iteratively and severe dependency of the parameters between different layers limits the learning performance, the hidden layer is non-parametric in ELM. This simple policy leads to the smallest training error and the smallest norm of weights, therefore ELM can achieve superior generation performance over other learning approaches for neural networks. ELM is able to improve the performance of single hidden layer neural network which is low and easy to be trapped in local minimums.

Denote the training sample as $(\mathbf{x}_i, \mathbf{t}_i)$, $i = 1, ..., N$, the input feature vectors $\mathbf{x} = [\mathbf{x}_1, \mathbf{x}_2, ..., \mathbf{x}_N]^T \in \mathbb{R}^{D \times N}$, and the label of the supervised sample output $\mathbf{t}_i = [t_{i1}, t_{i2}, ..., t_{iM}]^T \in \mathbb{R}^M$, where N is the sample number, D is the dimension size of the input sample feature vector, and M is the number of network output nodes those are used to solve multi-classification problems.

Denote the number of hidden layer nodes as L, the output of a hidden node indexed by i is

$$g(\mathbf{x}; \mathbf{w}_i, b_i) = g(\mathbf{x} \cdot \mathbf{w}_i + b_i). \tag{1}$$

where $i = 1, ..., N$, $\mathbf{w}_i$ is the input weight vector between the i-th hidden nodes and all input nodes, g is the activation function, and b_i is the bias of this node. A feature mapping function which connects the input layer and the hidden layer is

$$\mathbf{h}(\mathbf{x}) = [g(\mathbf{x}; \mathbf{w}_1, b_1), g(\mathbf{x}; \mathbf{w}_2, b_2), ..., g(\mathbf{x}; \mathbf{w}_L, b_L)]. \tag{2}$$

Denote the output weight between the i-th hidden node and the j-th output node as β_{ij}, where $i = 1, ..., L$, and $j = 1, ..., M$. The value of j-th output node can be obtained by

$$f_j(\mathbf{x}) = \sum_{i=1}^{L} \beta_{ij} \times g(\mathbf{x}; \mathbf{w}_i, b_i)). \tag{3}$$

Thus the output vector of the input sample $\mathbf{x}$ at he hidden layer can be described as

$$\mathbf{f}(\mathbf{x}) = [f_1(\mathbf{x}), f_2(\mathbf{x})..., f_M(\mathbf{x})] = \mathbf{h}(\mathbf{x})\boldsymbol{\beta}, \tag{4}$$

where

$$\boldsymbol{\beta} = \begin{bmatrix} \beta_1 \\ \vdots \\ \beta_L \end{bmatrix} = \begin{bmatrix} \beta_{11} & \cdots & \beta_{1M} \\ \vdots & \ddots & \vdots \\ \beta_{L1} & \cdots & \beta_{LM} \end{bmatrix}. \tag{5}$$

The above ELM calculation can be summed up as following. After randomly select the value of input weights $\mathbf{w}_i$ and the bias of the neural network b_i, we can obtain the output H of hidden layers, therefore the output weights β can be obtained. During the training, β is obtained based on solving an optimization problem. And during the recognition, the maxim f_j is selected as the ELM output class label.

3   ELM Based Ship Detection Method

A ship detection approach employing ELM classification for SAR images is proposed in this paper. We will discuss image pre-processing, feature extraction and network training of the proposed approach as follows.

3.1   Image Pre-processing

We used SAR image that is derived from TerraSAR-X images dataset [16]. SAR image is calibrated and geocoded for pre-processing. In this stage, the main aim is to extract ship candidate area with reducing alarm rate as much as possible. Pre-processing includes feature selection and image segmentation. Due to the ship shapes are regular, long and thin, selecting the appropriate length-width ratio as the given threshold can eliminate non-ship objects, such as irregular islands and clouds. After segmentation, we can remove non-target objects and gain ship candidate region. Then we use median filter to eliminate noise and enhance the accuracy of ship recognation. Finally we can cut out sample images based on the size of the ships to locate target areas and extract out all the ship samples and water samples with the size of 30 × 30 pixels.

Feature extraction is the extraction of ships and seawater texture. The texture are important information for the ship detection. To obtain more information, sample images processing tasks are employed to extract texture features. To get the texture information, a popular gray level co-occurrence matrix method [17] is employed. The element of the matrix is the coherent distribution for probability of a gray scale in constant distance. The matrix is obtained after scaning all the pixels with the reflection of co-occurrence time probability of related pixels in space. Therefore it can provide the joint probability distribution of the pixels. The gray level co-occurrence matrix is used for five texture parameters, they are entropy, energy, contrast, correlation and inverse difference moment.

3.2 Feature Extraction

Because ship has limited area, length and width range, we extracted the ship candidate area by selecting the appropriate ratio of the length-width and area size range. We not only segment target but also eliminate non-target objects. The following equation is used to calculate the ratio of length-width.

$$r = L_{MER}/W_{MER} \tag{6}$$

where r is the ratio of length-width, L is the length of the spindle direction, and W is the width of spindle direction. The ratio distinguishes between a rectangular objects and irregular objects.

Entropy. Since texture information is also important for ship detection, we use entropy as one of texture features. Entropy can provide the uniformity and complexity information of the texture, and it is calculated as

$$f_{entropy} = \sum_{i=0}^{L-1} \sum_{j=0}^{L-1} p(i,j) \times [-\ln p(i,j)] \tag{7}$$

where $p(i,j)$ is the element of the position (i,j) in gray level co-occurrence matrix which has been described in Sect. 3.1.

Contrast. Contrast feature i able to reflect the degree of the image sharpness and the depth of the texture groove. It defers the calculation of the intensity contrast linking pixel and its neighbor over the whole image. Contrast can be calculated as

$$f_{contrast} = \sum_{i=0}^{L-1} \sum_{j=0}^{L-1} (i-j)^2 \times p(i,j)^2. \tag{8}$$

Energy. Energy is the sum of square of elements in GLCM. It reflects the uniformity of the image gray scale and texture roughness. Energy is calculated as

$$f_{energy} = \sum_{i=0}^{L-1} \sum_{j=0}^{L-1} P(i,j)^2 \tag{9}$$

Correlation. Correlation measures the similarity of the spatial gray-level co-occurrence matrix elements in the row or column direction, reflecting the local gray correlation in the image. It is calculated as

$$f_{Correlation} = \frac{\sum_i \sum_j i \times j \times P(i,j) - \mu_x \times \mu_y}{\sigma_x^2 \times \sigma_y^2} \tag{10}$$

Inverse Difference Moment. It reflects the homogeneity of the image texture, and measures how much of the image texture changes. When its value become larger, the local texture is very uniform. The following is its calculation formula.

$$f_{Inverse\ difference\ moment} = \sum_{i=0}^{L-1} \sum_{j=0}^{L-1} \frac{P(i,j)}{1 + (i-j)^2} \tag{11}$$

3.3   Network Training

In our ship detection method in SAR using ELM network, the input layer is connected to the input feature vector which is texture features as described before. The output layer has one node used to mark ship or not. After defining the ELM network structure, the network can be used for sample training. The parameters of input weights $\mathbf{w}_i$ and biases b_i in ELM are randomly selected. Consequently the calculation of β is critical for ELM training.

Denote the actual output vector as $\mathbf{Y}$, the input vector $\mathbf{X}$, We can obtain the output vector from (3) as

$$\mathbf{Y} = \mathbf{H}\beta, \tag{12}$$

where

$$\mathbf{H} = \begin{bmatrix} \mathbf{h}(\mathbf{x}_1) \\ \vdots \\ \mathbf{h}(\mathbf{x}_N) \end{bmatrix}$$

$$= \begin{bmatrix} g(\mathbf{x}_1; \mathbf{w}_1, b_1) & \cdots & g(\mathbf{x}_1; \mathbf{w}_L, b_L) \\ \vdots & \ddots & \vdots \\ g(\mathbf{x}_N; \mathbf{w}_1, b_1) & \cdots & g(\mathbf{x}_N; \mathbf{w}_L, b_L) \end{bmatrix}, \tag{13}$$

and

$$\mathbf{Y} = \begin{bmatrix} \mathbf{y}_1 \\ \vdots \\ \mathbf{Y}_N \end{bmatrix} = \begin{bmatrix} y_{11} & \cdots & y_{1M} \\ \vdots & \ddots & \vdots \\ y_{N1} & \cdots & y_{NM} \end{bmatrix}. \tag{14}$$

The object of ELM method is to minimize two errors, they are the training error $||\mathbf{T} - \mathbf{H}\boldsymbol{\beta}||^2$ and the norm of output weight $||\boldsymbol{\beta}||$. This problem can be converted to an optimization problem as below

$$\min \quad \psi(\boldsymbol{\beta}, \boldsymbol{\xi}) = \frac{1}{2}||\boldsymbol{\beta}||^2 + \frac{C}{2}||\boldsymbol{\xi}||^2 \tag{15}$$

$$\text{s.t.} \quad \mathbf{H}\boldsymbol{\beta} = \mathbf{T} - \boldsymbol{\xi}. \tag{16}$$

where $\boldsymbol{\xi}$ is the output value error between the actual output and the desired output, and C is the regularization factor which is used to improve the training generalization performance with controlling the tradeoff between the closeness to the training data and the smoothness of the decision function. The above optimization problem can be solved employing Lagrange multiplier technique. When the matrix $(\mathbf{I}/C) + \mathbf{H}^T\mathbf{H}$ is not singular, solution $\boldsymbol{\beta}$ can be calculated as

$$\boldsymbol{\beta} = \left(\frac{\mathbf{I}}{C} + \mathbf{H}^T\mathbf{H}\right)^{-1} \mathbf{H}^T\mathbf{T}. \tag{17}$$

Otherwise, when the matrix $(\mathbf{I}/C) + \mathbf{H}\mathbf{H}^T$ is not singular, solution $\boldsymbol{\beta}$ can be calculated as

$$\boldsymbol{\beta} = \mathbf{H}^T \left(\frac{\mathbf{I}}{C} + \mathbf{H}\mathbf{H}^T\right)^{-1} \mathbf{T}, \tag{18}$$

where $\mathbf{I}$ is an identity matrix. In practice, when the number of training features of samples is greater than the one of hidden neurons, we use (17) to obtain the output weights, otherwise we use (18).

To improve the stability of ELM in calculating the output weights, an efficient solution is to find high quality mapping between input and hidden layers. RBF function is one of the most efficient mapping functions, and it used in our ELM based bubble defect detection method. $\mathbf{H}^T\mathbf{H}$ in (17) or $\mathbf{H}\mathbf{H}^T$ in (18) is called ELM kernel matrix, and $\mathbf{h}(\mathbf{x}_i) \cdot \mathbf{h}(\mathbf{x}_j)$ is ELM kernel. In our proposed method, the following Gaussian function is selected as the kernel

$$\phi(\mathbf{x}_i, \mathbf{x}_j) = \mathbf{h}(\mathbf{x}_i) \cdot \mathbf{h}(\mathbf{x}_j) = \exp\left(-\frac{||\mathbf{x}_i - \mathbf{x}_j||^2}{\sigma^2}\right). \tag{19}$$

The training process is performed as described above. After the training is finished, the trained ELM can be used for image detection in SAR.

4 Experimental Results

In our experiments, these SAR images acquired from TerraSAR-X Data Samples [16] have been radiometrically calibrated. Two sample images in our test dataset are illustrated in Fig. 1.

Some other usually used methods are assessed in our experiments to verify the efficiency of our proposed method. It has been widely validated that neural network based classification has poorer performance than SVM based one. Our test methods are K-nearest neighbors (KNN) [1], SVM [6], CNN [9] and ELM

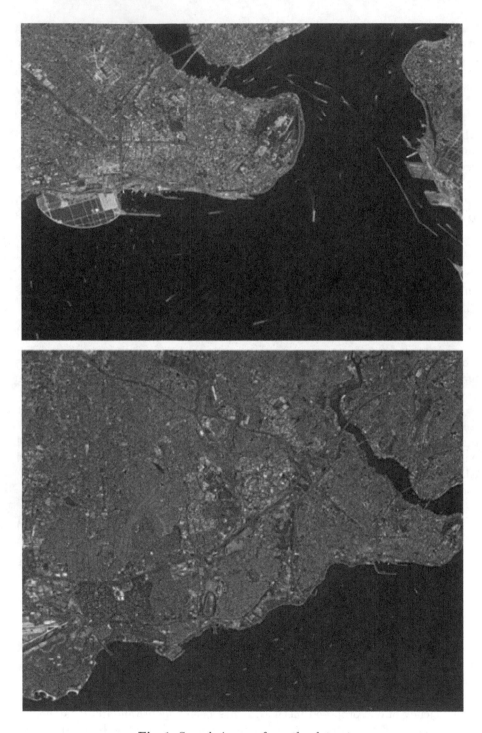

Fig. 1. Sample images from the dataset

methods. After testing the different parameters with experiments, we select the optimized parameters for the best performance from the allowed ranges employing optimization search. In our ELM based method, the number of hidden nodes is set to 200.

4.1 Accuracy

The comparisons of classification performance in a variety of sample numbers are performed. The training sample number is selected from 120 to 480 with the step of 120, and these 4 groups are marked as group A, B, C and D, respectively. Samples in each group are stochastically selected from the dataset, and half of the sample is selected from the ship images, and others from non-ship ones. Test sample data contains 10 ship samples and 10 seawater samples. Each experiment has been tested 10 times. The final test accuracy is the average of 10 test experiments.

The comparison of classification correction rate of different methods is listed in Table 1. And these experimental results are also illustrated in Fig. 2. As shown in the figure, with the increasement of training samples, the classification accuracy of our proposed method gradually increases as well. The classification accuracy is more prior to other methods when fewer training samples are employed. Our proposed ELM based method is able to keep the superior performance of accuracy and the faster speed with the different sample numbers. It means that our proposed ELM method has most satisfactory performance with varies of sample number.

Table 1. Classification accuracy of different methods

Samples number	Method	Accuracy	Time consumed (s)
A (480 samples)	KNN	0.850	0.002
	SVM	0.805	0.249
	CNN	0.350	11.975
	ELM	0.900	0.161
B (360 samples)	KNN	0.850	0.002
	SVM	0.765	0.167
	CNN	0.300	5.837
	ELM	0.880	0.140
C (240 samples)	KNN	0.700	0.002
	SVM	0.750	0.150
	CNN	0.350	4.780
	ELM	0.865	0.110
D (120 samples)	KNN	0.750	0.001
	SVM	0.680	0.024
	CNN	0.350	3.502
	ELM	0.870	0.060

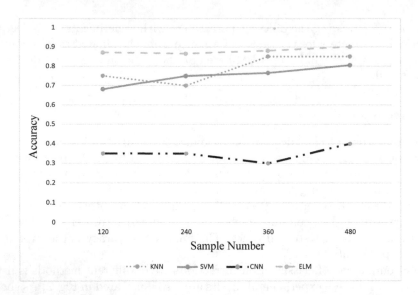

Fig. 2. Comparison of defect detection classification accuracy with different methods

4.2 Time Consumed

The speed is measured with the sum of training and test time, and the experimental results are also listed in Table 1. The time unit is seconds. The test data obtains 20 samples, which has 10 ship samples and 10 water samples. We performed the experiments with Matlab R2014a and Ubuntu 14.04 for python program on a computer with 64G RAM, 2.10 GHz E5-2620 CPU. And CNN method is tested with a GPU of GeForce GTX 1080 Ti. CNN has 50 iteration times for every training experiment. The data reveals that the proposed ELM algorithm is so fast that it can be employed in real time applications.

4.3 ROC and AUC

Receiver operating characteristics (ROC) curve and Area under the ROC curve (AUC) are widely used for classification performance comparison, and they are also employed in our experiments. We set the threshold varying from maximum to minimum and get the ROC curve. Interpreted as the probability that a classifier is able to distinguish a randomly chosen positive instance from a randomly chosen negative instance, AUC value is greater when the classification has good performance. The detailed ROC curves are illustrated in Fig. 3 in which the number of samples is 480. The curves of our proposed method are all on the above in the figures. It reveals that our proposed method has the best classification ability than other approaches. AUC value is listed in Table 2. Our proposed method obtain the greatest AUC value. All these experiments have shown that our proposed ELM based method has the best performance.

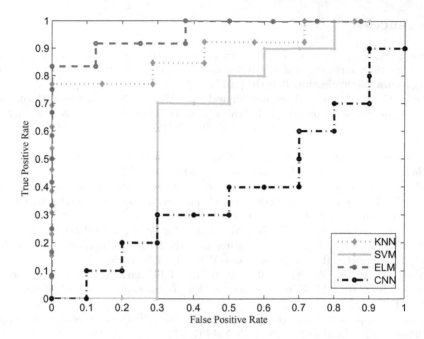

Fig. 3. ROC of different methods (sample number is 480).

Table 2. AUC of different methods

Samples number	KNN	SVM	CNN	ELM
480	0.747	0.500	0.390	0.833

5   Conclusions

In this work, a novel image processing application is developed to detect ship in SAR images. After the image processing and the feature extraction, ELM based classification is applied to detect ships in SAR images. Compared with other learning based classifiers, the proposed ELM based method can obtain better performance to detect ship. The proposed extreme learning machine based method is potential for object detection in other SAR applications. Research of the more efficient ELM based method with automatic feature selection will be studied in the future.

Acknowledgments. This work was partly supported by National Natural Science Foundation of China (No. 61371045).

References

1. Wang, S., Yang, S., Feng, Z., et al.: Fast ship detection of synthetic aperture radar images via multi-view features and clustering. In: International Joint Conference on Neural Networks, pp. 404–410 (2014)
2. Yang, G., Yu, J., Xiao, C., et al.: Ship wake detection for SAR images with complex backgrounds based on morphological dictionary learning. In: IEEE International Conference on Acoustics, Speech and Signal Processing, pp. 1896–1900. IEEE (2014)
3. Selvi, M.U., Kumar, S.S.: Sea object detection using shape and hybrid color texture classification. Commun. Comput. Inf. Sci. **204**, 19–31 (2011)
4. Martan-De-Nicols, J., Mata-Moya, D., Jarabo-Amores, M.P., et al.: Neural network based solutions for ship detection in SAR images. In: International Conference on Digital Signal Processing, pp. 1–6. IEEE (2013)
5. Khesali, E., Enayati, H., Modiri, M., et al.: Automatic ship detection in single-pol SAR images using texture features in artificial neural networks. Int. Archiv. Photogrammetry Remote Sens. **XL-1-W5**, 395–399 (2015)
6. Yang, X., Bi, F., Yu, Y., et al.: An effective false-alarm removal method based on OC-SVM for SAR ship detection. In: IET International Radar Conference, pp. 1–4. IET (2015)
7. Ma, L.: Support tucker machines based marine oil spill detection using SAR images. Indian J. Geo-Marine Sci. **45**, 1445–1449 (2016)
8. Ma, L., Hu, Y., Zhang, Y.: Support tucker machines based bubble defect detection of lithium-ion polymer cell sheets. Eng. Lett. **25**, 46–51 (2017)
9. Schwegmann, C.P., Kleynhans, W., Salmon, B.P., et al.: Very deep learning for ship discrimination in synthetic aperture radar imagery. In: 2016 IEEE International Geoscience and Remote Sensing Symposium, pp. 104–107. IEEE (2016)
10. Huang, G.B., Zhu, Q.Y., Siew, C.K.: Extreme learning machine: theory and applications. Neurocomputing **70**, 489–501 (2006)
11. Huang, G., Huang, G.B., Song, S., You, K.: Trends in extreme learning machines: a review. Neural Netw. **61**, 32–46 (2015)
12. Huang, G.B., Zhou, H., Ding, X., Zhang, R.: Extreme learning machine for regression and multiclass classification. IEEE Trans. Syst. Man Cybern. **2**, 513–529 (2016)
13. Wang, S., Deng, C., Lin, W., Huang, G.B.: NMF-based image quality assessment using extreme learning machine. IEEE Trans. Cybern. 255–258 (2016)
14. Yüksel, T.: Intelligent visual servoing with extreme learning machine and fuzzy logic. Expert Syst. Appl. **47**, 232–243 (2017)
15. Liu, X., Deng, C., Wang, S., Huang, G.B., Zhao, B., Lauren, P.: Fast and accurate spatiotemporal fusion based upon extreme learning machine. IEEE Geosci. Remote Sens. Lett. **13**, 2039–2043 (2016)
16. TerraSAR-X Data Samples. http://www.infoterra.de/free-sample-data
17. Benco, M., Hudec, R., Kamencay, P., et al.: An advanced approach to extraction of colour texture features based on GLCM. Int. J. Adv. Robot. Syst. **11**, article no 104 (2014)

Obtaining Ellipse Common Tangent Line Equations by the Rolling Tangent Line Method

Naizhang Feng, Teng Jiang, Shiqi Duan, and Mingjian Sun[✉]

School of Information and Electrical Engineering,
Harbin Institute of Technology, West Wenhua Road, 2, High-tech District,
Weihai 264209, Shandong, China
sunmingjian@hit.edu.cn

Abstract. In the field of image processing and machine vision, it is sometimes necessary to obtain common tangent line equations and tangent point coordinates from ellipses. A rolling tangent line method was proposed to obtain the 4 common tangent line equations and 8 tangent point coordinates from two ellipses in this paper. The principle of this method is simple and it is easy to program on a computer. Use this method to process two ellipse targets in an image and the experiment results show that the 4 common tangent equations and 8 tangent point coordinates can be obtained in high precision and the maximum execution time is less than 0.1 s.

Keywords: Image processing · Machine vision · Ellipse
Common tangent line

1 Introduction

In some engineering applications, it is necessary to obtain common tangent line equations and tangent point coordinates from two ellipses. For example, Mateos [1] used the tangent points as feature points for camera calibration. Guangjun [2] used the tangent points as feature points to measure the position and orientation of unmanned aerial vehicles.

In order to obtain the 4 tangent line equations and 8 tangent point coordinates, Zhang [2] proposed a method to solve an equation group which consists of two dual conic corresponding to the two ellipse equations. But the equation group is nonlinear and multivariate, it is not easy to solve by computers. Therefore, this method is not applicable to specific engineering practice. Xiaoxiang [3] proposed an iterative method to obtain tangent line equations from two ellipses. This method is sample and highly operational. It also converges quickly. However, in order to ensure convergence and accuracy, it needs to artificially adjust the position of the ellipses in the coordinate system so that the slope of the tangent line is approximately between 0.5 and 1.5. This makes this method no longer applicable to engineering applications with high autonomy requirements.

To solve the above problems, this paper proposes a rolling tangent line method, which can effectively obtain the 4 common tangent line equations and 8 tangent point coordinates from the two ellipses. Compared with the existing methods, this method

© ICST Institute for Computer Sciences, Social Informatics and Telecommunications Engineering 2018
X. Gu et al. (Eds.): MLICOM 2017, Part II, LNICST 227, pp. 569–576, 2018.
https://doi.org/10.1007/978-3-319-73447-7_61

has three advantages: (1) The principle of this method is simple, and it is easy to be achieved on a computer; (2) There is no iterative calculation, so this method executes fast; (3) The method has high stability and high precision. This paper will introduce the principle of this method in details, and the effectiveness of the proposed method is verified by experimental results.

2   Basic Principle of the Rolling Tangent Line Method

The general equation of an ellipse can be expressed in the form of formula (1).

$$x^2 + Axy + By^2 + Cx + Dy + E = 0. \tag{1}$$

The ellipse equation shown in formula (1) can be rewritten into a binomial form of homogeneous coordinates, as shown in formula (2). Formula (2) is equivalent to formula (1).

$$\begin{bmatrix} x & y & 1 \end{bmatrix} \begin{bmatrix} 1 & A/2 & C/2 \\ A/2 & B & D/2 \\ C/2 & D/2 & E \end{bmatrix} \begin{bmatrix} x \\ y \\ 1 \end{bmatrix} = 0. \tag{2}$$

Further, in order to facilitate analysis, the formula (2) is rewritten into the form of formula (3). In formula (3), d is the vector $[x\ y\ 1]^T$, which represents a point on the ellipse curve.

$$d^T M d = 0. \tag{3}$$

Now assume that there are two ellipses M_1 and M_2 on the image coordinate system. Using the rolling tangent line method to obtain the 4 tangent line equations can be implemented in three steps. Details are as follows:

Step 1: Generate tangent points on ellipse M_2.
Figure 1 shows a Diagrammatic sketch of an image coordinate system. Assuming that the equations for ellipses M_1 and M_2 are known, then tangent points will be generated on the ellipse M_2. Among all the tangent points, the top and the bottom tangent point,

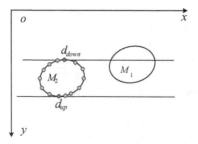

Fig. 1. Tangent points generated on ellipse M_2.

i.e. d_{down} and d_{up} in Fig. 1, will be generated at first. The tangent line through d_{down} or d_{up} is parallel to ox axis.

Assume that the coordinates of d_{down} and d_{up} are (x_{down}, y_{down}) and (x_{up}, y_{up}) respectively. We will use the coordinates of these two points to determine the coordinates of other tangent points.

Divide the interval $[y_{down}, y_{up}]$ into three sub-intervals. The first sub-interval is $[y_{down}, y_{down} + \delta y]$, and the y-coordinate of the tangent points in this interval are y_{down}, $y_{down} + \Delta_1$, $y_{down} + 2\Delta_1$, $y_{down} + 3\Delta_1$, $\cdots$, $y_{down} + \delta y$, respectively. The second sub-interval is $(y_{down} + \delta y, y_{up} - \delta y]$, and the y-coordinate of the tangent points in this interval are $y_{down} + \delta y + \Delta_2$, $y_{down} + \delta y + 2\Delta_2$, $y_{down} + \delta y + 3\Delta_2$, $\cdots$, $y_{up} - \delta y$ respectively. The third sub-interval is $(y_{up} - \delta y, y_{up}]$, and the y-coordinate of the tangent points in this interval are $y_{up} - \delta y + \Delta_3$, $y_{up} - \delta y + 2\Delta_3$, $y_{up} - \delta y + 3\Delta_3$, $\cdots$, y_{up} respectively. The δy is a small constant. The Δ_1, Δ_2, Δ_3 are small step lengths. In general, Δ_2 is much larger than Δ_1, and Δ_1 is equal to Δ_3. By dividing different intervals to determine the y-coordinate of the tangent point is to ensure the accuracy of the results and the execution speed of the method.

It is assumed that the y-coordinates of n tangent points are obtained by the above method. For any one of them, take y_i into the equation of ellipse M_2, we can get two x-coordinates, x_{i1} and x_{i2}, which locates on the left and right sides of the connection line between point d_{down} and point d_{up}. That is, each y_i corresponds to the two tangent points (x_{i1}, y_i) and (x_{i2}, y_i) on the ellipse M_2.

Step 2: Solve the tangent line equation for each tangent point generated on ellipse M_2. The coordinates of a tangent point d_i on ellipse M_2 is (x_i, y_i), corresponding to the homogeneous coordinate $[x_i, y_i, 1]^T$. Then a tangent line l_i on the ellipse M_2 that through d_i can be obtained by formula (4) in book [4].

$$l_i = M_2 d_i. \tag{4}$$

Starting at point d_{down}, arrive at point d_{up} in clockwise direction, and continue to go back to point d_{down} in clockwise direction, obtain the equation of the tangent line to each tangent point. N tangent line equations can be obtained in total. This process is like a tangent line rolling on the ellipse M_2, hence we call this method the rolling tangent line method. This process can also be shown in Fig. 2.

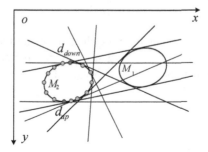

Fig. 2. Each tangent point generated on ellipse M_2 corresponds to a tangent line.

Step 3: Determine all the 4 tangent line equations by the deviation.

The tangent line equations for all tangent points generated on M2 has been obtained in step 2. If the tangent l_i on the ellipse M_2 is also tangent to the ellipse M_1, then the tangent l_i must satisfy the formula (5).

$$l_i^T M_1^{-1} l_i = 0. \tag{5}$$

Here, we define $l_i^T M_1^{-1} l_i$ as the deviation denoted by e. Further analysis shows that if l_i is the tangent line of M_2 but not the tangent line of M_1, then e is not equal to 0, and l_i farther away from M_1, the greater the absolute value of deviation e will be. When a tangent line rolls a circle along the ellipse M_2 from point d_{down}, the diagrammatic sketch that the absolute value of the deviation $|e|$ varies with the tangent line sequence number is shown in Fig. (3).

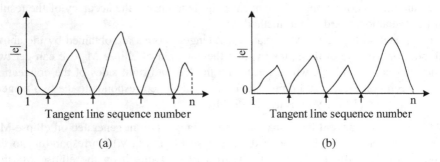

(a)   (b)

Fig. 3. Diagrammatic sketch that the absolute value of the deviation $|e|$ varies with the tangent line sequence number. (a) represents a general case, and (b) represents a special case.

In Fig. 3(a), the tangent lines corresponding to the 4 valleys between the two peaks indicated by the upper arrow are the common tangent lines. Figure 3(b) shows a special case. In special case, only 3 common tangent lines can be obtained directly. In order to obtain the fourth common tangent line, we can compare the two boundary points, then select the smaller one as the line sequence number corresponding to the fourth common tangent line. Further, we will use formula (6) to obtain the tangent point from the 4 common tangent lines and the ellipse M_1.

$$d = M_1 l. \tag{6}$$

The above three steps illustrates the procedure to obtain the common tangent line equations from two ellipses by the rolling tangent line method. In Sect. 3, we will verify the validity of the method through experiments.

3   Experiment and Results

The experiment was done on a laptop, in which the CPU is Intel Core i3-2350M and the memory size is 6 GB. Figure 4 is a 640 × 480 pixels image captured by a camera, which contains two ellipse targets. After a series of image processing algorithms [5– 10], we can get the equations of the outer contour curves of two ellipse targets, which are shown in the Fig. 4. In Fig. 4, the green curves represent the two ellipse and the crossings represent the center of the ellipse. Then, the rolling tangent line method will be used to obtain common tangent line equations and tangent points from the two ellipses.

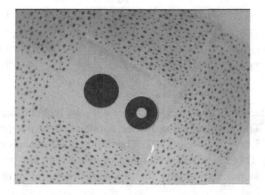

Fig. 4. A 640 × 480 pixels image contains two ellipse targets. In this figure, the green curves represent the two ellipse and the crossings represent the center of the ellipse. (Color figure online)

When writing a program to achieve the rolling tangent line method, we set the parameter δy to 1, Δ_1 and Δ_3 to 0.01, Δ_2 to 0.2. Using the rolling tangent line method generated 1314 tangent points in total, corresponding to 1314 tangent line. The curve

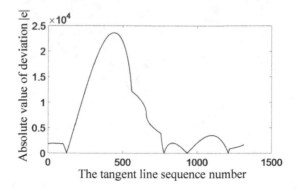

Fig. 5. The absolute value of the deviation $|e|$ varies with the tangent line sequence number. There are 4 valleys in this figure corresponding to the 4 common tangent lines.

Table 1. Tangent line equations obtained from the two ellipses

Tangent line sequence number	Tangent line equations
125	$21.95x - 38.44y + 1302.65 = 0$
779	$-21.115x + 38.89y - 5860.78 = 0$
934	$-44.36x + 9.18y + 10621.07 = 0$
1207	$-14.966x - 42.058y + 15065.51 = 0$

Table 2. Tangent point coordinates obtained from the two ellipses

Tangent point sequence number	Column coordinate	Row coordinate	Tangent point sequence number	Column coordinate	Row coordinate
1	260.60	182.17	5	283.47	214.11
2	367.61	243.80	6	300.49	295.20
3	213.01	265.30	7	252.57	269.04
4	323.25	326.20	8	330.75	240.60

that the absolute value of the deviation |e| varies with the tangent line sequence number is shown in Fig. 5. The tangent line sequence numbers corresponding to the common tangent lines are 125, 779, 934 and 1207. The detailed parameters of the four tangent lines are shown in Table 1. The coordinates of the 8 tangent points are shown in Table 2. Obtaining 4 common tangent line equations and 8 tangent point coordinates took a total of 0.077 s.

In order to intuitively observe the 4 common tangent lines and 8 tangent points obtained from the two ellipses, the tangent lines and the tangent points was marked in

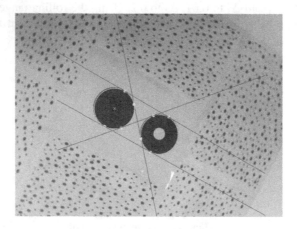

Fig. 6. The 4 tangent lines and 8 tangent points were marked in the image. The purple line represents tangent lines, and the cyan point represents tangent points. (Color figure online)

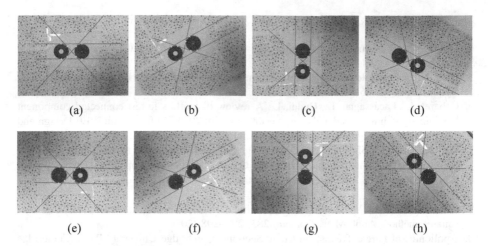

Fig. 7. The other 8 images and the corresponding processing results. Time consuming: (a) 0.062 s; (b) 0.048 s; (c) 0.065 s; (d) 0.046 s; (e) 0.068 s; (f) 0.051 s; (g) 0.047 s; (h) 0.058 s.

the image, as shown in Fig. 6. It can be seen that 4 common tangent lines and 8 tangent points was obtained in high precision.

In order to verify the stability of the rolling tangent line method, the other 8 images with ellipse targets were processed. The results are shown in Fig. 7. From the results shown in Fig. 7, we can see that regardless of how the ellipse object is distributed in the image coordinate system, the 4 common tangent lines and the 8 tangent points from the two ellipses can be stably and quickly obtained by using the rolling tangent method.

4   Conclusion

This paper presents a rolling tangent line method to obtain common tangent line equations and tangent point coordinates from two ellipses. The principle of this method is simple and it is easy to program on a computer. There is no iterative calculation, so this method can execute fast. The experimental results show that this method is stable and the common tangent line equations with the tangent point coordinates can be obtained in high precision. These advantages make the rolling tangent line method applicable for engineering practice.

References

1. Mateos, G.G.: A camera calibration technique using targets of circular features. In: 5th Ibero-America Symposium On Pattern Recognition (SIARP) (2000)
2. Guangjun, Z., Fuqiang, Z.: Position and orientation estimation method for landing of unmanned aerial vehicle with two circle based computer vision. Acta Aeronautica et Astronautica Sinica **26**(3), 344–348 (2005)

3. Xiaoxiang, Z.: Seek common tangent with the iterative method. Discipl. Explor. **5**, 28–29 (2015)
4. Hartley, R., Zisserman, A.: Multiple View Geometry in Computer Vision. Cambridge University Press, Cambridge (2003)
5. Otsu, N.: A threshold selection method from gray-level histograms. IEEE Trans. Syst. Man, Cybern. **9**(1), 62–66 (1979)
6. Cabaret, L., Lacassagne, L., Oudni, L.: A review of world's fastest connected component labeling algorithms: speed and energy estimation. In: 2014 Conference on IEEE Design and Architectures for Signal and Image Processing (DASIP), pp. 1–6 (2014)
7. Wu, K., Otoo, E., Shoshani, A.: Optimizing connected component labeling algorithms. In: Medical Imaging. International Society for Optics and Photonics, pp. 1965–1976 (2005)
8. Weiss, M.A.: Data Structures and Algorithm Analysis in C. Addison-Wesley, Reading (1997)
9. Amirfakhrian, M., Mafikandi, H.: Approximation of parametric curves by moving least squares method. Appl. Math. Comput. **283**, 290–298 (2016)
10. Apollonius of Perga: Treatise on Conic Sections. Cambridge University Press, Cambridge (2013)

On Sampling of Bandlimited Graph Signals

Mo Han, Jun Shi$^{(\boxtimes)}$, Yiqiu Deng, and Weibin Song

Communication Research Center, Harbin Institute of Technology,
Harbin 150001, China
junshi@hit.edu.cn

Abstract. The signal processing on graphs has been widely used in various fields, including machine learning, classification and network signal processing, in which the sampling of bandlimited graph signals plays an important role. In this paper, we discuss the sampling of bandlimited graph signals based on the theory of function spaces, which is consistent with the pattern of the Shannon sampling theorem. First, we derive an interpolation operator by constructing bandlimited space of graph signals, and the corresponding sampling operator is also obtained. Based on the relationship between the interpolation and sampling operators, a sampling theorem for bandlimited graph signals is proposed, and its physical meaning in the graph frequency domain is also given. Furthermore, the implementation of the proposed theorem via matrix calculation is discussed.

Keywords: Sampling · Signal processing on graphs · Graph signals

1 Introduction

With the rapid development of information technology, the demand for large-scale data processing is growing, such as signals from social, biological, and sensor networks. Different from traditional timeseries or images, these structured signals are interconnected. The underlying connectivities between data points naturally reside on the structure of graphs, which leads to the emerging field of signal processing on graphs. In recent years, the graph signal processing has been widely used in various application domains such as machine learning, classification and network signal processing [1,2].

The sampling theory plays a fundamental role in digital signal processing. The traditional Shannon sampling theorem bridges the continuous and discrete domains. Unlike traditional sampling, the sampling for graph signals is more challenging because the paradigm of leveraging frequency folding phenomenon cannot be defined for graph signal due to its irregular structure. Therefore, the sampling for graph signals has drawn lots of attention. Unfortunately, existing works on sampling of graph signals [4–7] do not reveal the clear physical meaning in the graph frequency domain, and the implementation of graph signal sampling and reconstruction is still not discussed in the literature. Towards this end,

© ICST Institute for Computer Sciences, Social Informatics and Telecommunications Engineering 2018
X. Gu et al. (Eds.): MLICOM 2017, Part II, LNICST 227, pp. 577–584, 2018.
https://doi.org/10.1007/978-3-319-73447-7_62

we propose a new derivation of the sampling for bandlimited graph signals based on the theory of function spaces. We first derive an interpolation operator by constructing bandlimited space of graph signals, and then obtain its corresponding sampling operator. Based on the relationship between these two operators, a sampling theorem for bandlimited graph signals is proposed. The physical meaning of the sampling and reconstruction process in the graph frequency domain is also given. Furthermore, the implementation of the proposed theorem via matrix calculation is presented. Finally, a numerical example of the derived results is given.

The rest of the paper is organized as follows. Some facts of signal processing on graphs are introduced in Sect. 2. Section 3 discusses the sampling for bandlimited signals defined on graph. Finally, a conclusion is made in Sect. 4.

2   Preliminaries

In this chapter, some basic concepts of discrete signal processing on graphs [1–3] are given, which are generalized from the traditional discrete signal processing.

Graph Signal. Discrete signal processing on graphs is focused on the signal with irregular and complex internal structure, which can be represented by a graph $G = (\mathcal{V}, A)$, where $\mathcal{V} = [v_0, v_1, \cdots, v_{N-1}]$ denotes the set of nodes and $A \in \mathbb{C}^{N \times N}$, the weighted adjacency matrix, means the *graph shift*. Given a graph representation $G = (\mathcal{V}, A)$, a *graph signal* is defined as the map on the graph nodes that assigns the signal coefficient $f_n \in \mathbb{C}$ to the node v_n. The edge weight $A_{m,n}$ between v_m and v_n can express the correlation and similarity between the signals defined on those two nodes. When the order of the nodes is determined, the graph signal can be represented by a vector

$$\mathbf{f} = [f_0 \ f_1 \ \cdots \ f_{N-1}]^T \in \mathbb{C}^N. \tag{1}$$

For simplicity, assume A can be completely decomposed as follows (unless A should be decomposed on a set of Jordan eigenvectors)

$$A = V \Lambda V^{-1} \tag{2}$$

where the columns of matrix V is the eigenvectors of A, and Λ is the diagonal matrix of corresponding eigenvalues $\lambda_0, \cdots, \lambda_{N-1}$ with $\lambda_0 >, \cdots, > \lambda_{N-1}$.

Graph Fourier Transform. Generally, a Fourier transform can achieve the expansion of a signal on a set of basis functions which are invariant to filtering. The eigenvectors (or the Jordan eigenvectors) of the graph shift A just satisfy the requirement [1,3], so the *graph Fourier transform* and the *inverse graph Fourier transform* can be respectively defined as

$$\hat{\mathbf{f}} = V^{-1} \mathbf{f} \tag{3}$$

$$f = V\hat{f}. \tag{4}$$

Eigenvalues $\lambda_0 >, \cdots, > \lambda_{N-1}$ denote the lowest to the highest frequencies of graph signals, with a descending order of the eigenvalues [3]. Eigenvectors of different frequencies correspond to different graph frequency components.

3   A Sampling Theorem of Bandlimited Graph Signals

For finite-dimentional discrete signal, sampling and interpolation mean the decrease and increase of the dimension of input signal. Thus the sampling and interpolation of a graph signal $f \in \mathbb{C}^N$ can be respectively expressed as

$$g = \Psi f \in \mathbb{C}^M \tag{5}$$

$$\tilde{f} = \Phi g = \Phi \Psi f = Pf \in \mathbb{C}^N, \tag{6}$$

where $M < N$, g is the sampled graph signal, and matrix $\Psi \in \mathbb{C}^{M \times N}$ and $\Phi \in \mathbb{C}^{N \times M}$ denote the sampling and interpolation operators respectively, and

$$P = \Phi\Psi \in \mathbb{C}^{N \times N} \tag{7}$$

with

$$\Psi^* = (\psi_0, \cdots, \psi_{M-1}) \in \mathbb{C}^{N \times M} \tag{8}$$

$$\Phi = (\phi_0, \cdots, \phi_{M-1}) \in \mathbb{C}^{N \times M} \tag{9}$$

where $\psi_i \in \mathbb{C}^N$ and $\phi_i \in \mathbb{C}^N$. If vectors $\psi_0, \cdots, \psi_{M-1}$ and $\phi_0, \cdots, \phi_{M-1}$ constitute two sets of basis of signal space $S_s = \text{span}\{\psi_0, \cdots, \psi_{M-1}\}$ and $S_i = \text{span}\{\phi_0, \cdots, \phi_{M-1}\}$, the sampling (5) and interpolation (6) can be regarded as the expansion and combination of signal f in the two spaces, where S_s and S_i represent the sampling and interpolation spaces respectively.

3.1   Sampling and Interpolation in Bandlimited Graph Signal Space

Similar to the Shannon theorem, for the possibility of perfect recovery, we consider bandlimited graph signals, i.e., the input signal f is in bandlimited space.

A graph signal f is called *bandlimited* when there exists a $K \in \{0, \cdots, N-1\}$ such that its graph Fourier transform $\hat{f}$ satisfies

$$\hat{f}_i = 0 \quad \text{for all} \quad i \geq K. \tag{10}$$

The smallest K is the *bandwidth* of f. All the graph signals in $\mathbb{C}^N$ with bandwidth of at most K can form a closed bandlimited subspace, represented by BL_K.

Perfect recovery equals to achieve $\tilde{f} = f$. Thus given $f \in \text{BL}_K$, $\tilde{f} \in \text{BL}_K$ must be satisfied. From (6) we can know $\tilde{f} \in S_i$, so the problem has been transformed into the construction of the bandlimited interpolation space which should satisfy:

$$S_i = \text{span}\{\phi_0, \cdots, \phi_{M-1}\} = \text{BL}_K. \tag{11}$$

The graph Fourier transform of interpolation operator Φ can be written as

$$
\begin{aligned}
\hat{\Phi} = V^{-1}\Phi &= (V^{-1}\phi_0, \cdots, V^{-1}\phi_{M-1}) \\
&= (\hat{\phi}_0, \cdots, \hat{\phi}_{M-1})
\end{aligned} \tag{12}
$$

where $\hat{\phi}_i$ is the graph Fourier transform of vector ϕ_i. For vector $u \in S_i$ with expansion coefficients $a_0, \cdots, a_{M-1}$ on basis $\phi_0, \cdots, \phi_{M-1}$, $\hat{u}$ is as follows

$$
\begin{aligned}
\hat{u} = V^{-1}u &= V^{-1}(\phi_0, \cdots, \phi_{M-1})(a_0, \cdots, a_{M-1})^T \\
&= (\hat{\phi}_0, \cdots, \hat{\phi}_{M-1})(a_0, \cdots, a_{M-1})^T \\
&= a_0\hat{\phi}_0 + \cdots + a_{M-1}\hat{\phi}_{M-1}
\end{aligned} \tag{13}
$$

where $\hat{\phi}_0, \cdots, \hat{\phi}_{M-1}$ form a new set of basis in graph frequency domain, and $\hat{u} \in \text{span}\{\hat{\phi}_0, \cdots, \hat{\phi}_{M-1}\}$. Thus if $\hat{\phi}_0, \cdots, \hat{\phi}_{M-1}$ satisfy (10), (11) holds true.

If $\hat{\phi}_0, \cdots, \hat{\phi}_{M-1}$ satisfy (10), then we have

$$
\begin{aligned}
\hat{\Phi} = \hat{\Phi}_{BL} = V^{-1}\Phi &= V^{-1}(\phi_0, \cdots, \phi_{M-1}) = (\hat{\phi}_0, \cdots, \hat{\phi}_{M-1}) \\
&= \left(\begin{pmatrix} \hat{\phi}_0(1) \\ \vdots \\ \hat{\phi}_0(K) \\ 0 \\ \vdots \\ 0 \end{pmatrix}, \cdots, \begin{pmatrix} \hat{\phi}_{M-1}(1) \\ \vdots \\ \hat{\phi}_{M-1}(K) \\ 0 \\ \vdots \\ 0 \end{pmatrix} \right) = \begin{pmatrix} \hat{\phi}_{01} & \cdots & \hat{\phi}_{(M-1)1} \\ \vdots & \ddots & \vdots \\ \hat{\phi}_{0K} & \cdots & \hat{\phi}_{(M-1)K} \\ 0 & \cdots & 0 \\ \vdots & \ddots & \vdots \\ 0 & \cdots & 0 \end{pmatrix} \\
&= \underbrace{\begin{pmatrix} Q \\ 0 \cdots 0 \\ \vdots \ddots \vdots \\ 0 \cdots 0 \end{pmatrix}}_{N \times M} = \underbrace{\begin{pmatrix} I_{K \times K} \\ 0 \cdots 0 \\ \vdots \ddots \vdots \\ 0 \cdots 0 \end{pmatrix}}_{N \times K} Q
\end{aligned} \tag{14}
$$

where I is the unit matrix, and the coefficient matrix $Q \in \mathbb{C}^{K \times M}$ includes all the nonzero frequency contents of bandlimited vectors $\hat{\phi}_0, \cdots, \hat{\phi}_{M-1}$:

$$
Q = \left(\begin{pmatrix} \hat{\phi}_0(1) \\ \vdots \\ \hat{\phi}_0(K) \end{pmatrix}, \cdots, \begin{pmatrix} \hat{\phi}_{M-1}(1) \\ \vdots \\ \hat{\phi}_{M-1}(K) \end{pmatrix} \right) = \begin{pmatrix} \hat{\phi}_{01} & \cdots & \hat{\phi}_{(M-1)1} \\ \vdots & \ddots & \vdots \\ \hat{\phi}_{0K} & \cdots & \hat{\phi}_{(M-1)K} \end{pmatrix}. \tag{15}
$$

And $V^{-1}V = I_{N \times N}$ is true, so we have

$$
V^{-1} \cdot V_{(K)} = \begin{pmatrix} I_{K \times K} \\ 0 \cdots 0 \\ \vdots \ddots \vdots \\ 0 \cdots 0 \end{pmatrix} \tag{16}
$$

where $V_{(K)} \in \mathbb{C}^{N \times K}$ denotes the first K columns of $V \in \mathbb{C}^{N \times N}$, and satisfies

$$V_{(K)} \cdot Q = V \left(\begin{pmatrix} \hat{\phi}_0(1) \\ \vdots \\ \hat{\phi}_0(K) \\ 0 \\ \vdots \\ 0 \end{pmatrix}, \cdots, \begin{pmatrix} \hat{\phi}_{M-1}(1) \\ \vdots \\ \hat{\phi}_{M-1}(K) \\ 0 \\ \vdots \\ 0 \end{pmatrix} \right) = V\hat{\Phi}_{BL} = \Phi. \tag{17}$$

Then combining (16) and (17), (14) can be expressed as

$$\hat{\Phi}_{BL} = \begin{pmatrix} Q \\ 0 \cdots 0 \\ \vdots \ddots \vdots \\ 0 \cdots 0 \end{pmatrix} = \begin{pmatrix} I_{K \times K} \\ 0 \cdots 0 \\ \vdots \ddots \vdots \\ 0 \cdots 0 \end{pmatrix} Q = V^{-1} \cdot V_{(K)} \cdot Q = V^{-1}\Phi \tag{18}$$

so that we can get

$$\Phi = V_{(K)}Q. \tag{19}$$

By (19), the interpolation operator Φ can be constructed uniquely using a given coefficient matrix Q, and simultaneously the interpolation space S_i satisfies (11).

The interpolation operator Φ can be built through (19), so the next step of perfect recovery is to find the corresponding sampling operator Ψ.

Under the sampling theory for finite-dimensional vectors discussed in [8], two requirements must be satisfied for perfect recovery: (1) input signal $f \in S_i = \text{span}\{\phi_0, ..., \phi_{M-1}\} = BL_K$; (2) $P = \Phi\Psi$ is a projection operator, satisfying

$$P^2 = P. \tag{20}$$

The first requirement can be guaranteed by (19) when given a graph signal $f \in BL_K$, and the second one (20) just implies the relation between Φ and Ψ.

From (7) and (19) we obtain

$$P = \Phi\Psi = V_{(K)}Q\Psi \tag{21}$$

so (20) can be written as

$$\begin{aligned} P^2 &= \Phi\Psi \cdot \Phi\Psi = V_{(K)}Q\Psi \cdot V_{(K)}Q\Psi \\ &= V_{(K)} \cdot (Q\Psi V_{(K)}) \cdot Q\Psi = V_{(K)} \cdot W_1 \cdot Q\Psi \\ &= V_{(K)}Q \cdot (\Psi V_{(K)}Q) \cdot \Psi = V_{(K)}Q \cdot W_2 \cdot \Psi \\ &= P = V_{(K)}Q\Psi \end{aligned} \tag{22}$$

where $W_1 = Q\Psi V_{(K)} \in \mathbb{C}^{K \times K}$ and $W_2 = \Psi V_{(K)}Q \in \mathbb{C}^{M \times M}$. To achieve $\tilde{f} = f \in BL_K$, sampled signal $g \in \mathbb{C}^M$ must include at least K graph frequencies to avoid the truncation error. Thus the dimension M should satisfy $M \geq K$. Then for $Q \in \mathbb{C}^{K \times M}$, rank $\left(W_2 = \Psi V_{(K)} Q\right) \leq$ rank $(Q) \leq K \leq M$; and $W_2 = I_{M \times M}$ only when $M = K$. So to make (22) true, $W_1 = I_{K \times K}$ should be satisfied, i.e.,

$$Q\Psi V_{(K)} = I_{K \times K}. \tag{23}$$

The relation between Φ and Ψ is given by (23). From (19) and (23), Φ and Ψ can be uniquely obtained. However, there are 3 unknowns in this problem: Φ, Ψ and Q, so one of them must be built first to fix the rest. For the feasibility and simplicity of sampling, we construct the interpolation operator Ψ first and conclude the following sampling theorem for graph signals.

Theorem 1. *For the sampling operator $\Psi \in \mathbb{C}^{M \times N}$ and interpolation operator $\Phi \in \mathbb{C}^{N \times M}$ of a bandlimited graph signal $f \in BL_K \in \mathbb{C}^N$, if $M \geq K$ and rank $(\Psi) \geq K$ are true, then the perfect recovery of f can be achieved, where M is the total sample number, with*

$$\Phi = V_{(K)} Q \quad and \quad Q\Psi V_{(K)} = I_{K \times K}. \tag{24}$$

The restriction of $M \geq K$ and rank $(\Psi) \geq K$ in Theorem 1 provides the instruction for building sampling operator $\Psi \in \mathbb{C}^{M \times N}$, and the results are varied. When this restriction is not satisfied or $f \notin BL_K$, perfect recovery is impossible due to the truncation error in the graph frequency domain.

By Theorem 1, the implementation steps for the sampling and interpolation of bandlimited graph signals are as follows:

(i) Select the total sample number M, satisfying $M \geq K$;
(ii) Build operator Ψ with rank $(\Psi) \geq K$ and sample the input signal: $g = \Psi f$;
(iii) Calculate Q using $Q\Psi V_{(K)} = I_{K \times K}$;
(iv) Obtain Φ by $\Phi = V_{(K)} Q$ and recover the signal: $\tilde{f} = \Phi \Psi f$.

3.2   Numerical Example

The perfect recovery of graph signals can be obtained via the given steps, and the choices of sampling operator Ψ are varied. Next, we take one of them as an example to demonstrate the validity of the proposed theorem.

We consider a 5-node graph with adjacency matrix

$$A = \begin{bmatrix} 0 & 1 & 0 & 0 & 1 \\ 1 & 0 & 1 & 0 & 1 \\ 0 & 1 & 0 & 0 & 1 \\ 0 & 0 & 0 & 0 & 1 \\ 1 & 1 & 1 & 1 & 0 \end{bmatrix} \tag{25}$$

and the corresponding inverse graph Fourier transform matrix is

$$V = \begin{bmatrix} 0.45 & 0.29 & 0.71 & 0.41 & 0.22 \\ 0.45 & 0.29 & 0 & -0.82 & 0.22 \\ 0.45 & 0.29 & 0.71 & 0.41 & 0.22 \\ 0.45 & -0.87 & 0 & 0 & 0.22 \\ 0.45 & 0 & 0 & 0 & -0.90 \end{bmatrix}. \tag{26}$$

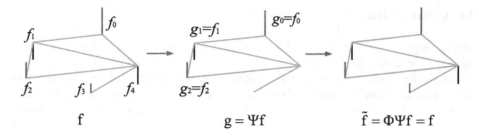

Fig. 1. Sampling and interpolation of graph signal $f = [f_0 \; f_1 \; f_2 \; f_3 \; f_4]^T$.

We input a graph signal f with bandwidth $K = 3$ as

$$f = \begin{bmatrix} 3.5643 & -2.2893 & 2.1501 & 1.2213 & -2.4374 \end{bmatrix}^T. \tag{27}$$

Without loss of generality, we let the number of samples be $M = K = 3$, and let $\text{rank}(\Psi) = K$. One possible sampling operator Ψ with simple form is

$$\Psi = \begin{bmatrix} 1 & 0 & 0 & 0 & 0 \\ 0 & 1 & 0 & 0 & 0 \\ 0 & 0 & 1 & 0 & 0 \end{bmatrix} \tag{28}$$

and we can obtain the following interpolation operator Φ by matrix calculation

$$\Phi = \begin{bmatrix} 1.0000 & -0.0000 & -0.0000 \\ 0.0000 & 1.0000 & 0.0000 \\ -0.0000 & 0.0000 & 1.0000 \\ 0.5411 & 0.8172 & 0.5411 \\ -0.9086 & -1.2033 & -0.9086 \end{bmatrix}. \tag{29}$$

Then we can get following sampled signal g and recovered signal $\tilde{f}$

$$g = \begin{bmatrix} 3.5643 & -2.2893 & 2.1501 \end{bmatrix}^T \tag{30}$$

$$\tilde{f} = \begin{bmatrix} 3.5643 & -2.2893 & 2.1501 & 1.2213 & -2.4374 \end{bmatrix}^T \tag{31}$$

where (31) implies the perfect recovery achieved and can be expressed as Fig. 1.

As mentioned above, the choices of the sampling operator Ψ are not unique. The following options of Ψ can also lead to perfect recovery

$$\Psi_1 = \begin{bmatrix} 1 & 0 & 0 & 0 & 0 \\ 0 & 0 & 1 & 0 & 0 \\ 0 & 0 & 0 & 0 & 1 \end{bmatrix} \quad \Psi_2 = \begin{bmatrix} 1 & 0 & 0 & 0 & 0 \\ 0 & 0 & 0 & 1 & 0 \\ 0 & 0 & 1 & 0 & 1 \end{bmatrix} \quad \Psi_3 = \begin{bmatrix} 2 & 0 & 0 & 0 & 0 \\ 1 & 2 & 3 & 4 & 0 \\ 0 & 0 & 1 & 0 & 10 \end{bmatrix} \tag{32}$$

as long as the restriction in Theorem 1 can be guaranteed.

4   Conclusion

In this paper, a new derivation for the sampling theorem of bandlimited graph signals is proposed based on the theory of function space. After introducing necessary preliminaries of signal processing on graphs, an interpolation operator is derived by constructing bandlimited space of graph signals, and the corresponding sampling operator is also obtained. On the basis of the relationship between the interpolation and sampling operators, a sampling theorem for bandlimited graph signals is obtained. Our proposed result states that perfect recovery is possible for bandlimited graph signals, and the theorem can be achieved easily in practice via matrix calculation, with the implementation given in the paper.

Acknowledgments. This work was supported in part by the National Natural Science Foundation of China under Grants 61501144 and 61671179, in part by the Fundamental Research Funds for the Central Universities under Grant 01111305, and in part by the National Basic Research Program of China under Grant 2013CB329003.

References

1. Sandryhaila, A., Moura, J.M.F.: Discrete signal processing on graphs. IEEE Trans. Sig. Process. **61**, 1644–1656 (2013)
2. Sandryhaila, A., Moura, J.M.F.: Big data analysis with signal processing on graphs: representation and processing of massive data sets with irregular structure. IEEE Sig. Process. Mag. **31**, 80–90 (2014)
3. Sandryhaila, A., Moura, J.M.F.: Discrete signal processing on graphs: frequency analysis. IEEE Trans. Sig. Process. **63**, 6510–6523 (2012)
4. Pesenson, I.Z.: Sampling in Paley-Wiener spaces on combinatorial graphs. Trans. Am. Math. Soc. **360**, 5603–5627 (2008)
5. Anis, A., Gadde, A., Ortega, A.: Towards a sampling theorem for signals on arbitrary graphs. In: IEEE International Conference on Acoustics, Speech and Signal Processing (ICASSP), pp. 3864–3868 (2014)
6. Wang, X., Liu, P., Gu, Y.: Local-set-based graph signal reconstruction. IEEE Trans. Sig. Process. **63**, 2432–2444 (2015)
7. Chen, S., Varma, R., Sandryhaila, A., et al.: Discrete signal processing on graphs: sampling theory. IEEE Trans. Sig. Process. **63**, 6510–6523 (2015)
8. Vetterli, M., et al.: Foundations of Signal Processing. Cambridge University Press, Cambridge (2014)

Data Association Based Passive Localization in Complex Multipath Scenario

Bing Zhao$^{(\boxtimes)}$ and Ganlin Hao

School of Information and Electronics, Beijing Institute of Technology, Beijing, China
{zhaobing,hglhust}@bit.edu.cn

Abstract. Complex scenarios are characterized by harsh multipath conditions. Recently, strong single reflections among multipath components (MPC) are proved to improve localization performance such as data-association (DA) and multipath components mitigation. We first propose a novel DA method, which figures out the relationship between the received signals and scatters based on an expectation maximization (EM) based Gaussian mixture model. Furthermore, sensors themselves often have uncertainties to be estimated, we propose a joint estimation method to obtain the final estimate. Simulation results show the effectiveness of the algorithm by considering sensors' uncertainties after demapping. As a result, the proposed algorithm can fit applications of large-scale wireless sensor networks (WSNs) in practice.

Keywords: Passive localization · Multipath components
Data association

1 Introduction

Wireless sensor networks (WSNs) [1] holds enough number of battery-powered sensors to transmit wireless signals and communicate with their neighbors. Sensors cooperatively estimate the state of one object by limited communication, ranging, and processing abilities. The idea of localization in WSNs has driven a myriad of applications like tracking, monitoring and control appliances [2].

In general, existing algorithms such as cooperative localization [3] and simultaneous localization and mapping (SLAM) [4] can work well in the desired line-of-sight (LOS) scenarios. However, in commercial shopping area, indoor, urban canyon or jungle scenario with scatters, these algorithms will experience severe performance declines, as each sensor may receive the same signals traveled from different paths in a time slot, i.e., multipath components (MPCs).

In [5], an iterative process is presented. Authors adopt time-of-arrival (TOA) measurements to estimate the ranging probability density function pdf. However, the static and i.i.d. assumptions of ranging pdf constrain its usage in practical scenarios. A TOA technique to utilize single reflections is presented in [6]. This research improves the performance but demands the whole map of layout and previous estimate to data-association (DA).

© ICST Institute for Computer Sciences, Social Informatics and Telecommunications Engineering 2018
X. Gu et al. (Eds.): MLICOM 2017, Part II, LNICST 227, pp. 585–594, 2018.
https://doi.org/10.1007/978-3-319-73447-7_63

In this paper, we propose a expectation maximization (EM) method in Gaussian mixture model to realize DA without the information of entire layout. Here we focus on an expectation maximization (EM) process in Gaussian mixture model. Gaussian mixture model is typically used in WSNs localization like [7].

This paper is organized as follows. Section 2 introduces the signal model. Section 3 involves EM algorithm with Gaussian Mixture model. Section 4 elaborates the proposed algorithm to estimate object's location, followed by a comprehensive simulations in Sect. 5. Finally, concluding remarks are made in Sect. 6.

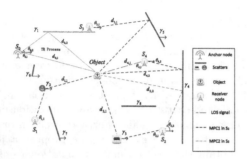

Fig. 1. A network with one anchor node S_0, N($= 4$) sensor nodes S_i and L ($= 8$) scatters with known number and tilt angles γ_k. S_0 sends a TR signal. Then each node i may receive several measurements $(d_{i,j})$.

2   System Model

We set a two-dimensional localization problem in Cartesian coordinate and this work focuses on real multipath scenarios like Fig. 1.

Generally, sensor S_0 is chosen as the reference sensor. Ranging measurement $d_{0,1}$ with the most accurate pseudo-range measurement is chosen to be a reference, which is calculated by $d = \hat{\tau}_{1,\text{TX}} \times c$. Then the i-th sensor obtains its j-th TDOA measurement $\Delta \tilde{d}_{i,j}$ with zero mean Gauss white noise as

$$\Delta \tilde{d}_{i,j} = d_{i,j} - d_{0,1} = \mathbf{g}(\hat{\theta}_{i,j}, \gamma_k)^T (\mathbf{q} - \bar{\mathbf{p}}_i) - \mathbf{g}(\hat{\theta}_{0,1}, \gamma_{S_0})^T (\mathbf{q} - \mathbf{p}_0) + \tilde{n}_{i,j} \quad (1)$$

where object's ground-truth position $\mathbf{q} \triangleq [x_q \ y_q]^T$, the i-th sensor's original position $\bar{\mathbf{p}}_i \triangleq [\bar{x}_i \ \bar{y}_i]^T$, where $i = 1, \cdots, N$. In practice, the sensors may change around their original positions. So we assume position's uncertainty $\Delta \mathbf{p}_i$ with Gaussian distribution, which will discuss later. k denotes the index of scatter associated to the measurement $d_{i,j}$, and γ_k is the known orientation of the k-th scatter. We further denote

$$\mathbf{g}(\hat{\theta}_{i,j}, \gamma_k) = \frac{1}{\cos(\hat{\theta}_{i,j} - \gamma_k)} [\cos \gamma_k, \sin \gamma_k]. \quad (2)$$

which is decided by geometric Topology. $\hat{\theta}_{i,j}$ is the AOA measurement of the j-th signal path at sensor i. With measurement noise, the estimated AOA measurement is used to replace $\theta_{i,j}$ as $\hat{\theta}_{i,j} = \theta_{i,j} + \eta_{i,j}$, where $\eta_{i,j}$ is noise with uniform distribution, i.e., $\mathcal{U}[-\eta^0, \eta^0]$.

3   Data Association Algorithm

In [5], the single reflection MPCs can be distinguished from the received waveform. Let $\Delta \tilde{\mathbf{d}}_i$ be the ranging block containing M_i measurements obtained in sensor i. Generally, the ranging measurements comes from the scatters and LOS components, but the sensor i doesn't know the probabilities which measurement stemming from which scatter or object directly from LOS path. Assuming every range estimate has a certain weight $\alpha_{i,j,k}$, we obtain the Gaussian mixture model as

$$p(\Delta \tilde{d}_{i,j}, \hat{\theta}_{i,j}|\mathbf{q}, \Delta \mathbf{p}_i, \theta_{i,j}) = p(\hat{\theta}_{i,j}|\theta_{i,j}) \sum_{k=1}^{K_j} \alpha_{i,j,k} \Phi(\Delta \tilde{d}_{i,j}|\mathbf{q}, \Delta \mathbf{p}_i, \theta_{i,j}) \qquad (3)$$

$$\Phi(\Delta \tilde{d}_{i,j}|\mathbf{q}, \Delta \mathbf{p}_i, \theta_{i,j}) = \frac{1}{\sqrt{2\pi}\sigma} \exp(-\frac{(\Delta \tilde{d}_{i,j} - \mu_k)^2}{2\sigma^2}) \qquad (4)$$

where $\alpha_{i,j,k} \geq 0$, $\sum_{k=1}^{K_j} \alpha_{i,j,k} = 1$. $\mathbf{q} = (x_q, y_q)$.

As the first received signals in each sensor has the probability that coming from LOS path instead of the single reflection (NLOS) path from the scatter $k(k \in L)$. L is the scatters' number. So sensor i's first signal has $L+1$ submodels in Gaussian mixture model as $K_j = L + 1(j = 1)$ or $K_j = L(j! = 1)$, $(L + 1)$th submodel means the LOS estimate.

The key to obtain the mapping information lies on the latent variable $\rho_{i,j,k}$, which means one measurement coming from one certain submodel k.

$$\rho_{i,j,k} = \begin{cases} 1 & \text{the measurement j coming from the model k} \\ 0 & \text{else} \end{cases}$$

where $\rho_{i,j,k} \in \{0, 1\}$.

Having range estimate $\Delta \tilde{d}_{i,j}$ and latent variables $\rho_{i,j,k}$, we obtain the complete data like $(\Delta \tilde{d}_{i,j}, \rho_{i,j,1}, \cdots, \rho_{i,j,K_j})$. From the model assumptions, $\tilde{\theta}_i$ is independent of other variables in $(\Delta \tilde{d}_{i,j}, \rho_{i,j,1}, \cdots, \rho_{i,j,K_j})$. Besides, scatter's horizontal angle and TDOA ranging measurements among sensors are also independent.

Here we express data's log likelihood function in the following align

$$\ln p(\Delta \hat{\mathbf{d}}, \hat{\boldsymbol{\theta}}, \boldsymbol{\rho}|\mathbf{x}) = \ln p(\{\{\{\Delta \hat{d}_{i,j}, \hat{\theta}_{i,j}, \rho_{i,j,k}, \}_{k=1}^{K_j}\}_{j=1}^{M_i}\}_{i=1}^{N}|\mathbf{x})$$

$$= \sum_{i=1}^{N} \sum_{j=1}^{M_i} \ln p(\hat{\theta}_{i,j}|\theta_{i,j}) + \ln p(\Delta \hat{\mathbf{d}}, \boldsymbol{\rho}|\mathbf{q}, \Delta \mathbf{p}, \boldsymbol{\theta}) \qquad (5)$$

where inaccurate sensors' positions $\bar{\mathbf{p}}$ are used to solve the mapping issue in subsection C, i.e. $\Delta\mathbf{p}$'s influence is negligible first.

For item $p(\Delta\hat{\mathbf{d}}, \boldsymbol{\rho}|\mathbf{q}, \Delta\mathbf{p}, \boldsymbol{\theta})$ in (5), we have a further mathematical expansion

$$
p(\Delta\hat{\mathbf{d}}, \boldsymbol{\rho}|\mathbf{q}, \Delta\mathbf{p}, \boldsymbol{\theta}) = \prod_{i=1}^{N}\prod_{j=1}^{M_i} p(\Delta\hat{d}_{i,j}, \rho_{i,1}, \rho_{i,2}, \cdots, \rho_{i,M_i}|\mathbf{q}, \Delta\mathbf{p}, \boldsymbol{\theta})
$$

$$
= \prod_{i=1}^{N}\prod_{j=1}^{M_i}\prod_{k=1}^{K_j} [\alpha_{i,j,k}\Phi(\Delta\hat{d}_{i,j}|\mathbf{q}, \Delta\mathbf{p}_i, \theta_{i,j})]^{\rho_{i,j,k}} \tag{6}
$$

Based on the TDOA and AOA method, each submodel is shown as

$$
\Phi(\Delta\hat{d}_{i,j}|\mathbf{q}, \Delta\mathbf{p}_i, \theta_{i,j}) = \frac{1}{\sqrt{2\pi}\sigma_i} \exp(-\frac{1}{2\sigma_i^2}(\Delta\hat{d}_{i,j} + \mathbf{g}(\hat{\theta}_{i,j}, \gamma_k)^T\bar{\mathbf{p}}_i - \mathbf{g}(\theta_0, \gamma_k)^T\mathbf{p}_1
$$
$$
- (\mathbf{g}(\hat{\theta}_{i,j}, \gamma_k) - \mathbf{g}(\theta_0, \gamma_k))^T\mathbf{q})^2
$$

Then the item in (6)'s log-likelihood function is

$$
\ln p(\Delta\hat{\mathbf{d}}, \boldsymbol{\rho}|\mathbf{q}, \Delta\mathbf{p}, \boldsymbol{\theta}) = \sum_{i=1}^{N}\sum_{j=1}^{M_i}\sum_{k=1}^{K_j} \tag{7}
$$
$$
\rho_{i,j,k}\left[\ln\alpha_{i,j,k} + \ln(\frac{1}{\sqrt{2\pi}}) - \ln\sigma_i - \frac{1}{2\sigma_i^2}(\Delta\hat{d}_{i,j} - \mu_{i,j})^2\right]
$$

where $\mu_{i,j} = \mathbf{g}(\hat{\theta}_{i,j}, \gamma_k)^T(\mathbf{q} - \mathbf{p}_i) - \mathbf{g}(\theta_0, \gamma_k)^T(\mathbf{q} - \mathbf{p}_0)$. We define n_k as the number of submodel k among all the measurements in sensors. So $n_k = \sum_{i=1}^{N}\sum_{j=1}^{M_i}\rho_{i,j,k}, \sum_{k=1}^{K_j} n_k = \mathbf{N}$. So (7) can be reformulated as

3.1   E Step of the EM Algorithm

In order to obtain Q function in lth iteration, we have

$$
\mathcal{Q}(\mathbf{x}, \mathbf{x}^l) = \mathrm{E}[\ln p(\Delta\hat{\mathbf{d}}, \hat{\boldsymbol{\theta}}, \boldsymbol{\rho}|\mathbf{x})|\boldsymbol{\rho}, \mathbf{q}^{(l)}, \Delta\mathbf{p}, \boldsymbol{\theta}] \tag{8}
$$
$$
= \mathrm{E}\Big\{ \sum_{i=1}^{N}\sum_{j=1}^{M_i} \ln p(\hat{\theta}_{i,j}|\theta_{i,j}) + \sum_{i=1}^{N}\sum_{j=1}^{M_i}\sum_{k=1}^{K_j} \rho_{i,j,k}
$$
$$
\left[\ln\alpha_{i,j,k} + \ln(\frac{1}{\sqrt{2\pi}}) - \ln\sigma_i - \frac{1}{2\sigma_i^2}(\Delta\hat{d}_{i,j} - \mu_k)^2\right]\Big\}
$$

We define $\mathrm{E}(\rho_{i,j,k})$ as $\hat{\rho}_{i,j,k}$.

$$
\hat{\rho}_{i,j,k}^{l+1} = \mathrm{E}(\rho_{i,j,k}) == \frac{\hat{\rho}_{i,j,k}^l\Phi(\Delta\hat{d}_{i,j}|\mathbf{q}^{l+1}, \Delta\mathbf{p}_i, \theta_{i,j})}{\sum_{k=1}^{K_j} \hat{\rho}_{i,j,k}^l\Phi(\Delta\hat{d}_{i,j}|\mathbf{q}^{l+1}, \Delta\mathbf{p}_i, \theta_{i,j})} \tag{9}
$$

where $\hat{\rho}_{i,j,k}^{l+1}$ names the possible weight of model k to the observed data $\Delta\hat{d}_{i,j}$.

Using $\hat{\rho}_{i,j,k} = \mathrm{E}(\rho_{i,j,k})$

$$
\mathcal{Q}(\mathbf{x}, \mathbf{x}^l) = \sum_{i=1}^{N}\sum_{j=1}^{M_i} \ln p(\hat{\theta}_{i,j}|\theta_{i,j}) \sum_{i=1}^{N}\sum_{j=1}^{M_i}\sum_{k=1}^{K_j} \hat{\rho}_{i,j,k}+
$$

$$
\left[\ln \alpha_{i,j,k} + \ln(\frac{1}{\sqrt{2\pi}}) - \ln \sigma_i - \frac{1}{2\sigma_i^2}(\Delta \hat{d}_{i,j} - \mu_{i,j})^2 \right] \quad (10)
$$

3.2 M Step of the EM Algorithm

After the E step, iterative M step for maximum $\mathcal{Q}$ is

$$
\mathbf{q}^{l+1} = \arg\max_{\mathbf{q}} \mathcal{Q}(\mathbf{q}, \mathbf{q}^l)
$$

After some manipulations, we can obtain

$$
\mathbf{q}_x^{l+1} = \frac{\sum_{i=1}^{N}\sum_{j=1}^{M_i}\sum_{k=1}^{K_j} \hat{\rho}_{i,j,k}^l(\Delta \hat{d}_{i,j}A_{i,j} - A_{i,j}B_{i,j}\mathbf{q}_y^{(l)} + A_{i,j}C_{i,j})/\sigma_i^2}{\sum_{i=1}^{N}\sum_{j=1}^{M_i}\sum_{k=1}^{K_j} \hat{\rho}_{i,j,k}A_{i,j}^2/\sigma_i^2} \quad (11)
$$

$$
\mathbf{q}_y^{l+1} = \frac{\sum_{i=1}^{N}\sum_{j=1}^{M_i}\sum_{k=1}^{K_j} \hat{\rho}_{i,j,k}^l(\Delta \hat{d}_{i,j}B_{i,j} - A_{i,j}B_{i,j}\mathbf{q}_x^{(l)} + B_{i,j}C_{i,j})/\sigma_i^2}{\sum_{i=1}^{N}\sum_{j=1}^{M_i}\sum_{k=1}^{K_j} \hat{\rho}_{i,j,k}B_{i,j}^2/\sigma_i^2} \quad (12)
$$

where $A_{i,j} = a_{i,j} - a_0, B_{i,j} = b_{i,j} - b_0, C_{i,j} = a_{i,j}\bar{x}_i + b_{i,j}\bar{y}_i - a_0 x_0 - b_0 y_0$, which $a_{i,j} = \frac{\cos\gamma_k}{\cos(\theta_{i,j}-\gamma_k)}$ $a_0 = \frac{\sin\gamma_k}{\cos(\theta_0-\gamma_k)}$ $b_{i,j} = \frac{\sin\gamma_k}{\cos(\theta_{i,j}-\gamma_k)}$ $b_0 = \frac{\sin\gamma_k}{\cos(\theta_0-\gamma_k)}$. This is a coarse position estimation without considering the AOAs' measurement errors and sensors' uncertainties, so we use it as the initial guess in the following section.

Furthermore, $\hat{\alpha}_{i,j,k}$ is obtained by $\hat{\mathbf{q}}$ and Laplace method under the constrain of $\sum_{k=1}^{K_j} \hat{\alpha}_{i,j,k} = 1$.

$$
\alpha_{i,j,k}^{l+1} = \arg\max_{\alpha_{i,j,k}} \mathcal{Q}(\alpha_{i,j,k}, \alpha_{i,j,k}^{(l)}) = \hat{\rho}_{i,j,k}^{l+1} \quad (13)
$$

where $k = 1, 2, \cdots, K_j$. Repeat this EM process N_{iter} times until log likelihood value are no longer changes obviously. The influence of $\Delta \boldsymbol{p}_i$ to mapping is discussed in simulations.

3.3 Demapping

After we obtain the coarse position of object, we use the updated Gaussian mixture model to realize the parameter evaluation, which means demapping. After calculation, if $\alpha_{i,j,k}$'s value is the biggest and exceed the empirical threshold in measurement $\Delta \hat{d}_{i,j}$, we choose the corresponding submodel to describe the likelihood distribution

$$
p(\Delta \hat{d}_{i,j}|\mathbf{q}, \Delta \mathbf{p}_i, \theta_{i,j}) = p(\hat{\theta}_{i,j}|\theta_{i,j}) \sum_{k=1}^{K_j} [\alpha_{i,j,k}\Phi(\Delta \tilde{d}_{i,j}|\mathbf{q}, \Delta \mathbf{p}_i, \theta_{i,j})]^{\rho_{i,j,k}} \quad (14)
$$

where $\rho_{i,j,k} = 1$ if and only if $\alpha_{i,j,k}$'s value is the biggest and exceed the threshold, otherwise, $\rho_{i,j,k} = 0$.

If $\rho_{i,j,k} = 1$ and $k \leq L$, the measurement is NLOS signal, else if the measurement is assumed LOS($\rho_{i,j,k} = 1$ and $k = L + 1$).

4   Centralized Algorithm

As sensors' position may move as time passes by. Here we further consider sensor position's uncertainty $\Delta\mathbf{p}_i$, which turns to be the parameter of interest in $\mathbf{p}_i = \bar{\mathbf{p}}_i + \Delta\mathbf{p}_i$. To further improve the positioning performance by joint estimation, we will update the sensor uncertainty's influence in (1) as

$$\Delta\hat{d}_{i,j} = \mathbf{g}(\hat{\theta}_{i,j}, \gamma_k)^T (\mathbf{q} - \bar{\mathbf{p}}_i) - \mathbf{g}(\theta_0, \gamma_k)^T (\mathbf{q} - \mathbf{p}_0) + \hat{n}_i \qquad (15)$$

Then we derive the likelihood function based on (14):

$$\tilde{p}(\Delta\hat{d}_{i,j}, \Delta\mathbf{p}_i | \mathbf{q}, \bar{\mathbf{p}}_i, \theta_{i,j}) = p(\hat{\theta}_{i,j} | \theta_{i,j}) \alpha''_{i,j,k_{i,j}} \tilde{\Phi}(\Delta\hat{d}_{i,j}, \Delta\mathbf{p}_i | \mathbf{q}, \bar{\mathbf{p}}_i, \theta_{i,j}). \qquad (16)$$

Since the measurements are independent to each other,

$$\tilde{p}(\Delta\hat{\mathbf{d}}, \Delta\mathbf{p}_i | \mathbf{q}, \mathbf{p}, \boldsymbol{\theta}) = \prod_{i \in \mathcal{N}} \prod_{j \in M_i} \tilde{p}(\Delta\hat{d}_{i,j}, \hat{\theta}_{i,j}, \Delta\mathbf{p}_i | \mathbf{q}, \bar{\mathbf{p}}_i, \theta_{i,j}). \qquad (17)$$

Here we define sets called $\mathcal{N} = \{1, 2, ..., N\}$ and $\mathcal{M}_i = \{1, 2, ..., M_i\}$. Since $\Delta\mathbf{p}_i$ is independent of other random variables in the complete data, we fix other interested parameters to obtain the new $\tilde{Q}$ function with the addition of $\Delta\mathbf{p}_i$ as

$$\tilde{Q}(\mathbf{q}, \mathbf{q}') = \mathrm{E}[\ln\tilde{p}(\Delta\hat{\mathbf{d}}, \Delta\mathbf{p}_i | \mathbf{q}, \mathbf{p}, \boldsymbol{\theta}) | \Delta\hat{\mathbf{d}}, \alpha'', \mathbf{q}'] \qquad (18)$$

$$= \sum_{i \in \mathrm{N}} \sum_{j \in M_i} \int p(\Delta\mathbf{p}_i | \Delta\hat{d}_{i,j}, \bar{\mathbf{p}}_i, \mathbf{q}') \times \ln\tilde{p}(\Delta\hat{d}_{i,j}, \Delta\mathbf{p}_i | \mathbf{q}, \bar{\mathbf{p}}_i, \theta_{i,j}) d\Delta\mathbf{p}_i$$

in which

$$\ln\tilde{p}(\Delta\hat{d}_{i,j}, \Delta\mathbf{p}_i | \mathbf{q}, \bar{\mathbf{p}}_i, \theta_{i,j}) = \ln p(\hat{\theta}_{i,j} | \theta_{i,j}) \alpha''_{i,j,k} + \ln\tilde{\Phi}(\Delta\hat{d}_{i,j}, \Delta\mathbf{p}_i | \mathbf{q}, \bar{\mathbf{p}}_i, \theta_{i,j})$$

Substitute the align into (18). The first item doesn't contain the parameter of interest $\mathbf{q}$ to realize Q function minimization, which can be dropped. $\tilde{Q}_i(\mathbf{q}, \mathbf{q}')$ can be reformulated as

$$\tilde{Q}_i(\mathbf{q}, \mathbf{q}') = \int p(\Delta\mathbf{p}_i | \Delta\hat{d}_{i,j}, \bar{\mathbf{p}}_i, \mathbf{q}') \times \ln\tilde{\Phi}(\Delta\tilde{d}_{i,j}, \Delta\mathbf{p}_i | \mathbf{q}, \bar{\mathbf{p}}_i, \theta_{i,j}) d\Delta\mathbf{p}_i \qquad (19)$$

By Bayes' rule, the posterior distribution of sensor i's position uncertainty in (19) is derived as

$$p(\Delta\mathbf{p}_i | \Delta\hat{d}_{i,j}, \bar{\mathbf{p}}_i, \mathbf{q}') \propto p(\Delta\mathbf{p}_i) \prod_{j \in M_i} p(\Delta\hat{d}_{i,j}, \hat{\theta}_{i,j} | \mathbf{q}, \bar{\mathbf{p}}_i, \Delta\mathbf{p}_i, \theta_{i,j}) \qquad (20)$$

Generally, the posterior distribution of sensor i's position uncertainty is intractable to be analyzed and calculated with low complexity, thus rendering the closed form of KullbackCLeibler divergence (KLD) as

$$D_{KL}(f \parallel p) = \int f(\Delta \mathbf{p}_i) \ln \frac{f(\Delta \mathbf{p}_i)}{p(\Delta \mathbf{p}_i)} d\Delta \mathbf{p}_i. \tag{21}$$

Single Reflections. Combining the updated model in (15), then the global $\Delta \mathbf{p}''$ with vector form can be expressed as

$$\Delta \mathbf{p}'' = \arg\min_{\Delta \mathbf{p}} \left\{ D_{KL}(\Delta \mathbf{p}; \boldsymbol{\alpha}'', \mathbf{q}', \hat{\boldsymbol{\theta}}) \right\} \tag{22}$$

As each sensor's uncertainty is i.i.d. with other sensors, the maximize the global $D_{KL}(\Delta \mathbf{p}; \boldsymbol{\alpha}'', \mathbf{q}', \hat{\boldsymbol{\theta}})$ is equivalent to obtain the extreme value in each $D_{KL}(\Delta \mathbf{p}_i; \boldsymbol{\alpha}_i'', \mathbf{q}', \hat{\boldsymbol{\theta}}_i)$.

The minimization of KLD can be derived by the partial derivatives of $D_{KL}(f \parallel p)$ with respect to $\Delta \bar{x}_i, \Delta \bar{y}_i$ and $\bar{\sigma}_{\Delta p_i}^2$ and setting the results are zeros. After some manipulations, we have $\Delta \mathbf{p}'' = (\Delta x_i'', \Delta y_i'')$, where

$$\Delta x_i'' = \frac{\frac{\Delta y_i'}{(1-\rho^2)\sigma_{\Delta x_i}\sigma_{\Delta y_i}} + \sum_{j=1}^{M_i} \frac{1}{\sigma_i^2}(E_{i,j} - a_{i,j}b_{i,j}\Delta y_i')}{\frac{1}{(1-\rho^2)\sigma_{\Delta x_i}^2} - \frac{1}{\sigma_i^2}\sum_{j=1}^{M_i} a_{i,j}^2}, \tag{23}$$

$$\Delta y_i'' = \frac{\frac{\Delta x_i'}{(1-\rho^2)\sigma_{\Delta x_i}\sigma_{\Delta y_i}} + \sum_{j=1}^{M_i} \frac{1}{\sigma_i^2}(F_{i,j} - a_{i,j}b_{i,j}\Delta x_i')}{\frac{1}{(1-\rho^2)\sigma_{\Delta y_i}^2} - \frac{1}{\sigma_i^2}\sum_{j=1}^{M_i} b_{i,j}^2} \tag{24}$$

$$\bar{\sigma}_{\mathbf{p}_i} = \sqrt{\frac{2(1-\rho^2)}{(1-\rho^2)\sigma_{\Delta x_i}^2\sigma_{\Delta y_i}^2 \sum_{j=1}^{M_i}(a_{i,j}^2 + b_{i,j}^2) + \sigma_i^2(\sigma_{\Delta x_i}^2 + \sigma_{\Delta y_i}^2)}} \sigma_i \sigma_{\Delta x_i} \sigma_{\Delta y_i} \tag{25}$$

Then $x_i'' = \bar{x}_i + \Delta x_i'', y_i'' = \bar{y}_i + \Delta y_i''$.

Finally, we derive the closed form of $\mathcal{Q}$ function of the j-th measurement in sensor i as

$$\tilde{\mathcal{Q}}_{i,j}(\mathbf{q}, \mathbf{q}') = \int f(\Delta \mathbf{p}_i | \Delta \hat{\mathbf{d}}_i, \bar{\mathbf{p}}_i, \mathbf{q}') \ln \tilde{\Phi}(\Delta \tilde{d}_{i,j}, \Delta \mathbf{p}_i | \mathbf{q}, \bar{\mathbf{p}}_i, \theta_{i,j}) d\Delta \mathbf{p}_i$$

$$= -\frac{1}{2\sigma_i^2} \Big[(a_{i,j} - a_0)^2 q_x^2 + (b_{i,j} - b_0)^2 q_y^2 - 2(a_{i,j} - a_0)$$

$$\mathrm{H}_{i,j}q_x - 2(b_{i,j} - b_0)\mathrm{H}_{i,j}q_y + 2\mathrm{K}_{i,j}q_x q_y \Big] + \mathcal{C} \tag{26}$$

where

$$\mathrm{H}_{i,j} = \Delta \tilde{d}_{i,j} + a_{i,j}x_i'' + b_{i,j}y_i'' - a_0 x_0 - b_0 y_0, \tag{27}$$

$$\mathrm{K}_{i,j} = a_{i,j}b_{i,j} + a_0 b_{i,j} + a_{i,j}b_0 + a_0 b_0. \tag{28}$$

For each sensor $i \in \mathrm{N_{LOS}}$ with M_i measurements, we obtain the global $\mathcal{Q}$ function as

$$
\tilde{\mathcal{Q}}(\mathbf{q}, \mathbf{q}') \propto -\sum_{i \in \mathrm{N_{LOS}}} \sum_{j=1}^{M_i} \frac{1}{2\sigma_i^2} \Big[(a_{i,j} - a_0)^2 q_x^2 + (b_{i,j} - b_0)^2 q_y^2 -
$$
$$
2(a_{i,j} - a_0) \mathrm{H}_{i,j} q_x - 2(b_{i,j} - b_0) \mathrm{H}_{i,j} q_y + 2 \mathrm{K}_{i,j} q_x q_y \Big] \tag{29}
$$

Finally, we can obtain the estimate of object like

$$
q_x'' = \frac{\sum_{i \in \mathrm{N_{NLOS}}} \sum_{j=1}^{M_i} \frac{1}{\sigma_i^2} \Big[(a_{i,j} - a_0) \mathrm{H}_{i,j} + \mathrm{K}_{i,j} q_y' \Big]}{\sum_{i \in \mathrm{N_{NLOS}}} \sum_{j=1}^{M_i} \frac{1}{\sigma_i^2} (a_{i,j} - a_0)^2} \tag{30}
$$

$$
q_y'' = \frac{\sum_{i \in \mathrm{N_{NLOS}}} \sum_{j=1}^{M_i} \frac{1}{\sigma_i^2} \Big[(b_{i,j} - b_0) \mathrm{H}_{i,j} + \mathrm{K}_{i,j} q_x' \Big]}{\sum_{i \in \mathrm{N_{NLOS}}} \sum_{j=1}^{M_i} \frac{1}{\sigma_i^2} (b_{i,j} - b_0)^2} \tag{31}
$$

5   Simulation Results

To evaluate the performance of the proposed algorithm in a centralized implementation, we realize the passive localization in a $100 \times 100 \, \mathrm{m}^2$ plane with one anchor node S_0 and four receiver node $S_1, S_2, \cdots, S_4$ as shown in Fig. 1. The parameters related to the simulations are summarized in Table 1. Each nodes' positions are $\mathbf{p}_1 = [20 \ 20]^T, \mathbf{p}_2 = [80 \ 30]^T, \mathbf{p}_3 = [60 \ 90]^T, \mathbf{p}_4 = [70 \ 70]^T$. The corresponding scatter orientations is $\boldsymbol{\gamma} = [0°, 86°, 150°, 90°, 111°, 55°, 135°, 11°]$. Furthermore, the ground-truth AOAs are $\boldsymbol{\theta} = [45°; 135°; -135° \ 18.4°; 0°; -170° \ -15.9°]$. In this simulation scenario, sensor nodes (S_1–S_4) received number of measurements ($|\mathcal{M}_1|$–$|\mathcal{M}_4|$) as $[1, 2, 1, 2]^T$ respectively.

We consider a Monte Carlo experiment with 1000 independent trials in Fig. 2. An initial guess of the proposed algorithm is tested according to the proposed data association method in Sect. 3. However, without considering sensors' uncertainties, the value of each submodel's weights are fluctuated and improve the risk of mismatch in demapping process. Therefore, the positioning performance of the data association method with different level of sensor position uncertainty is generally worse than the ideal case without uncertainties. We also estimate the position based on [5] for the comparison purpose. The error of [5] is larger than our method as the assumption that all the TDOA ranging have the same noise pdf. Compared with these five CDFs, the quality of demapping is reliable with uncertainties and effective than [5] even with uncertainties.

More precisely, we optimize the positioning performance including sensors' uncertainties by aligns (30) and (31) in Fig. 3. After sufficient number of iterations, we can figure out the location errors are smaller than Fig. 2 as we iteratively update the object and sensors' positions simultaneously. For comparable reasons, we also estimate the method in As TOA based method in [5] is valuable to the i.i.d. assumption, the performance will be worse considering sensors' uncertainties in Fig. 2's description.

Table 1. Major parameters in data association based algorithms.

Parameter	Note	Value
L×W	Space dimensions	$100\,\mathrm{m} \times 100\,\mathrm{m}$
$\mathbf{p}_0$	Anchor node S_1	$[10\,\mathrm{m}\ 70\,\mathrm{m}]^T$
$\mathbf{q}$	Object node	$[40\,\mathrm{m}\ 50\,\mathrm{m}]^T$
$\alpha_{i,j,k}$	Submodels' weight	$1/K_j$
$\Delta\mathbf{p}_i$	Sensor i's uncertainty	$\Delta\mathbf{p}_i \sim \mathcal{N}(0, \sigma_{\Delta p_i})$
$\sigma_{\Delta\hat{d}}$	Ranging std. deviation for $\Delta\hat{d}$	$1\,\mathrm{m}$
$\eta_{i,j}$	Ranging std. deviation for AOA	$\eta_{i,j} \sim \mathrm{Unif}[-3°, 3°]$
K_j	Submodels for first MPC	$K_1 = 6$
	Submodels for other MPCs	$K_j = 5, j \geq 1$

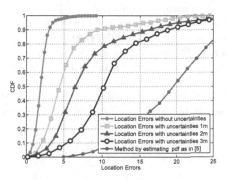

Fig. 2. Coarse location error based on different sensors' uncertainties.

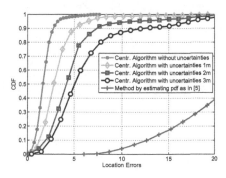

Fig. 3. Location errors based on proposed algorithm.

6   Conclusion

In this paper, we proposed a low complexity multipath aided algorithm to localization. For a further extension, we will study how to reduce the constrained known information to generalize the proposed algorithms and reduce the computational complexity.

References

1. Zhao, F., Guibas, L.J.: Wireless Sensor Networks: An Information Processing Approach. Morgan Kaufmann, Amsterdam (2004)
2. Gezici, S., Giannakis, G., Kobayashi, H., Molisch, A., Poor, H., Sahinoglu, Z.: Localization via ultra-wideband radios: a look at positioning aspects for future sensor networks. IEEE Sig. Process. Mag. **22**, 70–84 (2005)
3. Wymeersch, H., Lien, J., Win, M.Z.: Cooperative localization in wireless networks. In: Proceedings of IEEE, vol. 97, no. 2, pp. 427–450 (2009)
4. Grisetti, G., KuMmerle, R., Stachniss, C.: A tutorial on graph-based SLAM. IEEE Intell. Transp. Syst. Mag. **2**(4), 31–43 (2010)
5. Yin, F., Fritsche, C., Gustafsson, F., Zoubir, A.M.: TOA-based robust wireless geolocation and Cramr-Rao lower bound analysis in harsh LOS/NLOS environments. IEEE Trans. Sig. Process. **61**(9), 2243–2255 (2013)
6. Leitinger, E., Meissner, P., Rdisser, C.: Evaluation of position-related information in multipath components for indoor positioning. IEEE J. Sel. Areas Commun. **33**(11), 2313–2328 (2015)
7. Yin, F., Fritsche, C., Jin, D.: Cooperative localization in WSNs using Gaussian mixture modeling: distributed ECM algorithms. IEEE Trans. Sig. Process. **63**(6), 1448–1463 (2015)

Design and Implementation of Multi-channel Burst Frame Detector

Bing Zhao[✉]

School of Information and Electronics,
Beijing Institute of Technology, Beijing, China
zhaobing@bit.edu.cn

Abstract. In order to realize the frame detection of signals which have different unique word (UW) lengths in multi-channel receiver, multiple UWs correlation detection algorithm is proposed. The algorithm judges whether the decision variable is greater than the threshold according to the UW length, from large to small, to determine whether a valid header is presented. Monte Carlo simulation is used to analyze the feasibility of the algorithm. In addition, a barrel shift register bank structure is adopted in hardware implementation, which can reuse multipliers to calculate the square magnitude of the correlation value and the energy of differential signal while traversing UWs. Simulations show that the proposed algorithm improves the detection performance and results in an easy-to-implement and resources saving structure.

Keywords: Frame detection · Barrel shift register bank

1 Introduction

Burst communication has the advantages of anti-interference, low intercept, etc., which is widely used in frequency hopping communication and time division multiple access (TDMA) communication, and has become an important way of digital communication. Burst transmission signals usually have characteristics of short-term and burst, so the receiving equipment requires the ability to synchronize and capture quickly, and frame detection is the premise of other synchronization.

Although the commonly used algorithm of frame detection can detect the frame head, there still exists the problems in terms of accuracy or the range of application. Delay and correlate algorithm in [1–3] can detect the signal quickly, but it is not accurate due to the flat correlation peak. The algorithm in [4, 5] improves the performance of the delay and correlate algorithm. However, it improves the complexity and can not realize the frame detection quickly. In [6], the hard decision is adopted, but frame detection can not be realized with this method in low signal-to-noise ratio (SNR). The differential correlation detection algorithm in reference [7] is advantageous to the selection and judgement of the frame head because of the sharp output peak. None of the above methods has considered frame detection problems in the case of multiple UW lengths, so there is an urgent need for a highly scalable and highly practical frame detection method.

© ICST Institute for Computer Sciences, Social Informatics and Telecommunications Engineering 2018
X. Gu et al. (Eds.): MLICOM 2017, Part II, LNICST 227, pp. 595–602, 2018.
https://doi.org/10.1007/978-3-319-73447-7_64

In multi-channel burst receivers, signal frames of different channels may have different lengths of UW for different application conditions (such as SNR, frame length, modulation scheme, etc.). These UWs may have some of the same characteristics, the uniform use of the same UW length for detection will inevitably lead to the difference between detection length and UW length of some frame, and there will be two cases:

(i) If UW length is longer than the detection length, the UW is not fully utilized and the detection accuracy may be reduced.
(ii) UW length is less than the detection length which will introduce a certain interference and seriously affect the detection performance.

This paper proposes a correlation detection method for multiple UW lengths. The algorithm can adapt to the frame detection with different UW lengths, which provides accurate and reliable frame detection result for subsequent demodulation.

In addition, UW which is in different channels with the same length may also be different, and needs to be detected at the same time. The use of multiple correlators to detect different kinds of UWs will inevitably cause the multiplier resource waste. The structure of a barrel shift register group is adopted in this paper, which reduces the resource consumption and improves the versatility.

2   The UW Structure

Supposing that there are P kinds of UWs, and the length of each UW can be $L_1, L_2, \cdots L_N (L_1 < L_2 < \cdots < L_N)$. The structure of any kind of UWs is shown in Fig. 1, and the short UW is the interception of long UW.

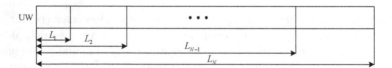

Fig. 1. UW structure of different lengths

3   Frame Detection Algorithm

3.1   Differential Correlation Detection Algorithm

Since the frequency and phase of the transmitter and the receiver are not the same, thereceived signal has a frequency and phase offset. In this regard, the effects of frequency offset and phase offset can be reduced by differential correlation. Assuming that the current received signal with ideal sampling is r_n, then r_n can be expressed as

$$r_n = a_n e^{j(2\pi n \Delta f T_{sam} + \Delta\theta)} \tag{1}$$

Where a_n is the signal transmitted, and $\Delta\theta$ is the phase offset. $\Delta f T_{sam}$ represents the normalized frequency offset. After differential operation, the differential signal can be written as

$$Y_n = r_n^* r_{n+q} = a_n^* a_{n+q} e^{j(2\pi q \Delta f T_{sam})} \tag{2}$$

Where q is the sampling ratio. We can see that the influence of $\Delta\theta$ is eliminated, and the phase deflection caused by the frequency offset is limited to $2\pi q \Delta f T_{sam}$. Similarly, do differential operation with UW b_n,

$$\alpha_n = b_n^* b_{n+1} \tag{3}$$

The decision variable of differential correlation detection algorithm can be expressed as

$$\Omega_n = \frac{|C_n|^2}{W_n} \tag{4}$$

where

$$C_n = \sum_{k=0}^{L-1} \alpha_k^* Y_{k+n} \tag{5}$$

and

$$W_n = \sum_{k=0}^{L-1} r_{n+q+k}^* r_{n+q+k} = \sum_{k=0}^{L-1} |r_{n+q+k}|^2 \tag{6}$$

The L in formula (5) and (6) is the UW length. Finally, if Ω_n is larger than the corresponding threshold ξ, output the frame head. Otherwise, repeat the above operation when the new data comes.

3.2 Multiple UWs Correlation Detection Algorithm

The correlation detection algorithm adopts one of the detection lengths uniformly, the algorithm proposed in this paper can adopt multiple detection lengths to detect from large to small, the algorithm implementation structure is shown in Fig. 2.

The UW structure is shown in Fig. 1, and the procedure of multiple UW correlation detection algorithm is summarized as follows :

step 1: calculate the decision variables $\Omega_{N,n}, \Omega_{N-1,n}, \cdots \Omega_{2,n}, \Omega_{1,n}$ with N kinds of UW lengths respectively according to the UW length from large to small by formula (4), and the corresponding threshold are $\xi_N, \xi_{N-1}, \cdots \xi_2, \xi_1$.

step 2: If $\Omega_{N,n}$ is larger than ξ_N, output the frame head; otherwise, go to the step 3;

step 3: If $\Omega_{N-1,n}$ is larger than ξ_{N-1}, output the frame head; otherwise, go to step 4;

$$\vdots$$

step N: If $\Omega_{2,n}$ is larger than ξ_2, output the frame head; otherwise, go to step N + 1;

step N + 1:   If $\Omega_{1,n}$ is larger than ξ_1, go to step N + 2; otherwise, wait for the new data and go to step 1;

step N + 2:   If $\Omega_{1,n}$ is larger than $\max\{\Omega_{1,n-1}, \Omega_{1,n+1}\}$, output the frame head; otherwise, wait the new data and go to step 1.

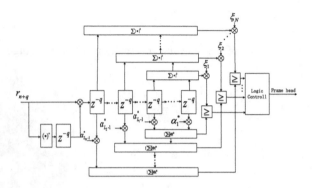

Fig. 2. The multiple UWs correlation algorithm implementation structure

4   Simulation Analysis

4.1   Theoretical Analysis

Based on the structure of the differential detector, we can sum up the frame detection into a binary hypothesis testing problem [8]. Suppose that the decision variable of the detector is Ω, we define H_1 when Ω is larger than the threshold ξ, otherwise H_0. And the probability density functions (PDF) of Ω can be expressed as $p_{\Omega|H_1}(\Omega)$ and $p_{\Omega|H_0}(\Omega)$. Therefore, the probability of correct detection P_d is

$$P_d = \int_\xi^\infty p_{\Omega|H_1}(\Omega)d\Omega \tag{7}$$

and the false alarm probability P_{fu} is

$$P_{fu} = \int_\xi^\infty p_{\Omega|H_0}(\Omega)d\Omega \tag{8}$$

We can give the expression of Ω, but calculating the PDF of Ω is very difficult. Hence, Monte Carlo simulation is adopted to observe P_d and P_{fu}. Figures 3 and 4 show the PDFs of Ω when UW length is 20 and 40, respectively.

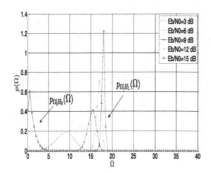

Fig. 3. The PDF of Ω (UW length = 20)

Fig. 4. The PDF of Ω (UW = 40)

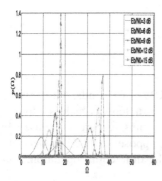

Fig. 5. $p_{\Omega|H_1}(\Omega)$ (UW length = 20 and 40)

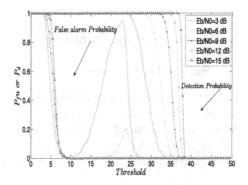

Fig. 6. The P_d and P_{fu} versus threshold

Figure 5 shows the $p_{\Omega|H_1}(\Omega)$ while detecting UW length of 20 and 40. From the results shown in Fig. 5, $p_{\Omega|H_1}(\Omega)$ in the case of length 20 and 40 can be well distinguished, so it is reasonable to detect the higher threshold first and then detect the lower threshold. With the simulation in Fig. 4 and formulas (7) and (8), we can get the P_d and P_{fu} as shown in Fig. 6. The threshold of the choice should ensure P_d is high while P_{fu} is low as far as possible which can refer to Fig. 6.

4.2 Simulation

To verify the effectiveness of the algorithm proposed, the two kinds of signals with UW length of 20 and 40 are simulated respectively. Both adopt QPSK modulation, over-sampling ratio is 4, SNR is 8 dB, the frequency offset is 7% and phase offset is $\pi/4$. Simulate the detection rate of 10000 frames sent, and compare with the differential correlation detection algorithm, the result is shown in Table 1. Besides, the threshold is selected by the simulation of the local optimal.

Referring to Table 1, using the detection length of 20 to detect signals with UW length of 40 will lead to a decline in frame detection rate. And using the detection

Table 1. Frame detection performance comparison.

Detection length	UW length	Threshold	Frame detection rate
20	20	10	0.9997
20	40	10	0.9993
40	40	18	1
40	20	18	0.2204
Algorithm proposed	20	10	0.9998
Algorithm proposed	40	18	1

length of 40 to detect signals with UW length of 20 will lead to frame head missed, which caused by a higher threshold. However, the multiple UWs correlation detection algorithm proposed in this paper can achieve the optimal detection at the same time.

5   Hardware Implementation

5.1   Barrel Shift Structure

In order to obtain the cross-correlation values with UWs of P kinds, the conventional parallel frame detector simultaneously instantiates P structures, which is complicated and resource consuming. In order to save the corresponding resources, we use a barrel shift register bank which is shown in Fig. 7. Suppose that UWs need to be cross-correlated are $\alpha_1, \alpha_2, \cdots \alpha_P$ of P kinds after the differential operation, and the length is L.

The register RAM_I and RAM_Q in Fig. 7 control the outputs of the real parts Yre and imaginary parts Yim of the differential signal Y_n respectively, and then do cross correlation calculation for the P kinds of UWs. Do correlation operation with α_1

Real part:

$$reg_{\alpha_1,I} = \sum_{k=0}^{L-1} Yre_{k+n}\alpha_{1,k}^* \tag{9}$$

Imaginary part:

$$reg_{\alpha_1,Q} = \sum_{k=0}^{L-1} Yim_{k+n}\alpha_{1,k}^* \tag{10}$$

Similarly do correlation operation with other kinds of UWs, the corresponding value $reg_{\alpha_2,I}, \cdots reg_{\alpha_P,I}$ and $reg_{\alpha_2,Q}, \cdots reg_{\alpha_P,Q}$ are obtained. The input ports of the multiplier M are $reg_{\alpha_1,I}$ and $reg_{\alpha_1,Q}$, the multiplication results can be expressed as :

$$M_1 = \left(reg_{\alpha_1,I} + jreg_{\alpha_1,Q}\right)\left(reg_{\alpha_1,I} - jreg_{\alpha_1,Q}\right) = \left|\sum_{k=0}^{L-1} \alpha_{1,k}^* Y_{k+n}\right|^2 \tag{11}$$

When the first barrel shift is performed after the complex multiplication operation, we do the complex multiplication operation again. Since the data in the register which connected to M has changed, M_1 will be the square magnitude of cross correlation value between data and α_2. Repeat the barrel shift and multiplication P times, all of the square magnitudes of cross correlation value between data and UWs can be obtained. Then the energy of Y_n. is obtained by controlling the input port of M according to (6). Using the energy of Y_n and the maximum value of P square magnitudes to calculate the decision variable according to (7). For multi-channel cases, the corresponding resource reuse can be accomplished by calculating corresponding values of different channels at different time periods. The only difference between the multi-channel implementation structure and Fig. 7 is that the front register will double.

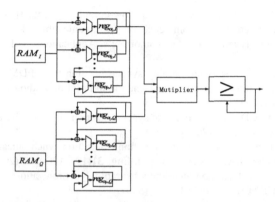

Fig. 7. Barrel shift register groups of single channel

5.2   Resource Evaluation

A burst frame detector for multi-channel is implemented in this paper. The related parameters are as follows: 15 channels, 4 different symbol rates, two kinds of UW lengths, and 17 types of UWs. Through the QUARTUS software synthesization, the resource usage of the module which calculates correlation value and energy value is shown in Table 2, where f represents the symbol rate, and the N means the number of channels. Referring to Table 2, only one multiplier is used in each case, that is, two $DSP36 \times 36$.

Table 2. Resource usage.

f/kBaud	N	$DSP36 \times 36$	ALMs	M4Ks	Combinational ALUTs
16.8	1	2	1013	4	1264
33.6	2	2	1257	9	1305
67.2	4	2	1829	18	1344
151.2	8	2	2888	29	1572

6 Conclusion

Aiming at the specific application environment of multi-channel burst frame detection, multiple UWs correlation detection algorithm and a barrel shift register bank structure are proposed in this paper to realize the frame detection. The simulation shows that the algorithm can improve the detector performance, and the structure can greatly save the multiplier and other resources to facilitate the realization of hardware circuits.

References

1. Sun, W., Song, J.: A frame synchronization algorithm in burst OFDM communication based on IEEE 802.11a (2011)
2. Schmidl, T.M., Cox, D.C.: Low-overhead, low-complexity [burst] synchronization for OFDM. In: IEEE International Conference on Communications, ICC 1996, Conference Record, Converging Technologies for Tomorrow's Applications, vol. 3, pp. 1301–1306 (1996)
3. Zhou, L., Saito, M.: A new symbol timing synchronization for OFDM based WLANs. In: IEEE International Symposium on Personal, Indoor and Mobile Radio Communications, vol. 2, pp. 1210–1214 (2004)
4. Wang, Y.Q., Yang, X.D.: A study of frame synchronization algorithm based on IEEE 802.16 standard. Appl. Sci. Technol. (2009)
5. Gao, Y., Jiao, L., Fengguo, M.A.: An efficient frame detection synchronization technology for IEEE 802.11a wireless LAN system. Comput. Eng. **31**(19), 120–122 (2005)
6. Cao, D., Wang, J.: Hard decision algorithms for rapid synchronization acquisition of bursty transmissions in CDMA. J. Tianjin Univ. (1999)
7. Nasraoui, L., Atallah, L.N., Siala, M.: An efficient synchronization method for OFDM systems in multipath channels. In: IEEE International Conference on Electronics, Circuits, and Systems, pp. 1152–1155 (2010)
8. Yang, D., Yan, C., Wang, H., et al.: Performance evaluation of different detectors for frame synchronization in DVB-S2 system. In: International Conference on Wireless Communications and Signal Processing, pp. 1–5. IEEE (2010)

Research on Cache Placement in ICN

Yu Zhang[1,2]([⊠]), Yangyang Li[1], Ruide Li[1], and Wenjing Sun[1]

[1] Beijing Institute of Technology, Beijing, China
{yuzhang,lyy_bl}@bit.edu.cn
[2] The Science and Technology on Information Transmission and Dissemination
in Communication Networks Laboratory, The 54th Research Institute of China
Electronics Technology Group Corporation, Shijiazhuang, China

Abstract. Ubiquitous in-network caching is one of key features of Information Centric Network, together with receiver-drive content retrieval paradigm, Information Centric Network is better support for content distribution, multicast, mobility, etc. Cache placement strategy is crucial to improving utilization of cache space and reducing the occupation of link bandwidth. Most of the literature about caching policies considers the overall cost and bandwidth, but ignores the limits of node cache capacity. This paper proposes a G-FMPH algorithm which takes into account both constrains on the link bandwidth and the cache capacity of nodes. Our algorithm aims at minimizing the overall cost of contents caching afterwards. The simulation results have proved that our proposed algorithm has a better performance.

Keywords: ICN · Steiner tree · Link cost · Cache placement · Group multicast

1 Introduction

Recently, with the rapid development of internet, network architecture based on contents gets the favor of researchers. The Palo Alto research center has put forward a landmark ICN network architecture CCN in 2007, which aims to provide an efficient and extensible content access application pattern for solving the insuperable internet traffic explosion problem [1]. ICN directly names the contents and doesn't focus on where the contents are causing the extensive concern of academic community [2]. Many research institutes carry out the research work of Information Centric Network, but the performance of many key technologies needs to be improved such as: caching strategy, routing mechanism, mobility and so on [3, 4].

A major feature of designing the ICN network architecture is in-network information caching, which has the advantages of improving the efficiency of contents distribution, distributing contents to the network edge, balancing the network bandwidth and load, etc. [5]. In recent years, researches on ICN network architecture have achieved substantial progress in the optimization methods, theoretical models and

Foundation Item: Science and Technology on Communication Networks Laboratory Foundation Project; Aerospace Field Pre-research Foundation Project (060501).

many other fields, but there are still a lot of problems to be solved. In ICN network, the redundant contents and the bandwidth consumption could be reduced through the content caching of nodes, this paper focus on how to select the cache nodes optimally, when requests returning to consumers. In the process of contents request returning to consumers, contents are stored on path nodes according to the cache management strategy. And the cache management strategy can be divided into two parts, i.e. cache placement policy and cache replacement policy. Appropriate cache placement is better support for content distribution, multicast, mobility, etc., therefore, the design of cache placement strategy is the key technic to performance of ICN. This paper mainly focuses on cache placement strategy.

Traditional algorithms generate a set of trees one by one, ignoring constrain of cache capacity which could lead to deterioration in performance, such as contents missing, larger delay, and network overload. In order to place contents effectively in the intermediate path nodes, we formulate cache placement as an extension of Group Steiner tree problem [6]. In our formulation, both the bandwidth and node's cache capacity are constrained, then meeting the needs of many-to-many data transmission and reception by establishing multiple Steiner tree.

2 Related Work

Recently, the way of communication in the network has been developed from one-to-one to one-to-many or many-to-many mode. So the research of multipoint communication has become an important topic in the field of network communication. Multipoint communication could be divided into two parts, i.e. "One-to-Many" and "Many-to-Many".

One-to-Many content distribution can be formulated as the minimum cost multicast tree problem, which is a typical NP-complete problem. There are some well-known algorithms such as MPH [7], Kou [8], Takahashi [9], Maxem-chuk [10] and Jingtao [11] algorithm, and their time complexity and the overall cost are much the same. Literature [12] proposes an improved MPH algorithm based on local search, which is called LSMPH (locally search minimum path cost heuristic), and its time complexity is low, but the total cost is generally greater than MPH algorithm. Literature [13] proposed a FMPH (Fast Minimum Path Cost Heuristic) algorithm aiming at solving the existing problems of MPH algorithm. The multicast tree established by FMPH algorithm is exactly the same as the tree by MPH algorithm, but FMPH algorithm improves the searching process of the shortest path node, so time complexity and the storage space will be reduced. Therefore, the Fast Minimum Path Cost Heuristic (FMPH) method can meet our need very well.

Many-to-Many content distribution problem is a typical group multicast routing problem (GMRP). At present, the researches on GMRP are still rare. Two methods can be generalized for solving the group multicast problem. The first method is to establish a tree for each set of multicast memberships, doing some coordination while building multiple trees so that the performance is optimal. Fei calls this method "Per-source-tree" [14]. Jia and Wang give a group multicast algorithm based on KMB algorithm called Jia and Wang's algorithm [6]. And then, Low and Wang give another algorithm based on TM [15] called GTM, whose performance is better compared with Jia and Wang's algorithm, but its traffic distribution is not fair enough. The same author gives a FTM based on the TM [16], which can fairly distribute the traffic, but the cost is higher. The other method is CBT (Core Based Tree), which only constructs one tree, then the root of the tree will be the center for multicasting to all member nodes, the minimum cost is extended to the group, Fei calls this method STGM [14]. However, when using CBT, the source has to pass through some of the edges connected with the kernel, which can cause congestion at these edges. At the same time, the selection of multicast kernel is crucial to the performance of the established group multicast trees.

On the actual network environment, the data packet may be sent to multiple destination nodes when it returns, meantime, many consumers may request different contents. In other words, the source node may also be the destination node, therefore, we need to further study to solve our problem based on the group multicast routing. In group multicast routing, each established tree must contain the given nodes set, but our model is to assign some given nodes sets and each established tree must contain the corresponding nodes set. So the first step is to establish the source nodes set, and then each source node will be in the given collection. Finally, in the optimal tree sets we build, each tree needs to contain those nodes which are in the collection, and the extra nodes contained in those tree are intermediate nodes which is used to cache contents.

3   Problem Formulation

The network model is a graph $G = (V, E)$, and the bandwidth $b(i, j) \geq 0$ is asymmetric, i.e. $b(i, j) \neq b(j, i)$, and then the edge from node i to node j is e_{ij}, so if $\forall e_{ij} \in E$, then $\forall e_{ji} \in E$, each edge in G has a link cost $c_{ij} > 0$. We define Bf_i is the cache threshold of each node.

Let $D(D \subseteq V, |D| = m)$, $D = \{d_1, d_2, \cdots, d_m\}$ is a group of source nodes in G, and then define $D' = \{D'_1, D'_2, \cdots D'_m\} \in G$ (d_i is the root of D'_i) is the group multicast sets. The bandwidth requirement for the nodes in D'_i is defined as $BW = \{bw_1, bw_2, \cdots bw_m\}$, and then we need to find a set of directed routing tree $\{T_1, T_2, \cdots T_m\}$, $T_i = (V_i, E_i)$ Assuming that all nodes in the optimal sets are collected to P, $P = \{p_1, p_2, \cdots p_q\} p_q \subseteq V_i$,so the following requirements are the constraints:

$$\min \sum_{k=1}^{m} \sum_{(i,j) \in T_k} c_{ij} X_{ij}^k, \qquad i \in V, j \in V \tag{1}$$

$$\sum_{k=1}^{m} bw_k X_{ij}^k \leq b(i, j), \forall e_{ij} \in E, X_{ij}^k = \begin{cases} 1, & e_{ij} \in E_k \\ 0, & else \end{cases} \tag{2}$$

$$\sum_{k=1}^{m} Y_r^{T_k} bw_k \leq Bf_r, \forall r \in P \tag{3}$$

In formula (1), it is used to ensure that the overall cost of the group multicast tree sets is optimal. In formula (2), it is used to constrain the total bandwidth of each edge. Formula (3) is the paper's key, it is used to constrain the node's cache threshold. A set of trees $\{T_1, T_2, \cdots T_m\}$ $(T_i(1 \leq i \leq m))$ which satisfies those constrains is our feasible solution called G-FMRP.

For the sake of contract, we should deal with the overall link cost of the algorithm ignoring the cache overflow of nodes, the following are constrains:

$$\Delta x = (\sum_{k=1}^{m} Y_r^{T_k} bw_k - Bf_r)/Bf_r \qquad (4)$$

The ratio of cache overflow is defined as Δx, if node r is belonging to the tree T_k, then $Y_r^{T_k} = 1$ else $Y_r^{T_k} = 0$, so the final overall cost for all trees is:

$$\cos t_{all} = \sum_{k=1}^{m} \sum_{(i,j) \in T_k} c_{ij} X_{ij}^k + \sum_{k=1}^{m} \sum_{r=1}^{q} \Delta x \cdot Y_r^{T_k} c_{T_k} \qquad (5)$$

4   The Proposed Algorithm

According to the above analyzing process, the first step of our proposed algorithm is to establish a multicast tree using FMPH algorithm, then generating a set of trees cooperatively based on the FMPH algorithm. We need to build group multicast trees, so we call it G-FMPH algorithm. The procedure stops if some saturated edges occurs when we build tree T_i, and then the saturated edges make up a set defined as E'. All trees (except T_i) have the saturated edges make up a set defined as M. Finally we will compare the alternative link cost of tree T_i with the most recently built tree (or trees), the smaller one will be changed to the alternative tree. Simultaneously, each multicast tree needs to determine whether the node cache constraints are satisfied or not, in order to ensure that the cache of each node isn't overflowed. If the tree does not satisfy the cache constraint, we will delete the overflowed node. Note: no saturated edge is used during adjustment. The details of G-FMPH are given in Fig. 1.

We take the topology in Fig. 2 to establish the group multicast trees. The number at both ends of each arrow indicates the available bandwidth in the corresponding direction, and then the number in the middle indicates the cost. Figures 3 and 4 illustrate the procedure of creating group multicast trees by G-FMPH. To better describe the treatment processing for cache overflow, we assume that the available bandwidth of nodes in the Fig. 2 is abundant. We suppose a situation where three different requests appear, and then when data packets return to consumers, we need to choose appropriate caching nodes. The source nodes set is denoted as $D = \{A, B, C\}$, and the destination nodes sets are denoted as $d_1 = \{B, C\}$, $d_2 = \{A, C\}$ and $d_3 = \{A, B\}$. The bandwidth requirement for each tree is $BW = \{2, 2, 3\}$ and the cache threshold of each node is 5 units.

Input: graph $G = (V, E)$ **, a set of source nodes** D_k **, bandwidth request** $BW = \{bw_1, bw_2, \cdots bw_m\}$

Output: a multicast tree $T_k(V_t, E_t)$ **,** $k \in D_k$

1 if G is not connected then stop

2 for each node $k \in D_k$

3   if (min $\{bw_1, bw_2, \cdots bw_m\}$ >the available bandwidth of the edge)

4   delete the edges and update G

5 if G is not connected then stop

6 compute shortest paths $V \rightarrow D_i$

7 for $i = 1$ to k

8   build multicast tree T_i using FMPH algorithm;

9   if there are overflowed nodes in T_i , delete the nodes and edges connecting with the nodes

10   if there are saturated edges in T_i

11   a set of saturated edges in T_i defined as E' , and then delete E' from G to get graph G'

12   compute shortest paths $V' \rightarrow D_i$

13   build alternative multicast tree T_i' using FMPH

14   compute the overhead $O_i = c(T_i') - c(T_i)$

15   multicast trees contain edges in E' make up a set M

16   for each tree $T_j \in M$

17   compute shortest paths $V' \rightarrow D_i$

18   build alternative multicast tree T_j' using FMPH

19   compute the overhead $O_j = c(T_j') - c(T_j)$

20   if $O_i > \sum_{T_j \in M} O_j$

21   T_i use the saturated edges; all the other trees $T_j \in M \rightarrow T_j'$

22   replace T_i by T_i' ; end if;

23   update the bandwidth status of all the edges and the cache of nodes;

24   end for;

25 end; (Procedure G-FMPH)

Fig. 1. G-FMPH algorithm

Here we only consider cache overflows of nodes to simplify the process.

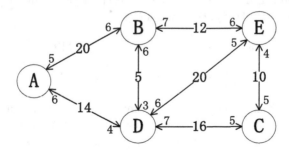

Fig. 2. A simple network topology

Starting from node A, the shortest path from A- > B is 19, which is smaller than A- > C (shortest path 30). The path is A- > D- > B and the path node is D, and then we need to update the available bandwidth of the used edges in the direction. The shortest path from D- > C is 16, which is smaller than the shortest path from A- > C (30). Therefore, the path D- > C is added to multicast tree. Finally, tree A is built shown in Fig. 3(a). The other two trees are built using the same method shown in Fig. 3(b) and 3 (c) respectively, ignoring the effect of cache overflow of node D.

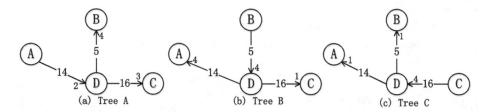

Fig. 3. An illustration of the traditional algorithm

The bandwidth requirement bw_1 and bw_2 is 4 units, and then bw_3 is 3 units, therefore, the cache of node D is overflowed when we build tree C. An alternative tree C' will be built using our proposed algorithm above. We will delete the node D and the edges connecting with node D when we build tree C', and then we build tree C' in graph G'. Finally, the group multicast trees are built in Fig. 4.

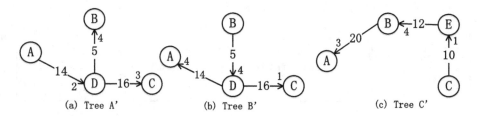

Fig. 4. An illustration of our proposed algorithm

Finally, compute the cost of trees established by using above two algorithms. The overall cost of traditional algorithm $\cos t_{tr}$ and our proposed algorithm $\cos t_{pr}$ are shown below calculated by formula (5) and formula (1).

$$\cos t_{tr} = \cos t_A + \cos t_B + \cos t_C = 119 \tag{6}$$

$$\cos t_{pr} = \cos t_A + \cos t_B + \cos t_{C'} = 112 \tag{7}$$

We can conclude that our proposed algorithm has smaller cost than the traditional one because of $\cos t_{pr} < \cos t_{tr}$, so our proposed algorithm has better performance. The difference of the overall cost between the two algorithms will increase as the number of group multicast trees grows.

5   Simulation

In order to assess our proposed algorithm's performance, the simulations are conducted. The topology is randomly generated, and the link between two nodes i and j is added by probability function:

$$P(i,j) = \lambda \exp(-d(i,j)/\rho L) \tag{8}$$

In formula (8), $d(i,j)$ is the distance between i and j, and then the maximum distance between any two nodes is defined as L. The range of the parameters λ and ρ is $0 < \lambda \leq 1$ and $0 < \rho \leq 1$. The average degree of nodes will be higher if we improve the value of λ, and then the density of shorter links compared with longer ones will be higher by decreasing the value of ρ, therefore, we can construct the network topology by modifying λ and ρ [17]. In our simulation, $\lambda = 0.3$ and $\rho = 0.15$. The cost from i to j is calculated by random integers (20, 50). The bandwidth is calculated by the formula (9):

$$b(i,j) = b_{\min} + r \bmod (b_{\max} - b_{\min}) \tag{9}$$

In formula (9), $b_{\max}$ is defined as the maximum bandwidth, $b_{\min}$ is defined as the minimum bandwidth. The bandwidth requirement of each tree is calculated by random integers (3, 5), and the cache threshold of each node is calculated by random integers (15, 20).

In the simulation, the overall cost is calculated by multicast trees. To insure the accuracy of the result, we simulate 10 times to get the average result.

Figure 5 shows the result of our proposed algorithm and traditional algorithm assigning $b_{\max} = 15$, $b_{\min} = 5$, $L = 200$ and the network size is 150. The abscissa and ordinate represent group size and network cost respectively. As the growth of the group multicast size, the gap becomes larger and larger. In the beginning, the group multicast size is small, therefore node cache may not be overflow, and then the overall cost of our proposed algorithm is the same as the traditional algorithm. But, many multicast trees are established as the growth of the group multicast size, this phenomenon may lead to cache overflow of partial nodes. Our proposed algorithm considers the cache overflow of nodes, but traditional algorithm ignores the cache overflow of nodes which will cause large additional overhead. Therefore, the overall cost of tradition algorithm is larger and the gap becomes larger as the growth of the group multicast size.

Figure 6 shows the result of our proposed algorithm and traditional algorithm assuming group size = 16. The abscissa and ordinate represent network size and network cost respectively. We can intuitively observe that the curve of traditional algorithm is higher than our proposed method. As the growth of network size, the gap becomes smaller. In the beginning, the network size is small, the group size that we assign is 16 which means we need to establish 16 trees, so we need to use many suboptimal paths and alternative trees because of constrains of bandwidth and cache, and then the overall cost is large. As the growth of the network size, node cache may not be overflowed, so the gap becomes smaller, finally two algorithms become nearly the same cost, which means there is no cache of nodes overflow.

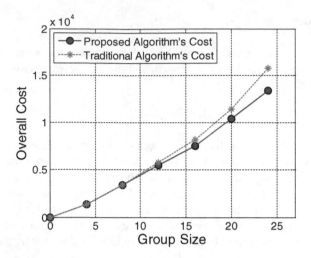

Fig. 5. Overall cost over group size

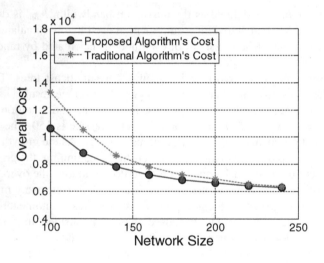

Fig. 6. Overall cost over network size

6   Conclusion

Traditional algorithms generate a set of trees one by one ignoring the limits of cache capacity which could lead to deterioration in performance, such as contents missing, larger delay, and network overload. Choosing appropriate caching placement policy is crucial to improving utilization of cache space and reducing the link cost when the data packet retrieval in ICN. In this paper, we use an extension of Steiner tree formulating the problem, and then we propose a G-FMPH algorithm which takes into account constrains of both available link bandwidth and the cache capacity limitation of nodes.

The simulation result shows that our algorithm has the superior performance over the traditional algorithm.

References

1. Jacobson, V., Smetters, D.K., Thornton, J.D., et al.: Networking named content. In: International Conference on Emerging Networking Experiments and Technologies, 55(1), pp. 1–12. ACM (2009)
2. Dannewitz, C., Golic, J., Ohlman, B., et al.: Secure naming for a network of information. In: INFOCOM IEEE Conference on Computer Communications Workshops, pp. 1–6. IEEE (2010)
3. Carofiglio, G., Gallo, M., Muscariello, L., et al.: Modeling data transfer in content-centric networking. In: Teletraffic Congress, pp. 111–118. IEEE (2011)
4. Muscariello, L., Carofiglio, G., Gallo, M.: Bandwidth and storage sharing performance in information centric networking. In: ACM SIGCOMM Workshop on Information Centric Networking, pp. 26–31. ACM (2011)
5. Shimizu, H., Asaeda, H., Jibiki, M., et al.: Content hunting for in-network cache: design and performance analysis. In: IEEE International Conference on Communications, pp. 3172–3177. IEEE (2014)
6. Jia, X., Wang, L.: A group multicast routing algorithm by using multiple minimum Steiner trees. Comput. Commun. 20(9), 750–758 (1997)
7. Winter, P.: Steiner problem in networks: a survey. IEEE Netw. 17, 129–167 (1987)
8. Kou, L., Markowsky, G., Berman, L.: A fast algorithm for Steiner trees. Acta Inf. 15, 141–145 (1981)
9. Wang, B., Hou, J.C.: Multicast routing and its QoS extension: problems, algorithms, and protocols. IEEE Netw. 14, 22–35 (2000)
10. Maxemchuk, N.F.: Video distribution on multicast networks. IEEE J. Sel. Areas Commun. 15(3), 357–372 (1997)
11. Jingtao, S.U., Lin, F., Zhou, X., et al.: Steiner tree based optimal resource caching scheme in fog computing. China Commun. 12(8), 161–168 (2015)
12. 李汉兵, 喻建平, 谢维信: 局部搜索最小路径费用算法[J]. 电子学报, 28(5), pp.92--95 (2000)
13. Guang-Min, H.U., Le-Min, L.I., Hong-Yan, A.N.: A fast heuristic algorithm of minimum cost tree. Acta Electronica Sinica 30(6), 880–882 (2002)
14. Fei, A., Duan, Z., Gerla, M.: Constructing shared-tree for group multicast with QoS constraints. In: Global Telecommunications Conference, pp. 2389–2394. IEEE (2001)
15. Low, C.P., Wang, N.: An efficient algorithm for group multicast routing with bandwidth reservation. Comput. Commun. 23(18), 1740–1746 (2000)
16. Wang, N., Low, C.P.: On finding feasible solutions to the group multicast routing problem. In: Pujolle, G., Perros, H., Fdida, S., Körner, U., Stavrakakis, I. (eds.) Networking 2000. LNCS, vol. 1815, pp. 213–227. Springer, Heidelberg (2000). https://doi.org/10.1007/3-540-45551-5_19
17. Waxman, B.M.: Routing of multipoint connections. IEEE J. Sel. Areas Commun. 6(9), 1617–1622 (1988)

The Digital Chaos Cover Transport and Blind Extraction of Speech Signal

Xinwu Chen, Yaqin Xie, and Erfu Wang[(✉)]

Key Laboratory of Electronics Engineering College, Heilongjiang University,
Xuefu Road 74, Harbin 150080, China
Cxw808@qq.com, 648427372@qq.com, efwang_612@163.com

Abstract. With its nonsense, non-detection and robustness, chaotic security technology is more widely used than cryptography in the field of secure communication. In this paper, under the background of digital era, wavelet transform is used to analyze the time-frequency energy concentration of Henon chaotic signal and speech signal, and with the Henon chaotic signal as carrier, the speech signal is hidden, which has important theoretical and practical significance to improve the self-security of the chaotic secure communication system. The speech signal, which chaos is hidden, is transmitted confidentially and it is effectively made to extract blindly at the receiving end. Then similarity coefficient is compared and analyzed under different SNR, which to verify the validity of the algorithm.

Keywords: Henon chaotic · Speech signal · Wavelet transform
Blind extraction · Masking

1 Introduction

Under the background of increasingly complex communication environment, information has become one of the most important strategic resources in today's society. In order to make the eavesdropper can not intercept the real and effective information, it is necessary to take the secure transmission of the speech signal. Meanwhile, the blind source separation technique could be used to extract the speech signal in the case of uncertain channel situation. The key point to secure the speech signal is the carrier signal which we take. In recent years, the emergence of digital chaos has provided an effective means for speech information hiding.

Compared with the traditional analog chaotic system, digital chaotic system [1–3] retaining the excellent characteristics of analog chaotic system, based on this, it strengthen the security and reliability of the system, improve the ability of anti-channel interference of chaotic system and the distortion of channel, and then improve the confidentiality and robustness of chaotic communication system. Under this background, based on the chaos signal processing, it has become a hot spot in the field of chaotic secure communication, and it has presented a more and more obvious intersection and fusion [4–6]. The application of the chaotic characteristics in the field of secure communication has become an emerging direction of research in recent years.

© ICST Institute for Computer Sciences, Social Informatics and Telecommunications Engineering 2018
X. Gu et al. (Eds.): MLICOM 2017, Part II, LNICST 227, pp. 612–621, 2018.
https://doi.org/10.1007/978-3-319-73447-7_66

Scholars between home and abroad have proposed many projects such as chaotic masking method, chaos switching method, chaotic modulation and other programs.

There are many scholars at home and abroad studied on the blind separation [7–11]. Some researchers took advantage of ICA algorithm to separate two different sounds from a non-accompaniment chorus recording, and realized blind separation in the background of multiple linearly mixed chaotic signals. Then some scholars used the geometric property of chaotic attractor and realized the separation of weak signal and chaotic interference by means of the concept of differential manifold tangent space. However, the above researches are based on analog signals. Neither do they take any advantage of digital technology, nor do they take the hidden and secure transmission of speech signals into account in the chaotic context.

2   Time Frequency Characteristics of Speech and Chaos

Chaos signal is easy to generate, and it possesses some characteristics, such as randomness and wide spectrum. So chaos signal is hard to decipher. Therefore, in this paper, with chaotic system as carrier, speech signal is hidden in chaos signal, which help information transmit confidentially. The Henon chaotic system is the most used to generate pseudo-random number sequence, and the theoretical basis is the sensitivity of chaotic dynamical systems to initial values and parameters.

The dynamic equation of Henon map is

$$\begin{cases} x_{n+1} = 1 + by_n - ax_n^2 \\ \quad y_{n+1} = x_n \end{cases}. \tag{1}$$

Henon chaotic system exhibits different states with different values of parameter x, y. In this paper, assuming initial value of the system is $x_0 = 0.4, y_0 = 0.4$, When $a = 1.4, b = 0.3$, the time domain waveform of Henon chaotic system could be gotten, which is shown in Fig. 1.

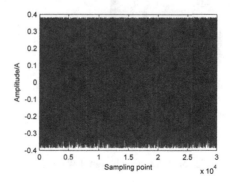

Fig. 1. Time domain waveform of Henon chaotic

In order to hide speech signal in chaos signal successfully, wavelet transform should be used to analyze the time-frequency characteristic of the chaotic signal. In Fig. 2, the energy distribution of the Henon chaotic system is relatively uniform. In the frequency range of 0–4000 Hz, the energy intensity is mainly about 0.4 J, but the speech signal is a small signal, and its energy and amplitude are relatively low, so the Henon chaotic system can be used as carrier to realize the concealment of the speech signal.

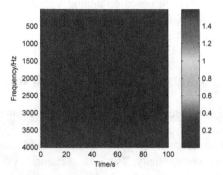

Fig. 2. Wavelet analysis of Henon

The speech signal could be gotten in our daily life. But in order to eliminate the interference of noise and ensure the validity and comparability of this algorithm, the voice bank, which embodies vowel phoneme, is selected. This paper takes the SA2 in the TIMIT voice bank as a hidden signal. As shown, the Fig. 3 is the waveform of SA2, while the Fig. 4 represents the time-frequency distribution of wavelet transform of SA2.

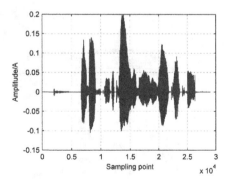

Fig. 3. SA2 speech signal waveform

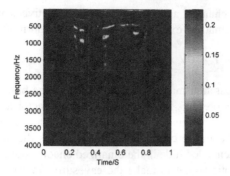

Fig. 4. Wavelet analysis of SA2 speech signal

From the wavelet analysis of the speech signal in Fig. 4, it could be seen that the power distribution of the speech signal is relatively wide, however, it is mainly concentrated in the frequency range of 500–1000 Hz.

3   System Model Establishment and Algorithm Evaluation Standard

3.1   The Establishment of the Model

In this paper, based on the digital processing, considering the speech signal which hide the chaotic signal which was blindly extract by the channel positive definite system. The system model can be abstracted as shown in Fig. 5:

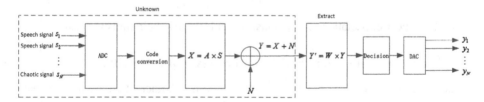

Fig. 5. The system model diagram

The mathematical expression of the model is

$$Y = A \times S + N. \tag{2}$$

Where A is an unknown channel of mixed matrix of $N \times N$, and $S = [s_1(t), s_2(t), \cdots, s_N(t)]^T$ represents N unknown source signal vectors. In order to achieve the purpose of signal secrecy transmission, one of the vectors selected as chaotic signal, while the others are the voice signals. After A/D conversion, the signals are mixed in the noisy channel, and N represents the additive white Gaussian noise in the channel. The mathematical expression of the separation model is

$$Y' = W \times Y = W \times A \times S + W \times N. \tag{3}$$

Where W is the separation matrix obtained by using the blind extraction algorithm at the receiver, and Y represents the observation signal vector at the receiving end.

In this paper, the speech signal as a hidden and extracted the desired signal, which needs digital coding. Then, the chaotic system is used as the hidden carrier, and the speech signal which is encoded hide in the binarized chaotic signal, with the help of the uncertainty of the chaotic signal to make the eavesdropper can not intercept the real information, so as to realize the purpose of confidential communication. The digital coding method of speech signal can be divided into two categories: waveform coding and parameter coding. Among them, Pulse Code Modulation (PCM) is one of the simplest and earliest methods of speech waveform coding. In this paper, the encoding of A law 13 segments is used to digitize the speech signals First, he voice signal is sampled, and set the sampling frequency $f_s = 8$ KHz, then the sampled values are quantized. Finally, a set of binary code pulse sequences is used to represent the quantized sampling values. The speech signal and the chaotic signal are mixed after the transmitter sends the A/D conversion to obtain the corresponding symbol sequence, meanwhile adds the additive white Gaussian noise N.

The receiver applies the classic fast ICA algorithm of the blind source separation theory to separate the mixed signal. The separation matrix and the normalized separation matrix expressions are

$$W^* = E\{Xg(W^TX)\} - E\{g'(W^TX)\}W$$
$$W = W^*/\|W^*\|. \tag{4}$$

Mathematical expectations in (4) must be replaced by their statistical values.

3.2   Evaluation Criteria and Simulation Process of the Algorithm

In this paper, the bit error rate (BER) and the similarity coefficient are used to evaluate the separation performance of the algorithm. The bit error rate is a measure of the accurate indicators which used to measure the data transmission over a specified period of time. The reason why the bit error emerged is due to the fact that in the signal transmission, the decay changes the voltage of the signal, thus the signal is destroyed during the process of transmission. While pulse, transmission equipment failure and other factors caused by noise, alternating current or lightning also will generate errors. The bit error rate is expressed as

$$P_e = \frac{1}{2}\left[1 - \mathrm{erf}\left(\frac{A}{\sqrt{2}\sigma_n}\right)\right]. \tag{5}$$

Where A is the peak of the signal, σ_n is the noise rms value. In the same probability of transmission and under the optimal threshold level, the total bit error rate of the bipolar base band system only depends on the ratio of A and σ_n, regardless of the type of signal being used, at the same probability of transmission and at the optimum threshold level. The correlation coefficient is used to measure the degree of similarity between the separation signal and the source signal. Assuming that S_j denotes the source signal and y_i' represents the separation signal. The mathematical expression of the similarity coefficient is

$$\xi_{ij} = \xi(S_j, y_i') = \frac{\left|\sum_{i=1}^{n} y_i'(t)S_j(t)\right|}{\sqrt{\sum_{i=1}^{n} (y_i')^2(t) \sum_{i=1}^{n} S_j^2(t)}}. \tag{6}$$

Where ξ_{ij} is regarded as a standard for verifying the performance of the separation algorithm. When $\xi_{ij} = 1$ means the two signals are fully correlated. When $\xi_{ij} = 0$ the two signals are completely independent. When ξ_{ij} become closer to 1 which indicates the higher the similarity between the source signal and the separation signal. The better the separation performance two signals are digitized and then mixed separation, after the chaotic system and the voice signal are selected, and then the D/A conversion of the separated symbol sequence is required to obtain the desired signal.

4   Simulation Experiment and Result Analysis

In this paper, the positive definite mixed model is considered, which is under the additive white Gaussian noise. At first, assuming that the signal-to-noise ratio of noise is $SNR = 18\,dB$, supposing $N = 2$, and then randomly generating a full-rank $(rank(A) = N)$ channel mixing matrix, which is

$$A = \begin{bmatrix} 0.6706 & 0.1977 \\ 0.5845 & 0.7163 \end{bmatrix}$$

In the processing of speech signal, at first, the simulative speech signal is processed by the encoding of A law 13 segments, which makes it develop into digital 0/1 sequence, and its sampling frequency is $f_s = 8\,KHz$. Then 8-bit quantification is adopted, and its quantized binary amplitude value is presented by a set of pulse sequences. Therefore the corresponding symbol sequence could be obtained and the output waveform could be finally decoded. In Fig. 6, it is the decoded waveform of SA2 speech signal, which compared with the waveform of the source signal in Fig. 1, and it is shown that the encoding method is successful in encoding the SA2 signal.

Also, chaos signal is digitized. Given the initial value of the Henon chaotic system, and the corresponding real valued sequence will be generated by its iterative equation. Since the mean of the real-valued sequence is $\mu=0.4980$, therefore, 0.5 is selected as

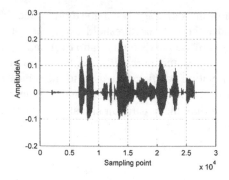

Fig. 6. SA2 speech signal decoding waveform

the criterion for quantization of the sequence, and the real-valued sequence is quantized into a 0/1 sequence.

In order to verify the successful concealment and confidential transmission of the speech signal, wavelet transform is applied to the mixed signal. The Figs. 7 and 8 show the wavelet analysis of mixed first signal and wavelet analysis of mixed second signal respectively. By comparing the wavelet analysis diagram of the chaotic signal and the speech signal (Figs. 2 and 4), the time-frequency distribution characteristic of the

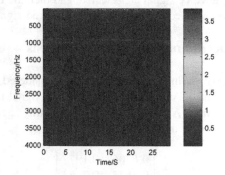

Fig. 7. Wavelet analysis of mixed first signal

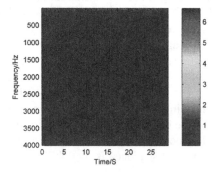

Fig. 8. Wavelet analysis of mixed second signal

speech signal is not displayed on the time-frequency analysis chart of the mixed signal, so the speech signal is successfully hidden.

The next step is to adopt the FastICA algorithm at the receiver to blindly separate the mixed signal. Because of the influence of channel and noise, the sequence after separation is a real-valued sequence, so it is necessary to convert the real-valued sequence into 0/1 sequence, and this simulation selects 0 as the decision threshold. For the probability and polarity of the opposite signal [12], the optimal decision criteria:

$$z(T) \underset{H_2}{\overset{H_1}{\gtrless}} = 0. \tag{7}$$

After the separated signal is converted into a 0/1 sequence by a threshold decision, it is necessary to verify the separation performance of the algorithm. The bit error rate and similarity coefficient are two criteria for evaluating the separation performance. When SNR = 18 dB, the BER of speech signal and chaotic signal are 6.5894×10^{-5} and 8.9978×10^{-4} respectively; Similarity coefficient matrix is:

$$C = \begin{bmatrix} 0.9783 & 0.0501 \\ 0.0217 & 0.9499 \end{bmatrix}$$

The matrix C can be seen that the first column has a maximum of 0.9783, while the second column is 0.9499, and the remaining numbers are close to zero. So it can be explained that when SNR = 18 dB, the algorithm realizes the blind separation of the speech signal hidden in the chaotic signal.

Finally, the separated speech coding sequence is converted to parallel output by serializer. And then its PCM decoding is reduced to an analog signal and the wavwrite function is used to save the speech signal into an audio file, which is affected by noise. Although there are some murmurs in the process, but the the content of talking of source language signal would be restored clearly. Figure 9 shows the Waveform of the SA2 speech signal, which has been decoded.

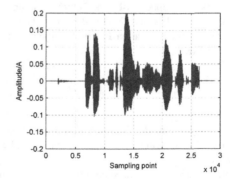

Fig. 9. Waveform of speech signal after mixed separation

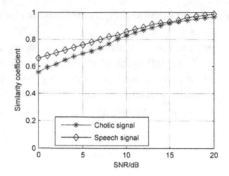

Fig. 10. Similarity coefficient of two kinds of signals with different SNR

Figure 10 is the curves of similarity coefficients of two signals at different SNR. It can be seen that with the increasing SNR, and the similarity coefficient shows a trend of growth. So it can verify the effectiveness of this separation algorithm.

5 Conclusion

Chaotic confidential transmission is widely used in a variety of security communications, and the chaotic hidden transmission of speech signals is one of the most basic problems. In this paper, based on the purpose of confidential transmission, the chaotic system is used to encrypt the speech signal on the basis of digitization. And compared with the traditional analog hybrid method, it is greatly improved from the aspects of confidentiality, robustness and reliability. The receiver adopts the FastICA, the classical algorithm in the blind source separation algorithm, to separate the mixed signal. And the separation performance of the proposed algorithm is verified by analyzing the BER and similarity coefficients, and comparing the auditory effects of the source and the separated signals. The follow-up work will study the hiding and separation of multi-channel speech signals in varied chaotic backgrounds.

Acknowledgments. This work was supported by the National Natural Science Foundation of China (grant 61571181), Postdoctoral Research Foundation of Heilongjiang Province (grant LBH-Q14136), and Graduate Student Innovation Research Project Foundation of Heilongjiang University (grant YJSCX2017-148HLJU).

References

1. Muthukumar, P., Balasubramaniam, P.: Feedback synchronization of the fractional order reverse butterfly-shaped chaotic system and its application to digital cryptography. Nonlinear Dyn. **74**(4), 1169–1181 (2013)
2. Stavrinides, S.G.: Digital chaotic synchronized communication system. J. Eng. Sci. Technol. Rev. **2**(1), 82–86 (2009)

3. Zhou, W.J.: Chaotic digital communication system based on field programmable gate array technology—design and implementation. Acta Physica Sinica **58**(1), 113–119 (2009)
4. Yang, T., Chua, L.O.: Impulsive stabilization for control and synchronization of chaotic systems: theory and application to secure communication. IEEE Trans. Circuits Syst. I Fundam. Theory App. **44**(10), 976–988 (1997)
5. Lin, T.C., Huang, F.Y., Du, Z.: Synchronization of fuzzy modeling chaotic time delay memristor-based Chua's circuits with application to secure communication. Int. J. Fuzzy Syst. **17**(2), 206–214 (2015)
6. Wang, B., Zhong, S.M., Dong, X.C.: On the novel chaotic secure communication scheme design. Commun. Nonlinear Sci. Numer. Simul. **39**, 108–117 (2016)
7. Brown, B.T., Zebrowski, P.M., Spencer, J.P.: Blind separation of instantaneous mixture of sources via the Gaussian mutual information criterion. Signal Process. **81**(4), 855–870 (2015)
8. Douglas, S.C.: Blind Signal Separation and Blind Deconvolution. CRC Press, New York (2002)
9. Mansour, A., Jutten, C., Loubaton, P.: Adaptive subspace algorithm for blind separation of independent sources in convolutive mixture. IEEE Trans. Signal Process. **48**(2), 583–586 (2013)
10. Yeredor, A.: Performance analysis of the strong uncorrelating transformation in blind separation of complex-valued sources. IEEE Trans. Signal Process. **60**(1), 478–483 (2012)
11. Bao, G., Ye, Z., Zhou, Y.: A compressed sensing approach to blind separation of speech mixture based on a two-layer sparsity model. IEEE Trans. Audio Speech Lang. Process. **21**(5), 899–906 (2013)
12. Bernard, S.: Digital Communications Fundamentals and Applications, 2nd edn. Publishing House of Electronics Industry, Beijing (2010)

A Multi-frame Image Speckle Denoising Method Based on Compressed Sensing Using Tensor Model

Ruofei Zhou, Gang Wang$^{(\boxtimes)}$, Wenchao Yang, Zhen Li, and Yao Xu

Harbin Institute of Technology, Harbin, China
zhouruofei0303@126.com, lizhen5301@126.com,
{gwang51,wenchaoy}@hit.edu.cn

Abstract. Due to the bad channel environment and poor image sampling equipment, images are often contaminated by noise in the process of collection, transmission and processing. Speckle noise, which is difficult and complex to eliminate, is one of the common noise appearing in image processing. Denoising methods based on Compressed Sensing (CS) technology have been proved as useful tools in suppressing speckle noise of single-frame images. However, temporal correlation in multi-frame images has not yet been utilized. Considering that the traditional denoising methods do not work satisfactorily in speckle noise reduction, a multi-frame image speckle denoising methods based on compressed sensing using tensor model is proposed. The first step is to use the third-order tensor to represent the blocks of image sequences, then the denoising tensor model is established according to the CS theory and the corresponding optimization problem is raised. The problem is divided into three parts: the sparse representation, the tensor dictionary update and the image reconstruction. A Kruskal tensor-based Orthogonal Matching Pursuit (OMP) and Candecomp/Parafac (CP) analysis are used to solve these problems and get the denoised image. At last, simulations are conducted to compare the CS method and traditional methods. It is shown that the CS-based multi-frame speckle denoising method performs well in noise variance and can significantly enhance the visual quality of the image.

Keywords: Compressing sensing · Multi-frame image · Image denoising
Tensor factorization

1 Introduction

In the course of the collecting and processing of images, it is inevitable that image signal is polluted by noise. As a result, image denoising has always been a research focus in the field of image processing. For ultrasound images and radar images, which are formed from the reflection of the sound wave and electromagnetic wave, shade and light image particles would be produced when two echoes reflected by the target are overlapped. That is how speckle noise comes out in images, on account of the echo interference and disturbance between dispersive wave beams.

In recent years, certain amounts of speckle denoising methods have been proposed, in which filter denoising is the most widely used. For example, Lee filter [1] and Kuan

© ICST Institute for Computer Sciences, Social Informatics and Telecommunications Engineering 2018
X. Gu et al. (Eds.): MLICOM 2017, Part II, LNICST 227, pp. 622–633, 2018.
https://doi.org/10.1007/978-3-319-73447-7_67

filter [2]. However, the size of filter window is difficult to choose. Although denoising effect turns out well, large size windows would lose most high frequency information. Small size windows fail in the ability of denoising, in spite of protecting detail information preferably. Aiming at solving this contradiction, several anisotropic diffusion have been presented, such as Perona-Malik Anisotropic Diffusion [3] (PMAD), Nonlinear Complex Diffusion Filter [4] (NCDF) and Speckle Reducing Anisotropic Diffusion [5] (SRAD). Nevertheless, these methods are likely to mix up image edges and speckle noises during edge detection.

A number of new speckle denoising methods have been suggested lately, for instance, Nonlinear Multi-scale Wavelet Diffusion [6] (NMWD) and Speckle Reduction Bilateral Filter [7] (SRBF). Compressed Sensing-based speckle denoising methods also perform well in speckle noise reduction of single-frame images. However, temporal correlation in multi-frame images has not yet been utilized.

In this paper, we focus on multi-frame image speckle denoising method based on Compressed Sensing using tensor model. Firstly, the third-order tensor is used to represent the blocks of image sequences. Not only is the information in spatial dimension kept, but also the information in temporal dimension is discovered. In the process of training the tensor sparse dictionary, temporal redundancy in video signals is utilized effectively. After the trained tensor sparse dictionary presents the images, output results will contain more information that is useful and noises will be separated extremely. The simulation results show that CS-based multi-frame speckle denoising method outperform traditional ways in terms of image quality and noise variance under the same conditions.

2 Speckle Denoising Tensor Model

2.1 Preliminaries

A tensor is also known as a multidimensional array, a higher dimensional form of data. A first-order tensor, as we know, is a vector. Moreover, a second-order tensor is a matrix. In addition, tensors of order three or higher are called higher-order tensors [8]. Multi-frame image cube is a typical third-order tensor. To distinguish higher order tensors from matrices, Higher-order tensors (order three or higher) are denoted by black letters. The nth order tensor is denoted by $\mathcal{A} \in \mathbb{R}^{I_1 \times I_2 \times \cdots I_N}$, and the number of all elements of $\mathcal{A}$ is $\prod_{j=1}^{N} I_j$. A third-order tensor is as shown in Fig. 1.

The outer product of two vectors U and V is:

$$U \otimes V = A = \begin{bmatrix} u_1 v_1 & u_1 v_2 & \cdots & u_1 v_n \\ u_2 v_1 & u_2 v_2 & \cdots & u_2 v_n \\ \vdots & \vdots & \ddots & \vdots \\ u_m v_1 & u_m v_2 & \cdots & u_m v_n \end{bmatrix} \tag{1}$$

where $U = (u_1, u_2, \cdots, u_m)$ and $V = (v_1, v_2, \cdots, v_n)$.

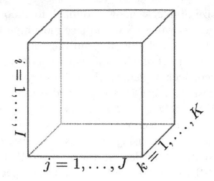

Fig. 1. A third-order tensor $\mathcal{A} \in \mathbb{R}^{I \times J \times K}$

And the Kronecker product of tensors $\mathcal{A}$ and $\mathcal{B}$ is defined by:

$$\mathcal{A} \otimes \mathcal{B} = \begin{bmatrix} a_{11}\mathcal{B} & a_{12}\mathcal{B} & \cdots & a_{1K}\mathcal{B} \\ a_{21}\mathcal{B} & a_{22}\mathcal{B} & \cdots & a_{2K}\mathcal{B} \\ \vdots & \vdots & \ddots & \vdots \\ a_{J1}\mathcal{B} & a_{J2}\mathcal{B} & \cdots & a_{JK}\mathcal{B} \end{bmatrix} \tag{2}$$

where $\mathcal{A} \in \mathbb{R}^{J \times K}$ and $\mathcal{B} \in \mathbb{R}^{M \times N}$.

After calculating the outer product, the number of dimensions of new tensor is the sum of two original tensors. For instance, $A \in R^{I_1 \times I_2 \times \cdots I_N}$ and $B \in R^{J_1 \times J_2 \times \cdots J_M}$, then $A \otimes B \in R^{I_1 \times I_2 \times \cdots I_N \times J_1 \times J_2 \times \cdots J_M}$. If N one-dimensional vector $K_i (i = 1, 2, \ldots, N)$, and the elements of each vector are $I_1, I_1, \ldots, I_N$, a N-order tensor $\mathcal{A}$ can be made up of these N one-dimensional vector $K_1 \circ K_2 \circ \cdots \circ K_N = \mathcal{A}$. The symbol "∘" represents the vector outer product. An N-way tensor is rank one if it can be written as the outer product of N vectors. The process, in turn, of factorizing a tensor into a sum of component rank-one tensors is called the rank-one decomposition of $\mathcal{A}$. Proportional coefficients are needed sometimes, and then rank-one decomposition is defined by:

$$\mathcal{A} = CK_1 \circ K_2 \circ \cdots \circ K_N \tag{3}$$

However, most tensors are not rank-one. The rank of a tensor $\mathcal{A}$, denoted rank $(\mathcal{A})$, is defined as the smallest number of rank-one tensors that generate $\mathcal{A}$ as their sum. For formula (4), rank $(\mathcal{A})$ equals to the minimum R.

$$\mathcal{A} = \sum_{i=1}^{R} C_i K_{i1} \circ K_{i2} \circ \cdots \circ K_{iN} \tag{4}$$

2.2   Tensor Decomposition and Tensor Recovery

In the course of image processing, image recovery is necessary because images are often polluted by noises for some reason, even some parts of images are lost on the receiving end. Using the characteristic low rank of images, images can be recovered by applying the low-rank recovery of matrices. In this way, the low-rank recovery method is applicable to recover any data that coincide the tensor model.

Kruskal decomposition and Tucker decomposition are two primary modes of tensor decomposition [9]. At first, Kruskal decomposition of a third-order tensor is introduced [10]. Consider a third-order tensor $\mathcal{X}$ of which the rank is R, i.e.,

$$\mathcal{X} = \sum_{i=1}^{R} \lambda_i \cdot a_i \circ b_i \circ \cdots \circ c_i \tag{5}$$

where A, B, C are rank-one component tensors of three directions, expressed as:

$$\begin{aligned} A &= [a_1, a_2, \ldots, a_R] \\ B &= [b_1, b_2, \ldots, b_R] \\ C &= [c_1, c_2, \ldots, c_R] \end{aligned} \tag{6}$$

So the Kruskal decomposition of $\mathcal{X}$ is illustrated in Fig. 2.

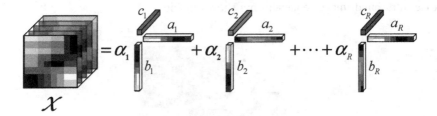

Fig. 2. Kruskal decomposition of a third-order tensor

The Tucker decomposition was first introduced by Tucker in [11] and refined in subsequent articles by Levin and Tucker. Let $\mathcal{X} \in \mathbb{R}^{X \times Y \times Z}$ be a three-way tensor and can be described as:

$$\begin{aligned} \mathcal{X} &= g \times_1 U \times_2 V \times_3 W \\ &= \sum_{r=1}^{R} \sum_{s=1}^{S} \sum_{t=1}^{T} g_{rst} u_r \circ v_s \circ w_t \end{aligned} \tag{7}$$

where $g \in \mathbb{R}^{R \times S \times T}$ is core tensor and $U \in \mathbb{R}^{X \times R}$, $V \in \mathbb{R}^{Y \times S}$, $W \in \mathbb{R}^{Z \times T}$ are three projection matrices of each direction.

The Tucker decomposition is a form of higher-order principal component analysis. It decomposes a tensor into a core tensor multiplied (or transformed) by a matrix along each mode. In some cases, the storage for the decomposed version of the tensor can be significantly smaller than for the original tensor. In the process of tensor recovery, original tensors can be generally recovered by arranging the coefficients of these components by values and adding the principal components.

So the Tucker decomposition of $\mathcal{X}$ is illustrated in Fig. 3.

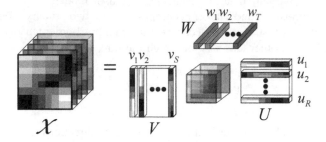

Fig. 3. Tucker decomposition of a third-order tensor

2.3   Multi-frame Image Denoising Tensor Model Based on CS

Because of the high sampling frequency in temporal dimension, contiguous frames are very similar in video data. As a result, there's a large amount of redundant information over each frame. In this paper, cardiac ultrasound video is used as research data. Cardiac ultrasound image sequences are shown in Fig. 4.

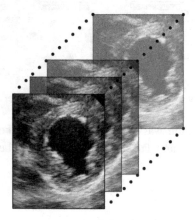

Fig. 4. Cardiac ultrasound image sequences

To begin with, images are divided into image blocks. After the sparse representation of these blocks, the integral image will be processed. The third-order Kruskal tensor model is introduced in the sparse representation of image block sequences, and the original images will be reconstructed by training the tensor dictionary. In this way, the loss of spatial information is avoided in the process of turning image blocks into one-dimensional signals. Meanwhile, the motional information of image blocks will be utilized for denoising by considering temporal information. The model can be generalized as:

$$\{\hat{\mathcal{X}}_k, \hat{\mathcal{D}}, \hat{A}\} = \arg \min_{\mathcal{D}, \alpha_{ijt}, \mathcal{X}} \lambda \left\| \frac{\mathcal{Y} - \mathcal{X}}{\sqrt{\mathcal{X}}} \right\|_F^2$$

$$+ \sum_{ij \in \Omega} \sum_{t=k-f+1}^{k+f-1} \mu_{ijt} \|\alpha_{ijt}\|_0 + \sum_{ij \in \Omega} \sum_{t=k-f+1}^{k+f-1} \|\mathcal{D}\alpha_{ijt} - R_{ijt}\mathcal{X}\|_F^2 \tag{8}$$

A third-order tensor representing noiseless image sequences is denoted by $\mathcal{X}$ The kth frame in $\mathcal{X}$ is denoted by $\mathcal{X}_k$, i.e. the noiseless form of the processing image. An image sequence that contains noise is denoted by $\mathcal{Y}$. An element of sparse coefficient matrix $A \in \mathbb{R}^{K \times N}$ is denoted by α_{ijt}, K is the number of atoms in dictionary and N equals to the number of blocks extracted from image sequences. The over-complete tensor dictionary is denoted by four-way tensor $\mathcal{D} \in \mathbb{R}^{m \times n \times f \times K}$, the estimation of kth noiseless frame is denoted by $\hat{\mathcal{X}}_k$, i.e. the resulting images after the process. When the optimal solution of this optimization problem is obtained, the over-complete tensor dictionary is denoted by $\hat{\mathcal{D}}$ and sparse coefficient matrix is denoted by $\hat{A}$. The position of blocks in integral image is denoted by μ_{ijt} and R_{ijt}, in which the elements are either 0 or 1.

To solve the optimization problem described by (8), we suggest two steps to get the results. Firstly, process the image block sequences and train the adaptive dictionary $\mathcal{D}$. Assuming that atoms of the tensor dictionary can represent each noiseless image sequence sparsely, we have $R_{ijt}\mathcal{X} = \mathcal{D}\alpha_{ijt}$. Then the optimization problem can be described as:

$$\left(\{\alpha_{ijt}\}^N, \mathcal{D}\right) = \arg \min_{\alpha_{ijt}, \mathcal{D}} \sum_{ij \in \Omega} \sum_{t=1}^T \left(\mu_{ijt} \|\alpha_{ijt}\|_0 + \left\| \frac{R_{ijt}\mathcal{Y} - \mathcal{D}\alpha_{ijt}}{\sqrt{\mathcal{D}\alpha_{ijt}}} \right\|_F^2 \right) \tag{9}$$

It is an optimization problem of two variate $\mathcal{D}$ and α_{ijt}, so sparse representation and dictionary update are involved in the solution. In the optimum iterative procedure of image sequences, $\mathcal{D}$ is fixed and corresponding sparse coefficient vector α_{ijt} is optimized. In the dictionary update, the optimized sparse coefficient matrix A is fixed and $\mathcal{D}$ is updated. Repeat this iteration until tensor dictionary $\mathcal{D}$, which corresponds to the processing image sequences, is obtained.

The second step is to define error rate of the sparse representation. Coefficient matrix A is expected to be more sparse under the premise that error rate of the sparse representation is less than a certain threshold value ε, i.e.

$$\min_{\alpha_{ijt}, \mathcal{D}} \|\alpha_{ijt}\|_0 \, s.t. \left\| \frac{R_{ijt}\mathcal{Y} - \mathcal{D}\alpha_{ijt}}{\sqrt{\mathcal{D}\alpha_{ijt}}} \right\|_2^2 \leq \varepsilon \tag{10}$$

The image denoising begins with the adaptive dictionary $\mathcal{D}$ and the sparsity is guaranteed in the above procedure. The optimization problem can finally be described as:

$$\hat{\mathcal{X}}_k = \arg\min_{\alpha_{ijt},\mathcal{X}} \lambda \left\|\frac{y-\mathcal{X}}{\sqrt{\mathcal{X}}}\right\|_2^2 + \sum_{ij\in\Omega} \sum_{t=k-f+1}^{k+f-1} \left\|\mathcal{D}\hat{\alpha}_{ijt} - R_{ijt}\mathcal{X}\right\|_2^2 \qquad (11)$$

3   Method and Algorithm

3.1   Sparse Representation

Due to the high sampling frequency in temporal dimension in the ultrasound video signal, we choose to collect the image block sequences that consists of the blocks in the same position from each image frame [12]. The data collecting process is shown in Fig. 5.

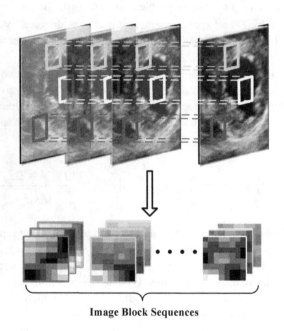

Image Block Sequences

Fig. 5. Image block sequences collecting process

The processed image block sequences contain the information in both spatial dimension and the temporal dimension, and they will be presented sparsely according to the tensor dictionary [13, 14]. To avoid the loss of information of images in either dimension, improved optimization algorithm based on tensor is proposed, called Kruskal Tensor Orthogonal Matching Pursuit (KTOMP).

The steps of KTOMP are summarized in Algorithm 1.

Algorithm 1 Kruskal Tensor Orthogonal Matching Pursuit

1: Input image block sequences with noise $R_{ijt}\mathcal{Y} \in \mathbb{R}^{m \times n \times f}$

2: Initialize projection matrix $D_1 \in \mathbb{R}^{m \times K}, D_2 \in \mathbb{R}^{n \times K}, D_3 \in \mathbb{R}^{f \times K}$, which are DCT matrices,

and $\mathcal{D}_k = 1 \times_1 D_1(:,k) \times_2 D_2(:,k) \times_3 D_3(:,k)$ where $1 \in \mathbb{R}^{1 \times 1 \times 1}$ and $k = 1, 2, ..., K$.

3: Optimum iterative procedure

Residue $R = R_{ijt}\mathcal{Y}$, $\alpha_{ijt} = \vec{0}$

while $\|\alpha_{ijt}\|_0 \le T_{max}$ & $\|R\|_F^2 \ge \varepsilon^2$ **do**

    Compute the projection $P = R \times_1 D_1' \times_2 D_2' \times_3 D_3'$ where $P \in \mathbb{R}^{K \times K \times K}$

    Search p_{max} in the diagonal of P and the corresponding atom order k_{max}

    Replace the residue with k_{max} th atom $\mathcal{D}_{k_{max}}$

    Compute residual image block

    $R = R - (p_{max} \cdot 1) \times_1 D_1(:,k_{max}) \times_2 D_2(:,k_{max}) \times_3 D_3(:,k_{max})$

    Update sparse coefficient vector $\alpha_{ijt}(k_{max}) = p_{max}$

end

4: Output sparse coefficient vector α_{ijt} corresponding to $R_{ijt}\mathcal{Y}$

3.2 Initialize Dictionary

In this paper, the dictionary is tensor dictionary and all the elements are rank-one because the data is three-dimensional. Assuming the image blocks and elements are tensors in space $\mathbb{R}^{m \times n \times f}$ and amount of elements is K. To begin with, three DCT matrices are required, i.e. $D_1 \in \mathbb{R}^{m \times K}$, $D_2 \in \mathbb{R}^{n \times K}$, $D_3 \in \mathbb{R}^{f \times K}$. Every atom in the dictionary is generated by normalizing these three matrices and make up a third-order tensor with the same column of each matrix. In this way, we obtain an initial DCT rank-one tensor dictionary, shown in Fig. 6.

3.3 Tensor Dictionary Update

The CANDECOMP/PARAFAC(CP) decomposition [15] is applied to update the tensor dictionary in this method. CP decomposition factorizes a tensor into a sum of

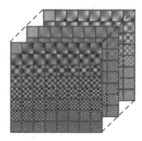

Fig. 6. Initial DCT rank-one tensor dictionary

component rank-one tensors so that atoms in initial dictionary may keep rank-one in the updating process. An error function is defined by:

$$E = \left\| \frac{\mathcal{Y} - \mathcal{D}A}{\sqrt{\mathcal{D}A}} \right\|_F^2 \tag{12}$$

The error function is defined as Frobenius-norm [16] of error tensors. Therefore, we can update the atoms of tensor dictionary by:

$$
\begin{aligned}
E &= \left\| \frac{\mathcal{Y} - \mathcal{D}A}{\sqrt{\mathcal{D}A}} \right\|_F^2 = \left\| \frac{\mathcal{Y} - \sum_{k=1}^{K} \mathcal{D}_k \alpha_T^k}{\sqrt{\mathcal{D}_k \alpha_T^k}} \right\|_F^2 \\
&= \left\| \frac{\left(\mathcal{Y} - \sum_{k \neq p} \mathcal{D}_k \alpha_T^k \right) - \mathcal{D}_p \alpha_T^p}{\sqrt{\sum_{k=1}^{K} \mathcal{D}_k \alpha_T^k}} \right\|_F^2 = \left\| \frac{E_p - \mathcal{D}_p \alpha_T^p}{\sqrt{\sum_{k=1}^{K} \mathcal{D}_k \alpha_T^k}} \right\|_F^2
\end{aligned}
\tag{13}
$$

$\mathcal{D}A$ will approach Y after multiple iteration, and the last step is to compute a CP decomposition of E_p in the denominator. In the end, we have optimum $\mathcal{D}_p$ and the corresponding sparse coefficient α_T^p.

3.4   Image Recovery

The optimization problem can be described as (11) and the output is the kth frame $\hat{\mathcal{X}}_k$. Analytic solution is difficult to obtain, so the problem is transformed into a easier one by introducing $\tilde{\lambda}$ as new coefficients. After derivation the solution is expressed as:

$$\hat{\mathcal{X}}_k = \left(\tilde{\lambda} I + \sum_{ij \in \Omega} \sum_{t=k-f+1}^{k} R_{ijt}^T R_{ijt} \right)^{-1} \left(\tilde{\lambda} \mathcal{Y}_k + \sum_{ij \in \Omega} \sum_{t=k-f+1}^{k} R_{ijt}^T D \hat{\alpha}_{ijt} \right) \tag{14}$$

4   Experimental Results

The proportionality coefficient of error rate ε and noise mean variance σ_n is denoted by C. Based on the previous studies, processed cardiac ultrasound images have better PSNR when $C = 8$. The size of image blocks is 8×8, because larger size makes sparse representation a time-consuming process, and smaller size leads to discontinuous blocks between frames. Experiments proved that 3 frames can meet the requirements. The detailed parameters of simulation are summarized in Table 1.

Table 1. Simulation parameters

Methods	Assumptions
Lee	Window size 5 × 5
Kuan	Window size 3 × 3
NCDF	Window size 3 × 3
SRAD	Initial value $Q_0 = 0.5$, $\Delta t = 0.1$
NMWD	Wavelet decomposition level $J = 3$, $\Delta t = 0.1$
SRBF	Window size 3 × 3
CS-based	Image block size 8 × 8, frame $f = 3$, $C = 8$

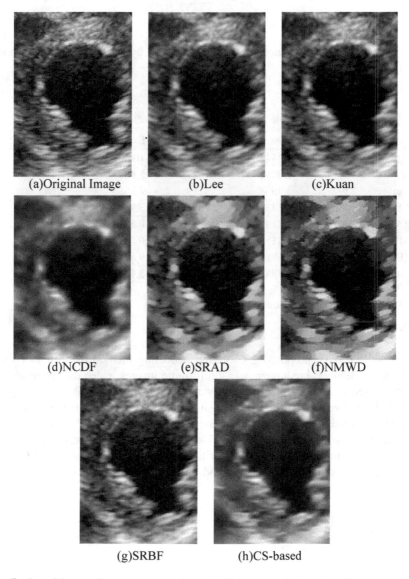

(a)Original Image   (b)Lee   (c)Kuan

(d)NCDF   (e)SRAD   (f)NMWD

(g)SRBF   (h)CS-based

Fig. 7. Denoising performance comparison of CS-based method and traditional methods

Figure 7 demonstrates the CS-based speckle denoising method has better performance in noise reduction and keeps more edge information.

The performance difference is difficult to tell by visual inspection so quantitative results is also required. We compute the remaining noise variance σ_n^2 in the processed images to compare the denoising ability of the methods above. For σ_n^2, lower is better. It is given by:

$$\sigma_n^2 = \frac{\sigma^2}{m} = \frac{\sum_{i=0}^{M-1}\sum_{j=0}^{N-1}[I(i,j) - \bar{I}(i,j)]^2}{\sum_{i=0}^{M-1}\sum_{j=0}^{N-1}I(i,j)} \tag{15}$$

The remaining noise variance of images processed by different methods are summarized in Table 2:

Table 2. Experimental results of σ_n^2

	Experiment 1	Experiment 2	Experiment 3	Experiment 4	Experiment 5
Original	9.2327	6.3542	7.7043	10.6013	9.3056
Lee	3.7621	2.0291	4.1677	5.4885	4.1175
Kuan	5.8392	3.4668	5.3789	7.2655	5.7603
NCDF	2.1080	1.1334	2.9522	3.9787	2.6482
SRAD	7.8007	2.2196	6.3844	8.3852	7.4011
NMWD	1.3690	1.4152	3.9535	6.0422	4.8639
SRBF	8.5283	3.6888	7.3209	9.5148	8.5044
CS-based	**0.3909**	**0.7888**	**2.2784**	**3.1959**	**1.8510**

5   Conclusion

In this paper, we have proposed a CS-based denoising method using tensor model. Considering the temporal redundancy in multi-frame images, video data is divided into image block sequences and represented by tensor models. In addition, an improved OMP based on Kruskal tensor decomposition is utilized in sparse representation. Aiming at the training problem of rank-one tensor dictionary, CP decomposition is applied in the tensor dictionary update. Using the trained dictionary, the noise is separated and the images are recovered in the end. Simulations show that CS-based method outperforms the traditional methods in both visual results and quantitative ones.

Acknowledgement. This work is supported in part by National Natural Science Foundation of China (No. 61671184, No. 61401120, No. 61371100) and National Science and Technology Major Project (No. 2015ZX03001041).

References

1. Lee, J.S.: Digital image enhancement and noise filtering by use of local statistics. IEEE Trans. Pattern Anal. Mach. Intell. **2**, 165–168 (1980)
2. Kuan, D.T., Sawchuk, A.A., Strand, T.C., et al.: Adaptive noise smoothing filter for images with signal-dependent noise. IEEE Trans. Pattern Anal. Mach. Intell. **2**, 165–177 (1985)
3. Perona, P., Malik, J.: Scale-space and edge detection using anisotropic diffusion. IEEE Trans. Pattern Anal. Mach. Intell. **12**(7), 629–639 (1990)
4. Yu, Y., Acton, S.T.: Speckle reducing anisotropic diffusion. IEEE Trans. Image Process. **11**(11), 1260–1270 (2002)
5. Yue, Y., Croitoru, M.M., Bidani, A., et al.: Nonlinear multiscale wavelet diffusion for speckle suppression and edge enhancement in ultrasound images. IEEE Trans. Med. Imaging **25**(3), 297–311 (2006)
6. Salinas, H.M., Fernández, D.C.: Comparison of PDE-based nonlinear diffusion approaches for image enhancement and denoising in optical coherence tomography. IEEE Trans. Med. Imaging **26**(6), 761–771 (2007)
7. Tamara, G., Brett, W.: Tensor decompositions and applications. SIAM Rev. **51**(3), 455–500 (2009)
8. Balocco, S., Gatta, C., Pujol, O., et al.: SRBF: speckle reducing bilateral filtering. Ultrasound Med. Biol. **36**(8), 1353–1363 (2010)
9. Caiafa, C.F., Cichocki, A.: Block sparse representations of tensors using kronecker bases. In: IEEE International Conference on Acoustics, Speech and Signal Processing (ICASSP), pp. 2709–2712. IEEE (2012)
10. Li, X., Shen, H., Zhang, L., Zhang, H., Yuan, Q., Yang, G.: Recovering quantitative remote sensing products contaminated by thick clouds and shadows using multitemporal dictionary learning. IEEE Trans. Geosci. Remote Sens. **52**(11), 7086–7098 (2014)
11. Lu, T., Li, S., Fang, L., Ma, Y., Benediktsson, J.A.: Spectral-spatial adaptive sparse representation for hyperspectral image denoising. IEEE Trans. Geosci. Remote Sens. **54**(1), 373–385 (2016)
12. Selesnick, I.: Total variation denoising via the moreau envelope. IEEE Signal Process. Lett. **24**(2), 216–220 (2017)
13. Lu, Z., Fu, Z., et al.: Learning from weak and noisy labels for semantic segmentation. IEEE Trans. Pattern Anal. Mach. Intell. **39**(3), 486–500 (2017)
14. Cao, Z., Gu, Y.: Sparse representation denoising framework for 3-D building reconstruction from airborne LiDAR data. IEEE J. Sel. Top. Appl. Earth Obs. Remote Sen. **9**(5), 1888–1900 (2016)
15. Rahmani, M., Atia, G.: High dimensional low rank plus sparse matrix decomposition. IEEE Trans. Signal Process. **65**(8), 2004–2019 (2017)
16. Qi, N., Shi, Y., et al.: Multi-dimensional sparse models. IEEE Trans. Pattern Anal. Mach. Intell. **40**(1), 163–178 (2017)

Frequency-Hopped Space-Time Coded OFDM over Time-Varying Multipath Channel

Fangfang Cheng, Jiyu Jin$^{(\boxtimes)}$, Guiyue Jin, Peng Li, and Jun Mou

School of Information Science and Engineering, Dalian Polytechnic University,
Dalian 116034, China
fangfangcheng25@163.com,
{jiyu.jin,guiyue.jin,lipeng,moujun}@dlpu.edu.cn

Abstract. In this paper, we proposed a frequency-hopped space-time coded orthogonal frequency-division multiplexing (FHST-OFDM) over time-varying multipath channels. Although OFDM is robust against frequency-selective fading channels, it is more vulnerable to the time-varying channels and has a higher peak-to-average power ratio (PAPR) than single-carrier systems. In space-time block coded OFDM (ST-OFDM), channel time variations cause not only the intertransmit-antenna interference (ITAI), but also the inter-carrier interference (ICI). In this paper, based on the analysis of the ITAI and ICI in ST-OFDM systems, the FHST-OFDM transmission scheme is proposed to reduce both ITAI, ICI, and PAPR simultaneously. By combining the Alamouti scheme and the frequency hopping, full data rate and frequency diversity can be achieved by the proposed FHST-OFDM over the time-varying multipath channels. Finally, simulation shows that the proposed FHST-OFDM scheme gets better performance over time varying channels.

Keywords: STBC · OFDM · Intercarrier interference (ICI)
Intertransmit-antenna interference (ITAI) · Time-varying channel

1 Introduction

In order to eliminate the detrimental influence of the channel fading and increase spectrum efficiency, both of the transmit diversity and the orthogonal frequency division multiplexing (OFDM) technologies have drawn a lot of attentions and exhibited great advantages in the next generation wireless communication systems.

Recently, transmit diversity has been studied extensively as a method of overcoming the detrimental effects of wireless fading channels because it is relatively easy to implement and multiple antennas at the base station are often available. One attractive approach of implementing transmit diversity is space-time block codes (STBCs) [1–3]. However, the orthogonal space-time block code (OSTBC) results in data rate loss if more than two transmit antennas are used [2]. The quasi-orthogonal space-time block code (QOSTBC) was proposed in [4, 5] to achieve full data rate at the cost of performance loss. Moreover, STBC are typically designed assuming that channel is quasi-static fading. However, in practice, the time-varying channel will

© ICST Institute for Computer Sciences, Social Informatics and Telecommunications Engineering 2018
X. Gu et al. (Eds.): MLICOM 2017, Part II, LNICST 227, pp. 634–646, 2018.
https://doi.org/10.1007/978-3-319-73447-7_68

destroy the orthogonality of signals among the transmit antennas and result in intertransmit-antenna interference (ITAI) in the STBCs.

Multi-antennas can be combined with OFDM to achieve spatial diversity and/or to increase spectral efficiency through spatial multiplexing. for the multi-antenna OFDM systems in frequency-selective channels, STBC schemes must be extended to include frequency element, forming space-time block coded OFDM (ST-OFDM) [6–9]. Similar to single antenna OFDM, ST-OFDM is also sensitive to the Doppler shift and frequency offsets that destroy the orthogonality among the subcarriers. In the OFDM systems with N_s subcarriers, the OFDM symbol duration is N_s, the number of subcarriers, times the modulated sampling period. Consequently, ITAI caused by channel time variations in ST-OFDM systems is more pronounced than that in single-carrier STBC systems. Interference cancellation schemes for ST-/QOST-OFDM over fast varying channel were proposed in [10–14] to mitigate the ITAI and/or Intercarrier interference (ICI). However, these interference cancellation schemes increase the computational load at the receiver.

The performance of a mobile communication system heavily relies on how well the system is designed to overcome the time-varying channel. In this paper, based on the analysis of the ITAI and ICI in ST-OFDM systems, a simple FHST-OFDM transmission scheme with four transmit antennas is proposed to mitigate the ITAI and ICI. Additionally, the peak-to-average power ratio (PAPR) is also been suppressed. In the proposed FHST-OFDM scheme, Alamouti STBC scheme and frequency hopping are adopted to provide full data rate and frequency diversity over the time-varying multipath channels. By using frequency hopping, only $N_s/2$ subcarriers are active in each time slot for each antenna. Therefore, the proposed FHST-OFDM experiences less ICI and it has a lower PAPR.

This paper is organized as follows. The system description is provided in Sect. 2. The proposed FHST-OFDM is derived in Sect. 3. Section 4 presents the simulation results and Sect. 5 concludes this paper.

Notation: In this paper, a boldface letter denotes a vector or matrix, which will be clear from the context; $\mathbf{I}_M$ denotes an $M \times M$ identity matrix. The superscript $(\cdot)^*$, $(\cdot)^T$, and $(\cdot)^H$ denote the complex conjugate, the transpose and the Hermitian transpose operators, respectively. $|\cdot|$, $E(\cdot)$ and var$(\cdot)$ represents absolute value, expectation and variance operators, respectively. $diag(\cdot)$ denotes the diagonal parts of a matrix. $\|\cdot\|_F$ and $tr(\cdot)$ denote the Frobenius norm and the trace of a matrix, respectively.

2 System Description

We focus on an ST-OFDM system with P transmit antennas, one receive antenna, and N_s subcarriers in the time-varying multipath channels. The input sequence $\{a(i), i = 0, ..., N_s P - 1\}$ is serial-to-parallel converted into P sequences, each of length N_s, as

$$a_p(k) = a(k + (p-1)N_s),$$
$$\text{for } p = 1, \ldots, P, \text{ and } k = 0, \ldots, N_s - 1. \tag{1}$$

Each sequences a_p (k) is then serial-to-parallel converted and mapped into the space-time coded matrix according to the ST-OFDM scheme.

Taking the inverse discrete Fourier transform (IDFT), the $N_s \times 1$ complex vector for each transmit antenna is converted into time-domain. The time-domain signals transmitted from the p-th antenna during the q-th OFDM symbol period can be expressed by

$$x_{p,q}(m) = \sum_{k=0}^{N_s-1} b_{p,q}(k) \cdot e^{j\frac{2\pi}{N_s}mk}, \tag{2}$$

$$m = 0, \ldots, N_s - 1, \text{ and } q = 1, \ldots, Q,$$

where $b_{p,q}(k)$ is the space-time encoded symbol for the p-th transmit antenna during the q-th symbol period on the k-th subcarrier, and Q denotes the block size of the space-time code. After the cyclic prefixes are added, the OFDM symbols are transmitted.

Since the channel is time-varying, the relationship between the channel coefficients for path l ($l = 0, \ldots, L - 1$) of antenna p at times nT_s (T_s is the sampling interval) and $(n + m) T_s$ during the q-th OFDM symbol period can be described by using the first-order autoregressive model as in [15, 16].

$$h_{p,q}(n+m, l) = \alpha_m h_{p,q}(n, l) + \beta_{p,q}(n+m, l), \tag{3}$$

where

$$\alpha_m = J_0(2\pi \cdot m f_d T_s), \tag{4}$$

and f_d is the Doppler shift, $J_0(\cdot)$ is the zeroth-order Bessel function of the first kind, $\beta_{p,q}$ (n, l) are independent (for different indexes p, q, l, and n) complex Gaussian random variables with zero mean and variance

$$\sigma_\beta^2 = \sigma_l^2 (1 - \alpha_m^2), \tag{5}$$

where σ_l^2 denotes the variance of the l-th path of the channel.

The received signal at the sampling time n can be given as

$$y_q(n) = \sum_{p=1}^{P} \sum_{l=0}^{L-1} h_{p,q}(n, l) x_{p,q}(n - \tau_l) + w_q(n), \tag{6}$$

where τ_l denotes the delay of the l-th path, $w_q(n)$ is complex additive white Gaussian noise (AWGN) with zero mean and variance of σ^2.

At the receiver, after removing the cyclic prefixes and performing FFT, the received signal on the m-th subcarrier can be given as

$$r_q(m) = \sum_{p=1}^{P} \sum_{k=0}^{N_s-1} \varphi_{p,q}(m,k) b_{p,q}(k) e^{-j\frac{2\pi}{N_s}mk} + v_q(m),$$

$$k = 0, \ldots, N_s - 1 \text{ and } q = 1, \ldots, Q, \tag{7}$$

where $v_q(m)$ denotes the FFT of additive white Gaussian noise, and

$$\varphi_{p,q}(m,k) = \sum_{l=0}^{L-1} \eta_{p,q,l}(m-k) e^{-j\frac{2\pi}{N_s}kl}, \tag{8}$$

$$\eta_{p,q,l}(m-k) = \frac{1}{N_s} \sum_{n=0}^{N_s-1} h_{p,q}(n,l) e^{-j\frac{2\pi}{N_s}(m-k)n}, \tag{9}$$

The notation $\eta_{p,q,l}(m-k)$ represents the FFT of the l-th path component between the p-th transmit antenna and the receive antenna during the q-th symbol period. Note that $\varphi_{p,q}(m,k)$, for $k \neq m$, denotes the ICI from the k-th subchannel to the m-th subchannel for the p-th transmit antenna, and $\varphi_{p,q}(m,k) = \varphi_{p,q}(m)$ for $k = m$. The more detailed interpretation of $\eta_{p,q,l}(m-k)$ and $\varphi_{p,q}(m,k)$ is provided in [17].

The received signals can be expressed in matrix form as

$$\mathbf{R}(m) = \mathbf{H}(m)\mathbf{A}(m) + \sum_{k=0, k \neq m}^{N_s-1} \mathbf{H}(m,k)\mathbf{A}(k) + \mathbf{V}(m),$$

$$\text{for } m = 0, \ldots, N_s - 1, \tag{10}$$

where $\mathbf{R}(m) = \left[r_1(m), r_2^*(m), \ldots, r_{Q-1}(m), r_Q^*(m) \right]^T$, $\mathbf{A}(m) = [a_1(m), \ldots, a_p(m), \ldots,$ $a_P(m)]^T$, and $\mathbf{V}(m) = \left[v_1(m), v_2^*(m), \ldots, v_{Q-1}(m), v_Q^*(m) \right]^T$, $\mathbf{H}(m)$ is the equivalent channel matrix with dimensions $Q \times P$. The second term on the right-hand side of (10) represents the ICI, and channel time-variations in $\mathbf{H}(m)$ induce ITAI.

$$\mathbf{C}_{\text{ITAI}}(m) = \mathbf{H}^H(m)\mathbf{H}(m) - \boldsymbol{\rho}(m), \tag{11}$$

where

$$\boldsymbol{\rho}(m) = diag\left(\mathbf{H}^H(m)\mathbf{H}(m)\right). \tag{12}$$

3 Frequency-Hopped Space-Time Code OFDM

In the ST-OFDM systems, the frequency-selective channel is converted into a collection of parallel frequency flat fading subchannels. Therefore, a space-time block code can be applied for each subcarrier. In general, the detector assumes that the channel does not change during a space-time coded OFDM symbol block. This is a critical restriction for OFDM compared to single carrier systems since the OFDM symbol duration is N_s times larger than the symbol duration in single carrier system. In ST-OFDM, the time-varying channels cause not only ITAI but also ICI among different subcarriers. Consequently, the performance of ST-OFDM will become poor under fast fading environments.

In this section, we present an FHST-OFDM equipped with four transmit antennas over time-varying channels. The block diagram of FHST-OFDM is given in Fig. 1. At the transmitter, the modulated symbols are space-time coded by using two STBC encoders. For antenna 1 and antenna 2, during the first and second symbol durations, the space-time coded symbols are transmitted on odd subcarriers, and during the third and fourth symbol durations, the space-time coded symbols are transmitted on even subcarriers. Contrarily, for antenna 3 and antenna 4, during the first and second symbol durations, the space-time coded symbols are transmitted on even subcarriers, and during the third and fourth symbol durations, the space-time coded symbols are transmitted on odd subcarriers. The space-time coded symbols are modulated by IFFT into OFDM symbols. After adding cyclic prefixes, the OFDM symbols are transmitted.

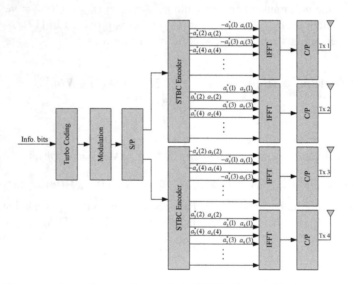

Fig. 1. Frequency hopped space-time coded OFDM scheme with 4 transmit antennas.

At the receiver, after removing the cyclic prefixes and performing FFT, the received signal vector on the even and odd subcarriers can be given as

$$\mathbf{R}_e(m) = \mathbf{H}_e(m)\mathbf{A}_e(m) + \sum_{k=0}^{N_s-2} \mathbf{H}_e(m, k)\mathbf{A}_e(k) + \mathbf{V}_e(m),$$

$$m, k = 0, 2, \ldots, N_s - 2$$

(13)

$$\mathbf{R}_o(m) = \mathbf{H}_o(m)\mathbf{A}_o(m) + \sum_{k=1}^{N_s-1} \mathbf{H}_o(m,k)\mathbf{A}_o(k) + \mathbf{V}_o(m),$$

$$m, \ k = 1, 3, \ldots, N_s - 1$$

(14)

where $\mathbf{H}_e(m)$ and $\mathbf{H}_o(m)$ are the equivalent channel matrices on the even and odd subcarriers, respectively, in the frequency domain, $\mathbf{A}_e(m)/\mathbf{A}_o(m)$ and $\mathbf{V}_e(m)/\mathbf{V}_o(m)$ are the transmitted signal and the noise vectors on the even/odd subcarriers.

3.1 ITAI Caused by Time-Varying Channels

As shown in Fig. 1, since the even and odd subcarriers on the different antennas are used alternately, there is no interference for the space-time coded symbols between two STBC encoders. However, in the time-varying channel, the channel coefficients will change in time, which may cause ITAI (11). Considering the time-varying characteristics of the channel, we analyze the ITAI of the proposed FHST-OFDM.

The equivalent channel matrix in (13) and (14) can be given as

$$\mathbf{H}_{e/o}(m) = \begin{pmatrix} \varphi_{p,1}(m) & \varphi_{p+1,1}(m) \\ -\varphi_{p+1,2}^*(m) & \varphi_{p,2}^*(m) \end{pmatrix}, \quad p = 1, 3$$

(15)

where $\varphi_{p,q}(m)$ ($\varphi_{p,q}(m, k) = \varphi_{p,q}(m)$, when $k = m$) denotes the channel frequency response on the m-th (even/odd) subcarrier for the p-th transmit antenna and the q-th ($q = 1, 2$) symbol time, and

$$\varphi_{p,2}(m) = \gamma \cdot \varphi_{p,1}(m) + \varepsilon_{p,1},$$

(16)

where $\varepsilon_{p,1}$ are independent complex Gaussian random variables with zero mean and variance

$$\sigma_\varepsilon^2 = 1 - |\gamma|^2,$$

(17)

and the channel correlation factor γ is given as

$$\gamma = J_0(2\pi \cdot f_d(N_s + c)T_s),$$

(18)

where c denotes the length of cyclic prefix.

According to (15), we represent (11) as (19)

$$
\begin{aligned}
\mathbf{C}_{\text{ITAI}}^{\text{FHST}}(m) = & \begin{pmatrix} |\varphi_{p,1}(m)|^2 + |\varphi_{p+1,2}(m)|^2 & \varphi_{p,1}^*(m)\varphi_{p+1,1}(m) - \varphi_{p,2}^*(m)\varphi_{p+1,2}(m) \\ \varphi_{p,1}(m)\varphi_{p+1,1}^*(m) - \varphi_{p,2}(m)\varphi_{p+1,2}^*(m) & |\varphi_{p+1,1}(m)|^2 + |\varphi_{p,2}(m)|^2 \end{pmatrix} \\
& - \begin{pmatrix} |\varphi_{p,1}(m)|^2 + |\varphi_{p+1,2}(m)|^2 & 0 \\ 0 & |\varphi_{p+1,1}(m)|^2 + |\varphi_{p,2}(m)|^2 \end{pmatrix} \\
& - \begin{pmatrix} 0 & \varphi_{p,1}^*(m)\varphi_{p+1,1}(m) - \varphi_{p,2}^*(m)\varphi_{p+1,2}(m) \\ \varphi_{p,1}(m)\varphi_{p+1,1}^*(m) - \varphi_{p,2}(m)\varphi_{p+1,2}^*(m) & 0 \end{pmatrix} \\
= & \begin{pmatrix} 0 & \mu_{12}(m) \\ \mu_{21}(m) & 0 \end{pmatrix}.
\end{aligned}
$$

(19)

Substituting (16) into (19), the magnitude of interference $\mu_{1,2}(m)$, $\mu_{2,1}(m)$ in (19) can be given as

$$
\mu_{1,2}(m) = \varphi_{p,1}^*(m)\varphi_{p+1,1}(m) \\
- \left[\gamma^* \varphi_{p,1}^*(m) + \varepsilon_{p+1}^*(m) \right] \left[\gamma\varphi_{p+1,1}(m) + \varepsilon_{p+1,1}(m) \right],
$$
(20)

$$
\mu_{2,1}(m) = \varphi_{p,1}(m)\varphi_{p+1,1}^*(m) \\
- \left[\gamma\varphi_{p,1}(m) + \varepsilon_{p,1}(m) \right] \left[\gamma^* \varphi_{p+1,1}^*(m) + \varepsilon_{p+1,1}^*(m) \right],
$$
(21)

where $\varepsilon_{p,q}(m)$ ($q = 1, 2$) has zero-mean and variance $1 - |\gamma|^2$, and we assume that $\varphi_{p,q}(m)$ is a complex Gaussian process with zero-mean and unit-variance. The variance of $\mu_{1,2}(m)$ and $\mu_{2,1}(m)$ can be given as

$$
\mathrm{var}\left(\mu_{1,2}(m)\right) = \mathrm{var}\left(\mu_{2,1}(m)\right) = 2\left(1 - |\gamma|^2\right),
$$
(22)

The variance of $|\varphi_{p,1}(m)|^2 + |\varphi_{p+1,2}(m)|^2$ and $|\varphi_{p+1,1}(m)|^2 + |\varphi_{p,2}(m)|^2$ in (19) can be given as

$$
\mathrm{var}\left(|\varphi_{p,1}(m)|^2 + |\varphi_{p+1,2}(m)|^2\right) \\
= \mathrm{var}\left(|\varphi_{p+1,1}(m)|^2 + |\varphi_{p,2}(m)|^2\right) = 2.
$$
(23)

Therefore, at each subcarrier, the signal to ITAI ratio of the FHST-OFDM is

$$
\mathrm{SIR}_{\mathrm{ITAI}}^{\mathrm{FHST}} = 1/\left(1 - |\gamma|^2\right),
$$
(24)

According to (18) and (24), the $\mathrm{SIR}_{\mathrm{ITAI}}^{\mathrm{FHST}}$ is the function of f_d and T_s, as

$$
\mathrm{SIR}_{\mathrm{ITAI}}^{\mathrm{FHST}} = f_{\mathrm{FHST}}(f_d, T_s).
$$
(25)

The equivalent channel matrix of QOST-OFDM can be given as

$$
\mathbf{H}_{\mathrm{QOST}} = \begin{pmatrix}
\varphi_{1,1}(m) & \varphi_{2,1}(m) & \varphi_{3,1}(m) & \varphi_{4,1}(m) \\
-\varphi_{2,2}^*(m) & \varphi_{1,2}^*(m) & -\varphi_{2,2}^*(m) & \varphi_{3,2}^*(m) \\
-\varphi_{3,3}^*(m) & -\varphi_{4,3}^*(m) & \varphi_{1,3}^*(m) & \varphi_{2,3}^*(m) \\
\varphi_{4,4}(m) & -\varphi_{3,4}(m) & -\varphi_{2,4}(m) & \varphi_{1,4}(m)
\end{pmatrix}.
$$
(26)

Similar to the above analysis, with four transmit antennas, the signal to ITAI ratio of QOST-OFDM at each subcarrier can be given as

$$
\mathrm{SIR}_{\mathrm{ITAI}}^{\mathrm{FHST}} = 1/\left(2 - \gamma^2 - \gamma^4\right) = f_{\mathrm{QOST}}(f_d, T_s).
$$
(27)

For QOST-OFDM, since the interference caused by the code structure is manipulated by a pairwise maximum-likelihood (ML) decoding scheme [4], only the interference caused by time-varying is considered in (27).

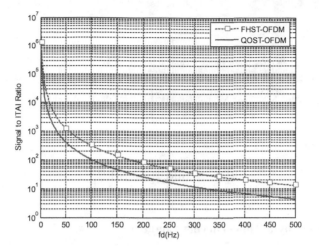

Fig. 2. Signal-to-ITAI ratio versus f_d.

As the functions of f_d, $\text{SIR}_{\text{ITAI}}^{\text{FHST}}$ and $\text{SIR}_{\text{ITAI}}^{\text{QOST}}$ are compared in Fig. 2. As shown in Fig. 2, in time-varying channels, as f_d increases, the signal-to-ITAI ratio of QOST-OFDM decreases more rapidly than that of the proposed FHST-OFDM scheme. Compared to QOST-OFDM, the block size of the proposed FHST-OFDM is two instead of four. Therefore the proposed FHST-OFDM scheme is less sensitive to the time-varying channels than the QOST-OFDM, and it obtains better performance than QOST-OFDM over time-varying multipath channels.

$$
\begin{aligned}
\text{SIR}_{\text{ICI, e}}^{\text{FHST}} &= \frac{E\left[\|\mathbf{H}_{\mathbf{e}}(m)\mathbf{A}_{\mathbf{e}}(m)\|_F^2\right]}{E\left[\left\|\sum_{k=0,k\neq m}^{N_s-2}\mathbf{H}_{\mathbf{e}}(m,k)\mathbf{A}_{\mathbf{e}}(m)\right\|_F^2\right]} \\[2mm]
&= \frac{tr\left(E\left[\mathbf{H}_{\mathbf{e}}(m)\mathbf{A}_{\mathbf{e}}(m)\mathbf{A}_{\mathbf{e}}^H(m)\mathbf{H}_{\mathbf{e}}^H(m)\right]\right)}{tr\left(E\left[\left(\sum_{k=0,k\neq m}^{N_s-2}\mathbf{H}_{\mathbf{e}}(m,k)\mathbf{A}_{\mathbf{e}}(m)\right)\left(\sum_{k=0,k\neq m}^{N_s-2}\mathbf{H}_{\mathbf{e}}(m,k)\mathbf{A}_{\mathbf{e}}(m)\right)^H\right]\right)} \\[2mm]
&= \frac{E[\boldsymbol{\rho}_{\text{FHST}}(m)]}{tr\left(E\left[\left(\sum_{k=0,k\neq m}^{N_s-2}\mathbf{H}_{\mathbf{e}}(m,k)\mathbf{A}_{\mathbf{e}}(m)\right)\left(\sum_{k=0,k\neq m}^{N_s-2}\mathbf{H}_{\mathbf{e}}(m,k)\mathbf{A}_{\mathbf{e}}(m)\right)^H\right]\right)} \\[2mm]
&= \frac{E\left[\sum_{q=1}^{2}\sum_{p=1}^{2}\left|\varphi_{p,q}(m)\right|^2\right]}{E\left[\sum_{k=0,\,k\neq m}^{N_s-2}\sum_{q=1}^{2}\sum_{p=1}^{2}\left|\varphi_{p,q}(m)\right|^2\right]}, \qquad m,\,k = 0,2,\ldots,N_s-2,
\end{aligned}
\tag{28}
$$

and

$$\text{SIR}_{\text{ICI,o}}^{\text{FHST}} = \frac{E\left[\sum\limits_{q=1}^{2}\sum\limits_{p=1}^{2}\left|\varphi_{p,q}(m)\right|^2\right]}{E\left[\sum\limits_{k=1,k\neq m}^{N_s-1}\sum\limits_{q=1}^{2}\sum\limits_{p=1}^{2}\left|\varphi_{p,q}(m)\right|^2\right]}, \qquad m,k=1,3,\ldots,N_s-1, \qquad (29)$$

respectively, and

$$\text{SIR}_{\text{ICI}}^{\text{FHST}} = \text{SIR}_{\text{ICI,e}}^{\text{FHST}} = \text{SIR}_{\text{ICI,o}}^{\text{FHST}}. \tag{30}$$

3.2   ICI Caused by a Time-Varying Channel

Compared with QOST-OFDM, the proposed FHST-OFDM uses half subcarriers and they are spaced twice as far apart. In each time slot, only $N_s/2$ subcarriers are used in FHST-OFDM, so we can reduce the interference from adjacent subcarriers. Hence, the proposed FHST-OFDM experiences less ICI than the QOST-OFDM.

When the channel is time-varying, channel variation within an OFDM symbol gives rise to ICI as shown in (10). From (10), the signal to ICI ratio of the proposed FHST-OFDM at each even and odd subcarrier can be given (28) and (29) at the bottom of the previous page.

According to (10) and (24), the signal to ICI of QOST-OFDM can be given as

$$
\begin{aligned}
\text{SIR}_{\text{ICI}}^{\text{QOST}} &= \frac{E\left[\left\|\mathbf{H}(m)\mathbf{A}_Q(m)\right\|_F^2\right]}{E\left[\left\|\sum\limits_{k=0,k\neq m}^{N_s-1}\mathbf{H}(m,k)\mathbf{A}_Q(m)\right\|_F^2\right]}\\[2ex]
&= \frac{tr\left(E\left[\mathbf{H}(m)\mathbf{A}_Q(m)\mathbf{A}_Q^H(m)\mathbf{H}^H(m)\right]\right)}{tr\left(E\left[\left(\sum\limits_{k=0,k\neq m}^{N_s-1}\mathbf{H}(m,k)\mathbf{A}_Q(m)\right)\left(\sum\limits_{k=0,k\neq m}^{N_s-1}\mathbf{H}(m,k)\mathbf{A}_Q(m)\right)^H\right]\right)}\\[2ex]
&= \frac{E\left[\boldsymbol{\rho}_{\text{QOST}}(m)\right]}{tr\left(E\left[\left(\sum\limits_{k=0,k\neq m}^{N_s-1}\mathbf{H}(m,k)\mathbf{A}_Q(m)\right)\left(\sum\limits_{k=0,k\neq m}^{N_s-1}\mathbf{H}(m,k)\mathbf{A}_Q(m)\right)^H\right]\right)}\\[2ex]
&= \frac{E\left[\sum\limits_{q=1}^{4}\sum\limits_{p=1}^{4}\left|\varphi_{p,q}(m)\right|^2\right]}{E\left[\sum\limits_{k=0,k\neq m}^{N_s-1}\sum\limits_{q=1}^{4}\sum\limits_{p=1}^{4}\left|\varphi_{p,q}(m)\right|^2\right]}.
\end{aligned}
\tag{31}
$$

Since only $N_s/2$ subcarriers are used in the proposed FHST-OFDM, with (30) and (31), we have

$$\frac{\text{SIR}_{\text{ICI}}^{\text{FHST}}}{\text{SIR}_{\text{ICI}}^{\text{QOST}}} = 2. \tag{32}$$

the signal to ICI ratio of the FHST-OFDM is two times that of QOST-OFDM.

3.3 PAPR Reduction

One of drawbacks of the OFDM system is the PAPR. Since the complex baseband OFDM signal is the combination of many sinusoids with different frequencies, the instantaneous power of the resulting signal may be larger than the average power of the OFDM signal, so the signal exhibits high peaks. When the fluctuant signal exceeds the linear region of a high power amplifier (HPA), saturation caused by the large peaks will induce intermodulation distortion clipping noise. This distortion deteriorates bit error rate (BER) performance and causes spectral leaking, resulting in out-band interference [18].

PAPR is defined as the ratio of the peak power to the average power of the OFDM signal, and it is given by

$$PAPR = 10 \log_{10}\left(\frac{P_{PEAK}}{P_{AVG}}\right) 10 \log_{10} N_s \quad \text{(dB)}. \tag{33}$$

where P_{PEAK} and P_{AVG} is the peak power and average power, respectively. In the proposed FHST-OFDM, at each time slot, only $N_s/2$ subcarriers are used. The peak and average power of the FHST-OFDM is $N_s^2/4$ (W), and $N_s/2$ (W), respectively. Therefore, PAPR reduction achieved by the proposed FHST-OFDM can be deduced as

$$PAPR_{RD} = 10 \log_{10} N_s - 10 \log_{10}\left(\frac{N_s^2/4}{N_s/2}\right) = 3 \quad \text{(dB)}. \tag{34}$$

4 Simulation Results

In this section, we demonstrate the performance through computer simulations. Simulations are carried out based on the ITU channel model as shown in Table 1. We assume that the OFDM systems equip four transmit antennas and one receive antenna, and employ the quaternary phase-shift keying (QPSK) modulation. The turbo coding with the channel code rate $1/2$, the constraint length of 4 bits, and 8 iterations are considered in our simulations. The available channel bandwidth is 10 MHz, which is divided into 1024 tones, and we use a 1024-point IFFT and a 2.3 GHz center frequency. Moreover, we assume that perfect channel state information (CSI) is available at the receiver, and the transmit antennas are separated sufficiently.

In Fig. 3, we compare the proposed FHST-OFDM and QOST-OFDM with vehicular speed $v = 5$ km/h and $v = 60$ km/h. Alamouti decoding scheme [1] is used for FHST-OFDM and a pairwise ML decoding scheme [4] is used for QOST-OFDM, respectively. For $v = 5$ km/h, the FHST-OFDM outperforms the QOST-OFDM about 2.5 dB in the case of BER $= 10^{-4}$. At a high signal-to-noise ratio (SNR), the signal to interference ratio (SIR) is the dominant factor to the system performance. Since the proposed FHST-OFDM suffers less ITAI and ICI than the QOST-OFDM, it outperforms QOST-OFDM especially in the high SNR region. When SNR > 20 dB, the QOST-OFDM approaches saturation due to the effect of the SIR. As mentioned above, the proposed FHST-OFDM suffers less ITAI and ICI than QOST-OFDM due to the smaller block size and frequency hopping (only $N_s/2$ subcarriers are used in each time slot), so a larger v makes the QOST-OFDM more vulnerable to time variations of the channel coefficients. As shown in Fig. 3, at $v = 60$ km/h, the BER performance of the QOST-OFDM is degraded more rapidly than that of the proposed FHST-OFDM.

Table 1. ITU vehicular A channel model

Relative delay (ns)	0	310	710	1090	1730	2510
Power delay profile (dB)	0	−1.0	−9.0	−10.0	−15.0	−20.0

Figure 4 compares the BER performance of the proposed FHST-OFDM and QOST-OFDM when the decision feedback equalizer (DFE) is used to perform interference cancellation in the receiver. As shown in Fig. 4, at $v = 60$ km/h, the proposed FHST-OFDM gets about 5.5 dB of performance gain compared to QOST-OFDM.

It should be mentioned that the frequency response might not be constant over N_s subcarriers in a multipath channel environment. Therefore, the proposed FHST-OFDM

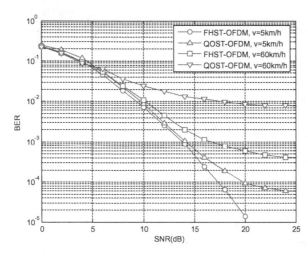

Fig. 3. BER performance for the proposed FHST-OFDM and QOST-OFDM with conventional decoding schemes.

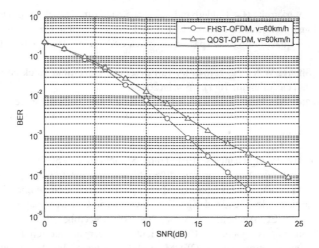

Fig. 4. BER performance for the proposed FHST-OFDM and QOST-OFDM with DFE at the receiver.

not only reduces the interference, but also achieves frequency diversity by using frequency hopping. Moreover, the FHST-OFDM can achieve a 3 dB PAPR reduction compared to QOST-OFDM since only $N_s/2$ subcarriers are used in each time slot.

5 Conclusion

In the ST-OFDM systems, time varying channel cause both the ITAI and ICI, which significantly degrade the BER performance. In this paper, we analyzed ITAI and ICI caused by channel variation, and a FHST-OFDM has been proposed. Compared with QOST-OFDM, the proposed FHST-OFDM is more robust against the time-varying channel. Frequency diversity can also be obtained over the multipath channel environment, and the proposed scheme gets lower PAPR than QOST-OFDM. Furthermore, since the proposed FHST-OFDM is a simple transmission scheme and no additional manipulation is needed at the receiver, it is attractive in low cost scenarios, such as the handset in the uplink of cellular networks.

Acknowledgements. This work supported by the Provincial Natural Science Foundation of Liaoning (Grant Nos. 20170540060 and 2015020031), Liaoning Provincial Department of Education Research Project (L2015043).

References

1. Alamouti, S.M.: A simple transmit diversity technique for wireless communications. IEEE J. Sel. Areas Commun. **16**(8), 1451–1458 (1998)
2. Tarokh, V., Jafarfarni, H., Calderband, A.R.: Space-time block codes from orthogonal designs. IEEE Trans. Inf. Theory **45**(5), 1456–1467 (1999)

3. Tarokh, V., Jafarkarni, H., Calderband, A.R.: Space-time block coding for wireless communications: performance results. IEEE J. Sel. Areas Commun. **17**(3), 451–460 (1987)
4. Jafarkarni, H.: A quasi-orthogonal space-time block code. IEEE Trans. Commun. **49**(1), 1–4 (2001)
5. Pham, V.B., Sheng, W.X.: No-zero-entry full diversity space-time block codes with linear receivers. Ann. Telecommun. **70**(1), 73–81 (2015)
6. Zhang, J., Zhang, M.: Error control coded space-time block coding for frequency-selective fading channels. In: First International Workshop On Education Technology and Computer Science, 2009, ETCS 2009, Wuhan, Hubei, China, March, pp. 923–926 (2009)
7. Liu, Z., Xin, Y., Giannakis, G.B.: Space-time-frequency coded OFDM over frequency-selective fading channels. IEEE Trans. Signal Process. **50**(10), 2465–2476 (2015)
8. Mudulodu, S., Paulraj, A.: A transmit diversity scheme for frequency selective fading channels. In: Proceedings of Globecom, vol. 2, pp. 1089–1093, November 2000
9. Lin, L.: Space-time block code design for Asymmetric-OFDM systems. In: Globecom Workshops 2012 IEEE, Anaheim, USA, pp. 204–209, December 2012
10. Groh, I., Dammann, A., Gentner, C.: Efficient inter-carrier interference mitigation for pilot-aided channel estimation in OFDM mobile systems. In: Vehicular Technology Conference (VTC Spring), 2011 IEEE 73rd, Yokohama, Japan, pp. 1–5, July. 2011
11. Stamoulis, A., Diggavi, S.N., Al-Dhahir, N.: Inter-carrier interference in MIMO OFDM. IEEE Trans. Signal Process. **50**(10), 2451–2464 (2002)
12. Chiu, Y.J., Chen, C.S., Chang, T.W.: Joint channel estimation and ISI47;ICI cancellation for MIMO OFDM systems. Int. J. Ad Hoc Ubiquitous Comput. **7**(2), 137–142 (2011)
13. Kim, J., Heath Jr., R.W., Power, E.J.: Receiver designs for Alamouti coded OFDM systems in fast fading channels. IEEE Trans. Commun. **4**(2), 550–559 (2005)
14. Zhang, Y., Liu, H.: Impact of time-selective fading on the performance of quasi-orthogonal space-time-coded OFDM systems. IEEE Trans. Commun. **54**, 251–260 (2006)
15. Tran, T.A., Sesay, A.B.: A generalized simplified ML decoder of orthogonal space-time block code for wireless communications over time-selective fading channels. In: Proceedings of IEEE Vehicular Technology Conference, pp. 1911–1915 (2002)
16. Ismail, B., Suvarna, M.: Estimation of linear regression model with correlated regressors in the presence of autocorrelation. Int. J. Stat. Appl. **6**(2), 35–39 (2016)
17. Hou, W.S., Chen, B.S.: ICI cancellation for OFDM communication systems in time-varying multipath fading channels. IEEE Press **4**(5), 2100–2110 (2005)
18. Miranda, J.P., Melgarejo, D., Mathilde, F.: Narrowband interference suppression in long term evolution systems. In: IEEE International Symposium on Personal, vol. 75, no. 4, pp. 64–72, June 2015

Dynamic Characteristic Analysis for Complexity of Continuous Chaotic Systems Based on the Algorithms of SE Complexity and C_0 Complexity

Xiaolin Ye, Jun Mou[✉], Zhisen Wang, Peng Li, and Chunfeng Luo

School of Information Science and Engineering, Dalian Polytechnic University,
Dalian 116034, China
{yexl,moujun,z_s_wang,lipeng,luocf}@dlpu.edu.cn

Abstract. In this paper, SE algorithm and C_0 algorithm were described in detail. The complexity characteristics of Lü chaotic system, Chua chaotic memristive system, Bao hyperchaotic system, Chen hyperchaotic system are analyzed based on SE algorithm and C_0 algorithm. We have compared with the dynamical characteristics of four systems by using the conventional dynamic analysis methods and the methods of complexity, the comparative results demonstrate that SE complexity and C_0 complexity can reflect the complexity of continuous chaotic systems accurately and effectually. Through the contrast for the complexity characteristics of two continuous chaotic systems and two continuous hyperchaotic systems, we can obtain that the varying trend of SE complexity and C_0 complexity have much well coherence, and it provides a dynamical analytical method for the research of chaos theory.

Keywords: SE complexity · C_0 complexity · Dynamic analysis
Chaotic system · Hyperchaotic system

1 Introduction

Chaos theory is a nonlinear dynamical science which has been thriving over the past decades. The application of chaos theory is more and more widely, especially in the information security areas [1–3]. The complexity is an ability of the chaotic system can generates random sequences, the value of complexity depend on the random degree with the sequences. Thus, the scientific community has been paying more and more attention to the algorithm of complexity in recent years.

The algorithms of complexity are generally divided into the algorithms based on behavioral complexity (FuzzyEn algorithm [4–6] and SCM algorithm [7, 8]) and the algorithms based on structural complexity (SE algorithm and C_0 algorithm). The larger the complexity of time series, the greater randomness, the more difficult the sequences are restored to the original sequences.

During mid-20th century, Kolmogorov et al. have expounded the concept of complexity, and at the same time they have put forward the Kolmogorov algorithm of complexity [9]. However, it is only a rough research. At that time, because of the

© ICST Institute for Computer Sciences, Social Informatics and Telecommunications Engineering 2018
X. Gu et al. (Eds.): MLICOM 2017, Part II, LNICST 227, pp. 647–657, 2018.
https://doi.org/10.1007/978-3-319-73447-7_69

limitations with science and technology, it can also not verify the correctness by using the computer. Until 1976, Lempel and Ziv presented the Limpel-Ziv algorithm [10] in their papers, and this algorithm is also the sublimation of the Kolmogorov algorithm. It is widely used in the fields of bio-medicine [11], weather forecasting [12] and cryptography [13]. In 1991, Pincus introduced the algorithm of approximate entropy (ApEn) [14]. Then in 2002, Bandt and Pompe developed the algorithm of permutation entropy (PE algorithm) [15], it is also the improvement of ApEn algorithm. Although these algorithms all can describe the complexity of continuous chaotic systems, but the Limpel-Ziv algorithm only estimates the time scale of chaotic sequences simply, and it needs coarse graining treatment for the non-pseudo-random sequences. When the ApEn algorithm is used to deal with the variations of different embedding dimensions, however, the problems of embedding dimensions and the resolution parameters will be involved during the process of calculation, and the calculated results are also affected by the subjective factors. At the same time, the calculated results of PE algorithm may be influenced by many factors too. These algorithms above are fast to the calculation of short sequences. While the length of the data increases to a certain amount, its calculated speed would slow down, and the practicality would be lower. Compared to the three algorithms, SE algorithm and C_0 algorithm are used to calculate the value of entropy based on Fourier transform (FFT). It not only has faster speed but also better reflect the structures of related sequence, and it can also measure the complexity of systems more effectively. Especially in the calculation of continuous stationary time series, the advantages of SE algorithm and C_0 algorithm are more obvious.

In this paper, we have analyzed the complexity characteristics of Lü chaotic system [16], Chua chaotic memristive system [17], Bao hyperchaotic system [18] and Chen hyperchaotic system [19] by using SE algorithm and C_0 algorithm. Then, theirs correctness were verified too. Through the dynamic contrastive analysis for two continuous chaotic systems and two continuous hyperchaotic systems, it shows that the superiority of SE complexity algorithm and C_0 complexity algorithm for calculating the continuous chaotic sequences. Meanwhile, we can also see that the chaotic systems have very rich dynamic characteristics. Finally, we compared and analyzed the maximum value and the average value of the four systems. The results shows that when we do the research of chaotic systems, the continuous chaotic systems and the continuous hyperchaotic systems are equivalent, there is no better or worse. All these above provided the theoretical source and the experimental basis for the application of chaotic theory.

2   SE Complexity Algorithm and C_0 Complexity Algorithm

2.1   SE Complexity Algorithm

At present, there are several algorithms for measuring the complexity of chaotic sequences. Among them, the SE [20–22] and C_0 [23–25] complexity algorithms have less parameters, faster calculation speed and higher accuracy. Spectral Entropy algorithm gets the corresponding Shannon entropy value based on the Fourier transform, the algorithm is described as follows:

(1) Remove the direct-current: using Eq. (1) to remove the DC part of pseudo-random sequence, which so that the spectrum can reflect the energy information of signal more accurately.

$$x(n) = x(n) - \bar{x} \tag{1}$$

where, $\bar{x} = (1/N) \sum_{n=0}^{N-1} x(n)$

(2) Do the discrete Fourier transform for Eq. (1)

$$X(k) = \sum_{n=0}^{N-1} x(n) e^{-j\frac{2\pi}{N}nk} = \sum_{n=0}^{N-1} x(n) W_N^{nk} \tag{2}$$

in which, $k = 0, 1, 2 \ldots, N - 1$

(3) Calculate the relative power spectrum: calculate the front half of $X(k)$, then we obtain the value of power spectrum in a certain frequency by using the Parseval theorem.

$$p(k) = \frac{1}{N} |X(k)|^2 \tag{3}$$

where, $k = 0, 1, 2 \ldots, N/2 - 1$, and the total power of sequence can be defined as:

$$P_{tot} = \frac{1}{N} \sum_{k=0}^{N/2-1} |X(k)|^2 \tag{4}$$

So, the probability of relative power spectrum can be expressed as:

$$P_k = \frac{p(k)}{P_{tot}} = \frac{\frac{1}{N} |X(k)|^2}{\frac{1}{N} \sum_{k=0}^{N/2-1} |X(k)|^2} = \frac{|X(k)|^2}{\sum_{k=0}^{N/2-1} |X(k)|^2} \tag{5}$$

where, $\sum_{k=0}^{N/2-1} P_k = 1$

(4) Using Eqs. (3), (4) and (5), and the Shannon entropy, we can obtain the Spectral Entropy (SE) of signal:

$$se = - \sum_{k=0}^{N/2-1} P_k \ln P_k \tag{6}$$

If $P_k = 0$ in Eq. (6), we will define $P_k \ln P_k = 0$. And, the value of spectrum entropy converges to $\ln(N/2)$. In order to comparison and analysis, the spectral entropy can be normalized. Then, we obtain the normalized spectral entropy:

$$SE(N) = \frac{se}{\ln(N/2)} \tag{7}$$

Through the formulas above, we can obtain that the more unevenly the power spectrum distribution of sequence, the more simple the structure of sequence, the smaller the corresponding measured value.

2.2 C_0 Complexity Algorithm

The main idea of C_0 complexity algorithm is to divide the sequence into the regular part and the irregular part, the proportion of irregular part is what we need. The computational steps as follows:

(1) Do the discrete fourier transform for the time series

$$X(k) = \sum_{n=0}^{N-1} x(n)e^{-\frac{2\pi}{N}nk} = \sum_{n=0}^{N-1} x(n)W_N^{nk} \tag{8}$$

where, $k = 0, 1, \ldots, N - 1$.

(2) Remove the regular part of Eq. (8), get the mean square value of $X(k)$:

$$G_N = \frac{1}{N}\sum_{k=0}^{N-1} |X(k)|^2 \tag{9}$$

The parameter r is added into Eq. (9), then retains the part which more than the r multiples of the mean square value, meanwhile set the remaining parts are zero, that is:

$$\tilde{X}(k) = \begin{cases} X(k), & |X(k)|^2 > rG_N \\ 0, & |X(k)|^2 < rG_N \end{cases} \tag{10}$$

(3) Do the Fourier inverse transform for Eq. (10)

$$\tilde{x}(n) = \frac{1}{N}\sum_{k=0}^{N-1} \tilde{X}(k)e^{\frac{2\pi}{N}nk} = \frac{1}{N}\sum_{k=0}^{N-1} \tilde{X}(k)W_N^{-nk} \tag{11}$$

Where, $n = 0, 1, \ldots, N - 1$

(4) With Eq. (11), the measure of C_0 complexity is defined as:

$$C_0(r,N) = \sum_{n=0}^{N-1} |x(n) - \tilde{x}(n)| \tag{12}$$

The C_0 complexity algorithm is calculated based on the fast Fourier transform algorithm, which deleted the regular part of the sequence, and retained the irregular part. The larger proportion of irregular part the sequence has, the higher value of complexity.

3 Dynamical Analysis of Continuous Chaotic Systems

3.1 Dynamic Analysis of Lü Chaotic System

Lü chaotic system is described as follows:

$$\begin{cases} \dot{x} = a(y - x) \\ \dot{y} = cy - xz \\ \dot{z} = xy - bz \end{cases} \tag{13}$$

The mathematical model of Lü chaotic system is the simplest structure in the groups of Lorenz system. Setting the initial value is (1, 1, 1), and the time step is 0.001 s. We calculate the complexity characteristics by using SE algorithm and C_0 algorithm. When the parameters $a = 36$, $b = 3$, $c = 20$, the steady-state values of Lyapunov exponents are $LE_1 = 1.3657$, $LE_2 = 0$, $LE_3 = -20.3620$. In this case, we can calculate the corresponding Lyapunov dimension is 2.0671. The phase diagrams of chaotic attractor in Lü system as shown in Fig. 1. With the parameter b changing, the system is in chaotic state, periodic state, stable point state and so on. It shows that the algorithms of SE complexity and C_0 complexity can reflect the complexity of continuous chaotic systems accurately and effectually (Fig. 2).

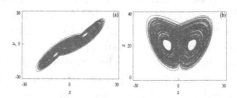

Fig. 1. Chaotic attractor of Lü system: (a) x-y plane (b) x-z plane

3.2 Dynamic Analysis of Chua Memristive Chaotic System

The Chua chaotic circuit is a classical circuit system, it is also a very hot circuit model of the scientific community in recent years. The Chua chaotic oscillation circuit is realized by using the parallel connection of a flue-controlled memristor and a negative conductance.

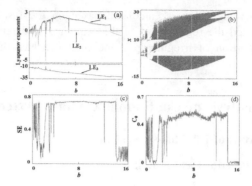

Fig. 2. Dynamic characteristics of Lü system: (a) Lyapunov exponents spectrum (b) bifurcation diagram (c) SE complexity (d) C_0 complexity

The equations of Chua circuit system is:

$$\begin{cases} \dot{x} = a[y - x + dx - W(w)x] \\ \dot{y} = x - y + z \\ \dot{z} = -by - cz \\ \dot{w} = x \end{cases} \tag{14}$$

In which,

$$q(w) = gw + hw^3, \ W(w) = dq(w)/dw = g + 3hw^2 \tag{15}$$

Setting the initial value of Eq. (14) is $(0.1, -0.1, 0.1, 0.1)$, the time step is 0.001 s. The complexity of x sequence is calculated by using SE algorithm and C_0 algorithm. When $a = 10$, $b = 100/7$, $c = 0.1$, $d = 9/7$, $g = 1/7$, $h = 2/7$, the steady-state values of Lyapunov exponents spectrum are $LE_1 = 0.2935$, $LE_2 = 0$, $LE_3 = 0$, $LE_4 = -3.3719$. Thus, the corresponding Lyapunov dimension is 3.0893. The Lyapunov exponents spectrum in Chua chaotic system is shown as Fig. 5(a). The path of the system into the chaotic state can be clearly seen from Fig. 5(b). All of these above show that the algorithms of SE complexity and C_0 complexity are right and effective dynamic analysis methods (Figs. 3 and 4).

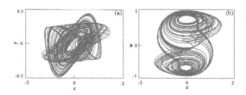

Fig. 3. Chaotic attractor of Chua memristive system: (a) x-y plane (b) x-w plane

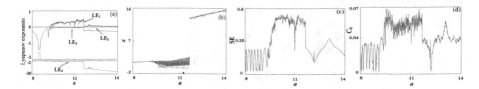

Fig. 4. Dynamic characteristics of Chua memristive system: (a) Lyapunov exponents spectrum (b) bifurcation diagram (c) SE complexity (d) C_0 complexity

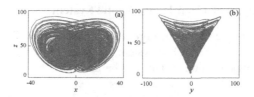

Fig. 5. Chaotic attractor of Bao hyperchaotic system: (a) x-z plane (b) y-z plane

3.3 Dynamic Analysis of Bao Hyperchaotic System

To generate a hyperchaotic signal from an autonomous dissipative system, the state equation of the system must satisfy the following two basic conditions: (1) The dimension of the state equation must be at least four, and the order of the state equation must be at least two. (2) The system has at least two positive Lyapunov exponents, and the sum of all the exponents is less than 0. So, the method of obtaining the hyperchaotic system is that adding a state feedback controller to the 3D continuous chaotic system. The 4D Bao hyperchaotic circuit by adding a state controller to the 3D Bao chaotic circuit.

According to the voltage-current characteristic relation of the circuit and the mathematically treated, we can get the mathematical model of Bao hyperchaotic system is:

$$\begin{cases} \dot{x} = a(x - y) \\ \dot{y} = xz - cy + w \\ \dot{z} = x^2 - bz \\ \dot{w} = d(x + y) \end{cases} \tag{16}$$

Setting the initial value of Eq. (16) is (10, 10, 10, 10), the time step is 0.01 s. When a = 20, b = 4, c = 32, d = 4, the steady-state values of Lyapunov exponents spectrum are $LE_1 = 2.0722$, $LE_2 = 0.0750$, $LE_3 = 0$, $LE_4 = -26.3259$, and the corresponding Lyapunov dimension is 3.0816. There are two positive Lyapunov exponents, so the system is a hyperchaotic system. With the parameter d varying, the system goes into the chaotic state from the hyperchaotic state. We can observed from the Fig. 6 that SE complexity and C_0 complexity also can precisely reflect the dynamical characteristics as the same to the conventional dynamic analysis methods.

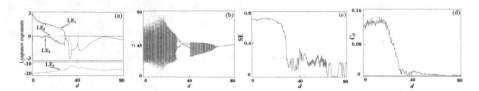

Fig. 6. Dynamic characteristics of Bao hyperchaotic system: (a) Lyapunov exponents spectrum (b) bifurcation diagram (c) SE complexity (d) C_0 complexity

3.4 Dynamic Analysis of Chen Hyperchaotic System

Chen system belongs to the groups of Lorenz system too. A feedback term is added to the equations of the classical 3D Chen system, and then we can get a 4D hyperchaotic Chen system. Chen hyperchaotic system can be described as follows:

$$\begin{cases} \dot{x} = a(y - x) + w \\ \dot{y} = dx - xz + cy \\ \dot{z} = xy - bz \\ \dot{w} = yz + ew \end{cases} \tag{17}$$

Let the initial value of Eq. (17) is (1, 0, 1, 0), the time step is 0.01 s. The complexity of x sequence is calculated by using SE algorithm and C_0 algorithm. When a = 35, b = 3, c = 12, d = 7, e = 0.083, the steady-state values of Lyapunov exponents spectrum are LE_1 = 0.3745, LE_2 = 0.0405, LE_3 = 0, LE_4 = −26.3259. We can calculate the corresponding Lyapunov dimension is 3.0158. The system has two positive Lyapunov exponents under the certain conditions, so it is a hyperchaotic system. When the parameter c varying, the state of system changing within periodic state, chaotic state and hyperchaotic state. The results of dynamic analysis in Fig. 10 are correspondence, it also shows that SE algorithm and C_0 algorithm are very correct and necessary for the dynamical analysis of the chaotic system (Figs. 7 and 8).

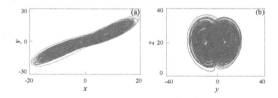

Fig. 7. Chaotic attractor of Chen hyperchaotic system: (a) x-y plane (b) y-z plane

3.5 Analysis of Complexity Characteristics for Continuous Chaotic Systems

Using the SE complexity algorithm and C_0 complexity algorithm, the complexity of four different continuous chaotic systems are compared and analyzed. The maximum value of complexity and the average value of complexity as shown in Table 1. We can

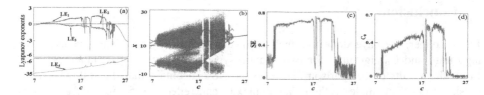

Fig. 8. Dynamic characteristics of Chen hyperchaotic system: (a) Lyapunov exponents spectrum (b) bifurcation diagram (c) SE complexity (d) C_0 complexity

Table 1. Analysis of complexity characteristics for continuous chaotic systems

	SE_{max}	$\overline{SE}$	C_{0max}	$\overline{C_0}$
Lü chaotic system	0.7318	0.5834	0.5598	0.3756
Chua chaotic system	0.4593	0.2422	0.0677	0.0382
Bao hyperchaotic system	0.7195	0.3432	0.1415	0.0426
Chen hyperchaotic system	0.7428	0.4948	0.6220	0.2838

obtain that the maximum value of complexity generated in Chen hyperchaotic system, the maximum average value of complexity generated in Lü chaotic system. And the minimum value of complexity generated in Chua memristive chaotic system, the minimum average value of complexity generated in Chua memristive chaotic system too. Through the comparative analysis to the Lü chaotic system and the Bao hyperchaotic system, we can see that the value of complexity in hyperchaotic system is not necessarily greater than that in chaotic system. Thus, the relationship of size of complexity in the different systems cannot be determined. The Table 2 shows the complexity of continuous chaotic systems in the chaotic state and the hyperchaotic state. Through the comparative analysis for the complexity of Chen hyperchaotic system in the chaotic state and in the hyperchaotic state, we can know that for a same system, the value of complexity in the hyperchaotic state is not necessarily greater than that in chaotic state. All the results show that the size of complexity for the different states in different chaotic systems can also not be determined. But, the varying tendencies of SE complexity and C0 complexity are basically consistent.

Table 2. Analysis of complexity characteristics in the chaotic state and the hyperchaotic state

System		SE_{max}	$\overline{SE}$	C_{0max}	$\overline{C_0}$
Lü chaotic system	Chaotic state	0.7318	0.6662	0.5598	0.4436
Chua chaotic system	Chaotic state	0.4593	0.4027	0.0677	0.0449
Bao hyperchaotic system	Chaotic state	0.6877	0.6160	0.1209	0.0740
	Hyperchaotic state	0.7195	0.7026	0.1415	0.1260
Chen hyperchaotic system	Chaotic state	0.7428	0.6839	0.6220	0.4714
	Hyperchaotic state	0.6623	0.6313	0.3810	0.3041

4   Conclusion

In this paper, we have done the analysis of complexity characteristics by using SE algorithm and C_0 algorithm for two chaotic systems and two hyperchaotic systems. From the results of comparison and analysis, we can obtain that the following conclusions: (1) SE complexity and C_0 complexity can reflect the complexity of continuous chaotic systems accurately and effectually. (2) For the different systems, the value of complexity in hyperchaotic system is not necessarily greater than that in chaotic system. For the same system, the value of complexity in hyperchaotic state is not necessarily greater than that in chaotic state. Generally, the maximum value of complexity generated in the chaotic state or the hyperchaotic state. The complexity characteristic of chaotic system is its inherent property, which is decided by the variation of parameters and the selection of initial value. Therefore, when we choose the chaotic system to study, the chaotic state and the hyperchaotic state all can be used as the experimental subjects, there is no better or worse. That is to say, when we choose the research object, the chaotic system and the hyperchaotic system are equivalent. (3) The varying tendency of SE complexity and C_0 complexity are basically consistent. Because they all reflect the complexity of sequence based on Fourier transform. However, the difference which between the specific value of two algorithms is larger, this is determined by the algorithm itself. (4) The value of complexity varying within a certain range, that is the complexity of continuous chaotic system has boundedness. This is one of the inherent characteristics with chaotic system. The research based on complexity characteristics of SE algorithm and C_0 algorithm, which provide a relevant theoretical basis and an experimental guidance for the applications of cryptography, secure communication and information security.

Acknowledgements. This work supported by the Provincial Natural Science Foundation of Liaoning (Grant Nos. 20170540060 and 2015020031), Science and Technology Project of Dalian, China (2015A11GX011).

References

1. Mou, J., Wang, Z.S., Kang, L.: Synchronous control of unified chaotic system based on stated observer and its application in secure communication. J. Dalian Polytech. Univ. **27**(2), 162–166 (2008)
2. Sun, K.H., Liu, W., Zhang, T.S.: Implementation of a chaos encryption algorithm. J. Comput. Appl. **23**(1), 15–17 (2003)
3. Zhang, Y.C., Wang, S.J., Li, Y.: Detection of encrypted data-flow based on entropy. Comput. Digit. Eng. **42**(4), 555–558 (2014)
4. Chen, W.T., Zhuang, J., Yu, W.X., et al.: Measuring complexity using Fuzzyen, ApEn and Sampen. Med. Eng. Phys. **31**(1), 61–68 (2009)
5. Sun, K.H., He, S.B., Yin, L.Z., et al.: Application of Fuzzyen algorithm to the analysis of complexity of chaotic sequence. Acta Phys. Sin. **61**(13), 130507 (2012)
6. Chen, X.J., Li, Z., Bai, B.M., et al.: A new complexity metric of chaotic pseudorandom sequences based on Fuzzy entropy. J. Electron. Inf. Technol. **33**(5), 1198–1203 (2011)

7. Sun, K.H., He, S.B., Sheng, L.Y.: Complexity analysis of chaotic sequence based on the intensive statistical complexity algorithm. Acta Phys. Sin. **60**(2), 2406–2411 (2011)
8. Larrondo, H.A., Gonzalez, C.M., Martin, M.T., et al.: Intensive statistical complexity measure of pseudorandom number generators. Phys. Stat. Mech. Appl. **356**(1), 133–138 (2005)
9. Kolmogorov, A.N.: Three approaches for defining the concept of information quantity. Prob. Inf. Transm. **1**(1), 3–11 (1965)
10. Lempel, A., Ziv, J.: On the complexity of finite sequence. IEEE Trans. Inf. Theory **22**(1), 75–81 (1976)
11. Eviatar, H., Somorjai, R.L.: A fast, simple active contour algorithm for biomedical images. Pattern Recogn. Lett. **17**(9), 969–974 (1996)
12. Gneiting, T., Raftery, A.E.: Weather forecasting with ensemble methods. Science **310**(5746), 248–249 (2005)
13. Liao, X.F., Yue, B., Zhou, Q., et al.: A field programmable gate array implementation of an image encryption algorithm based on a discrete chaotic map. J. Chongqing Univ. **31**(10), 1189–1193 (2008)
14. Pincus, S.M.: Approximate entropy (ApEn) as a complexity measure. Chaos **5**(1), 110–117 (1995)
15. Bant, C., Pompe, B.: Permutation entropy: a natural complexity measure for time series. Phys. Rev. Lett. **88**(17), 1741–1743 (2002)
16. Lü, J.H., Chen, G.R.: A new chaotic attractor coined. Int. J. Bifurcat. Chaos **12**(3), 659–661 (2011)
17. Bao, B.C., Liu, Z., Xu, J.P.: Dynamical analysis of memristor chaotic oscillator. Acta Phys. Sin. **59**(6), 3785–3793 (2010)
18. Bao, B.C., Liu, Z., Xu, J.P.: New chaotic system and its hyperchaos generation. Syst. Eng. Electron. **20**(6), 1179–1187 (2009)
19. Li, Y.X., Tang, W.K.S., Chen, G.R.: Generating hyperchaos via state feedback control. Int. J. Bifurcat. Chaos **15**(10), 3367–3375 (2011)
20. Sun, K.H., He, S.B., He, Y., Yin, L.Z.: Complexity analysis of chaotic pseudo-random sequences based on spectral entropy algorithm. Acta Phys. Sin. **62**(1), 709–712 (2013)
21. Staniczenko, P.P.A., Lee, C.F., Jones, N.S.: Rapidly detecting disorder in rhythmic biological signals: a spectral entropy measure to identify cardiac arrhythmias. Phys. Rev. Stat. Nonlinear Soft Matter Phys. **79**(1), 100–115 (2009)
22. Dong, Y.Q., Tan, G.Q., Sun, K.H., He, S.B.: Applications of spectral entropy and wavelet entropy algorithm for structure complexity analysis of chaotic sequence. J. Chin. Comput. Syst. **35**(2), 348–352 (2014)
23. Chen, F., Xu, J.H., Gu, F.J., et al.: Dynamic process of information transmission complexity in humaxbrains. Biol. Cybern. **83**(4), 355–366 (2000)
24. Cai, Z.J., Sun, J.: Modified C_0 complexity and application. J. Fudan Univ. **47**(6), 791–796 (2008)
25. Sun, K.H., He, S.B., Zhu, C.X., He, Y.: Analysis of chaotic complexity characteristics based on C_0 algorithm. Tien Tzu HsuehPao/Acta Electronica Sin. **41**(9), 1765–1771 (2013)

Design and Implemention of an Emulation Node for Space Network Protocol Testing

Sichen Zhao, Yuan Fang[✉], Wenfeng Li[✉], and Kanglian Zhao[✉]

School of Electronic Science and Engineering, Nanjing University,
Nanjing 210023, China
zsc199405606@outlook.com, {yfang,zhaokanglian}@nju.edu.cn,
leewf_cn@hotmail.com

Abstract. This paper proposed a scheme to design and implement an embedded emulation node, which provided an approach to emulate a precision network environment for the measurement of network protocols in the space information network. The design scheme employed the Beaglebone black (BBB) board which owns the approximate hardware performance as a satellite has, ported the real-time operating system RTEMS to BBB board, and then loaded the ION-DTN on it. We established the RTEMS development environment on BBB board, and then designed and implemented the network adapter driver associated with BBB board for RTEMS. The emulation results show that the designed emulation node is stable and reliable. With the DTN protocol stack working properly on emulation node, the function and performance of the designed emulation node can meet the requirements of space network protocol tests.

Keywords: DTN · RTEMS · Satellite emulation node

1 Introduction

A Space Information Network (SIN) is the network system based on space platforms, such as geostationary (GEO) satellites, medium earth orbit (MEO) satellites, low earth orbit (LEO) satellites, stratospheric balloons, etc., which can obtain, transmit and process space information in real time. Its goal is for the increasingly demand of information sharing among the connected heterogeneous networks, and the efficient data delivery in SIN.

Due to the harsh transmission conditions in space communication environment, such as the long propagation delay, high loss of data, frequent link disruptions, dynamic changes of the network infrastructure, the condition or environment of space networking is quite different to that of terrestrial network. It is

This work is supported by the National Natural Science Foundation of China (No. 61401194), the Fundamental Research Funds for the Central Universities (021014380064) and the Priority Academic Program Development of Jiangsu Higher Education Institutions.

© ICST Institute for Computer Sciences, Social Informatics and Telecommunications Engineering 2018
X. Gu et al. (Eds.): MLICOM 2017, Part II, LNICST 227, pp. 658–667, 2018.
https://doi.org/10.1007/978-3-319-73447-7_70

necessary to carry out the research on basic theory and key technologies for SIN before they are directly employed in space networking. While some of the existing network simulators can provide flexible, scalable network Emulations, e.g. Open-Net and NS-2, they are just discrete event-driven state simulators which only create an open Emulation environment, and can not generate real data stream inside the network as the actual network does. This greatly limits the emulation to satisfy many experimental requirements of the network applications.

For research on SIN, we can construct a measurement platform to create the scenarios as the environment of space networking. Generally, we employ a PC as a satellite node in the emulation platform. However, the performance of PC hardware is much better than that of satellite hardware which would cause deviations of the emulation results in some measurements.

To eliminate such effects, this paper studies how to design and implement an embedded emulation node to provide an approach to emulate a precision network environment for the measurement of network protocols in SIN.

2   General Scheme Design

As mentioned before, it is important to develop an emulation node with similar properties owned by the satellite, which can improve the authenticity of the space networking environment for SIN protocol measurements.

In this paper, we develop the emulation node in SIN based on Beaglebone Black (BBB) embedded core board [1], which can provide the approximate hardware performance as a satellite does.

BBB board is a low cost embedded core board developed by TI company. The board hardware specification includes a TI AM335x [2] series ARM processor running at 1 GHz, 512 MB of DDR3 RAM and 4 GB of flash memory. Its standard ports include 1 × RJ-45 interface for 100 Mbit LAN, 1 × USB 2.0 host and client, 1 × SDIO (for SD memory cards), etc. Compared with the PC, its hardware resources are closer to those of a satellite. It is more suitable for the hardware platform of the satellite emulation node.

To ensure that the satellite works reliably in the harsh space environment, and can deal with the emergencies instantaneously, stability and timeliness are specific requirements for the satellite operating system. Therefore, real-time operating system replaces Linux or Windows operating system and becomes the priority of the satellite operating system.

RTEMS [3] is a hard real-time embedded operating system developed by the United States military. It has been widely used in communications, aerospace, industrial control, military and other fields. Table 1 shows the performance comparison between RTEMS and other systems.

As listed in Table 1, compared with the time-sharing operating system Linux and the real-time operating system VxWorks, RTEMS works with higher reliability and better real-time nature [4]. So far, RTEMS has been running on THEMIS, REXUS 5 rockets and other aircraft [5]. Hence, RTEMS is chosen as the operation system of the satellite emulation node in our scheme.

Table 1. Performance comparison between RTEMS and other systems [6]

	Interrupt delay		Context transfer	
	System load balancing			
	Max	Average	Max	Average
RtLinux	13.5	1.7	33.1	8.7
RTEMS	14.9	1.3	16.4	2.2
VxWorks	13.1	2.0	19.0	3.1
	Heavy load			
RtLiunx	196.8	2.1	193.9	11.2
RTEMS	19.2	2.4	213	10.4
VxWorks	25.2	2.9	38.8	9.5

It has been proved that TCP protocol works inefficiently when it is directly employed in space networking. Currently, the delay-/disruption-tolerant networking (DTN) originated from the deep space communications is widely recognized as the most suitable technology to be employed in space networking. Many research problems will focus on the studies of DTN protocols and their uses in space networking. Thus, DTN protocol stacks will be ported to the emulation node. Since the ION-DTN developed by the California Institute of Technology's Jet Dynamics Laboratory (JPL) is a implementation of the DTN network protocol architecture, we consider porting the ION-DTN to the operating system of the emulation node.

The general design scheme of the emulation node is shown in Fig. 1. The Beaglebone Black embedded core board is used as the hardware development platform. The satellite operating system selects RTEMS real-time operating system and runs ION-DTN on it to realize the data transmission based on the DTN stack.

Since RTEMS does not provide a network adapter driver for the BBB broad, one of the difficulties in this scheme is to develop the network adapter driver for RTEMS on BBB broad. In addition, the architecture of ION-DTN is more complex, and how to port the ION-DTN on RTEMS is also one of the difficulties. Hence, to complete the design scheme of the emulation node proposed in this paper, the following problems should be solved:

- Development of network adapter driver for BBB board;
- Transplantation of ION-DTN protocol stack;
- Development application for ION internetworking.

3 Establishment of RTEMS Development Environment

The development and operation of embedded applications are carried out on different machines. So first of all, we need establish a cross-development environment. Embedded development environment software is usually composed of operating system, compiler, debugger and so on.

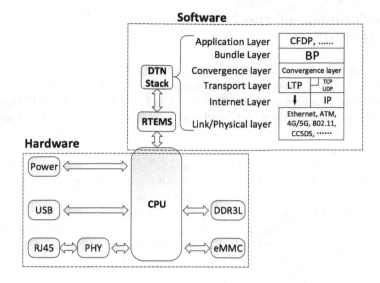

Fig. 1. System general program design

Development environment of the design scheme is based on Ubuntu 16.04 64-bit and RTEMS 4.11.

Download the latest version of RTEMS from official website. Its open source code already contains Beaglebone Black's BSP. The work approach [8] is shown in Fig. 2.

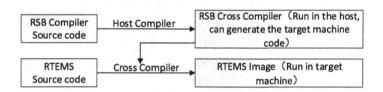

Fig. 2. Development diagram

RTEMS-Source-Build (RSB) is RTEMS official cross compiler. First configure the RSB to match the development environment and the RTEMS. Then run the bootstrap script file in the root directory of the source code. After that, RTEMS kernel trimming and configuration can be implemented by running the configuration file. For example, the parameter "-target" is set to compile the target, and thus "-target = beaglebonblack" indicates the target is BBB board; The parameter "Cenable" indicates that a function is enabled, so that "Cenable-networking" can enable the network protocol stack function.

After the configuration and cross-compiling aforementioned, RTEMS system image for BBB board can be achieved and transplanted on BBB board by the command "Make install" [10].

4 Development of the Network Adapter Driver for RTEMS

Since RTEMS does not have the network adapter driver associated with BBB board, we need design and implement its network adapter driver before other application transplantation. Consider the implementation of U-Boot and FreeBSD driver as references. Although the implementation of U-Boot network driver is simple and easily understood, we cannot duplicate its implementation to RTEMS since it should also obey the open source protocol GPL3. As the network protocol stack of RTEMS is developed from TCP/IP protocol stack of FreeBSD, the API function of RTEMS's protocol is similar to that of FreeBSD. Thus, it is convenient for porting driver. In addition, the development of FreeBSD is according to the BSD open source protocol, which allows the code modification done by the developers arbitrarily. The details of the implementation for the network adapter driver on RTEMS is described in Fig. 3 [11].

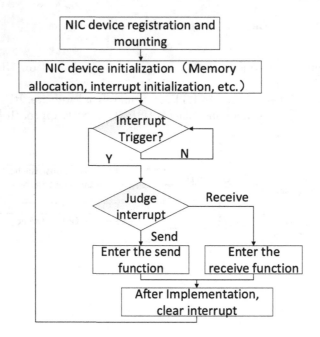

Fig. 3. Network adapter workflow

The transplantation of the network adapter driver is according to the following steps.

- Registration and mounting for network adapter;
- Operation of the initial configuration on network adapter;
- Implemention of interrupt on network adapter;

– Implemention of transceiver on network adapter;
– Function test on network adapter;
– Application test on network adapter.

Some key issues should be noted in the process of development. For example, BBB board fulfills the network adapter management via the TI instruction "CPSW". Then interface function associated with the network adapter registration is named "cpsw attach", and it will be called by the network usage or the system initialization. Usually, CPU is authorised to read data from cache first. However, the transmission method adopted by DMA is directly transmitting data via memory. Thus, it is important for DMA that the operation on the data cache should be disabled while data exchanged with the network adapter.

After the development of network adapter driver, we carry out its functional test by the instruction set "shell" integrated with RTEMS.

5   ION-DTN Transplantation

5.1   DTN Protocol Stack Transplantation

DTN, as an overlay networking architecture, is widely recognized as the most suitable technology to be employed in space networking. Therefore, many researchers focus on the studies of the heterogeneous protocol stacks and overlay networking of DTN for their use in space networking. ION-DTN developed by JPL is one of the implementation for DTN. We thus transplant ION-DTN to RTEMS in our emulation node scheme.

The DTN protocol stack has been described in Fig. 2. As the fact that the source code of ION-DTN already contains the Makefile file and the application for RTEMS, transplantation can be implemented by the Makefile file modification.

First of all, configure the environment variable in the Makefile to make it suitable for the development environment. The objective of Makefile is to generate "ion.exe" file. The source files include ICISOURCES, LTPSOURCES, BPSOURCES, TESTSOURCES, etc. If one wants to add a new function, the source file list needs to be modified, e.g. entering a new source file into the list. Suppose that the node expects to provide the ability of the space router, the function of BP packet transmitting-receiving in Bundle layer will be added on list.

In addition, RTEMS static library should be also added in the Makefile file, because the interface function between Bundle layer and OSI protocol layer needs the support of sockets integrated with RTEMS. After that, the "ion.exe" file is generated once again, and then converted into an image. Burn it to the SD card, BBB board thus can boot from such SD card.

5.2   Application for ION Internetworking

Interplanetary Overlay Network (ION) is an implementation of the space internetworking based on DTN protocol stack. Its data flow processing is shown in Fig. 4 [12].

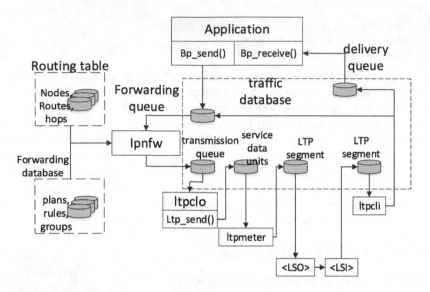

Fig. 4. ION data stream

The source code of ION-DTN contains a demo file, ionrtems.c, which implements the loopback function of the BP package. However, it only transfers data packets between the Bundle layer, which does not involve using the RTEMS network protocol and the physical layer Ethernet frames.

After reconfiguration aforementioned, the pseudoshell function in ionrtems.c file is modified to obtain the command "bpdriver" and "bpcounter" as follows.

```
bpdriver -1000 ipn:1.1 ipn:3.1 -1000
bpcounter ipn:3.1
```

where the first parameter of bpdriver indicates the size of the bp packet, e.g. 1000 is 1000 KB, the second and third arguments indicate the source node and the destination node respectively, and the last argument indicates the number of the bp packets. The parameter of bpcounter indicates the source node. With the help of these two commands, the entire protocol stack is enabled to send and receive BP packets successfully.

6   Emulation Results and Discussion

According to the scheme proposed in this paper, we implement the development of emulation node network adapter driver, ION-DTN protocol stack transplantation and application for ION internetworking.

The performance of our designed emulation node will be evaluated via the following experiments. Most of our emulation parameters are listed in Table 2.

We use ping as the diagnostic tool to test the reachability of our emulation node on the network. Taking our designed emulation node as the destination

Table 2. Emulation parameters

Parameter	Setting/Value
Space Router Hardware	BBB Platform
Bandwidth Limit	100 Mbps
Liunx host PC	Ubuntu 16.04
BP Hosted Transport	No
ACK Packet Size/bytes	70
LTP Block Size/bytes	240
LTP Segment Size/bytes	1400
MTU Size/bytes	1500
Number of samples	Independent test 8 times

BP: Bundle protocol layer MTU: Maximum transfer unit

host, we send Internet Control Message Protocol (ICMP) Echo Request packets to the target host from a Linux host and wait for the ICMP Echo Replies.
Figure 5 is the output of running ping on Linux for sending 50 probes to the target node. It lists the statistics of the entire test and the red line in Fig. 5 indicates
the value of average round trip time (RTT). In this experiment, the first RTT
spent the longest time since the source host at first needs to go through ARP
broadcasting via the router to find the physical address corresponding to the target host IP address. The value of other RTTs was fluctuated around the average
slightly which indicates the emulation node network adapter working stably.

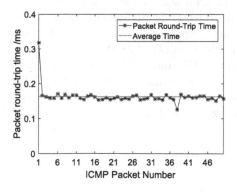

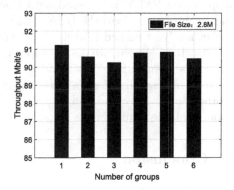

Fig. 5. The Emulation node sends ICMP packets

Fig. 6. FTP test

Further, we develop an FTP server program to test the transmission ability
of our embedded emulation node. Here, function rtems_initialize_ftpd is called
to initialize the ftp, and the structure rtems_ftpd_configuration is used for the
corresponding parameters configuration, including ftp port, the maximum number of connections, etc. The tests had been done after setup the FTP server

on RTEMS, and the measurement results are illustrated in Fig. 6. It shows that uplink rate of network adapter on BBB board is about 32 Mb/s and the downlink rate is 90 Mb/s, which are approximate to the rate available at network adapter on BBB board.

As can be seen from Fig. 6, the transfer rate is maintained at 90 Mbps, the network adapter has a good performance.

No.	Source	Destinatior	Protocol	Lengtt	Info
1	10.0.0.3	10.0.0.4	LTP Segme	94	ipn:1.1 > ipn:2.1
2	10.0.0.4	10.0.0.3	LTP Segme	55	Report segment
3	10.0.0.3	10.0.0.4	LTP Segme	60	Report ack segment
4	10.0.0.4	10.0.0.3	LTP Segme	118	ipn:2.0 > ipn:1.0
5	10.0.0.3	10.0.0.4	LTP Segme	60	Report segment
6	10.0.0.4	10.0.0.3	LTP Segme	48	Report ack segment
No.	Source	Destinatior	Protocol	Lengtt	Info
3	10.0.0.3	10.0.0.4	Bundle	84	ipn:1.1 > ipn:2.1
5	10.0.0.3	10.0.0.4	Bundle	181	ipn:1.1 > ipn:2.1
7	10.0.0.3	10.0.0.4	Bundle	181	ipn:1.1 > ipn:2.1
9	10.0.0.3	10.0.0.4	Bundle	181	ipn:1.1 > ipn:2.1

Fig. 7. BP, LTP, CFDP protocol

Finally, we do experiments to test whether the DTN protocol stack working properly on RTEMS. We send data from our emulation node to a Linux host, and both of them load the DTN protocol for data transmission. In the tests, a packet analyzer named Wireshark runs on the Linux host to capture the packets transmitted between two nodes, and some of the results are illustrated in Fig. 7. As can be seen in Fig. 7, two nodes can employ BP and LTP protocol for data delivery successfully. It shows that the embedded emulation node can load DTN protocol effectively and run it properly, which makes our designed emulation node meet the requirements for space network protocol testing.

7   Conclusion

This paper proposed a scheme to design and implement an embedded emulation node, which provided an approach to emulate a precision network environment for the measurement of network protocols in the space information network. The design scheme uses the Beaglebone Black (BBB) embedded core board owned the approximate hardware performance as a satellite has, ports the real-time operating system RTEMS to BBB board, and then loads and runs the ION-DTN on it. The experiment results show that the function and performance of the designed emulation node can meet the requirements for space network protocol testing.

References

1. Beaglebone Black User Manual. https://cdn.sparkfun.com/datasheets/Dev/Beagle
2. AM335x Sitara Processors Users Guide. http://www.ti.com.cn/cn/lit/er/sprz360i/sprz360i.pdf
3. RTEMS Ada Users Guide. https://www.rtems.org/
4. Faxin, Y.: Comparison and analysis of commonly used embedded real-time operation. J. Comput. Appl. **4**, 761–764 (2006)
5. Dong, J., Li, Y., Yang, Q., Zhai, J.: Real time evaluation of embedded operating system oriented to space system. J. Comput. Eng. Des. **1**, 114–120 (2013)
6. Sun, L.: A comparative study of four popular embedded real-time operating systems-VxWorks, QNX, ucLinux, RTEMS. J. Comput. Appl. Softw. **8**, 196–197 (2007)
7. Zhou, J.: Research on key technologies of space integrated information network based on DTN. D. ACM SIGBED Rev. **11**, 20–25 (2014)
8. Yang, H.: Porting of RTEMS embedded operating system. J. Softw. **12**, 108–113 (2015)
9. Bloom, G., Sherrill, J.: Scheduling and thread management with RTEMS. J. ACM SIGBED Rev. **11**, 20–25 (2014)
10. Fan, C., Gui, X.: Development of RTEMS real-time system board support package. J. Appl. Single Chip Microcomput. Embed. Syst. **6**, 35–38 (2005)
11. Huazhong, W., Chen, H.: Design of Network Driver Based on RTEMS. J. Electron. World **2**, 129–130 (2014)
12. ION.pdf. http://ipnsig.org/wp-content/uploads/2015/05/Whats-new-in-ION.pdf

Optimization Spiking Neural P System
for Solving TSP

Feng Qi and Mengmeng Liu$^{(\boxtimes)}$

Shandong Normal University, Jinan, China
qfsdnu@126.com, 1783797657@qq.com

Abstract. Spiking neural P systems are a class of distributed and parallel computing models that incorporate the idea of spiking neurons into P systems. Membrane computing (MC) combining with evolutionary computing (EC) is called evolutionary MC. In this work, we will combine SNPS with heuristic algorithm to solve the travelling salesman problem. To this aim, an extended spiking neural P system (ESNPS) has been proposed. A certain number of ESNPS can be organized into OSNPS. Extensive experiments on TSP have been reported to experimentally prove the viability and effectiveness of the proposed neural system.

Keywords: OSNPS · GA · Membrane algorithm · TSP

1 Introduction

Membrane computing is one of the recent branches of natural computing. The obtained models are distributed and parallel computing devices, usually called P systems. There are three main classes of P systems investigated: cell-like P systems [1], tissue-like P systems [2] and neural-like P systems [3]. Spiking Neural P system (SNPS, for short) is a class of neural-like P systems, which are inspired by the method of biological neuron processing information and communicating with others by means of electrical spikes. Evolutionary computing (EC) is based in Darwin's theory of evolution, simulating the evolution process and structuring a kind of heuristic optimization algorithms with characteristics of self-organization, adaptive and self-learning, such as genetic algorithm, ant colony optimization, particle swarm optimization and so on.

MC combining with EC is called evolutionary membrane computing [4], in which the membrane algorithm is a research direction. Membrane algorithm is a kind of hybrid optimization algorithm which combines the structure of membrane system, evolution rules, calculation mechanism and the principle of evolutionary computation.

The research on the membrane algorithm can be dated back to 2004 and Nishida combined a membrane structure with the way of tabu search to solve the traveling salesman problems [5]. In 2008, a one-level membrane structure combining with a quantum-inspired evolutionary algorithm was put forward to solve knapsack problems [6]. In 2013, a tissue membrane system was used to solve parameter optimization problems [7]. These investigations indicate the feasibility of the P systems for multifarious optimization problems. But, at present, the membrane algorithm is mainly

© ICST Institute for Computer Sciences, Social Informatics and Telecommunications Engineering 2018
X. Gu et al. (Eds.): MLICOM 2017, Part II, LNICST 227, pp. 668–676, 2018.
https://doi.org/10.1007/978-3-319-73447-7_71

focused on the cell-like P system and tissue-like P system. The research of membrane algorithm on the neural-like P system is relatively few. In 2014, Professor Zhang designed an optimization spiking neural P system [8], which can be used to solve the knapsack problem-a famous NP complete problem. The results show that the design optimization spiking neural P system has obvious advantages in solving knapsack problems.

The Traveling Salesman Problem (TSP) is a widely studied NP-hard combinatorial problem, and it's famous for being difficult to solve. So, it is meaningful both in theory and applications to develop techniques to solve such problems. In this paper, we combine SNPS and genetic algorithm (GA) to solve the TSP. First, we design the optimization SNPS (OSNPS), achieving the connection between the GA algorithm and the membrane system. Second, we implement our ideas on the platform MATLAB. The ideas of this article not only contribute to the membrane algorithm of the neural-like P system, but also find a new way to solve the TSP.

2   Related Background

Generally, an SNP system is composed of neurons, spikes, synapses, and rules. Neurons may contain a number of spikes, spiking rules and forgetting rules, and directed connections between neurons and neurons are accomplished by synapses. A neuron can send information to its neighboring neurons by using the spiking rule. By using the forgetting rule, a number of spikes will be removed from the neuron, and thus they are removed from the system.

An SNP system of degree $m \geq 1$ is a construct of the form:

$$\prod = (O, \sigma_1, \sigma_2, \cdots \sigma_m, \text{syn}, \text{in}, \text{out})$$

Where

- $o = \{a\}$ is the alphabet, a is spike;
- $\sigma_1, \sigma_2, \cdots \sigma_m$ are neurons of the form $\sigma_i = (n_i, R)$ with $1 \leq i \leq m$. n_i is a natural number representing the initial number of spikes in neuron σ_i; R is set of rules in each neuron of the following forms:

  (a) $E/a^c \rightarrow a; d$ is the spiking rule, where E is the regular expression over $\{a\}$; (c and d are integer and $c \geq 1, d \geq 0$)
  (b) $a^s \rightarrow \lambda$ is the forgetting rule, with the restriction that for any $s \geq 1$ and any spiking rule $E/a^c \rightarrow a; d, a^s \notin L(E)$, where $L(E)$ is set of regular languages associated with regular expression E and λ is the empty string;

- $\text{syn} \subseteq \{1, 2, ..., m\} \times \{1, 2, ..., m\}$ is set of synapses between neurons, where $i \neq j$, $z \neq 0$ for each $(i, j) \in \text{syn}$, and for each $(i, j) \in \{1, 2, ..., m\} \times \{1, 2, ..., m\}$ there is at most one synapse (i, j) in syn.
- $\text{In}, \text{out} \in \{1, 2, ..., m\}$ indicate the input and output neurons respectively.

In SNP systems, spiking rules $(E/a^c \rightarrow a; d)$ can be applied in any neuron as follows: if neuron σ_i contains k spikes a with $a^k \in L(E)$ and $k \geq c$, the spiking rule $E/a^c \rightarrow a; d$ is enabled to be applied. By using the rule, c spikes a are consumed, thus $k - c$ spikes a remain in the neuron σ_i, and after d time units, one spike a is sent to all neurons σ_j such that $(i, j) \in$ syn. For any spiking rule, if $E = a^c$, the rule is simply written as $a^c \rightarrow a; d$ and if $d = 0$, we can omit it, and then the spiking rules can be written as $a^c \rightarrow a$.

Rules of the form $a^s \rightarrow \lambda, s \geq 1$ are forgetting rules with the restriction $a^s \notin L(E)$ (that is to say, a neuron cannot apply the spiking rules and forgetting rules at the same moment), where $L(E)$ is a set of regular languages associated with regular expression E. λ is the empty string. If neuron σ_i contains exactly s spikes, the forgetting rule $a^s \rightarrow \lambda$ can be executed, and then s spikes are removed from the neuron.

The TSP is a class of problem that finding a shortest closed tour visiting each city once and only once. Given a set $\{c_1, c_2, \ldots c_n\}$ of n cities and symmetric distance $d(c_i, c_j)$ which gives the distance between city c_i and c_j, the goal is to find a permutation π of these n cities that minimizes the following function:

$$\sum_{i=1}^{n-1} d\left(c_{\pi(i)}, c_{\pi(i+1)}\right) + d\left(c_{\pi(n)}, c_{\pi(1)}\right) \tag{1}$$

3   OSNPS for TSP

3.1   The Structure of OSNPS

The SNPS can be represented graphically. A directed graph is used to represent the structure: the neurons connect with each other by the synapses; the output neuron emits spikes to the environment using outgoing synapse.

Inspired by the fact that spiking neural P system can generate string languages or spike trains [9], an extended spiking neural P system (ESNPS, for short) has been proposed to produce a binary string, and corresponding probability string is used to represent a chromosome. An ESNPS of degree $m \geq 1$ is shown in Fig. 1.

Each ESNPS consists of m neurons. $\sigma_1, \sigma_2, \ldots \sigma_m$ are neurons of the form $\sigma_i = (1, R_i, P_i)$ with $1 \leq i \leq m$, where $R_i = \{r_i^1, r_i^2\}$ ($r_i^1 = \{a \rightarrow a\}$ and $r_i^2 = \{a \rightarrow \lambda\}$) is a set of rules and $P_i = \{p_i^1, p_i^2\}$ is a set of probabilities, where p_i^1 and p_i^2 are the selection probabilities of rules r_i^1 and r_i^2 respectively, and $p_i^1 + p_i^2 = 1$. If the ith neuron spikes, we get its output 1 and probability p_i^1, otherwise, we get its output 0 and p_i^2. That is to say we get 1 by probability p_i^1 and we get 0 by probability p_i^2.

For example, as for an ESNPS of degree m = 5, its probability matrix is shown in below. If we get the spike train [0 0 1 1 0], then the corresponding probability vector is [0.49 0.65 0.42 0.79 0.45].

$$\begin{bmatrix} p_i^1 & 0.51 & 0.35 & 0.42 & 0.79 & 0.55 \\ p_i^2 & 0.49 & 0.65 & 0.58 & 0.21 & 0.45 \end{bmatrix}$$

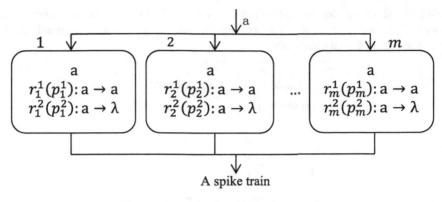

Fig. 1. An example of ESNPS structure

From Fig. 2, we can see that a certain number of ESNPS can be organized into OSNPS by introducing a guider to adjust the selection probabilities and adding a subsystem (σ_{m+1} and σ_{m+2}) to be the spikes supplier. OSNPS consists of H ESNPS, ESNPS$_1$, ESNPS$_2$..., ESNPS$_H$. Each ESNPS is identical (Fig. 1) and the operation steps are illustrated in Subsect. 3.2. Thus, each ESNPS outputs a spike train at each moment of time, and then OSNPS will output H binary string, and we can get the corresponding probability matrix.

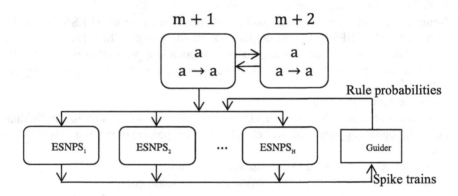

Fig. 2. The structure of OSNPS

In the OSNPS, $\sigma_{m+1} = \sigma_{m+2} = (1, \{a \rightarrow a\})$, σ_{m+1} and σ_{m+2} spike at each time, send spike to each ESNPS and reload each other continuously. We record the spike train matrix T_t (t is current evolution generation) outputted by OSNPS and the corresponding probability matrix P_t. If we can adjust the probabilities, we can control the outputted matrix. In this paper, we put GA algorithm as the guider algorithm to adjust the probability.

We introduce the idea of smallest position value (SPV) [10] method into the genetic algorithm and we give a Table 1 to explain this encoding and decoding method. We put 2 4 1 3 5 as the city sequence.

Table 1. An example of SPV

Dimension j	Position P_{ij}	Sequence
1	0.65	2
2	0.32	4
3	0.87	1
4	0.46	3
5	0.21	5

The input of the guider is a spike train T_t with $H \times m$ bits. The output of the guider is the rule probability matrix $P_t = \left[p_{ij} \right]_{H \times m}$, which is made up of the rule probabilities of H ESNPS. Where p_{ij} is the probability of spiking rule or forgetting rule. For example, as for an ESNPS of degree m = 5, one of the vectors mentioned above [0.49 0.65 0.42 0.79 0.45] could be a part of the P_t.

3.2   The Operation Steps

1. Initialize system parameters;
2. Neuron σ_{m+1} and neuron σ_{m+2} spike and supply neurons for H ESNPS. At the same time, H ESNPS spike and output spike training matrix T_t(0–1matrix);
3. Put T_t into the guider and rearrange it as corresponding probability matrix P_t; We put P_t as the initial population of GA and convert P_t to real matrix M_t by using the SPV idea;
4. Calculate fitness function;
5. Selection operation: Roulette wheel selection algorithm and optimal individual preservation strategy are used; we select the first ten percent of the best individual to save;
6. Cross operation: Adopting OX crossover algorithm;
7. Mutation operation: Using transposition mutation techniques;
8. Judge whether the termination condition (the max generation) is met or not. If it reached, output the final result, end; otherwise $t = t + 1$ and go to step 9;
9. We combine the updated probability matrix P_t with the corresponding 0–1 matrix T_t to update the probability of each ESNPS and go to step 1;

In the implementation process of OSNPS, each of the neuron in ESNPS according to the rules of probability to spike spiking rules or forgetting rules, which will increase the population diversity (Fig. 3).

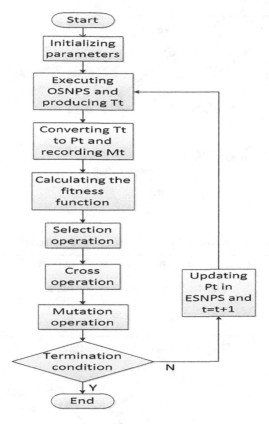

Fig. 3. The system flow diagram

4 Experimental Results

In this section, our system was implemented using matlab and tested on a personal PC with Pentium IV 3.0 GHz CPU and 512 MB memory. The population size is taken as 30; Crossover probability $p_c = 0.8$ and the mutation probability $p_m = 0.2$. The maximum iteration number N is taken as 500. Since OSNPS mainly uses the combination of SNPS and GA algorithm, we make a contrast experiment between the improved GA algorithm in the guider and the OSNPS system (Figs. 4 and 5).

Through experiments, we can see that when the number of cities is 30, the results of OSNPS are better than guider algorithm, but OSNPS find the optimum in 402 generation and guider algorithm in 247 generation (Fig. 6).

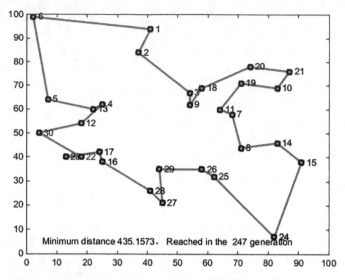

Fig. 4. 30 cities in guider algorithm

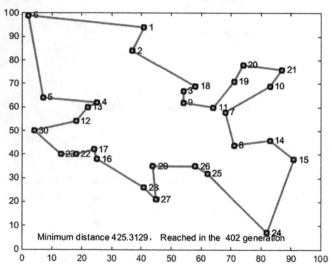

Fig. 5. 30 cities in OSNPS

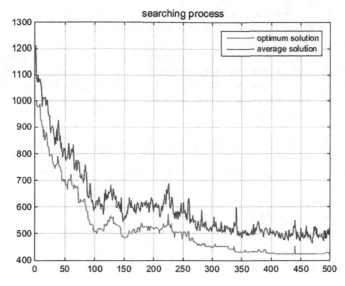

Fig. 6. The searching process of OSNPS

5 Conclusion

In this paper, we proposed the OSNPS for solving the TSP. The OSNPS achieve the connection between the GA algorithm and the membrane system. Experimental results show that the OSNPS can effectively solve TSP and prevent GA algorithm from falling into local optimum. The ideas of this article not only contribute to the membrane algorithm of the neural-like P system, but also find a new way to solve the TSP.

Certainly, the OSNPS has some drawbacks in solving the TSP. When the scale of the problem is getting bigger and bigger, the advantage of OSNPS is increasingly obscure and the system need more time to solve problems than standard GA. So the future work is to improve the SNP system or GA algorithm to optimize experimental results.

Acknowledgment. This work was supported by the Natural Science Foundation of China (No. 61502283). Natural Science Foundation of China (No. 61472231).

References

1. Păun, G.: Computing with membranes. J. Comput. Syst. Sci. **61**(1), 108–143 (2000)
2. Freund, R., Păun, G., Pérez-Jiménez, M.J.: Tissue-like P systems with channel-states. Theor. Comput. Sci. **330**, 101–116 (2005)
3. Ionescu, M., Păun, G., Yokomori, T.: Spiking neural P systems. Fund. Inform. **71**(2), 279–308 (2006)
4. Zhang, G., Gheorghe, M., Pan, L., et al.: Evolutionary membrane computing: a comprehensive survey. Inf. Sci. **279**(1), 528–551 (2014)

5. Nishida, T.Y.: An application of P systems: a new algorithm for NP-complete optimization problems. In: Proceedings of 8th World Multi-Conference Systems, Cybernetics and Informatics, pp. 109–112 (2004)

6. Zhang, G.X., Gheorghe, M., Wu, C.Z.: A quantum-inspired evolutionary algorithm based on P systems for knapsack problem. Fund. Inform. **87**(1), 93–116 (2008)

7. Zhang, G., Cheng, J., Gheorghe, M., Meng, Q.: A hybrid approach based on differential evolution and tissue membrane systems for solving constrained manufacturing parameter optimization problems. Appl. Soft Comput. **13**(3), 1528–1542 (2013)

8. Zhang, G., Rong, H., Neri, F., et al.: An optimization spiking neural P system for approximately solving combinatorial optimization problems. Int. J. Neural Syst. **24**(05), 1440006 (2014)

9. Reeves, C.R.: A genetic algorithm for flowshop sequencing. Comput. Oper. Res. **22**(1), 5–13 (1995)

10. Chen, H., Freund, R., Ionescu, M., et al.: On string languages generated by spiking neural P systems. Fund. Inform. **75**(75), 141–162 (2007)

Author Index

Printed in the United States
By Bookmasters